MW01258524

Kawasaki Ninja ZX-7R and ZX-9R
Service and Repair Manual

by Mark Coombs and Phil Mather

Models covered
Ninja ZX-7R (ZX750P). 748 cc. 1996 to 2003
Ninja ZX-9R (ZX900B). 899 cc. 1994 to 1997
Ninja ZX-9R (ZX900C). 899 cc. 1998 to 1999
Ninja ZX-9R (ZX900E). 899 cc. 2000 to 2001
Ninja ZX-9R (ZX900F). 899 cc. 2002 to 2004

Note: Does not cover the ZX-7RR (ZX750N)

(3721 - 360 - 1AE2)

© Haynes Group Limited 2005

A book in the **Haynes Service and Repair Manual Series**

ISBN **978 1 78521 296 3**

British Library Cataloguing in Publication Data
A catalogue record for this book is available from the British Library.

Library of Congress Control Number 2005920361

Haynes Group Limited
Haynes North America, Inc

www.haynes.com

Contents

LIVING WITH YOUR KAWASAKI NINJA

Introduction

Daily (pre-ride) checks

MAINTENANCE

Routine maintenance and servicing

Contents

REPAIRS AND OVERHAUL

Engine, transmission and associated systems

Chassis and bodywork components

Electrical system

Wiring diagrams

REFERENCE

Index

Kawasaki
The Green Meanies

by Julian Ryder

Kawasaki Heavy Industries

Kawasaki is a company of contradictions. It is the smallest of the big four Japanese manufacturers but the biggest company, it was the last of the four to make and market motorcycles yet it owns the oldest name in the Japanese industry, and it was the first to set up a factory in the USA. Kawasaki Heavy Industries, of which the motorcycle operation is but a small component, is a massive company with its heritage firmly in the old heavy industries like shipbuilding and railways; nowadays it is as much involved in aerospace as in motorcycles.

In fact it may be because of this that Kawasaki's motorcycles have always been quirky, you get the impression that they are designed by a small group of enthusiasts who are given an admirably free hand. More realistically, it may be that Kawasaki's designers have experience with techniques and materials from other engineering disciplines. Either way, Kawasaki have managed to be the factory who surprise us more than the rest. Quite often, they do this by totally ignoring a market segment the others are scrabbling over, but more often they hit us with pure, undiluted performance.

The origins of the company, and its name, go back to 1878 when Shozo Kawasaki set up a dockyard in Tokyo. By the late 1930s, the company was making its own steel in massive steelworks and manufacturing railway locos and rolling stock. In the run up to war, the Kawasaki Aircraft Company was set up in 1937 and it was this arm of the now giant operation that would look to motorcycle engine manufacture in post-war Japan.

They bought their high-technology experience to bear first on engines which were sold on to a number of manufacturers as original equipment. Both two- and four-stroke units were made, a 58 cc and 148 cc OHC unit. One of the customer companies was Meihatsu Heavy Industries, another company within the Kawasaki group, which in 1961 was shaken up and renamed Kawasaki Auto Sales. At the same time, the Akashi factory which was to be Kawasaki's main production facility until the Kobe earthquake of 1995, was opened. Shortly afterwards, Kawasaki took over the ailing Meguro company, Japan's oldest motorcycle maker, thus instantly obtaining a range of bigger bikes which were marketed as Kawasaki-Meguros. The following year, the first bike to be made and sold as a Kawasaki was produced, a 125 cc single called the B8 and in 1963 a motocross version, the B8M appeared.

The three cylinder two-stroke 750

Model development

Kawasaki's first appearance on a road-race circuit came in 1965 with a batch of disc-valve 125 twins. They were no match for the opposition from Japan in the shape of Suzuki and Yamaha or for the fading force of the factory MZs from East Germany. Only after the other Japanese factories had pulled out of the class did Kawasaki win, with British rider Dave Simmonds becoming World 125 GP Champion in 1969 on a bike that looked astonishingly similar to the original racer. That same year Kawasaki reorganised once again, this time merging three companies to form Kawasaki Heavy Industries. One of the new organisation's objectives was to take motorcycle production forward and exploit markets outside Japan.

KHI achieved that target immediately and set out their stall for the future with the astonishing and frightening H1. This three-cylinder air-cooled 500 cc two-stroke was arguably the first modern pure performance bike to hit the market. It hypnotised a whole generation of motorcyclists who'd never before encountered such a ferocious, wheelie inducing power band or such shattering straight-line speed allied to questionable handling. And as for the 750 cc version ...

The triples perfectly suited the late '60s, fitting in well with the student demonstrations of 1968 and the anti-establishment ethos of the Summer of Love. Unfortunately, the oil crisis would put an end to the thirsty strokers but Kawasaki had another high-performance ace up their corporate sleeve. Or rather they thought they did.

The 1968 Tokyo Show saw probably the single most significant new motorcycle ever made unveiled: the Honda CB750. At Kawasaki it caused a major shock, for they also had a 750 cc four, code-named New York Steak, almost ready to roll and it was a double, rather than single, overhead cam motor. Bravely, they took the decision to go ahead - but with the motor taken out to 900 cc. The result was the Z1, unveiled at the 1972 Cologne Show. It was a bike straight out of the same mould as the H1, scare stories spread about unmanageable power, dubious straight-line stability and frightening handling, none of which stopped the sales graph rocketing upwards and led to the coining of the term 'superbike'. While rising fuel prices cut short development of the big two-strokes, the Z1 went on to found a dynasty, indeed its genes can still be detected in Kawasaki's latest products like the ZZ-R1100 (Ninja ZX-11).

This is another characteristic of the way Kawasaki operates. Models quite often have very long lives, or gradually evolve. There is no major difference between that first Z1 and the air-cooled GPz range. Add water-cooling and you have the GPZ900, which in turn metamorphosed into the GPZ1000RX and then the ZX-10 and the ZZ-R1100. Indeed, the

The first Superbike, Kawasaki's 900 cc **Z1**

One of the two-stroke engined KH and KE range - the KE100B

The GT750 - a favourite hack for despatch riders

last three models share the same 58 mm stroke. The bikes are obviously very different but it's difficult to put your finger on exactly why.

Other models have remained effectively untouched for over a decade: the KH and KE single-cylinder air-cooled two-stroke learner bikes, the GT550 and 750 shaft-drive hacks favoured by big city despatch riders and the GPz305 being prime examples. It's only when they step outside the performance field that Kawasakis seems less sure. Their first factory

The high-performance ZXR750

customs were dire, you simply got the impression that the team that designed them didn't have their heart in the job. Only when the Classic range appeared in 1995 did they get it right.

Racing success

Kawasaki also have a more focused approach to racing than the other factories. The policy has always been to race the road bikes and with just a couple of exceptions that's what they've done. Even Simmonds' championship winner bore a strong resemblance to the twins they were selling in the late '60s and racing versions of the 500 and 750 cc triples were also sold as over-the-counter racers, the H1R and H2R. The 500 was in the forefront of the two-stroke assault on MV Agusta but wasn't a Grand Prix winner. It was the 750 that made the impact and carried the factory's image in F750 racing against the Suzuki triples and Yamaha fours.

The factory's decision to use green, usually regarded as an unlucky colour in sport, meant its bikes and personnel stood out and the phrase 'Green Meanies' fitted them perfectly. The Z1 motor soon became a full 1000 cc and powered Kawasaki's assault in F1 racing, notably in endurance which Kawasaki saw as being most closely related to its road bikes.

That didn't stop them dominating 250 and 350 cc GPs with a tandem twin two-stroke in the late '70s and early '80s, but their path-breaking monocoque 500 while a race winner never won a world title. When Superbike arrived, Kawasaki's road 750s weren't as track-friendly as the opposition's out-and-out race replicas. This makes Scott Russell's World title on the ZXR750 in 1993 even more praiseworthy, for the homologation bike, the ZXR750RR, was much heavier and much more of a road bike than the Italian and Japanese competition.

The company's Supersport 600 contenders have similarly been more sports-tourers than race-replicas, yet they too have been competitive on the track. Indeed, the flagship bike, the ZZ-R1100, is most definitely a sports tourer capable of carrying two people and their luggage at high speed in comfort all day and then doing it again the next day. Try that on one of the race replicas and you'll be in need of a course of treatment from a chiropractor.

Through doing it their way Kawasaki developed a brand loyalty for their performance bikes that kept the Z1's derivatives in production until the mid-'80s and turned the bike into a classic in its model life. You could even argue that the Z1 lives on in the shape of the 1100 Zephyr's GPz1100-derived motor. And that's another Kawasaki invention, the retro bike. But when you look at what many commentators refer to as the retro boom, especially in Japan, you find that it is no such thing. It is the Zephyr boom. Just another example of Japan's most surprising motorcycle manufacturer getting it right again.

The Ninja ZX-7R and ZX-9R

You might be forgiven for thinking that the Kawasaki ZX-7R and ZX-9R were on a hiding to nothing, commercially that is. After all, the 750 was always going to be compared to the race-replica Suzuki GSX-R750 and the 900 started off in direct competition to the FireBlade and then found itself in the same marketing niche as the Yamaha R1. On paper, both bikes are longer and heavier than the opposition and yet both bikes have sold well over their model lives despite not being as radical as the opposition. A clever trick, and typically Kawasaki.

The ZX-9R did not get off to the best of starts in life. The B1 version of 1994 was heavily criticised for its rear suspension and some road testers seemed confused as to which niche the bike should be slotted into. Some even went as far as to label it a sports tourer, which is stretching a point. Sure the Kawasaki was distinctly porkier than the opposition but on the road very few people noticed. What they did notice was the enormous waves of power that pushed the plot along in typical big Kawasaki fashion.

The original ZX-9R (the ZX900B) didn't change much (apart from gaining six-piston calipers) until the ZX900C1 arrived in 1998. This was really a totally new motorcycle. The old B-model shed vast amounts of weight from both motor and chassis as Kawasaki gleefully announced that they'd turned it into a real FireBlade beater. Total weight loss was over 27 kg with the motor shrunk as well. The stroke was shortened, valve operation changed from rocker arm to direct actuation, engine covers were made from magnesium and there was even a titanium silencer. The engine became a stressed member of the chassis which meant frame downtubes could

The Ninja ZX-9R ZX900B model

be done away with, and the rest of the cycle parts received the same sort of attention to detail as the motor in the quest for reduced weight. If the first ZX-9R had had this spec it would have been as revolutionary as the FireBlade was in its day or the R1 was when it appeared. Its power-to-weight ratio didn't cause front pages to be held, but once again, the spec didn't tell the whole story. On paper, the opposition looked to have the advantage but roadtests showed that the ZX-9R was at least on a par with the rest and probably made it easier to live with than most big-bore hyperbikes. The reason? Power; lots of it. All the way from 3000 rpm to the 12,000 red line with a surge at 8000. Sure the ZX-9R is big, but it's big in the way that Kawasaki flagships always have been, with loads of

presence and as much grunt as you could want.

The ZX-7R was also bigger and heavier than its natural opposition in the 750 Supersports stakes – which means the Suzuki GSX-R750 – when it appeared in 1996 but it hasn't suffered for that. It is a direct descendant of the ZXR750 with a shorter stroke motor (44.7 as opposed to 47.3 mm), bigger forks, and, conversely, slightly longer wheelbase. The chassis was stiffened up and lightened and used the engine as a stressed member. It also had the benefit of being stunningly good looking with the frontal aspect dominated by big Ram Air intakes each side of the headlights. The differences from the 750 Suzuki leap off the spec sheet: the green bike is bigger, longer and heavier, has less radical steering geometry, and makes less power.

The result is a much less single-minded machine, although it's still very much a supersportster. The GSX-R is Suzuki's homologation bike for Superbike racing whereas the stock ZX-7R doesn't have to do that job. For that there is the ZX-7RR. Note that extra R, it denotes a bank of flat-slide carbs, close-ratio box, multi-adjustable chassis, race suspension, brakes, and a much higher price tag, But you don't need the 'double-R' for the road, in fact the slide carbs make it so lumpy it's unrideable on the street. The bog-stock ZX-7R makes a very civilised sportster with grunt all through the rev range and an impeccable front end. And when compared with most other supersportsters, not only does it have grab rails it can actually carry a pillion passenger in relative comfort. That's a significant fact that tells you a lot about the bike; it's designed for the real world and in the real world you often want to carry a passenger. Happily, if you want to have fun on your own there is more room than usual on a sportster as well.

The Ninja ZX-9R ZX900E model

Model development

Ninja ZX-7R

The Ninja ZX-7R P1 was introduced in 1996.

The engine was a liquid cooled four-cylinder with double overhead camshafts driven by chain from the right-hand end of the crankshaft. Four valves per cylinder were operated by bucket-type followers. The crankcases were two-piece, split horizontally, with a separate cylinder block fitted with dry cylinder liners.

Drive was transmitted to the six-speed gearbox through a hydraulically-operated, six spring multi-plate clutch, and to the rear wheel by chain and sprockets.

A ram air system ducted air from openings in the front of the fairing on either side of the twin head lights, to the air filter housing. Fuel was pressure fed to four 38 mm flat slide Keihin CV carburettors, and a secondary air injection system reduced the level of unburned hydrocarbons in the exhaust gasses. The alternator was externally mounted on the left-hand side of the engine unit.

The chassis comprised a twin-spar aluminium alloy frame with a bolt-on rear sub-frame and box-section swingarm. Front suspension was by upside-down, three-way adjustable telescopic forks and rear suspension was by a rising rate, three-way adjustable mono-shock with piggy-back gas reservoir.

Braking was by twin, semi-floating discs with six piston Tokico calipers at the front and a single disc with a two piston Nissin caliper at the rear.

Technically the ZX-7R P series remained the same throughout its production run, the only changes being to the colour scheme.

Ninja ZX-9R

The Ninja ZX-9R B1 was introduced in 1994.

The 900 cc engine design was based on the race replica ZXR 750 – a liquid cooled four-cylinder with chain-driven double overhead camshafts. Cylinder stroke and crankpin diameter were increased and the crankcases strengthened. Four valves per cylinder were operated by rocker arms. The crankcases were two-piece, split horizontally, with a separate cylinder block fitted with dry cylinder liners.

Drive was transmitted to the six-speed gearbox through a hydraulically-operated, six spring multi-plate clutch, and to the rear wheel by chain and sprockets.

A ram air system ducted air from an opening in the front of the fairing below the head light unit, to the air filter housing. Fuel was pressure fed to four 40 mm flat slide Keihin CV carburettors, and a secondary air injection system reduced the level of unburned hydrocarbons in the exhaust gasses. The alternator was externally mounted on the left-hand side of the engine unit behind the cylinders.

The chassis comprised a twin-spar aluminium alloy frame with a bolt-on front downtubes and rear sub-frame and box-section swingarm. Front suspension was by upside-down, three-way adjustable telescopic forks and rear suspension was by a rising rate, three-way adjustable mono-shock with remote gas reservoir.

Braking was by twin, semi-floating discs with four piston Tokico calipers at the front and a single disc with a single piston Nissin caliper at the rear.

The Ninja ZX-9R B3 was introduced in

1996. The designs of the transmission shafts and rear suspension rising rate linkage were revised, and six piston calipers were fitted to the front brakes.

The Ninja ZX-9R C1 was introduced in 1998. A new, wider, cylinder bore dimension allowed larger valves to be fitted and valve actuation was by bucket-type followers. The alternator was located on the left-hand end of the crankshaft and the designs of the clutch and transmission shafts were revised. Magnesium engine covers and a titanium silencer were fitted. Front suspension was by conventional telescopic forks and a new design of rear shock with piggy-back gas reservoir was fitted. A redesigned frame had a welded-on rear sub-frame and incorporated the engine unit as a stressed member, dispensing with the front downtubes.

The Ninja ZX-9R E1 was introduced in 2000. A closed-deck cylinder block was fitted and the compression ratio raised to 12.2:1. The design of the transmission shafts was revised and semi-flat slide Keihin carburettors were fitted. A redesigned windshield and twin headlights were fitted. The rear sub-frame was bolted-on and the rear tyre width increased.

The Ninja ZX-9R F1 was introduced in 2002. Two additional upper engine mountings were added and the rear rubber mountings were dispensed with. A new, braced swingarm, revised rising rate suspension linkage and new rear shock were fitted. Nissin four piston calipers were fitted to the front brakes. The exhaust silencer was redesigned internally and all market models were fitted with a catalytic converter. The seat cowling and front mudguard were restyled.

Bike spec

Weights and dimensions

Wheelbase
ZX-7R . . . . .1435 mm
ZX-9R B . . . . .1440 mm
ZX-9R C, E and F . . . . .1415 mm
Overall length
ZX-7R . . . . .2090 mm
ZX-9R B . . . . .2085 mm
ZX-9R C and E . . . . .2050 mm
ZX-9R F . . . . .2065 mm
Overall height
ZX-7R . . . . .1130 mm
ZX-9R B . . . . .1165 mm
ZX-9R C, E and F . . . . .1155 mm
Overall width
ZX-7R . . . . .740 mm
ZX-9R . . . . .730 mm

Seat height
ZX-7R . . . . .790 mm
ZX-9R B, C and E . . . . .810 mm
ZX-9R F . . . . .815 mm
Ground clearance
ZX-7R . . . . .105 mm
ZX-9R . . . . .160 mm
Dry weight
ZX-7R . . . . .203 kg
ZX-7R (California models) . . . . .204 kg
ZX-9R B . . . . .215 kg
ZX-9R B (California models) . . . . .216 kg
ZX-9R C and E . . . . .183 kg
ZX-9R C and E (California models) . . . . .186 kg
ZX-9R F . . . . .186 kg
ZX-9R F (California models) . . . . .189 kg

Engine

Type . . . . .Liquid cooled, in-line 4-cylinder
Capacity
ZX-7R . . . . .748 cc
ZX-9R . . . . .899 cc
Bore
ZX-7R . . . . .73.0 mm
ZX-9R B . . . . .73.0 mm
ZX-9R C, E and F . . . . .75.0 mm
Stroke
ZX-7R . . . . .44.7 mm
ZX-9R B . . . . .53.7 mm
ZX-9R C, E and F . . . . .50.9 mm
Compression ratio
ZX-7R 11.5:1
ZX-9R B and C 11.5:1
ZX-9R E and F 12.2:1
Camshafts . . . . .DOHC, chain driven

Valves . . . . .4 valves per cylinder
Fuel system
ZX-7R . . . . .4 x Keihin CVKD38 carburettors
ZX-9R E . . . . .4 x Keihin CVRD40 carburettors
ZX-9R B, C and F . . . . .4 x Keihin CVKD40 carburettors
Clutch . . . . .Wet multi-plate, hydraulically operated
Transmission . . . . .6 speed constant mesh
Final drive
Chain
ZX-7R . . . . .RK 525ROZ2 (110 links)
ZX-9R B . . . . .EK 50UV-X (112 links)
ZX-9R C and E . . . . .EK 525UVX (110 links)
ZX-9R F . . . . .EK 525UVXL2 (110 links)
Sprockets
ZX-7R . . . . .16 tooth front/43 tooth rear
ZX-9R . . . . .16 tooth front/41 tooth rear

Chassis

Type . . . . .Twin spar, aluminium alloy
Rake
ZX-7R . . . . .25.0°
ZX-9R . . . . .24.0°
Trail
ZX-7R . . . . .99.0 mm
ZX-9R . . . . .97.0 mm
Front suspension
Type
ZX-7R . . . . .3-way adjustable upside-down forks
ZX-9R B model . . . . .3-way adjustable upside-down forks
ZX-9R C, E and F models . . . . 3-way adjustable telescopic forks
Travel . . . . .120 mm
Adjustments . .Spring pre-load, compression and rebound damping
Rear suspension
Type . . . . .Rising rate with monoshock
Travel
ZX-7R . . . . 130 mm
ZX-9R . . . . 135 mm
Adjustments . .Spring pre-load, compression and rebound damping

Tyre sizes
ZX-7R
Front . . . . .120/70 ZR 17 58W
Rear . . . . .190/50 ZR 17 73W
ZX-9R
Front . . . . .120/70 ZR 17 58W
Rear
B and C . . . . .180/55 ZR 17 73W
E and F . . . . .190/50 ZR 17 73W
Brakes
Front
ZX-7R . . . . .2 x discs with six-piston calipers
ZX-9R B1 and B2 . . . . .2 x discs with four-piston calipers
ZX-9R B3, B4, C and E . . . . . . .2 x discs with six-piston calipers
ZX-9R F . . . . .2 x discs with four-piston calipers
Rear
ZX-7R . . . . .Single disc with two-piston caliper
ZX-9R . . . . .Single disc with single-piston caliper

Acknowledgements

Our thanks are due to Kawasaki Motors (UK) Ltd for permission to reproduce certain illustrations used in this manual. We would also like to thank Paul Branson Motorcycles of Yeovil and GT Motorcycles of Yeovil who supplied the machines featured in the illustrations throughout this manual. NGK Spark Plugs (UK) Ltd supplied the colour spark plug condition photos and the Avon Rubber Company supplied information on tyre fitting.

The introduction 'Kawasaki – The Green Meanies' was written by Julian Ryder.

About this manual

The aim of this manual is to help you get the best value from your motorcycle. It can do so in several ways. It can help you decide what work must be done, even if you choose to have it done by a dealer; it provides information and procedures for routine maintenance and servicing; and it offers diagnostic and repair procedures to follow when trouble occurs.

We hope you use the manual to tackle the work yourself. For many simpler jobs, doing it yourself may be quicker than arranging an appointment to get the motorcycle into a dealer and making the trips to leave it and pick it up. More importantly, a lot of money can be saved by avoiding the expense the shop must pass on to you to cover its labour and overhead costs. An added benefit is the sense of satisfaction and accomplishment that you feel after doing the job yourself.

References to the left or right side of the motorcycle assume you are sitting on the seat, facing forward.

We take great pride in the accuracy of information given in this manual, but motorcycle manufacturers make alterations and design changes during the production run of a particular motorcycle of which they do not inform us. No liability can be accepted by the authors or publishers for loss, damage or injury caused by any errors in, or omissions from, the information given.

It is the policy of the Publisher to actively protect its Copyrights and Trade Marks. Legal action will be taken against anyone who unlawfully copies the cover or contents of this Manual. This includes all forms of unauthorised copying including digital, mechanical, and electronic in any form. Authorisation from the Publisher will only be provided expressly and in writing. Illegal copying will also be reported to the appropriate statutory authorities.

Identification numbers

Engine and frame numbers

The frame serial number is stamped into the right side of the steering head. The engine number is stamped onto the top of the crankcase, directly above the clutch, and is visible from the right side of the machine. Both of these numbers should be recorded and kept in a safe place so they can be given to law enforcement officials in the event of a theft.

The frame serial number and engine serial number should also be kept in a handy place (such as with your driver's licence) so they are always available when purchasing or ordering parts for your machine.

The model code (e.g. ZX-9R B1) can be determined from the engine and frame serial numbers in the accompanying table for UK and US markets. Engine and frame number details are not available for other markets. Note that the ZX-9R C is known as the ZX-9R D in Germany and Switzerland.

Model	Year	Initial engine number	Initial frame number
UK Models			
ZX-7R P1	1996	ZX750NE000001 on	JKAZX750PPA000001 to 013000
ZX-7R P2	1997	ZX750NE000001 on	JKAZX750PPA013001 to 025000
ZX-7R P3	1998	ZX750NE000001 on	JKAZX750PPA025001 to 036000
ZX-7R P4	1999	ZX750NE000001 on	JKAZX750PPA036001 to 047000
ZX-7R P5	2000	ZX750NE000001 on	JKAZX750PPA047001 on
ZX-7R P6	2001	ZX750NE000001 on	JKAZX750PPA053001 on
ZX-7R P7	2002/3	ZX750NE000001 on	JKAZX750PPA058001 on
ZX-9R B1	1994	ZX900BE000001 on	ZX900B-000001 to 018000
ZX-9R B2	1995	ZX900BE000001 on	ZX900B-018001 to 028000
ZX-9R B3	1996	ZX900BE000001 on	ZX900B-028001 to 038000
ZX-9R B4	1997	ZX900BE000001 on	ZX900B-038001 on
ZX-9R C1	1998	ZX900CE000001 on	JKAZX900CCA000001 to 026000
ZX-9R C2	1999	ZX900CE000001 on	JKAZX900CCA026001 on
ZX-9R E1	2000	ZX900CE000001 on	JKAZX900CEA000001 on
ZX-9R E2	2001	ZX900CE000001 on	JKAZX900EEA021001 on
ZX-9R F1	2002	ZX900CE000001 on	JKAZX900EFA035001 on
ZX-9R F2	2003/4	ZX900CE000001 on	JKAZX900EFA040001 on
US models			
ZX-7R P1	1996	ZX750NE000001 on	JKAZXDP1✓TA000001 to 013000
ZX-7R P2	1997	ZX750NE000001 on	JKAZXDP1✓VA013001 to 025000
ZX-7R P3	1998	ZX750NE000001 on	JKAZXDP1✓WA025001 to 036000
ZX-7R P4	1999	ZX750NE000001 on	JKAZXDP1✓VA036001 to 047000
ZX-7R P5	2000	ZX750NE000001 on	JKAZXDP1✓YA047001 on
ZX-7R P6	2001	ZX750NE000001 on	JKAZXDP1✓1A053001 on
ZX-7R P7	2002	ZX750NE000001 on	JKAZXDP1✓2A058001 on
ZX-9R B1	1994	ZX900BE000001 on	JKAZX2B1✓RA000001 to 018000
ZX-9R B2	1995	ZX900BE000001 on	JKAZX2B1✓SA018001 to 028000
ZX-9R B3	1996	ZX900BE000001 on	JKAZX2B1✓TA028001 to 038000
ZX-9R B4	1997	ZX900BE000001 on	JKAZX2B1✓VA038001 on
ZX-9R C1	1998	ZX900CE000001 on	JKAZX2C1✓WA000001 to 026000
ZX-9R C2	1999	ZX900CE000001 on	JKAZX2C1✓WA026001 on
ZX-9R E1	2000	ZX900CE000001 on	JKAZX2E1✓YA000001 on
ZX-9R E2	2001	ZX900CE000001 on	JKAZX2E1✓1A021001 on
ZX-9R F1	2002	ZX900CE000001 on	JKAZX2F1✓2A000001 on
ZX-9R F2	2003	ZX900CE000001 on	JKAZX2F1✓3A006001 on

Buying spare parts

Once you have found all the identification numbers, record them for reference when buying parts. Since the manufacturers change specifications, parts and vendors (companies that manufacture various components on the machine), providing the ID numbers is the only way to be reasonably sure that you are buying the correct parts.

Whenever possible, take the worn part to the dealer so direct comparison with the new component can be made. Along the trail from the manufacturer to the parts shelf, there are numerous places that the part can end up with the wrong number or be listed incorrectly.

The two places to purchase new parts for your motorcycle – the accessory store and the franchised dealer – differ in the type of parts they carry. While dealers can obtain virtually every part for your motorcycle, the accessory dealer is usually limited to normal high wear items such as shock absorbers, tune-up parts, various engine gaskets, cables, chains, brake parts, etc. Rarely will an accessory outlet have major suspension components, cylinders, transmission gears, or cases.

Used parts can be obtained for considerably less than new ones, but you can't always be sure of what you're getting. Once again, take your worn part to the breaker for direct comparison.

Whether buying new, used or rebuilt parts, the best course is to deal directly with someone who specialises in parts for your particular make.

The engine number is stamped in the top of the crankcase on the right-hand side of the engine

The frame number is stamped in the right-hand side of the steering head . . .

. . . and repeated on the VIN plate on the right-hand side of the frame

Professional mechanics are trained in safe working procedures. However enthusiastic you may be about getting on with the job at hand, take the time to ensure that your safety is not put at risk. A moment's lack of attention can result in an accident, as can failure to observe simple precautions.

There will always be new ways of having accidents, and the following is not a comprehensive list of all dangers; it is intended rather to make you aware of the risks and to encourage a safe approach to all work you carry out on your bike.

Asbestos

● Certain friction, insulating, sealing and other products - such as brake pads, clutch linings, gaskets, etc. - contain asbestos. Extreme care must be taken to avoid inhalation of dust from such products since it is hazardous to health. If in doubt, assume that they do contain asbestos.

Fire

● Remember at all times that petrol is highly flammable. Never smoke or have any kind of naked flame around, when working on the vehicle. But the risk does not end there - a spark caused by an electrical short-circuit, by two metal surfaces contacting each other, by careless use of tools, or even by static electricity built up in your body under certain conditions, can ignite petrol vapour, which in a confined space is highly explosive. Never use petrol as a cleaning solvent. Use an approved safety solvent.

● Always disconnect the battery earth terminal before working on any part of the fuel or electrical system, and never risk spilling fuel on to a hot engine or exhaust.

● It is recommended that a fire extinguisher of a type suitable for fuel and electrical fires is kept handy in the garage or workplace at all times. Never try to extinguish a fuel or electrical fire with water.

Fumes

● Certain fumes are highly toxic and can quickly cause unconsciousness and even death if inhaled to any extent. Petrol vapour comes into this category, as do the vapours from certain solvents such as trichloro-ethylene. Any draining or pouring of such volatile fluids should be done in a well ventilated area.

● When using cleaning fluids and solvents, read the instructions carefully. Never use materials from unmarked containers - they may give off poisonous vapours.

● Never run the engine of a motor vehicle in an enclosed space such as a garage. Exhaust fumes contain carbon monoxide which is extremely poisonous; if you need to run the engine, always do so in the open air or at least have the rear of the vehicle outside the workplace.

The battery

● Never cause a spark, or allow a naked light near the vehicle's battery. It will normally be giving off a certain amount of hydrogen gas, which is highly explosive.

● Always disconnect the battery ground (earth) terminal before working on the fuel or electrical systems (except where noted).

● If possible, loosen the filler plugs or cover when charging the battery from an external source. Do not charge at an excessive rate or the battery may burst.

● Take care when topping up, cleaning or carrying the battery. The acid electrolyte, evenwhen diluted, is very corrosive and should not be allowed to contact the eyes or skin. Always wear rubber gloves and goggles or a face shield. If you ever need to prepare electrolyte yourself, always add the acid slowly to the water; never add the water to the acid.

Electricity

● When using an electric power tool, inspection light etc., always ensure that the appliance is correctly connected to its plug and that, where necessary, it is properly grounded (earthed). Do not use such appliances in damp conditions and, again, beware of creating a spark or applying excessive heat in the vicinity of fuel or fuel vapour. Also ensure that the appliances meet national safety standards.

● A severe electric shock can result from touching certain parts of the electrical system, such as the spark plug wires (HT leads), when the engine is running or being cranked, particularly if components are damp or the insulation is defective. Where an electronic ignition system is used, the secondary (HT) voltage is much higher and could prove fatal.

Remember...

✗ **Don't** start the engine without first ascertaining that the transmission is in neutral.

✗ **Don't** suddenly remove the pressure cap from a hot cooling system - cover it with a cloth and release the pressure gradually first, or you may get scalded by escaping coolant.

✗ **Don't** attempt to drain oil until you are sure it has cooled sufficiently to avoid scalding you.

✗ **Don't** grasp any part of the engine or exhaust system without first ascertaining that it is cool enough not to burn you.

✗ **Don't** allow brake fluid or antifreeze to contact the machine's paintwork or plastic components.

✗ **Don't** siphon toxic liquids such as fuel, hydraulic fluid or antifreeze by mouth, or allow them to remain on your skin.

✗ **Don't** inhale dust - it may be injurious to health (see Asbestos heading).

✗ **Don't** allow any spilled oil or grease to remain on the floor - wipe it up right away, before someone slips on it.

✗ **Don't** use ill-fitting spanners or other tools which may slip and cause injury.

✗ **Don't** lift a heavy component which may be beyond your capability - get assistance.

✗ **Don't** rush to finish a job or take unverified short cuts.

✗ **Don't** allow children or animals in or around an unattended vehicle.

✗ **Don't** inflate a tyre above the recommended pressure. Apart from overstressing the carcass, in extreme cases the tyre may blow off forcibly.

✔ **Do** ensure that the machine is supported securely at all times. This is especially important when the machine is blocked up to aid wheel or fork removal.

✔ **Do** take care when attempting to loosen a stubborn nut or bolt. It is generally better to pull on a spanner, rather than push, so that if you slip, you fall away from the machine rather than onto it.

✔ **Do** wear eye protection when using power tools such as drill, sander, bench grinder etc.

✔ **Do** use a barrier cream on your hands prior to undertaking dirty jobs - it will protect your skin from infection as well as making the dirt easier to remove afterwards; but make sure your hands aren't left slippery. Note that long-term contact with used engine oil can be a health hazard.

✔ **Do** keep loose clothing (cuffs, ties etc. and long hair) well out of the way of moving mechanical parts.

✔ **Do** remove rings, wristwatch etc., before working on the vehicle - especially the electrical system.

✔ **Do** keep your work area tidy - it is only too easy to fall over articles left lying around.

✔ **Do** exercise caution when compressing springs for removal or installation. Ensure that the tension is applied and released in a controlled manner, using suitable tools which preclude the possibility of the spring escaping violently.

✔ **Do** ensure that any lifting tackle used has a safe working load rating adequate for the job.

✔ **Do** get someone to check periodically that all is well, when working alone on the vehicle.

✔ **Do** carry out work in a logical sequence and check that everything is correctly assembled and tightened afterwards.

✔ **Do** remember that your vehicle's safety affects that of yourself and others. If in doubt on any point, get professional advice.

● If in spite of following these precautions, you are unfortunate enough to injure yourself, seek medical attention as soon as possible.

Engine/transmission oil level check

Before you start:

✔ Start the engine and allow it to reach normal operating temperature.
Caution: Do not run the engine in an enclosed space such as a garage or workshop.
✔ Stop the engine and support the motorcycle on its sidestand. Allow it to stand undisturbed for a few minutes to allow the oil level to stabilise. Make sure the motorcycle is on level ground.

✔ The oil level is viewed through the window in the clutch cover on the right-hand side of the engine. Wipe the glass clean before inspection to make the check easier.

Bike care:

● If you have to add oil frequently, you should check whether you have any oil leaks. If there is no sign of oil leakage from the joints and gaskets the engine could be burning oil (see *Fault Finding*).

The correct oil

● Modern, high-revving engines place great demands on their oil. It is very important that the correct oil for your bike is used.
● Always top up with a good quality oil of the specified type and viscosity and do not overfill the engine.

Oil type	API grade SE, SF or SG
Oil viscosity	SAE 10W40, 10W50, 20W40 or 20W50

1 With the motorcycle held vertical, check the oil level in the inspection window at the bottom of the clutch cover. The level should lie between the upper and lower level marks (arrowed).

2 The oil filler cap is located at the top of the clutch cover. Unscrew the cap to add oil.

3 Add the specified oil to bring the oil level to the upper level mark on the inspection window but do not overfill. Once the level is correct, securely refit the filler cap ensuring its O-ring is in place.

Coolant level check

⚠ *Warning: DO NOT remove the filler neck pressure cap to add coolant. Topping up is done via the coolant reservoir tank filler. DO NOT leave open containers of coolant about, as it is poisonous.*

Before you start:

✔ Make sure you have a supply of coolant available (a mixture of 50% distilled water and 50% corrosion inhibited ethylene glycol anti-freeze is needed).

✔ Always check the coolant level when the engine is cold.
Caution: Do not run the engine in an enclosed space such as a garage or workshop.
✔ Ensure the motorcycle is held vertical whilst checking the coolant level. Make sure the motorcycle is on level ground.

Bike care:

● Use only the specified coolant mixture. It is important that anti-freeze is used in the system all year round, and not just in the winter. Do not top the system up using only water, as the system will become too diluted.
● Do not overfill the reservoir tank. If the coolant is significantly above the F (full) level line at any time, the surplus should be siphoned or drained off to prevent the possibility of it being expelled out of the overflow hose.
● If the coolant level falls steadily, check the system for leaks (see Chapter 1). If no leaks are found and the level continues to fall, it is recommended that the machine is taken to a Kawasaki dealer for a pressure test.

1 The coolant reservoir is located on the right-hand side of the machine on ZX-7R and ZX-9R B models and the left side on ZX-9R C, E and F models. The coolant F (full) and L (low) level lines are visible on the rear of the reservoir.

2 If the coolant level does not lie between the F (full) and L (low) markings, unscrew the reservoir cap.

3 Top the coolant level up with the recommended coolant mixture then securely fit the cap to the reservoir.

Brake and clutch fluid level checks

The clutch fluid level check only applies to the ZX-7R and ZX-9R B models.

⚠️ **Warning: Hydraulic fluid can harm your eyes and damage painted surfaces, so use extreme caution when handling and pouring it and cover surrounding surfaces with rag. Do not use fluid that has been standing open for some time, as it absorbs moisture from the air which can cause a dangerous loss of braking effectiveness.**

Before you start:

✔ Ensure the motorcycle is held vertical whilst checking the levels. Make sure the motorcycle is on level ground.

✔ Make sure you have the correct hydraulic fluid. DOT 4 is recommended.

✔ Wrap a rag around the reservoir being worked on to ensure that any spillage does not come into contact with painted surfaces.

Bike care:

● The fluid in the front and rear brake master cylinder reservoirs will drop slightly as the brake pads wear down.

● If any fluid reservoir requires repeated topping-up this is an indication of an hydraulic leak somewhere in the system, which should be investigated immediately.

● Check for signs of fluid leakage from the hydraulic hoses and components – if found, rectify immediately.

● Check the operation of both brakes before taking the machine on the road; if there is evidence of air in the system (spongy feel to lever or pedal), it must be bled as described in Chapter 7.

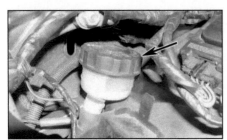

7 If the level is below the LOWER level line, remove the seats (see Chapter 8). Unscrew the reservoir cap (arrowed) and remove the diaphragm plate and diaphragm.

ZX-9R B models

1 The front brake and the clutch fluid levels are checked in the same way. With the reservoir as level as possible, check that the fluid level is above the LOWER level line (arrowed) on the inspection window.

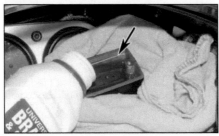

3 Top up with new DOT 4 hydraulic fluid, until the level is just below the upper level mark; this mark is in the form of a line cast on the inside of the reservoir front face (arrowed). Do not overfill the reservoir, and take care to avoid spills (see **Warning** above).

5 The rear brake fluid level is visible through the cut-out in the right side cover.

8 Top up with new DOT 4 hydraulic fluid, until the level is just below the UPPER level line. Do not overfill the reservoir, and take care to avoid spills (see **Warning** above).

2 If the level is below the LOWER level line, remove the two reservoir cover screws and remove the cover, the diaphragm plate and the diaphragm.

4 When the fluid level is correct, clean and dry the diaphragm, fold it into its compressed state and install it. Ensure that the diaphragm is correctly seated before installing the plate and cover. Tighten the cover screws securely and wipe off any spilt fluid.

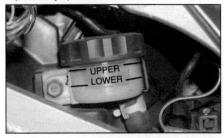

6 The fluid level must be between the UPPER and LOWER level lines.

9 When the fluid level is correct, clean and dry the diaphragm, fold it into its compressed state and install it. Ensure that the diaphragm is correctly seated before installing the plate and cap, tightening it securely. Install the seats (see Chapter 8).

ZX-7R and ZX-9R C, E and F models

1 To check the front brake fluid level (and clutch fluid level on ZX-7R models), ensure the reservoir is as level as possible, then check that the fluid level is between the UPPER and LOWER level lines on the side of the reservoir.

2 If the level is below the LOWER level line, undo the retaining screw and lift off the reservoir cap retaining plate. Unscrew the reservoir cap and remove the diaphragm plate and diaphragm.

3 Top up with new DOT 4 hydraulic fluid, until the level is just below the UPPER level mark; do not overfill the reservoir, and take care to avoid spills (see **Warning** above).

4 When the fluid level is correct, clean and dry the diaphragm, fold it into its compressed state and install it. Ensure that the diaphragm is correctly seated before installing the plate and cap, tightening it securely. Fit the cap retaining plate and securely tighten its screw. Wipe off any spilt fluid.

5 The rear brake fluid level must also be between the UPPER and LOWER level lines on the reservoir (ZX-9R shown).

6 On ZX-7R models the level lines are visible through the cut-out in the right-hand side cover; remove the seats (see Chapter 8) to gain access to the reservoir.

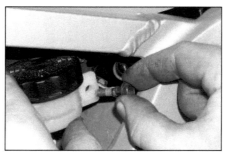

7 Unscrew the reservoir cap and remove the diaphragm plate and diaphragm. Note that the reservoir mounting bolt must be removed on ZX-9R models to permit topping up.

8 Top up with new DOT 4 hydraulic fluid until the level is just below the UPPER level line, then clean and dry the diaphragm, fold it into its compressed state and install it. Ensure that the diaphragm is correctly seated before installing the plate and cap, tightening it securely. On ZX-7R models install the seats (see Chapter 8).

Tyre checks

The correct pressures:
● The tyres must be checked when **cold**, not immediately after riding. Note that low tyre pressures may cause the tyre to slip on the rim or come off. High tyre pressures will cause abnormal tread wear and unsafe handling.
● Use an accurate pressure gauge.
● Proper air pressure will increase tyre life and provide maximum stability and ride comfort.

Tyre pressures	
Front	36 psi (2.5 Bar)
Rear	41 psi (2.9 Bar)

Tyre care:
● Check the tyres carefully for cuts, tears, embedded nails or other sharp objects and excessive wear. Operation of the motorcycle with excessively worn tyres is extremely hazardous, as traction and handling are directly affected.
● Check the condition of the tyre valve and ensure the dust cap is in place.
● Pick out any stones or nails which may have become embedded in the tyre tread. If left, they will eventually penetrate through the casing and cause a puncture.
● If tyre damage is apparent, or unexplained loss of pressure is experienced, seek the advice of a tyre fitting specialist without delay.

Tyre tread depth:
● At the time of writing UK law requires that tread depth must be at least 1 mm over 3/4 of the tread breadth all the way around the tyre, with no bald patches. Many riders, however, consider 2 mm tread depth minimum to be a safer limit. Kawasaki recommend a minimum of 2 mm on the front tyre and 3 mm on the rear tyre if the motorcycle is to be ridden at speeds in excess of 80 mph (130 kmh).
● Many tyres now incorporate wear indicators in the tread. Identify the triangular pointer or 'TWI' mark on the tyre sidewall to locate the indicator bar and renew the tyre if the tread has worn down to the bar.

1 Check the tyre pressures when the tyres are **cold** and keep them properly inflated.

2 Measure tread depth at the centre of the tyre using a tread depth gauge.

3 Tyre tread wear indicator bar and its location marking (usually either an arrow, a triangle or the letters TWI) on the sidewall (arrowed).

Suspension, steering and final drive checks

Suspension and Steering:
● Check that the front and rear suspension operate smoothly without binding.
● Check that the suspension is adjusted as required.

● Check that the steering moves smoothly from lock-to-lock.

Final drive:
● Check that the drive chain slack isn't excessive, and adjust if necessary (see Chapter 1).
● If the chain looks dry, lubricate it (see Chapter 1).

Legal and safety checks

Lighting and signalling:
● Take a minute to check that the headlight, tail light, brake light, instrument lights and turn signals all work correctly.
● Check that the horn sounds when the switch is operated.
● A working speedometer graduated in mph is a statutory requirement in the UK.

Safety:
● Check that the throttle grip rotates smoothly and snaps shut when released, in all steering positions. Also check for the correct amount of freeplay (see Chapter 1).
● Check that the engine shuts off when the kill switch is operated.
● Check that sidestand return spring holds the stand securely up when retracted.

Fuel:
● This may seem obvious, but check that you have enough fuel to complete your journey. If you notice signs of fuel leakage – rectify the cause immediately.
● Ensure you use the correct grade unleaded fuel – see Chapter 4 Specifications.

Chapter 1
Routine maintenance and servicing

Contents

Degrees of difficulty

Easy, suitable for novice with little experience		Fairly easy, suitable for beginner with some experience		Fairly difficult, suitable for competent DIY mechanic		Difficult, suitable for experienced DIY mechanic		Very difficult, suitable for expert DIY or professional	

Engine

Cylinder identification	1-2-3-4 (from left to right)
Engine idle speed	
ZX-7R and ZX-9R B models	
California models	1300 ± 100 rpm
All other models	1100 ± 100 rpm
ZX-9R C and E models	1100 ± 100 rpm
ZX-9R F models	1100 ± 50 rpm
Spark plugs	
ZX-7R models	NGK CR9E or Nippondenso U27ESR-N
ZX-9R models	NGK CR9EK or Nippondenso U27ETR
Electrode gap	0.7 to 0.8 mm
Valve clearances (COLD engine)	
ZX-7R models	
Intake	0.17 to 0.25 mm
Exhaust	0.22 to 0.31 mm
ZX-9R B models	
Intake	0.18 to 0.23 mm
Exhaust	0.21 to 0.26 mm
ZX-9R C, E and F models	
Intake	0.15 to 0.24 mm
Exhaust	0.22 to 0.31 mm
Cylinder compression	
ZX-7R models	149 to 228 psi (10.5 to 16.0 bar)
ZX-9R B models	139 to 213 psi (9.8 to 15.0 bar)
ZX-9R C, E and F models	155 to 236 psi (10.9 to 16.5 bar)
Oil pressure (at 4000 rpm)	
ZX-7R models	46 to 54 psi (3.2 to 3.8 bar) at 80°C (176°F)
ZX-9R B models	44 to 53 psi (3.1 to 3.7 bar) at 80°C (176°F)
ZX-9R C, E and F models	17 to 26 psi (1.2 to 1.8 bar) at 90°C (194°F)

Cycle parts

Drive chain slack	
ZX-7R models	
Standard	30 to 35 mm
Maximum	40 mm
Minimum	30 mm
ZX-9R B models	
Standard	10 to 15 mm
Maximum	15 mm
Minimum	10 mm
ZX-9R C and E models	
Standard	20 to 35 mm
Maximum	40 mm
Minimum	20 mm
ZX-9R F models – standard	27 to 33 mm
Drive chain length over 20 links	317.5 to 318.2 mm
Service limit	323 mm
Brake pedal height	
ZX-7R models	70 mm approx.
ZX-9R models	43 mm approx.
Throttle cable freeplay	2 to 3 mm
Choke cable freeplay	2 to 3 mm
Clutch cable freeplay – ZX-9R C, E and F models	2 to 3 mm
Tyre pressures and tyre tread depth	see *Daily (pre-ride) checks*

Recommended lubricants and fluids

Engine/transmission oil type	API grade SF or SG motor oil
Engine/transmission oil viscosity	SAE 10W40, 10W50, 20W40 or 20W50
Engine/transmission oil capacity	
ZX-7R models	
Oil change	3.0 litres
Oil and filter change	3.1 litres
After overhaul (dry engine, new oil filter)	3.6 litres

Recommended lubricants and fluids (continued)

Engine/transmission oil capacity (continued)
  ZX-9R B models
    Oil change .... 3.4 litres
    Oil and filter change .... 3.5 litres
    After overhaul (dry engine, new oil filter) .... 4.0 litres
  ZX-9R C, E and F models
    Oil change .... 3.1 litres
    Oil and filter change .... 3.3 litres
    After overhaul (dry engine, new oil filter) .... 3.8 litres
Coolant type .... 50% distilled water, 50% corrosion inhibited ethylene glycol anti-freeze

Coolant capacity (including reservoir)
  ZX-7R models .... 2.6 litres
  ZX-9R B models .... 2.4 litres
  ZX-9R C, E and F models .... 2.9 litres
Front fork oil .... see Chapter 6
Brake fluid .... DOT 4
Clutch fluid – ZX-7R and ZX-9R B models .... DOT 4
Drive chain .... SAE 80 or 90 gear oil or aerosol chain lubricant for O-ring chains
Steering head bearings .... Multi-purpose grease
Wheel bearings (unsealed) .... Multi-purpose grease
Swingarm pivot bearings
  ZX-7R and ZX-9R B models .... Molybdenum disulphide grease
  ZX-9R C, E and F models .... Multi-purpose grease
Suspension linkage bearings
  ZX-7R and ZX-9R B models .... Molybdenum disulphide grease
  ZX-9R C, E and F models .... Multi-purpose grease
Oil/dust seal lips .... Multi-purpose grease
Brake lever/pedal pivots .... Multi-purpose grease or dry film lubricant
Clutch lever pivot .... Silicone grease or dry film lubricant
Cables .... Cable lubricant or 10W40 motor oil
Sidestand pivots .... Engine oil
Throttle grip .... Multi-purpose grease or dry film lubricant

Torque wrench settings

Bottom yoke fork clamp bolt
  ZX-7R and ZX-9R B models .... 28 Nm
  ZX-9R C, E and F models .... 20 Nm
Oil filter
  ZX-7R and ZX-9R B models .... 10 Nm
  ZX-9R C, E and F models .... 27 Nm
Oil pan drain plug .... 20 Nm
Oil passage plug – ZX-9R C, E and F models .... 20 Nm
Oil pipe fitting bolt – ZX-9R B models .... 10 Nm
Rear wheel axle
  ZX-7R and ZX-9R B models .... 145 Nm
  ZX-9R C models .... 110 Nm
  ZX-9R E models .... 125 Nm
  ZX-9R F models .... 127 Nm
Steering stem nut
  ZX-7R models .... 54 Nm
  ZX-9R B and C models .... 39 Nm
  ZX-9R E and F models .... 49 Nm
Spark plugs .... 13 Nm

All ZX-7R models and UK/Europe ZX-9R B3/B4 models

Note: *The daily (pre-ride) checks outlined in the owner's manual cover those items which should be inspected on a daily basis. Always perform the pre-ride inspection at every maintenance interval (in addition to the procedures listed). The intervals listed below are the intervals recommended by the manufacturer for each particular operation during the model years covered in this manual. Your owner's manual may have slightly different intervals for some items.*

Daily (pre-ride)
☐ See *'Daily (pre-ride) checks'* at the beginning of this manual.

After the initial 600 miles (1000 km)
Note: *This check is usually performed by a dealer after the first 600 miles (1000 km) from new. Thereafter, maintenance should be carried out according to the following intervals.*
☐ Change the engine oil and filter (Section 17).
☐ Check the operation of the braking system and brake light switch (Section 9).
☐ Check the steering head bearings (Section 10).
☐ Check the tightness of all nuts, bolts and fasteners (Section 22).
☐ Check the engine idle speed (Section 23).

Every 400 miles (600 km)
☐ Clean and lubricate the drive chain (Section 1).

Every 600 miles (1000 km)
☐ Check and adjust drive chain freeplay (Section 2).

Every 4000 miles (6000 km) or six months
☐ Check the spark plugs (Section 3).
☐ Check the air suction valves (Section 4).
☐ Check the evaporative emission control system (California models only) (Section 5).
☐ Change the engine oil (Section 6).
☐ Check for drive chain wear and stretch and sprocket wear (Section 7).
☐ Check the brake pads for wear (Section 8).
☐ Check the operation of the braking system and brake light switch (Section 9).
☐ Check the steering head bearings (Section 10).
☐ Check the wheel and tyre condition, and the tyre tread depth (Section 11).

Every 8000 miles (12,000 km) or twelve months
☐ Check the valve clearances (Section 12).
☐ Clean the air filter element (Section 13).
☐ Check carburettor synchronisation (Section 14).
☐ Check and lubricate the stands, lever pivots and cables (Section 15).
☐ Check throttle/choke cable operation and freeplay (Section 16).
☐ Change the engine oil and renew the oil filter (Section 17).
☐ Check the cooling system (Section 18).
☐ Check the fuel hoses and system components (Section 19).
☐ Check the front and rear suspension (Section 20).
☐ Re-grease the swingarm and suspension linkage bearings (Section 21).
☐ Check the tightness of all nuts and bolts (Section 22).
☐ Check the engine idle speed (Section 23).

Every 16,000 miles (24,000 km) or two years
☐ Change the brake fluid (Section 24).
☐ Change the clutch fluid (Section 25).
☐ Re-grease the steering head bearings (Section 26).
☐ Change the front fork oil (Section 27).
☐ Change the coolant (Section 28).

Every four years
☐ Renew the brake master cylinder and caliper seals (Section 29).
☐ Renew the clutch master cylinder and slave cylinder seals (Section 30).

Non-scheduled maintenance
☐ Check the battery (Section 31).
☐ Check the headlight aim (Section 32).
☐ Check the wheel bearings (Section 33).
☐ Check the cylinder compression (Section 34).
☐ Check the engine oil pressure (Section 35).

US ZX-9R B models and UK/Europe ZX-9R B1/B2 models

Note: *The daily (pre-ride) checks outlined in the owner's manual cover those items which should be inspected on a daily basis. Always perform the pre-ride inspection at every maintenance interval (in addition to the procedures listed). The intervals listed below are the intervals recommended by the manufacturer for each particular operation during the model years covered in this manual. Your owner's manual may have slightly different intervals for some items.*

Daily (pre-ride)
- [ ] See *'Daily (pre-ride) checks'* at the beginning of this manual.

After the initial 500 miles (800 km)
Note: *This check is usually performed by a dealer after the first 500 miles (800 km) from new. Thereafter, maintenance should be carried out according to the following intervals.*
- [ ] Check the valve clearances (Section 12).
- [ ] Clean the air filter element (Section 13).
- [ ] Check throttle/choke cable operation and freeplay (Section 16).
- [ ] Change the engine oil and filter (Section 17).
- [ ] Check the evaporative emission control system (California models only) (Section 5).
- [ ] Check carburettor synchronisation (Section 14).
- [ ] Check the operation of the braking system and brake light switch (Section 9).
- [ ] Check the steering head bearings (Section 10).
- [ ] Check the tightness of all nuts, bolts and fasteners (Section 22).
- [ ] Check the engine idle speed (Section 23).

Every 200 miles (300 km)
- [ ] Clean and lubricate the drive chain (Section 1).

Every 500 miles (800 km)
- [ ] Check and adjust drive chain freeplay (Section 2).

Every 3000 miles (5000 km) or six months
- [ ] Check the spark plugs (Section 3).
- [ ] Check the air suction valves (Section 4).
- [ ] Check the evaporative emission control system (California models only) (Section 5).
- [ ] Renew the fuel filter (Section 36).
- [ ] Check for drive chain wear and stretch and sprocket wear (Section 7).
- [ ] Check the brake pads for wear (Section 8).
- [ ] Check the operation of the braking system and brake light switch (Section 9).
- [ ] Check the steering head bearings (Section 10).
- [ ] Check the wheel and tyre condition, and the tyre tread depth (Section 11).
- [ ] Check carburettor synchronisation (Section 14).
- [ ] Check and lubricate the stands, lever pivots and cables (Section 15).
- [ ] Check the engine idle speed (Section 23).

Every 6000 miles (10,000 km) or twelve months
- [ ] Check the valve clearances (Section 12).
- [ ] Clean the air filter element and air vent filter (Section 13).
- [ ] Check throttle/choke cable operation and freeplay (Section 16).
- [ ] Change the engine oil and the oil filter (Section 17).
- [ ] Check the cooling system (Section 18).
- [ ] Check the fuel hoses and system components (Section 19).
- [ ] Check the front and rear suspension (Section 20).
- [ ] Re-grease the swingarm and suspension linkage bearings (Section 21).
- [ ] Check the tightness of all nuts and bolts (Section 22).

Every 12,000 miles (20,000 km) or two years
- [ ] Renew the air filter element and air vent filter (Section 37).
- [ ] Change the brake fluid (Section 24).
- [ ] Change the clutch fluid (Section 25).
- [ ] Re-grease the steering head bearings (Section 26).

Every 18,000 miles (30,000 km) or two years
- [ ] Change the front fork oil (Section 27).
- [ ] Change the coolant (Section 28).

Every two years
- [ ] Renew the brake master cylinder and caliper seals (Section 29).
- [ ] Renew the clutch master cylinder and slave cylinder seals (Section 30).

Every four years
- [ ] Renew the brake hoses (Section 38).
- [ ] Renew the clutch hose (Section 39).
- [ ] Renew the fuel hoses (Section 40).

Non-scheduled maintenance
- [ ] Check the battery (Section 31).
- [ ] Check the headlight aim (Section 32).
- [ ] Check the wheel bearings (Section 33).
- [ ] Check the cylinder compression (Section 34).
- [ ] Check the engine oil pressure (Section 35).

ZX-9R C, E and F models

Note: The daily (pre-ride) checks outlined in the owner's manual cover those items which should be inspected on a daily basis. Always perform the pre-ride inspection at every maintenance interval (in addition to the procedures listed). The intervals listed below are the intervals recommended by the manufacturer for each particular operation during the model years covered in this manual. Your owner's manual may have slightly different intervals for some items.

Daily (pre-ride)
☐ See *'Daily (pre-ride) checks'* at the beginning of this manual.

After the initial 600 miles (1000 km)
Note: This check is usually performed by a dealer after the first 600 miles (1000 km) from new. Thereafter, maintenance should be carried out according to the following intervals.
☐ Change the engine oil and filter (Section 17).
☐ Check and adjust drive chain freeplay (Section 2).
☐ Check the evaporative emission control system (California models only) (Section 5).
☐ Check the operation of the braking system and brake light switch (Section 9).
☐ Check the steering head bearings (Section 10).
☐ Check throttle/choke cable operation and freeplay (Section 16).
☐ Check the tightness of all nuts, bolts and fasteners (Section 22).
☐ Check the engine idle speed (Section 23).
☐ Check the operation of the clutch (Section 41).

Every 400 miles (600 km)
☐ Clean and lubricate the drive chain (Section 1).

Every 600 miles (1000 km)
☐ Check and adjust drive chain freeplay (Section 2).

Every 4000 miles (6000 km) or six months
☐ Check the spark plugs (Section 3).
☐ Check the air suction valves (Section 4).
☐ Check the evaporative emission control system (California models only) (Section 5).
☐ Change the engine oil (Section 6).
☐ Check for drive chain wear and stretch and sprocket wear (Section 7).
☐ Check the brake pads for wear (Section 8).
☐ Check the operation of the braking system and brake light switch (Section 9)
☐ Check the steering head bearings (Section 10).
☐ Check the wheel and tyre condition, and the tyre tread depth (Section 11).
☐ Check the operation of the clutch (Section 41).

Every 8000 miles (12,000 km) or twelve months
☐ Check the valve clearances (Section 12).
☐ Clean the air filter element and the air vent filter (Section 13).
☐ Check carburettor synchronisation (Section 14).
☐ Check and lubricate the stands, lever pivots and cables (Section 15).
☐ Check throttle/choke cable operation and freeplay (Section 16).
☐ Change the engine oil and renew the oil filter (Section 17).
☐ Check the cooling system (Section 18).
☐ Check the fuel hoses and system components (Section 19).
☐ Check the front and rear suspension (Section 20).
☐ Re-grease the swingarm and suspension linkage bearings (Section 21).
☐ Check the tightness of all nuts and bolts (Section 22).
☐ Check the engine idle speed (Section 23).

Every 16,000 miles (24,000 km) or two years
☐ Change the brake fluid (Section 24).
☐ Re-grease the steering head bearings (Section 26).
☐ Change the front fork oil (Section 27).
☐ Change the coolant (Section 28).

Every four years
☐ Renew the brake master cylinder and caliper seals (Section 29).

Non-scheduled maintenance
☐ Check the battery (Section 31).
☐ Check the headlight aim (Section 32).
☐ Check the wheel bearings (Section 33).
☐ Check the cylinder compression (Section 34).
☐ Check the engine oil pressure (Section 35).

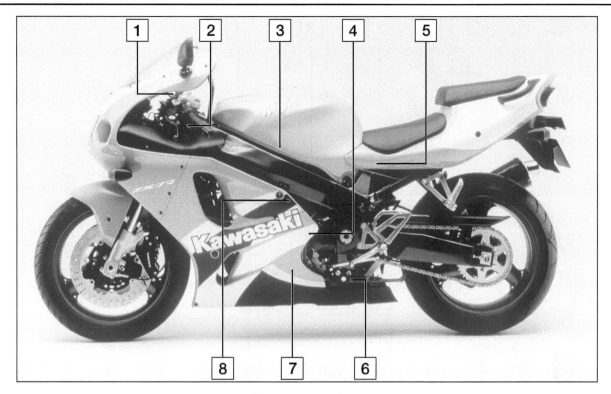

**Component locations –
ZX-7R models**

1 Clutch fluid reservoir
2 Steering head bearing
  adjuster
3 Air filter

4 Clutch slave cylinder
5 Battery
6 Engine oil drain bolt
7 Coolant drain bolt

8 Idle speed adjuster
9 Rear brake fluid reservoir
10 Coolant reservoir
11 Radiator pressure cap

12 Front brake fluid reservoir
13 Engine oil filter
14 Oil level window
15 Oil filler cap

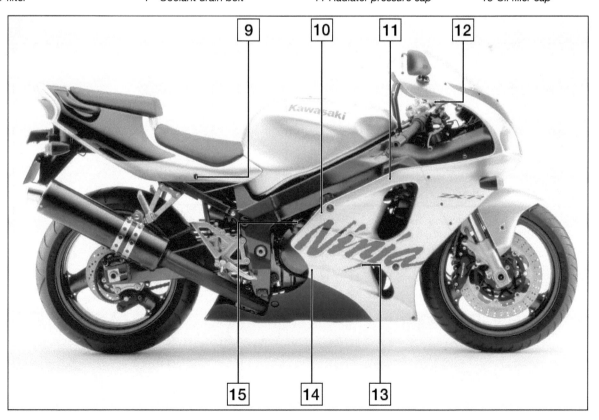

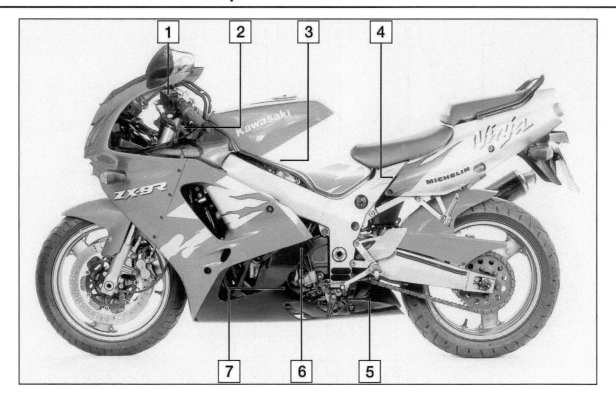

**Component locations –
ZX-9R B models**

1 Clutch fluid reservoir	4 Battery	8 Rear brake fluid reservoir	12 Front brake fluid reservoir
2 Steering head bearing adjuster	5 Engine oil drain bolt	9 Idle speed adjuster	13 Engine oil filter
	6 Clutch slave cylinder	10 Oil filler cap	14 Engine oil window
3 Air filter	7 Coolant drain bolt	11 Radiator pressure cap	15 Coolant reservoir

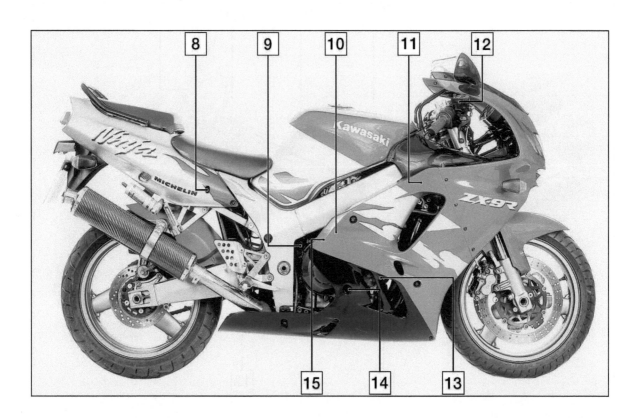

**Component locations –
ZX-9R C, E and F models**

1 Clutch cable upper adjuster
2 Steering head bearing
   adjuster
3 Air filter
4 Coolant reservoir
5 Battery
6 Engine oil drain bolt
7 Idle speed adjuster
8 Coolant drain bolt
9 Rear brake fluid reservoir
10 Clutch cable lower adjuster
11 Front brake fluid reservoir
12 Radiator pressure cap
13 Engine oil filter
14 Engine oil window
15 Engine oil filler cap

Introduction

1 This Chapter is designed to help the home mechanic maintain his/her motorcycle for safety, economy, long life and peak performance.

2 Deciding where to start or plug into the routine maintenance schedule depends on several factors. If the warranty period on your motorcycle has just expired, and if it has been maintained according to the warranty standards, you may want to pick up routine maintenance as it coincides with the next mileage or calendar interval. If you have owned the machine for some time but have never performed any maintenance on it, then you may want to start at the nearest interval and include some additional procedures to ensure that nothing important is overlooked. If you have just had a major engine overhaul, then you may want to start the maintenance routine from the beginning. If you have a used machine and have no knowledge of its history or maintenance record, you may desire to combine all the checks into one large service initially and then settle into the maintenance schedule prescribed.

3 Before beginning any maintenance or repair, the machine should be cleaned thoroughly, especially around the oil filter, spark plugs, valve cover, seat cowling, etc. Cleaning will help ensure that dirt does not contaminate the engine and will allow you to detect wear and damage that could otherwise easily go unnoticed.

4 Certain maintenance information is sometimes printed on decals attached to the motorcycle. If the information on the decals differs from that included here, use the information on the decal.

Maintenance procedures

1 Drive chain – cleaning and lubrication

Interval

US ZX-9R B models and UK/Europe ZX-9R B1 and B2 models – every 200 miles (300 km)
All other models – every 400 miles (600 km)

1 Support the machine on an auxiliary stand so that the rear wheel is off the ground. Rotate the rear wheel whilst cleaning and lubricating the chain to access all the links.

2 Wash the chain in paraffin (kerosene), then wipe it off and allow it to dry, using compressed air if available. If the chain is excessively dirty, it should be removed from the machine and allowed to soak in the paraffin (see Chapter 6).

Caution: Don't use petrol, solvent or other cleaning fluids which might damage the internal sealing properties of the chain. Don't use high-pressure water. The entire process shouldn't take longer than ten minutes – If It does, the O-rings in the chain rollers could be damaged.

3 The best time to lubricate the chain is after the motorcycle has been ridden, as when the chain is warm the lubricant penetrates the joints between the side plates better than when cold.

1.4 Apply the oil to the top of the lower run where the sideplates overlap

4 Apply the specified lubricant (see Specifications at the beginning of the Chapter) to the area where the side plates overlap – not to the middle of the rollers – covering the inside edge as well as the outside **(see illustration)**. After applying the lubricant, let it soak in for a few minutes before wiping off any excess.

> **HAYNES HiNT** *Apply lubricant to the top of the lower chain run – centrifugal force will work it into the chain when the bike is moving.*

2 Drive chain – check and adjustment

Interval:

US ZX-9R B models and UK/Europe ZX-9R B1 and B2 models – every 500 miles (800 km)
All other models – every 600 miles (1000 km)

Check

1 A neglected drive chain won't last long and can quickly damage the sprockets. Routine chain adjustment will ensure maximum chain and sprocket life.

2 To check the chain, shift the transmission into neutral and make sure the ignition switch is OFF. Rotate the rear wheel until the chain is positioned with the tightest point at the centre of its bottom run, then place the machine on its sidestand. Make sure that the adjuster is in the same position on each side relative to the notches in the swingarm.

3 Measure the amount of freeplay on the chain's bottom run at a point midway between the two sprockets; on ZX-9R B models, take the measurement at the rear of the lower edge of the swingarm chainguard. Compare your measurement to the value listed in this Chapter's Specifications **(see illustration)**. Since the chain will rarely wear evenly, rotate the rear wheel so that another section of chain can be checked; do this several times to check the entire length of chain. In some cases where lubrication has been neglected, corrosion and galling may cause the links to bind and kink, which effectively shortens the chain's length. If the chain is tight between the sprockets, rusty or kinked, or if any of the pins are loose or the rollers damaged, it's time to renew it. If you find a tight area, mark it with felt pen or paint, and repeat the measurement after the bike has been ridden. If the chain's still tight in the same area, it may be damaged or worn. Because a tight or kinked chain can damage the transmission output shaft bearing, it's a good idea to renew it.

Adjustment

4 Rotate the rear wheel until the chain is positioned with the tightest point at the centre of its bottom run, then place the machine on its sidestand.

5 Remove the split pin from the rear axle nut, then slacken the nut **(see illustration)**.

6 Slacken the adjuster locknut on each side of the swingarm, then turn the adjusters evenly until the amount of freeplay specified at the beginning of the Chapter is obtained at the centre of the bottom run of the chain. If the chain was too tight and the adjusters have been turned in to create slack, kick the back of the rear tyre to ensure all the created slack has been taken up. Following chain

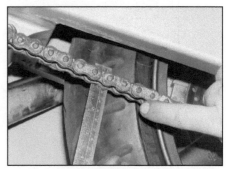

2.3 Push up on the chain and measure the slack

2.5 Slacken the rear axle nut

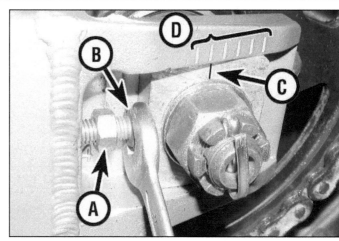

2.6 Slacken the locknut (A) and then turn the adjuster (B). Make sure that the alignment mark (C) on the adjuster is in the same position in relation to the marks on the swingarm (D)

adjustment, check that the mark on the top of each chain adjuster marker is in the same position in relation to the marks on the swingarm **(see illustration)**. It is important that each adjuster aligns with the same notch; if not, the rear wheel will be out of alignment with the front.

7 If there is a discrepancy in the chain adjuster positions, adjust one of the chain adjusters so that its position is exactly the same as the other. Check the chain freeplay as described above and readjust if necessary.

8 Tighten the axle nut to the torque setting specified at the beginning of the Chapter, then tighten the adjuster locknuts securely **(see**

illustration)**. Fit a new split pin onto the axle nut **(see illustration)**.

3 Spark plugs – gap check and adjustment

Interval:

US ZX-9R B models and UK/Europe ZX-9R B1 and B2 models – every 3000 miles (5000 km)
All other models – every 4000 miles (6000 km)

1 Make sure your spark plug socket is the correct size (16 mm hex) before attempting to remove the plugs – a suitable one is supplied in the motorcycle's tool kit, which is stored under the seat.

2 Remove the air filter housing (see Chapter 4).

3 Clean the area around the plug caps to prevent any dirt falling into the spark plug channels. If required, move aside or detach the vacuum valve components to improve access.

4 On ZX-7R and ZX-9R B models, check that the cylinder location is marked on each plug lead, then pull the spark plug cap off each spark plug **(see illustration)**.

5 On ZX-9R C, E and F models, disconnect the wiring connector from each ignition coil and remove the coils from the engine **(see illustrations)**.

6 On all models, using either the plug removing tool supplied in the bike's toolkit or a socket-type wrench, unscrew the plugs from the cylinder head **(see illustration)**. Lay each plug out in relation to its cylinder; if either plug shows up a problem, it will then be easy to identify the troublesome cylinder.

7 Inspect the electrodes for wear. Both the centre and side electrodes should have square edges and the side electrode(s) (ZX-9R standard spark plugs have twin side electrodes) should be

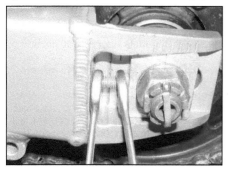

2.8a Tighten the adjuster locknuts securely

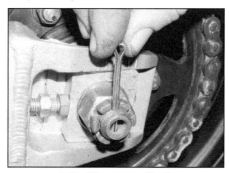

2.8b Fit a new split pin

3.4 Remove the spark plug cap (ZX-7R and ZX-9R B models)

3.5a Disconnect the wiring connector . . .

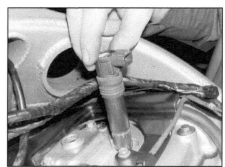

3.5b . . . and remove the ignition coils

3.6 Remove the spark plugs

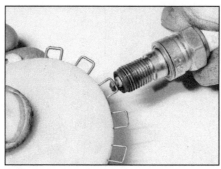

3.10a Using a wire-type gauge to measure the spark plug electrode gap

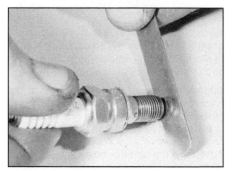

3.10b Using a feeler gauge to measure the spark plug electrode gap

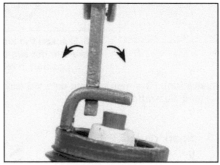

3.10c Adjust the electrode gap by bending the side electrode only

of uniform thickness. Look for excessive deposits and evidence of a cracked or chipped insulator around the centre electrode. Compare your spark plugs to the colour spark plug reading chart at the end of this manual. Check the threads, the washer and the ceramic insulator body for cracks and other damage.

8 If the electrodes are not excessively worn, and if the deposits can be easily removed with a wire brush, the plugs can be re-gapped and re-used (if no cracks or chips are visible in the insulator). If in doubt concerning the condition of the plugs, renew them, as the expense is minimal.

9 Cleaning spark plugs by sandblasting is permitted, provided you clean the plugs with a high flash-point solvent afterwards.

10 Before installing the plugs, make sure they are the correct type and heat range and check the gap between the electrodes (they are not pre-set on new plugs). For best results, use a

wire-type gauge rather than a flat (feeler) gauge to check the gap **(see illustrations)**. Compare the gap to that specified and adjust as necessary. If the gap must be adjusted, bend the side electrode only and be very careful not to chip or crack the insulator nose **(see illustration)**. Make sure the washer is in place before installing each plug.

11 Since the cylinder head is made of aluminium, which is soft and easily damaged, thread the plugs into the heads, turning the tool by hand. Once the plugs are finger-tight, the job can be finished with a spanner on the tool or a with socket drive. Tighten the plugs an additional 1/4 to 1/2 turn, or as directed on the manufacturer's packaging. If a torque wrench can be fitted to the socket/wrench, tighten the plugs to the specified torque.

12 On ZX-7R and ZX-9R B models, reconnect the spark plug caps, making sure they are securely connected to the correct cylinder.

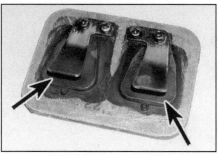

4.2 Check the reeds (arrowed) and their contact areas on the air suction valve for damage and wear as described

HAYNES HiNT *As the plugs are quite recessed, slip a short length of hose over the end of the plug to use as a tool to thread it into place. The hose will grip the plug well enough to turn it, but will start to slip if the plug begins to cross-thread in the hole – this will prevent damaged threads. Stripped plug threads in the cylinder head can be repaired with a thread insert – see Section 2 of Tools and Workshop Tips in the Reference section.*

13 On ZX-9R C, E and F models, fit the ignition coils to the plugs and securely reconnect each wiring connector to its correct coil (see Chapter 5).

14 On all models, install the air filter housing (see Chapter 4).

4 Air suction valve – check

Interval:

> US ZX-9R B models and UK/Europe ZX-9R B1 and B2 models – every 3000 miles (5000 km)
> All other models – every 4000 miles (6000 km)

1 Remove the secondary air injection system air suction valves as described in Chapter 4.

2 Check the valve reeds for cracks, warpage and any other damage or deterioration **(see illustration)**. Also check the contact areas between the reeds and the reed holders, and the holders themselves. Any carbon deposits or other foreign particles can be cleaned off using a high flash-point solvent. Renew the reed valve assemblies if there is any doubt about their condition. Also check the condition of the upper and lower gaskets, and renew them if necessary.

3 Install the valves as described in Chapter 4.

5 Evaporative emission control (EVAP) system – check (California models)

Interval:

> ZX-9R B models – every 3000 miles (5000 km)
> All other models – every 4000 miles (6000 km)

Periodically check the charcoal canister and its hoses for signs of damage; the seats, side covers/seat cowling and fuel tank will have to be removed to do this properly (see Chapters 4 and 8). If any component shows signs of damage it must be renewed. Refer to Chapter 4 for further information.

6 Engine – oil change

Interval:

> US ZX-9R B models and UK/Europe ZX-9R B1 and B2 models – not specified
> All other models – every 4000 miles (6000 km)

 Warning: Be careful when draining the oil, as the exhaust pipes, the engine, and the oil itself can cause severe burns.

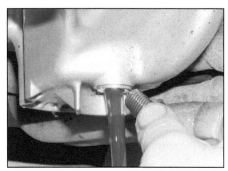

6.4 Remove the oil drain plug

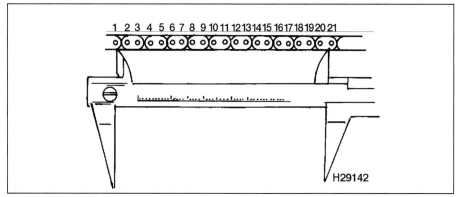

7.2 Measure the distance between 21 pins as shown, to determine chain stretch

1 Consistent routine oil changes are the single most important maintenance procedure you can perform on a motorcycle. The oil not only lubricates the internal parts of the engine, transmission and clutch, but also acts as coolant, cleaner, sealant, and protectant. Because of these demands, the oil takes a terrific amount of abuse and should be renewed often with new oil of the recommended grade and type (see Specifications at the beginning of this Chapter).

 HiNT *Saving a little money on the difference between good and cheap oils won't pay off if the engine is damaged as a result.*

2 Before changing the oil, warm up the engine so the oil will drain easily.

3 Support the motorcycle upright using an auxiliary stand, and position a clean drain tray below the engine. Unscrew the oil filler cap on the clutch cover to vent the crankcase and to act as a reminder that there is no oil in the engine.

4 Next, unscrew the oil drain plug from the bottom of the engine and allow the oil to flow into the drain tray **(see illustration)**. Check the condition of the drain plug sealing washer. If it is damaged or deformed, discard it and use a new one.

 HiNT *To help determine whether any abnormal or excessive engine wear is occurring, place a strainer between the engine and the drain tray so that any debris in the oil is filtered out and can be examined. If there are flakes or chips of metal in the oil, then something is drastically wrong internally and the engine will have to be disassembled for inspection and repair. If there are pieces of fibre-like material in the oil, the clutch is experiencing excessive wear and should be checked.*

5 When the oil has completely drained, fit the sealing washer over the drain plug, using a new one if necessary, then fit the plug to the oil pan and tighten it to the torque setting specified at the beginning of the Chapter.

Avoid overtightening, as damage to the sump will result.

6 Refill the crankcase to the proper level using the recommended type and amount of oil, as emphasised above. With the motorcycle on its wheels and held vertical, the oil level should lie between the upper and lower level lines on the inspection window in the clutch cover (see *Daily (pre-ride) checks*). Install the filler cap. Start the engine and let it run for two or three minutes (make sure that the oil pressure light extinguishes after a few seconds). Shut it off, wait a few minutes, then check the oil level. If necessary, add more oil to bring the level up to the high level line on the inspection window. Check around the drain plug for leaks.

7 The old oil drained from the engine cannot be re-used and should be disposed of properly. Check with your local refuse disposal company, disposal facility or environmental agency to see whether they will accept the used oil for recycling. Don't pour used oil into drains or onto the ground.

 *Note: It is antisocial and illegal to dump oil down the drain. To find the location of your nearest oil recycling bank in the UK, call this number free. In the USA, note that any oil supplier must accept used oil for recycling.*

0800 66 33 66

7 **Drive chain and sprockets –** wear check

Interval:
  US ZX-9 R B models and UK/Europe ZX-9R B1 and B2 models – every 3000 miles (5000 km)
  All other models – every 4000 miles (6000 km)

1 Check the entire length of the chain for damaged rollers, cracked sideplates, loose links and pins, and renew the chain if damage is found. If the chain has reached the end of its adjustment, it must be renewed.

2 The amount of chain stretch can be measured and compared to the stretch limit specified at the beginning of the Chapter. Remove the screws securing the chainguard to the swingarm and remove the guard, noting how it fits. Hang a 10 kg (22 lb) weight from the bottom run of the chain. Measure along the top run the length of 21 pins (from the centre of the 1st pin to the centre of the 21st pin) and compare the result with the service limit specified at the beginning of the Chapter **(see illustration)**. Rotate the rear wheel so that several sections of the chain are measured. If any of the measurements exceeds the service limit the chain and sprockets must be renewed as a set. **Note:** *Never install a new chain on old sprockets, and never use the old chain if you install new sprockets – renew the chain and sprockets as a set*

3 Remove the engine sprocket cover (see Chapter 6). Check the teeth on the engine sprocket and the rear wheel sprocket for wear **(see illustration)**.

4 Inspect the drive chain slider on the swingarm for excessive wear and renew it if necessary (see Chapter 6).

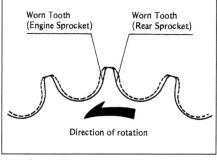

7.3 Check the teeth on both sprockets to determine whether they are excessively worn

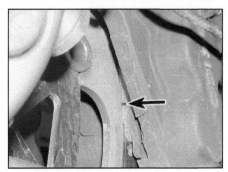

8.1a Front brake pad wear indicator groove (arrowed)

8 Brake pad –
wear check

Interval:

> **US ZX-9R B models and UK/Europe ZX-9R B1 and B2 models – every 3000 miles (5000 km)**
> **All other models – every 4000 miles (6000 km)**

1 A quick check of the brake pads can be made without removing them from the caliper. The amount of pad wear can be judged by looking at the pads from the front or rear of

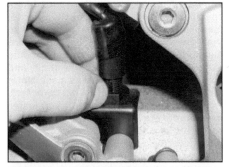

9.5 Hold the switch and turn the adjusting nut as required

the caliper. A cutout in the friction material indicates the wear limit **(see illustrations)**.

2 If either pad has worn down to, or beyond, the cutout/grooves in the friction material, both pads must be renewed as a set. If the pads are dirty, or if you are in doubt as to the amount of friction material remaining, remove them for inspection (see Chapter 7). **Note:** *Some after-market pads may use different indicators to those on the original equipment as shown.*

3 Refer to Chapter 7 for details of pad renewal.

9 Brake system –
check

Interval:

> **US ZX-9R B models and UK/Europe ZX-9R B1 and B2 models – every 3000 miles (5000 km)**
> **All other models – every 4000 miles (6000 km)**

1 A routine general check of the brake system will ensure that any problems are discovered and remedied before the rider's safety is jeopardised.

2 Check the brake lever and pedal for loose connections, improper or rough action, excessive play, bends, and other damage. Renew any damaged parts with new ones (see Chapter 7).

3 Make sure all brake fasteners are tight. Check the brake pads for wear (see Section 8) and make sure that the fluid level in the reservoirs is correct (see *Daily (pre-ride) checks*). Look for leaks at the hose connections and check for cracks in the hoses. If the lever or pedal is spongy, bleed the brakes (see Chapter 7).

4 Make sure the brake light operates when the front brake lever is depressed. The front brake light switch is not adjustable. If it fails to operate properly, check it (see Chapter 9).

5 Make sure the brake light is activated after about 10 mm of brake pedal travel or just

8.1b Rear brake pad wear indicator cut-out (arrowed)

before the rear brake takes effect. If adjustment is necessary, hold the switch and turn the adjusting nut on the switch body until the brake light is activated when required **(see illustration)**. If the switch doesn't operate the brake lights, check it (see Chapter 9).

6 Check the position of the brake pedal. Kawasaki recommend that the distance from the pedal tip to the top of the rider's footrest should be as specified at the beginning of the Chapter. If the pedal height is incorrect, or if the rider's preference is different, slacken the clevis locknut on the master cylinder pushrod, then turn the pushrod using a spanner on the hex at the top of the rod until the pedal is at the correct or desired height **(see illustrations)**. If access to the pushrod is too restricted, remove the footrest bracket mounting bolts, then draw the bracket away from the frame, taking care not to twist or strain the brake hoses (see Chapter 6). On completion tighten the locknut securely. Adjust the rear brake light switch after adjusting the pedal height (see Step 5).

7 The front brake lever has a span adjuster which alters the distance of the lever from the handlebar. Pull the lever away from the handlebar and turn the adjuster dial until the setting which best suits the rider is obtained. There are four positions; align the number for the setting required with the triangular mark on the lever bracket.

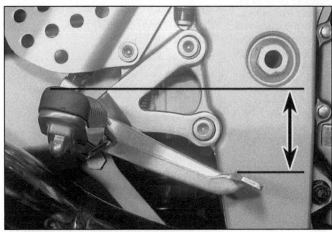

9.6a Measure the distance between the pedal tip and the top of the footrest as shown

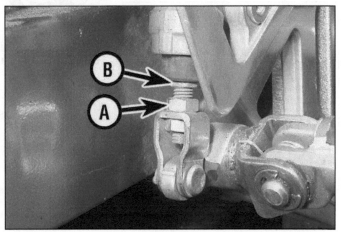

9.6b Slacken the locknut (A) and turn the pushrod using the hex (B)

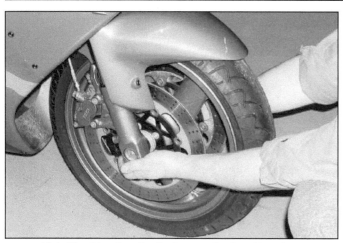

10.4 Checking for play in the steering head bearings

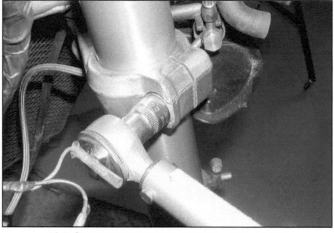

10.5 Slacken the bottom yoke fork clamps bolts

10 Steering head bearings – check and adjustment

Interval:

US ZX-9R B models and UK/Europe ZX-9R B1 and B2 models – every 3000 miles (5000 km)
All other models – every 4000 miles (6000 km)

1 This motorcycle is equipped with tapered-roller type or caged ball steering head bearings which can become dented, rough or loose during normal use of the machine. In extreme cases, worn or loose steering head bearings can cause steering wobble – a condition that is potentially dangerous.

Check

2 Place the motorcycle on an auxiliary stand. Raise the front wheel off the ground either by having an assistant push down on the rear, or by removing the lower fairing panels (see Chapter 8) and placing a support under the engine.
3 Point the front wheel straight ahead and slowly move the handlebars from side to side. Any dents or roughness in the bearing races will be felt and the bars will not move smoothly and freely. With the wheel pointing straight ahead, tap the end of each bar in turn. The handlebars should travel to the full-lock position under the force of gravity alone. If not, and it is not due to interference from wiring or cables, the bearings are overtight.
4 Next, grasp the fork sliders and try to move them forward and backward **(see illustration)**. Any looseness in the steering head bearings will be felt as front-to-rear movement of the forks. If play is felt in the bearings, adjust the steering head as follows.

 Freeplay in the fork due to worn fork bushes can be misinterpreted for steering head bearing play – do not confuse the two.

Adjustment

5 Remove the upper fairing (see Chapter 8) and the air filter housing (see Chapter 4). Slacken the steering stem nut, then slacken the bottom yoke fork clamp bolts **(see illustration)**.
6 If necessary, to improve access unbolt the upper fairing/rear view mirror bracket from the frame and remove it from the bike. On ZX-9R E and F models, remove the air filter intake duct cover brackets from the bracket mounting rubbers noting that the left- and right-hand brackets are different. On all other models, recover the collars from the bracket mounting rubbers.
7 Using a suitable C-spanner or drift located in one of the notches in the adjuster ring locknut, slacken the locknut. Now initially slacken the adjuster ring, then tighten or slacken it a little bit at a time as required until all freeplay in the forks is removed, yet the steering is able to move freely from side to side. Do not turn the adjuster ring more than 1/8 turn at a time. The object is to set the adjuster ring so that the bearings are under a very light loading, just enough to remove any freeplay. Tighten the locknut against the adjuster ring finger-tight only.
Caution: Take great care not to apply excessive pressure because this will cause premature failure of the bearings.
8 If the bearings cannot be set up properly, or if there is any binding, roughness or notchiness, they will have to be removed for inspection or renewal (see Chapter 6).
9 With the bearings correctly adjusted, tighten the steering stem nut and the fork clamp bolts to the torque settings specified at the beginning of the Chapter.
10 Re-check the bearing adjustment as described above and re-adjust if necessary.
11 Where necessary, ensure the mounting rubbers and collars/mounting brackets (as applicable) are correctly positioned, then fit the fairing/rear view mirror bracket to the frame.
12 Install the air filter housing (see Chapter 4) and the upper fairing (see Chapter 8).

11 Wheels and tyres – general check

Interval:

US ZX-9R B models and UK/Europe ZX-9R B1 and B2 models – every 3000 miles (5000 km)
All other models – every 4000 miles (6000 km)

Tyres

1 Check the tyre condition and tread depth thoroughly – see *Daily (pre-ride) checks*.

Wheels

2 Cast wheels are virtually maintenance free, but they should be kept clean and checked periodically for cracks and other damage. Also check the wheel runout and alignment (see Chapter 7). Never attempt to repair damaged cast wheels; they must be renewed if damaged. Check the valve rubber for signs of damage or deterioration and have it renewed if necessary. Also, make sure the valve stem cap is in place and tight.

12 Valve clearances – check and adjustment

Interval:

US ZX-9R B models and UK/Europe ZX-9R B1 and B2 models – every 6000 miles (10,000 km)
All other models – every 8000 miles (12,000 km)

Check

1 The engine must be completely cool for this maintenance procedure, so let the machine sit overnight before beginning.
2 Remove the cylinder head cover (see Chapter 2A or 2B).

12.6 Turn the engine using a socket on the rotor hex until the T 1.4 mark aligns with the crankcase lug index mark

12.8 The cam lobes should look like this

3 Remove the spark plugs to allow the engine to be turned over more easily (see Section 3).

4 Make a chart or sketch of all four valve positions so that a note of each clearance can be made against the relevant valve.

5 Remove the pick-up coil cover from the right-hand end of the crankshaft (see Chapter 5).

6 On ZX-7R and ZX-9R B models, using a socket or spanner on the timing rotor hex, rotate the crankshaft clockwise until the 'T' mark of Nos. 1 and 4 cylinders is aligned with the index mark on the crankcase lug at the base of the rotor **(see illustration)**. **Note:** *Always turn the engine in the normal direction of rotation (clockwise – viewed from the right-hand end of the engine).*

Caution: Never turn the engine over on the timing rotor Allen bolt. Always use the timing rotor hex.

7 On ZX-9R C, E and F models, using a socket or spanner on the timing rotor bolt, rotate the crankshaft clockwise until the 'T' mark of Nos. 1 and 4 cylinders is aligned with the crankcase mating surface join located to the rear of the rotor **(see illustration 9.10 in Chapter 2B)**. **Note:** *Always turn the engine in the normal direction of rotation (clockwise – viewed from the right-hand end of the engine).*

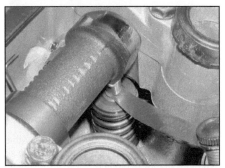

12.11a Insert the feeler gauge between the rocker arm and the shim

8 On all models, with the crankshaft positioned as described, either No. 1 or No. 4 cylinder will be at top dead centre (TDC) on the compression stroke. To determine which one is, check the position of the cam lobes on No. 1 cylinder **(see illustration)**. If they are facing away from each other and are not depressing the valves, No. 1 cylinder is at TDC on the compression stroke. If the cam lobes on No. 1 cylinder are facing each other and are depressing the valves, the lobes on No. 4 cylinder will be facing away from each other and No. 4 is at TDC on the compression stroke.

9 With No. 1 cylinder at TDC on the compression stroke, the following valves can be checked.

 a) No. 1 cylinder intake and exhaust valves.
 b) No. 2 cylinder exhaust valves.
 c) No. 3 cylinder intake valves.

10 With No. 4 cylinder at TDC on the compression stroke, the following valves can be checked.

 a) No. 2 cylinder intake valves.
 b) No. 3 cylinder exhaust valves.
 c) No. 4 cylinder intake and exhaust valves.

11 Insert a feeler gauge of the same thickness as the correct valve clearance (see Specifications at the beginning of this Chapter). On ZX-9R B models insert the feeler gauge between the rocker arm and shim of each valve **(see illustration)** and, on all other models, insert the gauge between the cam lobe and follower of each valve. Check that the gauge is a firm sliding fit – you should feel a slight drag when you pull the gauge out. If not, use the feeler gauges to obtain the exact clearance. Record the measured clearance on the chart **(see illustrations)**.

12 Rotate the engine so that the timing rotor turns through 360° and measure the valve clearance of the remaining valves using the method described in Step 11.

13 When all clearances have been measured and charted, identify whether the clearance

on any valve falls outside that specified and adjust it as described below.

14 Once all the valve clearances are known to be correct, lubricate all bearing surfaces with clean engine oil, then fit the cylinder head cover (see Chapter 2A or 2B) and install the spark plugs (see Section 3).

15 Fit the pick-up coil cover (Chapter 5) and check the engine oil level (see *Daily (pre-ride) checks*) before starting the engine.

Adjustment

> **HAYNES HiNT**
>
> *If more than one valve clearance requires adjustment, before ordering all new shims, check that the shim sizes required are not fitted to any of the other valves being adjusted. Shims can be swapped between valves and this will cut down on the number of new shims required. Retain all old shims in a safe place as they may come in handy when the valve clearances are next adjusted.*

ZX-9R B models

16 On ZX-9R B models, the valve clearances can be adjusted without removing the camshafts. Adjustment for each valve is as follows.

17 With the camshafts correctly positioned (see Steps 8 to 10) so that the valve requiring adjustment is in the checking position, slide the rocker arm sideways along its shaft, then pivot it downwards. Slowly release the rocker arm and allow it to rest against the side of the valve spring.

18 Remove the shim from the top of the valve using a magnet or a pair of pliers.

Caution: Take great care not to drop the shim down into the engine as it is removed.

12.11b Inlet valve selection chart (ZX-7R models) — INSTALL THE SHIM OF THIS THICKNESS (mm)

VALVE CLEARANCE MEASUREMENT — PART No. (92180 -)	1014	1016	1018	1020	1022	1024	1026	1028	1030	1032	1034	1036	1038	1040	1042	1044	1046	1048	1050	1052	1054
MARK	50	55	60	65	70	75	80	85	90	95	00	05	10	15	20	25	30	35	40	45	50
THICKNESS (mm)	2.50	2.55	2.60	2.65	2.70	2.75	2.80	2.85	2.90	2.95	3.00	3.05	3.10	3.15	3.20	3.25	3.30	3.35	3.40	3.45	3.50
0.00 ~ 0.01					2.50	2.55	2.60	2.65	2.70	2.75	2.80	2.85	2.90	2.95	3.00	3.05	3.10	3.15	3.20	3.25	3.30
0.02 ~ 0.06				2.50	2.55	2.60	2.65	2.70	2.75	2.80	2.85	2.90	2.95	3.00	3.05	3.10	3.15	3.20	3.25	3.30	3.35
0.07 ~ 0.11			2.50	2.55	2.60	2.65	2.70	2.75	2.80	2.85	2.90	2.95	3.00	3.05	3.10	3.15	3.20	3.25	3.30	3.35	3.40
0.12 ~ 0.16		2.50	2.55	2.60	2.65	2.70	2.75	2.80	2.85	2.90	2.95	3.00	3.05	3.10	3.15	3.20	3.25	3.30	3.35	3.40	3.45
0.17 ~ 0.25	SPECIFIED CLEARANCE/NO CHANGE REQUIRED																				
0.26 ~ 0.30	2.55	2.60	2.65	2.70	2.75	2.80	2.85	2.90	2.95	3.00	3.05	3.10	3.15	3.20	3.25	3.30	3.35	3.40	3.45	3.50	
0.31 ~ 0.35	2.60	2.65	2.70	2.75	2.80	2.85	2.90	2.95	3.00	3.05	3.10	3.15	3.20	3.25	3.30	3.35	3.40	3.45	3.50		
0.36 ~ 0.40	2.65	2.70	2.75	2.80	2.85	2.90	2.95	3.00	3.05	3.10	3.15	3.20	3.25	3.30	3.35	3.40	3.45	3.50			
0.41 ~ 0.45	2.70	2.75	2.80	2.85	2.90	2.95	3.00	3.05	3.10	3.15	3.20	3.25	3.30	3.35	3.40	3.45	3.50				
0.46 ~ 0.50	2.75	2.80	2.85	2.90	2.95	3.00	3.05	3.10	3.15	3.20	3.25	3.30	3.35	3.40	3.45	3.50					
0.51 ~ 0.55	2.80	2.85	2.90	2.95	3.00	3.05	3.10	3.15	3.20	3.25	3.30	3.35	3.40	3.45	3.50						
0.56 ~ 0.60	2.85	2.90	2.95	3.00	3.05	3.10	3.15	3.20	3.25	3.30	3.35	3.40	3.45	3.50							
0.61 ~ 0.65	2.90	2.95	3.00	3.05	3.10	3.15	3.20	3.25	3.30	3.35	3.40	3.45	3.50								
0.66 ~ 0.70	2.95	3.00	3.05	3.10	3.15	3.20	3.25	3.30	3.35	3.40	3.45	3.50									
0.71 ~ 0.75	3.00	3.05	3.10	3.15	3.20	3.25	3.30	3.35	3.40	3.45	3.50										
0.76 ~ 0.80	3.05	3.10	3.15	3.20	3.25	3.30	3.35	3.40	3.45	3.50											
0.81 ~ 0.85	3.10	3.15	3.20	3.25	3.30	3.35	3.40	3.45	3.50												
0.86 ~ 0.90	3.15	3.20	3.25	3.30	3.35	3.40	3.45	3.50													
0.91 ~ 0.95	3.20	3.25	3.30	3.35	3.40	3.45	3.50														
0.96 ~ 1.00	3.25	3.30	3.35	3.40	3.45	3.50															
1.01 ~ 1.05	3.30	3.35	3.40	3.45	3.50																
1.06 ~ 1.10	3.35	3.40	3.45	3.50																	
1.11 ~ 1.15	3.40	3.45	3.50																		
1.16 ~ 1.20	3.45	3.50																			
1.21 ~ 1.25	3.50																				

12.11c Exhaust valve selection chart (ZX-7R models) — INSTALL THE SHIM OF THIS THICKNESS (mm)

VALVE CLEARANCE MEASUREMENT — PART No. (92180 -)	1014	1016	1018	1020	1022	1024	1026	1028	1030	1032	1034	1036	1038	1040	1042	1044	1046	1048	1050	1052	1054
MARK	50	55	60	65	70	75	80	85	90	95	00	05	10	15	20	25	30	35	40	45	50
THICKNESS (mm)	2.50	2.55	2.60	2.65	2.70	2.75	2.80	2.85	2.90	2.95	3.00	3.05	3.10	3.15	3.20	3.25	3.30	3.35	3.40	3.45	3.50
0.00 ~ 0.01						2.50	2.55	2.60	2.65	2.70	2.75	2.80	2.85	2.90	2.95	3.00	3.05	3.10	3.15	3.20	3.25
0.02 ~ 0.06					2.50	2.55	2.60	2.65	2.70	2.75	2.80	2.85	2.90	2.95	3.00	3.05	3.10	3.15	3.20	3.25	3.30
0.07 ~ 0.11				2.50	2.55	2.60	2.65	2.70	2.75	2.80	2.85	2.90	2.95	3.00	3.05	3.10	3.15	3.20	3.25	3.30	3.35
0.12 ~ 0.16			2.50	2.55	2.60	2.65	2.70	2.75	2.80	2.85	2.90	2.95	3.00	3.05	3.10	3.15	3.20	3.25	3.30	3.35	3.40
0.17 ~ 0.21		2.50	2.55	2.60	2.65	2.70	2.75	2.80	2.85	2.90	2.95	3.00	3.05	3.10	3.15	3.20	3.25	3.30	3.35	3.40	3.45
0.22 ~ 0.31	SPECIFIED CLEARANCE/NO CHANGE REQUIRED																				
0.32 ~ 0.36	2.55	2.60	2.65	2.70	2.75	2.80	2.85	2.90	2.95	3.00	3.05	3.10	3.15	3.20	3.25	3.30	3.35	3.40	3.45	3.50	
0.37 ~ 0.41	2.60	2.65	2.70	2.75	2.80	2.85	2.90	2.95	3.00	3.05	3.10	3.15	3.20	3.25	3.30	3.35	3.40	3.45	3.50		
0.42 ~ 0.46	2.65	2.70	2.75	2.80	2.85	2.90	2.95	3.00	3.05	3.10	3.15	3.20	3.25	3.30	3.35	3.40	3.45	3.50			
0.47 ~ 0.51	2.70	2.75	2.80	2.85	2.90	2.95	3.00	3.05	3.10	3.15	3.20	3.25	3.30	3.35	3.40	3.45	3.50				
0.52 ~ 0.56	2.75	2.80	2.85	2.90	2.95	3.00	3.05	3.10	3.15	3.20	3.25	3.30	3.35	3.40	3.45	3.50					
0.57 ~ 0.61	2.80	2.85	2.90	2.95	3.00	3.05	3.10	3.15	3.20	3.25	3.30	3.35	3.40	3.45	3.50						
0.62 ~ 0.66	2.85	2.90	2.95	3.00	3.05	3.10	3.15	3.20	3.25	3.30	3.35	3.40	3.45	3.50							
0.67 ~ 0.71	2.90	2.95	3.00	3.05	3.10	3.15	3.20	3.25	3.30	3.35	3.40	3.45	3.50								
0.72 ~ 0.76	2.95	3.00	3.05	3.10	3.15	3.20	3.25	3.30	3.35	3.40	3.45	3.50									
0.77 ~ 0.81	3.00	3.05	3.10	3.15	3.20	3.25	3.30	3.35	3.40	3.45	3.50										
0.82 ~ 0.86	3.05	3.10	3.15	3.20	3.25	3.30	3.35	3.40	3.45	3.50											
0.87 ~ 0.91	3.10	3.15	3.20	3.25	3.30	3.35	3.40	3.45	3.50												
0.92 ~ 0.96	3.15	3.20	3.25	3.30	3.35	3.40	3.45	3.50													
0.97 ~ 1.01	3.20	3.25	3.30	3.35	3.40	3.45	3.50														
1.02 ~ 1.06	3.25	3.30	3.35	3.40	3.45	3.50															
1.07 ~ 1.11	3.30	3.35	3.40	3.45	3.50																
1.12 ~ 1.16	3.35	3.40	3.45	3.50																	
1.17 ~ 1.21	3.40	3.45	3.50																		
1.22 ~ 1.26	3.45	3.50																			
1.27 ~ 1.31	3.50																				

PRESENT SHIM — Example

PART No. (92180 -)	1014	1016	1018	1020	1022	1024	1026	1028	1030	1032	1034	1036	1038	1040	1042	1044	1046	1048	1050	1052	1054
MARK	50	55	60	65	70	75	80	85	90	95	00	05	10	15	20	25	30	35	40	45	50
THICKNESS (mm)	2.50	2.55	2.60	2.65	2.70	2.75	2.80	2.85	2.90	2.95	3.00	3.05	3.10	3.15	3.20	3.25	3.30	3.35	3.40	3.45	3.50

VALVE CLEARANCE MEASUREMENT (Inlet)

Clearance	2.50	2.55	2.60	2.65	2.70	2.75	2.80	2.85	2.90	2.95	3.00	3.05	3.10	3.15	3.20	3.25	3.30	3.35	3.40	3.45	3.50
0.00 ~ 0.03					2.50	2.55	2.60	2.65	2.70	2.75	2.80	2.85	2.90	2.95	3.00	3.05	3.10	3.15	3.20	3.25	3.30
0.04 ~ 0.08				2.50	2.55	2.60	2.65	2.70	2.75	2.80	2.85	2.90	2.95	3.00	3.05	3.10	3.15	3.20	3.25	3.30	3.35
0.09 ~ 0.13			2.50	2.55	2.60	2.65	2.70	2.75	2.80	2.85	2.90	2.95	3.00	3.05	3.10	3.15	3.20	3.25	3.30	3.35	3.40
0.14 ~ 0.17		2.50	2.55	2.60	2.65	2.70	2.75	2.80	2.85	2.90	2.95	3.00	3.05	3.10	3.15	3.20	3.25	3.30	3.35	3.40	3.45
0.18 ~ 0.23	SPECIFIED CLEARANCE/NO CHANGE REQUIRED																				
0.24 ~ 0.28	2.55	2.60	2.65	2.70	2.75	2.80	2.85	2.90	2.95	3.00	3.05	3.10	3.15	3.20	3.25	3.30	3.35	3.40	3.45	3.50	
0.29 ~ 0.33	2.60	2.65	2.70	2.75	2.80	2.85	2.90	2.95	3.00	3.05	3.10	3.15	3.20	3.25	3.30	3.35	3.40	3.45	3.50		
0.34 ~ 0.38	2.65	2.70	2.75	2.80	2.85	2.90	2.95	3.00	3.05	3.10	3.15	3.20	3.25	3.30	3.35	3.40	3.45	3.50			
0.39 ~ 0.43	2.70	2.75	2.80	2.85	2.90	2.95	3.00	3.05	3.10	3.15	3.20	3.25	3.30	3.35	3.40	3.45	3.50				
0.44 ~ 0.48	2.75	2.80	2.85	2.90	2.95	3.00	3.05	3.10	3.15	3.20	3.25	3.30	3.35	3.40	3.45	3.50					
0.49 ~ 0.53	2.80	2.85	2.90	2.95	3.00	3.05	3.10	3.15	3.20	3.25	3.30	3.35	3.40	3.45	3.50						
0.54 ~ 0.58	2.85	2.90	2.95	3.00	3.05	3.10	3.15	3.20	3.25	3.30	3.35	3.40	3.45	3.50							
0.59 ~ 0.63	2.90	2.95	3.00	3.05	3.10	3.15	3.20	3.25	3.30	3.35	3.40	3.45	3.50								
0.64 ~ 0.68	2.95	3.00	3.05	3.10	3.15	3.20	3.25	3.30	3.35	3.40	3.45	3.50									
0.69 ~ 0.73	3.00	3.05	3.10	3.15	3.20	3.25	3.30	3.35	3.40	3.45	3.50										
0.74 ~ 0.78	3.05	3.10	3.15	3.20	3.25	3.30	3.35	3.40	3.45	3.50											
0.79 ~ 0.83	3.10	3.15	3.20	3.25	3.30	3.35	3.40	3.45	3.50												
0.84 ~ 0.88	3.15	3.20	3.25	3.30	3.35	3.40	3.45	3.50													
0.89 ~ 0.93	3.20	3.25	3.30	3.35	3.40	3.45	3.50														
0.94 ~ 0.98	3.25	3.30	3.35	3.40	3.45	3.50															
0.99 ~ 1.03	3.30	3.35	3.40	3.45	3.50																
1.04 ~ 1.08	3.35	3.40	3.45	3.50																	
1.09 ~ 1.13	3.40	3.45	3.50																		
1.14 ~ 1.18	3.45	3.50																			
1.19 ~ 1.23	3.50																				

INSTALL THE SHIM OF THIS THICKNESS (mm)

12.11d Inlet valve selection chart (ZX-9R B models)

PRESENT SHIM — Example

PART No. (92180 -)	1014	1016	1018	1020	1022	1024	1026	1028	1030	1032	1034	1036	1038	1040	1042	1044	1046	1048	1050	1052	1054
MARK	50	55	60	65	70	75	80	85	90	95	00	05	10	15	20	25	30	35	40	45	50
THICKNESS (mm)	2.50	2.55	2.60	2.65	2.70	2.75	2.80	2.85	2.90	2.95	3.00	3.05	3.10	3.15	3.20	3.25	3.30	3.35	3.40	3.45	3.50

VALVE CLEARANCE MEASUREMENT (Exhaust)

Clearance	2.50	2.55	2.60	2.65	2.70	2.75	2.80	2.85	2.90	2.95	3.00	3.05	3.10	3.15	3.20	3.25	3.30	3.35	3.40	3.45	3.50
0.00 ~ 0.05					2.50	2.55	2.60	2.65	2.70	2.75	2.80	2.85	2.90	2.95	3.00	3.05	3.10	3.15	3.20	3.25	3.30
0.06 ~ 0.10				2.50	2.55	2.60	2.65	2.70	2.75	2.80	2.85	2.90	2.95	3.00	3.05	3.10	3.15	3.20	3.25	3.30	3.35
0.11 ~ 0.15			2.50	2.55	2.60	2.65	2.70	2.75	2.80	2.85	2.90	2.95	3.00	3.05	3.10	3.15	3.20	3.25	3.30	3.35	3.40
0.16 ~ 0.20		2.50	2.55	2.60	2.65	2.70	2.75	2.80	2.85	2.90	2.95	3.00	3.05	3.10	3.15	3.20	3.25	3.30	3.35	3.40	3.45
0.21 ~ 0.26	SPECIFIED CLEARANCE/NO CHANGE REQUIRED																				
0.27 ~ 0.31	2.55	2.60	2.65	2.70	2.75	2.80	2.85	2.90	2.95	3.00	3.05	3.10	3.15	3.20	3.25	3.30	3.35	3.40	3.45	3.50	
0.32 ~ 0.36	2.60	2.65	2.70	2.75	2.80	2.85	2.90	2.95	3.00	3.05	3.10	3.15	3.20	3.25	3.30	3.35	3.40	3.45	3.50		
0.37 ~ 0.41	2.65	2.70	2.75	2.80	2.85	2.90	2.95	3.00	3.05	3.10	3.15	3.20	3.25	3.30	3.35	3.40	3.45	3.50			
0.42 ~ 0.46	2.70	2.75	2.80	2.85	2.90	2.95	3.00	3.05	3.10	3.15	3.20	3.25	3.30	3.35	3.40	3.45	3.50				
0.47 ~ 0.51	2.75	2.80	2.85	2.90	2.95	3.00	3.05	3.10	3.15	3.20	3.25	3.30	3.35	3.40	3.45	3.50					
0.52 ~ 0.56	2.80	2.85	2.90	2.95	3.00	3.05	3.10	3.15	3.20	3.25	3.30	3.35	3.40	3.45	3.50						
0.57 ~ 0.61	2.85	2.90	2.95	3.00	3.05	3.10	3.15	3.20	3.25	3.30	3.35	3.40	3.45	3.50							
0.62 ~ 0.66	2.90	2.95	3.00	3.05	3.10	3.15	3.20	3.25	3.30	3.35	3.40	3.45	3.50								
0.67 ~ 0.71	2.95	3.00	3.05	3.10	3.15	3.20	3.25	3.30	3.35	3.40	3.45	3.50									
0.72 ~ 0.76	3.00	3.05	3.10	3.15	3.20	3.25	3.30	3.35	3.40	3.45	3.50										
0.77 ~ 0.81	3.05	3.10	3.15	3.20	3.25	3.30	3.35	3.40	3.45	3.50											
0.82 ~ 0.86	3.10	3.15	3.20	3.25	3.30	3.35	3.40	3.45	3.50												
0.87 ~ 0.91	3.15	3.20	3.25	3.30	3.35	3.40	3.45	3.50													
0.92 ~ 0.96	3.20	3.25	3.30	3.35	3.40	3.45	3.50														
0.97 ~ 1.01	3.25	3.30	3.35	3.40	3.45	3.50															
1.02 ~ 1.06	3.30	3.35	3.40	3.45	3.50																
1.07 ~ 1.11	3.35	3.40	3.45	3.50																	
1.12 ~ 1.16	3.40	3.45	3.50																		
1.17 ~ 1.21	3.45	3.50																			
1.22 ~ 1.26	3.50																				

INSTALL THE SHIM OF THIS THICKNESS (mm)

12.11e Exhaust valve selection chart (ZX-9R B models)

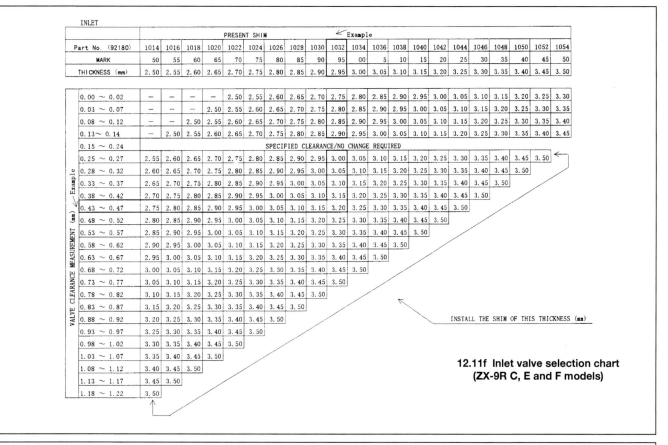

INLET — 12.11f Inlet valve selection chart (ZX-9R C, E and F models)

PRESENT SHIM ← Example

Part No. (92180)	1014	1016	1018	1020	1022	1024	1026	1028	1030	1032	1034	1036	1038	1040	1042	1044	1046	1048	1050	1052	1054
MARK	50	55	60	65	70	75	80	85	90	95	00	5	10	15	20	25	30	35	40	45	50
THICKNESS (mm)	2.50	2.55	2.60	2.65	2.70	2.75	2.80	2.85	2.90	2.95	3.00	3.05	3.10	3.15	3.20	3.25	3.30	3.35	3.40	3.45	3.50

VALVE CLEARANCE MEASUREMENT (mm):

Clearance																					
0.00 ~ 0.02	—	—	—	—	2.50	2.55	2.60	2.65	2.70	2.75	2.80	2.85	2.90	2.95	3.00	3.05	3.10	3.15	3.20	3.25	3.30
0.03 ~ 0.07	—	—	—	2.50	2.55	2.60	2.65	2.70	2.75	2.80	2.85	2.90	2.95	3.00	3.05	3.10	3.15	3.20	3.25	3.30	3.35
0.08 ~ 0.12	—	—	2.50	2.55	2.60	2.65	2.70	2.75	2.80	2.85	2.90	2.95	3.00	3.05	3.10	3.15	3.20	3.25	3.30	3.35	3.40
0.13 ~ 0.14	—	2.50	2.55	2.60	2.65	2.70	2.75	2.80	2.85	2.90	2.95	3.00	3.05	3.10	3.15	3.20	3.25	3.30	3.35	3.40	3.45
0.15 ~ 0.24	SPECIFIED CLEARANCE/NO CHANGE REQUIRED																				
0.25 ~ 0.27	2.55	2.60	2.65	2.70	2.75	2.80	2.85	2.90	2.95	3.00	3.05	3.10	3.15	3.20	3.25	3.30	3.35	3.40	3.45	3.50	
0.28 ~ 0.32	2.60	2.65	2.70	2.75	2.80	2.85	2.90	2.95	3.00	3.05	3.10	3.15	3.20	3.25	3.30	3.35	3.40	3.45	3.50		
0.33 ~ 0.37	2.65	2.70	2.75	2.80	2.85	2.90	2.95	3.00	3.05	3.10	3.15	3.20	3.25	3.30	3.35	3.40	3.45	3.50			
0.38 ~ 0.42	2.70	2.75	2.80	2.85	2.90	2.95	3.00	3.05	3.10	3.15	3.20	3.25	3.30	3.35	3.40	3.45	3.50				
0.43 ~ 0.47	2.75	2.80	2.85	2.90	2.95	3.00	3.05	3.10	3.15	3.20	3.25	3.30	3.35	3.40	3.45	3.50					
0.48 ~ 0.52	2.80	2.85	2.90	2.95	3.00	3.05	3.10	3.15	3.20	3.25	3.30	3.35	3.40	3.45	3.50						
0.53 ~ 0.57	2.85	2.90	2.95	3.00	3.05	3.10	3.15	3.20	3.25	3.30	3.35	3.40	3.45	3.50							
0.58 ~ 0.62	2.90	2.95	3.00	3.05	3.10	3.15	3.20	3.25	3.30	3.35	3.40	3.45	3.50								
0.63 ~ 0.67	2.95	3.00	3.05	3.10	3.15	3.20	3.25	3.30	3.35	3.40	3.45	3.50									
0.68 ~ 0.72	3.00	3.05	3.10	3.15	3.20	3.25	3.30	3.35	3.40	3.45	3.50										
0.73 ~ 0.77	3.05	3.10	3.15	3.20	3.25	3.30	3.35	3.40	3.45	3.50											
0.78 ~ 0.82	3.10	3.15	3.20	3.25	3.30	3.35	3.40	3.45	3.50												
0.83 ~ 0.87	3.15	3.20	3.25	3.30	3.35	3.40	3.45	3.50													
0.88 ~ 0.92	3.20	3.25	3.30	3.35	3.40	3.45	3.50														
0.93 ~ 0.97	3.25	3.30	3.35	3.40	3.45	3.50															
0.98 ~ 1.02	3.30	3.35	3.40	3.45	3.50																
1.03 ~ 1.07	3.35	3.40	3.45	3.50																	
1.08 ~ 1.12	3.40	3.45	3.50																		
1.13 ~ 1.17	3.45	3.50																			
1.18 ~ 1.22	3.50																				

INSTALL THE SHIM OF THIS THICKNESS (mm)

EXHAUST — 12.11g Exhaust valve selection chart (ZX-9R C, E and F models)

PRESENT SHIM ← Example

Part No. (92180)	1014	1016	1018	1020	1022	1024	1026	1028	1030	1032	1034	1036	1038	1040	1042	1044	1046	1048	1050	1052	1054
MARK	50	55	60	65	70	75	80	85	90	95	00	5	10	15	20	25	30	35	40	45	50
THICKNESS (mm)	2.50	2.55	2.60	2.65	2.70	2.75	2.80	2.85	2.90	2.95	3.00	3.05	3.10	3.15	3.20	3.25	3.30	3.35	3.40	3.45	3.50

VALVE CLEARANCE MEASUREMENT (mm):

Clearance																					
0.00 ~ 0.04	—	—	—	—	—	2.50	2.55	2.60	2.65	2.70	2.75	2.80	2.85	2.90	2.95	3.00	3.05	3.10	3.15	3.20	3.25
0.05 ~ 0.09	—	—	—	—	2.50	2.55	2.60	2.65	2.70	2.75	2.80	2.85	2.90	2.95	3.00	3.05	3.10	3.15	3.20	3.25	3.30
0.10 ~ 0.14	—	—	—	2.50	2.55	2.60	2.65	2.70	2.75	2.80	2.85	2.90	2.95	3.00	3.05	3.10	3.15	3.20	3.25	3.30	3.35
0.15 ~ 0.19	—	—	2.50	2.55	2.60	2.65	2.70	2.75	2.80	2.85	2.90	2.95	3.00	3.05	3.10	3.15	3.20	3.25	3.30	3.35	3.40
0.20 ~ 0.21	—	2.50	2.55	2.60	2.65	2.70	2.75	2.80	2.85	2.90	2.95	3.00	3.05	3.10	3.15	3.20	3.25	3.30	3.35	3.40	3.45
0.22 ~ 0.31	SPECIFIED CLEARANCE/NO CHANGE REQUIRED																				
0.32 ~ 0.34	2.55	2.60	2.65	2.70	2.75	2.80	2.85	2.90	2.95	3.00	3.05	3.10	3.15	3.20	3.25	3.30	3.35	3.40	3.45	3.50	
0.35 ~ 0.39	2.60	2.65	2.70	2.75	2.80	2.85	2.90	2.95	3.00	3.05	3.10	3.15	3.20	3.25	3.30	3.35	3.40	3.45	3.50		
0.40 ~ 0.44	2.65	2.70	2.75	2.80	2.85	2.90	2.95	3.00	3.05	3.10	3.15	3.20	3.25	3.30	3.35	3.40	3.45	3.50			
0.45 ~ 0.49	2.70	2.75	2.80	2.85	2.90	2.95	3.00	3.05	3.10	3.15	3.20	3.25	3.30	3.35	3.40	3.45	3.50				
0.50 ~ 0.54	2.75	2.80	2.85	2.90	2.95	3.00	3.05	3.10	3.15	3.20	3.25	3.30	3.35	3.40	3.45	3.50					
0.55 ~ 0.59	2.80	2.85	2.90	2.95	3.00	3.05	3.10	3.15	3.20	3.25	3.30	3.35	3.40	3.45	3.50						
0.60 ~ 0.64	2.85	2.90	2.95	3.00	3.05	3.10	3.15	3.20	3.25	3.30	3.35	3.40	3.45	3.50							
0.65 ~ 0.69	2.90	2.95	3.00	3.05	3.10	3.15	3.20	3.25	3.30	3.35	3.40	3.45	3.50								
0.70 ~ 0.74	2.95	3.00	3.05	3.10	3.15	3.20	3.25	3.30	3.35	3.40	3.45	3.50									
0.75 ~ 0.79	3.00	3.05	3.10	3.15	3.20	3.25	3.30	3.35	3.40	3.45	3.50										
0.80 ~ 0.84	3.05	3.10	3.15	3.20	3.25	3.30	3.35	3.40	3.45	3.50											
0.85 ~ 0.89	3.10	3.15	3.20	3.25	3.30	3.35	3.40	3.45	3.50												
0.90 ~ 0.94	3.15	3.20	3.25	3.30	3.35	3.40	3.45	3.50													
0.95 ~ 0.99	3.20	3.25	3.30	3.35	3.40	3.45	3.50														
1.00 ~ 1.04	3.25	3.30	3.35	3.40	3.45	3.50															
1.05 ~ 1.09	3.30	3.35	3.40	3.45	3.50																
1.10 ~ 1.14	3.35	3.40	3.45	3.50																	
1.15 ~ 1.19	3.40	3.45	3.50																		
1.20 ~ 1.24	3.45	3.50																			
1.25 ~ 1.29	3.50																				

INSTALL THE SHIM OF THIS THICKNESS (mm)

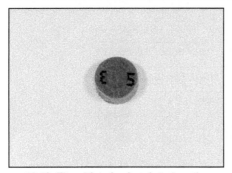

12.19 The shim size is printed on the underside of the shim

12.27a Lift out the follower . . .

12.27b . . . and remove the shim

19 A size mark should be stamped on the face of the shim **(see illustration)** – refer to the shim selection charts for reference. If the mark is not visible the shim thickness will have to be measured. It is recommended that the shim is measured anyway to check that it has not worn. Shims are available in 0.05 mm increments from 2.50 mm to 3.50 mm.

20 Using the appropriate shim selection chart, find where the measured valve clearance and existing shim thickness values intersect and read off the shim size required. Obtain the correct shim, then lubricate it with engine oil and fit it into its recess in the top of the valve.

21 Ensure the shim is correctly seated, then carefully pivot the rocker arm back and slide it into position between the camshaft and the shim.

22 Repeat the process for any other valve requiring adjustment until all the clearances are correctly set.

23 Rotate the crankshaft through a few rotations to settle all disturbed components in position, then check all the valve clearances again.

24 Once all the valve clearances are known to be correct, lubricate all bearing surfaces with clean engine oil, then fit the cylinder head cover (see Chapter 2A) and install the spark plugs (see Section 3).

25 Fit the pick-up coil cover (Chapter 5) and check the engine oil level (see *Daily pre-ride checks*) before starting the engine.

ZX-7R models and ZX-9R C, E and F models

26 If any of the clearances need to be adjusted the camshafts must be removed as described in Chapter 2A or 2B (as applicable).

27 With the camshafts removed, lift out the follower of the first valve to be adjusted out of the cylinder head and remove the shim **(see illustrations)**. Note that the shim is likely to stick to the inside of the follower, so take great care not to lose it as the follower is removed. **Note:** *Only remove one follower and shim at a time to avoid getting the followers and shims mixed up.*

28 A size mark should be stamped on the face of the shim – refer to the shim selection charts for reference. If the mark is not visible the shim thickness will have to be measured. It is recommended that the shim is measured anyway to check that it has not worn. Shims are available in 0.05 mm increments from 2.50 mm to 3.50 mm.

29 Using the appropriate shim selection chart, find where the measured valve clearance and existing shim thickness values intersect and read off the shim size required. Obtain the correct shim, then lubricate it with engine oil and fit it into its recess in the top of the valve. Lubricate the follower with clean engine, then install it in the cylinder head, making sure its enters its bore squarely.

30 Repeat the process for any other valve requiring adjustment until all the clearances are correctly set, then install the camshafts (see Chapter 2A or 2B).

13 Air filter element and vent filter(s) – cleaning

Interval:

> **US ZX-9R B models and UK/Europe ZX-9R B1 and B2 models – every 6000 miles (10,000 km)**
> **All other models – every 8000 miles (12,000 km)**

Caution: If the machine is continually ridden in dusty conditions, this task should be carried out more frequently.

Air filter element cleaning

1 Remove the fuel tank (see Chapter 4).

2 On ZX-7R models, disconnect the vacuum control valve and vent valve hoses from the front of the air filter housing cover **(see illustration)**.

3 On all models, unscrew the bolts securing the air filter cover to the filter housing, noting the correct fitted location of any wiring clamps (where fitted) **(see illustration)**.

4 Remove the cover and withdraw the filter element assembly from the housing **(see illustration)**. Check the filter cover seal for signs of damage or deterioration and renew if necessary.

5 Noting each component's correct fitted location, unclip the upper sections of the element holder, then separate the wire gauze

13.2 Disconnect the vacuum control valve and the vent valve hoses

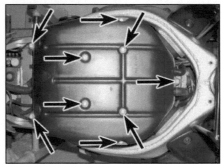

13.3 Undo the air filter cover bolts

13.4 Remove the filter element

and filter element from the lower section **(see illustration)**.

6 Soak the element in a high flash-point solvent until it is clean, then if compressed air is available, use it to dry the element, directing the air from the bottom upwards. Otherwise, dry it by shaking it or leaving it in the open air for a while.

7 Check the element, gauze and its holder for signs of damage. If the element is torn or cannot be cleaned, renew it. The filter element should be renewed after every five cleanings, regardless of its apparent condition.

8 Soak a clean lint-free rag in engine oil, then smear the rag over the upper (grey) side of the filter element.

9 Once the filter element upper surface is covered with oil, fit the element to the lower holder, ensuring its grey surface is uppermost. Seat the wire gauze on the top of the filter element, then clip the upper section of the holder onto the lower section.

10 Prior to refitting the element assembly, remove the plug from the base of the air filter housing drain hose, located on the left-hand side of the engine. Allow all the water/oil to drain completely from the hose, then securely refit the plug to the hose end.

11 Seat the filter element assembly correctly in the housing then, making sure the seal is in position, install the housing cover. Fit the cover retaining bolts, ensuring all the wiring clamps (where fitted) are correctly positioned, and tighten securely. On ZX-7R models, securely reconnect the vacuum and vent hoses to the cover.

12 On ZX-9R models, clean the air vent filter(s) (see Steps 14 to 18).

13 On completion, install the fuel tank (see Chapter 4).

Air vent filter cleaning – ZX-9R models

14 On ZX-9R models, the air vent filter(s) should also be cleaned at the same time as the main filter element.

15 On UK and US (except California) ZX-9R B models, two vent filters are fitted. Remove the air filter housing (see Chapter 4) to gain access to the filters which are fitted to the carburettor vent hoses **(see illustration)**.

16 On all other models, a single vent filter is fitted. The filter is located in between the headstock of the frame and the air filter intakes of the upper fairing. Where necessary, remove the retaining screws and clip(s) securing each air filter housing intake duct cover in position and remove both the left- and right-hand covers to gain access to the valve.

17 Release the retaining clips and disconnect the vent valve from its hoses, noting which way around it is fitted. Clean the filter by directing compressed air through it from the carburettor side to the fairing side. Check the filter for signs of damage. If it is torn or cannot be cleaned, renew it. The vent filter should be renewed after every five cleanings.

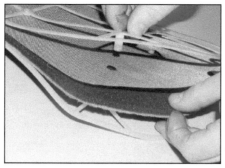

13.5 Separate the filter components

18 Once the filter is clean, fit it to the bike making sure it is the correct way around, then install any components removed for access.

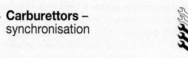

14 Carburettors – synchronisation

Interval:

> **US ZX-9R B models and UK/Europe ZX-9R B1 and B2 models – every 3000 miles (5000 km)**
> **All other models – every 8000 miles (12,000 km)**

⚠️ *Warning: Petrol (gasoline) is extremely flammable, so take extra precautions when you work on any part of the fuel system. Don't smoke or allow open flames or bare light bulbs near the work area, and don't work in a garage where a natural gas-type appliance is present. If you spill any fuel on your skin, rinse it off immediately with soap and water. When you perform any kind of work on the fuel system, wear safety glasses and have a fire extinguisher suitable for a Class B type fire (flammable liquids) on hand.*

⚠️ *Warning: Take great care not to burn your hand on the hot engine unit when accessing the gauge take-off points on the cylinder head. Do not allow exhaust gases to build up in the work area; either perform the check outside or use an exhaust gas extraction system.*

14.2 Carburettor vacuum gauge set-up and synchronisation adjustment

13.15 Air vent filters

1 Carburettor synchronisation is simply the process of adjusting the carburettors so that they pass the same amount of fuel/air mixture to each cylinder. This is done by measuring the vacuum produced in each cylinder. Carburettors that are out of synchronisation will result in increased fuel consumption, increased engine temperature, less than ideal throttle response and higher vibration levels. Before synchronising the carburettors, make sure the valve clearances are properly set and the spark plugs are in good condition (see Sections 12 and 3).

2 To synchronise the carburettors, you will need a set of four vacuum gauges or calibrated tubes (manometer) to indicate engine vacuum **(see illustration)**. **Note:** *Because of the nature of the synchronisation procedure and the need for special instruments, most owners leave the task to a Kawasaki dealer.*

3 Start the engine and let it run until it reaches normal operating temperature, then shut it off.

4 Remove the fuel tank (see Chapter 4).

5 The take-off point for each cylinder is located at the base of the cylinder head intake port, directly beneath the carburettor intake rubber **(see illustration)**. Depending on model, the take-off port will have either a blanking bolt or an adapter fitting screwed into it. Where a blanking bolt is fitted, slacken and remove the bolt and its sealing washer, then screw an adapter fitting securely into the threaded hole. Where an adapter is already fitted, disconnect the blanking cap or vacuum hose from the adapter, noting the correct routing of all hoses.

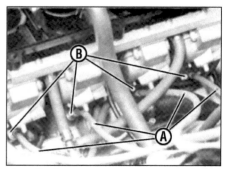

14.5 Typical vacuum gauge pipes (A) and take-off points (B)

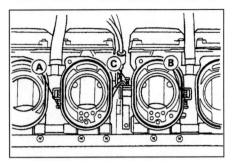

14.10a Synchronising screws for left side pair (A), right side pair (B) and centre screw (C)

14.10b Synchronisation screw detail

6 Connect the gauge hoses to the adapters. Make sure there are no air leaks, as false readings will result.

7 Arrange a temporary fuel supply, either by using a small temporary tank or by using extra long fuel pipes to the now-remote fuel tank. Alternatively, position the tank on a suitable base on the motorcycle, taking care not to scratch any paintwork, and making sure that the tank is safely and securely supported.

8 Start the engine and let it idle. If the gauges are fitted with damping adjustment, set this so that the needle flutter is just eliminated but so that they can still respond to small changes in pressure.

9 The vacuum readings for all of the cylinders should be the same. If the vacuum readings vary, remove the air filter housing (see Chapter 4) and proceed as follows.

10 The carburettors are adjusted by turning the synchronising screws situated in between each carburettor, in the throttle linkage **(see illustrations)**. **Note:** *Do not press down on the screws whilst adjusting them, otherwise a*

false reading will be obtained. First synchronise the pair of left-side carburettors, using the screw located between Nos. 1 and 2 carburettors. Once both left-side carburettor readings are the same, synchronise the pair of right-side carburettors, using the screw located between Nos. 3 and 4 carburettors. Finally synchronise the left-side carburettors with the right-side carburettors, using the centre synchronising screw located between Nos. 2 and 3 carburettors. When all the carburettors are synchronised, open and close the throttle quickly to settle the linkage, and recheck the gauge readings, readjusting if necessary.

11 When the adjustment is complete, recheck the vacuum readings, then adjust the idle speed (see Section 23) until the idle speed listed in this Chapter's Specifications is obtained. Install the air filter housing (see Chapter 4) and recheck the adjustment.

12 Detach the temporary fuel supply and remove the vacuum gauges and adapters.

13 Reconnect the vacuum hose/blanking cap correctly to each adapter, or fit a new sealing washer to the blanking bolt and securely fit the bolt to the intake port threaded hole.

14 Install the fuel tank (see Chapter 4).

15 Stands, pivots and cables – lubrication

Interval:

US ZX-9R B models and UK/Europe ZX-9R B1 and B2 models – every 3000 miles (5000 km)
All other models – every 8000 miles (12,000 km)

Pivot points

1 Since the controls, cables and various other components of a motorcycle are exposed to the elements, they should be lubricated periodically to ensure safe and trouble-free operation.

2 The footrests, clutch and brake levers, brake pedal, and sidestand pivots should be lubricated frequently. In order for the lubricant to be applied where it will do the most good, the component should be disassembled.

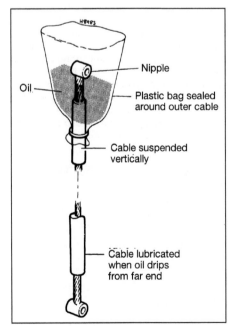

15.3 Lubricating a cable with a makeshift funnel and motor oil

However, if chain and cable lubricant is being used, it can be applied to the pivot joint gaps and will usually work its way into the areas where friction occurs. If motor oil or light grease is being used, apply it sparingly as it may attract dirt (which could cause the controls to bind or wear at an accelerated rate). **Note:** *One of the best lubricants for the control lever pivots is a dry-film lubricant (available from many sources by different names).*

Cables

3 To lubricate the cables, disconnect the relevant cable at its upper end, then lubricate the cable with a cable oiler clamp, or if one is not available, using the set-up shown **(see illustration)**. See Chapter 4 for the choke and throttle cable removal procedures. On ZX-9R C and E models, see Chapter 2B for the clutch cable removal procedure.

16 Throttle and choke cable – check

Interval:

US ZX-9R B models and UK/Europe ZX-9R B1 and B2 models – every 6000 miles (10,000 km)
All other models – every 8000 miles (12,000 km)

Throttle cables

1 Make sure the throttle grip rotates easily from fully closed to fully open with the front wheel turned at various angles. The grip should return automatically from fully open to fully closed when released.

2 If the throttle sticks, this is probably due to a cable fault. Remove the cables (see Chapter 4) and lubricate them (see Section 15). Install the cables, making sure they are correctly routed. If this fails to improve the operation of the throttle, the cables must be renewed. Note that, in very rare cases, the fault could lie in the carburettors rather than the cables, necessitating the removal of the carburettors and inspection of the throttle linkage (see Chapter 4).

3 With the throttle operating smoothly, check for a small amount of freeplay in the cables, measured in terms of the amount of twistgrip rotation before the throttle opens, and compare the amount to that listed in this Chapter's Specifications **(see illustration)**. If it's incorrect, adjust the cables to correct it.

4 Freeplay adjustments can be made at the throttle end of the cable. Loosen the locknut on the accelerator cable where it leaves the handlebar. Turn the adjuster until the specified amount of freeplay is obtained (see this Chapter's Specifications), then retighten the locknut.

5 If the adjuster has reached its limit of

16.3 Check the amount of freeplay in the twistgrip

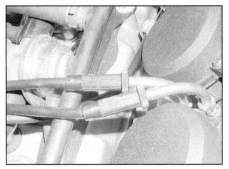

16.5 Throttle cable adjusters – carburettor end

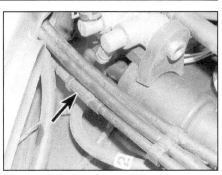

16.9 Choke cable adjuster

adjustment, reset it so that the freeplay is at a maximum, then remove the air filter housing (see Chapter 4) to gain access to the cable adjuster at the carburettor end **(see illustration)**. Slacken the adjuster locknuts, then fully back off both adjusters to obtain maximum freeplay. Ensure the throttle grip is fully closed, then use the decelerator (closing) cable adjuster to remove all freeplay from the cable, without placing the cable under any strain. Once the decelerator cable is correctly set, use the accelerator (opening) cable adjuster to correctly set the twistgrip freeplay. Once the freeplay is correctly set, securely tighten both the adjuster locknuts. Future adjustments can now be made at the throttle grip end. If the cables cannot be adjusted as specified, renew them (see Chapter 4). Once adjustment is correct, install the air filter housing (see Chapter 4).

⚠️ **Warning: Turn the handlebars all the way through their travel with the engine idling. Idle speed should not change. If it does, the cables may be routed incorrectly. Correct this condition before riding the bike.**

6 Check that the throttle twistgrip operates smoothly and snaps shut quickly when released.

Choke cable

7 If the choke does not operate smoothly, this is probably due to a cable fault. Remove the cable (see Chapter 4) and lubricate it (see Section 15). Install the cable, routing it so that it takes the smoothest route possible.
8 Check for a small amount of freeplay (see Specifications) in the cable before the plungers in the carburettors move.
9 Freeplay adjustments are made at the adjuster located midway along the cable **(see illustration)**; remove the air filter housing for access to the adjuster (see Chapter 4). Loosen the locknut and turn the adjuster until the specified amount of freeplay is obtained (see Specifications), then retighten the locknut. If this fails to improve the operation of the choke, the cable must be renewed. Note that in very rare cases the fault could lie in the carburettors rather than the cable, necessitating the removal of the carburettors and inspection of the choke valves (see Chapter 4).

17 Engine – oil and filter change

Interval:

> US ZX-9R B models and UK/Europe ZX-9R B1 and B2 models – every 6000 miles (10,000 km)
> All other models – every 8000 miles (12,000 km)

⚠️ **Warning: Be careful when draining the oil, as the exhaust pipes, the engine, and the oil itself can cause severe burns.**

Note: *Oil filter removal and installation is far easier with a filter wrench, either the Kawasaki service tool (57001-1249) or a pattern alternative (available from most good motorcycle accessory dealers). The wrench will also allow the new filter to be tightened to the specified torque.*

1 Consistent routine oil and filter changes are the single most important maintenance procedure you can perform on a motorcycle. The oil not only lubricates the internal parts of the engine, transmission and clutch, but it also acts as coolant, cleaner, sealant, and protectant. Because of these demands, the oil takes a terrific amount of abuse and should be changed often with new oil of the recommended grade and type (see Specifications at the beginning of this Chapter).

HAYNES HiNT *Saving a little money on the difference in cost between a good oil and a cheap oil won't pay off if the engine is damaged.*

2 Before changing the oil, warm up the engine so that the oil will drain easily.
3 On ZX-7R and ZX-9R B models, remove the left-hand side lower fairing panel and, on ZX-9R C, E and F models, remove the lower fairing (see Chapter 8).
4 Support the motorcycle on an auxiliary stand, so that it is upright, and position a clean drain tray below the engine. Unscrew the oil filler cap from the right-hand crankcase

cover to vent the crankcase and to act as a reminder that there is no oil in the engine.
5 Next, unscrew the oil drain plug from the oil pan on the bottom of the engine and allow the oil to flow into the drain tray **(see illustration 6.4)**. Check the condition of the sealing

HAYNES HiNT *To help determine whether any abnormal or excessive engine wear is occurring, place a strainer between the engine and the drain tray so that any debris in the oil is filtered out and can be examined. If there are flakes or chips of metal in the oil, then something is drastically wrong internally and the engine will have to be disassembled for inspection and repair. If there are pieces of fibre-like material in the oil, the clutch is experiencing excessive wear and should be checked.*

washer on the drain plug and obtain a new one if it is damaged or worn.
6 When the oil has completely drained, fit the plug to the oil pan, using a new sealing washer if necessary, and tighten it to the specified torque. Avoid overtightening, as damage to the oil pan will result.
7 On ZX-9R B models, in order to gain the necessary clearance required to remove the oil filter, it will be necessary to disconnect the cylinder head oil pipe from the crankcase. Unscrew the retaining bolt and free the pipe from the crankcase **(see illustration)**. Recover the O-ring from the pipe end fitting and discard it; a new one will be needed.

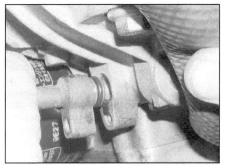

17.7 Unscrew the retaining bolt and free the oil pipe from the crankcase

17.8 With the use of a filter wrench, remove the oil filter

17.9 Apply a smear of clean engine oil to the rubber seal

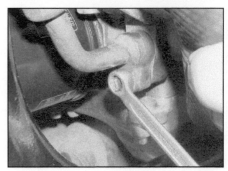

17.10 Tighten the retaining bolt to the specified torque

8 On all models, place the drain tray below the oil filter. Unscrew the oil filter using a filter wrench or a strap wrench and tip any residue oil into the drain tray (see illustration). Wipe clean the oil filter mating surface on the oil cooler.

9 Smear clean engine oil onto the rubber seal on the new filter (see illustration), then manoeuvre the filter into position. Screw the filter onto the oil cooler and tighten it to the specified torque.

10 On ZX-9R B models, fit the new O-ring to the oil pipe end fitting and lubricate it with a smear of engine oil. Ease the pipe into position in the crankcase and tighten its retaining bolt to the specified torque (see illustration).

11 On all models, refill the engine to the proper level (see *Daily (pre-ride) checks*) using the recommended type and amount of oil, as emphasised above. With the motorcycle resting on its wheels and held upright, the oil level should lie between the upper and lower level lines on the inspection window on the right crankcase cover (see *Daily (pre-ride) checks*). Install the filler cap. Start the engine and let it run for two or three minutes (make sure that the oil pressure light extinguishes after a few seconds). Shut it off, wait a few minutes, then check the oil level. If necessary, add more oil to bring the level up to the upper level line on the inspection window. Check around the oil filter and drain plug for leaks before installing the fairing panel (see Chapter 8).

12 The old oil drained from the engine cannot be re-used and should be disposed of properly. Check with your local refuse disposal company, disposal facility or environmental agency to see whether they will accept the used oil for recycling. Don't pour used oil into drains or onto the ground.

Note: It is antisocial and illegal to dump oil down the drain. To find the location of your nearest oil recycling bank in the UK, call this number free. In the USA, note that any oil supplier must accept used oil for recycling.

0800 66 33 66

18 Cooling system – check

Interval:

US ZX-9R B models and UK/Europe ZX-9R B1 and B2 models – every 6000 miles (10,000 km)
All other models – every 8000 miles (12,000 km)

⚠️ *Warning: The engine must be cool before beginning this procedure.*

1 On ZX-7R and ZX-9R B models, undo the retaining screws securing the right-hand side air filter housing intake duct cover in position and remove the cover to gain access to the pressure cap. Remove the lower fairing panels (see Chapter 8).

2 On ZX-9R C, E and F models, remove the lower fairing and middle panels (see Chapter 8).

3 The entire cooling system should be checked for evidence of leakage. Examine each rubber coolant hose along its entire length. Look for cracks, abrasions and other damage. Squeeze each hose at various points. They should feel firm, yet pliable, and return to their original shape when released. If they are dried out or hard, renew them.

4 Check for evidence of leaks at each cooling system joint. Tighten the hose clips carefully to prevent future leaks.

5 Check the radiator for leaks and other damage. Leaks in the radiator leave tell-tale scale deposits or coolant stains on the

18.7 Radiator pressure cap

outside of the core below the leak. If leaks are noted, remove the radiator (see Chapter 3) and have it repaired at a radiator shop or replace it with a new one.

Caution: Do not use a liquid leak-stopping compound to try to repair leaks.

6 Check the radiator fins for mud, dirt and insects, which may impede the flow of air through the radiator. If the fins are dirty, force water or low pressure compressed air through the fins from the backside. If the fins are bent or distorted, straighten them carefully with a screwdriver.

7 Remove the pressure cap by turning it anti-clockwise until it reaches a stop (see illustration). If you hear a hissing sound (indicating that there is still pressure in the system), wait until it stops. Now press down on the cap and continue turning it until it can be removed. Check the condition of the coolant in the system. If it is rust-coloured or if accumulations of scale are visible, drain, flush and refill the system with new coolant (See Section 28). Check the cap seal for cracks and other damage. If in doubt about the pressure cap's condition, have it tested by a dealer service department or renew it. Install the cap by turning it clockwise until it reaches the first stop, then push down on the cap and continue turning until it can turn no further.

8 Check the antifreeze content of the coolant with an antifreeze hydrometer. Sometimes coolant looks like it's in good condition, but might be too weak to offer adequate protection. If the hydrometer indicates a weak mixture, drain, flush and refill the system (see Section 28).

9 If the coolant level is consistently low, and no evidence of leaks can be found, have the entire system pressure checked by a Kawasaki dealer service department or motorcycle shop.

10 On UK (and most European) models, a filter is incorporated in the cooling system to prevent the carburettor coolant passages from getting blocked. To ensure adequate coolant flow around the carburettor this filter must be cleaned regularly (at least once a year, preferably before the start of the winter season). On ZX-7R and ZX-9R B models the filter is located on the right-hand end of the cylinder head (see illustration) and, on ZX-9R

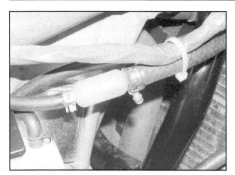

**18.10a Coolant filter
(ZX-7R and ZX-9R B models)**

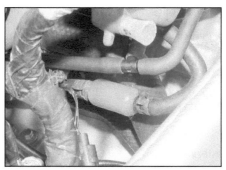

**18.10b Coolant filter
(ZX-9R C and E models)**

19.5 In-line fuel filter

C, E and F models, it is located underneath the carburettors (remove the fuel tank to gain access – see Chapter 4) **(see illustration)**. Clamp the coolant hoses on each side of the filter, then release the retaining clip and disconnect the larger bore hose from the filter housing. Withdraw the filter element from its housing and clean it, using compressed air or a suitable solvent. Ensure the filter element is clean and undamaged (renew the element if necessary), then fit it back in its housing and securely reconnect the coolant hose. Wash off any traces of spilt coolant.

11 On all models, ensure the pressure cap is correctly installed, then fit the fairing panels as described in Chapter 8.

---

19 Fuel system – check

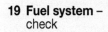

Interval:

> **US ZX-9R B models and UK/Europe ZX-9R B1 and B2 models – every 6000 miles (10,000 km)**
> **All other models – every 8000 miles (12,000 km)**

⚠️ *Warning: Petrol (gasoline) is extremely flammable, so take extra precautions when you work on any part of the fuel system. Don't smoke or allow open flames or bare light bulbs near the work area, and don't work in a garage where a natural gas-type appliance is present. If you spill any fuel on your skin, rinse it off immediately with soap and water. When you perform any kind of work on the fuel system, wear safety glasses and have a fire extinguisher suitable for a Class B type fire (flammable liquids) on hand.*

1 Remove the fuel tank (see Chapter 4).
2 Check the tank, the fuel tap, and the fuel hoses and vacuum hoses for signs of leakage, deterioration or damage; in particular check that there is no leakage from the fuel hoses. Renew any hoses which are cracked or deteriorated.
3 If the carburettor gaskets are leaking, the carburettors should be disassembled and rebuilt using new gaskets and seals (see Chapter 4).

4 The fuel tap should be removed from the tank (see Chapter 4) so that its filters can be inspected. Clean the tap filters to remove all traces of dirt and fuel sediment. Check the gauze for signs of damage and renew if necessary (check for availability – it may be necessary to renew the whole tap). Install the tap as described in Chapter 4.
5 Inspect the in-line fuel filter fitted in the fuel pipe from the tank to the fuel pump **(see illustration)**. The filter should be clean, undamaged and free of residue, otherwise a new one should be fitted (see Chapter 4).
6 Check the secondary air injection system hoses, linking the control valve assembly to the suction valves, for signs of damage or deterioration, and renew if necessary (see Chapter 4).
7 On completion, install the fuel tank.

---

20 Suspension – check

Interval:

> **US ZX-9R B models and UK/Europe ZX-9R B1 and B2 models – every 6000 miles (10,000 km)**
> **All other models – every 8000 miles (12,000 km)**

1 The suspension components must be maintained in top operating condition to ensure rider safety. Loose, worn or damaged suspension parts decrease the motorcycle's stability and control.

20.7a Checking for play in the swingarm bearings

Front suspension

2 While standing alongside the motorcycle, apply the front brake and push on the handlebars to compress the forks several times. See if they move up and down smoothly without binding. If binding is felt, the forks should be disassembled and inspected (see Chapter 6).
3 Inspect the front forks around the dust seal for signs of oil leakage. If leakage is evident, the fork seals must be renewed (see Chapter 6).
4 Check the tightness of all suspension nuts and bolts to be sure none have worked loose.

Rear suspension

5 Inspect the rear shock for fluid leakage and tightness of its mountings. If leakage is found, the shock should be renewed (see Chapter 6).
6 With the aid of an assistant to support the bike, compress the rear suspension several times. It should move up and down freely without binding. If any binding is felt, the worn or faulty component must be identified and renewed. The problem could be due to either the shock absorber, the suspension linkage components or the swingarm components.
7 Support the motorcycle on an auxiliary stand so that the rear wheel is off the ground. Grab the swingarm and attempt to rock it from side to side **(see illustration)** – there should be no discernible movement at the rear. If there is a little movement or a slight clicking can be heard, inspect the tightness of all the rear suspension mounting bolts and nuts, referring to the torque settings specified at the beginning of Chapter 6, and re-check for movement. Next, grasp the top of the rear wheel and pull it upwards **(see illustration)** – there should be no discernible freeplay before the shock absorber begins to compress. Any freeplay felt in either check indicates worn bearings in the suspension linkage or swingarm, or worn shock absorber mountings. The worn components must be renewed (see Chapter 6).
8 To make an accurate assessment of the swingarm bearings, remove the rear wheel (see Chapter 7) and the bolt securing the suspension linkage assembly to the swingarm (see Chapter 6). Grasp the rear of the swingarm with one hand and place your other hand at the junction of the swingarm and the

20.7b Checking for play in the suspension and linkage

frame. Try to move the rear of the swingarm from side to side. Any wear (play) in the bearings should be felt as movement between the swingarm and the frame at the front. If there is any play the swingarm will be felt to move forward and backward at the front (not from side to side). Next, move the swingarm up and down through its full travel. It should move freely, without any binding or rough spots. If any play in the swingarm is noted or if the swingarm does not move freely, the bearings must be removed for inspection or renewal (see Chapter 6).

21 Swingarm and suspension linkage bearings – re-greasing

Interval:

US ZX-9R B models and UK/Europe ZX-9R B1 and B2 models – every 6000 miles (10,000 km)
All other models – every 8000 miles (12,000 km)

1 Over a period of time, the grease will harden or dirt will penetrate the bearing due to failed dust seals.
2 On ZX-9R E and F models, all the swingarm and suspension linkage pivots are equipped with a grease nipple to enable lubrication to be easily carried out using a grease gun. Fill the grease gun with multi-purpose grease and lubricate each pivot generously. Wipe off the old grease which is forced out by the new grease.

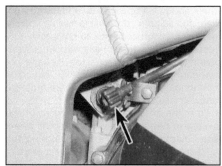

23.3a Idle speed adjusting screw (ZX-9R B models)

3 On all other models, the swingarm and suspension linkage pivots are not equipped with grease nipples. Remove the swingarm and suspension linkage as described in Chapter 6 for greasing of the bearings.

22 Nuts and bolts – tightness check

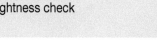

Interval:

US ZX-9R B models and UK/Europe ZX-9R B1 and B2 models – every 6000 miles (10,000 km)
All other models – every 8000 miles (12,000 km)

1 Since vibration of the machine tends to loosen fasteners, all nuts, bolts, screws, etc. should be periodically checked for proper tightness.
2 Pay particular attention to the following:
Footrest and stand bolts
Engine mounting bolts
Shock absorber and suspension linkage bolts and swingarm pivot bolts
Handlebar clamp bolts
Front axle bolt and axle clamp bolts
Front fork clamp bolts (top and bottom yoke)
Rear wheel nut
Brake caliper mounting bolts
Brake hose banjo bolts and caliper bleed valves
Brake disc bolts and rear sprocket nuts
Exhaust system bolts/nuts
3 If a torque wrench is available, use it along with the torque specifications at the beginning of this and other Chapters.

23 Idle speed – check and adjustment

Interval:

US ZX-9R B models and UK/Europe ZX-9R B1 and B2 models – every 3000 miles (5000 km)
All other models – every 8000 miles (12,000 km)

1 The idle speed should be checked and adjusted before and after the carburettors are synchronised (balanced) and when it is obviously too high or too low. Before adjusting the idle speed, make sure the valve clearances and spark plug gaps are correct. Also, turn the handlebars back and forth and see if the idle speed changes as this is done. If it does, the throttle cables may not be adjusted correctly, or may be worn out. This is a dangerous condition that can cause loss of control of the bike. Be sure to correct this problem before proceeding.
2 The engine should be at normal operating temperature, which is usually reached after 10 to 15 minutes of stop-and-go riding. Support

the motorcycle upright on an auxiliary stand, and make sure the transmission is in neutral.
3 With the engine idling in neutral, adjust the idle speed by turning the adjusting screw in or out until the idle speed listed in this Chapter's Specifications is obtained. The idle speed adjusting screw is located above the clutch cover on the right-hand side of the engine on ZX-9R B models **(see illustration)**, and above the sprocket cover on the left-hand side of the engine on all other models **(see illustration)**.
4 Snap the throttle open and shut a few times, then recheck the idle speed. If necessary, repeat the adjustment procedure.
5 If a smooth, steady idle cannot be achieved, the fuel/air mixture may be incorrect (see Chapter 4) or the carburettors may need synchronising (see Section 14). Also check the air suction valves (see Section 4).

24 Brakes – fluid change

Interval:

US ZX-9R B models and UK/Europe ZX-9R B1 and B2 models – every 12,000 miles (20,000 km)
All other models – every 16,000 miles (24,000 km)

Note: *To prevent damage to the paint from spilled brake fluid, always cover the fuel tank when working on the front brake master cylinder, and the surrounding components when working on the rear brake fluid reservoir.*
1 The procedure is similar to that for the bleeding of each brake as described in Chapter 7, except that the fluid reservoir should be emptied by siphoning before starting, using a clean poultry baster or similar, and allowance should be made for the old fluid to be expelled when bleeding a section of the circuit.
2 Working as described, open the bleed valve and pump the lever/pedal gently. Be careful to keep the master cylinder reservoir topped up to above the LOWER level at all times or air may enter the system and greatly increase the length of the task. Continue pumping until new fluid can be seen emerging from the bleed valve.

23.3b Idle speed adjusting screw (all models except ZX-9R B models)

HAYNES HINT *Old hydraulic fluid is usually much darker in colour than the new, making it easy to distinguish the two.*

3 When the new fluid is seen to be emerging, hold the lever/pedal and tighten the bleed valve to the specified torque (see Chapter 7). Where necessary, repeat the operation on the other bleed valve until all old hydraulic fluid has been renewed.

4 When the operation is complete, wash off all traces of spilt fluid, then top-up the reservoir fluid level (see *Daily (pre-ride) checks*).

5 Check the operation of the brakes before riding the motorcycle.

25 Clutch – fluid change (ZX-7R and ZX-9R B models)

Interval:

US ZX-9R B models and UK/Europe ZX-9R B1 and B2 models – every 12,000 miles (20,000 km)
All other models – every 16,000 miles (24,000 km)

Note: *To prevent damage to the paint from spilled brake fluid, always cover the fuel tank when working on the clutch master cylinder.*

1 The procedure is similar to that for the bleeding of the clutch hydraulic system as described in Chapter 2A, except that the fluid reservoir should be emptied by siphoning before starting, using a clean poultry baster or similar, and allowance should be made for the old fluid to be expelled when bleeding a section of the circuit.

2 Working as described, open the bleed valve and pump the lever gently. Be careful to keep the master cylinder reservoir topped up to above the LOWER level at all times, or air may enter the system and greatly increase the length of the task. Continue pumping until new fluid can be seen emerging from the bleed valve.

HAYNES HINT *Old hydraulic fluid is usually much darker in colour than the new, making it easy to distinguish the two.*

3 When the new fluid is seen to be emerging, hold the lever and tighten the bleed valve to the specified torque (see Chapter 2A).

4 When the operation is complete, wash off all traces of spilt fluid then top-up the reservoir fluid level (see *Daily (pre-ride) checks*).

5 Check the operation of the clutch before riding the motorcycle.

28.4 Drain the coolant

26 Steering head bearings – re-greasing
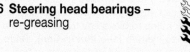

Interval:

US ZX-9R B models and UK/Europe ZX-9R B1 and B2 models – every 12,000 miles (20,000 km)
All other models – every 16,000 miles (24,000 km)

1 Over a period of time the grease will harden or may be washed out of the bearings by incorrect use of jet washes.

2 Disassemble the steering head for re-greasing of the bearings. Refer to Chapter 6 for details.

27 Front forks – oil change
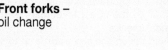

Interval:

US ZX-9R B models and UK/Europe ZX-9R B1 and B2 models – every 18,000 miles (30,000 km)
All other models – every 16,000 miles (24,000 km)

1 Fork oil degrades over a period of time and loses its damping qualities and should therefore be regularly changed.

2 On ZX-7R and ZX-9R B models, with both forks removed, drain all the oil from the first fork as described in Steps 3 to 9 of Section 7

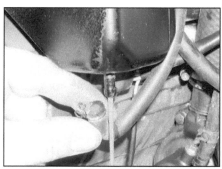

28.5 Disconnect the hose from the coolant reservoir

of Chapter 6 (It is not necessary to dismantle the fork completely), then fill it with fresh oil as described in Steps 33 to 44. Repeat the operation on the other fork, then fit both forks to the motorcycle (see Chapter 6).

3 On ZX-9R C, E and F models, with both forks removed, drain all the oil from the first fork as described in Steps 47 to 52 of Section 7 of Chapter 6 (It is not necessary to dismantle the fork completely), then fill it with fresh oil as described in Steps 70 to 77. Repeat the operation on the other fork, then fit both forks to the motorcycle (see Chapter 6).

28 Cooling system – draining, flushing and refilling

Interval:

US ZX-9R B models and UK/Europe ZX-9R B1 and B2 models – every 18,000 miles (30,000 km)
All other models – every 16,000 miles (24,000 km)

⚠ *Warning: Allow the engine to cool completely before performing this maintenance operation. Also, don't allow antifreeze to come into contact with your skin or the painted surfaces of the motorcycle. Rinse off spills immediately with plenty of water. Antifreeze is highly toxic if ingested. Never leave antifreeze lying around in an open container or in puddles on the floor; children and pets are attracted by its sweet smell and may drink it. Check with your local authority about antifreeze disposal facilities in your area. Antifreeze is also combustible, so don't store it near open flames.*

Draining

1 On ZX-7R and ZX-9R B models, undo the retaining screws securing the right-hand side air filter housing intake duct cover in position and remove the cover to gain access to the pressure cap **(see illustration 18.7)**. Remove the lower fairing panels (see Chapter 8).

2 On ZX-9R C, E and F models, remove the lower fairing and middle panels (see Chapter 8).

3 On all models, remove the pressure cap from the filler neck by turning it anti-clockwise until it reaches a stop. If you hear a hissing sound (indicating there is still pressure in the system), wait until it stops. Now press down on the cap and continue turning the cap until it can be removed.

4 Position a suitable container beneath the water pump on the left-hand side of the engine. Remove the coolant drain plug and its sealing washer and allow the coolant to drain completely from the system **(see illustration)**.

5 To drain the system completely, disconnect the hose from the base of the coolant reservoir and allow its contents to drain into the container **(see illustration)**.

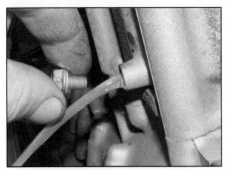

28.6 Cylinder block drain plug

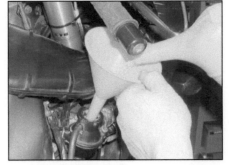

28.15 Refilling the cooling system

28.16 Unscrew the bleed screw

6 On ZX-9R C, E and F models, there is also a drain plug on the left-hand end of the front of the cylinder block. If necessary, remove the drain plug and its sealing washer and allow the coolant to drain completely from the cylinder block **(see illustration)**.

Flushing

7 Flush the system with clean tap water by inserting a garden hose into the filler neck. Allow the water to run through the system until it is clear and flows cleanly out of the drain hole(s). If the radiator is extremely corroded, remove it (see Chapter 3) and have it cleaned at a radiator shop. Also rinse out the coolant reservoir.

8 Clean the drain hole(s), then install the drain plug(s) using the old sealing washer(s).

9 Fill the cooling system with clean water mixed with a flushing compound. Make sure the flushing compound is compatible with aluminium components, and follow the manufacturer's instructions carefully.

10 Start the engine and allow it to reach normal operating temperature. Let it run for about ten minutes.

11 Stop the engine. Let it cool for a while, then cover the pressure cap with a heavy rag and turn it anti-clockwise to the first stop, releasing any pressure that may be present in the system. Once the hissing stops, push down on the cap and remove it completely.

12 Drain the system once again.

13 Fill the system with clean water and repeat the procedure in Steps 9 to 12.

Refilling

14 Fit a new sealing washer to the drain plug, then fit the drain plug to the water pump and tighten it securely. Securely reconnect the hose to the base of the coolant reservoir. On ZX-9R C, E and F models, where necessary, also fit a new sealing washer to the cylinder block drain plug, then fit the plug and tighten it securely

15 Fill the system with the proper coolant mixture (see this Chapter's Specifications) **(see illustration)**. **Note:** *Pour the coolant in slowly to minimise the amount of air entering the system.*

16 On ZX-7R and ZX-9R B models, when the system is full (all the way up to the top of the

filler neck) fit the pressure cap. Release the dust cap, then slacken the bleed valve on the water pump to bleed any trapped air from the cooling system **(see illustration)**. Once the coolant flowing out of the valve is free of air bubbles, tighten the valve securely and refit the dust cap. Remove the pressure cap and top the coolant level up before securely fitting the pressure cap again.

17 On ZX-9R C, E and F models, when the system is full (all the way up to the top of the filler neck), start the engine and allow it to idle to bleed any trapped air from the cooling system. Once no more air bubbles can be seen to be emerging from the coolant, switch off the engine. Top the coolant level back up to the top of the filler neck, then securely fit the pressure cap.

18 On all models, top up the coolant reservoir to the upper level mark (see *Daily (pre-ride) checks*).

19 Start the engine and warm it up to normal operating temperature and check for leaks.

20 Let the engine cool, then check the coolant level in the reservoir and top up if necessary (see *Daily (pre-ride) checks*).

21 Install the fairing panels (see Chapter 8).

22 Do not dispose of the old coolant by pouring it down the drain. Instead pour it into a heavy plastic container, cap it tightly and take it into an authorised disposal site or service station – see **Warning** at the beginning of this Section.

29 Brake master cylinder and caliper seals – renewal

Interval:
> **US ZX-9R B models and UK/Europe ZX-9R B1 and B2 models – every 2 years**
> **All other models – every 4 years**

Brake seals will deteriorate over a period of time and lose their effectiveness, leading to sticking operation or fluid loss, or allowing the ingress of air and dirt. Remove the master cylinders and calipers and renew all seals as described in Chapter 7.

30 Clutch master cylinder and slave cylinder seals – renewal (ZX-7R and ZX-9R B models)

Interval:
> **US ZX-9R B models and UK/Europe ZX-9R B1 and B2 models – every 2 years**
> **All other models – every 4 years**

Clutch master and slave cylinder seals will deteriorate over a period of time and lose their effectiveness, leading to sticking operation or fluid loss, or allowing the ingress of air and dirt. Remove the master cylinder and slave cylinder and renew all seals as described in Chapter 2A.

31 Battery – check

1 All models covered in this manual are fitted with a sealed battery, which is maintenance-free. **Note:** *Do not attempt to remove the battery caps to check the electrolyte level or battery specific gravity. Removal will damage the caps, resulting in electrolyte leakage and battery damage.* All that should be done is to check periodically that its terminals are clean and tight and that the casing is not damaged or leaking. See Chapter 9 for further details.

2 If the machine is not in regular use, disconnect the battery and give it a refresher charge every month to six weeks, as described in Chapter 9.

32 Headlight aim – check and adjustment

Note: *An improperly adjusted headlight may cause problems for oncoming traffic or provide poor, unsafe illumination of the road ahead. Before adjusting the headlight aim, be sure to consult with local traffic laws and regulations. Machines in use in the UK should refer to MOT Test Checks in the Reference section.*

1 The headlight beam can be adjusted both

horizontally and vertically. Before making any adjustment, check that the tyre pressures are correct and the suspension is adjusted as required. Make any adjustments to the headlight aim with the machine on level ground, with the fuel tank half full and with an assistant sitting on the seat. If the bike is usually ridden with a passenger on the back, have a second assistant to do this.

2 On ZX-7R models, there are separate adjusters for each light. Horizontal adjustments are made by turning the adjusters on the bottom of the headlight casing (located in between the bulbs) and vertical adjustments are made using the adjusters which are fitted to the top of the headlight casing (located in the left- and right-hand upper corners of the casing). The adjusters can be turned using a Philips screwdriver.

3 On ZX-9R B models horizontal adjustments are made by turning the adjuster on the left-hand upper corner of the headlight casing with a Philips screwdriver (see illustration) and vertical adjustments are made using the adjuster which is fitted to the right-hand lower corner of the headlight casing (see illustration). Note: European (except UK) models have separate adjusters for each bulb.

4 On ZX-9R C models, vertical adjustments are made by turning the adjuster knob on the left-hand side of the headlight casing, just below the level of the bulb (see illustration). Horizontal adjustments are made using the adjusters located on the left- and right-hand side of the headlight casing, just above the level of the bulb (see illustration).

5 On ZX-9R E and F models, there are separate adjusters for each light. Horizontal adjust-ments are made by turning the adjuster knobs located above each bulb on its outside, and vertical adjustments are made by turning the adjuster knobs located below each bulb on its inside.

33 Wheel bearings – check

Support the motorcycle upright using an auxiliary stand. Check for any play in the bearings by pushing and pulling the wheel against the hub. Also rotate the wheel and check that it rotates smoothly. If any play is detectable in the hub, or if the wheel does not rotate smoothly (and this is not due to brake or transmission drag), the wheel bearings must be removed and inspected for wear or damage (see Chapter 7).

34 Cylinder compression – check

1 Amongst other things, poor engine performance may be caused by leaking valves, incorrect valve clearances, a leaking

32.3a Horizontal adjuster (ZX-9R B models)

head gasket, or worn pistons, rings and/or cylinder walls. A cylinder compression check will help pinpoint these conditions and can also indicate the presence of excessive carbon deposits in the cylinder heads.

2 The only tools required are a compression gauge and a spark plug wrench. A compression gauge with a threaded adapter for the spark plug hole is preferable to the type which requires hand pressure to maintain a tight seal. Depending on the outcome of the initial test, a squirt-type oil can may also be needed.

3 Ensure the valve clearances are correctly set (see Section 12), then check the compression pressures using the information given in *Fault Finding Equipment* in the *Reference* section.

35 Engine – oil pressure check

1 The oil pressure warning light should come on when the ignition switch is turned ON and extinguish soon after the engine is started – this serves as a check that the warning light bulb is sound. If the oil pressure light comes on whilst the engine is running, low oil pressure is indicated – stop the engine immediately and carry out an oil level check *(see Daily (pre-ride) checks)*.

2 An oil pressure check must be carried out if the warning light comes on when the engine is running yet the oil level is good (Step 1). It can also provide useful information about the condition of the engine's lubrication system.

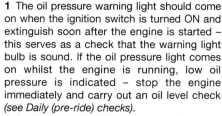

32.4a Vertical adjuster (ZX-9R C models)

32.3b Vertical adjuster (ZX-9R B models)

3 To check the oil pressure, a suitable gauge and adapter will be needed. Kawasaki dealers use a pressure gauge (57001-164) and adapter (57001-1033).

4 On ZX-7R and ZX-9R B models, remove the oil pressure switch (see Chapter 9) and screw the adapter and pressure gauge securely into the crankcase threads.

5 On ZX-9R C, E and F models, remove the lower fairing (see Chapter 8). Unscrew the plug from the oil passage located underneath the pick-up coil cover on the right-hand side of the crankcase and screw the gauge and adapter securely into the crankcase threads.

6 On all models, check the engine oil level *(see Daily (pre-ride) checks)* and top up to the upper level mark.

7 Start the engine and warm it up to the normal operating temperature, ensuring that there is no oil leakage from the pressure gauge and adapter.

8 Once the engine is at operating temperature, increase the engine speed briefly to 4000 rpm whilst watching the gauge reading. The oil pressure should be similar to that given in the Specifications at the start of this Chapter. Once the pressure reading has been obtained, stop the engine and allow it to cool.

9 If the pressure is significantly lower than the standard, either the pressure relief valve is stuck open, the oil pump is faulty, the oil strainer or filter is blocked, or there is other engine damage. Begin diagnosis by checking the oil filter, strainer and relief valve, then the oil pump (see Chapter 2A or 2B). If those items are not faulty, it is possible that the

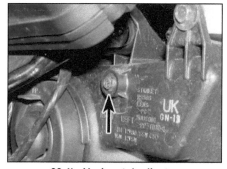

32.4b Horizontal adjuster (ZX-9R C models)

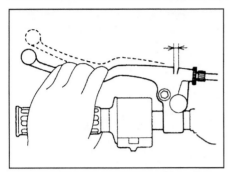

41.1 Measure the amount of freeplay between the clutch lever and the bracket as shown

bearing oil clearances are excessive and the engine needs to be overhauled.

10 If the pressure is too high, either an oil passage is clogged, the relief valve is stuck closed or the wrong grade of oil is being used.

11 On ZX-7R and ZX-9R B models, remove the pressure gauge and adapter from the engine and install the oil pressure switch (see Chapter 9).

12 On ZX-9R C, E and F models remove the pressure gauge and adapter from the engine. Apply a smear of sealant (Kawasaki recommend the use of Kawasaki Bond 56019-120) to the threads of the oil passage plug, then fit it to the crankcase and tighten to the specified torque.

13 On all models, check the engine oil level *(see Daily (pre-ride) checks)* and top-up to the upper level mark.

14 On completion, start the engine and check for leaks.

36 Fuel filter – renewal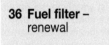

Interval:

US ZX-9R B models and UK/Europe ZX-9R B1 and B2 models – every 3000 miles
All other models – no specified interval
Renew the fuel filter as described in Chapter 4.

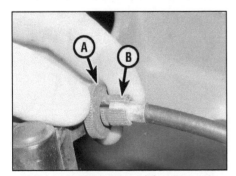

41.2 Loosen the locknut (A) and turn the adjuster (B) as required

37 Air filter element and vent filter(s) – renewal

Interval:

US ZX-9R B models and UK/Europe ZX-9R B1 and B2 models – every 12,000 miles (20,000 km) or 5 cleanings
All other models – no specified interval
Renew the air filter element and air vent filter(s) as described in Section 13.

38 Brake hoses – renewal

Interval:

US ZX-9R B models and UK/Europe ZX-9R B1 and B2 models – every 4 years
All other models – no specified interval
The hoses will deteriorate with age and should then be renewed. Refer to Chapter 7 for details, noting that new banjo union sealing washers must be used.

39 Clutch hose – renewal (ZX-7R and ZX-9R B models)

Interval:

US ZX-9R B models and UK/Europe ZX-9R B1 and B2 models – every 4 years
All other models – no specified interval
The hose will deteriorate with age and should then be renewed. Refer to Chapter 2A for details noting that new banjo union sealing washers must be used.

40 Fuel hoses – renewal

Interval:

US ZX-9R B models and UK ZX-9R B1 and B2 models – every 4 years
All other models – no specified interval
⚠ *Warning: Petrol (gasoline) is extremely flammable, so take extra precautions when you work on any part of the fuel system. Don't smoke or allow open flames or bare light bulbs near the work area, and don't work in a garage where a natural gas-type appliance is present. If you spill any fuel on your skin, rinse it off immediately with soap and water. When you perform any kind of work on the fuel system, wear safety glasses and have a fire extinguisher suitable for a Class B type fire (flammable liquids) on hand.*

1 The fuel hoses should be renewed, regardless of their condition.

2 Remove the fuel tank (see Chapter 4) and renew all the hoses connecting the fuel tap, fuel pump, fuel filter and carburettors. If necessary, remove the fuel pump and/or filter to improve access to the hoses. Ensure all new hoses are securely held in position with their retaining clips.

3 On completion, install the fuel tank, then run the engine and check that there are no leaks before taking the machine out on the road.

41 Clutch – check and adjustment (ZX-9R C, E and F models)

1 Periodic adjustment of the clutch cable is necessary to compensate for wear in the clutch plates and stretch of the cable. Check that the amount of freeplay at the clutch lever is within the specifications listed at the beginning of the Chapter **(see illustration)**. If adjustment is required, it can be made at either end of the cable or at the clutch end.

2 To adjust the freeplay at the lever, loosen the locknut (C models only) and turn the adjuster in or out until the required amount of freeplay is obtained **(see illustration)**. To increase freeplay, turn the adjuster clockwise. To reduce freeplay, turn the adjuster anti-clockwise. On C models, tighten the locknut securely once the adjuster is correctly set.

3 If all the adjustment has been taken up at the lever, reset the adjuster so that there are 5 to 6 mm of threads visible between the adjuster head and the locknut (C models) or between the adjuster and clutch cable bracket (E and F models). Pull back the rubber boot on the adjuster at the clutch end of the cable and fully slacken the locknut **(see illustration)**. Pull the outer cable so that it is tight and tighten the cable adjuster nut against the bracket. Securely tighten the cable locknut, then locate the rubber boot correctly on the cable end. Now set the correct amount of freeplay using the adjuster at the clutch lever end of the cable as

41.3 Fully slacken the locknut on the clutch end of the cable

described in Step 2. Subsequent adjustments can be made using the lever adjuster only, until all the adjustment has been taken up once more. If all the adjustment on both adjusters has been taken up, renew the cable (see Chapter 2B).

4 Push the release lever on the clutch cover forward until it stops. At this point the angle between the release lever and the cable should be approximately 60°. If not, and the cable

freeplay is set correctly, the clutch should be inspected for wear (see Chapter 2B).

5 On C models, the clutch lever has a span adjuster which alters the distance of the lever from the handlebar **(see illustration)**. Pull the lever away from the handlebar and turn the adjuster dial until the setting which best suits the rider is obtained. There are five positions. Align the number for the setting required with the triangular mark on the lever bracket.

41.5 The clutch lever span adjuster

Notes

Chapter 2 Part A:
Engine, clutch and transmission ZX-7R and ZX-9R B models

Contents

Degrees of difficulty

Easy, suitable for novice with little experience	Fairly easy, suitable for beginner with some experience	Fairly difficult, suitable for competent DIY mechanic	Difficult, suitable for experienced DIY mechanic	Very difficult, suitable for expert DIY or professional 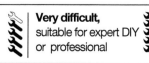

Specifications

General

Capacity	
ZX-7R models	748 cc
ZX-9R B models	899 cc
Bore	73.0 mm
Stroke	
ZX-7R models	44.7 mm
ZX-9R B models	53.7 mm
Compression ratio	11.5 to 1
Cylinder identification	1-2-3-4 (from left to right)
Firing order	1-2-4-3

Camshaft and followers/rocker arms

Intake cam lobe height	
ZX-7R models	
Standard	37.246 to 37.354 mm
Service limit	37.150 mm
ZX-9R B models	
Standard	36.667 to 36.807 mm
Service limit	36.560 mm
Exhaust cam lobe height	
ZX-7R models	
Standard	35.446 to 35.554 mm
Service limit	35.350 mm
ZX-9R B models	
Standard	36.480 to 36.620 mm
Service limit	36.380 mm
Camshaft journal OD	
ZX-7R models	
Standard	23.930 to 23.952 mm
Service limit	23.900 mm
ZX-9R B models	
Nos. 1 and 4 bearings	
Standard	23.930 to 23.952 mm
Service limit	23.900 mm
Nos. 2 and 3 bearings	
Standard	23.900 to 23.922 mm
Service limit	23.870 mm
Camshaft bearing cap ID	
Standard	24.000 to 24.021 mm
Service limit	24.080 mm
Camshaft bearing oil clearance	
ZX-7R models	0.048 to 0.091 mm
ZX-9R B models	
Nos. 1 and 4 bearings	0.048 to 0.091 mm
Nos. 2 and 3 bearings	0.078 to 0.121 mm
Camshaft runout	
Standard	Less than 0.02 mm
Service limit	0.10 mm
Rocker arm bore ID – ZX-9R B models	
Standard	12.000 to 12.018 mm
Service limit	12.050 mm
Rocker arm shaft OD – ZX-9R B models	
Standard	11.966 to 11.984 mm
Service limit	11.940 mm
Camchain 20-link length	
ZX-7R models	
Standard	155.5 to 155.8 mm
Maximum	157.8 mm
ZX-9R models	
Standard	127.0 to 127.36 mm
Maximum	128.9 mm

Cylinder head

Maximum warpage	0.05 mm

Valves and valve springs

Intake valve stem OD

    Standard . . . . 4.475 to 4.490 mm

    Service limit . . . . 4.460 mm

Exhaust valve stem OD

    Standard . . . . 4.455 to 4.470 mm

    Service limit . . . . 4.440 mm

Valve stem runout

    Standard . . . . Less than 0.01 mm

    Service limit . . . . 0.05 mm

Valve head thickness

    Intake valve

        Standard . . . . 0.50 mm

        Service limit . . . . 0.25 mm

    Exhaust valve

        Standard . . . . 0.80 mm

        Service limit . . . . 0.50 mm

Valve guide ID – intake and exhaust

    Standard . . . . 4.500 to 4.512 mm

    Service limit . . . . 4.580 mm

Valve seat width . . . . 0.5 to 1.0 mm

Valve spring free length

    ZX-7R models

        Inner spring

            Standard . . . . 36.47 mm

            Service limit . . . . 34.80 mm

        Outer spring

            Standard . . . . 41.39 mm

            Service limit . . . . 39.70 mm

    ZX-9R B models

        Standard . . . . 41.8 mm

        Service limit . . . . 40.1 mm

Cylinder block

Cylinder bore ID

    Standard . . . . 73.000 to 73.012 mm

    Service limit . . . . 73.100 mm

Cylinder-to-piston clearance . . . . 0.042 to 0.070 mm

Maximum gasket face warpage . . . . 0.05 mm

Taper and out-of-round limits . . . . Not specified

Pistons

Piston OD (measured 5 mm up from base of skirt)

    Standard . . . . 72.948 to 72.958 mm

    Service limit . . . . 72.800 mm

Piston ring groove width

    Top ring

        Standard . . . . 0.84 to 0.86 mm

        Service limit . . . . 0.94 mm

    Second (middle) ring

        Standard . . . . 0.82 to 0.84 mm

        Service limit . . . . 0.92 mm

    Oil control ring . . . . Not specified

Piston rings

Top and second (middle) ring thickness

    Standard . . . . 0.77 to 0.79 mm

    Service limit . . . . 0.70 mm

Top ring-to-groove clearance

    Standard . . . . 0.05 to 0.09 mm

    Service limit . . . . 0.19 mm

Second (middle) ring-to-groove clearance

    Standard . . . . 0.03 to 0.07 mm

    Service limit . . . . 0.17 mm

Top ring end gap

    Standard . . . . 0.20 to 0.35 mm

    Service limit . . . . 0.65 mm

Piston rings (continued)

Second (middle) ring end gap
    Standard .... 0.40 to 0.55 mm
    Service limit .... 0.85 mm
Oil control ring
    Standard .... 0.20 to 0.70 mm
    Service limit .... 1.00 mm

Clutch

Friction plate thickness .... Not specified
Steel plate thicknesses .... 2.0, 2.3, 2.6 mm
Friction and plain plate warpage
    Standard .... Less than 0.2 mm
    Service limit .... 0.3 mm
Clutch spring free length
    ZX-7R models
        Standard .... 34.7 mm
        Service limit .... 33.5 mm
    ZX-9R B models
        Standard .... 42.9 mm
        Service limit .... 40.9 mm
Clutch pressure plate freeplay check – see text (Section 17)
    With original friction plates .... 0.15 to 0.75 mm
    With new friction plates .... 0.05 to 0.35 mm

Alternator drive chain

Drive chain 20-link length
    Standard .... 158 to 159.2 mm
    Service limit
        ZX-7R models .... 161.0 mm
        ZX-9R B models .... 159.8 mm

Crankshaft and connecting rods

Crankshaft runout
    Standard .... Less than 0.02 mm
    Service limit .... 0.05 mm
Crankshaft endfloat
    Standard .... 0.05 to 0.20 mm
    Service limit .... 0.40 mm
Connecting rod big-end bearing side clearance
    Standard .... 0.13 to 0.38 mm
    Service limit .... 0.6 mm
Connecting rod crankpin bore ID
    ZX-7R models
        Unmarked .... 37.000 to 37.008 mm
        Size group 0 .... 37.009 to 37.016 mm
    ZX-9R B models
        Unmarked .... 38.000 to 38.008 mm
        Size group 0 .... 38.009 to 38.016 mm
Crankshaft crankpin OD
    ZX-7R models
        Unmarked .... 33.984 to 33.992 mm
        Size group 0 .... 33.993 to 34.000 mm
    ZX-9R B models
        Unmarked .... 34.984 to 34.992 mm
        Size group 0 .... 34.993 to 35.000 mm
Connecting rod bearing oil clearance
    Standard .... 0.036 to 0.066 mm
    Service limit .... 0.10 mm
Connecting rod bearing insert thicknesses
    Brown .... 1.475 to 1.480 mm
    Black (ZX-7R) or unmarked (ZX-9R B) .... 1.480 to 1.485 mm
    Blue .... 1.485 to 1.490 mm
Connecting rod bolt stretch limits (bolt length measurement tightening method – see text, Section 31)
    Original connecting rod .... 0.20 to 0.32 mm
    New connecting rod .... 0.24 to 0.36 mm
Crankcase main bearing bore ID
    ZX-7R models
        Unmarked .... 35.000 to 35.008 mm
        Size group 0 .... 35.009 to 35.016 mm

Crankshaft and connecting rods (continued)

Crankcase main bearing bore ID (continued)
   ZX-9R B models
      Unmarked . . . . 36.000 to 36.008 mm
      Size group 0 . . . . 36.009 to 36.016 mm
Crankshaft main bearing journal OD
   ZX-7R models
      Unmarked . . . . 31.984 to 31.992 mm
      Size group 1 . . . . 31.993 to 32.000 mm
   ZX-9R B models
      Unmarked . . . . 32.984 to 32.992 mm
      Size group 1 . . . . 32.993 to 33.000 mm
Main bearing oil clearance
   Standard . . . . 0.020 to 0.044 mm
   Service limit . . . . 0.07 mm
Main bearing insert thicknesses
   Brown . . . . 1.490 to 1.494 mm
   Black (ZX-7R) or unmarked (ZX-9R B) . . . . 1.494 to 1.498 mm
   Blue . . . . 1.498 to 1.502 mm

Oil pump and pressure relief valves

Oil pressure (at 4000 rpm)
   ZX-7R models . . . . 46 to 54 psi (3.3 to 3.8 bar) at 80°C (176°F)
   ZX-9R B models . . . . 44 to 53 psi (3.1 to 3.7 bar) at 90°C (194°F)
Oil pressure relief valve opening pressure
   ZX-7R models . . . . Not specified
   ZX-9R B models . . . . 63 to 85 psi (4.4 to 6.0 bar)

Transmission

Gear ratios (No. of teeth)
   ZX-7R models
      1st 2.857:1 (40/14)
      2nd 2.000:1 (36/18)
      3rd 1.619:1 (34/21)
      4th 1.391:1 (32/23)
      5th 1.222:1 (33/27)
      6th 1.103:1 (32/29)
   ZX-9R B models
      Early (B1) models
         1st 2.857:1 (40/14)
         2nd 2.055:1 (37/18)
         3rd 1.650:1 (33/20)
         4th 1.391:1 (32/23)
         5th 1.222:1 (33/27)
         6th 1.103:1 (32/29)
      Later (B2 on) models
         1st 2.785:1 (39/14)
         2nd 2.000:1 (36/18)
         3rd 1.619:1 (34/21)
         4th 1.391:1 (32/23)
         5th 1.222:1 (33/27)
         6th 1.103:1 (32/29)
Primary drive ratio
   ZX-7R models 1.754:1 (93/53)
   ZX-9R B models 1.534:1 (89/58)
Gear selector fork groove width
   Standard . . . . 6.05 to 6.15 mm
   Service limit . . . . 6.25 mm
Selector fork end thickness
   Standard . . . . 5.9 to 6.0 mm
   Service limit . . . . 5.8 mm
Selector fork guide pin diameter
   Standard . . . . 7.9 to 8.0 mm
   Service limit . . . . 7.8 mm
Selector drum groove width
   Standard . . . . 8.05 to 8.20 mm
   Service limit . . . . 8.30 mm

Torque wrench settings – ZX-7R models

Alternator drive chain tensioner bolts	12 Nm
Alternator drive coupling bolt	25 Nm
Alternator driveshaft bearing plate bolts	12 Nm
Camchain rear guide pivot bolt	25 Nm
Camchain tensioner	
Mounting bolts	12 Nm
Cap bolt	8 Nm
Camshaft bearing cap bolts	12 Nm
Clutch assembly	
Centre nut	130 Nm
Drum bolts	8 Nm
Spring bolts	9 Nm
Spring guides	25 Nm
Clutch cover bolts	10 Nm
Clutch hydraulic hose banjo fitting bolts	25 Nm
Clutch lever pivot bolt nut	6 Nm
Clutch master cylinder mounting bolts	11 Nm
Clutch slave cylinder bleed valve	8 Nm
Connecting rod bearing cap bolt nuts	
Bolt length measurement method	See text (Section 31)
Torque tightening method	
New connecting rod assembly (using bolts and nuts supplied with the rod)	
Stage 1	18 Nm
Stage 2	Angle-tighten a further 120°
New connecting rod assembly (using the bolts supplied with the rod but other new nuts)	
Stage 1	20 Nm
Stage 2	Angle-tighten a further 120°
Original connecting rod assembly (using new bolts and the original nuts)	
Stage 1	24 Nm
Stage 2	Angle-tighten a further 120°
Original connecting rod assembly (using new bolts and nuts)	
Stage 1	25 Nm
Stage 2	Angle-tighten a further 120°
Crankcase bolts	
9 mm (main bearing) bolts	44 Nm
8 mm bolts	
Long (115 mm) bolt	27 Nm
All other bolts	25 Nm
Crankcase breather cover bolts	10 Nm
Cylinder head cover bolts	10 Nm
Cylinder head bolts	
6 mm bolts	12 Nm
10 mm bolts	
Stage 1 (first)	20 Nm
Stage 2 (final)	44 Nm
Cylinder head/block sound damper bolts	10 Nm
Engine mountings	
Threaded collars	10 Nm
Mounting bolts	59 Nm
Threaded collar locknuts	49 Nm
Gearchange mechanism	
Cover bolts	10 Nm
Cover screws	5 Nm
Stopper arm pivot bolt	10 Nm
Centralising spring locating pin	42 Nm
Oil cooler centre bolt	49 Nm
Oil cooler centre bolt filter adapter	25 Nm
Oil filter	10 Nm
Oil pan bolts	10 Nm
Oil pan drain plug	20 Nm
Oil pipe bolts	
Alternator drive shaft pipe	12 Nm
Crankcase-to-cylinder head pipe	10 Nm
Transmission oil spray pipe	12 Nm
Oil pressure relief valve	15 Nm
Oil pump retaining bolts	12 Nm
Selector drum bearing retaining plate bolts	12 Nm
Selector drum cam centre bolt	12 Nm
Starter one-way clutch holder bolts	12 Nm

Torque wrench settings – ZX-9R models

Alternator drive chain tensioner bolts	12 Nm
Alternator drive coupling bolt	25 Nm
Alternator driveshaft bearing plate bolts	12 Nm
Camchain rear guide pivot bolt	25 Nm
Camchain tensioner	
Mounting bolts	12 Nm
Cap bolt	8 Nm
Camshaft bearing cap bolts	12 Nm
Clutch assembly	
Centre nut	135 Nm
Spring bolts	9 Nm
Spring guides	25 Nm
Clutch cover bolts	10 Nm
Clutch hydraulic hose banjo fitting bolts	25 Nm
Clutch lever pivot bolt nut	6 Nm
Clutch master cylinder mounting bolts	11 Nm
Clutch slave cylinder bleed valve	8 Nm
Connecting rod bearing cap bolt nuts	
Bolt length measurement method	See text (Section 31)
Torque tightening method	
New connecting rod assembly (using bolts and nuts supplied with the rod)	
Stage 1	18 Nm
Stage 2	Angle-tighten a further 120°
New connecting rod assembly (using bolts supplied with the rod but other new nuts)	
Stage 1	20 Nm
Stage 2	Angle-tighten a further 120°
Original connecting rod assembly (using new bolts and the original nuts)	
Stage 1	24 Nm
Stage 2	Angle-tighten a further 120°
Original connecting rod assembly (using new bolts and nuts)	
Stage 1	25 Nm
Stage 2	Angle-tighten a further 120°
Crankcase bolts	
9 mm (main bearing) bolts	44 Nm
8 mm bolts	27 Nm
6 mm bolts	20 Nm
Cylinder block sound damper bolts	10 Nm
Cylinder head bolts	
6 mm bolts	12 Nm
10 mm bolts	
Stage 1 (first)	20 Nm
Stage 2 (final)	
Original bolts	49 Nm
New bolts	54 Nm
Cylinder head coolant pipe bolts	12 Nm
Cylinder head cover bolts	10 Nm
Cylinder head left end cover bolts	5 Nm
Engine mountings	
Frame downtube bolts and nuts	44 Nm
Front mounting and bracket nuts and bolts	44 Nm
Rear mountings	
Threaded collars	10 Nm
Threaded collar locknuts	49 Nm
Mounting bolt nuts	59 Nm
Gearchange mechanism	
Cover bolts	10 Nm
Cover screws	5 Nm
Stopper arm pivot bolt	10 Nm
Neutral positioning arm pivot nut	10 Nm
Centralising spring locating pin	25 Nm
Oil cooler centre bolt	49 Nm
Oil cooler centre bolt filter adapter	25 Nm
Oil filter	10 Nm
Oil pan bolts	12 Nm
Oil pan drain plug	20 Nm

Torque wrench settings – ZX-9R models (continued)

Oil pipe bolts
    Alternator driveshaft pipe . . . . 12 Nm
    Crankcase-to-cylinder head pipe
        Cylinder head end banjo bolt . . . . 34 Nm
        Crankcase end bolt . . . . 10 Nm
    Transmission oil spray pipe . . . . 12 Nm
Oil pressure relief valve . . . . 15 Nm
Oil pump retaining bolts . . . . 12 Nm
Selector drum bearing retaining plate bolts . . . . 12 Nm
Selector drum cam centre bolt . . . . 12 Nm
Selector fork shaft retaining plate bolt . . . . 12 Nm
Starter one-way clutch holder bolts . . . . 12 Nm

1 General information

The engine/transmission unit is of the water-cooled, in-line, four-cylinder design, installed transversely across the frame. The engine/transmission unit is constructed in aluminium alloy, with the crankcase being divided horizontally. The crankcase incorporates a wet sump, pressure-fed lubrication system, and houses a dual rotor oil pump.

The sixteen valves are operated by double overhead camshafts, which are chain driven off the right-hand end of the crankshaft. On ZX-7R engines, the valves are operated by bucket-type followers and, on ZX-9R B engines, the valves are operated by rocker arms. Valve clearances are adjusted via shims fitted between the top of the valve stem and the follower/rocker arm (as applicable).

The alternator is situated directly behind the cylinder block, on the left-hand side, and is chain-driven off the rear of the clutch. The alternator chain also drives the oil pump drive gear, which in turn operates the water pump via the oil pump shaft. The starter clutch is incorporated on the alternator driveshaft.

The hydraulically-operated clutch is of the wet multi-plate type and is driven off the right-hand end of the crankshaft by the primary drive gear. The transmission is of the six-speed constant mesh type. Final drive to the rear wheel is by chain and sprockets, the drive sprocket being mounted on the left-hand end of the output shaft.

2 Operations possible with the engine in the frame

The components and assemblies listed below can be removed without having to remove the engine/transmission assembly from the frame. If, however, a number of areas require attention at the same time, removal of the engine is recommended.

Starter motor (see Chapter 9)

Alternator (see Chapter 9)
Water pump (see Chapter 3)
Cylinder head cover
Camchain tensioner and guides
Camshafts and followers – ZX-7R engine
Camshafts – ZX-9R B engine
Clutch assembly
Alternator chain and tensioner
Oil pan
Oil pump and pressure relief valves
Oil cooler
Gearchange mechanism components

3 Operations requiring engine removal

It is necessary to remove the engine/transmission assembly from the frame to enable the following components to be removed.

Rocker arms and shafts – ZX-9R B engine
Cylinder head
Cylinder block
Pistons and rings
Crankshaft and bearings
Connecting rods and bearings
Camchain
Alternator driveshaft and starter clutch
Transmission shafts
Selector drum and forks

4 Major engine repair – general note

1 It is not always easy to determine when, or if, an engine should be completely overhauled, as a number of factors must be considered.
2 High mileage is not necessarily an indication that an overhaul is needed, whilst low mileage, on the other hand, does not preclude the need for an overhaul. Frequency of servicing is probably the single most important consideration. An engine that has regular and frequent oil and filter changes, as well as other required maintenance, will most likely give many miles of reliable service. Conversely, a neglected engine, or one which has not been run-in properly, may require an

overhaul very early in its life.
3 Exhaust smoke and excessive oil consumption are both indications that piston rings and/or valve guides are in need of attention, although make sure that the fault is not due to oil leakage.
4 If the engine is making obvious knocking or rumbling noises, the connecting rod and/or main bearings are probably at fault.
5 Loss of power, rough running, excessive valve train noise and high fuel consumption rates may also point to the need for an overhaul, especially if they are all present at the same time. If a complete tune-up does not remedy the situation, major mechanical work is the only solution.
6 An engine overhaul generally involves restoring the internal parts to the specifications of a new engine. The piston rings and main and connecting rod bearings are usually renewed, and the cylinder bores honed, during a major overhaul. Generally, the valve seats are re-ground, since they are usually in less than perfect condition at this point. The end result should be a like-new engine that will give as many trouble-free miles as the original.
7 Before beginning the engine overhaul, read through the related procedures to familiarise yourself with the scope and requirements of the job. Overhauling an engine is not all that difficult, but it is time-consuming. Plan on the motorcycle being tied up for a minimum of two weeks. Check on the availability of parts and make sure that any necessary special tools, equipment and supplies are obtained in advance.
8 Most work can be done with typical workshop hand tools, although a number of precision measuring tools are required for inspecting parts to determine if they must be renewed. Often a dealer will handle the inspection of parts and offer advice concerning reconditioning and renewal. As a general rule, time is the primary cost of an overhaul so it does not pay to install worn or substandard parts.
9 As a final note, to ensure maximum life and minimum trouble from a rebuilt engine, everything must be assembled with care in a spotlessly clean environment.

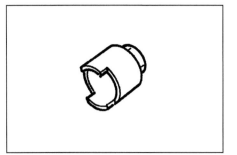

5.0 This special tool is required to loosen and tighten the locknuts on the engine mounting adjusters

5 Engine – removal and installation

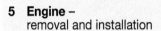

Caution: The engine is very heavy. Engine removal and installation should be carried out with the aid of at least one assistant; personal injury or damage could occur if the engine falls or is dropped. A mechanical or hydraulic floor jack should be used to support and lower or raise the engine, if possible.

Note: *A special socket will be needed to slacken/tighten the engine mounting threaded collar locknuts. If the Kawasaki service tool (57001-1347) is not available, a suitable alternative can be made by cutting a spare socket (approximately 24 mm in size) as shown* **(see illustration).**

Removal

1 Support the bike securely upright using an auxiliary stand so that it cannot be knocked over during this procedure. Work can be made easier by raising the machine on an hydraulic ramp or a suitable platform to a comfortable working height (see *Tools and Workshop Tips* (Section 1) in the *Reference* section).

Caution: Ensure the bike is securely supported before proceeding.

2 If the engine is dirty, particularly around its mountings, wash it thoroughly before starting any major dismantling work. This will make

5.8 Remove the bolt and slip the lever off the shaft

work much easier and rule out the possibility of caked-on lumps of dirt falling into some vital component.

3 Remove the complete fairing (see Chapter 8).

4 Remove the battery (see Chapter 9).

5 Drain the engine oil (see Chapter 1).

6 Drain the cooling system (see Chapter 1) and remove the radiator and coolant reservoir (see Chapter 3).

7 Remove the fuel tank, air filter housing, carburettors and complete exhaust system (see Chapter 4).

8 Note the correct fitted position of the gearchange lever on its shaft (make alignment marks if necessary), then unscrew the clamp bolt and free the gearchange lever from the engine **(see illustration).**

9 Remove the front sprocket (see Chapter 6) and position the clutch slave cylinder clear of the engine.

10 Remove the ignition coils (see Chapter 5) and proceed as described under the relevant sub-heading.

ZX-7R models

11 Referring to Chapter 4, remove the secondary air injection system control valve and the carburettor vent valve.

12 Unscrew the retaining bolts and remove the baffle plate and insulation pad from the top of the cylinder head cover **(see illustrations).**

13 Slacken the retaining clips securing the thermostat housing hoses to the cylinder

5.12a Unscrew the retaining bolts and remove the baffle plate . . .

head pipe and oil cooler, and disconnect both hoses. Unscrew the mounting bolt and remove the thermostat housing assembly from the bike, taking care not to lose the housing collars and mounting rubbers **(see illustration).**

14 Unbolt the radiator mounting bracket and remove it from the front of the crankcase.

15 Trace the wiring back from the ignition pick-up coil cover/oil pressure switch, the alternator and the neutral switch to the connectors located on top of the crankcase. Note the correct routing of all the wiring, then disconnect all the connectors so that the wiring is free to be removed with the engine.

16 Unscrew the bolt and free the earth (ground) lead from the top of the crankcase.

17 Lift the rubber cover and unscrew the nut securing the starter motor cable to the motor. Free the cable from the motor, noting its correct routing, and position it clear of the engine.

18 At this point, position an hydraulic or mechanical jack under the engine with a block of wood between the jack head and sump. Make sure the jack is centrally positioned so that the engine will not topple when the last mounting bolt is removed. Take the weight of the engine on the jack **(see illustration).**

19 Slacken and remove the left and right upper mounting bolts securing the cylinder head to the frame, and remove the nuts **(see illustration).**

20 Using the special socket (Kawasaki service tool No. 57001-1347) or a suitable

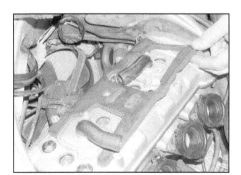

5.12b . . . and insulation pad

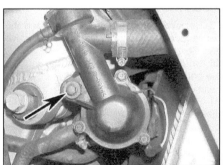

5.13 Thermostat mounting bolt

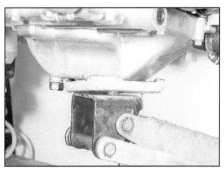

5.18 Support the engine with a jack; place a block of wood between the jack and sump to protect the sump

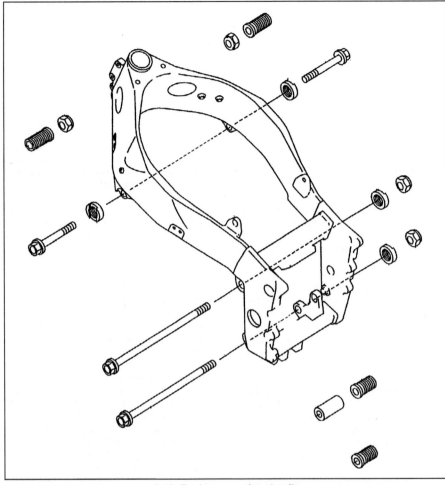

5.19 Engine mounting details (ZX-7R models)

home-made alternative, slacken the upper mounting bolt collar locknuts then fully back-off both threaded collars **(see illustration 5.0)**.
21 Slacken and remove the nuts from the upper and lower rear mounting bolts, then loosen both the mounting collar locknuts.
22 Ensure the engine is securely supported, then withdraw both rear mounting bolts and fully back-off the threaded collars. Recover the spacer, which is fitted to the upper mounting bolt between the left-hand side of the engine and the frame.

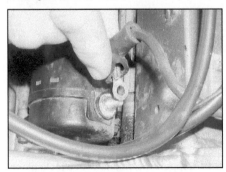

5.30 Free the starter motor cable

23 The engine is now free to be lowered out of the frame. Check that all relevant wiring, cables and hoses are disconnected and secured well clear, then carefully lower the engine out of position (see *Caution* at the start of this Section). As the engine is lowered out of position, note that it will be necessary to free the drive chain from the output shaft.
24 With the aid of an assistant, lift the engine unit off the jack and move it carefully to the work surface.

ZX-9R B models

25 Remove the fuel pump assembly and the secondary air injection system control valve (see Chapter 4).
26 Unscrew the retaining bolts and remove the baffle plate from the front of the cylinder head cover **(see illustration)**.
27 Slacken the retaining clip securing the thermostat housing hose to the cylinder head pipe and disconnect the hose. Unscrew the mounting bracket bolts and remove the thermostat housing assembly from the bike.
28 Trace the wiring back from the ignition pick-up coil cover/oil pressure switch, the alternator, the neutral switch and the sidestand switch to the connectors located on

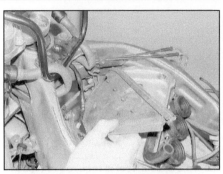

5.26 Unscrew the retaining bolts and remove the baffle plate

5.29 Unscrew the bolt and free the earth (ground) lead from the top of the crankcase

top of the crankcase. Note the correct routing of all the wiring, then disconnect all the connectors so that the wiring is free to be removed with the engine.
29 Unscrew the bolt and free the earth (ground) lead from the top of the crankcase **(see illustration)**.
30 Lift the rubber cover and unscrew the nut securing the starter motor cable to the motor **(see illustration)**. Free the cable from the motor, noting its correct routing, and position it clear of the engine.
31 Slacken and remove the bolts and nuts securing the frame downtubes to the mounting brackets on the front of the crankcase **(see illustration)**.
32 Unscrew the mounting bolts and nuts securing the downtubes to the main frame

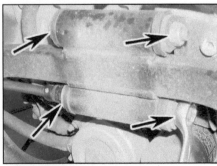

5.31 Slacken and remove the bolts and nuts securing the downtubes to the mounting brackets on the front of the crankcase

5.32a Left downtube upper mounting (right side similar)

5.32b Right downtube lower mounting (left side similar)

5.32c Remove the downtubes brackets from the crankcase

(see illustrations) and remove the downtube assembly from the bike. Unscrew the bolts securing the downtube brackets to the crankcase and remove both brackets (see illustration).

33 At this point, position an hydraulic or mechanical jack under the engine with a block of wood between the jack head and sump.

Make sure the jack is centrally positioned so that the engine will not topple when the last mounting bolt is removed. Take the weight of the engine on the jack.

34 Slacken and remove the nuts from the engine upper and lower rear mounting bolts (see illustration).

35 Using the special socket (Kawasaki service tool No. 57001-1347) or a suitable home-made alternative, slacken the rear mounting bolt collar locknuts.

36 Ensure the engine is securely supported, then withdraw both rear mounting bolts and fully back-off the threaded collars. Recover the spacer, which is fitted to the upper mounting bolt between the left side of the engine and the frame.

37 The engine is now free to be lowered out of the frame. Check that all relevant wiring, cables and hoses are disconnected and secured well clear, then carefully lower the engine out of position (see *Caution* at the start of this Section). As the engine is lowered out of position, note that it will be necessary to free the drive chain from the output shaft.

38 With the aid of an assistant, lift the engine unit off the jack and move it carefully to the work surface.

Installation

ZX-7R models

39 Ensure all the engine mounting threaded collars are fully backed-off to provide maximum clearance for the engine (see illustration).

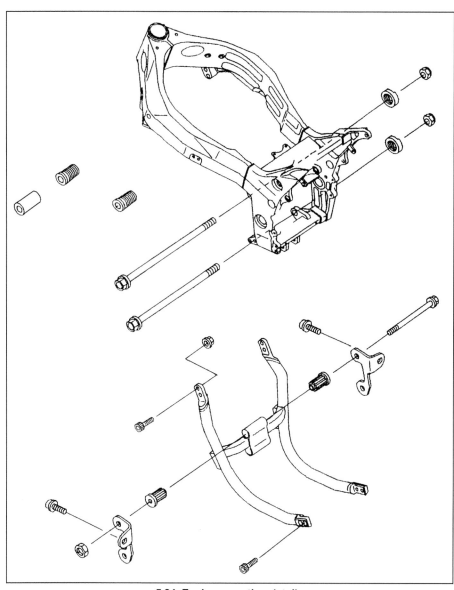

5.34 Engine mounting details (ZX-9R B models)

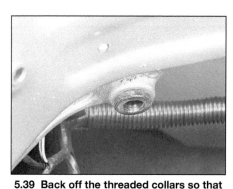

5.39 Back off the threaded collars so that they look like this when viewed from inside the frame

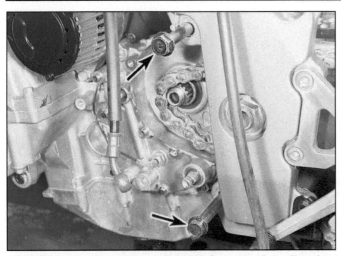

5.42 Withdraw the rear mounting bolts just enough to allow the threaded collars to be screwed in

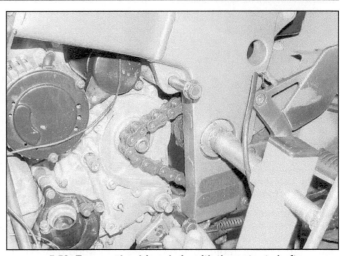

5.50 Engage the drive chain with the output shaft

40 With the aid of an assistant, place the engine unit on top of the jack and block of wood. Carefully raise the engine unit into position in the frame, engaging the drive chain with the output shaft as it is lifted. Make sure no wires, cables or hoses become trapped between the engine and the frame.

41 Insert the spacer between the engine rear upper mounting and left-hand side of the frame, then insert both the upper and lower rear mounting bolts from the left-hand side of the bike.

42 Insert both the front mounting bolts, then partially withdraw the rear mounting bolts (see illustration) just enough to allow the threaded collars to be screwed in. Tighten both rear mounting threaded collars to the specified torque setting, then slide the mounting bolts fully back into position.

43 Remove the front mounting bolts and screw both the front mounting threaded collars in until they contact the cylinder head. Ensure the cylinder head is centrally positioned between the frame sections and check that both front mounting bolts can be easily inserted. Once the engine is correctly positioned, tighten both the left-hand and right-hand front threaded collars to the specified torque setting. Note: The cylinder head must not contact the frame.

44 Fit the left-hand and right-hand front mounting bolts and nuts and tighten them lightly.

45 Fit the nuts to the rear mounting bolts and tighten them to the specified torque setting.

46 Tighten the front mounting bolts to the specified torque.

47 Once all the mounting bolts are tightened, go round and tighten all the threaded collar locknuts to the specified torque.

48 The remainder of the installation procedure is the reverse of removal, noting the following points.

a) Make sure all wires, cables and hoses are correctly routed and connected, and secured by the relevant clips or ties.

b) Tighten all nuts and bolts to the specified torque settings (where given) and renew all gaskets and O-rings disturbed on removal.

c) Adjust the throttle and choke cable freeplay (see Chapter 1).

d) Adjust the drive chain (see Chapter 1).

e) Refill the engine with oil and coolant (see Chapter 1).

f) Prior to installing the lower fairing panels, start the engine and check that there are no signs of coolant/oil leakage.

ZX-9R B models

49 Ensure the engine rear mounting threaded collars are fully backed-off to provide maximum clearance for the engine (see illustration 5.39).

50 With the aid of an assistant, place the engine unit on top of the jack and block of wood. Carefully raise the engine unit into position in the frame, engaging the drive chain with the output shaft as it is lifted (see illustration). Make sure no wires, cables or hoses become trapped between the engine and the frame.

51 Insert the spacer between the engine rear upper mounting and left-hand side of the frame, then insert both the upper and lower rear mounting bolts from the left-hand side of the bike (see illustration).

52 Apply sealant to the threads of the mounting bolts and fit the front mounting brackets to the crankcase. Tighten the bolts only lightly at this stage.

53 Manoeuvre the downtube assembly into position and tighten its mounting bolts and nuts to the specified torque. Insert the engine front mounting bolts and nuts, tightening them lightly only at this stage.

54 Withdraw the rear engine mounting bolts approximately 55 mm, so that they are clear of the threaded collars, then tighten both threaded collars to the specified torque. Once both collars are correctly tightened, secure them in position by tighten the collar locknuts to the specified torque (see illustration).

55 Fully insert the rear mounting bolts, then fit the nuts and tighten them to the specified torque.

56 Tighten the engine front mounting bolts to the specified torque then tighten the bolts securing the mounting brackets to the crankcase to the specified torque.

57 The remainder of the installation procedure is the reverse of removal, noting the following points.

a) Make sure all wires, cables and hoses are correctly routed and connected, and secured by the relevant clips or ties.

b) Tighten all nuts and bolts to the specified

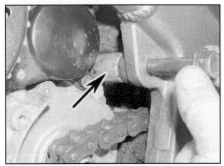

5.51 Insert the spacer between the engine rear upper mounting

5.54 Tighten the collar locknuts

torque settings (where given) and renew all gaskets and O-rings disturbed on removal.
c) *Adjust the throttle and choke cable freeplay (see Chapter 1).*
d) *Adjust the drive chain (see Chapter 1).*
e) *Refill the engine with oil and coolant (see Chapter 1).*
f) *Prior to installing the lower fairing panels, start the engine and check that there are no signs of coolant/oil leakage.*

6 Engine disassembly and reassembly – general information

Disassembly

1 Before disassembling the engine, the external surfaces of the unit should be thoroughly cleaned and degreased. This will prevent contamination of the engine internals, and will also make working a lot easier and cleaner. A high flash-point solvent, such as paraffin (kerosene) can be used or, better still, a proprietary engine degreaser. Use old paintbrushes and toothbrushes to work the solvent into the various recesses of the engine casings. Take care to exclude solvent or water from the electrical components and intake and exhaust ports.

 Warning: The use of petrol (gasoline) as a cleaning agent should be avoided because of the risk of fire.

2 When clean and dry, arrange the unit on the workbench, leaving a suitable clear area for working. Gather a selection of small containers and plastic bags so that parts can be grouped together in an easily identifiable manner. Some paper and a pen should be on hand for making notes and writing labels, to be attached where necessary. A supply of clean shop towels is also required.
3 Before commencing work, read through the appropriate section to familiarise yourself with the procedure. It should be noted that great force is seldom required when removing engine components (if it is, it will be specified). If a component is reluctant to be removed, this is often indicative of an incorrect approach or removal method. If in any doubt, re-check with the text.
4 When disassembling the engine, keep 'mated' parts together (including gears, cylinders, pistons, valves, etc. that have been in contact with each other during engine operation). These 'mated' parts must be re-used or renewed as an assembly.
5 Engine/transmission disassembly should be done in the following general order, with reference to the appropriate Sections.
Remove the camshafts
Remove the cylinder head
Remove the cylinder block
Remove the pistons
Remove the starter motor and alternator (see Chapter 9)

7.4 Remove the six cylinder head bolts and sealing washers

Remove the clutch
Remove the alternator chain
Remove the gearchange mechanism
Remove the oil pan
Remove the oil pump and pressure relief valves
Separate the crankcase halves
Remove the crankshaft
Remove the connecting rods
Remove the transmission shafts
Remove the selector drum and forks

Reassembly

6 Reassembly is accomplished by reversing the general disassembly sequence.

7 Cylinder head cover – removal and installation

Note: *The cylinder head cover can be removed with the engine in the frame.*

Removal

ZX-7R models

1 Remove the carburettors, secondary air injection system control valve and the carburettor vent valve (see Chapter 4). On California models, it will also be necessary to remove the evaporative emission control system control valve.
2 Disconnect the spark plug caps and position them clear of the cover.
3 Unscrew the retaining bolts and remove the

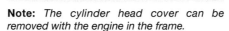

7.12a Apply a small bead of sealant to the semi-circular cutouts

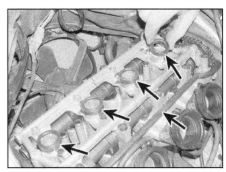

7.5 Recover the main seal from the head and the four seals from the spark plug apertures

baffle plate and insulation pad from the top of the cylinder head cover **(see illustrations 5.12a & 5.12b)**.
4 Slacken and remove the six cylinder head cover bolts and lift off the sealing washers **(see illustration)**.
5 Carefully lift off the cylinder head cover and recover the main seal from the head and the four seals from the spark plug apertures **(see illustration)**. Renew any seal which shows signs of damage or deterioration. Check the condition of the camchain guide fitted to the inside of the cover; if it shows signs of wear or damage, it must be renewed.
6 Whilst the cover is removed, check the condition of the O-rings on the upper ends of the four air suction tubes and renew them if they show signs of damage or deterioration. If the O-rings need replacing, pull out the suction tubes and check the condition of the lower O-rings (there are two on each tube), replacing them if necessary.

ZX-9R B models

7 Remove the carburettors and secondary air injection system control valve (see Chapter 4). On California models, it will also be necessary to remove the evaporative emission control system control valve.
8 Remove the ignition HT coils (Chapter 5).
9 Unscrew the retaining bolt and remove the baffle plate from the front of the cylinder head cover **(see illustration 5.26)**.
10 Remove the cylinder head cover as described in Steps 4 to 6.

Installation

ZX-7R models

11 If the air suction tubes have been removed, fit new O-rings to the upper and two lower grooves on each tube. Lubricate the O-rings with a smear of engine oil and push the tubes firmly into their cylinder head locations, ensuring that each one is fitted with its two O-rings at the bottom.
12 Ensure the cylinder head, camshaft cap and cover mating surfaces are clean and dry, then apply a small bead of sealant to the semi-circular cutouts on each end of the cylinder head **(see illustration)**. Also apply a small bead of sealant (Kawasaki recommend

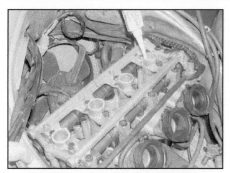

7.12b Apply a small bead of sealant to each of the spark plug apertures

the use of Kawasaki Bond 56019-120) to each of the spark plug aperture **(see illustration)** mating surfaces on the camshaft caps.

13 Fit the main seal to the cylinder head and install the four spark plug aperture seals on the camshaft caps.

14 Ensure the air suction tube upper O-rings are all correctly installed and lubricate them with a smear of engine oil to aid installation.

15 Ensure the camchain guide is correctly fitted to the cylinder head cover then manoeuvre the cover into position. Align the cover with the air suction tubes and seat in on the cylinder head.

16 Fit the sealing washers with their flat metal surfaces facing upwards and install the cover bolts, tightening them to the specified torque.

17 Fit the insulation pad and baffle plate to the cover and securely tighten its retaining bolts.

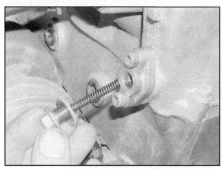

8.3 Remove the cap bolt and washer and withdraw the tensioner spring

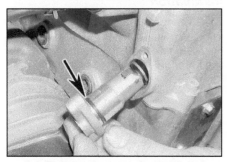

8.4 Remove the mounting bolts and withdraw the tensioner. Remove and renew the O-ring (arrowed)

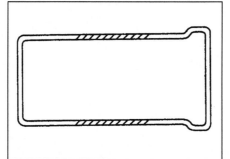

7.20 Apply sealant to the shaded areas (see text)

18 Securely fit the plug caps, ensuring the HT leads are correctly routed.

19 Install the secondary air injection system control valve, the vent valve and the carburettors as described in Chapter 4. On California models ensure the evaporative emission system control valve is correctly installed.

ZX-9R B models

20 Install the cover as described in Steps 11 to 16 noting that it will also be necessary to apply sealant to the cylinder head surface and the upper surface of the main seal in the areas shown in the accompanying illustration **(see illustration)**.

21 Seat the baffle plate correctly in position and securely tighten its retaining bolt.

22 Install the ignition HT coils (see Chapter 5).

23 Fit the secondary air injection valve and the carburettors (see Chapter 4). On California models, ensure the evaporative emission system control valve is correctly installed.

---

8 Camchain tensioner and guides – removal and installation

Note: *The camchain tensioner and guides can be removed with the engine in the frame.*
Caution: The tensioner plunger locks in place as it extends. Once the tensioner bolts have been loosened, the tensioner must be removed from the engine and the plunger reset before the bolts are

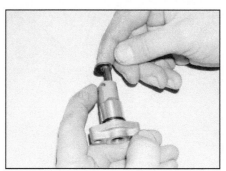

8.5 Checking the tensioner operation

tightened. If the tensioner bolts are slackened and then retightened without resetting the tensioner plunger, the camchain could be overtensioned, resulting in serious engine damage.

Camchain tensioner

Removal

1 Remove the fuel tank and carburettors (see Chapter 4).
2 Remove the pick-up coil cover from the right-hand end of the crankshaft (see Chapter 5).
3 Slacken and remove the cap bolt and washer from the tensioner body and withdraw the tensioner spring **(see illustration)**.
4 Slacken and remove the mounting bolts, then withdraw the tensioner from the rear of the cylinder head. Remove the O-ring from the tensioner body and discard it; a new one should be used on installation **(see illustration)**.
Caution: DO NOT turn the engine over during removal of the camchain tensioner.
5 Check the operation of the tensioner by pushing the plunger fully back into the tensioner (see Step 7) and then extending it slowly. As the plunger extends, the stopper should click, and lock firmly into each of the plunger teeth, preventing the plunger from being pushed back into the body. If this is not the case, the tensioner assembly should be renewed **(see illustration)**.

Installation

6 Remove all traces of locking compound from the tensioner retaining bolt threads and ensure that the cylinder head and tensioner mating surfaces are clean and dry.
7 Release the stopper and push the plunger fully back into the tensioner body.
8 Fit a new O-ring to the groove in the tensioner body and lubricate it with a smear of engine oil to aid installation.
9 Ease the tensioner into position, making sure the plunger stopper is at the top. Apply a few drops of locking compound to the threads of each bolt **(see illustration)** then fit the bolts, tightening them to the specified torque.
10 Insert the spring into the tensioner then fit the washer and cap bolt, tightening it to the specified torque.

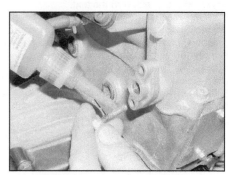

8.9 Apply a few drops of locking compound to the thread of each bolt

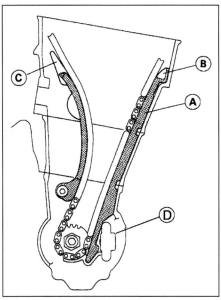

8.15 Camchain guide locations

A Front guide
B Front guide protection
C Rear guide
D Pick-up coil

11 Using a socket or spanner on the timing rotor hex, rotate the crankshaft clockwise a few rotations. As the crankshaft is rotated, the tensioner should be heard to click as the plunger extends and takes up the camchain slack.

12 Install the pick-up coil cover (see

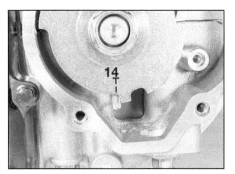

9.4a Align the 'T' mark for Nos. 1 & 4 cylinders with the index mark on the crankcase

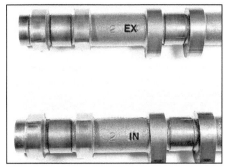

9.4b The camshafts are marked 'IN' (intake) and 'EX' (exhaust)

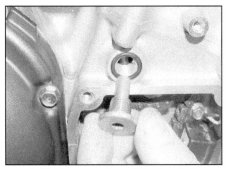

8.18 Unscrew the guide pivot bolt

Chapter 5), then fit the carburettors and fuel tank (see Chapter 4).

Camchain front guide

Removal

13 Remove the camshafts (see Section 9 or 10 – as applicable).
14 Using a pair of pointed-nose pliers, lift the guide and manoeuvre it out of position.

Installation

15 Manoeuvre the guide into position, ensuring its lower end is correctly seated in the lug on the lower crankcase (located between the crankshaft and pick-up coil). Seat the upper end of the guide against the cylinder head **(see illustration)**.
Caution: Serious engine damage could result if the guide is not correctly located.
16 Install the camshafts (see Section 9 or 10).

Camchain rear guide

Removal

17 Remove the camshafts (see Section 9 or 10 – as applicable).
18 Retain the guide with a pair of pointed nose pliers, then unscrew the guide pivot bolt from the crankcase **(see illustration)**.

Remove the bolt and lift out the guide. Discard the pivot bolt O-ring; a new one should be used on installation.

Installation

19 Lower the guide down into position and align its pivot with the crankcase bolt hole.
20 Fit a new O-ring, then install the pivot bolt, ensuring that it passes through the guide pivot, and tighten it to the specified torque.
21 Check the rear guide pivots freely on its bolt, then install the camshafts (Section 9 or 10).

9 Camshafts and followers (ZX-7R models) – removal, inspection and installation

Note: *The camshafts and followers can be removed with the engine in the frame.*

Removal

1 Disconnect the battery negative terminal (see Chapter 9).
2 Remove the cylinder head cover as described in Section 7.
3 Remove the pick-up coil cover from the right-hand end of the crankshaft (see Chapter 5).
4 Using a socket or spanner on the timing rotor hex, rotate the crankshaft clockwise until the 'T' mark of Nos. 1 and 4 cylinders is aligned with the index mark on the crankcase lug at the base of the rotor **(see illustration)**. Check the position of the 'IN' mark on the intake camshaft sprocket and the 'EX' mark on the exhaust camshaft sprocket **(see illustration)** (if the engine is in the frame, the view will be obscured by the frame; on some engines, there will be marks on the rear of each sprocket which can be used instead); the marks should be facing away from each other and should both be aligned with the cylinder head upper surface **(see illustration)**.

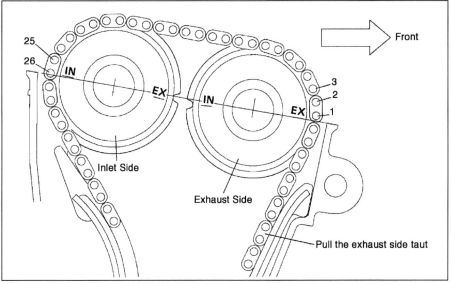

9.4c Position the camshaft like this

9.8a Support the cam chain so it won't drop into the engine . . .

9.8b . . . if the chain is allowed to drop and bunch up like this, turning the crankshaft could cause damage

9.9 Install new bearing cap O-rings

If the camshaft marks are not correctly positioned, rotate the crankshaft through another 360° (one complete turn) to position them as described. **Note:** *Always turn the engine in the normal direction of rotation (clockwise – viewed from the right-hand end of the engine).*

Caution: Never turn the engine over on the timing rotor Allen bolt. Always use the timing rotor hex.

5 Once the camshafts are correctly positioned, remove the camchain tensioner (see Section 8).

Caution: Do not rotate the crankshaft once the camchain tensioner has been removed.

6 Working in the **reverse** of the tightening sequence **(see illustration 9.35)**, loosen the camshaft bearing cap bolts by a quarter of a turn at a time to gently relieve valve spring pressure on the cap assembly. Whilst slackening the bolts, make sure that the cap assembly lifts squarely away from the cylinder head and does not stick on the locating dowels. Once spring pressure is relieved, remove all the bolts (noting the locations of the four longer bolts) and lift off the bearing cap assembly, taking care not to lose the locating dowels. If necessary, separate the two halves of the assembly and recover the joining collars and O-rings.

Caution: If the bearing cap bolts are carelessly loosened and the caps do not come squarely away from the head, they are likely to break. If this happens the complete cylinder head assembly must be renewed; the bearing caps are matched to

the cylinder head and cannot be renewed separately.

7 Remove the half-ring from each camshaft bearing outer race.

8 Lift out the camshafts from the cylinder head, noting that they are not interchangeable; the exhaust camshaft has a groove on its left-hand end, whereas the intake camshaft doesn't **(see illustration 9.4b)**. During camshaft removal, either wire the chain up or pass an object through it to prevent it falling down into the crankcase **(see illustration)**. **Note:** *If it is necessary to rotate the crankshaft whilst the camshafts are removed, always pull the chain taut before rotating the crankshaft. If the chain is not held taut, it will become wedged between the crankshaft sprocket and crankcase lug, resulting in chain/casing damage* **(see illustration)**.

9 Remove the O-rings which are fitted to the cylinder head spark plug apertures **(see illustration)** and pull out the oil pipe from the left end of the cylinder head. Discard all O-rings; new ones should be used on installation.

10 If the followers are to be removed, obtain a container with sixteen compartments and label the compartments 1 – 16.

11 Using a magnet, lift each follower out of the cylinder head and store it in its corresponding compartment in the container. Note that the shim is likely to stick to the inside of the follower, so take great care not to lose it as the follower is removed. Remove the shims and store each one with its respective follower.

Inspection

HAYNES HiNT *Before renewing a damaged cylinder head or camshafts, check out any local machine shops specialising in motorcycle engine work, as it may be possible to save the (considerable) cost of a new component. If the bearing surfaces in the cylinder head or caps are damaged, these can sometimes be bored out to accept bearing inserts. In the case of the camshafts, it may be possible for cam lobes to be welded, reground and hardened.*

12 Inspect the cam bearing surfaces, looking for score marks, deep scratches and evidence of pitting. Check the camshaft lobes for heat discoloration (blue appearance), score marks, chipped areas, flat spots and pitting **(see illustration)**. Spin the bearing on the right-hand end of the camshaft and check for signs of roughness or freeplay. If the bearing is worn or damaged, the camshaft must be renewed; bearing renewal is not possible.

13 Camshaft runout can be checked by supporting each end bearing of the camshaft on V-blocks and measuring any runout at the centre bearing using a dial gauge. If the runout exceeds the specified limit, the camshaft must be renewed.

14 Measure the height of each lobe with a micrometer and compare the results to the lobe height service limit listed in this Chapter's Specifications **(see illustration)**. If damage is noted or wear is excessive, the camshaft must be renewed.

15 The camshaft bearing oil clearance should then be checked. There are two possible ways of checking this, the first is by direct measurement (see Step 16) and the second by the use of a product known as Plastigauge (see Steps 17 to 20).

16 If the first method is to be used, make sure the locating dowels are in position, then fit the camshaft bearing cap assembly to the head. Install the bearing cap bolts and, working in the specified sequence, tighten them evenly and progressively to the specified torque (see Steps 34 and 35).

9.12 Check the camshaft lobes for wear – here's a good example of damage which will require repair or renewal

9.14 Measuring cam lobe height

9.18 Lay a strip of Plastigauge on the camshaft journal, parallel to the camshaft centreline

9.19 Compare the width of the crushed Plastigauge with the scale on the container

9.20 Measuring the cam bearing journal diameter

Measure the diameter of each bearing journal and calculate the oil clearance by subtracting the camshaft bearing journal diameter from the bearing holder journal diameter. Compare the measurements obtained with the service limit given in the Specifications at the start of this Chapter.

17 If the second method is to be used, clean the camshafts and the bearing surfaces in the cylinder head and bearing caps with a clean, lint-free cloth. Ensure all the shims and followers are correctly installed, then make sure that the crankshaft is correctly positioned with pistons Nos. 1 and 4 at TDC (see Step 4). Engage the camshafts with the camchain and lay them in place in the cylinder head, as described in Steps 30 and 31.

18 Cut strips of Plastigauge and lay one piece on each bearing journal, parallel with the camshaft axis **(see illustration)**. Make sure the locating dowels are all installed, then fit the half-ring to each camshaft bearing. Install the bearing cap assembly, ensuring the camshafts are not rotated at all, and tighten the retaining bolts to the specified torque as described in Steps 34 and 35 (ignore the instruction about the oil pipe).

19 Now unscrew the bolts (see Step 6) and carefully lift off the camshaft bearing assembly, again making sure the camshafts are not rotated. To determine the oil clearance, compare the crushed Plastigauge (at its widest point) on each journal to the scale printed on the Plastigauge container **(see illustration)**.

20 Compare the results to this Chapter's Specifications. If the oil clearance is greater than specified, measure the diameter of the cam bearing journal with a micrometer **(see illustration)**. If the journal diameter is less than the specified limit, replace the camshaft with a new one and recheck the clearance. If the clearance is still too great, renew the cylinder head assembly.

21 Check the camshaft sprockets for signs of damage such as chipped or missing teeth. If damage is found the camshaft must be renewed.

22 Check each follower for signs of wear or damage to its outer surface and renew any damaged ones. If any follower shows signs of

damage, also check its cylinder head bore for similar wear; any serious damage will require either extensive engineering work, or replacement of the cylinder head with a new one.

Installation

HAYNES HiNT *If the engine is in the frame, use a scriber/marker pen to make timing marks on the rear of each camshaft sprocket corresponding accurately with those on the front of each sprocket. The rear marks will be much easier to use, since they will not be obscured by the frame.*

23 If the camshaft bearing cap assembly halves were separated, fit new sealing rings to the joining collar grooves. Lubricate the O-rings with engine oil and install them in one of the castings, then carefully join the two halves of the casting.

24 Fit each shim to the top of its correct valve, making sure it is correctly seated in the valve spring retainer. **Note:** *It is most important that the shims are returned to their original valves, otherwise the valve clearances will be inaccurate.*

25 Lubricate each follower with clean engine oil, then install each one in its original location in the cylinder head, making sure it enters its bore squarely.

26 Fit a new O-ring to each of the four spark plug apertures.

9.34a Make sure the bearing cap dowels are in place . . .

27 Fit a new O-ring to the groove on each end of the oil pipe (there is no need to fit an O-ring to the innermost groove of the two lower grooves). Lubricate both O-rings with a smear of engine oil, then fit the oil pipe to the cylinder head, making sure that the end with the two grooves is at the bottom.

28 Ensure both the camchain guides are correctly installed, then apply a smear of clean engine oil to the cylinder head camshaft bearings and followers.

29 Check that the crankshaft is correctly positioned with pistons Nos. 1 and 4 at TDC (see Step 4). **Note:** *If it is necessary to rotate the crankshaft, pull the chain taut before rotating the crankshaft, to prevent it becoming wedged between the crankshaft sprocket and the crankcase lug.*

30 Pull the front run of the camchain taut and engage the exhaust camshaft (see Step 8 for identification details) with the chain so that the 'EX' mark on the sprocket is at the front and is level with the cylinder head upper surface when the camshaft is seated in position.

31 Once the exhaust camshaft is correctly positioned, starting with the camchain link pin located directly above the sprocket 'EX' mark, count back along the camchain until you come to the 26th pin back from the mark. Engage the intake camshaft with the chain so that its sprocket 'IN' mark is aligned with this 26th link pin **(see illustration 9.4c)**. Seat the inlet camshaft correctly in the head and check that its 'IN' mark is at the rear and is level with the cylinder head upper surface.

32 Ensure the crankshaft timing mark and both camshaft sprocket timing marks are correctly positioned before proceeding.

33 Fit a half-ring to the groove in each camshaft bearing and lubricate the camshaft journals and lobes with clean engine oil.

34 Ensure all the locating dowels are in position, then fit the camshaft bearing cap assembly to the cylinder head **(see illustration)**. Ensure the bearing cap is correctly engaged with the oil pipe, as are the camshaft bearing half-rings **(see illustration)**, then install the retaining bolts, noting that the four longer bolts are fitted in the locating dowel locations (1, 4, 5 and 7 in the tightening sequence).

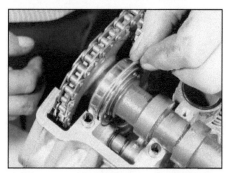

9.34b . . . and install the camshaft bearing half rings

35 Working in the specified sequence **(see illustration)**, tighten the bolts by a quarter of a turn at a time to gradually draw the camshaft bearing cap down into position. Whilst tightening the bolts, make sure that the bearing cap assembly is being pulled squarely down onto the cylinder head and is not sticking on the locating dowels. Once the camshaft bearing cap is in contact with the head, go round again in the specified sequence and tighten the bolts to the specified torque setting.

Caution: If the bolts are carelessly tightened and the bearing cap assembly is not drawn squarely onto the head, it is likely to break. If this happens the complete cylinder head assembly must be renewed; the camshaft bearing cap is matched to the cylinder head and cannot be renewed separately.

36 Insert a wooden dowel in through the camchain tensioner aperture and push firmly on the camchain rear guide to remove all slack from the camchain (the front and top run of the chain should now be taut).
37 Check the crankshaft 'T' mark of Nos. 1 and 4 cylinders is still correctly aligned with the index mark on the crankcase lug **(see illustration 9.4a)** and the camshaft sprocket marks are correctly aligned with the cylinder head upper surface **(see illustration 9.4c)**. If any of the marks aren't correctly positioned, unbolt the camshaft bearing cap assembly from the cylinder head and repeat the operations in Steps 29 to 37.

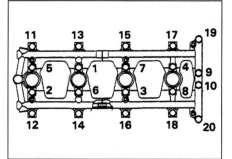

9.35 Bearing cap bolts tightening sequence

38 Once all the marks are correctly positioned, fit the camchain tensioner (Section 8).
39 Rotate the crankshaft several times to settle all disturbed components into position, then check and, if necessary, adjust the valve clearances as described in Chapter 1.
40 Lubricate all bearing surfaces with clean engine oil, then fit the cylinder head cover (Section 7).
41 Install the pick-up coil cover (Chapter 5) and reconnect the battery.
42 Check the engine oil level (see *Daily (pre-ride) checks*) before starting the engine.

10 Camshafts and rocker arms (ZX-9R B models) – removal, inspection and installation

Note: *It will be necessary to remove the engine to enable the camshaft and rocker arms to be removed. The camshafts can be removed with the engine in the frame, but it will be necessary to make accurate timing marks on the rear of each sprocket prior to installation (the frame completely obscures the timing marks on the front of the sprockets).*

Removal

1 Remove the engine from the frame (see Section 5).
2 Remove the cylinder head cover (see Section 7).
3 Remove the pick-up coil cover from the right-hand end of the crankshaft (see Chapter 5).

4 Using a socket or spanner on the timing rotor hex, rotate the crankshaft clockwise until the 'T' mark of Nos. 1 and 4 cylinders is aligned with the index mark on the crankcase lug at the base of the rotor **(see illustration)**. Check the position of the timing marks on the intake and exhaust camshaft sprockets; the marks should be facing away from each other and both be aligned with the cylinder head upper surface **(see illustration)**. If the camshaft marks are not correctly positioned, rotate the crankshaft through another 360° (one complete turn) to position them as described. **Note:** *Always turn the engine in the normal direction of rotation (clockwise – viewed from the right-hand end of the engine).*
Caution: Never turn the engine over on the timing rotor Allen bolt. Always use the timing rotor hex.
5 Once the camshafts are correctly positioned, remove the camchain tensioner (see Section 8).
Caution: Do not rotate the crankshaft once the camchain tensioner has been removed.
6 Working in a spiral pattern from the outside inwards, slacken the camshaft bearing cap retaining bolts by a quarter of a turn at a time, to relieve the pressure of the valve springs on the bearing caps gradually and evenly. Whilst slackening the bolts, make sure that the caps lift squarely away from the cylinder head and do not stick on the locating dowels. Once the valve spring pressure has been relieved, the bolts can be fully unscrewed and removed along with the caps; the bearing caps are numbered (1 to 4 from left to right, the right-hand end cap has no number but is easily identified) to ensure they are correctly positioned on refitting. Take care not to lose the locating dowels.
Caution: If the bearing cap bolts are carelessly slackened, the bearing caps might break. If any bearing cap breaks then the complete cylinder head assembly must be renewed; the bearing caps are matched to the head and are not available separately.
7 Remove the half-ring from each camshaft bearing outer race **(see illustration)**.
8 Lift out the camshafts from the cylinder head. Note that the camshafts are different

10.4a Align the 'T' mark for Nos. 1 & 4 cylinders with the index mark on the crankcase

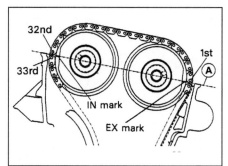

10.4b Check the position of the timing marks

10.7 Remove the half-ring from each camshaft outer race

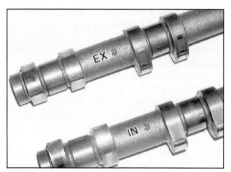

10.8 The camshafts are marked 'IN' (intake) and 'EX' (exhaust)

10.9 Remove and renew the spark plug aperture O-rings

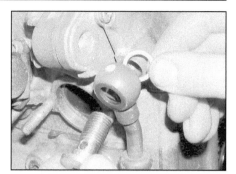

10.10 Unscrew the banjo bolt

10.11 Unscrew the bolts and remove the cover from the left-hand end of the cylinder head

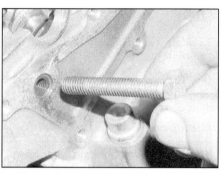

10.12a Screw an 8 x 1.25 mm bolt (at least 20 mm in length) into the end of the shaft . . .

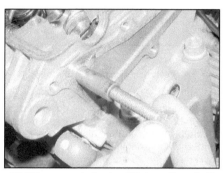

10.12b . . . and slowly withdraw the shaft from the head

and must not be swapped; the exhaust camshaft is marked 'EX' and the intake camshaft marked 'IN' **(see illustration)**. During removal of the camshafts, either wire the chain up or pass an object through it to prevent it falling down into the crankcase **(see illustration 9.8a)**. **Note:** *If it is necessary to rotate the crankshaft whilst the camshafts are removed, always pull the chain taut before rotating the crankshaft. If the chain is not held taut, it will become wedged between the crankshaft sprocket and the crankcase lug, resulting in chain/casing damage* **(see illustration 9.8b)**.

9 Remove the O-rings which are fitted to the cylinder head spark plug apertures **(see illustration)** and discard them; new ones should be used on installation.
10 If the rocker shafts and arms are to be removed, unscrew the banjo bolt connecting the oil hose to the cover on the left-hand end of the cylinder head **(see illustration)**. Remove the sealing washer and O-ring from the bolt and discard them; new ones should be used on installation.
11 Unscrew the bolts and remove the cover from the left-hand end of the cylinder head **(see illustration)**. Discard the cover seal; a

new one should be used on installation.
12 Starting with the intake rocker arm shaft, screw an 8 x 1.25 mm bolt (at least 20 mm in length) into the end of the shaft. Slowly withdraw the shaft from the head and remove the springs and rocker arms as they are freed from the shaft end **(see illustrations)**. Note the correct fitted location of each spring and rocker arm as it is removed **(see illustrations)** and keep them in the correct fitted order. Once the rocker arm shaft is removed, slide the arms and springs onto the shaft for safe-keeping, keeping them in the correct order.

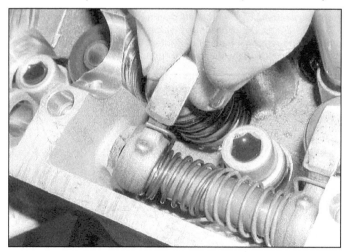

10.12c Remove the rocker arm . . .

10.12d . . .and the springs

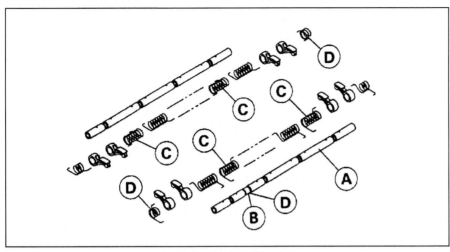

10.13 Rocker identification

A Inlet rocker shaft   B Groove   C Red paint   D Blue paint

13 Remove the exhaust rocker arm shaft, springs and rocker arms as described in Step 12. Store the shaft assemblies separately to ensure that all components are refitted in their original locations. **Note:** *The rocker arm shafts are different and are not interchangeable. The intake rocker arm shaft can be identified by its groove and blue paint mark (see illustration), the exhaust shaft has no groove or marking. The springs are also colour-coded.*

14 Obtain a container which is divided into sixteen compartments and label them 1 – 16. Using a magnet, lift each shim out from its

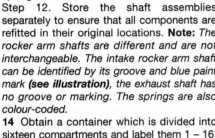

10.17 Measuring the height of the camshaft lobe

spring retainer and store it in its corresponding compartment in the container.

Inspection

Before renewing a damaged cylinder head or camshafts, check out any local machine shops specialising in motorcycle engine work, as it may be possible to save the (considerable) cost of a new component. If the bearing surfaces in the cylinder head or caps are damaged, these can sometimes be bored out to accept bearing inserts. In the case of the camshafts, it may be possible for cam lobes to be welded, reground and hardened.

15 Inspect the cam bearing surfaces, looking for score marks, deep scratches and evidence of pitting. Check the camshaft lobes for heat discoloration (blue appearance), score marks, chipped areas, flat spots and pitting. Spin the bearing on the right-hand end of the camshaft and check for signs of roughness or freeplay. If the bearing is worn or damaged, the camshaft must be renewed; bearing renewal is not possible.

16 Camshaft runout can be checked by

supporting each end bearing of the camshaft on V-blocks, and measuring any runout at the centre bearing using a micrometer. If the runout exceeds the specified limit the camshaft must be renewed.

17 Measure the height of each lobe with a micrometer and compare the results to the lobe height service limit listed in this Chapter's Specifications **(see illustration)**. If damage is noted or wear is excessive, the camshaft must be renewed.

18 The camshaft bearing oil clearance should then be checked. There are two possible ways of checking this, the first is by direct measurement (see Step 19) and the second by the use of a product known as Plastigauge (see Steps 20 to 23).

19 If the first method is to be used, make sure the locating dowels are in position **(see illustration)** then fit the camshaft bearing caps to the head, ensuring they are all correctly positioned. Install the bearing cap bolts and tighten them evenly and progressively to the specified torque **(see illustration)** (see Steps 38 to 40 – ignoring the instruction about the half-rings). Measure the diameter of each bearing journal **(see illustration)** and calculate the oil clearance by subtracting the camshaft bearing journal diameter from the bearing holder journal diameter. Compare the measurements obtained with the service limit given in the Specifications at the start of this Chapter.

20 If the second method is to be used, clean the camshafts and the bearing surfaces in the cylinder head and bearing caps with a clean, lint-free cloth. Ensure all the shims and rocker arms followers are correctly installed, then make sure that the crankshaft is correctly positioned with pistons Nos. 1 and 4 at TDC (see Step 4). Engage the camshafts with the camchain and lay them in place in the cylinder head, as described in Steps 33 and 34.

21 Cut strips of Plastigauge and lay one piece on each bearing journal parallel with the camshaft axis. Make sure the locating dowels are all installed, then fit the half-ring to each camshaft bearing. Install the bearing caps, ensuring that the camshafts are not rotated at all, and tighten the retaining bolts to the specified torque, as described in Steps 38 to 40.

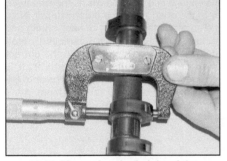

10.19a Make sure the locating dowels are in position

10.19b Tightening the bearing cap bolts to the specified torque

10.19c Measuring the camshaft journal

22 Now unscrew the bolts (see Step 6) and carefully lift off the camshaft bearing assembly, again making sure the camshafts are not rotated. To determine the oil clearance, compare the crushed Plastigauge (at its widest point) on each journal to the scale printed on the Plastigauge container **(see illustrations 9.18 & 9.19)**.

23 Compare the results to this Chapter's Specifications. If the oil clearance is greater than specified, measure the diameter of the cam bearing journal with a micrometer. If the journal diameter is less than the specified limit, replace the camshaft with a new one and recheck the clearance. If the clearance is still too great, renew the cylinder head assembly.

24 Check the camshaft sprockets for signs of damage such as chipped or missing teeth. If damage is found, the camshaft must be renewed.

25 Check each rocker arm for signs of wear or damage to its follower surface and inspect the rocker arm and shaft bearing surfaces for wear ridges and scoring. If the necessary measuring equipment is available, measure the inside diameter of the rocker arm and the outside diameter of the rocker shaft at the point where the rocker pivots, and compare the results to the service limits given in the Specifications. Renew all worn components.

Installation

> **HAYNES HiNT**
> *If the engine is in the frame, use a scriber/marker pen to make timing marks on the rear of each camshaft sprocket corresponding accurately with those on the front of each sprocket. The rear marks will be much easier to use, since they will not be obscured by the frame.*

26 Fit each shim to the top of its correct valve, making sure it is correctly seated in the valve spring retainer. **Note:** *It is most important that the shims are returned to their original valves, otherwise the valve clearances will be inaccurate.*

27 Starting with the exhaust shaft (see Step 13 for shaft and spring identification details), lubricate the shaft and rocker arm bearing surfaces with clean engine oil. Locate the shaft in the cylinder head, ensuring its sealed end goes in first (threaded end facing the left), and slide it into position, fitting the springs and rocker arms in their original fitted locations as you go. Ensure the spring longer ends are positioned against the cylinder head surface and engage the rocker arms with the spring end shorter ends before locating them on the shaft. Once all components are correctly fitted, push the rocker shaft fully home and check that all rocker arms are held firmly in contact with the shims by the springs.

28 Install the intake rocker shaft, springs and rocker arms as described in Step 27.

29 Ensure both rocker shafts are pushed fully

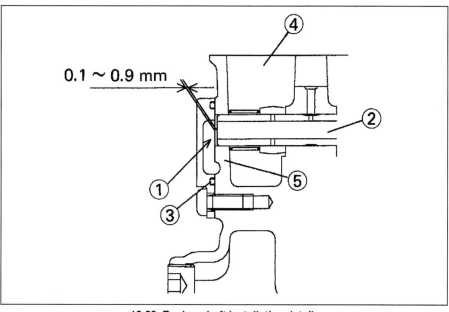

10.29 Rocker shaft installation details

| 1 | Left cylinder head cover | 2 | Rocker shaft | 4 | Cylinder head |
| | | 3 | O-ring | 5 | Rocker shaft support |

home (their ends should be recessed 0.1 to 0.9 mm below the cover mating surface) then clean and dry the head and cover mating surfaces **(see illustration)**. Fit a new seal to the cover groove and fit the cover to the left end of the cylinder head. Ensure the cover is correctly seated, then install the cover retaining bolts, tightening them evenly and progressively to the specified torque in a diagonal sequence.

30 Fit a new O-ring to the oil pipe banjo bolt **(see illustration)** and position a new sealing washer between the oil pipe and cylinder head cover. Fit the oil pipe banjo bolt and tighten it to the specified torque.

31 Ensure both the camchain guides are correctly fitted, then apply a smear of clean engine oil to the cylinder head camshaft bearings and followers.

32 Check that the crankshaft is correctly positioned with pistons Nos. 1 and 4 at TDC (see Step 4). **Note:** *If it is necessary to rotate the crankshaft, pull the chain taut before rotating the crankshaft to prevent it becoming wedged between the crankshaft sprocket and crankcase lug.*

33 Pull the front run of the camchain taut and engage the exhaust camshaft (see Step 8 for identification details) with the chain so that the timing mark on the sprocket is at the front and is level with the cylinder head upper surface when the camshaft is seated in position.

34 Once the exhaust camshaft is correctly positioned, starting with the camchain link pin located directly above the sprocket timing mark, count back along the camchain until you come to the 32nd and 33rd pins from the mark. Engage the intake camshaft with the chain so that its sprocket timing mark is positioned in between the 32nd and 33rd pins

(see illustration 10.4b). Seat the inlet camshaft correctly in the head and check that its timing mark is at the rear and is level with the cylinder head upper surface.

35 Ensure the crankshaft timing mark, and both camshaft sprocket timing marks, are correctly positioned before proceeding.

36 Fit a new O-ring to each of the four spark plug apertures.

37 Fit a half-ring to the groove in each camshaft bearing and lubricate the camshaft journals and lobes with clean engine oil.

38 Ensure all the locating dowels are in position, then fit the right camshaft bearing cap. Ensure the bearing cap is correctly engaged with the camshaft bearing half-rings, then install the retaining bolts.

39 Ensure the locating dowels are all in position, then refit the remaining camshaft bearing caps and the retaining bolts in their original locations on the cylinder head **(see illustration)**. The caps are numbered (1 to 4) from left to right and all bearing cap numbers should be at the front.

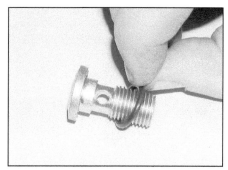

10.30 Fit a new O-ring on to the oil pipe banjo bolt

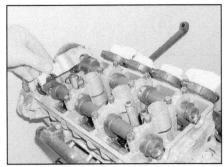

10.39 Refit the camshaft bearing caps

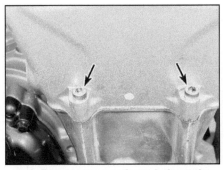

11.6 Remove the two 6 mm bolts at the end of the cylinder head (arrowed)

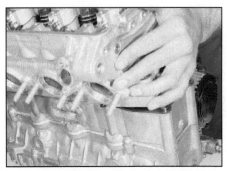

11.9 Lift the cylinder head off

40 Tighten all the bearing cap bolts by hand only then, working in a spiral pattern from the centre outwards, tighten the bolts by a quarter of a turn at a time to gradually impose the pressure of the valve springs on the bearing caps. Repeat this sequence until all bearing caps are in contact with the cylinder head, then go round and tighten the camshaft retaining bolts to the specified torque.

Caution: If the bearing cap bolts are carelessly tightened, the bearing caps might break. If any bearing cap breaks then the complete cylinder head assembly must be renewed; the bearing caps are matched to the head and are not available separately.

41 Insert a wooden dowel through the camchain tensioner aperture and push firmly on the camchain rear guide to remove all slack from the camchain (the front and top run of the chain should now be taut).

42 Check the crankshaft 'T' mark of Nos. 1 and 4 cylinders is still correctly aligned with the index mark on the crankcase lug and the camshaft sprocket marks are correctly aligned with the cylinder head upper surface (see Step 4). If any of the marks aren't correctly positioned, unbolt the camshaft bearing caps from the cylinder head and repeat the operations in Steps 33 to 42.

43 Once all the marks correctly positioned, fit the camchain tensioner (Section 8).

44 Rotate the crankshaft several times to settle all disturbed components into position, then check and, if necessary, adjust the valve clearances as described in Chapter 1.

45 Lubricate all bearing surfaces with clean

engine oil, then fit the cylinder head cover (Section 7).

46 Install the pick-up coil cover (Chapter 5) and reconnect the battery.

47 Check the engine oil level (see *Daily (pre-ride) checks*) before starting the engine.

11 Cylinder head –
removal and installation

Note: *It will be necessary to remove the engine from the frame to enable the cylinder head to be removed.*

Caution: The engine must be completely cool before beginning this procedure, or the cylinder head may become warped.

Removal

1 Remove the engine from the frame (see Section 5) and proceed as described under the sub-heading appropriate to your model.

ZX-7R models

2 Remove the camshafts and followers (see Section 9).

3 Remove the camchain front guide (see Section 8).

4 Unscrew the retaining bolt and free the oil pipe union from the left-hand end of the cylinder head. Remove the O-ring from the union and discard it; a new one must be used on refitting.

5 Unscrew the three bolts and remove the sound damper cover and damper from the right-hand end of the cylinder block/head.

6 Slacken and remove the two 6 mm bolts from the right-hand end of the cylinder head **(see illustration)**.

7 Working in the **reverse** of the tightening sequence **(see illustration 11.25)**, slacken the ten 10 mm cylinder head bolts by half a turn at a time. Once all pressure is released from the bolts, fully unscrew them and remove them along with their sealing washers.

> **HAYNES HiNT**
> *There are three different lengths of 10 mm cylinder head bolts. To avoid confusion during install-ation, remove the bolts and washers and store them in a cardboard template, in their correct fitted locations.*

8 Free the cylinder head from the cylinder block. If it is stuck, tap around the joint faces of the cylinder head with a soft-faced mallet to free the head. Don't attempt to free the head by inserting a screwdriver between the head and cylinder block – you will damage the sealing surfaces.

Caution: If the cylinder block is not being removed, great care must be taken not to disturb the cylinder base gasket as the head is freed from the block. If the base gasket joint is disturbed, the block must be removed and the gasket renewed before the cylinder head is installed. Otherwise there is a risk of oil leakage from the base gasket joint.

9 Lift the cylinder head from the engine **(see illustration)**. As the cylinder head is removed, pass the camchain down through the head, then either wire the chain up or pass an object through it to prevent it falling down into the crankcase.

10 Remove the old head gasket and discard it. If they are loose, remove the cylinder head locating dowels from the cylinder head/block and store them with the head for safe-keeping **(see illustrations)**.

11 Check the cylinder head gasket and the mating surfaces on the cylinder head and block for signs of leakage, which could indicate warpage. Check the flatness of the head as described in Section 13.

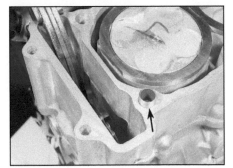

11.10a There's a dowel at the right front corner (arrowed) . . .

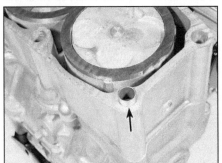

11.10b . . . and at the left front corner (arrowed)

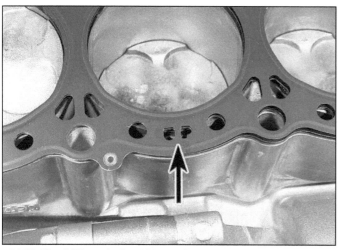

11.20 The 'UP' mark should be upright when the head gasket is installed

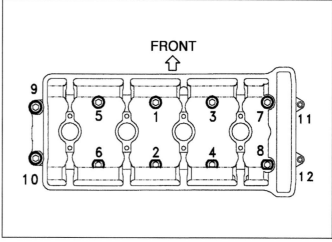

11.25 Cylinder head bolt TIGHTENING sequence

ZX-9R B models

12 Remove the camshafts (see Section 10).

13 Remove the camchain front guide (see Section 8).

14 Unscrew the banjo bolt securing the oil hose to the cover on the left-hand end of the cylinder head **(see illustration 10.10)**. Remove the sealing washer and O-ring from the bolt and discard them; new ones should be used on installation.

15 Unscrew the bolts and remove the cover from the left-hand end of the cylinder head. Discard the cover seal; a new one should be used on installation **(see illustration 10.11)**.

16 If the cylinder is being disassembled and overhauled, remove the rocker shafts, arms and springs (see Section 10); they can be left in position if no work is being carried out on the head.

17 Remove the cylinder head as described in Steps 6 to 11.

Installation

ZX-7R models

18 Clean all traces of old gasket material from the cylinder head and block. If a scraper is used, take care not to scratch or gouge the soft aluminium. Also ensure that none of the gasket material is allowed to fall into the cylinder bores, oil passages or water jacket. As a precaution, it is recommended that the cylinder head coolant pipe O-rings are renewed before the head is installed.

19 Ensure both cylinder head and block mating surfaces are clean, and fit the locating dowels to the cylinder block (if removed). Apply a smear of engine oil to the surface of each cylinder bore.

20 Fit the new head gasket over the locating dowels making sure its the right way up **(see illustration)**.

21 Carefully manoeuvre the cylinder head into position, passing the camchain up through the cylinder head tunnel, and lower it onto the locating dowels. Once the head is

correctly seated, either wire the camchain up or pass an object through it to prevent it falling down into the crankcase.

22 Lubricate both sides of the cylinder head bolt washers with clean engine oil, then install the bolts in their original locations in the cylinder head. The correct locations are as follows.

a) 151 mm long bolts – fitted in locations 1, 2, 4, 6 and 8 in the tightening sequence.

b) 165 mm long bolts – fitted in locations 3, 5 and 7 in the tightening sequence.

c) 137 mm long bolts – fitted in locations 9 and 10 in the tightening sequence.

23 Ensure that all 10 mm bolts and sealing washers are correctly positioned, then tighten them all by hand.

24 Fit the two 6 mm cylinder head bolts and tighten by hand.

25 Working in the specified sequence **(see illustration)**, tighten the ten 10 mm cylinder head bolts to the specified Stage 1 (first) torque setting.

26 Once the 10 mm bolts have been tightened to the Stage 1 (first) torque, go round again in the specified sequence and tighten the bolts to the Stage 2 (final) torque setting.

27 With the 10 mm bolts correctly tightened, tighten the two 6 mm bolts (Nos. 11 and 12 in the tightening sequence) to their specified torque setting.

28 Remove all traces of locking compound from the sound damper cover bolts, then apply a drop of fresh locking compound to the threads of each bolt. Fit the sound damper and cover to the right-hand end of the block/head, tightening its retaining bolts to the specified torque.

29 Fit a new O-ring to the oil pipe union groove and lubricate it with a smear of engine oil. Ease the union back into the left-hand end of the cylinder head and tighten its retaining bolt to the specified torque.

30 Install the camchain front guide

(Section 8) then fit the followers and camshafts (Section 9).

31 Install the engine (see Section 5).

ZX-9R B models

32 Carry out the operations described in Steps 18 to 21, ensuring that the cylinder head gasket is installed with its 'UP' marking facing upwards,

33 Lubricate both sides of the cylinder head bolt washers with clean engine oil, then install the bolts and washers in their original locations in the cylinder head. The correct locations are as follows.

a) 182 mm long bolts – fitted in locations 1, 3, 5 and 7 in the tightening sequence.

b) 164 mm long bolts – fitted in locations 2, 4, 6 and 8 in the tightening sequence (these bolts can be easily identified by the flats on the sides of the bolt heads).

c) 146 mm long bolts – fitted in locations 9 and 10 in the tightening sequence.

Note: *The two 146 mm long bolts are fitted with thinner (2.3 mm thick) sealing washers than those fitted to the other eight bolts (4.5 mm thick).*

34 Ensure all 10 mm bolts and sealing washers are correctly positioned then tighten them all by hand.

35 Fit the two 6 mm cylinder head bolts and tighten them by hand.

36 Working in the specified sequence **(see illustration 11.25),** tighten the ten 10 mm cylinder head bolts to the specified Stage 1 (first) torque setting.

37 Once the 10 mm bolts have been tightened to the Stage 1 (first) torque, go round again in the specified sequence and tighten the bolts to the Stage 2 (final) torque setting.

38 With the 10 mm bolts correctly tightened, tighten the two 6 mm bolts (Nos. 11 and 12 in the tightening sequence) to their specified torque setting.

39 Where necessary, install the rocker arms, springs and shafts (see Section 10).

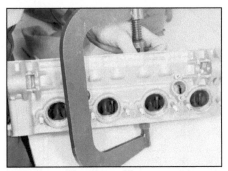

13.5a Install a valve spring compressor . . .

13.5b . . . compress the spring and remove the collets . . .

13.5c . . . the valve spring retainer . . .

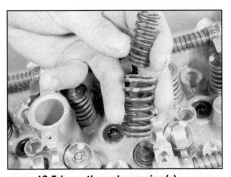

13.5d . . . the valve spring(s) . . .

13.5e . . . the spring seat . . .

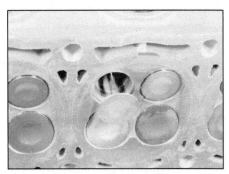

13.5f . . . and the valve

40 Ensure both rocker shafts are pushed fully home (their ends should be recessed 0.1 to 0.9 mm below the cover mating surface), then clean and dry the head and cover mating surfaces **(see illustration 10.29)**.
41 Fit a new seal to the cover groove and fit the cover to the left-hand end of the cylinder head. Ensure the cover is correctly seated, then install the retaining bolts, tightening them evenly and progressively to the specified torque in a diagonal sequence.
42 Fit a new O-ring to the oil pipe banjo bolt and position a new sealing washer between the pipe and cylinder head cover. Fit the oil pipe banjo bolt and tighten it to the specified torque.
43 Install the camchain front guide (Section 8) then fit the camshafts (Section 9).
44 Install the engine (see Section 5).

12 Valves/valve seats/ valve guides – servicing

1 Because of the complex nature of this job and the special tools and equipment required, most owners leave servicing of the valves, valve seats and valve guides to a professional.
2 The home mechanic can, however, remove the valves from the cylinder head, clean and check the components for wear and assess the extent of the work needed and, unless a valve service is required, grind in the valves (see Section 13).
3 The dealer or motorcycle engineer will remove the valves and springs, renew the

valves and guides, recut the valve seats, check and renew the valve springs, spring retainers and collets (as necessary), renew the valve seals and reassemble the valve components.
4 After the valve service has been performed, the head will be in like-new condition. When the head is returned, be sure to clean it again very thoroughly before installation on the engine to remove any metal particles or abrasive grit that may still be present from the valve service operations. Use compressed air, if available, to blow out all the holes and passages.

13 Cylinder head and valves – disassembly, inspection and reassembly

1 As mentioned in the previous section, valve servicing, valve seat re-cutting and valve guide renewal should be left to a dealer or motorcycle engineer. However, disassembly, cleaning and inspection of the valves and related components can be done (if the necessary special tools are available) by the home mechanic. This way no expense is incurred if the inspection reveals that overhaul is not required at this time.
2 To disassemble the valve components without the risk of damaging them, a valve spring compressor is absolutely necessary. If the special tool is not available, have a dealer service department or motorcycle repair shop handle the entire process of disassembly, inspection, service or repair (if required) and reassembly of the valves.

Disassembly

3 Before proceeding, arrange to label and store the valves along with their related components in such a way that they can be returned to their original locations without getting mixed up. A good way to do this is obtain a container which is divided into compartments, and to label each compartment with the identity of the valve which will be stored in it (ie number of cylinder, intake or exhaust side, inner or outer valve). Alternatively, labelled plastic bags will do just as well.
4 If not already done, clean all traces of old gasket material from the cylinder head. If a scraper is used, take care not to scratch or gouge the soft aluminium.

> **HAYNES HiNT** *Refer to Tools and Workshop Tips (Section 7) for details of gasket removal methods.*

5 Compress the valve spring(s) on the first valve with a spring compressor, making sure it is correctly located onto each end of the valve assembly. Do not compress the spring(s) any more than is absolutely necessary. Remove the collets, using either needle-nose pliers, tweezers, a magnet or a screwdriver with a dab of grease on it. Carefully release the valve spring compressor and remove the spring retainer – noting which way up it fits – the springs (ZX-7R models) or spring (ZX-9R B models), the spring seat, and the valve from the head **(see illustrations)**. If the valve binds in the guide (i.e. it won't pull through), push it back into the head and deburr the area

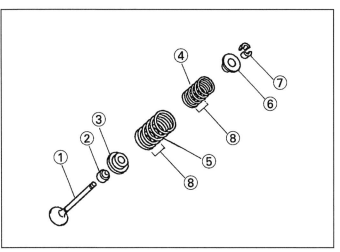

**13.5g Valve details
(ZX-7R model)**

1 Valve stem
2 Oil seal
3 Spring seat
4 Inner valve spring
5 Outer valve spring
6 Valve spring retainer
7 Collets
8 Tightly wound coils

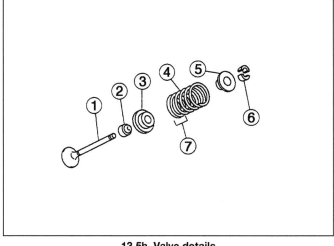

**13.5h Valve details
(ZX-9R B model)**

1 Valve stem
2 Oil seal
3 Spring seat
4 Spring
5 Retainer
6 Collets
7 Tightly wound coil

around the collet groove with a very fine file or whetstone **(see illustrations)**.

6 Repeat the procedure for the remaining valves. Remember to keep the parts for each valve together, and separate from the other valves, so that they can be reinstalled in the same location.

7 Once the valves have been removed and labelled, pull the valve stem seals off the top of the valve guides with pliers and discard them (the old seals should never be reused).

8 Next, clean the cylinder head with solvent and dry it thoroughly. Compressed air will speed the drying process and ensure that all holes and recessed areas are clean.

9 Clean all the valve springs, collets, retainers and spring seats with solvent and dry them thoroughly. Do the parts from one valve at a time so that no mixing of parts between valves occurs.

10 Scrape off any deposits that may have formed on the valve, then use a motorised wire brush to remove deposits from the valve heads and stems. Again, make sure the valves do not get mixed up.

Inspection

11 Inspect the head very carefully for cracks and other damage. If cracks are found, a new head will be required. Check the cam bearing surfaces for wear and evidence of seizure. Check the camshafts for wear as well (see Section 9 or 10).

12 On ZX-7R models, inspect the outer surfaces of the cam followers for evidence of scoring or other damage. If a follower is in poor condition, it is probable that the bore in which it works is also damaged. Check for clearance between the followers and their bores. If the bores are seriously out-of-round or tapered, the cylinder head and the followers must be renewed.

13 Using a precision straight-edge and a feeler gauge set to the warpage limit listed in

the specifications at the beginning of the Chapter, check the head gasket mating surface for warpage **(see illustration)**. Refer to *Tools and Workshop Tips* (Section 3*)* in the *Reference* section for details of how to use the straight-edge.

14 Examine the valve seats in the combustion chamber. If they are pitted, cracked or burned, the head will require work beyond the scope of the home mechanic. Measure the valve seat width and compare it to this Chapter's Specifications **(see illustration)**. If it exceeds the service limit, or if it varies around its circumference, valve overhaul is required. If available, use Engineers blue to determine the extent of valve seat wear. Uniformly coat the seat with the Engineers blue, then install the valve and rotate it back and forth using a lapping tool. Remove the valve and check whether the ring of blue on the valve is uniform and continuous around the valve, and is of the correct width as specified.

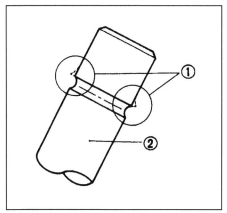

**13.5i Check the area around the collet
groove for burrs**

1 Burrs (removed)   2 Valve stem

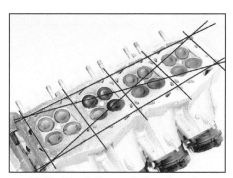

**13.13 Check the gasket surface for
flatness with a straight edge and feeler
gauge; measure in the directions shown**

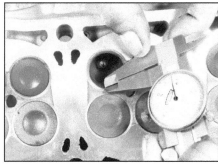

13.14 Measuring valve seat width

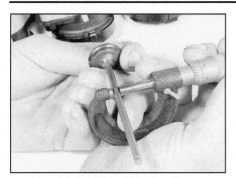

13.15a Measuring valve stem diameter

13.15b Measure the valve guide inside diameter with a hole gauge . . .

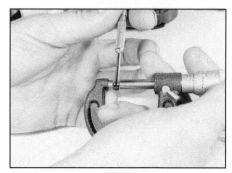

13.15c . . . then measure the gauge with a micrometer

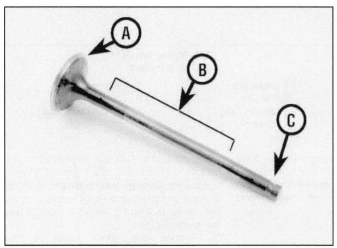

13.16a Check the valve face (A), stem (B) and collet groove (C) for wear and damage

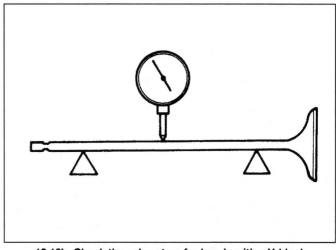

13.16b Check the valve stem for bends with a V-block (or V-blocks, as shown here) and a dial indicator

15 Measure the valve stem diameter **(see illustration)**. Clean the valve guides to remove any carbon build-up, then measure the inside diameters of the guides (at both ends and at the centre of the guide) with a small-bore gauge and micrometer **(see illustrations)**. The guides are measured at the ends and at the centre to determine if they are worn in a bell-mouth pattern (more wear at the ends). If the valve stem or guide is worn beyond its limit, or if the guide is worn unevenly, it must be renewed.

16 Carefully inspect each valve face for cracks, pits and burned spots. Check the valve stem and the collet groove area for cracks. Rotate the valve and check for any obvious indication that it is bent. Check the end of the stem for pitting and excessive wear **(see illustrations)**. The presence of any of the above conditions indicates the need for valve servicing. The stem end can be ground down, provided that the amount of stem above the collet groove after grinding is sufficient.

17 Check the end of each valve spring for wear and pitting. Measure the spring free length and compare it to that listed in the specifications **(see illustration)**. If any spring is shorter than specified it has sagged and must be renewed. Also place the spring upright on a flat surface and check it for bend

by placing a ruler against it **(see illustration)**. If the bend in any spring is excessive, it must be renewed.

18 Check the spring retainers and collets for obvious wear and cracks. Any questionable parts should not be reused, as extensive damage will occur in the event of failure during engine operation.

19 If the inspection indicates that no overhaul work is required, the valve components can be reinstalled in the head.

Reassembly

20 Unless a valve service has been performed, before installing the valves in the head they

13.16c Measure the valve head margin thickness

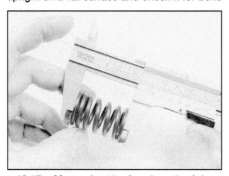

13.17a Measuring the free length of the valve spring

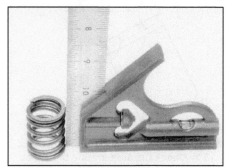

13.17b Checking the valve springs for squareness

should be ground-in (lapped) to ensure a positive seal between the valves and seats. This procedure requires coarse and fine valve-grinding compound and a valve-grinding tool. If a grinding tool is not available, a piece of rubber or plastic hose can be slipped over the valve stem (after the valve has been installed in the guide) and used to turn the valve.

21 Apply a small amount of coarse grinding compound to the valve face, then slip the valve into the guide **(see illustration)**. **Note:** *Make sure each valve is installed in its correct guide and be careful not to get any grinding compound on the valve stem.*

22 Attach the grinding tool (or hose) to the valve and rotate the tool between the palms of your hands. Use a back-and-forth motion (as though rubbing your hands together), rather than a circular motion (ie so that the valve rotates alternately clockwise and anti-clockwise rather than in one direction only). Lift the valve off the seat and turn it at regular intervals to distribute the grinding compound properly. Continue the grinding procedure until the valve face and seat contact area is of uniform width, and unbroken around the entire circumference of the valve face and seat **(see illustrations)**.

23 Carefully remove the valve from the guide and wipe off all traces of grinding compound. Use solvent to clean the valve and wipe the seat area thoroughly with a solvent soaked cloth.

24 Repeat the procedure with fine valve grinding compound, then repeat the entire procedure for the remaining valves.

25 Fit the spring seat for the first valve in place in the cylinder head, then install the new valve stem seal onto the guide. Use an appropriate size deep socket to push the seal over the end of the valve guide until it is felt to clip into place. Don't twist or cock it, or it will not seal properly against the valve stem. Also, don't remove it again or it will be damaged.

26 Coat the valve stem with engine oil, then install it into its guide, rotating it slowly to avoid damaging the seal. Check that the valve moves up and down freely in the guide.

27 On ZX-7R models, install the inner and outer springs, ensuring both springs are fitted with their closer-wound coils facing down into the cylinder head. Ensure both springs are correctly located on the seat, then fit the spring retainer, with its shouldered side facing down so that it fits into the top of the springs.

28 On ZX-9R B models, install the valve spring with its closer-wound coils facing down into the cylinder head. Ensure the spring is correctly located on the seat, then fit the spring retainer, with its shouldered side facing down so that it fits into the top of the spring.

29 On all models, apply a small amount of grease to the collets to help hold them in place. Compress the spring(s) with the valve spring compressor and install the collets **(see illustration)**. When compressing the spring(s), depress only as far as is absolutely necessary to slip the collets into place. Make certain that the collets are securely locked in the retaining

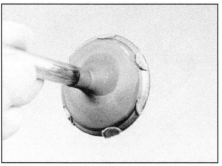

13.21 Apply the lapping compound very sparingly, in small dabs, to the valve face

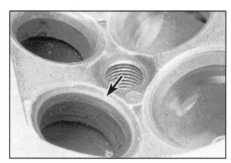

13.22b . . . and the seat should be the specified width (arrowed) with a smooth, unbroken appearance

groove, then carefully release the spring compressor.

30 Repeat the procedure for the remaining valves. Remember to keep the parts for each valve together, and separate from the other valves, so that they can be reinstalled in the same location.

31 Support the cylinder head on blocks so that the valves cannot contact the workbench top, then very gently tap each of the valve stems with a soft-faced hammer. This will help seat the collets in their grooves.

> **HAYNES HINT** *Check for proper sealing of the valves by pouring a small amount of solvent into each of the valve ports. If the solvent leaks past any valve into the combustion chamber area the valve grinding operation on that valve should be repeated.*

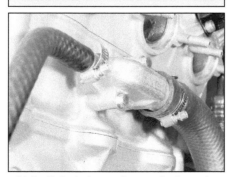

14.4a Unbolt the coolant outlet from the cylinder block . . .

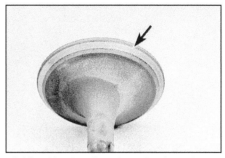

13.22a After lapping, the valve face should exhibit a uniform, unbroken contact pattern (arrowed) . . .

13.29 A dab of grease will hold the collets in place while the spring compressor is released

14 Cylinder block – removal, inspection and installation

Note: *It will be necessary to remove the engine from the frame to enable the cylinder block to be removed.*

Removal

1 Remove the engine from the frame (see Section 5).

2 Remove the cylinder head (see Section 11).

3 Remove the camchain rear guide (see Section 8).

4 Slacken the retaining clip(s) and detach the hose(s) from the coolant outlet union on the front of the cylinder block. Undo the retaining bolts and remove the coolant outlet and seal. Discard the seal; a new one should be used on installation **(see illustrations)**.

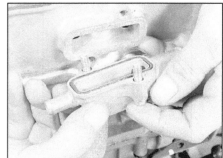

14.4b . . . and renew its seal

14.6 Lift the cylinder block off the crankcase

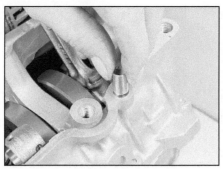

14.7a There's a dowel at the left-hand front corner . . .

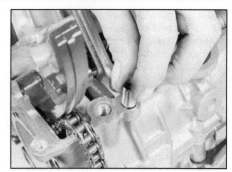

14.7b . . . and at the right-hand front corner

5 Free the cylinder block from the crankcase. If it is stuck, tap around its perimeter with a soft-faced hammer. Don't attempt to prise the block and the crankcase apart, as you will ruin the sealing surfaces.

6 Carefully lift the block off the crankcase **(see illustration)**, passing the camchain down through the block tunnel. Prior to freeing the pistons from their bores, stuff the crankcase mouth with clean. lint-free cloth to prevent any debris from falling into the crankcase.

7 Remove the cylinder block base gasket and discard it. If the locating dowels are a loose fit, remove them from the block/crankcase and store them with the block for safe-keeping **(see illustrations)**.

Inspection

8 Check the cylinder bores carefully for scratches and score marks.

9 Using the appropriate precision measuring tools, check each cylinder bore diameter. Measure 10 mm down from the top of the bore and 60 mm down from the top of the bore, parallel to the crankshaft axis **(see illustration)**. Next, measure each cylinder's diameter at the same two locations across the crankshaft axis. Compare the results to this Chapter's Specifications. If the cylinder bores are tapered, out-of-round, worn beyond the specified limits, or badly scuffed or scored, new pistons and

cylinder liners will have to be fitted (Kawasaki do not manufacture oversize pistons). **Note:** *Cylinder liner renewal should be entrusted to a Kawasaki dealer or a workshop equipped with the necessary tools and facilities.*

10 As an alternative, if the precision measuring tools are not available, a dealer service department or motorcycle repair shop will make the measurements and offer advice concerning servicing of the cylinder bores.

11 If the cylinder bores are in reasonably good condition and not worn to the outside of the limits, and if the piston-to-cylinder clearances can be maintained properly (see Section 15), then the cylinder liners do not have to be renewed; hone the bores and fit new piston rings.

12 To perform the honing operation you will need the proper size flexible hone with fine stones, or a 'bottle brush'-type hone, plenty of light oil or honing oil, some clean rags and an electric drill motor. Hold the cylinder block in a vice (cushioned with soft jaws or wood blocks) when performing the honing operation. Mount the hone in the drill motor, compress the stones and slip the hone into the cylinder. Lubricate the cylinder thoroughly, turn on the drill and move the hone up and down in the cylinder bore at a pace which will produce a fine crosshatch pattern on the cylinder wall with the crosshatch lines intersecting at approximately a 60° angle **(see illustration)**. Be sure to use plenty of lubricant and do not take off any more material than is absolutely necessary to produce the desired effect. Do not withdraw the hone from the cylinder while it is running. Instead, shut off the drill and continue moving the hone up and

down in the cylinder until it comes to a complete stop, then compress the stones and withdraw the hone. Wipe the oil out of the cylinder and repeat the procedure on the remaining cylinder. Remember, do not remove too much material from the cylinder bore. If you do not have the tools, or do not desire to perform the honing operation, a dealer service department or motorcycle repair shop will generally do it for a reasonable fee.

13 Next, the cylinder bores must be thoroughly washed with warm soapy water to remove all traces of the abrasive grit produced during the honing operation. Be sure to run a brush through the bolt holes and flush them with running water. After rinsing, dry the cylinder bores thoroughly and apply a coat of light, rust-preventative oil to all machined surfaces.

Installation

Note: *Cylinder block installation will be considerably easier with access to a set of piston ring compressors.*

14 Obtain two lengths of 10 mm threaded rod, approximately 200 mm in length; or, alternatively, obtain two of the longer cylinder head bolts and cut their heads off. These can be used to ensure the cylinder block is lowered squarely onto the pistons.

15 Ensure the crankcase and cylinder block mating surfaces are clean and dry, then install the locating dowels in the crankcase.

16 Manoeuvre the new base gasket over the pistons and seat it on the locating dowels, ensuring that it is fitted the correct way up **(see illustration)**.

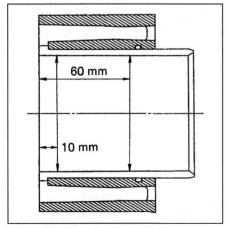

14.9 Measure the diameter 10 mm and 60 mm from the top, in front-to-rear and side-to-side directions

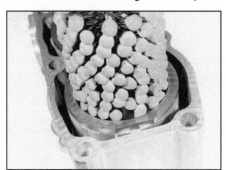

14.12 Honing the cylinders with a 'bottle brush'-type hone

14.16 Install the cylinder block base gasket and both dowels on the crankcase

14.20 The cylinder block can be installed over the rings without ring compressors, but compressors are recommended

17 Screw the two 10 mm rods/bolts into the diagonally-opposite outer cylinder head bolt threads to form the guides for the cylinder block.
18 Ensure that the piston ring end gaps are all correctly spaced (see Section 16), then lubricate the rings with clean engine oil. If a set of piston ring compressors is available, fit the compressors to the pistons and clamp the rings in position.
19 Position the crankshaft so that all pistons are level, then lubricate the cylinder bores with plenty of clean engine oil.
20 With the aid of an assistant, carefully lower the cylinder block down over the guide rods/bolts and seat the piston crowns in the base of the liners **(see illustration)**. Ensure all four pistons remain square, then gently ease the cylinder block onto the pistons until the bottom of the cylinder liners slides down past the piston rings.
Caution: If piston ring compressors are not being used, ensure the piston rings do not snag and break as the pistons enter the cylinder liners. The base of each cylinder liner is chamfered to ease installation – but great care is still needed.
21 Once all four sets of pistons are correctly located in their bores, remove the piston ring compressors (where fitted) and pass the camchain up through the cylinder block tunnel. Slide the block fully down the pistons, seating it on the locating dowels, and wire the camchain up or pass an object through it to prevent it falling down into the crankcase.
22 Fit a new seal to the coolant outlet groove

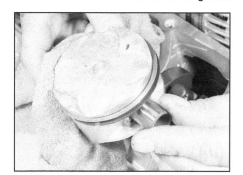

15.6a Push the piston pin out

15.4 Mark the top of each piston with its cylinder number

and fit the outlet to the front of the block. Ensure the seal is correctly fitted, then securely tighten the coolant outlet union bolts. Reconnect the hose(s) to the outlet and securely tighten the retaining clip(s).
23 Fit the camchain rear guide (Section 8).
24 Remove the guide bolts and install the cylinder head (Section 11).
25 Fit the engine to the frame (Section 5).

15 Pistons – removal, inspection and installation

Note: It will be necessary to remove the engine from the frame in order for the pistons to be removed.

Removal

1 Remove the engine from the frame (see Section 5).
2 Remove the cylinder head and block (see Sections 11 and 14).
3 Before removing the pistons from the rods, stuff a clean, lint-free cloth into each crankcase hole, around the connecting rods. This will prevent the circlips from falling into the crankcase if they are inadvertently dropped.

15.5 Wear eye protection and prise the circlip out of its groove with a pointed tool

4 Using a sharp scriber (or a marker pen if the piston is clean enough), mark the number of each piston on its crown **(see illustration)**. Each piston should also have an arrow or triangular mark pointing towards the front of the engine. If not, scribe an arrow into the piston crown before removal.
5 Support the piston and prise one of the circlips out with a small, flat-bladed screwdriver and discard it; circlips must never be re-used **(see illustration)**.
6 Push the piston pin out from the opposite end to free the piston from the rod **(see illustration)**. You may have to deburr the area around the groove to enable the pin to slide out (use a triangular file for this procedure). If the pin won't come out, you can fabricate a piston pin removal tool from a long bolt, a nut, a piece of tubing and washers **(see illustration)**. Repeat the procedure for the remaining pistons.

Inspection

7 Before the inspection process can be carried out, the pistons must be cleaned and the old piston rings removed.
8 Using a piston ring removal and installation tool, carefully remove the rings from the pistons **(see illustration)**. Do not nick or gouge the pistons in the process.

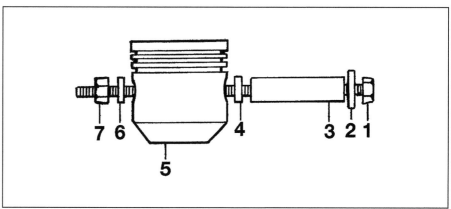

15.6b If the pins won't come out with hand pressure, this removal tool can be fabricated from readily-available parts

1 Bolt	3 Pipe (A)	5 Piston	7 Nut (B)
2 Washer	4 Padding (A)	6 Washer (B)	

A Large enough for piston pin to fit inside   B Small enough to fit through piston pin bore

15.8 Remove the piston rings with a ring removal and installation tool

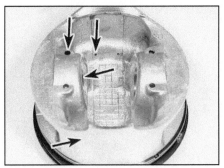

15.13 Check the piston pin bore and the skirt for wear, and make sure the oil holes are clear (arrowed)

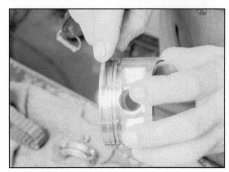

15.15 Measure the piston ring-to-groove clearance with a feeler gauge

9 Scrape all traces of carbon from the tops of the pistons. A hand-held wire brush or a piece of fine emery cloth can be used once most of the deposits have been scraped away. Do not, under any circumstances, use a wire brush mounted in a drill motor to remove deposits from the pistons; the piston material is soft and will be eroded away by the wire brush.

10 Use a piston ring groove cleaning tool to remove any carbon deposits from the ring grooves. If a tool is not available, a piece broken off an old ring will do the job. Be very careful to remove only the carbon deposits. Do not remove any metal and do not nick or gouge the sides of the ring grooves.

11 Once the deposits have been removed, clean the pistons with solvent and dry them thoroughly. Make sure the oil return holes below the oil ring grooves are clear.

12 If the pistons are not damaged or worn excessively (normal piston wear appears as even, vertical wear on the thrust surfaces of the piston and slight looseness of the top ring in its groove) and if the cylinders liners are not to be renewed, new pistons will not be necessary. New piston rings, on the other hand, should always be used when an engine is rebuilt and the bores should be honed (see Section 14).

13 Carefully inspect each piston for cracks around the skirt, at the pin bosses and at the ring lands **(see illustration)**.

14 Look for scoring and scuffing on the thrust faces of the skirt, for holes in the piston crown and burned areas at the edge of the crown. If the skirt is scored or scuffed, the engine may have been suffering from overheating and/or abnormal combustion, which caused excessively high operating temperatures. The oil pump and oil cooler should be checked thoroughly. A hole in the piston crown – admittedly, an extreme condition – is an indication that abnormal combustion (pre-ignition) has been occurring. Burned areas at the edge of the piston crown are usually evidence of spark knock (detonation). If any of the above problems exist, the causes must be corrected or the damage will occur again.

15 Measure the piston ring-to-groove clearance by fitting a new piston ring in the ring groove and slipping a feeler gauge in beside it **(see illustration)**. Check the clearance at three or four locations around the groove. Be sure to use the correct ring for each groove; they are different (see Section 16). If the clearance is greater than the service limit, new pistons will have to be used when the engine is reassembled.

16 Calculate the piston-to-bore clearance by measuring the bore (see Section 14) and the piston diameter. Make sure that the pistons and cylinders are correctly matched. Measure the piston across the skirt on the thrust faces at a 90° angle to the piston pin, 5 mm up from the bottom of the skirt **(see illustration)**. Subtract the piston diameter from the bore diameter to obtain the clearance. If it is greater than specified in the Specifications at the beginning of this Chapter, new pistons and cylinder liners will have to be fitted (Kawasaki do not manufacture oversize pistons).

17 Apply clean engine oil to the pin, insert it into the piston and check for freeplay by rocking the pin back-and-forth. If the pin is loose, new pistons and pins must be installed.

18 Install the rings on the pistons as described in Section 16.

Installation

19 Check that each piston has one new circlip fitted to it and that it is correctly seated

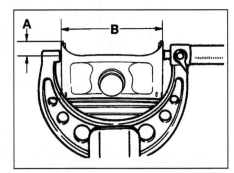

15.16 Measure the piston diameter with a micrometer

A 5 mm (0.2 inch) from bottom of piston
B Piston diameter

in the piston groove with its end gap away from the removal notch in the piston. Insert the piston pin from the opposite side. If it is a tight fit, the piston should be warmed first. If the original pistons are being installed, use the marks made on disassembly to ensure each piston is fitted in its correct location.

20 Lubricate the piston pin and connecting rod small-end bores with clean engine oil.

21 Stuff a clean, lint-free cloth into each crankcase hole, around the connecting rods. This will prevent the circlips from falling into the crankcase if they are inadvertently dropped.

22 Fit the piston to its respective connecting rod, making sure that the arrow or triangular mark on the crown of the piston is pointing towards the front of the engine.

23 Push the piston pin through both piston bosses and the connecting rod bore. If necessary,s the pin can be tapped carefully into position, using a hammer and suitable drift, whilst supporting the connecting rod and piston. Secure the piston pin in position with a second new circlip, making sure it is correctly seated in the piston groove with its end gap away from the removal notch in the piston.

24 Once all pistons are correctly installed, fit the cylinder block and head (Sections 14 and 11).

25 Install the engine in the frame (Section 5).

16 Piston rings – installation

1 Before installing new piston rings, their end gaps must be checked.

2 Lay out the new ring sets so that the same rings will be matched with the same piston and cylinder during the end gap measurement procedure and engine assembly.

3 Insert the top ring into the bottom of the first cylinder and square it up with the cylinder walls by pushing it in with the top of the piston. The ring should be about 25 mm up from the base of the cylinder liner. To measure the end gap, slip a feeler gauge between the ends of the ring and compare the measurement to that given in the

16.3 Check the piston ring end gap with a feeler gauge

16.7a Installing the oil ring expander – make sure the ends don't overlap

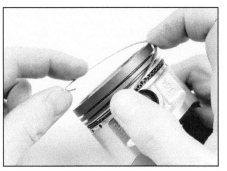

16.7b Installing an oil ring side rail – don't use a ring installation tool to do this

Specifications at the beginning of this Chapter **(see illustration)**.

4 If the gap is larger or smaller than specified, double check to make sure that you have the correct rings before proceeding.

5 Repeat the procedure for each ring that will be installed in the first cylinder and for each ring in the remaining cylinders. Remember to keep the rings, pistons and cylinders matched up.

6 Once the ring end gaps have been checked/corrected, the rings can be installed on the pistons.

7 The oil control ring (lowest on the piston) is installed first. It is composed of three separate components. Slip the expander into the groove, then install the lower side rail **(see**

illustrations). Do not use a piston ring installation tool on the oil ring side rails as they may be damaged. Instead, place one end of the side rail into the groove between the expander and the ring land. Hold it firmly in place and slide a finger around the piston while pushing the rail into the groove. Next, install the upper side rail in the same manner.

8 After the three oil ring components have been installed, check to make sure that both the upper and lower side rails can be turned smoothly in the ring groove.

9 Install the second (middle) ring next **(see illustration)**. **Note:** *The second ring and top ring are different and cannot be interchanged. The second ring is easily identified by its tapered outer edge.* To avoid breaking the ring, use a piston ring installation tool and make sure that the ring is fitted the correct way up with its widest point at the bottom and its identification mark (RN) facing up **(see illustration)**. Fit the ring into the middle groove on the piston. Do not expand the ring any more than is necessary to slide it into place.

10 Finally, install the top ring in the same manner. Make sure the identification mark (R) is facing up.

11 With the piston rings correctly installed, check that each ring is free to rotate easily in its groove. Check the ring-to-groove clearance of each ring using feeler gauges and check that the clearance is within the specified range, then position the ring end gaps as shown **(see illustration)**.

12 Repeat the procedure for the remaining pistons and rings.

17 Clutch – removal, inspection and installation

Note: *The clutch assembly can be removed with the engine in the frame. If the engine has been removed, a clutch centre holding tool will be required to enable the centre nut to be slackened (see Step 11).* **(see illustrations overleaf)**

Removal

1 Remove the lower fairing panels (see Chapter 8).

2 Drain the engine oil (see Chapter 1). Once the oil has drained, fit a new sealing washer to the drain plug and tighten it to the specified torque.

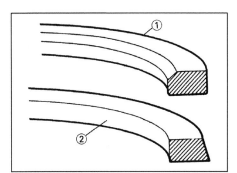

16.9a The top and second (middle) rings can be distinguished by their profiles

1   Top ring
2   Second (middle) ring

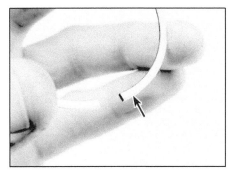

16.9b The marks on the rings (arrowed) must face up when the rings are installed on the pistons

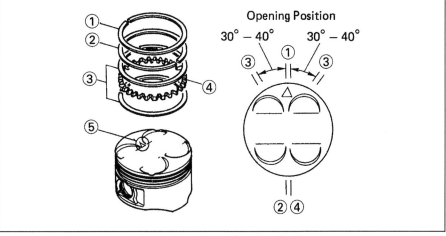

16.11 Ring gap positioning details

1   Top ring
2   Second (middle) ring
3   Oil ring side rails

4   Oil ring expander
5   Arrowhead mark (points to front of engine)

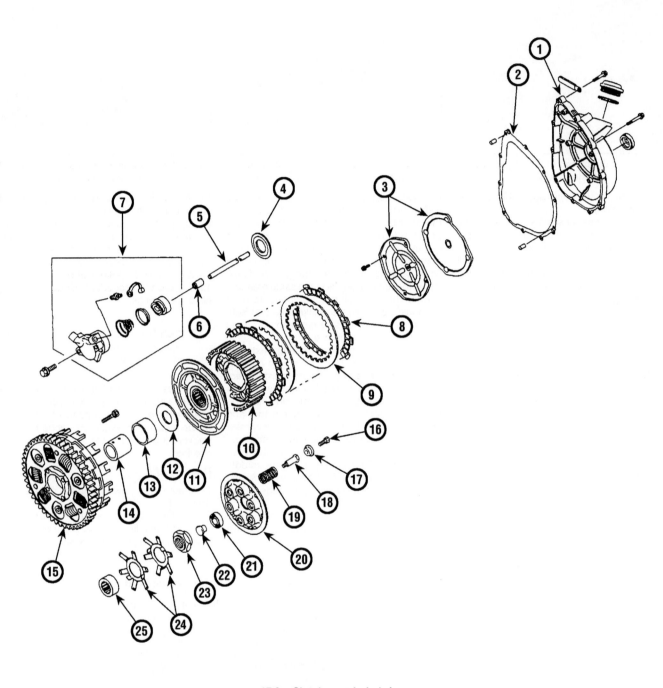

**17.0a Clutch – exploded view
(ZX-7R model)**

1 Clutch cover
2 Gasket
3 Damper and damper cover
4 Collar
5 Clutch pushrod
6 Pushrod end piece
7 Slave cylinder
8 Friction plates

9 Plain plates
10 Clutch centre
11 Inner plate
12 Spacer
13 Needle bearing
14 Bush
15 Clutch drum
16 Pressure plate bolt
17 Spring seat

18 Post
19 Spring
20 Pressure plate
21 Ball bearing
22 Push piece
23 Clutch centre nut
24 Torque limiter springs
25 Splined spacer

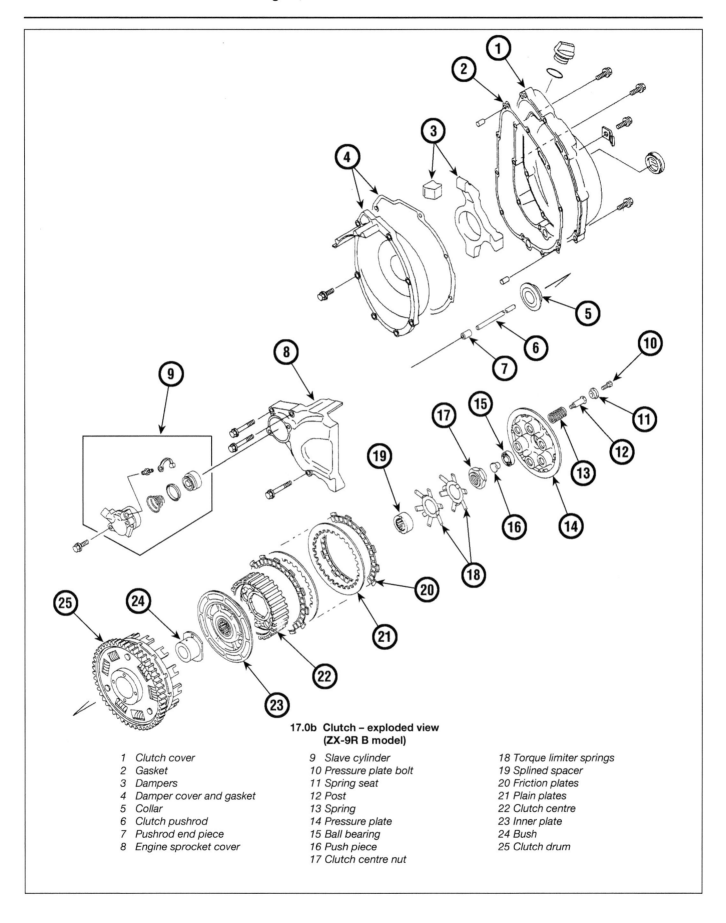

17.0b Clutch – exploded view (ZX-9R B model)

1 Clutch cover
2 Gasket
3 Dampers
4 Damper cover and gasket
5 Collar
6 Clutch pushrod
7 Pushrod end piece
8 Engine sprocket cover

9 Slave cylinder
10 Pressure plate bolt
11 Spring seat
12 Post
13 Spring
14 Pressure plate
15 Ball bearing
16 Push piece
17 Clutch centre nut

18 Torque limiter springs
19 Splined spacer
20 Friction plates
21 Plain plates
22 Clutch centre
23 Inner plate
24 Bush
25 Clutch drum

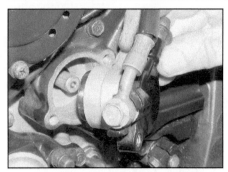

17.3 Removing the slave cylinder

Caution Retain the slave cylinder piston with a cable tie to prevent it being accidentally expelled whilst the cylinder is removed

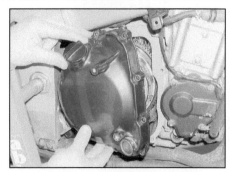

17.5a Removing the clutch cover (ZX-7R model shown)

3 Unscrew the clutch slave cylinder bolts and free the cylinder from the sprocket cover **(see illustration)**. Remove the end piece from the pushrod end. **Note:** *There is no need to disconnect the hydraulic hose from the cylinder.*
Caution: Do not operate the clutch lever whilst the cylinder is detached. To prevent the piston being accidentally expelled, retain it with a cable passed through the cylinder mounting bolts holes and securely tightened around the cylinder (see illustration).
4 Remove the coolant reservoir (see Chapter 3).
5 Working in a criss-cross pattern, evenly slacken and remove the clutch cover retaining bolts **(see illustration)**. On ZX-7R models, note the correct fitted location of the wiring clamp **(see illustration)** and, on ZX-9R B

models, note the correct fitted location of the idle speed adjuster retaining bracket **(see illustration)**. Lift the cover away from the engine, and be prepared to catch any residual oil which may be released as the cover is removed.
6 Remove the clutch cover gasket and discard it. Note the two locating dowels fitted to the crankcase; remove these for safe-keeping if they are loose.
7 Working in a criss-cross pattern, gradually slacken the clutch spring retaining bolts until spring pressure is released. Unscrew the bolts and remove them along with the collars and springs **(see illustration)**.
Caution: Do not operate the clutch lever

from this point in the removal procedure.
8 Remove the pressure plate from the clutch and recover the pushrod guide from the plate bearing.
9 Withdraw the pushrod from the centre of the input shaft **(see illustration)**.
10 Withdraw the clutch friction plates and plain plates **(see illustrations)**.
11 To slacken the clutch centre nut the input shaft/clutch centre must be locked in one of the following ways.
a) *If the engine is in the frame, lock the clutch through the transmission by selecting top gear and applying the rear brake hard whilst the nut is slackened.*
b) *Retain the clutch centre with Kawasaki service tool (No. 57001-1243) (see illustration) or a universal clutch centre holding tool (available from most good motorcycle accessory dealers).*

17.5b Wiring clamp (ZX-7R models)

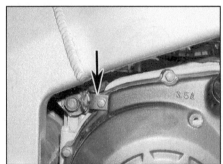

17.5c The idle speed adjuster bracket

17.7 Remove the clutch spring retaining bolts

17.9 Withdraw the pushrod

17.10a Remove the friction plates . . .

17.10b . . . and plain plates

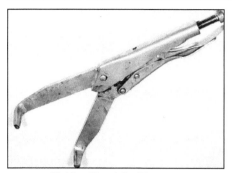

17.11a Clutch locking tool

Alternatively, a clutch centre holding tool can be fabricated from some steel strap, bent at the ends and bolted together in the middle (see illustration) (see also Tool Tip).

12 Remove the centre nut and discard it; a new one must be used on installation.

13 Remove both the torque limiter springs, noting their correct fitted locations **(see illustration)**.

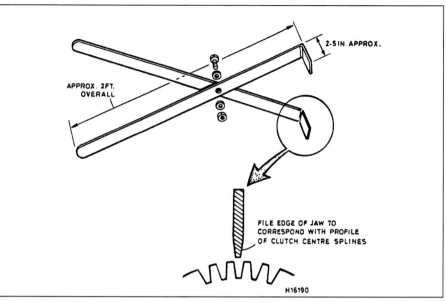

17.11b Home-made version of Kawasaki clutch holding tool

TOOL TiP

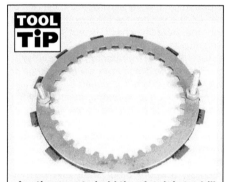

Another way to hold the clutch is to drill holes in a friction plate and a steel plate and bolt them together as they would be when installed. Slip the bolted plates into their installed positions; the clutch hub will be locked to the clutch housing. Shift the transmission into a low gear and have an assistant hold the rear brake on. Unscrew the nut and remove it

14 Remove the clutch centre and splined spacer and slide the inner plate off of the input shaft **(see illustrations)**. Continue as described under the relevant sub-heading.

ZX-7R models

15 Slide the washer off the input shaft **(see illustration)**.

16 Slacken and remove the bolts securing the clutch drum to the alternator drive chain sprocket.

17 Slide the needle roller bearing out from the centre of the drum and remove the drum from the engine **(see illustration)**. Leave the centre bush in position in the alternator drive chain sprocket. **Note:** *If the centre bush is removed from the sprocket, it will be necessary to reset the alternator drive chain lower tensioner before sliding it back into position. Once the bush is in position, the lower tensioner can be released.*

17.13 Removing the torque limiter springs

17.14a Remove the clutch centre . . .

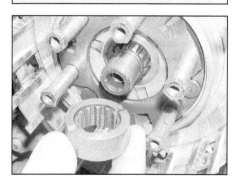

17.14b . . . the splined spacer . . .

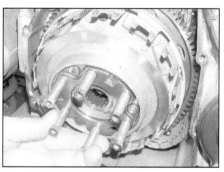

17.14c . . . and the inner plate

17.15 Slide off the washer from the input shaft

17.17 Removing the needle roller bearing

17.20 Check the metal plates for warpage

17.24 Check the pressure plate bearing and push piece for wear or damage

ZX-9R B models

18 Withdraw the centre bush from the clutch drum, then free the drum from the alternator drive chain sprocket and remove it from the engine. The bush has two threaded holes to ease installation. Screw a 6 mm bolt into one of the holes and use the bolt to draw out the bush.

Inspection

19 After an extended period of service, the clutch friction plates will wear and promote clutch slip. Check for warpage using a flat surface and feeler gauges. If any plate exceeds the maximum permissible amount of warpage, or shows signs of wear, all friction plates must be renewed as a set.
20 The plain plates should not show any signs of excess heating (bluing). Check for warpage using a flat surface and feeler gauges (see illustration). If any plate exceeds the maximum permissible amount of warpage, or shows signs of bluing, all plain plates must be renewed as a set. Note: *Plain plates are available in three different thicknesses (2.0, 2.3 and 2.6 mm) to enable the pressure plate freeplay to be correctly set (see Steps 29 to 34). Ensure that the new plates ordered are the same thickness as those being renewed.*
21 Inspect the clutch assembly for burrs and indentations on the edges of the protruding tangs of the friction plates and/or slots in the edge of the clutch drum with which they engage. Similarly check for wear between the inner tangs of the plain plates and the slots in

the clutch centre. Wear of this nature will cause clutch drag and slow disengagement during gear shifting, since the plates will snag when the pressure plate is lifted. With care, a small amount of wear can be corrected by dressing with a fine file, but if this is excessive the worn components must be renewed.
22 Check the clutch centre cams and their slots in the inner plate for signs of wear or damage and renew worn components as necessary.
23 Inspect the input shaft, centre bush and clutch drum bearing surfaces for signs of wear and damage. If any component shows signs of wear or damage, it must be renewed. On ZX-7R models, also check the needle roller bearing for wear or damage.
24 Check the clutch pressure plate bearing for wear (see illustration). Ensure that the inner race of the bearing spins freely without any sign of roughness and that there is no freeplay between the inner and outer races or the outer race and plate. If necessary, renew the bearing by driving the old bearing out of the plate and tapping the new bearing into position, using a hammer and suitable tubular drift which bears only on the bearing's outer race.
25 Measure the free length of each clutch spring (see illustration). If any one has settled to less than the service limit, the clutch springs must be renewed as a set.
26 Inspect the torque limiter springs for signs of wear or damage (see illustration). Ensure the three inner locating tabs and the six outer fingers of each spring are all intact and undamaged. Renew the springs if there is any doubt about their condition (it is

recommended that they are renewed, regardless of their apparent condition).
27 Check the pushrod for signs of damage and straightness by rolling it on a flat surface. Renew the pushrod if it is bent.

Installation

28 If a new pressure plate, new friction plates or new plain plates are being installed, then Kawasaki recommend that the clutch pressure plate freeplay should be checked as described in Steps 29 to 34; this will ensure that the torque limiter mechanism housed in the rear of the clutch drum has the full operating range. If not, the freeplay check is not necessary; continue as described in Step 35 onwards. Note: *If the clutch pressure plate freeplay is insufficient, the clutch lever will feel spongy or will 'pulsate' when it is pulled in and, if it is excessive, the engine braking effect when the clutch is released will be harsh. If either of these conditions were noted prior to removal, then the freeplay should be checked before the clutch is installed.*
29 In order to check the clutch pressure plate freeplay, a spare input shaft and bearing assembly will be required; if these are not available have the check carried out by a Kawasaki dealer.
30 Clamp the spare input shaft and bearing vertically in a vice equipped with soft jaws (clutch end of the shaft uppermost).
31 On ZX-7R models, remove the alternator drive chain sprocket, needle roller bearing, centre bush and spacer from the input shaft (see Section 21) and install them in their correct fitted order on the spare input shaft. Remove all traces of oil and install the following components on the shaft.
 a) *Clutch drum and bearing (Steps 36 and 37 – don't put locking compound on bolts).*
 b) *Washer and inner plate (Step 38).*
 c) *Clutch centre (Step 40).*
 d) *Friction and plain plates (Step 43).*
 e) *Pressure plate (Step 45).*
32 On ZX-9R B models, remove the alternator drive chain sprocket and its shouldered bush (see Section 21) and fit them to the spare input shaft. Remove all traces of oil and install the following components on the shaft.
 a) *Clutch drum and centre bush (Step 53).*

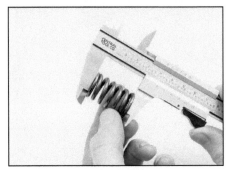

17.25 Measure the clutch spring free length

17.26 Inspect the torque limiter springs

b) *Inner plate (Step 54).*
c) *Clutch centre (Step 40).*
d) *Friction and plain plates (Step 43).*
e) *Pressure plate (Step 45).*

33 Ensure all the clutch components are correctly assembled, then position a dial gauge so that it is in contact with the centre of the pressure plate **(see illustration)**. Gently rotate the clutch drum back and forth whilst measuring the up-and-down movement of the pressure plate; this reading is the pressure plate freeplay measurement. Compare the reading obtained to that given in the Specifications. If it is not within the specified limits, renew all the friction plates and repeat the check. If the reading is still not within the specified limits, adjust the freeplay by removing one of the clutch plain plates and replacing it with one of a different thickness (plain plates are available in three thicknesses; 2.0, 2.3 and 2.6 mm) and repeat the check.

34 Once the pressure plate freeplay is correctly set, remove all the components from the input shaft and install the alternator drive chain sprocket components back on the engine (see Section 21). Reassemble the clutch as follows.

ZX-7R models

35 Prior to installation, ensure the alternator drive chain and sprockets are correctly installed and the chain is correctly tensioned (see Section 21).

36 Remove all traces of locking compound from the threads of the clutch drum bolts, then manoeuvre the drum into position. Engage the drum gear with the crankshaft primary drive gear and align the drum holes with the alternator drive chain sprocket pegs. Ensure the drum is correctly located, lubricate the needle roller bearing with clean engine oil, then carefully slide it into position.

37 Apply a drop of locking compound to each of the drum retaining bolts, then install both bolts, tightening them to the specified torque.

38 Slide the washer along the input shaft, then install the clutch inner plate. Ensure all the clutch spring guides are securely screwed into the inner plate. If any guide is loose, remove it and clean its threads. Apply a drop of locking compound to the guide threads, then refit it to the inner plate, tightening it to the specified torque.

39 Ensure the oil grooves of the splined spacer are on the inside (facing the inner plate) and slide the spacer onto the shaft.

40 Fit the clutch centre, aligning its cams with the inner plate slots.

41 Fit the first torque limiter spring, engaging its inner tabs in the clutch centre slots, then fit the second torque limiter spring engaging its inner tabs in the three remaining centre slots.

42 Fit the new clutch centre nut and tighten it to the specified torque setting, whilst holding the clutch centre using the method employed on removal.

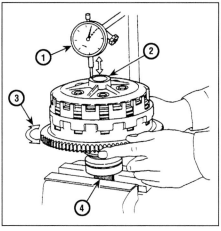

17.33 Measuring the clutch free play

1 *Dial gauge*
2 *Clutch spring plate raised centre*
3 *Moving the clutch housing back and forth*
4 *Drive shaft*

43 Install the first friction plate, aligning its tangs with the slots in the clutch drum, then slide on one of the plain plates, engaging its inner tangs with the slots in the clutch centre. Install all the remaining friction and plain plates alternately, noting that the outer friction plate must be fitted so that its tangs are engaged with the cutouts in the drum housing, not the slots **(see illustration)**. **Note:** *If new clutch plates are being fitted, apply a coating of engine oil to their surfaces to prevent seizure.*

44 Insert the pushrod into the centre of the input shaft.

45 Lubricate the pressure plate bearing with clean engine oil, then fit the pushrod guide to the bearing. Lubricate the bearing surfaces of the guide and pushrod tip with molybdenum disulphide grease, then fit the pressure plate, ensuring its inner tangs are correctly engaged with the clutch centre.

46 Fit the clutch springs and install the collars and retaining bolts. Gradually tighten the bolts evenly in a criss-cross pattern until they are all tightened to the specified torque.

47 Fit the end piece to the left end of the pushrod. Ensure the mating surfaces are

17.43 Engage the tangs (arrowed) with the cutouts

clean and dry, then remove the cable tie (where fitted) and fit the slave cylinder, tightening its retaining bolts securely. Check the operation of the clutch before proceeding.

48 Ensure the mating surfaces are clean and dry, then apply a smear of sealant (Kawasaki recommend the use of Kawasaki Bond 56019-120) to the area of the crankcase mating surface on each side of the crankcase half joints. Fit both locating dowels to the crankcase and locate the new gasket on the dowels **(see illustration)**.

49 Manoeuvre the clutch cover into position and locate it on the dowels.

50 Apply thread locking compound to the two clutch cover bolts fitted to the front holes located above and below the crankcase half joint, then install all the bolts, making sure the wiring clamp/idle speed adjuster bracket (as applicable) is correctly positioned. Tighten all bolts by hand, then go round and tighten them evenly and progressively to the specified torque setting.

51 Fill the engine with the correct type and amount of oil, as described in Chapter 1.

52 Install the coolant reservoir (see Chapter 3), then fit the lower fairing panel (see Chapter 8).

ZX-9R B models

53 Prior to installation, ensure the alternator drive chain and sprockets are correctly installed and the chain is correctly tensioned (see Section 21).

54 Lubricate the clutch drum bush with clean engine oil, then manoeuvre the drum into position. Engage the clutch drum with the crankshaft primary drive gear and align its holes with the alternator drive chain sprocket pegs. Ensure the drum is correctly engaged with the sprocket, then slide the centre bush into position, aligning its flats with the clutch drum cutout.

55 Install the clutch inner plate. Ensure all the clutch spring guides are securely screwed into the inner plate. If any guide is loose, remove it and clean its threads. Apply a drop of locking compound to the guide threads before refitting it to the inner plate and tightening it to the specified torque.

56 Install the remaining components as described in Steps 39 to 52.

17.48 Locating the gasket on to the dowels

18.3 Unplug the clutch switch connector

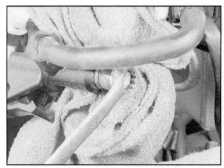

18.4 Undo the clutch hose banjo bolt

18.5a Remove the master cylinder mounting bolts . . .

18 Clutch master cylinder –
removal, overhaul and installation

1 If the master cylinder is leaking fluid, or if the clutch does not function and bleeding does not help (see Section 20), then master cylinder overhaul is recommended.
2 Before disassembling the master cylinder, read through the entire procedure and make sure that you have obtained all the new parts required. You will also need some new brake fluid, clean rags and internal circlip pliers.
Caution: Disassembly, overhaul and reassembly of the master cylinder must be done in a spotlessly clean work area to avoid contamination and possible failure of
the brake hydraulic system components. To prevent damage to the paint from spilled hydraulic fluid, always cover the fuel tank and fairing panels when working on the master cylinder.

Removal

3 Disconnect the electrical connector(s) from the clutch switch **(see illustration)**.
4 Note the correct fitted location of the clutch hose end fitting then unscrew the banjo bolt and separate the hose from the master cylinder **(see illustration)**. Plug the hose end, or wrap a plastic bag tightly around it, to minimise fluid loss and prevent dirt entering the system. Discard the sealing washers, as new ones must be used on installation.
5 On ZX-7R models, unscrew the bolts and remove the master cylinder mounting clamp,
then undo the fluid reservoir mounting bolt and remove the master cylinder and reservoir assembly from the bike **(see illustrations)**. Unscrew the reservoir cap, then lift out the diaphragm plate and the rubber diaphragm and empty the reservoir contents into a suitable container.
6 On ZX-9R B models, unscrew the mounting clamp bolts and remove the master cylinder from the handlebar. Remove the reservoir cover retaining screws and lift off the cover, the diaphragm plate and the rubber diaphragm and empty the reservoir contents into a suitable container.

Overhaul

7 Unscrew the locknut from the clutch lever pivot screw, then remove the screw and lever from the master cylinder **(see illustrations)**.

18.5b . . . and separate the master cylinder from the clamp

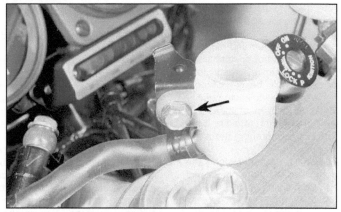

18.5c Remove the reservoir mounting bolt (arrowed)

18.7a Remove the pivot screw locknut (arrowed) . . .

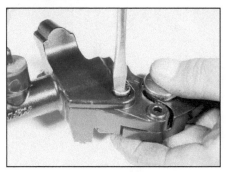

18.7b . . . undo the pivot screw . . .

18.7c . . . and remove the clutch lever and pivot bushing

On ZX-9R B models, take care not to lose the pivot bush from the lever.
8 Undo the screw and remove the clutch switch from the master cylinder **(see illustration)**.
9 Carefully remove the dust boot and push-rod from the end of the master cylinder bore.

10 Using circlip pliers, remove the circlip then pull out the washer, piston assembly, primary cup and spring, noting how they fit.

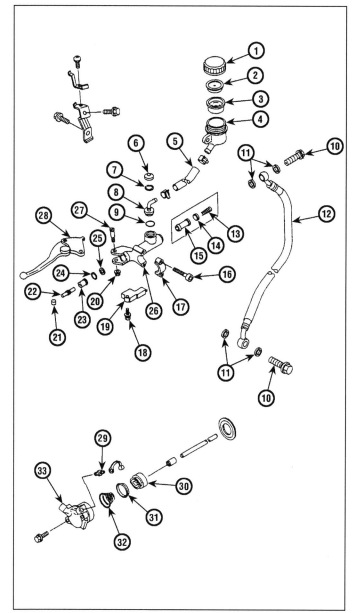

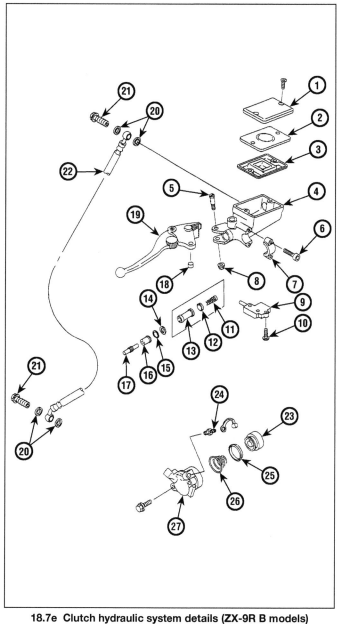

18.7d Clutch hydraulic system details (ZX-7R models)

1 Reservoir cap	13 Spring	24 Snap ring
2 Retainer	14 Primary cup	25 Washer
3 Diaphragm	15 Piston	26 Master cylinder
4 Fluid reservoir	16 Clamp bolt	body
5 Fluid feed hose	17 Clamp	27 Pivot screw
6 Rubber cap	18 Clutch switch	28 Clutch lever
7 Snap ring	screw	29 Bleed valve
8 Fluid feed	19 Clutch switch	30 Slave cylinder
fitting	20 Pivot screw	piston
9 O-ring	locknut	31 Piston seal
10 Banjo bolt	21 Pivot bushing	32 Spring
11 Sealing washers	22 Pushrod	33 Slave cylinder
12 Fluid hose	23 Rubber boot	body

18.7e Clutch hydraulic system details (ZX-9R B models)

1 Reservoir lid	10 Clutch switch	20 Sealing washers
2 Retainer	screw	21 Banjo bolt
3 Diaphragm	11 Spring	22 Fluid feed hose
4 Master cylinder	12 Primary cup	23 Slave cylinder
body/reservoir	13 Piston	piston
5 Pivot screw	14 Washer	24 Bleed valve
6 Clamp bolt	15 Snap ring	25 Piston seal
7 Clamp	16 Rubber boot	26 Spring
8 Pivot screw	17 Pushrod	27 Slave cylinder
locknut	18 Pivot bushing	body
9 Clutch switch	19 Clutch lever	

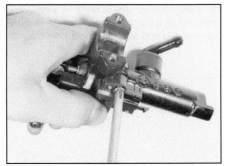

18.8 Remove the clutch switch

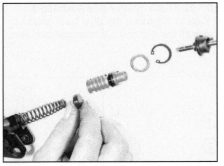

18.10 Remove the washer, piston, primary cup and spring

Lay the parts out in the correct fitted order to prevent confusion during reassembly **(see illustration)**.

11 If necessary on ZX-7R models, ease the dust cap out from the master cylinder fluid reservoir union port. Remove the circlip, then separate the reservoir union and master cylinder and recover the O-ring.

12 Clean all parts with clean brake fluid or denatured alcohol. If compressed air is available, use it to dry the parts thoroughly (make sure it's filtered and unlubricated). *Caution: Do not, under any circumstances, use a petroleum-based solvent to clean master cylinder parts.*

13 Check the master cylinder bore for corrosion, scratches, nicks and score marks. If damage or wear is evident, the master cylinder must be renewed. If the master cylinder is in poor condition, then the slave cylinder should be checked as well. Check that the fluid inlet and outlet ports in the master cylinder are clear. Inspect the reservoir cover rubber diaphragm and renew it if it is damaged or has deteriorated.

14 The piston assembly, primary cup and spring are supplied together as an assembly; all other components can be ordered individually. Renew all rubber components, regardless of their apparent condition.

15 Lubricate the new primary cup with clean brake fluid and fit it to the tapered end of the new spring. Insert the assembly into the master cylinder so that the primary cup is towards the piston.

16 Lubricate the new piston and seal assembly with clean brake fluid. Ensure the assembly is

the correct way round, then carefully ease it into the master cylinder, making sure the seal lips do not turn inside out as they slip into the bore. Fit the new washer, then depress the piston and install the circlip, making sure that it locates in the master cylinder groove.

17 Fit the new rubber dust boot to the push-rod ensuring that the rounded end of the pushrod is facing inwards. Lubricate the push-rod ends with silicone grease, then fit the pushrod and boot assembly to the master cylinder, locating the boot lip in the piston bore groove.

18 Fit the clutch switch to the master cylinder and securely tighten its retaining screw.

19 Fit the lever, ensuring it engages correctly with the pushrod end, then install the pivot screw. Securely tighten the pivot screw, then fit the locknut and tighten it to the specified torque.

20 On ZX-7R models, fit the new O-ring to the master cylinder and seat the reservoir fluid union in position. Secure the union in position with the circlip, then slide the dust cap into position.

Installation

21 On ZX-7R models, locate the master cylinder on the handlebar and fit the mounting clamp with its arrow mark facing upwards. Align the master cylinder mounting clamp split with the punch mark on the top of the handlebar, then tighten the mounting clamp upper bolt to the specified torque followed by the lower bolt. Fit the fluid reservoir to its mounting bracket and securely tighten its retaining bolt.

22 On ZX-9R B models, locate the master cylinder on the handlebar and fit the mounting clamp with its arrow mark facing upwards. Position the master cylinder so that its clamp upper split is located 5 mm to the rear of the handlebar switch split, then tighten first the mounting clamp upper bolt, then the lower one, to the specified torque.

23 On all models, position a new sealing washer on each side of the clutch hose end fitting, then connect the hose to the master cylinder. Ensure the hose end fitting is correctly positioned against its stop, then tighten the banjo bolt to the specified torque.

24 Connect the wiring to the clutch switch.

25 Fill the fluid reservoir with specified fluid as described in *Daily (pre-ride) checks*. Refer to Section 20 of this Chapter and bleed the air from the hydraulic system.

26 Ensure the fluid level is correct, then fit the reservoir rubber diaphragm, diaphragm plate and cap/cover (as applicable).

27 Thoroughly check the operation of the clutch before riding the motorcycle.

---

19 Clutch slave cylinder – removal, overhaul and installation

Caution: Disassembly, overhaul and reassembly of the slave cylinder must be done in a spotlessly clean work area to avoid contamination and possible failure of the brake hydraulic system components.

Removal

1 Remove the left lower fairing panel as described in Chapter 8.

2 Note the correct fitted location of the clutch hose end fitting, then unscrew the banjo bolt and separate the hose from the slave cylinder. Plug the hose end, or wrap a plastic bag tightly around it, to minimise fluid loss and prevent dirt entering the system. Discard the sealing washers as new ones must be used on installation.

3 Unscrew the clutch slave cylinder bolts and remove the cylinder from the sprocket cover **(see illustration)**. If necessary, remove the end cap from the clutch pushrod and withdraw the pushrod from the engine.

Overhaul

4 Clean the exterior of the cylinder with denatured alcohol or brake system cleaner.

5 Withdraw the piston from the cylinder **(see illustration)**.

19.3 Remove the slave cylinder from the engine sprocket cover

19.5 Remove the piston from the slave cylinder

 If the piston cannot be withdrawn by hand, it can be pushed out by applying compressed air to the clutch hose union hole. Only low pressure should be required, such as is generated by a foot pump, and wrap the slave cylinder in a wad of rag to prevent the piston being forcibly expelled.

6 Recover the spring from the cylinder, noting which way round it is fitted.

7 Carefully remove the fluid seal from the piston, noting which way round it is fitted.

8 Clean all parts with clean brake fluid or denatured alcohol. If compressed air is available, use it to dry the parts thoroughly (make sure it is filtered and unlubricated). *Caution: Do not, under any circumstances, use a petroleum-based solvent to clean master cylinder parts.*

9 Inspect the cylinder bore and piston for signs of corrosion, nicks and burrs and loss of plating. If surface defects are present, the cylinder assembly must be renewed. If the cylinder is in bad shape, the master cylinder should also be checked. No specifications are given to check piston and bore wear.

10 Lubricate the new piston fluid seal with clean fluid. Fit the seal to the piston groove, making sure it is fitted the correct way round with its wider end facing away from the piston.

11 Fit the spring to the cylinder, with its tapered end facing the piston.

12 Lubricate the piston with clean fluid and install it in the cylinder bore. Make sure the spring remains correctly positioned and take great care to ensure the fluid seal is not damaged as it enters the bore. Using your thumbs, push the piston all the way in, making sure it enters the bore squarely.

Installation

13 Where necessary, apply a smear of molybdenum disulphide grease to the pushrod ends, then insert the rod into position and refit its end cap.

14 Ensure the mating surfaces are clean and dry, then fit the clutch slave cylinder to the cover. Install the retaining bolts and tighten them securely.

15 Position a new sealing washer on each side of the clutch hose end fitting, then connect the hose to the slave cylinder. Ensure the hose end fitting is correctly positioned against its stop, then tighten the banjo bolt to the specified torque.

16 Fill the master cylinder reservoir with the recommended clutch fluid (see *Daily (pre-ride) checks*) and bleed the hydraulic system as described in Section 20.

17 Check for leaks and thoroughly test the operation of the clutch before installing the fairing panel.

20 Clutch system – bleeding
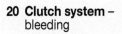

Caution: To prevent damage to the paint from spilled hydraulic fluid, always cover the fuel tank and fairing panels when working on the master cylinder.

1 Bleeding the clutch is simply the process of removing all the air bubbles from the clutch master cylinder, the hose and the slave

21.3 Remove the alternator chain lower tensioner

cylinder. Bleeding is necessary whenever a hydraulic connection is loosened, when a component or hose is renewed, or when the master cylinder or slave cylinder is overhauled. Leaks in the system may also allow air to enter, but leaking fluid will reveal their presence and warn you of the need for repair.

2 To bleed the clutch, you will need some new DOT 4 hydraulic fluid, a length of clear vinyl or plastic tubing, a small container partially filled with clean hydraulic fluid, some rags and a spanner to fit the slave cylinder bleed valve.

3 Remove the left side lower fairing panel (see Chapter 8) to gain access to the slave cylinder bleed valve.

4 Remove the master cylinder reservoir cap/cover (as applicable) and remove the diaphragm plate and diaphragm (see *Daily (pre-ride) checks*). Slowly pump the clutch lever a few times until no air bubbles can be seen floating up from the holes in the bottom of the reservoir. This bleeds the air from the master cylinder end of the line. Loosely refit the reservoir cap/cover **(see illustrations 18.7d or 18.7e)**.

5 Pull the dust cap off the slave cylinder bleed valve. Attach one end of the clear vinyl or plastic tubing to the bleed valve and submerge the other end in the brake fluid in the container.

6 Remove the reservoir cover and check the fluid level. Do not allow the fluid level to drop below the lower mark during the bleeding process.

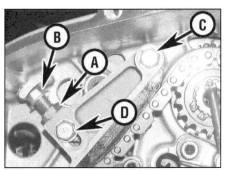

21.4 Slacken the locknut (A), screw in the adjuster bolt (B) and remove the pivot bolt (C) and the set bolt (D)

7 Carefully pump the clutch lever three or four times and hold it in while opening the bleed valve. When the valve is opened, fluid will flow out of the cylinder into the clear tubing.

8 Retighten the bleed valve, then release the clutch lever gradually. Repeat the process until no air bubbles are visible in the fluid leaving the valve, and the clutch action feels smooth and progressive.

9 Disconnect the bleeding equipment, then tighten the bleed valve to the specified torque and install the dust cap.

10 Top the fluid level up to the upper level mark (see *Daily (pre-ride) checks*), then install the diaphragm, diaphragm plate and reservoir cap/cover. Wipe up any spilled fluid and check the system for leaks before installing the fairing panel (see Chapter 8). **Note:** *Failure to bleed satisfactorily after a reasonable repetition of the bleeding procedure may be due to worn master cylinder seals.*

21 Alternator drive chain and tensioners – adjustment, removal, inspection and installation

Note: *The alternator drive chain and tensioners can be removed with the engine in the frame.*

Adjustment

1 If the alternator drive chain is noisy in operation, it can be adjusted as follows.

2 Remove the clutch assembly as described in Section 17.

3 Unscrew the retaining bolts and remove the alternator chain lower tensioner **(see illustration)**.

4 Slacken the chain upper tensioner locknut and screw in the adjuster bolt so the chain becomes slack. Unscrew the mounting bolts and remove the tensioner from the crankcase **(see illustration)**. **Note:** *Ensure the starter motor idler gear shaft remains fully in position whilst the tensioner is removed. If the shaft is withdrawn, the idler gear will drop into the crankcase and the crankcase halves will have to be separated to enable the gear to be refitted.*

5 Remove all traces of locking compound from the threads of the upper and lower tensioner mounting bolts.

6 Apply a drop of locking compound to the threads of the mounting bolts and install the upper tensioner, tightening its mounting bolts lightly only. Slowly unscrew the tensioner adjuster bolt until the point is reached where all slack is removed from the drive chain without placing the chain under any tension. Tighten both the mounting bolts to the specified torque, then recheck the chain tension. If all is well, ensure the adjuster bolt is in firm contact with the crankcase, then hold it stationary and securely tighten its locknut. *Caution: Do not overtighten the drive chain, as this will cause premature wear.*

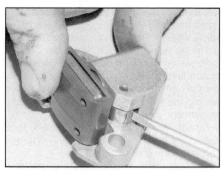

21.7 Release the stopper and push the plunger fully back into the tensioner body

7 Release the lower tensioner stopper and push the plunger fully back into the tensioner body. Hold the plunger in the fully retracted position and fit the lower tensioner to the crankcase **(see illustration)**. Apply a drop of locking compound to the tensioner bolts, fit the bolts, then tighten them to the specified torque.
8 Install the clutch assembly (see Section 17).

Removal

9 Remove the clutch assembly (see Section 17).
10 Unscrew the retaining bolts and remove the alternator chain lower tensioner.
11 Slacken the drive chain upper tensioner locknut and screw in the adjuster bolt so the chain becomes slack. Unscrew the mounting bolts and remove the tensioner from the crankcase (see Note in Step 4).

21.13a Remove the circlip from the oil pump sprocket . . .

21.14 . . . slide off the sprockets and chain . . .

21.12 Remove the alternator driveshaft oil pipe (arrowed)

12 Unscrew the retaining bolt and remove the alternator driveshaft oil pipe **(see illustration)**. Remove the O-ring from the oil pipe and discard it; a new one will be needed on installation.
13 Using circlip pliers, remove the circlips securing the sprockets to the oil pump and alternator driveshafts **(see illustrations)**.
14 Free the oil pump sprocket and the alternator driven sprocket from their shafts and remove all the sprockets and chain as an assembly **(see illustration)**.
15 Remove the chain guide from the crankcase **(see illustration)**.
16 On ZX-7R models, remove the drive sprocket bearing and centre bush from the input shaft, then slide off the spacer, noting which way around it is fitted.
17 On ZX-9R B models, slide the drive sprocket shouldered bush off the input shaft, noting which way round it is fitted.

21.13b . . . and the alternator driven sprocket . . .

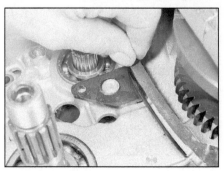

21.15 . . . then remove the chain guide

Inspection

18 Check the sprocket teeth for wear or damage. Check the drive pegs in the alternator drive sprocket for looseness, wear or damage. Check the chain for wear, damage or loose pins. Renew the sprockets and chain as a set if any defects are found. The amount of chain wear can be assessed by pulling it tight and measuring a twenty-link length (distance between 21 link pins) section **(see illustration)**. Repeat this check along several different sections of the chain and compare the results to those given in the specifications. If any section exceeds the specified limit, the drive chain must be renewed.
19 Check the alternator driveshaft oil pipe for clogging. Flush it with clean solvent and blow it out with compressed air, if available.
20 Check the tensioner guides and the chain guide for score marks or excessive wear. Renew the tensioners or the guide if defects are found.
21 Check the latch on the lower tensioner for wear or damage and renew the tensioner if defects are found.

Installation

22 On ZX-7R models, fit the spacer to the input shaft, ensuring its stepped surface is facing inwards. Lubricate all bearing surfaces with clean engine oil, then slide the centre bush and drive sprocket bearing onto the input shaft.
23 On ZX-9R B models, lubricate all bearing surfaces with clean engine oil, then fit the drive sprocket shouldered bush to the input shaft with its shoulder facing outwards.
24 On all models, fit the drive chain guide to the crankcase, locating it on the oil pipe boss.
25 Fit the drive sprocket to the input shaft ensuring its drive pegs are facing outwards.
26 Locate the oil pump drive sprocket on the driveshaft splines.
27 Engage the drive chain with the oil pump and drive sprockets, then engage the alternator driven sprocket with the chain and locate it on the alternator driveshaft splines.
28 Ensure the drive sprocket is correctly located, then secure the oil pump and alternator driven sprockets in position with the circlips.

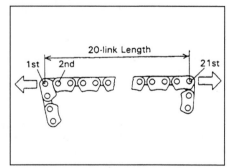

21.18 Check the chain wear

21.31 The chain and sprockets should look like this when assembled

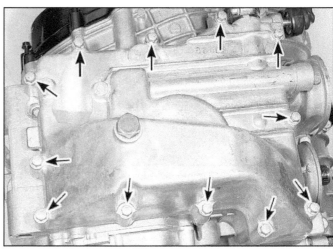

22.5a Remove the oil pan bolts (arrowed) . . .

29 Remove all traces of locking compound from the threads of the oil pipe bolt. Fit a new O-ring on the oil pipe, lubricating it with a smear of engine oil, and ease the pipe into position in the crankcase. Apply a drop of locking compound to the threads of the pipe retaining bolt and tighten it to the specified torque.

30 Install the tensioners and adjust the chain tension as described in Steps 5 to 7.

31 Once the chain is correctly adjusted **(see illustration)**, install the clutch assembly (see Section 17).

22 Oil pan –
removal and installation

Note: *The oil pan can be removed with the engine in the frame. Some of the following procedures are shown with the engine removed for clarity.*

Removal

1 Remove the radiator as described in Chapter 3.

2 Remove the exhaust system as described in Chapter 4.

3 Drain the engine oil as described in Chapter 1 and proceed as described under the sub-heading appropriate to your model.

ZX-7R models

4 Working in a criss-cross pattern, gradually loosen the oil pan retaining bolts.

5 Remove all the bolts and lower the oil pan away from the crankcase bolts **(see illustrations)**. If the engine is in the frame, note that as the oil pan is removed, the oil pump pick-up strainer may fall out of position. Recover the oil pan gasket and O-ring and discard them; new ones must be used on installation.

6 If it was not released when the oil pan was removed, remove the oil pump pick-up strainer from the base of the engine. Remove the seal from the pick-up; a new one will be needed for installation.

7 Ease the oil pipe carefully out from the base of the crankcase, taking great care not to bend it. Remove the O-ring from each oil pipe fitting and discard them; new ones must be used on installation **(see illustration)**.

8 Clean the pick-up strainer mesh in solvent. Check it for clogging or splitting and renew if necessary. Ensure the oil pipe is undamaged and unblocked.

ZX-9R B models

9 Slacken and remove the bolts and nuts securing the frame downtubes to the mounting brackets on the front of the crankcase (See Step 31 of Section 5).

10 Unscrew the mounting bolts and nuts securing the downtubes to the main frame and remove the downtube assembly from the bike.

11 Slacken the retaining clips and remove the hose connecting the union on the right side of the oil pan to the base of the crankcase **(see illustration)**.

12 Remove the oil pan as described in Steps 4 to 8.

Installation

13 Ensure all mating surfaces are clean and dry.

14 Fit a new O-ring to each oil pipe fitting groove. Lubricate the O-rings with clean engine oil, then ease the pipe into position in the crankcase.

15 Fit a new oil pump pick-up strainer seal to the crankcase **(see illustration)**, making sure its flange is facing the strainer. Fit the strainer, ensuring the cast tab on the crankcase is

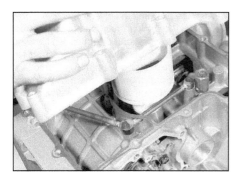

22.5b . . . and lift the oil pan off the engine

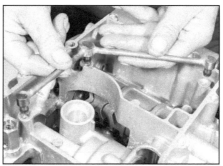

22.7 Work the three O-rings clear of the crankcase passages and lift the oil pipe out

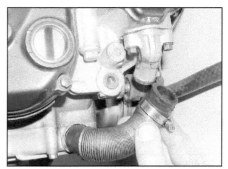

22.11 Remove the hose connecting the union to the crankcase

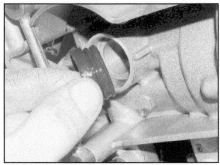

22.15a Fit the new oil pump pick-up strainer seal to the crankcase

22.15b Align the strainer's notch with the cast tab on the crankcase

22.17 Install a new gasket on the crankcase

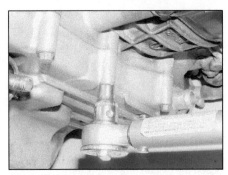

22.18 Tighten all the oil pan retaining bolts to the specified torque

correctly positioned in the strainer's notch **(see illustration)**.
16 Fit the new oil pan O-ring to the recess in the base of the crankcase, ensuring its flat

surface is against the crankcase. Use a dab of grease to hold the O-ring in position.
17 Locate the new gasket on the crankcase **(see illustration)**, then fit the oil pan. Ensure

the O-ring is still correctly seated in its crankcase recess, then insert all the retaining bolts and tighten them by hand.
18 Working in a criss-cross pattern, tighten all the oil pan retaining bolts to the specified torque setting **(see illustration)**.
19 On ZX-9R B models, fit the hose connecting the oil pan to the crankcase and securely tighten its retaining clips. Install the frame downtubes and fit all its mounting nuts and bolts, tightening them by hand only. Tighten the downtube to main frame nuts and bolts to the specified torque first, then tighten the engine front mounting bolts to the specified torque.
20 On all models, install the exhaust system and radiator as described in Chapters 4 and 3.
21 Fill the engine with the correct type and quantity of oil as described in *Daily (pre-ride) checks*. Start the engine and check for leaks.
22 If all is well, check the oil and coolant levels, then install the fairing panels as described in Chapter 8.

23 Oil pump – removal, inspection and installation

Note: *The oil pump can be removed with the engine in the frame.*

Removal

1 Remove the clutch (see Section 17).
2 Remove the alternator drive chain and sprockets (see Section 21).
3 Unscrew the three oil pump retaining bolts **(see illustration)**.
4 Firmly grasp the oil pump driveshaft and withdraw the pump assembly from the crankcase, taking care not to lose the locating pin. If the (main pump) outer rotor remains in its housing, remove it and fit it to the rear of the pump, keeping it the correct way round **(see illustrations)**.

Inspection

Note: *The pump has two sets of rotors. The thinner set circulates oil around the oil cooler and the thicker set functions as the main oil pump supply to the engine.*
5 Wash the oil pump in solvent, then dry it off.
6 Remove the thicker (main pump) outer rotor from the rear of the pump, noting which way round it is fitted. Slide out the driveshaft to enable the inner rotor drive pin to be removed **(see illustration)**, then slide the thicker (main pump) inner rotor off the end of the driveshaft, noting which way around it is fitted.
7 Remove the locating pin and slide the pump cover off the driveshaft **(see illustrations)**.
8 Withdraw the driveshaft and remove the thinner (oil cooler) inner and outer rotors from the pump body, noting which way round they are fitted.

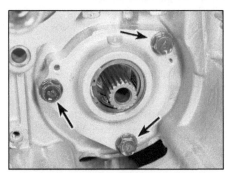

23.3 Remove the oil pump mounting bolts

23.4a Pull on the shaft to detach the oil pump from the crankcase . . .

23.4b . . . the outer main rotor (arrowed) may remain in the engine when the pump is removed

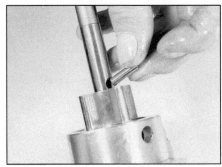

23.6 Remove the drive pin from the pump shaft

23.7a Remove the locating pin . . .

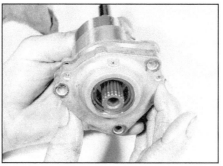

23.7b . . . and remove the pump cover

23.10 Renew the bearing

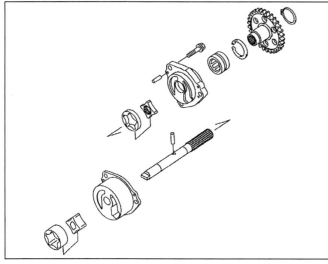

23.12 Oil pump detail

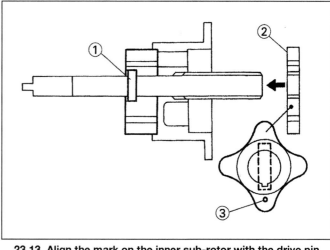

23.13 Align the mark on the inner sub-rotor with the drive pin

1 Pin   2 Inner rotor   3 Punch mark

9 Check the pump housings and rotors for scoring and wear and renew all worn components (all parts are available individually). If any component is badly worn or damaged, it is a good idea to install a new oil pump assembly.

10 Inspect the pump cover bearing and the bearing surface of the sprocket for wear and damage and renew if necessary. To renew the bearing, extract the circlip from the cover, then press out the bearing **(see illustration)**. Install the new bearing, aligning its oilway with the oil hole in the cover, and secure it in position with the circlip.

11 If the pump is good, make sure all components are clean and lubricate them with clean engine oil. Reassemble the pump as follows, ensuring all rotors are fitted the same way round as was noted on removal. **Note:** *If any rotor is fitted the wrong way around, the rate of pump wear will be accelerated.*

12 Insert the driveshaft into the pump body and slide the thicker (main pump) inner rotor onto the rear of the shaft. Insert the drive pin into the driveshaft and locate the pin in the inner rotor slot **(see illustration)**.

13 Fit the thinner (oil cooler) inner rotor to the driveshaft, aligning its punch mark with the driveshaft pin **(see illustration)**, then fit the thinner outer rotor.

14 Align the pump cover with the pump body and insert the locating pin.

15 Fit the thicker (main pump) outer rotor to the rear of the pump, ensuring it is the correct way round.

Installation

16 Remove all traces of locking compound from the threads of the oil pump retaining bolts.

17 Lubricate the pump assembly with clean engine oil and check that the pump driveshaft rotates freely. **Note:** *Ensure the driveshaft pin is correctly located in the thicker (main pump) inner rotor slot. To prevent the pin dropping out, grasp the driveshaft and pull it outwards to keep the pin forced into its slot during installation.*

18 Ensure the locating pin is fitted to the pump, then manoeuvre the pump assembly into position. Align the oil pump driveshaft dog with the slot in the water pump shaft and the locating pin with the crankcase hole and seat the pump assembly correctly in position.

19 Apply a drop of locking compound to the retaining bolt threads, then install the bolts and tighten them to the specified torque.

20 Check the pump driveshaft rotates freely, then install the alternator drive chain and sprockets and the clutch assembly (see Sections 21 and 17).

24 Oil pressure relief valves – removal, inspection and installation

Note: *The oil pressure relief valves can be removed with the engine in the frame.*

Removal

1 Remove the oil pan (see Section 22).

2 Unscrew the oil pressure relief valves and remove them from the base of the crankcase **(see illustration)**.

24.2 Unscrew the oil pressure relief valves (arrowed) from the crankcase

25.4 Loosen the clips (arrowed) and disconnect the coolant hoses

25.5 Remove the oil cooler bolt

25.7 Seat the cooler on the crankcase, engaging the locating lug (arrowed) with the peg on the crankcase

Inspection

3 Clean each valve with solvent and dry it, using compressed air if available.
4 Using a wood or plastic tool, depress the steel ball inside each valve and see if it moves smoothly. Make sure it returns to its seat completely. If it doesn't, replace the valve with a new one (don't attempt to disassemble and repair it).

Installation

5 Remove all traces of locking compound from the relief valve threads.
6 Apply a drop of locking compound to the threads of each valve, then fit the valves to the crankcase and tighten them to the specified torque.
Caution: Ensure no locking compound is allowed to enter the valve bore, as this will cause the valve to stick and prevent it functioning correctly.
7 Install the oil pan (see Section 22).

25 Oil cooler – removal and installation

Removal

Note: *Access to the oil cooler is poor with the exhaust system in position.*
1 Remove the lower and inner fairing panels

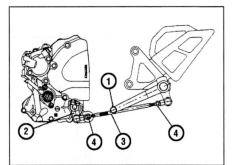

26.0 Shift pedal details (ZX-7R models)

1 Shift pedal	3 Shift rod
2 Shift lever	4 Locknuts

(see Chapter 8).
2 Drain the engine oil (see Chapter 1). Once the oil has drained, fit a new sealing washer to the drain plug and tighten it to the specified torque.
3 Drain the cooling system (see Chapter 1).
4 Slacken the retaining clips and disconnect the coolant hoses from the oil cooler unions **(see illustration)**. Note: *If access to the clips is poor, they can be slackened and disconnected once the centre bolt has been removed.*
5 Unscrew the centre bolt and remove the oil cooler from the front of the crankcase **(see illustration)** Recover the sealing washer from the bolt, and the O-ring fitted between the cooler and the crankcase, and discard them both; new ones must be used on installation.

Installation

6 Ensure the oil cooler and crankcase mating surfaces are clean and dry, then fit a new O-ring to the groove in the rear of the oil cooler.
7 Manoeuvre the oil cooler into position, ensuring the O-ring remains correctly positioned. Seat the cooler on the crankcase, engaging its locating lug with the peg on the crankcase **(see illustration)**.
8 Apply clean engine oil to the underside of the head and threads of the centre bolt then fit the new sealing washer. Screw the bolt into the oil cooler and tighten it to the specified torque setting. **Note:** *New oil cooler centre bolts are supplied without the oil filter adapter. Obtain a new oil filter adapter, apply locking*

26.5 Unscrew the clamp bolt and free the linkage from the engine

compound to its last few threads then screw it into the centre bolt, tightening it to the specified torque.
9 Reconnect the coolant hoses to the oil cooler and securely tighten the retaining clips.
10 Fill the engine with the correct type and quantity of oil (see Chapter 1).
11 Refill the cooling system (see Chapter 1).
12 Start the engine and check for leaks. If all is well, check the oil and coolant levels, then install the fairing panels as described in Chapter 8.

26 Gearchange mechanism – removal, inspection and installation

ZX-7R models

Note: *The gearchange mechanism components can be removed with the engine in the frame* **(see illustration)**.

Removal

1 Remove the front sprocket (see Chapter 6).
2 Remove the rear wheel (see Chapter 7).
3 Drain the engine oil (see Chapter 1).
4 Remove the water pump (see Chapter 3).
5 Note the correct fitted position of the gearchange lever linkage on the shaft (make alignment marks if necessary). Ensure the transmission is in neutral, then unscrew the clamp bolt and free the linkage from the engine **(see illustration)**.
6 Withdraw the clutch pushrod and end cap from the engine.
7 Undo the two screws and free the neutral switch from the gearchange mechanism cover. Recover the switch O-ring and discard it; a new one should be used on installation. Remove the neutral switch contact and spring from the end of the selector drum for safe-keeping.
8 Free the final drive chain from the output shaft and position it clear of the gearchange mechanism cover.
9 Slacken and remove the gearchange mechanism cover retaining screws and bolts **(see illustrations)**.

26.9a Remove the cover bolts and screws (arrowed) . . .

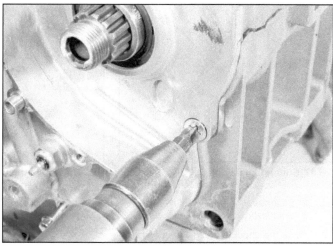

26.9b . . . use an impact driver on the screws

10 Remove all traces of dirt from the gearchange shaft, then slide the cover off the shaft and remove it from the engine **(see illustration)**. Recover the outer washer from the gearshift shaft and store it with the cover for safe-keeping. If the cover locating dowels are loose, remove them and store them with the cover (note that the upper dowel is fitted with an O-ring) **(see illustrations)**.

11 Remove the gasket and discard it; a new one must be used on refitting.

12 Remove the gearchange shaft assembly from the engine, complete with its inner shouldered spacer **(see illustration)**.

13 Unscrew the pivot bolt and remove the shouldered washer, selector drum stopper arm, washer and spring, noting the correct fitted location of each component.

Inspection

14 Check the gearchange shaft for straightness and damage to the splines. If the shaft is bent or the splines are damaged, the shaft must be renewed. Inspect the shaft centralising spring and the change lever return springs for signs of damage and renew as necessary. Also check that the centralising spring locating pin in the casing is securely tightened. If it is loose, remove it and apply a suitable thread-locking compound before installing and tightening it to the specified torque.

15 Inspect the stopper arm components, paying particular attention to the arm spring, and renew any defective item.

16 Check the condition of the oil seals and the gearchange shaft needle roller bearing in the cover. To renew an oil seal, lever the old seal carefully out of position with a flat-bladed screwdriver, then press the new one into position, ensuring its sealing lip is facing inwards. If the needle roller bearing requires renewal, remove the oil seal and note the correct fitted location of the bearing before pressing/drifting it out of position. The new bearing should be pressed or drawn into its

bore rather than driven into position to prevent possible damage. In the absence of a press, a suitable drawbolt arrangement can be made up as described in *Tools and Workshop Tips* (Section 5) in the *Reference* section. Ensure the bearing is correctly positioned in its bore, then press the new oil seal into position.

Installation

17 Remove all traces of locking compound from the threads of the stopper arm pivot bolt and the gearchange mechanism cover screws.

26.10a Take off the cover . . .

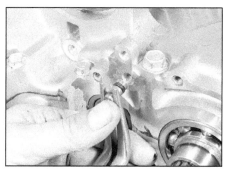

26.10c . . . and the upper dowel (which has an O-ring)

18 Apply a drop of locking compound to the threads of the stopper arm pivot bolt, then fit the shouldered washer so that its shoulder is facing inwards (towards the stopper arm). Locate the stopper arm on the shouldered washer, ensuring it is the correct way round, then fit the washer and spring. Manoeuvre the assembly into position and screw in the pivot bolt a few turns. Locate the stopper arm correctly on the selector drum cam and pivot bolt collar, then tighten the pivot bolt to the specified torque. Ensure the stopper arm pivots smoothly and is securely held against the selector drum cam by its spring before proceeding.

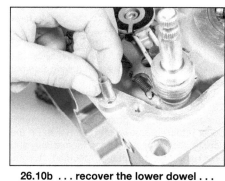

26.10b . . . recover the lower dowel . . .

26.12 Remove the gearchange shaft assembly from the engine

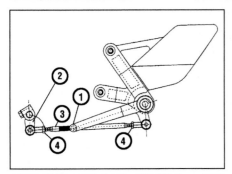

26.32 Shift pedal details (ZX-9R B models)

1	*Shift pedal*	*3*	*Shift rod*
2	*Shift lever*	*4*	*Locknuts*

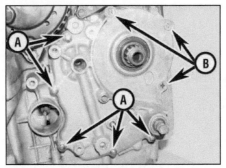

26.36 Remove the cover retaining bolts (A) and screws (B)

26.39 Recover the outer washer from the shaft

19 Ensure the shouldered spacer is correctly fitted (with its flat surface innermost) to the inner end of the gearchange shaft and locate the shaft in its crankcase bore. Align the shaft centralising spring with its locating pin and push the shaft fully into position, engaging its fork with the selector drum cam.

20 Ensure the upper locating dowel O-ring is in good condition (renew it if not) and lubricate it with a smear of engine oil. Fit the lower dowel to the crankcase and fit the upper dowel so that its O-ring is innermost (closed end of the dowel on the outside).

21 Ensure the mating surfaces are clean and dry and apply a smear of sealant (Kawasaki recommend the use of Kawasaki Bond 56019-120) to the area of the crankcase mating surfaces on each side of the crankcase half joints

22 Locate the new gasket on the dowels.

23 Fit the outer washer to the gearchange shaft.

24 Lubricate the oil seal lips with a smear of multi-purpose grease. Carefully slide the cover along the gearshift shaft (taking care not to damage the oil seal lips), over the output shaft and locate it on the dowels.

25 Apply a drop of locking compound to the threads of all the gearchange mechanism cover retaining screws (not the bolts). Fit the screws and bolts and tighten them evenly and progressively to their specified torque settings.

26 Fit the spring and contact in the end of the selector drum. Fit a new O-ring to the neutral switch, then fit the switch to the cover, tightening its retaining screws securely.

27 Lubricate the pushrod ends with molybdenum disulphide grease. Insert the pushrod into the crankcase and fit the end cap.

28 Engage the gearchange lever linkage with the shaft splines so the lever is correctly positioned. Fit the clamp bolt to the linkage and tighten it securely.

29 Fit the rear wheel and front sprocket (see Chapters 6 and 7).

30 Fit the water pump (see Chapter 3).

31 Refill the engine with clean oil and refill the cooling system (see Chapter 1).

32 Start the engine and check for leaks. If all is well, check the oil and coolant levels, then install the fairing panels as described in Chapter 8.

ZX-9R B models

Note: *The gearchange mechanism components can be removed with the engine in the frame (see illustration). In order to allow the cover to be removed from the engine, it is necessary to withdraw the swingarm pivot shaft. Bear this in mind when supporting the bike before removing the rear wheel (see Chapter 6).*

Removal

33 Carry out the operations described in Steps 1 to 6.

34 Disconnect the wiring connector from the neutral light switch.

35 Referring to Chapter 6, remove the swingarm pivot shaft and the shock absorber upper mounting bolt. Move the swingarm slightly to the rear so that the drive chain is positioned clear of the gearchange mechanism cover. **Note:** *There is no need to remove the swingarm completely.*

36 Slacken and remove the gearchange mechanism cover retaining screws and bolts **(see illustration)**.

37 Remove all traces of dirt from the gearchange shaft, then slide the cover off the shaft and remove it from the engine. Take care not to lose the rubber plug which is fitted to the inside of the cover.

38 Remove the gasket and discard it; a new one must be used on refitting. If the cover locating dowels are loose, remove them and store them with the cover (note that the upper dowel is fitted with an O-ring).

39 Recover the outer washer from the gearchange shaft and store it with the cover for safe-keeping **(see illustration)**.

40 Remove the gearchange shaft assembly from the engine, complete with its shouldered spacer. **(see illustration)**

41 On early (B1) models, slacken and remove the nut and shouldered outer washer and remove the neutral position lever, spring and inner washer **(see illustrations)**. **Note:** *The neutral positioning lever is not fitted to later models.*

42 On all models, using a pair of pointed-

26.40 Remove the gearchange shaft

26.41a Remove the neutral position lever . . .

26.41b . . . the spring . . .

26.41c . . . and the inner washer

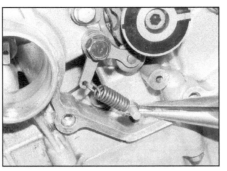

26.42a Unhook the spring from the crankcase pin . . .

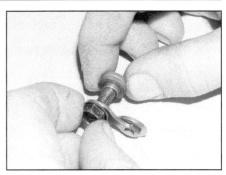

26.42b . . . and remove the pivot bolt from the stopper arm

nose pliers, carefully unhook the selector drum stopper arm spring from its crankcase pin and unhook it from the arm **(see illustration)**. Unscrew the pivot bolt and remove the selector drum stopper arm and its shouldered spacer, noting the correct fitted location of each component **(see illustration)**.

Inspection

43 See Steps 14 to 16.

Installation

44 Remove all traces of locking compound from the threads of the stopper arm pivot bolt and the gearchange mechanism cover screws and bolts.

45 Position the stopper arm the right way round and locate it on the shouldered spacer. Apply a drop of locking compound to the threads of the stopper arm pivot bolt, then fit the assembly to the crankcase, tightening the pivot bolt to the specified torque. Ensure the stopper arm pivots smoothly then fit the spring to the arm and hook it over the crankcase pin. Ensure the stopper arm is securely held against the selector drum cam by its spring before proceeding.

46 On early (B1) models, ensure the neutral positioning arm stud is securely screwed into the crankcase, then fit the inner washer to the stud. Locate the spring on the crankcase collar and engage the neutral positioning arm with the hooked end of the spring. Fit the shouldered washer with its shoulder facing inwards and screw on the nut. Locate the neutral position arm on the selector drum cam and tighten the retaining nut whilst aligning its

pivot end with the outer washer shoulder. Tighten the nut to the specified torque then check the arm is free to pivot smoothly and is securely held against the cam by its spring.

47 On all models, ensure the shouldered spacer is correctly fitted (with its flat surface innermost) to the inner end of the gearchange shaft and locate the shaft in its crankcase bore. Align the shaft centralising spring with its locating pin and push the shaft fully into position, engaging its fork with the selector drum cam.

48 Ensure the upper locating dowel O-ring is in good condition (renew it if not) and lubricate it with a smear of engine oil. Fit the lower dowel to the crankcase and fit the upper dowel so that its O-ring is innermost (closed end of the dowel on the outside).

49 Ensure the mating surfaces are clean and dry and apply a smear of sealant (Kawasaki recommend the use of Kawasaki Bond 56019-120) to the area of the crankcase mating surface on each side of the crankcase half joints. **(see illustration)**

50 Locate the new gasket on the dowels **(see illustration)**.

51 Fit the outer washer to the gearshift shaft.

52 Fit the rubber plug to the hole on the inside of the mechanism cover **(see illustration)**.

53 Lubricate the oil seal lips with a smear of multi-purpose grease. Carefully slide the cover along the gearshift shaft, taking care not to damage the oil seal lips, over the output shaft. Ensure the rubber plug is still correctly fitted to the cover, then locate the cover on the dowels.

54 Apply a drop of locking compound to the threads of all the gearchange mechanism cover screws and the three bolts installed in the front locations (but not the two lower bolts). Fit all the cover retaining screws and bolts and tighten them evenly and progressively to their specified torque settings.

55 Move the swingarm back into position and fit its pivot shaft and the shock absorber upper mounting bolt. Tighten all fixings to their specified torque settings (see Chapter 6).

56 Reconnect the neutral switch wiring connector.

57 Carry out the remainder of installation as described in Steps 27 to 32.

27 Crankcase – separation and reassembly

Separation

1 To examine and repair or renew the crankshaft, the connecting rods and bearings and transmission components, the crankcase must be split into two parts.

2 To enable the crankcases to be split, the engine must first be removed from the frame (see Section 5) and the following components removed, with reference to the relevant Sections.

  a) Camshafts.*
  b) Cylinder head.*
  c) Cylinder block.*
  d) Pistons.*

26.49 Apply sealant to each side of the crankcase half-joints

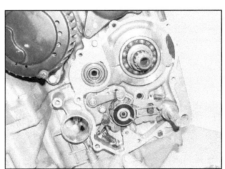

26.50 Fit a new gasket

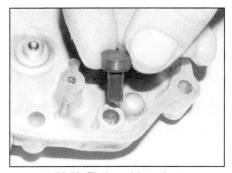

26.52 Fit the rubber plug

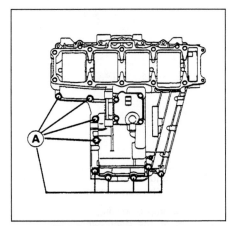

27.4 Crankcase upper bolts (ZX-7R models)

A 8 mm

e) Clutch.
f) Oil pan.
g) Alternator drive chain and sprockets.
h) Gearchange mechanism components.
i) Alternator (Chapter 9).
j) Starter motor (Chapter 9).
k) Ignition system pick-up coil and rotor (Chapter 5).

If no work is to be carried out on the crankshaft, the cylinder head and camshafts can remain in situ.

3 With all the relevant components removed proceed as follows.

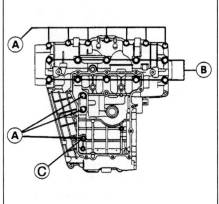

27.5 Crankcase lower bolts (ZX-7R models)

A 8 mm   C Long
B 9 mm   (115 mm)

ZX-7R models

4 With the crankcase the right way up, slacken and remove the nine 8 mm bolts from the top of the upper crankcase half **(see illustration)**. **Note:** *As each bolt is removed, store it in its relative position in a cardboard template of the crankcase halves. This will ensure that each bolt is returned to its original location on reassembly.*
5 Turn the crankcase upside down, and unscrew the seven 8 mm bolts located along the front edge of the lower crankcase and the three 8 mm bolts located down the right-hand side **(see illustration)** (see Note in Step 4).

6 Working in the reverse of the tightening sequence (numbers cast on lower crankcase **(see illustration)**. Refer to Step 27), gradually slacken the ten 9 mm (main bearing) bolts. Once all the bolts are loose, unscrew and remove them (see Note in Step 4).
7 Carefully lift the lower crankcase half off, leaving the crankshaft and transmission shafts in the upper half of the crankcase **(see illustration)**. As the lower half is lifted away take care not to dislodge or lose any main bearing inserts. **Note:** *If it won't come away easily, make sure all fasteners have been removed. Don't prise the crankcase mating surfaces apart, or they will leak; initial separation can be achieved by tapping gently with a soft-faced mallet.*
8 Remove the three locating dowels from the upper crankcase half and the crankshaft left end sealing plug **(see illustrations)**.
9 Remove the oil nozzle and its O-ring from the upper crankcase half, noting which way around it is fitted **(see illustration)**. Also recover the O-ring which is fitted to the oilway located directly behind the crankshaft centre main bearing.

ZX-9R B models

10 With the crankcase the right way up, slacken and remove the seven 6 mm bolts and the two 8 mm bolts from the top of the upper crankcase half **(see illustration)**. **Note:** *As each bolt is removed, store it in its relative position in a cardboard template of the crankcase halves. This will ensure that each bolt is returned to its original location on reassembly.*

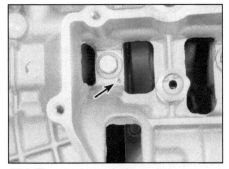

27.6 The crankcase bolt numbers are cast in the crankcase (arrowed)

27.7 Lift the lower crankcase half off the upper half

27.8a There's a dowel at the cam chain end of the crankshaft . . .

27.8b . . . and at the seal end . . .

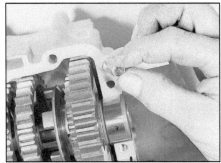

27.8c . . . and one near the transmission output shaft

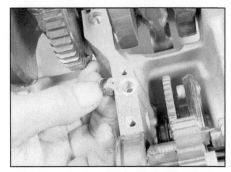

27.9 Remove the oil nozzle and its O-ring

11 Turn the crankcase upside down, and unscrew the eight 6 mm bolts (six located along the front edge and two located down the right-hand side) and the single 8 mm bolt from the lower crankcase **(see illustration)** (see Note in Step 10).

12 Working in the reverse of the tightening sequence (numbers cast on lower crankcase **(see illustration 27.6)**. Refer to Step 39), gradually slacken the ten 9 mm (main bearing) bolts **(see illustration 27.11)**. Once all the bolts are loose, unscrew and remove them (see Note in Step 10).

13 Carefully lift the lower crankcase half off, leaving the crankshaft and transmission shafts in the upper half of the crankcase. As the lower half is lifted away take care not to dislodge or lose any main bearing inserts. **Note:** *If it won't come away easily, make sure all fasteners have been removed. Don't prise the crankcase mating surfaces apart, or they will leak; initial separation can be achieved by tapping gently with a soft-faced mallet.*

14 Remove the three locating dowels from the upper crankcase half and the crankshaft left end sealing plug.

15 Remove the oil nozzle and its O-ring from the upper crankcase half, noting which way round it is fitted.

Reassembly

ZX-7R models

16 Check that the transmission shafts, crankshaft and camchain, alternator shaft and starter clutch components are correctly installed in the upper crankcase half, as described in Sections 30 to 33. Ensure the selector drum and forks are correctly fitted to the lower crankcase half, as described in Section 36.

17 Remove all traces of sealant from the crankcase mating surfaces, taking care not to let any fall into the case.

18 Check that all components are installed and that they can rotate smoothly and easily.

19 Lubricate the transmission shafts and crankshaft with clean engine oil, then use a rag soaked in high flash-point solvent to wipe over the gasket surfaces of both halves to remove all traces of oil.

20 Make sure the oil nozzle hole is clear, then fit the nozzle to the upper crankcase half so

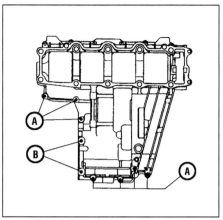

27.10 Crankcase upper bolts (ZX-9R B models)

A 6 mm   B 8 mm

that its larger diameter internal bore is facing towards the lower crankcase. Fit a new O-ring to the oil nozzle, ensuring it is correctly located in the crankcase recess **(see illustration)**.

21 Fit a new O-ring to the oilway located directly behind the crankshaft centre main bearing and install the three locating dowels in the upper crankcase half.

22 Ensure the crankcase half mating surfaces are clean and dry, then fit the new sealing cap to the upper crankcase, on the left end of the crankshaft.

23 Apply a thin smear of suitable sealant (Kawasaki recommend the use of Kawasaki Bond 56019-120) **(see illustration)** to the areas of the lower crankcase half mating surface **(see illustration)**.
Caution: Do not use an excessive amount of sealant, as it will ooze out when the case halves are assembled and may obstruct oil passages and prevent the bearings from seating.

24 Check the position of the selector drum cam, selector forks and transmission shafts – make sure they're in the neutral position.

25 Make sure that the main bearing inserts are in position and carefully install the lower crankcase half on the upper half. The selector forks must engage with their respective slots in the transmission gears as the halves are joined.

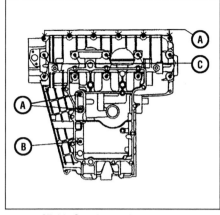

27.11 Crankcase lower bolts (ZX-9R B models)

A 6 mm   B 8 mm   C 9 mm

26 Check that the lower crankcase half is correctly seated and that all shafts are free to rotate.
Caution: If the casings are not correctly seated, remove the lower crankcase half and investigate the problem. Do not attempt to pull them together using the crankcase bolts, as the casing will crack and be ruined.

27 Install the ten 9 mm (main bearing) bolts and tighten them all by hand. Note the number cast next to each 9 mm (main bearing) bolt on the lower crankcase; these numbers are the tightening sequence. Working in the correct sequence, go round and tighten each of the 9 mm bolts to approximately half its specified torque setting, then go round again in the specified sequence and tighten them to the full specified torque setting.

28 Fit the ten 8 mm bolts in their original locations in the lower crankcase and tighten them all by hand. Tighten the long (115 mm) bolt to its specified torque first, then tighten the remaining bolts to the specified torque **(see illustration 27.5)**.

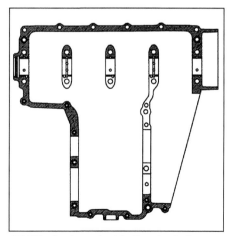

27.23b Apply sealant to the shaded areas

27.20 Install the oil nozzle and a new O-ring

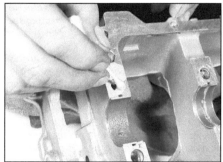

27.23a Apply silicone sealant to the crankcase mating surfaces

29 Turn the crankcase over so that it is upright.
30 Fit the nine 8 mm upper crankcase bolts in their original locations and tighten them evenly and progressively to the specified torque **(see illustration 27.4)**.
31 With all crankcase fasteners tightened, check that the crankshaft and transmission shafts rotate smoothly and easily. If there are any signs of undue stiffness or of any other problem, the fault must be rectified before proceeding further.
32 Install all other removed assemblies in the reverse of the sequence given in Step 2.

ZX-9R B models

33 Carry out the operations described in Steps 16 to 20.
34 Ensure the crankcase half mating surfaces are clean and dry, then fit the new sealing cap to the upper crankcase, on the left-hand end of the crankshaft.
35 Apply a thin smear of suitable sealant (Kawasaki recommend the use of Kawasaki Bond 56019-120) to the areas of the lower crankcase half mating surface shown in **illustration 27.23b**.
Caution: Do not use an excessive amount of sealant, as it will ooze out when the case halves are assembled and may obstruct oil passages and prevent the bearings from seating.
36 Check the position of the selector drum cam, selector forks and transmission shafts – make sure they're in the neutral position.
37 Make sure that the main bearing inserts are in position and carefully install the lower crankcase half on the upper half. The selector forks must engage with their respective slots in the transmission gears as the halves are joined.
38 Check that the lower crankcase half is correctly seated and that all shafts are free to rotate.
Caution: If the casings are not correctly seated, remove the lower crankcase half and investigate the problem. Do not attempt to pull them together using the crankcase bolts, as the casing will crack and be ruined.
39 Install the ten 9 mm (main bearing) bolts and tighten them all by hand. Note the number cast next to each 9 mm (main bearing) bolt on the lower crankcase; these numbers are the tightening sequence. Working in the correct sequence, go round and tighten each of the 9 mm bolts to approximately half its specified torque setting, then go round again in the specified sequence and tighten them to the full specified torque setting.
40 Fit the eight 6 mm bolts and the single 8 mm bolt in their original locations and tighten them all by hand **(see illustration 27.11)**. Tighten the 8 mm bolt to its specified torque first, then tighten the 6 mm bolts to the specified torque.
41 Turn the crankcase over so that it is upright.

42 Fit the seven 6 mm bolts and the two 8 mm upper crankcase bolts in their original locations and tighten them all by hand **(see illustration 27.10)**. Tighten the 8 mm bolts to their specified torque first then tighten the 6 mm bolts to their specified torque.
43 With all crankcase fasteners tightened, check that the crankshaft and transmission shafts rotate smoothly and easily. If there are any signs of undue stiffness or of any other problem, the fault must be rectified before proceeding further.
44 Install all other removed assemblies in the reverse of the sequence given in Step 2.

28 Crankcase components – inspection and servicing

1 After the crankcases have been separated and the crankshaft and transmission components have been removed, the crankcases should be cleaned thoroughly with new solvent and dried with compressed air.

Warning: Wear eye protection when using compressed air!

2 On ZX-7R models, unbolt the breather cover from the top of the upper crankcase and discard its gasket. Thoroughly clean the breather aperture and the inside of the cover and remove all traces of locking compound from the bolt threads.
3 On all models, remove any oil passage plugs that haven't already been removed. All oil passages should be blown out with compressed air.
4 Check the transmission oil spray pipe is clear and all its oil holes are unblocked. If necessary, undo the retaining bolt and remove the pipe from the crankcase. On installation, remove all traces of locking compound from the retaining bolt threads and install the pipe. Apply a drop of fresh locking compound to the retaining bolt threads, then fit it and tighten it to the specified torque.
5 All traces of old gasket sealant should be removed from the mating surfaces. Minor damage to the surfaces can be cleaned up with a fine sharpening stone or grindstone.
Caution: Be very careful not to nick or gouge the crankcase mating surfaces, or leaks will result. Check both crankcase halves very carefully for cracks and other damage.
6 All threaded holes must be clean, to ensure accurate torque readings during reassembly. To clean the threads, run the correct-size tap into each of the holes to remove rust, corrosion, thread locking compound or sealant, and to restore damaged threads. If possible, use compressed air to clear the holes of debris produced by this operation. A good alternative is to inject aerosol-applied water-dispersant lubricant into each hole, using the long spout usually supplied.

Warning: Wear eye protection when cleaning out these holes in this way!

7 Small cracks or holes in aluminium castings may be repaired with an epoxy resin adhesive as a temporary measure. Permanent repairs can only be effected by argon-arc welding, and only a specialist in this process is in a position to advise on the economy or practical aspect of such a repair. If any damage is found that can't be repaired, renew the crankcase halves as a set.
8 Damaged threads can be economically reclaimed by using a diamond section wire insert, of the Helicoil type, which is easily fitted after drilling and re-tapping the affected thread. Sheared studs or screws can usually be removed with screw extractors, which consist of a tapered, left thread screw of very hard steel. These are inserted into a pre-drilled hole in the stud, and usually succeed in dislodging the most stubborn stud or screw.

> **HAYNES HINT**
> *Refer to Tools and Workshop Tips (Section 2) in the Reference section for details of thread repair methods and using screw extractors.*

9 Apply silicone sealant to the threads of the oil passage plugs, then fit them to the cases, tightening them securely.
10 On ZX-7R models, fit a new gasket to the upper crankcase breather aperture and fit the breather cover. Apply a drop of locking compound to each cover retaining bolt, then fit the bolts, tightening them to the specified torque. **Note:** *The breather gasket tab will mean that a little force will be needed to align the gasket holes with those of the crankcase as the bolts are installed.*

29 Main and connecting rod bearings – general note

1 Even though main and connecting rod bearings are generally replaced with new ones during the engine overhaul, the old bearings should be retained for close examination, as they may reveal valuable information about the condition of the engine.
2 Bearing failure occurs mainly because of lack of lubrication, the presence of dirt or other foreign particles, overloading the engine, and/or corrosion. Regardless of the cause of bearing failure, it must be corrected before the engine is reassembled, to prevent it from happening again.
3 When examining the bearings, remove the main bearings from the case halves and the rod bearings from the connecting rods and caps and lay them out on a clean surface in the same general position as their location on the crankshaft journals. This will enable you to match any noted bearing problems with the corresponding crankshaft journal.

4 Dirt and other foreign particles get into the engine in a variety of ways. It may be left in the engine during assembly or it may pass through filters or breathers. It may get into the oil and from there into the bearings. Metal chips from machining operations and normal engine wear are often present. Abrasives are sometimes left in engine components after reconditioning operations such as cylinder honing, especially when parts are not thoroughly cleaned using the proper cleaning methods. Whatever the source, these foreign objects often end up imbedded in the soft bearing material and are easily recognised. Large particles will not imbed in the bearing and will score or gouge the bearing and journal. The best prevention for this cause of bearing failure is to clean all parts thoroughly and keep everything spotlessly clean during engine reassembly. Frequent and regular oil and filter changes are also recommended.

5 Lack of lubrication, or lubrication breakdown, has a number of interrelated causes. Excessive heat (which thins the oil), overloading (which squeezes the oil from the bearing face) and oil leakage or throw-off from excessive bearing clearances, worn oil pump or high engine speeds, all contribute to lubrication breakdown. Blocked oil passages will also starve a bearing and destroy it. When lack of lubrication is the cause of bearing failure, the bearing material is wiped or extruded from the steel backing of the bearing. Temperatures may increase to the point where the steel backing and the journal turn blue from overheating.

6 Riding habits can have a definite effect on bearing life. Full throttle low speed operation, or lugging (labouring) the engine, puts very high loads on bearings, which tend to squeeze out the oil film. These loads cause the bearings to flex, which produces fine cracks in the bearing face (fatigue failure). Eventually the bearing material will loosen in pieces and tear away from the steel backing. Short trip riding leads to corrosion of bearings, as insufficient engine heat is produced to drive off the condensed water and corrosive gases produced. These products collect in the engine oil, forming acid and sludge. As the oil is carried to the engine bearings, the acid attacks and corrodes the bearing material.

7 Incorrect bearing installation during engine assembly will lead to bearing failure as well. Tight fitting bearings which leave insufficient bearing oil clearances result in oil starvation. Dirt or foreign particles trapped behind a bearing insert result in high spots on the bearing which lead to failure.

8 To avoid bearing problems, clean all parts thoroughly before reassembly, double check all bearing clearance measurements and lubricate the new bearings with clean engine oil during installation.

30 Crankshaft and main bearings – removal, inspection and installation

Removal

1 Separate the crankcase halves as described in Section 27.

2 Lift the crankshaft out of the upper crankcase half, taking care not to dislodge the bearing inserts, and remove the camchain from the crankshaft.

3 The main bearing inserts can be removed from the crankcase halves by pushing their centres to the side, then lifting them out **(see illustration)**. Keep the bearing inserts in order.

Inspection

General information

4 Remove the connecting rods from the crankshaft (see Section 31).

5 Clean the crankshaft with solvent, using a small cleaning brush to scrub out the oil passages. If available, blow the crank dry with compressed air.

6 Refer to Section 29 and examine the main bearing inserts. If they are scored, badly scuffed or appear to have been seized, new bearings must be installed. Always renew the main bearings as a set. If they are badly damaged, check the corresponding crankshaft journal. Evidence of extreme heat, such as discoloration, indicates that lubrication failure has occurred. Be sure to thoroughly check the oil pump and pressure relief valves as well as all oil holes and passages before reassembling the engine.

7 The crankshaft journals should be given a close visual examination, paying particular attention where damaged bearing inserts have been discovered. If the journals are scored or pitted in any way, a new crankshaft will be required. Note that undersizes are not available, precluding the option of re-grinding the crankshaft.

8 Set the crankshaft on V-blocks and check the runout with a dial indicator touching the centre main bearing journal, comparing your

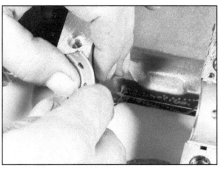

30.3 Push the centres of the bearing inserts sideways and rotate them out of their webs

findings with this Chapter's Specifications. If the runout exceeds the limit, renew the crankshaft.

Bearing selection

9 The main bearing running clearance is controlled in production by selecting one of three grades of bearing insert. The grades are indicated by a colour-code marked on the edge of each insert (this colour-code may no longer be visible on the original bearings). In order, from the thickest to the thinnest, the insert grades are: Blue, Black (ZX-7R models) or unmarked (ZX-9R B models) and Brown. New bearing inserts are selected as follows, using the crankshaft journal and crankcase main bearing bore size group markings.

10 The standard crankshaft (main bearing) journal diameter is divided into two size groups to allow for manufacturing tolerances. The size group of each journal can be determined by examining the crankshaft web next to each journal **(see illustration)**. There will either be a No. 1 marking, or no marking at all. **Note:** *Ignore the '0' markings (where present) as these refer to the crankpin journals (see Section 31).* If the equipment is available, the size group can be checked by direct measurement.

11 The crankcase main bearing bore diameters are also divided into two size groups to allow for manufacturing tolerances. The size group of each main bearing bore can be determined by checking the tab(s) on the

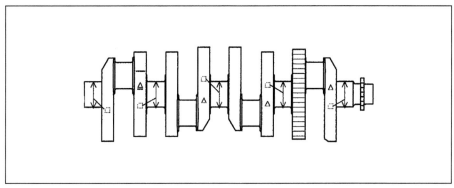

30.10 Main bearing journal diameter size group locations

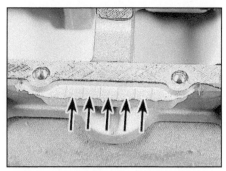

30.11 Main bearing bore diameter size group locations

30.15 Nos. 2 and No. 4 bearing inserts have oil grooves (arrowed)

front of the upper crankcase half (see illustration). There will either be an '0' marking or no marking at all for each of the main bearing bores. If the equipment is available, the size group can be checked by direct measurement.

12 Match the relevant crankshaft code with its crankcase code and select a new set of bearing inserts using the relevant following table.

ZX-7R models

Journal size	Bore size	Bearing insert
1	0	Brown
1	None	Black
None	0	Black
None	None	Blue

ZX-9R B models

Journal size	Bore size	Bearing insert
1	0	Brown
1	None	Unmarked
None	0	Unmarked
None	None	Blue

Oil clearance check

13 Whether new bearing inserts are being fitted or the original ones are being re-used, the main bearing oil clearance should be checked prior to reassembly.

14 Clean the backs of the bearing inserts and the bearing locations in both crankcase halves.

15 Press the bearing inserts into their locations, ensuring that the tab on each insert engages in the notch in the crankcase. Make sure the bearings are fitted in the correct locations and take care not to touch any insert's bearing surface with your fingers. Note that Nos. 2 and 4 bearing inserts have oil grooves (see illustration), whereas Nos. 1, 3 and 5 bearings are plain.

16 There are two possible ways of checking the oil clearance. The first method is by direct measurement (see Step 17 and 23) and the second by the use of a product known as Plastigauge (see Steps 18 to 23).

17 If the first method is to be used, with the main bearing inserts in position, carefully lower the lower crankcase half onto the upper half. Make sure that the selector forks (if fitted) engage with their respective slots in the transmission gears as the halves are joined. Check that the lower crankcase half is correctly seated, then install the ten 9 mm (main bearing) bolts in their original locations. **Note:** *Do not tighten the crankcase bolts if the casing is not correctly seated.* Working in the sequence marked on the crankcase, tighten all the bolts to approximately half the specified torque setting, then go round and tighten them to the full specified torque (see Step 27 of Section 27). Measure the internal diameter of each assembled pair of bearing inserts. If the diameter of each corresponding crankshaft journal is measured and then subtracted from the bearing internal diameter, the result will be the main bearing oil clearance.

18 If the second method is to be used, ensure the main bearing inserts are correctly fitted and that the inserts and crankshaft are clean and dry. Lay the crankshaft in position in the upper crankcase.

19 Cut several lengths of the appropriate size Plastigauge (they should be slightly shorter than the width of the crankshaft journal). Place a strand of Plastigauge on each (cleaned) crankshaft journal (see illustration).

20 Carefully lower the lower crankcase half onto the upper half. Make sure that the selector forks (if fitted) engage with their respective slots in the transmission gears as the halves are joined. Check that the lower crankcase half is correctly seated, then install the ten 9 mm (main bearing) bolts in their original locations. **Note:** *Do not tighten the crankcase bolts if the casing is not correctly seated.* Working in the sequence marked on the crankcase, tighten all the bolts to approximately half the specified torque setting then go round and tighten them to the full specified torque (see Step 27 of Section 27). Make sure that the crankshaft is not rotated as the bolts are tightened (see illustration).

21 Slacken and remove the crankcase bolts, working in the reverse of the sequence marked on the crankcase, then carefully lift off the lower crankcase half, making sure the Plastigauge is not disturbed.

22 Compare the width of the crushed Plastigauge on each crankshaft journal to the scale printed on the Plastigauge envelope to obtain the main bearing oil clearance (see illustration).

23 If the clearance is not within the specified limits, the bearing inserts may be the wrong grade (or excessively worn, if the original inserts are being re-used). Before deciding that different grade inserts are needed, make sure that no dirt or oil was trapped between the bearing inserts and the crankcase halves when the clearance was measured. If the clearance is excessive, even with new inserts (of the correct size), the crankshaft journal is worn and the crankshaft should be renewed.

24 On completion, carefully scrape away all traces of the Plastigauge material from the crankshaft journal and bearing inserts; use a fingernail or other object which is unlikely to score the inserts.

30.19 Lay a strip of Plastigauge along the bearing journal, parallel to the crankshaft centre line

30.20 Lay the lower crankcase half on the upper crankcase half and DO NOT rotate the crankshaft

30.22 Measure the width of the crushed Plastigauge with the scale on the envelope

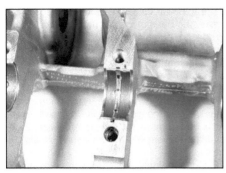

30.26 Make sure the tabs on the bearing inserts fit into the notches on the casing

Installation

25 Clean the backs of the bearing inserts and the bearing recesses in both crankcase halves. If new inserts are being fitted, ensure that all traces of the protective grease are cleaned off. Wipe the inserts and crankcase halves dry with a lint-free cloth.

26 Press the bearing inserts into their locations. Make sure the tab on each insert engages in the notch in the casing **(see illustration)**. Make sure the bearings are fitted in the correct locations and take care not to touch any insert's bearing surface with your fingers. Note that Nos. 2 and 4 bearing inserts have oil grooves **(see illustration 30.15)**, whereas Nos. 1, 3 and 5 bearings are plain.

27 Lubricate the bearing inserts in the upper crankcase with clean engine.

28 Ensure the connecting rods are correctly fitted to the crankshaft (see Section 31).

31.2 Check the connecting rod side clearance with a feeler gauge

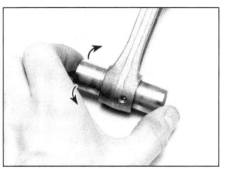

31.6 Checking the piston pin and connecting rod bore for wear

29 Locate the camchain on the crankshaft sprocket, then lower the crankshaft into position in the upper crankcase.

30 Reassemble the crankcase halves as described in Section 27.

31 Connecting rods and bearings – removal, inspection and installation

Note: *New connecting rod bearing cap bolts will be need on installation. The nuts can be re-used but we recommend that they are also renewed.*

Removal

1 Remove the crankshaft (see Section 30).

2 Before removing the connecting rods from the crankshaft measure the side clearance of each rod with a feeler gauge **(see illustration)**. If the clearance is greater than the service limit listed in this Chapter's Specifications, the rod will have to be renewed with a new one.

3 Using paint or a suitable marker pen, mark the relevant cylinder number on each connecting rod and bearing cap.

4 Unscrew the bearing cap nuts **(see illustration)** and remove the first connecting rod and bearing cap, complete with the bearing inserts, from the crankshaft. Immediately install the bearing cap and nuts on the connecting rod, so that they are kept together as a matched set.

5 Remove the remaining three connecting rods in the same way.

31.4 Remove the bearing cap nuts

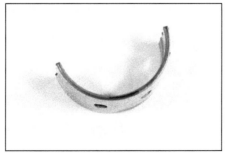

31.10 Bearing thickness is indicated by a colour code painted on the side of the bearing

Inspection

General information

6 Check the connecting rods for cracks and other obvious damage. Lubricate the piston pin for each rod, install it in its original rod and check for play. If it wobbles, renew the connecting rod and/or the pin **(see illustration)**.

7 Refer to Section 29 and examine the connecting rod bearing inserts. If they are scored, badly scuffed or appear to have been seized, new bearings must be installed. Always renew the bearings in the connecting rods as a set. If they are badly damaged, check the corresponding crankpin. Evidence of extreme heat, such as discoloration, indicates that lubrication failure has occurred. Be sure to thoroughly check the oil pump and pressure relief valves, as well as all oil holes and passages before reassembling the engine.

8 Have the rods checked for twist and bending at a dealer service department or other motorcycle repair shop.

9 If a connecting rod is to renewed, be sure to state what weight group it is when ordering. Each connecting rod is marked with a weight code (in the form of a letter) which is stamped across the connecting rod/bearing cap joint. To minimise vibration, Kawasaki recommend that each pair of rods (Nos. 1 and 2 rods are treated as a pair, as are Nos. 3 and 4 rods) should be of the same weight group.

Bearing selection

10 The connecting rod bearing running clearance is controlled in production by selecting one of three grades of bearing insert. The grades are indicated by a colour-code marked on the edge of each insert (this colour-code may no longer be visible on the original bearings) **(see illustration)**. In order, from the thickest to the thinnest, the insert grades are: Blue, Black (ZX-7R models) or unmarked (ZX-9R B models) and Brown. New bearing inserts are selected as follows, using the crankpin and connecting rod size group markings.

11 The standard crankpin journal diameter is divided into two size groups to allow for manufacturing tolerances. The size group of each journal can be determined by examining the crankshaft web next to each journal **(see illustration)**. There will either be an '0'

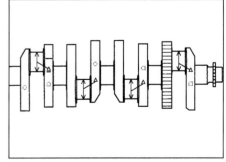

31.11 Crankpin journal diameter size group locations

marking or no marking at all. **Note:** *Ignore the No. 1 markings (where present) as these refer to the main bearing journals (see Section 30).* If the equipment is available, the size group can be checked by direct measurement.

12 The connecting rod bore diameters are also divided into two size groups to allow for manufacturing tolerances. The size group of each main bearing bore can be determined by inspecting the weight group letter which is stamped across the connecting rod/bearing cap joint **(see illustration)**. If the letter is on its own (not surrounded by a circle), the rod has no marking and if the letter is surrounded by a circle the rod is in size group 0. If the equipment is available, the size group can be checked by direct measurement **(see illustration)**.

13 Match the relevant connecting rod code with its crankshaft code and select a new set of bearing inserts using the relevant following table.

ZX-7R models

Connecting rod size group marking	Crankpin size group marking	Bearing insert required
None	0	Brown
None	None	Black
0	0	Black
0	None	Blue

ZX-9R B models

Connecting rod size group marking	Crankpin size group marking	Bearing insert required
None	0	Brown
None	None	Unmarked
0	0	Unmarked
0	None	Blue

Oil clearance check

14 Whether new bearing inserts are being fitted or the original ones are being re-used, the connecting rod bearing oil clearance should be checked prior to reassembly.

15 Clean the backs of the bearing inserts and the bearing locations in both the connecting rod and bearing cap.

16 Press the bearing inserts into their locations, ensuring that the tab on each insert engages the notch in the connecting rod/bearing cap. Make sure the bearings are fitted in the correct locations and take care not to touch any insert's bearing surface with your fingers.

17 There are two possible ways of checking the oil clearance. The first method is by direct measurement (see Steps 18 and 21) and the second by the use of a product known as Plastigauge (see Steps 19 to 21).

18 If the first method is to be used, fit the bearing cap to the connecting rod, with the bearing inserts in place. Make sure the cap is fitted the correct way round, so that the connecting rod and bearing cap weight/size markings are correctly aligned. Tighten the cap retaining nuts to the specified Stage 1

31.12a The weight group letter can be found stamped across the connecting rod/bearing cap joint

torque setting and then through the specified Stage 2 angle (see Steps 35 and 36) (use the original bearing cap bolts and nuts for the check, not the new ones) and measure the internal diameter of each assembled pair of bearing inserts. If the diameter of each corresponding crankpin journal is measured and then subtracted from the bearing internal diameter, the result will be the connecting rod bearing oil clearance.

19 If the second method is to be used, cut lengths of the appropriate size Plastigauge (they should be slightly shorter than the width of the crankpin). Place a strand of Plastigauge on each (cleaned) crankpin journal and fit the (clean) piston/connecting rod assemblies, inserts and bearing caps. Make sure the cap is fitted the correct way round, so that the connecting rod and bearing cap weight/size markings are correctly aligned. Fit the cap retaining nuts (use the original bearing cap bolts and nuts for the check, not the new ones) and tighten them first to the specified Stage 1 torque setting and then through the specified Stage 2 angle (see Steps 35 and 36) whilst ensuring that the connecting rod does not rotate. Take care not to disturb the Plastigauge. Slacken the bearing cap nuts and remove the connecting rod assemblies, again taking great care not to rotate the connecting rod.

20 Compare the width of the crushed Plastigauge on each crankpin to the scale printed on the Plastigauge envelope to obtain the connecting rod bearing oil.

31.12b Measure the diameter of the connecting rod with a telescoping gauge, then measure the gauge

21 If the clearance is not within the specified limits, the bearing inserts may be the wrong grade (or excessively worn if the original inserts are being re-used). Before deciding that different grade inserts are needed, make sure that no dirt or oil was trapped between the bearing inserts and the connecting rod or bearing cap when the clearance was measured. If the clearance is excessive, even with new inserts (of the correct size), the crankpin is worn and the crankshaft should be renewed.

22 On completion, carefully scrape away all traces of the Plastigauge material from the crankpin and bearing inserts using a fingernail or other object which is unlikely to score the inserts.

Installation

23 Thoroughly clean the new bearing cap bolts and nuts in a high-flash point solvent to remove all traces of the protective anti-rust compound from their threads. Allow the bolts to dry completely (use compressed air if available). **Note:** *If the bolt length measuring method is to be used to tighten the bearing cap nuts, carefully centre-punch the centre of each new bolt head and end at this stage to ensure accuracy when measuring the bolt length (see Step 30).*

24 Carefully tap the original bearing cap bolts out from the connecting rod, taking great care not damage the connecting rod itself. **Note:** *This is not necessary if new connecting rods are being fitted, as they are supplied complete with new bolts and nuts.*

25 Insert the new bolts into the connecting rod, aligning their heads with the connecting rod cutouts, and tap them fully into position.

26 Clean the backs of the bearing inserts and the bearing bores in both the connecting rod and bearing cap. If new inserts are being fitted, ensure that all traces of the protective grease are cleaned off using paraffin (kerosene). Wipe dry the inserts and connecting rods with a lint-free cloth.

27 Apply a thin smear of molybdenum disulphide grease to the top of the connecting rod bearing bore, then press the bearing inserts into their locations. Make sure the tab on each insert engages the notch in the connecting rod or bearing cap. Make sure the bearings are fitted in the correct locations.

28 Ensure the bearing inserts and crankpin are clean, then lubricate them liberally with clean engine oil.

29 Ensure the connecting rod and bearing cap mating surfaces are clean and dry. Fit the connecting rod to the crankshaft and install the bearing cap, making sure the cap is fitted the correct way round so that the connecting rod and bearing cap weight/size markings are correctly aligned. If the original connecting rod is being reused, use the identification marks made to ensure it is fitted to its original crankpin and is the same way round as was noted prior to removal.

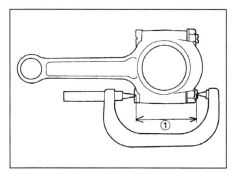

31.32 Measure the connecting rod bolt length (1) after the bolts are tightened

30 Lubricate the threads of the new bearing cap bolts and the seating surface of the nuts with clean engine oil. Screw the nuts onto the bolts, tightening them by hand only. Kawasaki give two possible tightening methods for the bearing cap bolts; the bolt length measuring method and the torque tightening method. They state that the bolt length measuring method is the more accurate of the two (and also the most complicated) but either method can be used.

Bolt length measuring tightening method

31 Accurately measure the length of each bearing cap bolt with a point micrometer, locating the point tips in the centre-punched indents. Note the exact length of each bolt.
32 Tighten both nuts to the specified Stage 1 torque and recheck the length of each bolt. From this point, tighten both nuts evenly a

little at a time, checking the length of each bolt regularly after each tightening. Continue this procedure until both bolts have stretched by the specified amount (aim to get the stretch in the middle of specified limits). The bearing cap nuts are now correctly tightened **(see illustration)**.
Caution: If either of the nuts is overtightened and a bolt is stretched beyond the specified limit, the connecting rod must be removed and the bearing cap bolts discarded. Fit two more new bolts and repeat the installation procedure. Never use a bearing cap bolt which has been overstretched, as it could break in use, leading to serious engine damage.
33 Check the connecting rod pivots freely on its crankpin and check the side clearance before proceeding (see Step 2).
34 Install the three remaining assemblies in the same way. Where new connecting rods are being installed, ensure that the connecting rod weight/size markings are all facing the same way.

Torque tightening method

35 Ensure both nuts are hand-tight, then tighten each one to the specified Stage 1 torque setting.
36 Once both nuts have been tightened to the specified stage, tighten each nut through the specified Stage 2 angle. To ensure accuracy, either of the following methods can be used.
a) Use an angle-measuring gauge to ensure each nut is tightened through the specified angle.

b) Use the corners of the nut to measure the tightening angle (the corners are spaced 60° apart). Using paint or a suitable marker pen, make a dot on one of the corners of each nut and a corresponding dot on the connecting rod itself. Rotate the nut accurately through the specified angle, so that the second corner back from the mark on the nut is aligned with the mark made on the connecting rod.
37 Check the connecting rod pivots freely on its crankpin and check the side clearance before proceeding (see Step 2).
38 Install the three remaining assemblies in the same way. Where new connecting rods are being installed, ensure that the connecting rod weight/size markings are all facing the same way.

32 Alternator driveshaft and starter clutch – removal, inspection and installation

Removal

1 Remove the engine from the frame (see Section 5).
2 Remove the alternator (see Chapter 9).
3 Remove the ignition system pick-up coil (see Chapter 5).
4 Hold the crankshaft using a socket or spanner on the timing rotor hex (do not use the rotor Allen bolt to hold the crankshaft), then slacken the alternator drive coupling retaining bolt **(see illustration 32.9a)**.
5 Separate the crankcase halves as described in Section 27. **Note:** *If no work is being carried out on the crankshaft, the camshafts and cylinder head do not need to be removed.*
6 Remove the transmission shafts from the upper crankcase (see Section 34).
7 Unscrew the retaining bolt and remove the transmission oil spray pipe from the upper crankcase **(see illustrations)**.
8 Slide out the shaft and manoeuvre the starter motor idler gear out from the upper crankcase **(see illustration)**.
9 Unscrew the retaining bolt and washer and remove the alternator drive coupling from the driveshaft **(see illustrations)**.

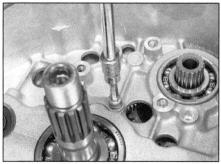

32.7a Remove the Allen bolt . . .

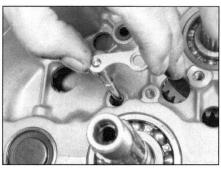

32.7b . . . and pull the oil pipe out of the crankcase

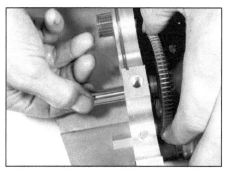

32.8 Pull out the idler gear shaft and lift out the gear

32.9a Remove the bolt . . .

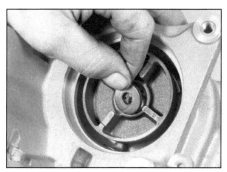

32.9b . . . the washer . . .

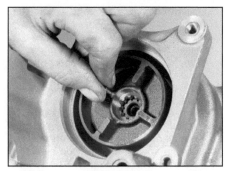

32.9c . . . and the alternator coupling

32.10 Remove the Allen bolts and take off the bearing retaining plate

32.11 Withdraw the alternator driveshaft . . .

10 Unscrew the two bolts and remove the alternator driveshaft bearing retaining plate from the upper crankcase **(see illustration)**.
11 Partially withdraw the alternator

32.12 . . . slide out the spacer, then remove the alternator driveshaft and lift out the starter clutch

driveshaft, then slide out the spacer which is fitted between the starter clutch and the crankcase **(see illustration)**.
12 Slide the alternator driveshaft fully out of position and lift out the starter clutch assembly, noting which way round it is fitted **(see illustration)**.

Inspection

Alternator driveshaft

13 Inspect the driveshaft and coupling for signs of wear or damage and check both the driveshaft bearings (one on the driveshaft and the other in the crankcase) spin freely and easily with no sign of roughness. Renew worn/damaged components as necessary **(see illustrations)**.

Starter motor clutch and idler gear

14 Inspect the starter clutch driven gear and

idler gear teeth and renew them as a set if any teeth are chipped or missing **(see illustration)**. Check the idler gear shaft and bearing surfaces for signs of wear or damage, and renew them if necessary. Hold the starter motor clutch hub and attempt to turn the driven gear back and forth **(see illustration)**. It should rotate freely in one direction and not at all in the other. If the driven gear turns freely in both directions, or is locked solid, dismantle the starter clutch and inspect the components as follows.
15 Remove the circlip and lift off the outer thrust washer, then ease the driven gear out of position. Remove the needle roller bearing and inner thrust washer from the hub **(see illustrations)**. Clamp the hub in a vice, then unscrew the six retaining bolts. Separate the holder, one-way clutch and hub assembly, noting the correct fitted location of each component.

32.13a Check the alternator shaft bearings for looseness, roughness or noise . . .

32.13b . . . there is one on each end of the shaft

32.14a Check the idler gear for worn or damaged teeth and for looseness on it's shaft

32.14b Hold the starter clutch and try to rotate the gear

32.15a Remove the circlip . . .

32.15b . . . the thrust washer . . .

32.15c . . . the starter clutch gear . . .

32.15d . . . and the needle roller bearing

32.19a Place the starter clutch in the engine . . .

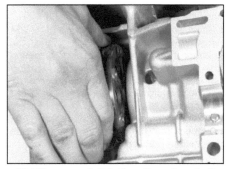

32.19b . . . and slide the alternator shaft partway in

32.20 Install the spacer and push the alternator shaft the rest of the way in

32.23 Position the idler gear in the case and install its shaft

16 Inspect the one-way clutch rollers and driven gear contact surfaces for signs of wear and scoring. The one-way clutch rollers should be unmarked, with no signs of wear such as pitting or flat spots. Check the needle roller bearing, hub and driven gear contact surfaces for wear or scoring. Renew worn components as necessary.

17 On reassembly, remove all traces of locking compound from the threads of the holder bolts, then lubricate all components with clean engine oil. Fit the one-way clutch to the rear of the holder, ensuring its flange is correctly seated in the holder recess, then assemble the holder and clutch with the hub. Apply locking compound to the holder bolt threads, then fit them and tighten to the specified torque. Fit the inner thrust washer to the hub centre and slide on the needle roller bearing. Ease the driven gear into position, then fit the outer thrust washer and secure all components in position with the circlip. Ensure the circlip is correctly seated in the hub groove, then check the operation of the starter clutch (see Step 14).

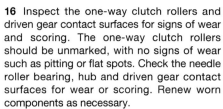

Installation

18 Ensure the alternator driveshaft bearings are correctly fitted to the shaft and crankcase. Remove all traces of locking compound from the bearing retaining plate and oil spray pipe bolt threads.

19 Fit the starter clutch assembly (clutch hub outermost) in location in the upper crankcase

and insert the alternator driveshaft. Locate the clutch hub on the splines and partially insert the driveshaft **(see illustrations)**.

20 Insert the spacer in between the starter clutch driven gear and the crankcase, then push the driveshaft fully into position **(see illustration)**.

21 Apply locking compound to the threads of the bolts, then fit the alternator driveshaft bearing retaining plate, tightening the bolts to the specified torque.

22 Fit the alternator drive coupling to the shaft and install the retaining bolt and washer.

23 Slide the idler gear into position and engage it with the driven gear teeth. Lubricate the idler gear shaft with clean engine oil, then slide it in through the gear **(see illustration)**. Check that the idler gear and driven gear rotate freely in one direction but lock on the alternator driveshaft when rotated in the opposite direction.

24 Install the transmission oil spray pipe in the crankcase. Apply a drop of locking compound to the retaining bolt threads, then fit the oil pipe bolt, tightening it to the specified torque.

25 Install the transmission shafts and reassemble the crankcase halves (see Sections 34 and 27).

26 Retain the crankshaft timing rotor (see Step 4), then tighten the alternator drive coupling bolt to the specified torque.

27 Install the pick-up coil (Chapter 5) and alternator (Chapter 9), then fit the engine to the frame as described in Section 5.

33 Camchain – removal, inspection and installation

Removal

1 Remove the engine from the frame (see Section 5).

2 Separate the crankcase halves as described in Section 27. **Note:** *If no work is being carried out on the crankshaft, the cylinder head does not need to be removed (just remove the camshafts).*

3 Disengage the camchain from the crankshaft sprocket and manoeuvre it out of position.

Inspection

4 Check the camchain for wear or damage, such as tight or loose link pins, and renew it if there is any doubt about its condition. The amount of chain wear can be assessed by pulling it tight and measuring a twenty-link length (distance between 21 link pins) section. Repeat this check along several different sections of the chain and compare the results to those given in the specifications. If any section exceeds the specified limit, the camchain must be renewed **(see illustration 21.18)**.

Installation

5 Manoeuvre the camchain in position and engage it correctly with the crankshaft sprocket.

6 Reassemble the crankcase halves (Section 27) and install the engine (Section 5).

34.3a Lift out the input shaft . . .

34.3b . . . and the output shaft

34.6 Make sure the dowel pins and bearing half rings are in position

34 Transmission shafts –
removal and installation

Removal

1 Remove the engine from the frame (see Section 5).
2 Separate the crankcase halves as described in Section 27. **Note:** *If no work is being carried out on the crankshaft, the camshafts and cylinder head do not need to be removed.*
3 Lift the input shaft and output shaft out of the crankcase **(see illustrations)**.
4 Recover the bearing half-rings and dowel

When disassembling the transmission shafts, place the parts on a long rod, or thread a wire through them to keep them in order and facing in the proper direction

pins (one each for both input and output shafts) and store them with the transmission shafts for safe-keeping.
5 If necessary, the transmission shafts can be disassembled and inspected for wear or damage, as described in Section 35.

Installation

6 Install the input and output shaft bearing half-rings and dowel pins in the upper crankcase **(see illustration)**.
7 Lower the output shaft into position in the crankcase half. As the shaft is fitted, align the bearing groove with the half-ring and engage the needle roller bearing race hole with the dowel pin. On ZX-7R models, also ensure that the bearing outer race locating pin is correctly seated in its recess in the crankcase.
8 Lower the input shaft into position in the upper crankcase, aligning its bearing groove

35.2a Remove the circlip . . .

with the half-ring and the needle roller bearing race hole with the dowel pin.
9 Make sure both transmission shafts are correctly seated.
Caution: If either of the half-rings or dowel pins (or the output shaft bearing locating pin – ZX-7R models) are not correctly located, the crankcase halves will not seat correctly.
10 Position the gears in the neutral position and check that the shafts are free to rotate freely before proceeding further.

35 Transmission shafts –
disassembly, inspection and reassembly

1 Remove the shafts from the casing as described in Section 34 (see *Haynes Hint*).

Input shaft

Disassembly

Note: *Discard all circlips; new ones must be used on reassembly.*
2 Using circlip pliers, remove the circlip from the left-hand end of the shaft, then slide off the needle roller bearing outer race, bearing and thrust washer **(see illustrations)**.
3 Slide off the 2nd gear, noting which way around it is fitted **(see illustration)**.
4 Remove the 6th gear, followed by its splined bushing and thrust washer **(see illustrations)**.
5 Remove the second circlip, using a suitable pair of circlip pliers **(see illustration)**.

35.2b . . . the outer race . . .

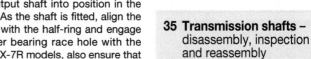

35.2c . . . the needle roller bearing . . .

35.2d . . . and then the thrust washer

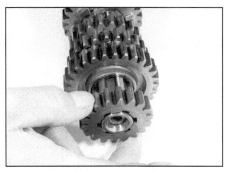

35.3 Remove second gear

35.4a Remove sixth gear . . .

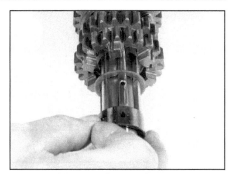

35.4b . . . its bushing . . .

6 Remove the 3rd/4th gear, noting which way around it is fitted **(see illustration)**.
7 Remove the third circlip, using a suitable pair of circlip pliers **(see illustration)**.
8 Slide off the splined thrust washer, followed by the 5th gear and 5th gear bushing **(see illustrations)**.

Inspection

9 Wash all the components in clean solvent and dry them off.
10 Check the gear teeth for cracking and other obvious damage. Check the gear bushings and the surface in the inner diameter of each gear for scoring or heat discoloration. If the gear or bushing is damaged, renew it.
11 Inspect the dogs and the dog holes in the gears for excessive wear. Renew the paired gears as a set, if necessary.
12 The shaft is unlikely to sustain damage unless the engine has seized – placing an

unusually high loading on the transmission – or the machine has covered a very high mileage. Check the surface of the shaft, especially where a pinion turns on it, and renew the shaft if it has scored or picked up. Inspect the threads of the shafts and check them for trueness by setting them up in V-blocks and measuring any runout with a dial gauge. Damage of any kind can only be cured by renewal.
13 Check that the outer race of the bearing fitted to the shaft rotates freely and has no sign of freeplay between its inner and outer races. If the bearing requires renewal, a bearing puller will be required to pull the bearing off. Note which way round the bearing is fitted, then remove it from the shaft. Ensure the new bearing is fitted the right way round, then press/drift it fully onto the shaft, using a tubular spacer which bears only on the inner race of the bearing.

35.4c . . . and its thrust washer

Reassembly

14 Before reassembly, lubricate all components with engine oil **(see illustration)**. **Note:** *Always use new circlips on reassembly and ensure each circlip is fitted with its ends*

35.5 Remove the circlip

35.6 Slide off the third/fourth gears

35.7 Remove the circlip

35.8a Remove the thrust washer . . .

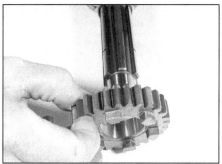

35.8b . . . fifth gear . . .

35.8c . . . and the bushing

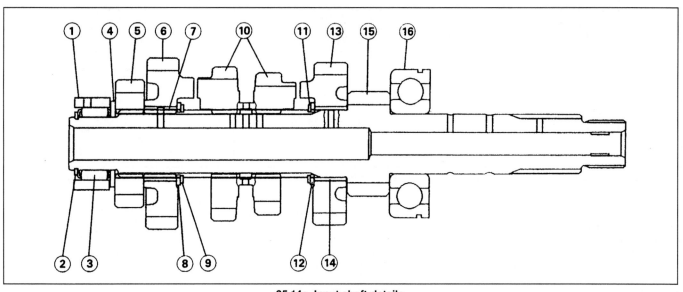

35.14a Input shaft details

1 *Bearing outer race*	5 *Second gear*	9 *Circlip*	13 *Fifth gear*
2 *Circlip*	6 *Sixth gear*	10 *Third/forth gear*	14 *Bushing*
3 *Needle bearing*	7 *Bushing*	11 *Circlip*	15 *First gear/input shaft*
4 *Thrust washer*	8 *Washer*	12 *Washer*	16 *Bearing*

positioned in one of the shaft grooves. When fitting splined bushes/gears, always align one of the component's oil holes with one of the shaft oilways **(see illustrations)**.

15 Slide on the 5th gear bushing, then fit the 5th gear with its dogs facing away from the 1st gear. Fit the splined thrust washer and secure the 5th gear components in position

with a new circlip, ensuring it is correctly located in the input shaft groove.

16 Install the 3rd/4th gear with its smaller 3rd gear facing the 5th gear. Engage the gear on the shaft splines, aligning its oil hole with the shaft oilway.

17 Fit the second new circlip to the shaft, making sure it is correctly located in the shaft

groove.

18 Slide on the splined thrust washer and 6th gear splined bushing, aligning the bushing oil hole with the shaft oilway. Fit the 6th gear so that its dogs are facing the 3rd/4th gear.

19 Fit the 2nd gear followed by the thrust washer.

20 Oil the needle roller bearing assembly liberally, and install the bearing and outer race on the end of the shaft. Secure the bearing in position with a new circlip, making sure it is correctly located in the shaft groove.

Output shaft

Disassembly

Note: *Discard all circlips; new ones must be used on reassembly.*

21 Slide the needle roller bearing outer race and bearing off the right-hand end of the output shaft **(see illustrations)**.

22 Remove the thrust washer followed by the 1st gear, noting which way round it is fitted **(see illustrations)**.

35.14b Align the oil hole in the fifth gear bushing with the oil hole in the shaft . . .

35.14c . . . and do the same for the sixth gear bushing

35.21a Remove the bearing outer race . . .

35.21b . . . and the needle roller bearing

35.22a Remove the thrust washer . . .

23 Hold the output shaft vertically and rotate the shaft rapidly back and forth to force the positive neutral finder mechanism steel balls into the 5th gear. Once all the balls are in the gear, carefully slide the 5th gear off the shaft, noting which way round it is fitted, and recover the three steel balls **(see illustration)**.
24 Remove the circlip with a suitable pair of circlip pliers and slide off the splined washer **(see illustrations)**.
25 Slide off the 3rd gear and then the 4th gear, noting which way round each one is fitted. Continue as described under the sub-heading appropriate to your model.

ZX-7R models
26 Slide off the 3rd/4th gear bushing followed by the thrust washer.
27 Remove the 6th gear, noting which way around it is fitted.
28 The 2nd gear and bushing is removed from the left-hand end of the output shaft. Remove the bearing and collar (see Step 34), then slide the 2nd gear and bushing off from the shaft. **Note:** *The bearing must be renewed whenever it is removed; never refit a used bearing.*

ZX-9R B models
29 Slide off the 3rd/4th gear splined bushing, followed by the splined thrust washer.
30 Remove the second circlip with a suitable pair of circlip pliers.
31 Remove the 6th gear, noting which way round it is fitted.
32 Remove the third circlip, then slide off splined thrust washer.
33 Remove the 2nd gear, noting which way round it is fitted, and slide off the 2nd gear bushing.

Inspection

34 Refer to Steps 9 to 13. If the bearing is being removed (see Step 13) from the left-hand end of the shaft, note that the collar will be drawn off at the same time. If the collar surface is marked it must be renewed; the collar runs in the oil seal lip and any damage could lead to oil leakage. Fit the bearing as described (Step 13) then press/drift the collar fully onto the shaft.

Reassembly

35 Before reassembly, lubricate all components with engine oil **(see illustrations)**. **Note:** *Always use new circlips on reassembly and ensure each circlip is fitted with its ends positioned in one of the shaft grooves* (see Section 2 of *Tools and Workshop Tips* in the *Reference* section). *When fitting splined bushes/gears, always align one of the component's oil holes with one of the shaft oilways* **(see illustrations 35.14b and 35.14c)**.

ZX-7R models
36 Where necessary, slide the 2nd gear bushing onto the left-hand end of the output shaft, aligning its oil hole with that of the shaft. Fit the 2nd gear so that the side on which its gear teeth protrude is facing the 6th gear. Install the new bearing and collar (see Step 34).

35.22b . . . and the first gear

35.23 Removing fifth gear

35.24a Remove the circlip . . .

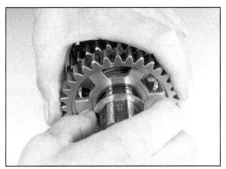

35.24b . . . and the splined washer

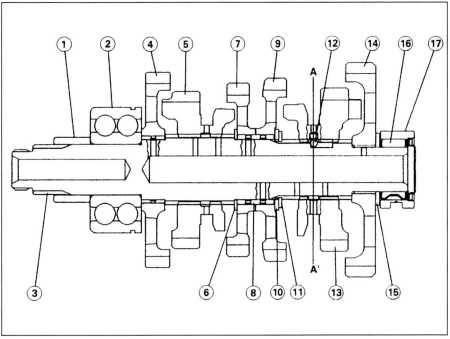

35.35a Output shaft details (ZX-7R models)

1 Collar	7 Fourth gear	13 Fifth gear
2 Ball bearing	8 Bushing	14 First gear
3 Output shaft	9 Third gear	15 Thrust washer
4 Second gear	10 Toothed washer	16 Needle bearing
5 Sixth gear	11 Circlip	17 Bearing outer race
6 Toothed washer	12 Steel ball	

A-A Fifth gear (cross-section) Refer to illustration 35.35b

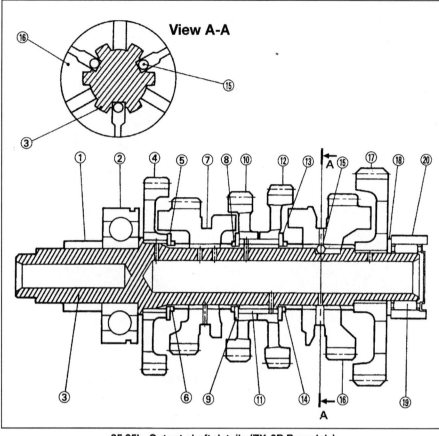

View A-A

35.35b Output shaft details (ZX-9R B models)

1 Collar	8 Circlip	15 Steel ball
2 Ball bearing	9 Toothed washer	16 Fifth gear
3 Output shaft	10 Fourth gear	17 First gear
4 Second gear	11 Bushing	18 Thrust washer
5 Toothed washer	12 Third gear	19 Needle roller bearing
6 Circlip	13 Toothed washer	20 Bearing outer race
7 Sixth gear	14 Circlip	

A-A Fifth gear (cross-section)

37 Fit the 6th gear to the right end of the shaft, so that its selector fork groove is facing away from the 2nd gear. Align the gear oil hole with the shaft oilway and slide the gear onto the shaft.

38 Fit the thrust washer and slide on the

3rd/4th gear bushing. Continue as described in Steps 43 to 48.

ZX-9R B models

39 Slide on the 2nd gear bushing and install the 2nd gear with its flat surface facing the output shaft bearing. Fit the splined thrust

washer and secure the 2nd gear components with a new circlip, making sure it is correctly located in the output shaft groove.

40 Fit the 6th gear to the shaft so that its selector fork groove is facing away from the 2nd gear. Align the gear oil hole with the shaft oilway and slide the gear onto the shaft.

41 Fit a second new circlip ensuring it is correctly located in the shaft groove.

42 Slide on the splined thrust washer, then align the 3rd/4th gear splined bushing oil hole with the shaft oilway and slide it along the shaft. Continue as described in Steps 43 to 48.

All models

43 Fit the 4th gear so that the side on which its gear hub protrudes the most is facing away from the 6th gear.

44 Fit the 3rd gear so that the side on which its gear hub protrudes the most is facing the 4th gear. Slide on the splined thrust washer and secure the 3rd/4th gear components in position with a new circlip, ensuring it is correctly located in the output shaft groove.

45 Position the shaft assembly vertically in a vice, with its right-hand end uppermost.

46 Hold the 5th gear vertically so that its selector fork groove is facing downwards (towards the 3rd gear), then insert the three positive neutral finder steel balls into the three smaller holes in the 5th gear (the larger holes are oil holes) **(see illustration)**. Ensure that all three balls are in position in the gear, then align the balls with the cutouts on the output shaft and lower the gear onto the shaft **(see illustration)**. Shake the gear/shaft to release the balls and gently pull on the 5th gear to check that the positive neutral finder balls are correctly located in the shaft grooves.

⚠ **Warning: Do not be tempted to use grease to hold the steel balls in the gear as this will prevent the positive neutral finder mechanism from functioning correctly.**

47 Install the 1st gear with its flat surface facing away from the 5th gear, then fit the thrust washer.

48 Lubricate the needle roller bearing assembly and fit the bearing and outer race to the end of the output shaft **(see illustration)**.

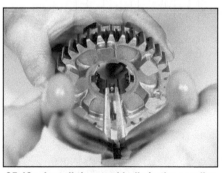

35.46a Install the steel balls in the smaller holes in the gear . . .

35.46b . . . and align the steel balls with the shaft slots (arrowed) when installing the gear

35.48 The assembled output shaft should look like this

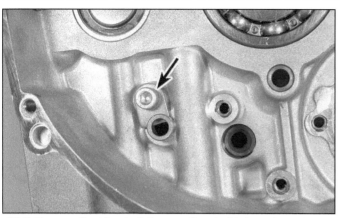

36.7 Remove the Allen bolt (arrowed) and withdraw the selector fork shaft

36.8 Remove the Allen bolts (arrowed) from the selector drum retaining plate

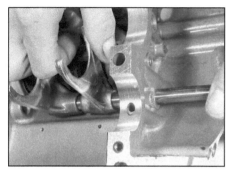

36.9a Support the selector forks and slide out the selector rod . . .

36.9b . . . then support the remaining selector fork and slide out the other selector rod

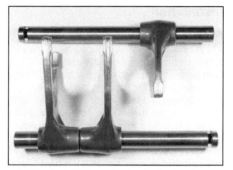

36.9c Install the selector forks back on their rods to ensure correct reassembly

36 Selector drum and forks – removal, inspection and installation

Removal

1 Separate the crankcase halves as described in Section 27.

ZX-7R models

2 Undo the retaining bolts and remove the selector drum bearing retaining plate from the left-hand side of the lower crankcase half.

3 Withdraw the selector fork front shaft slowly and remove the centre selector fork from the crankcase as it is released from the end of the shaft.

4 Withdraw the selector fork rear shaft from the crankcase and recover the left- and right-hand selector forks as they are released. **Note:** *All the selector forks are different; if necessary, make identification marks on them to avoid confusion on installation.*

5 Remove the selector drum and bearing from the crankcase.

6 If necessary, clamp the selector drum in a vice equipped with soft jaws, then slacken and remove the cam centre bolt. Remove the cam and bearing from the drum and recover the locating pin. Also, take care not to lose any of the selector mechanism pins from the cam.

ZX-9R B models

7 Unscrew the bolt securing the rear selector fork shaft retaining plate to the right-hand side of the lower crankcase **(see illustration)**. Withdraw the selector fork rear shaft from the crankcase and recover the left- and right-hand selector forks as they are released. **Note:** *All the selector forks are different; if necessary, make identification marks on them to avoid confusion on installation.*

8 Undo the retaining bolts and remove the selector drum bearing retaining plate from the left-hand side of the lower crankcase half **(see illustration)**.

9 Withdraw the selector fork front shaft slowly

36.10 Remove the selector drum from the crankcase

and remove the centre selector fork from the crankcase as it is released from the end of the shaft **(see illustrations)**.

10 Remove the selector drum and bearing from the crankcase **(see illustration)**.

11 If necessary, clamp the selector drum in a vice equipped with soft jaws, then slacken and remove the cam centre bolt. Remove the neutral switch contact and locating pin, then remove the cam and bearing from the drum and recover its locating pin.

Inspection

12 The selector forks and shaft should be closely inspected to ensure that they are not badly damaged or worn **(see illustration)**.

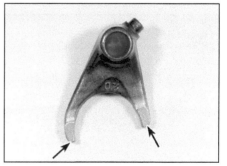

36.12 Check the selector forks for wear and damage, especially at the fork ears (arrowed)

13 Measure the width of both fork ends and the internal diameter of the shaft bore. If either fork end or the shaft bore has worn beyond its service limit the selector fork(s) must be renewed.

14 The selector fork shafts can be checked for trueness by rolling them along a flat surface. A bent shaft will cause difficulty in selecting gears and make the gearshift action heavy. If the shaft is bent it must be renewed.

15 Inspect the selector drum grooves and selector fork guide pins for signs of wear or damage. If either component shows signs of damage or has worn beyond the specified limits, the selector fork(s) and drum must be renewed **(see illustration)**.

16 Check that the selector drum bearing rotates freely and there is no sign of freeplay between its inner and outer race. Renew the bearing, if worn.

Installation

ZX-7R models

17 Where necessary, remove all traces of locking compound from the threads of the cam centre bolt threads. Fit the bearing to the drum and insert the locating pin into the drum hole. Ensure all the selector mechanism pins are in position, then fit the cam to the drum, aligning its cutout with the locating pin. Apply a drop of locking compound to the bolt, then fit it and tighten to the specified torque.

18 Remove all traces of locking compound from the selector drum bearing plate bolt threads. Lubricate the selector drum bearing and grooves with clean engine oil and insert the selector drum and bearing into position in the crankcase.

19 Apply a smear of engine oil to the selector fork shafts and slide them partially into the crankcase (both shafts are the same).

20 The selector forks are all different and are not interchangeable. The centre fork (fitted to the front shaft) is easily identified as it is the shortest fork of the three. The left- and right-hand forks (fitted to the rear shaft) are both of similar appearance, but they must be installed with their wider shaft ends facing towards each other.

21 Locate the centre fork pin in its groove in the selector drum, then slide the front shaft in through the fork and fully into position.

22 Locate the left fork pin in its groove in the selector drum and slide in the selector fork shaft

until it engages the fork. Repeat the process for the right-hand fork and push the shaft fully home. Check that the wider section of each fork's shaft end is facing towards the other fork, to ensure both forks are correctly fitted.

23 Manoeuvre the selector drum bearing retaining plate into position and engage it with the slots in the selector fork shafts. Apply locking compound to the threads of the retaining plate bolts, then fit the bolts and tighten them to the specified torque.

24 Join the crankcase halves as described in Section 27.

ZX-9R B models

25 Where necessary, remove all traces of locking compound from the threads of the cam centre bolt threads. Fit the bearing to the drum and insert the locating pin into the drum hole. Fit the cam to the drum, aligning its cutout with the locating pin, then fit the second locating pin and install the neutral switch contact. Apply a drop of locking compound to the centre bolt, then fit it and tighten to the specified torque.

26 Install the selector forks and shafts as described in Steps 18 to 22 (it will be necessary to fit the right-hand fork before the left-hand fork on the rear shaft).

27 Manoeuvre the selector drum bearing retaining plate into position and engage it with the slot in the front selector fork shaft. Apply locking compound to the threads of the retaining plate bolts, then fit the bolts and tighten them to the specified torque.

28 Locate the selector fork rear shaft retaining plate with the slot in the right-hand end of the shaft. Apply locking compound to the threads then fit the retaining plate bolt and tighten it to the specified torque **(see illustration)**.

29 Join the crankcase halves as described in Section 27.

37 Initial start-up after overhaul

Note: *Do not install the inner and lower fairing panels until after the engine has been run.*

1 Make sure the engine oil and coolant levels are correct (see *Daily (pre-ride) checks*).

2 Turn on the ignition switch and crank the engine over with the starter to prime the lubrication system of the engine.

⚠️ *Warning: Operate the starter in 5-second bursts with at least a 15-second wait in between operations. This will prevent the starter motor and battery overheating and becoming damaged.*

3 Make sure there is fuel in the tank then start the engine and allow it to idle slowly.

⚠️ *Warning: If the oil pressure warning light does not go off immediately, or soon after the engine starts (a delay of a few seconds is usual), or it comes on while the engine is*

running, stop the engine immediately and investigate the cause.

4 Once the oil pressure warning light goes out, bleed the air from the cooling system (see Chapter 1) and top-up the radiator and coolant reservoir fluid levels.

5 Warm the engine up to normal operating temperature whilst checking carefully for oil and coolant leaks. Check the operation of the clutch and transmission, then switch off the engine.

6 Make sure the transmission and controls, especially the brakes, function properly before road testing the machine. Refer to Section 38 for the recommended running-in procedure.

7 Upon completion of the road test, and after the engine has cooled down completely, check the engine oil and the coolant level in both the radiator and reservoir before installing the fairing panels.

38 Recommended running-in procedure

1 Any rebuilt engine needs time to run in, even if parts have been installed in their original locations. For this reason, treat the machine gently for the first few miles, to make sure oil has circulated throughout the engine and any new parts installed have started to seat.

2 Even greater care is necessary if the engine has been fitted with new cylinder liners and pistons, or a new crankshaft. In the case of new cylinder liners and pistons, the engine will have to be run in as if the machine were new. This means greater use of the transmission and a restraining hand on the throttle until at least 500 miles (800 km) have been covered. There is no point in keeping to any set speed limit – the main idea is to keep from labouring (lugging) the engine and to increase performance gradually until the 500 mile (800 km) mark is reached. These recommendations can be lessened to an extent when only a new crankshaft is installed. Experience is the best guide, since it is easy to tell when an engine is running freely.

3 If a lubrication failure is suspected, stop the engine immediately and try to find the cause. If an engine is run without oil, even for a short period of time, irreparable damage will occur.

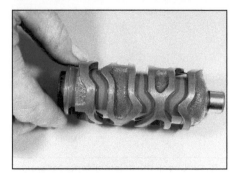

36.15 Check the grooves on the selector drum for wear, especially at the points

36.28 The selector rods and forks should look like this when assembled

Chapter 2 Part B:
Engine, clutch and transmission
ZX-9R C, E and F models

Contents

Degrees of difficulty

Easy, suitable for novice with little experience	Fairly easy, suitable for beginner with some experience	Fairly difficult, suitable for competent DIY mechanic	Difficult, suitable for experienced DIY mechanic	Very difficult, suitable for expert DIY or professional

Specifications

General

Capacity	899 cc
Bore	75.0 mm
Stroke	50.9 mm
Compression ratio	
C models	11.5 to 1
E and F models	12.2 to 1
Cylinder identification	1-2-3-4 (from left to right)
Firing order	1-2-4-3

Camshaft and followers

Intake cam lobe height
    Standard . . . .   37.143 to 37.257 mm
    Service limit . . . .   37.040 mm
Exhaust cam lobe height
    Standard . . . .   36.643 to 36.757 mm
    Service limit . . . .   36.540 mm
Camshaft journal OD
    Standard . . . .   23.950 to 23.972 mm
    Service limit . . . .   23.920 mm
Camshaft bearing cap ID
    Standard . . . .   24.000 to 24.021 mm
    Service limit . . . .   24.080 mm
Camshaft bearing oil clearance . . . .   0.028 to 0.071 mm
Camshaft runout
    Standard . . . .   Less than 0.02 mm
    Service limit . . . .   0.10 mm
Camchain 20-link length
    Standard . . . .   127.00 to 127.36 mm
    Service limit . . . .   128.90 mm

Cylinder head

Maximum warpage . . . .   0.05 mm

Valves and valve springs

Intake valve stem OD
    Standard . . . .   4.475 to 4.490 mm
    Service limit . . . .   4.460 mm
Exhaust valve stem OD
    Standard . . . .   4.455 to 4.470 mm
    Service limit . . . .   4.440 mm
Valve stem runout
    Standard . . . .   Less than 0.01 mm
    Service limit . . . .   0.05 mm
Valve head thickness
    Intake valve
        Standard . . . .   0.50 mm
        Service limit . . . .   0.25 mm
    Exhaust valve
        Standard . . . .   0.80 mm
        Service limit . . . .   0.50 mm
Valve guide ID – intake and exhaust
    Standard . . . .   4.500 to 4.512 mm
    Service limit . . . .   4.580 mm
Valve seat width . . . .   0.5 to 1.0 mm
Valve spring free length
    Intake valve
        Inner spring
            Standard . . . .   34.6 mm
            Service limit . . . .   33.0 mm
        Outer spring
            Standard . . . .   38.6 mm
            Service limit . . . .   37.4 mm
    Exhaust valve
        Inner spring
            Standard . . . .   35.3 mm
            Service limit . . . .   32.7 mm
        Outer spring
            Standard . . . .   39.2 mm
            Service limit . . . .   38.1 mm

Cylinder block

Cylinder bore ID
    C models
        Standard . . . .   75.000 to 75.012 mm
        Service limit . . . .   75.100 mm
    E and F models
        Standard . . . .   74.970 to 74.982 mm
        Service limit . . . .   75.100 mm

Cylinder block (continued)

Cylinder-to-piston clearance
    C models . . . .   0.040 to 0.067 mm
    E and F models . . . .   0.010 to 0.037 mm
Maximum gasket face warpage . . . .   0.05 mm
Taper and out-of-round limits . . . .   Not specified

Pistons

Piston OD (measured 5 mm up from base of skirt)
    Standard . . . .   74.945 to 74.960 mm
    Service limit . . . .   74.790 mm
Piston ring groove width
    Top ring
        Standard . . . .   0.83 to 0.85 mm
        Service limit . . . .   0.93 mm
    Second (middle) ring
        Standard . . . .   0.82 to 0.84 mm
        Service limit . . . .   0.92 mm
    Oil control ring . . . .   Not specified

Piston rings

Top and second (middle) ring thickness
    Standard . . . .   0.77 to 0.79 mm
    Service limit . . . .   0.70 mm
Top ring-to-groove clearance
    Standard . . . .   0.04 to 0.08 mm
    Service limit . . . .   0.18 mm
Second (middle) ring-to-groove clearance
    Standard . . . .   0.03 to 0.07 mm
    Service limit . . . .   0.17 mm
Top ring end gap
    Standard . . . .   0.20 to 0.35 mm
    Service limit . . . .   0.60 mm
Second (middle) ring end gap
    Standard . . . .   0.35 to 0.50 mm
    Service limit . . . .   0.80 mm
Oil control ring . . . .   Not specified

Clutch

Friction plate thickness . . . .   2.72 to 2.88 mm
Steel plate thicknesses . . . .   2.0, 2.3, 2.6 mm
Friction and plain plate warpage
    Standard . . . .   Less than 0.2 mm
    Service limit . . . .   0.3 mm
Clutch spring free length
    Standard . . . .   73.49 mm
    Service limit . . . .   69.90 mm
Clutch plate assembly thickness – see text . . . .   48.4 to 49.0 mm

Crankshaft and connecting rods

Crankshaft runout
    Standard . . . .   Less than 0.02 mm
    Service limit . . . .   0.05 mm
Crankshaft endfloat
    Standard . . . .   0.05 to 0.20 mm
    Service limit . . . .   0.40 mm
Connecting rod big-end bearing side clearance
    Standard . . . .   0.13 to 0.38 mm
    Service limit . . . .   0.58 mm
Connecting rod crankpin bore ID
    Unmarked . . . .   38.000 to 38.008 mm
    Size group 0 . . . .   38.009 to 38.016 mm
Crankshaft crankpin OD
    Unmarked . . . .   34.984 to 34.992 mm
    Size group 0 . . . .   34.993 to 35.000 mm
Connecting rod bearing oil clearance
    Standard . . . .   0.036 to 0.066 mm
    Service limit . . . .   0.10 mm

Crankshaft and connecting rods (continued)

Connecting rod bearing insert thicknesses

Brown	1.475 to 1.480 mm
Black or unmarked	1.480 to 1.485 mm
Blue	1.485 to 1.490 mm

Connecting rod bolt stretch limits (bolt length measurement tightening procedure – see text)

Original connecting rod	0.20 to 0.32 mm
New connecting rod	0.24 to 0.36 mm

Crankcase main bearing bore ID

Unmarked	36.000 to 36.008 mm
Size group 0	36.009 to 36.016 mm

Crankshaft main bearing journal OD

Unmarked	32.984 to 32.992 mm
Size group 1	32.993 to 33.000 mm

Main bearing oil clearance

Standard	0.020 to 0.044 mm
Service limit	0.07 mm

Main bearing insert thicknesses

Brown	1.490 to 1.494 mm
Black	1.494 to 1.498 mm
Blue	1.498 to 1.502 mm

Oil pump and pressure relief valves

Oil pressure (at 4000 rpm)	17 to 26 psi (1.2 to 1.8 bar) at 90°C (194°F)
Oil pressure relief valve opening pressure	Not specified

Transmission

Gear ratios (no. of teeth)

1st	2.571:1 (36/14)
2nd	1.941:1 (33/17)
3rd	1.556:1 (28/18)
4th	1.333:1 (28/21)
5th	1.200:1 (24/20)
6th	1.095:1 (23/21)
Primary drive ratio	1.714:1 (84/49)

Gear selector fork groove width

Standard	6.05 to 6.15 mm
Service limit	6.25 mm

Selector fork end thickness

Standard	5.9 to 6.0 mm
Service limit	5.8 mm

Selector fork guide pin diameter

Standard	6.9 to 7.0 mm
Service limit	6.8 mm

Selector drum groove width

Standard	7.05 to 7.20 mm
Service limit	7.30 mm

Torque wrench settings

Camchain rear guide pivot bolt	25 Nm

Camchain tensioner bolts

C models	11 Nm
E and F models	10 Nm
Camshaft bearing cap bolts	12 Nm

Clutch assembly

Centre nut	135 Nm
Spring bolts	9 Nm
Clutch cover bolts	11 Nm

Connecting rod bearing cap bolt nuts

Bolt length measurement method	See text

Torque tightening method

New connecting rod assembly (using bolts and nuts supplied with the rod)

Stage 1	18 Nm
Stage 2	Angle-tighten a further 120°

New connecting rod assembly (using the bolts supplied with the rod but other new nuts)

Stage 1	20 Nm
Stage 2	Angle-tighten a further 120°

Torque wrench settings (continued)

Connecting rod bearing cap bolt nuts (continued)
  Torque tightening method
    Original connecting rod assembly (using new bolts and the original nuts)

Stage 1	24 Nm
Stage 2	Angle-tighten a further 120°

    Original connecting rod assembly (using new bolts and nuts)

Stage 1	25 Nm
Stage 2	Angle-tighten a further 120°

Crankcase bolts
  9 mm (main bearing) bolts

Shorter bolts (1 to 6 in tightening sequence)	42 Nm
Longer bolts (7 to 10 in tightening sequence)	47 Nm
8 mm bolts	27 Nm
7 mm bolts	20 Nm
6 mm bolts	12 Nm
Crankcase breather plate bolts	10 Nm
Cylinder head cover bolts	10 Nm
Cylinder head cover baffle plate bolts	11 Nm

Cylinder head bolts

6 mm bolts	12 Nm

  10 mm bolts

Stage 1 (first)	20 Nm

    Stage 2 (final)

Original bolts	49 Nm
New bolts	54 Nm

Engine mountings
  C models

Mounting bolts	44 Nm
Mounting bolt collar clamp bolts	23 Nm
Rear upper mounting bracket to frame bolts	23 Nm

  E and F models

Mounting bolts	44 Nm

    Threaded collar locknuts

E models	49 Nm
F models	59 Nm
Rear upper mounting bracket to frame bolts	25 Nm

Gearchange mechanism
  C and F models

Stopper arm pivot bolt	10 Nm
Centralising spring locating pin	30 Nm

  E models

Stopper arm pivot bolt	12 Nm
Centralising spring locating pin	27 Nm
Oil cooler centre bolt	78 Nm
Oil filter	27 Nm

Oil pan bolts

C models	11 Nm
E and F models	12 Nm
Oil pan drain plug	20 Nm
Oil pipe retaining plate bolts	12 Nm
Oil pressure relief valve	15 Nm

Selector drum

Bearing retaining plate bolt	12 Nm
Bearing retaining plate screw	6 Nm
Cam centre bolt	12 Nm
Starter one-way clutch holder bolts	12 Nm

Water pump

Cover bolts	11 Nm
Impeller bolt	10 Nm

1 General information

The engine/transmission unit is of the water-cooled, in-line, four-cylinder design, installed transversely across the frame. The engine/transmission unit is constructed in aluminium alloy with the crankcase being divided horizontally. The crankcase incorporates a wet sump, pressure fed lubrication system, and houses a dual rotor oil pump

The sixteen valves are operated by double overhead camshafts which are chain driven off the right end of the crankshaft. The valves are operated by bucket-type followers and valve clearances are adjusted via shims fitted between the top of the valve stem and the follower.

The cable-operated clutch is of the wet multi-plate type and is driven off the right end of the crankshaft by the primary drive gear. The transmission is of the six-speed constant mesh type. Final drive to the rear wheel is by chain and sprockets, the drive sprocket being mounted on the left end of the output shaft.

The alternator is situated on the left end of the crankshaft; the rear of the alternator rotor incorporates the starter clutch assembly. The water pump is driven by the oil pump which is gear-driven off the rear of the clutch assembly.

2 Operations possible with the engine in the frame

The components and assemblies listed below can be removed without having to remove the engine/transmission assembly from the frame. If however, a number of areas require attention at the same time, removal of the engine is recommended.

> Starter motor (see Chapter 9)
> Alternator (see Chapter 9)
> Water pump (see Chapter 3)
> Cylinder head cover
> Camchain tensioner and guides
> Camshafts and followers
> Clutch assembly
> Starter clutch and idler gear
> Oil pan
> Oil pump, drive gear and pressure relief valve
> Oil cooler
> Gearchange mechanism components
> Selector drum and forks*

*Selector drum and fork removal and installation is possible with the engine in the frame but is very awkward. The operation is much easier if the engine is removed and turned upside-down – see Section 24.

3 Operations requiring engine removal

It is necessary to remove the engine/transmission assembly from the frame to enable the following components to be removed.

> Cylinder head
> Cylinder block
> Pistons and rings
> Crankshaft and bearings
> Connecting rods and bearings
> Camchain
> Transmission shafts

4 Major engine repair – general note

1 It is not always easy to determine when or if an engine should be completely overhauled, as a number of factors must be considered.
2 High mileage is not necessarily an

indication that an overhaul is needed, while low mileage, on the other hand, does not preclude the need for an overhaul. Frequency of servicing is probably the single most important consideration. An engine that has regular and frequent oil and filter changes, as well as other required maintenance, will most likely give many miles of reliable service. Conversely, a neglected engine, or one which has not been run in properly, may require an overhaul very early in its life.
3 Exhaust smoke and excessive oil consumption are both indications that piston rings and/or valve guides are in need of attention, although make sure that the fault is not due to oil leakage.
4 If the engine is making obvious knocking or rumbling noises, the connecting rod and/or main bearings are probably at fault.
5 Loss of power, rough running, excessive valve train noise and high fuel consumption rates may also point to the need for an overhaul, especially if they are all present at the same time. If a complete tune-up does not remedy the situation, major mechanical work is the only solution.
6 An engine overhaul generally involves restoring the internal parts to the specifications of a new engine. The piston rings and main and connecting rod bearings are usually renewed and the cylinder bores honed during a major overhaul. Generally the valve seats are re-ground, since they are usually in less than perfect condition at this point. The end result should be a like new engine that will give as many trouble-free miles as the original.
7 Before beginning the engine overhaul, read through the related procedures to familiarise yourself with the scope and requirements of the job. Overhauling an engine is not all that difficult, but it is time consuming. Plan on the motorcycle being tied up for a minimum of two weeks. Check on the availability of parts and make sure that any necessary special tools, equipment and supplies are obtained in advance.
8 Most work can be done with typical workshop hand tools, although a number of precision measuring tools are required for inspecting parts to determine if they must be renewed. Often a dealer will handle the inspection of parts and offer advice concerning reconditioning and renewal. As a

general rule, time is the primary cost of an overhaul so it does not pay to install worn or substandard parts.
9 As a final note, to ensure maximum life and minimum trouble from a rebuilt engine, everything must be assembled with care in a spotlessly clean environment.

5 Engine – removal and installation

Caution: The engine is very heavy. Engine removal and installation should be carried out with the aid of at least one assistant; personal injury or damage could occur if the engine falls or is dropped. A mechanical or hydraulic floor jack should be used to support and lower or raise the engine if possible.

Note: *On E and F models, a special socket will be needed to slacken/tighten the engine mounting threaded collar locknuts. If the Kawasaki service tool (57001-1450) or a pattern equivalent is not available, a suitable alternative can be made by cutting a spare socket (approximately 24 mm in size) as shown* (see illustration).

Removal

1 Support the bike securely upright using an auxiliary stand so it can't be knocked over during this procedure. Work can be made easier by raising the machine to a suitable working height on an hydraulic ramp or a suitable platform (see Section 1 of *Tools and Workshop Tips* in the *Reference* section).
Caution: Ensure the bike is securely supported before proceeding.
2 If the engine is dirty, particularly around its mountings, wash it thoroughly before starting any major dismantling work. This will make work much easier and rule out the possibility of caked on lumps of dirt falling into some vital component.
3 Remove the complete fairing (see Chapter 8).
4 Remove the battery (see Chapter 9).
5 Drain the engine oil (see Chapter 1).
6 Drain the cooling system (see Chapter 1) and remove the radiator and coolant reservoir (see Chapter 3).
7 Remove the fuel tank, air filter housing, fuel pump and filter assembly, carburettors and complete exhaust system (see Chapter 4).
8 Note the correct fitted position of the gearchange lever on its shaft (make alignment marks if necessary) then unscrew the clamp bolt and free the gearchange lever from the engine.
9 Remove the front sprocket (see Chapter 6 Section 16).
10 Remove the ignition coils (see Chapter 5).
11 Referring to Chapter 4, remove the secondary air injection system control valve. On California models also remove the evaporative emission system vacuum valve.

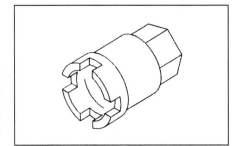

5.0 Engine mount nut wrench

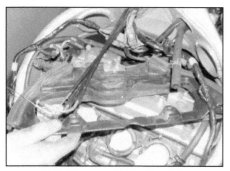

5.12 Remove the baffle plate

5.13a Slacken the clutch cable locknut

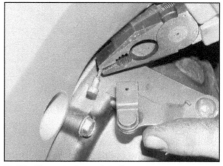

5.13b Detach the cable from the release arm

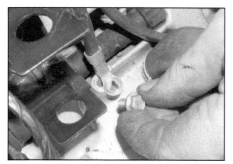

5.15 Free the earth to ground lead

5.16 Unscrew the starter motor cable

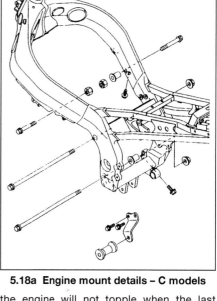

5.18a Engine mount details – C models

12 Unscrew the retaining bolts and remove the baffle plate, complete with sealing strips, from the top of the cylinder head cover **(see illustration)**.
13 Referring to Section 17, slacken the clutch cable locknut **(see illustration)** and adjuster nut then free the lower end of the cable from its mounting bracket and detach the inner cable from the release arm **(see illustration)**.
14 Trace the wiring back from the ignition pick-up coil cover/oil pressure switch, the alternator, the neutral switch and the sidestand switch to the connectors located on top of the crankcase. Note the correct routing of all wiring then disconnect all the

connectors so the wiring is free to be removed with the engine. On C models also disconnect the cam sensor wiring connector.
15 Unscrew the bolt and free the earth (ground) lead from the top of the crankcase **(see illustration)**.
16 Lift the rubber cover and unscrew the nut securing the starter motor cable to the motor. Free the cable from the motor, noting its correct routing, and position it clear of the engine **(see illustration)**.
17 At this point, position a hydraulic or mechanical jack under the engine with a block of wood between the jack head and sump. Make sure the jack is centrally positioned so

the engine will not topple when the last mounting bolt is removed. Take the weight of the engine on the jack.
18 Slacken and remove the left and right upper mounting bolts **(see illustrations)**, which secure the cylinder head to the frame, and remove the nuts. Note that on ZX-9R F models there are four upper mounting bolts.
19 Unscrew the nuts from the upper and lower rear mounting bolts.
20 Slacken the bolts securing the upper rear mounting bracket to the inside of the right frame section **(see illustration)**.

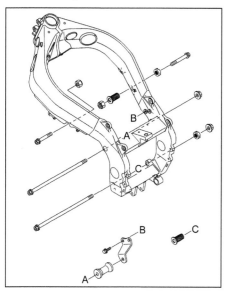

5.18b Engine mount details – E models

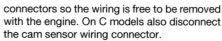
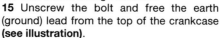

5.18c Engine mount details – F models

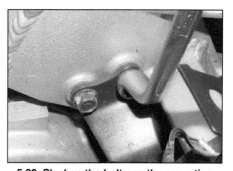

5.20 Slacken the bolts on the mounting bracket

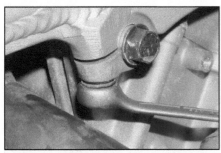

5.21a Slacken the clamp bolts on the right upper mounting . . .

5.21b . . . and the rear lower mounting

21 On C models, slacken the clamp bolts on the right upper mounting and right side of the rear lower mounting so the mounting collars are free to slide easily in the frame (see illustrations).

22 On E and F models, using the special socket (Kawasaki service tool 57001-1450) or suitable alternative, slacken the mounting bolt collar locknuts and back-off the threaded collars to provide maximum clearance between the engine unit and the frame (see illustrations).

23 On all models, ensure the engine is securely supported then withdraw both rear mounting bolts. Recover the spacer which is fitted to the rear upper mounting bolt, between the left side of the engine and frame.

24 The engine is now free to be lowered out of the frame. Check that all relevant wiring, cables and hoses are disconnected and secured well clear, then carefully lower the engine out of position (see *Caution* at the start of this Section). As the engine is lowered out of position, note that it will be necessary to free the drive chain from the output shaft.

25 With the aid of an assistant lift the engine unit off the jack and move it carefully to the work surface. On C and E models, note the location of the rear upper mounting rubbers and renew them if necessary (see Section 25). On F models, note the spacers fitted in the rear upper mounting bolt location in the engine case and remove them for safekeeping if they are loose.

Installation
C models

26 Ensure the rear upper mounting bracket bolts are loose and both the right front and rear lower mounting collars are inserted fully

into the frame to provide maximum clearance for the engine (see illustration 5.18a).

27 With the aid of an assistant place the engine unit on top of the jack and block of wood. Carefully raise the engine unit into position in the frame, engaging the drive chain with the output shaft as it is lifted. Make sure no wires, cables or hoses become trapped between the engine and the frame.

28 Insert the spacer in between the engine rear upper mounting and left side of the frame then insert both the upper and lower rear mounting bolts from the left side of the bike. Screw the nuts onto the bolts, tightening them lightly only at this stage.

29 Fit the upper mounting bolt nuts to the cylinder head and install the bolts (see illustration).

30 Tighten both the right and left upper bolts and the upper and lower rear mounting bolts to the specified torque setting.

31 Once all the mounting bolts have been tightened, tighten the rear lower mounting bolt collar clamp bolt and the right upper mounting bolt collar clamp bolts to the specified torque.

32 Tighten the rear upper mounting bracket to frame bolts to the specified torque.

33 The remainder of the installation procedure is the reverse of removal, noting the following points.

a) Make sure all wires, cables and hoses are correctly routed and connected, and secured by the relevant clips or ties.
b) Tighten all nuts and bolts to the specified torque settings (where given) and renew all gaskets and O-rings disturbed on removal.
c) Adjust the throttle and choke cable freeplay (see Chapter 1).

d) Adjust the drive chain (see Chapter 1).
e) Adjust the clutch cable (see Chapter 1).
f) Refill the engine with oil and coolant (see Chapter 1).
g) Prior to installing the lower fairing panels start the engine and check that there are no signs of coolant/oil leakage.

E models

34 Ensure the rear upper mounting bracket bolts are loose and both the engine mounting threaded collars are fully backed-off to provide maximum clearance for the engine (see illustration 5.18b).

35 With the aid of an assistant place the engine unit on top of the jack and block of wood. Carefully raise the engine unit into position in the frame, engaging the drive chain with the output shaft as it is lifted. Make sure no wires, cables or hoses become trapped between the engine and the frame.

36 Insert the spacer in between the engine rear upper mounting and left side of the frame then insert both the upper and lower rear mounting bolts from the left side of the bike.

37 Fit the nuts to the cylinder head then install both the upper mounting bolts, tightening them lightly only.

38 Partially withdraw the rear lower mounting bolt just enough to allow the threaded collar to be screwed in. Securely tighten the rear lower mounting threaded collar to remove all clearance from between the frame, crankcase and collar then fully insert the rear lower mounting bolt again.

39 Fit the nuts to the upper and lower rear mounting bolts and tighten both bolts and the upper left mounting bolt to the specified torque.

40 Tighten the rear lower mounting bolt threaded collar locknut to the specified torque, using the special socket.

41 Remove the right upper mounting bolt and securely tighten the upper threaded collar to remove all clearance between the cylinder head and frame. Install the mounting bolt again and tighten it to the specified torque then tighten the threaded collar locknut to the specified torque.

42 Once all mounting bolts are correctly tightened, tighten the bolts securing the upper rear mounting bracket to the frame to the specified torque setting.

43 The remainder of the installation procedure is the reverse of removal (see Step 33).

5.22a Slacken the mounting bolt collar locknuts . . .

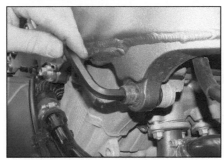

5.22b . . . and back-off the threaded collars

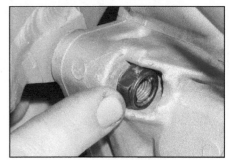

5.29 Install the upper mounting bolt nuts to the cylinder head

F models

44 Ensure the rear upper mounting bracket bolts are loose and the collars for the mounting bolts are fully backed-off to provide maximum clearance for the engine **(see illustration 5.18c)**. If removed, install the left and right-hand spacers in the rear upper mounting bolt location in the engine case.

45 Follow the procedure in Step 35, then insert the lower rear mounting bolt from the left side of the bike.

46 Insert both left-hand upper mounting bolts, the right-hand upper rear mounting bolt and the upper rear mounting bolt.

47 Turn the mounting collar on the lower rear mounting bolt to remove any clearance between the left-hand side of the crankcase and the frame and the right-hand side of the crankcase and the collar. Tighten the left-hand upper rear mounting bolt, and the upper and lower rear mounting bolts to the torque setting specified at the beginning of the Chapter. Tighten the locknut on the lower rear mounting bolt collar to the specified torque.

48 Temporarily remove the right-hand upper rear mounting bolt, then turn the mounting collar to remove any clearance between the engine and the collar. Install the mounting bolt and tighten it to the specified torque, then tighten the collar locknut to the specified torque.

49 Temporarily remove the left-hand upper front mounting bolt, then turn the left and right-hand upper front mounting collars to remove any clearance between the engine and the collars. Install the upper front mounting bolts and tighten them to the specified torque, then tighten the collar locknuts to the specified torque.

50 Tighten the bolts securing the rear upper mounting bracket to the frame to the specified torque.

51 The remainder of the installation procedure is the reverse of removal (see Step 33).

6 Engine disassembly and reassembly – general information

Disassembly

1 Before disassembling the engine, the external surfaces of the unit should be thoroughly cleaned and degreased. This will prevent contamination of the engine internals, and will also make working a lot easier and cleaner. A high flash-point solvent, such as paraffin (kerosene) can be used, or better still, a proprietary engine degreaser. Use old paint-brushes and toothbrushes to work the solvent into the various recesses of the engine casings. Take care to exclude solvent or water from the electrical components and intake and exhaust ports.

 Warning: The use of petrol (gasoline) as a cleaning agent should be avoided because of the risk of fire.

2 When clean and dry, arrange the unit on the workbench, leaving suitable clear area for working. Gather a selection of small containers and plastic bags so that parts can be grouped together in an easily identifiable manner. Some paper and a pen should be on hand to permit notes to be made and labels attached where necessary. A supply of clean shop towels is also required.

3 Before commencing work, read through the appropriate section so that some idea of the necessary procedure can be gained. When removing various engine components it should be noted that great force is seldom required, unless specified. In many cases, a component's reluctance to be removed is indicative of an incorrect approach or removal method. If in any doubt, re-check with the text.

4 When disassembling the engine, keep 'mated' parts together (including gears, cylinders, pistons, valves, etc. that have been in contact with each other during engine operation). These 'mated' parts must be re-used or renewed as an assembly.

5 Engine/transmission disassembly should be done in the following general order with reference to the appropriate Sections.

Remove the camshafts
Remove the cylinder head
Remove the cylinder block
Remove the pistons
Remove the starter motor and alternator (see Chapter 9)
Remove the clutch
Remove the gearchange mechanism
Remove the oil pan
Remove the oil pump and pressure relief valve
Separate the crankcase halves
Remove the crankshaft
Remove the connecting rods
Remove the transmission shafts
Remove the selector drum and forks

7.5 Remove the cylinder head cover bolts

Reassembly

6 Reassembly is accomplished by reversing the general disassembly sequence.

7 Cylinder head cover – removal and installation

Note: *The cylinder head cover can be removed with the engine in the frame.*

Removal

1 Remove the carburettors and secondary air injection system control valve (see Chapter 4). On California models, it will also be necessary to remove the evaporative emission control system control valve.

2 Remove the complete fairing (see Chapter 8) then withdraw the air filter housing intake duct tubes which pass through the frame cutouts.

3 Remove the ignition HT coils (see Chapter 5).

4 Unscrew the retaining bolts and remove the baffle plate **(see illustration 5.12)**, complete with its rubber sealing strips, from the top of the cylinder head cover. If necessary, undo the radiator upper mounting bolts (see Chapter 3) and pivot the radiator forwards slightly to gain the necessary clearance required to manoeuvre the plate out of position.

5 Slacken and remove the six cylinder head cover bolts and lift off sealing washers **(see illustration)**.

6 Carefully lift off the cylinder head cover, taking care not to lose the four locating dowels. Recover the main seal from head and four seals from the spark plug apertures **(see illustrations)**. Renew any seal which shows

7.6a Lift off the cylinder head, taking care not to lose . . .

7.6b . . . the four locating dowels

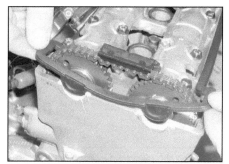

7.6c Recover the main seal . . .

7.6d ... and the four seals from the spark plug apertures

7.8 Apply a small bead of sealant to the semi-circular cutouts

signs of damage or deterioration. If the locating dowels are loose, remove them and store them with the cover for safe-keeping.

Installation

7 Ensure the cylinder head, camshaft cap and cover mating surfaces are clean and dry.
8 Apply a small bead of sealant (Kawasaki recommend the use of Kawasaki Bond 56019-120) to the semi-circular cutouts on each end of the cylinder head then fit the main seal to the cylinder head **(see illustration)**.
9 Ensure the four locating dowels are in position then install the four spark plug aperture seals on the cylinder head.
10 Manoeuvre the cover into position and seat in on the cylinder head.
11 Fit the sealing washers with their flat metal surfaces facing upwards and install the cover bolts, tightening them to the specified torque.
12 Fit the baffle plate, complete with all its sealing strips, to the cover and tighten its retaining bolts to the specified torque. Where necessary, fit the radiator upper mounting bolts and tighten

them to the specified torque (see Chapter 3).
13 Install the ignition HT coils (see Chapter 5).
14 Locate the air filter housing duct tubes in the frame cutouts then install the fairing (see Chapter 8).
15 Fit the secondary air injection valve and the carburettors (see Chapter 4). On California models ensure the evaporative emission system control valve is correctly installed.

8 Camchain tensioner and guides – removal and installation

Caution: The tensioner plunger locks in place as it extends. Once the tensioner bolts have been loosened, the tensioner must be removed from the engine and the plunger reset before the bolts are tightened. If the tensioner bolts are slackened and then retightened without resetting the tensioner plunger, the camchain could be overtensioned, resulting in serious engine damage.

Camchain tensioner

Removal

1 Remove the carburettors (see Chapter 4).
2 Slacken and remove the cap bolt and washer from the tensioner body and withdraw the tensioner spring and rod **(see illustrations)**.
3 Slacken and remove the mounting bolts then withdraw the tensioner from the rear of the cylinder head **(see illustration)**. Remove the O-ring from the tensioner body and discard it; a new one should be used on installation.
Caution: DO NOT turn the engine over whilst the camchain tensioner is removed.
4 Check the operation of the tensioner by pushing the plunger fully back into the tensioner **(see illustration)** and then extending it slowly (see Step 5). As the plunger extends, the stopper should `click' and lock firmly into each of the plunger teeth, preventing the plunger from being pushed back into the body. If this is not the case, the tensioner assembly should be renewed.

Installation

5 Release the stopper and push the plunger fully back into the tensioner body. Slowly extend the plunger from the stopper mechanism and set it so the stopper is engaged with the 5th tooth on the plunger (count the number of `clicks' emitted as the plunger is extended, the plunger will be correctly set after the 5th `click') **(see illustration)**.
6 Fit a new O-ring to the groove in the tensioner body and lubricate it with a smear of engine oil to aid installation.
7 Ensure the plunger is correctly set (stopper on 5th tooth) then fit the tensioner to the cylinder head, making sure the plunger stopper is at the top. Fit the tensioner mounting bolts and tighten them to the specified torque **(see illustration)**.

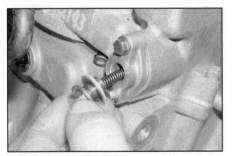

8.2a Remove the cap bolt ...

8.2b ... and withdraw the spring and rod

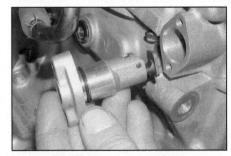

8.3 Withdraw the tensioner

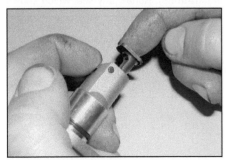

8.4 Push the plunger back into the tension body

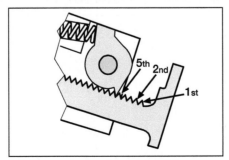

8.5 Ensure the tensioner is set (stopper on the 5th tooth)

8.7 Fit the tensioner mounting bolts

8.13 Remove the two camchain guide bolts

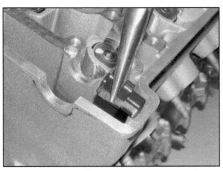

8.19 Remove the camchain front guide

8.20 Position the lower end on to the lug

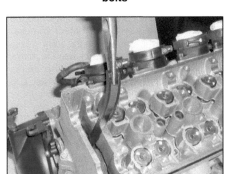

8.23a Retain the guide . . .

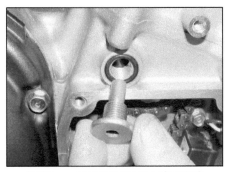

8.23b . . . and remove the pivot bolt

8 Insert the rod into the centre of the tensioner spring then install both components in the tensioner body. Fit the washer and cap bolt, tightening it securely.
9 Using a socket or spanner on the timing rotor bolt, rotate the crankshaft a few rotations in a clockwise direction. As the crankshaft is rotated, the tensioner should be heard to 'click' as the plunger extends and takes up the camchain slack.
10 Install the carburettors (see Chapter 4).

Camchain upper guide

Removal

11 Remove the camchain tensioner as described in Steps 1 to 4.
12 Remove the cylinder head cover (see Section 7).
13 Undo the two bolts and remove the upper guide from the top of the camshaft bearing caps **(see illustration)**.
14 Inspect the guide for signs of wear or damage and renew if necessary.

Installation

15 Fit the guide to the top of the camshaft bearing caps and tighten its retaining bolts to the specified torque.
16 Install the cylinder head cover (see Section 7).
17 Fit the camchain tensioner as described in Steps 6 to 11.

Camchain front guide

Removal

18 Remove the camshafts (see Section 9).
19 Using a pair of pointed-nose pliers, lift the

guide until it is just clear of its lower locating lug (behind the timing rotor) then rotate it 90° clockwise and manoeuvre it out of position **(see illustration)**.

Installation

20 Manoeuvre the guide into position and seat its lower end correctly in the lug on the lower crankcase (located in between the crankshaft and pick-up coil) **(see illustration)**. Seat the upper end of the guide against the cylinder head.
Caution: Serious engine damage could result if the guide is not correctly located.
21 Install the camshafts (see Section 9).

Camchain rear guide

Removal

22 Remove the camshafts (see Section 9).
23 Retain the guide with a pair of pointed nose pliers then unscrew the guide pivot bolt from the crankcase. Remove the bolt and lift out the

9.4a Setting the engine at TDC (ZX-9R C models)

guide. Discard the pivot bolt O-ring, a new one should be used on installation **(see illustrations)**.

Installation

24 Lower the guide down into position and align its pivot with the crankcase bolt hole.
25 Fit a new O-ring then install the pivot bolt, ensuring it passes through the guide pivot, and tighten it to the specified torque.
26 Check the rear guide pivots freely on its bolt then install the camshafts (Section 9).

9 Camshafts and followers – removal, inspection and installation

Removal

1 Disconnect the battery negative terminal (see Chapter 9).
2 Remove the cylinder head cover as described in Section 7.
3 Remove the pick-up coil cover from the right end of the crankshaft (see Chapter 5). Proceed as described under the relevant sub-heading.

C models

4 Using a socket or spanner on the timing rotor bolt, rotate the crankshaft clockwise until the 'T' mark of Nos. 1 and 4 cylinders is aligned with the crankcase mating surface join located to the rear of the rotor **(see illustration)**. Check the position of the 'IN' mark on the intake camshaft sprocket and the 'EX' mark on the exhaust camshaft sprocket **(see illustration)**; the marks should be facing

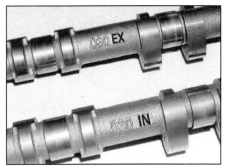

9.4b Identification marks on the camshafts (removed from the engine for clarity)

9.6a Slacken the bearing cap bolts

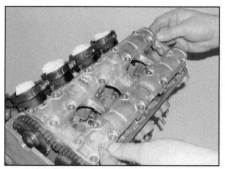

9.6b Lift off the bearing cap

9.9a Remove the follower . . .

9.9b . . . and also the shim

away from each other and both be aligned with the cylinder head upper surface. If the camshaft marks are not correctly positioned, rotate the crankshaft through another 360° (one complete turn) to position them as described. **Note:** *Always turn the engine in the normal direction of rotation (clockwise – viewed from the right end of the engine).*

5 Once the camshafts are correctly positioned, remove the camchain tensioner (see Section 8).

Caution: Do not rotate the crankshaft once the camchain tensioner has been removed.

6 Working in a spiral pattern from the outside inwards, slacken the camshaft bearing cap retaining bolts by a quarter of a turn at a time, to relieve the pressure of the valve springs on the bearing cap assembly gradually and evenly. Whilst slackening the bolts make sure

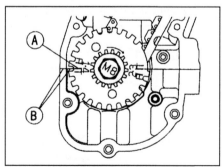

9.10 Setting the engine to TDC
(ZX-9R E and F models)

A TDC mark   B Timing mark

that the cap assembly lifts squarely away from the cylinder head and does not stick on the locating dowels **(see illustration)**. Once the valve spring pressure has been relieved, remove all the bolts (noting the locations of the two longer bolts) and the camchain upper guide. Lift off the bearing cap assembly, taking care not to lose the locating dowels **(see illustration)**.

Caution: If the bearing cap bolts are carelessly loosened and the cap assembly does not come squarely away from the head, it is likely to break. If this happens the complete cylinder head assembly must be renewed; the bearing cap assembly is matched to the cylinder head and cannot be renewed separately.

7 Lift out the camshafts from the cylinder head, noting that they are not interchangeable; the exhaust camshaft is marked '030 EX' and the intake camshaft '030 IN' **(see illustration 9.4b)**. Whilst the camshafts are removed, either wire the chain up or pass an object through it to prevent it falling down into the crankcase. **Note:** *If it is necessary to rotate the crankshaft whilst the camshafts are removed, always pull the chain taut before rotating the crankshaft. If the chain is held not taut, it will become wedged between the crankshaft sprocket and crankcase lug resulting in chain/casing damage.*

8 If the followers are to be removed, obtain a container which is divided into sixteen compartments and label each compartment with the number of its corresponding valve in the cylinder head.

9 Using a magnet, lift each follower out of the cylinder head and store it in its corresponding compartment in the container. Note that the shim is likely to stick to the inside of the follower so take great care not to lose it as the follower is removed. Remove the shims and store each one with its respective follower **(see illustrations)**.

E and F models

10 Using a socket or spanner on the timing rotor bolt, rotate the crankshaft clockwise until the 'T' mark of Nos. 1 and 4 cylinders is aligned with the crankcase mating surface join located to the rear of the rotor **(see illustration)**. Check the position of the 'IN' mark on the intake camshaft sprocket and the 'EX' mark on the exhaust camshaft sprocket (if the engine is in the frame, the front marks will be obscured by the frame – use the marks on the rear of the sprockets); the marks should be facing away from each other and both be aligned with the cylinder head upper surface. If the camshaft marks are not correctly positioned, rotate the crankshaft through another 360° (one complete turn) to position them as described. **Note:** *Always turn the engine in the normal direction of rotation (clockwise – viewed from the right end of the engine).*

11 Working in the **reverse** of the tightening sequence **(see illustration 9.42)**, loosen the camshaft bearing cap bolts by a quarter of a turn at a time to gently relieve valve spring pressure on the caps. Whilst slackening the bolts make sure that each cap lifts squarely away from the cylinder head and does not stick on the locating dowels. Once spring pressure is relieved, remove all the bolts (noting the locations of the four longer bolts) and lift off the bearing caps, taking care not to lose the locating dowels. Note that the bearing caps are different and are not interchangeable; the exhaust camshaft bearing cap is marked 'EX' and the intake camshaft bearing cap 'IN'.

Caution: If the bearing cap bolts are carelessly loosened and the caps do not come squarely away from the head, they are likely to break. If this happens the complete cylinder head assembly must be renewed; the bearing caps are matched to the cylinder head and cannot be renewed separately.

12 Remove the camshafts and followers as described in Steps 7 to 9.

Inspection

 Before renewing the camshafts or cylinder head because of damage, check with local machine shops specialising in motorcycle engine work. In the case of the camshafts, it may be possible for cam lobes to be welded, reground and hardened, at a cost far lower than that of a new camshaft. If

the bearing surfaces in the cylinder head or caps are damaged, it may be possible for them to be bored out to accept bearing inserts. Due to the cost of new components it is recommended that all options be explored.

13 Inspect the cam bearing surfaces, looking for score marks, deep scratches and evidence of pitting. Check the camshaft lobes for heat discoloration (blue appearance), score marks, chipped areas, flat spots and pitting.
14 Camshaft runout can be checked by supporting each end bearing of the camshaft on V-blocks, and measuring any runout at the centre bearing using a dial gauge. If the runout exceeds the specified limit the camshaft must be renewed.
15 Measure the height of each lobe with a micrometer and compare the results to the lobe height service limit listed in this Chapter's Specifications **(see illustration)**. If damage is noted or wear is excessive, the camshaft must be renewed.
16 The camshaft bearing oil clearance should then be checked. There are two possible ways of checking this, the first method by direct measurement (see Steps 17 and 21) and the second by the use of a product known as Plastigauge (see Steps 17 to 21).
17 If the first method is to be used, make sure the locating dowels are in position then fit the camshaft bearing cap(s) to the head. Install the bearing cap bolts and tighten them evenly and progressively to the specified torque (see Steps 31 and 32 for C models or Steps 41 and 42 for E and F models). Measure the diameter of each bearing journal and calculate the oil clearance by subtracting the camshaft bearing journal diameter from the bearing holder journal diameter. Compare the measurements obtained with the service limit given in the Specifications at the start of this Chapter.
18 If the second method is to be used, clean the camshafts and the bearing surfaces in the cylinder head and bearing caps with a clean, lint-free cloth. Ensure all the shims and followers are correctly installed then make sure that the crankshaft is correctly positioned with pistons Nos. 1 and 4 at TDC (see Step 4). Engage the camshafts with the camchain and lay them in place in the cylinder head as described in Steps 28 and 29.
19 Cut strips of Plastigauge and lay one piece on each bearing journal, parallel with the camshaft axis. Make sure the locating dowels are all installed then fit the half-ring to each camshaft bearing. Install bearing cap(s), ensuring the camshafts are not rotated at all, and tighten the retaining bolts to the specified torque (see Steps 31 and 32 for C models or Steps 41 and 42 for E and F models).
20 Now unscrew the bolts (see Step 6 for C models and Step 11 for E and F models) and carefully lift off the camshaft bearing cap(s), again making sure the camshafts are

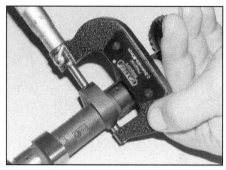

9.15 Measure the height of each lobe

not rotated. To determine the oil clearance, compare the crushed Plastigauge (at its widest point) on each journal to the scale printed on the Plastigauge container.
21 Compare the results to this Chapter's Specifications. If the oil clearance is greater than specified, measure the diameter of the cam bearing journal with a micrometer. If the journal diameter is less than the specified limit, renew the camshaft with a new one and recheck the clearance. If the clearance is still too great, renew the cylinder head assembly.
22 Check the camshaft sprockets for signs of damage such as chipped or missing teeth. If damage is found the camshaft must be renewed.
23 Check each follower for signs of wear or damage to its outer surface and renew any damaged followers. If any follower shows signs of damage, check its cylinder head bore for similar wear; any serious damage will

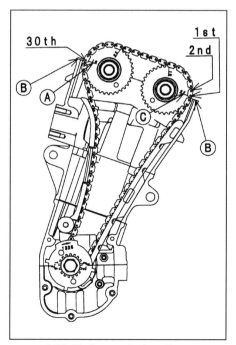

9.29 Timing marks locations

A 'IN' mark
B Cylinder head timing marks
C 'EX' mark

either require a renewal cylinder head or extensive engineering work.

Installation

24 Fit each shim to the top of its correct valve making sure it is correctly seated in the valve spring retainer. **Note:** *It is most important that the shims are returned to their original valves otherwise the valve clearances will be inaccurate.*
25 Lubricate each follower with clean engine oil then install each one in its original location in the cylinder head, making sure its enters its bore squarely.
26 Ensure both the camchain guides are correctly installed then apply a smear of clean engine oil to the cylinder head camshaft bearings and followers.
27 Check that the crankshaft is correctly positioned with pistons Nos. 1 and 4 at TDC (see Step 4) then proceed as described under the relevant sub-heading. **Note:** *If it is necessary to rotate the crankshaft, pull the chain taut before rotating the crankshaft to prevent it becoming wedged between crankshaft sprocket and crankcase lug.*

C models

 HAYNES HINT *If the engine is in the frame, use a scriber/marker pen to make timing marks on the rear of each camshaft sprocket which accurately correspond with those of the front of each sprocket. The rear marks will be much easier to use since they will not be obscured by the frame.*

28 Pull the front run of the camchain taut and engage the exhaust camshaft (see Step 7 for identification details) with the chain so that the 'EX' mark on the sprocket is at the front and is level with the cylinder head upper surface when the camshaft is seated in position.
29 Once the exhaust camshaft is correctly positioned, starting with the camchain link pin located directly above the sprocket 'EX' mark, count back along the camchain until you come to the 30th and 31st pins back from the mark. Engage the intake camshaft with the chain so that its 'IN' mark is positioned in between the 30th and 31st pins **(see illustration)**. Seat the inlet camshaft correctly in the head and check that its 'IN' mark is at the rear and is level with the cylinder head upper surface.
30 Ensure the crankshaft timing mark and both camshaft sprocket timing marks are correctly positioned before proceeding.
31 Ensure the locating dowels are in position then fit the camshaft bearing cap assembly to the cylinder head. Install the retaining bolts and the upper camchain guide, noting that the two longer bolts are fitted in the locating dowel locations (indicated by triangular marks cast on the bearing cap).
32 Tighten all the bearing cap bolts by hand

only then, working in a spiral pattern from the centre outwards, tighten the bolts by a quarter of a turn at a time to gradually draw the camshaft bearing cap assembly into position. Whilst tightening the bolts make sure that the bearing cap assembly is being pulled squarely down onto the cylinder head and is not sticking on the locating dowels. Once the camshaft bearing cap is in contact with the head, go around again in the same sequence and tighten the bolts to the specified torque setting.

Caution: If the bolts are carelessly tightened and the bearing cap assembly is not drawn squarely onto the head, it is likely to break. If this happens the complete cylinder head assembly must be renewed; the camshaft bearing cap assembly is matched to the cylinder head and cannot be renewed separately.

33 Insert a wooden dowel in through the camchain tensioner aperture and push firmly on the camchain rear guide to remove all slack from the camchain (the front and top run of the chain should now be taut).

34 Check the crankshaft 'T' mark of Nos. 1 and 4 cylinders is still correctly aligned with the crankcase mating surface join located to the rear of the rotor and the camshaft sprocket marks are correctly aligned with the cylinder head upper surface (see Step 4). If any of the marks aren't correctly positioned, unbolt the camshaft bearing cap assembly from the cylinder head and repeat the operations in Steps 27 to 33.

35 Once all the marks correctly positioned **(see illustration 9.29)**, fit the camchain tensioner (Section 8).

36 Rotate the crankshaft through a few rotations to settle all disturbed components in position then check and, if necessary, adjust the valve clearances as described in Chapter 1.

37 Lubricate all bearing surfaces with clean engine oil then fit the cylinder head cover (Section 7).

38 Install the pick-up coil cover (Chapter 5) and reconnect the battery.

39 Check the engine oil level (see *Daily(pre-ride) checks)* before starting the engine.

E and F models

40 Engage the camshafts with the camchain as described in Steps 28 to 30.

41 Ensure the locating dowels are in position then fit the camshaft bearing caps in their original locations on the cylinder head (intake camshaft cap in marked 'IN' and the exhaust 'EX'). Install the retaining bolts and the upper camchain guide, noting that the four longer bolts are fitted in the locating dowel locations (indicated by triangular marks cast on the bearing caps).

42 Working in the specified sequence **(see illustration)**, tighten all the bearing cap bolts by hand only then, working in a spiral pattern from the centre outwards, tighten the bolts by a quarter of a turn at a time to gradually draw

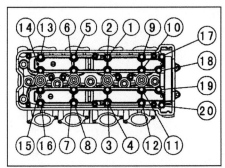

9.42 Camshaft bearing cap tightening sequence

the camshaft bearing caps into position. Whilst tightening the bolts make sure that the bearing caps are being pulled squarely onto the cylinder head and are not sticking on the locating dowels. Once both camshaft bearing caps are in contact with the head, go around again in the same sequence and tighten the bolts to the specified torque setting.

Caution: If the bolts are carelessly tightened and the bearing caps are not drawn squarely onto the head, they are likely to break. If this happens the complete cylinder head assembly must be renewed; the camshaft bearing caps are matched to the cylinder head and cannot be renewed separately.

43 Insert a wooden dowel in through the camchain tensioner aperture and push firmly on the camchain rear guide to remove all slack from the camchain (the front and top run of the chain should now be taut).

44 Check the crankshaft 'T' mark of Nos. 1 and 4 cylinders is still correctly aligned with the crankcase mating surface join located to the rear of the rotor and the camshaft sprocket marks are correctly aligned with the cylinder head upper surface (see Step 10). If any of the marks aren't correctly positioned, unbolt the camshaft bearing cap assembly from the cylinder head and repeat the operations in Steps 40 to 43.

45 Once all the marks correctly positioned, fit the camchain tensioner (Section 8).

46 Rotate the crankshaft through a few rotations to settle all disturbed components in position then check and, if necessary, adjust

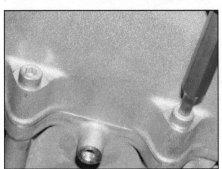

10.6 Remove the two 6 mm bolts

the valve clearances as described in Chapter 1.

47 Lubricate all bearing surfaces with clean engine oil then fit the cylinder head cover (Section 7).

48 Install the pick-up coil cover (Chapter 5) and reconnect the battery.

49 Check the engine oil level (see *Daily (pre-ride) checks)* before starting the engine.

---

10 Cylinder head – removal and installation

Note: It will be necessary to remove the engine from the frame to enable the cylinder head to be removed.
Caution: The engine must be completely cool before beginning this procedure or the cylinder head may become warped.

Removal

1 Remove the engine from the frame (see Section 5).

2 Remove the camshafts and followers (see Section 9).

3 Remove the camchain front guide (see Section 8).

4 Disconnect the wiring connector from the coolant temperature sensor on the rear of the head.

5 Release the retaining clip and disconnect the coolant hose from the thermostat housing.

6 Slacken and remove the two 6 mm bolts from the right end of the cylinder head **(see illustration)**.

7 Working in the **reverse** of the tightening sequence **(see illustration 10.20)**, slacken the ten 10 mm cylinder head bolts by half a turn at a time. Once all pressure is released from the bolts, fully unscrew them and remove along with their sealing washers (all bolts are the same).

8 Free the cylinder head from the cylinder block. If it is stuck, tap around the joint faces of the cylinder head with a soft-faced mallet to free the head. Don't attempt to free the head by inserting a screwdriver between the head and cylinder block – you'll damage the sealing surfaces.

Caution: If the cylinder block is not being removed, great care must be taken not to disturb the cylinder base gasket as the head is freed from the block. If the base gasket joint is disturbed, the block must be removed and the gasket renewed before the cylinder head is installed. Otherwise there is a risk of oil leakage from the base gasket joint.

9 Lift the cylinder head off from the engine **(see illustration)**. As the cylinder head is removed, pass the camchain down through the head then either wire the chain up or pass an object through it to prevent it falling down into the crankcase **(see illustration)**.

10 Remove the oil pipe which is fitted to the right end of the cylinder block **(see**

10.9a Lift the cylinder head off the engine

10.9b Wire up the chain to prevent it from falling into the crankcase

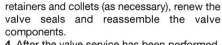

10.10 Remove the oil pipe

illustration). Remove the O-rings from oil pipe and discard them, new ones will be needed on installation.

11 Remove the old head gasket and discard it. If they are loose, remove the cylinder head locating dowels from the cylinder head/block and store them with the head for safe-keeping.

12 Check the cylinder head gasket and the mating surfaces on the cylinder head and block for signs of leakage, which could indicate warpage. Check the flatness of the head as described in Section 12.

Installation

13 Clean all traces of old gasket material from the cylinder head and block. If a scraper is used, take care not to scratch or gouge the soft aluminium. Also ensure that none of the gasket material is allowed to fall into the cylinder bores, oil passages or water jacket.

14 Ensure both cylinder head and block mating surfaces are clean and fit the locating dowels to the cylinder block (if removed). Apply a smear of engine oil to the surface of each cylinder bore.

15 Fit the new head gasket over the locating dowels making sure its the right way up (see illustration).

16 Fit a new O-ring to the groove on each end of the oil pipe. Lubricate both O-rings with a smear of engine oil then ease the pipe fully into position in the cylinder block.

17 Carefully manoeuvre the cylinder head into position, passing the camchain up through the cylinder head tunnel, and lower it into position. Ensure the oil pipe is correctly located in its cylinder head bore then seat the head on the dowels. Either wire the camchain up or pass an object through it to prevent it falling down into the crankcase.

18 Lubricate both sides of the cylinder head bolt washers with clean engine oil. Install all the 10 mm bolts and washers in their original locations (all bolts are the same) and tighten them all by hand.

19 Fit the two 6 mm cylinder head bolts and tighten by hand.

20 Working in the specified sequence (see illustration), tighten the ten 10 mm cylinder head bolts to the specified Stage 1 (first) torque setting.

21 Once the 10 mm bolts have been tightened to the Stage 1 (first) torque, go around again in the specified sequence and tighten the bolts to the Stage 2 (final) torque setting.

22 With the 10 mm bolts correctly tightened, tighten the two 6 mm bolts (numbers 11 and 12 in the tightening sequence) to their specified torque setting.

23 Reconnect the coolant temperature sensor wiring connector and refit the hose to the thermostat housing.

24 Install the camchain front guide (Section 8) then fit the followers and camshafts (Section 9).

25 Install the engine (see Section 5).

11 Valves/valve seats/ valve guides – servicing

1 Because of the complex nature of this job and the special tools and equipment required, most owners leave servicing of the valves, valve seats and valve guides to a professional.

2 The home mechanic can, however, remove the valves from the cylinder head, clean and check the components for wear and assess the extent of the work needed, and, unless a valve service is required, grind in the valves (see Section 12).

3 The dealer or motorcycle engineer will remove the valves and springs, renew the valves and guides, recut the valve seats, check and renew the valve springs, spring

retainers and collets (as necessary), renew the valve seals and reassemble the valve components.

4 After the valve service has been performed, the head will be in like-new condition. When the head is returned, be sure to clean it again very thoroughly before installation on the engine to remove any metal particles or abrasive grit that may still be present from the valve service operations. Use compressed air, if available, to blow out all the holes and passages.

12 Cylinder head and valves – disassembly, inspection and reassembly

1 As mentioned in the previous section, valve servicing, valve seat re-cutting and valve guide renewal should be left to a dealer or motorcycle engineer. However, disassembly, cleaning and inspection of the valves and related components can be done (if the necessary special tools are available) by the home mechanic. This way no expense is incurred if the inspection reveals that overhaul is not required at this time.

2 To disassemble the valve components without the risk of damaging them, a valve spring compressor is absolutely necessary. If the special tool is not available, have a dealer service department or motorcycle repair shop handle the entire process of disassembly, inspection, service or repair (if required) and reassembly of the valves.

10.15 Fit a new cylinder head gasket

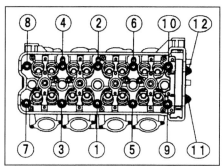

10.20 Tighten the cylinder head bolts in the correct sequence

12.5a Depress the spring . . .

12.5b . . . and remove the collets

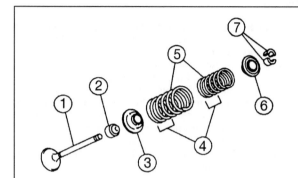

12.5c Valve components

1 Valve stem
2 Oil seal
3 Spring seat
4 Closed coil end
5 Valve springs
6 Retainer
7 Collets

Disassembly

3 Before proceeding, arrange to label and store the valves along with their related components in such a way that they can be returned to their original locations without getting mixed up. A good way to do this is obtain a container which is divided into compartments, and to label each compartment with the identity of the valve which will be stored in it (ie number of cylinder, intake or exhaust side, inner or outer valve). Alternatively, labelled plastic bags will do just as well.

4 If not already done, clean all traces of old gasket material from the cylinder head. If a scraper is used, take care not to scratch or gouge the soft aluminium.

 HAYNES HINT *Refer to Section 7 of Tools and Workshop Tips for details of gasket removal methods.*

5 Compress the valve springs on the first valve with a spring compressor, making sure it is correctly located onto each end of the valve assembly. Do not compress the springs any more than is absolutely necessary. Remove the collets, using either needle-nose pliers, tweezers, a magnet or a screwdriver with a dab of grease on it. Carefully release the valve spring compressor and remove the spring retainer, noting which way up it fits, the springs, the spring seat, and the valve from the head. If the valve binds in the guide (won't pull through), push it back into the head and deburr the area around the collet groove with a very fine file or whetstone (see illustrations).

6 Repeat the procedure for the remaining valves. Remember to keep the parts for each valve together and separate from the other valves so they can be reinstalled in the same location.

7 Once the valves have been removed and labelled, pull the valve stem seals off the top of the valve guides with pliers and discard

them (the old seals should never be reused).
8 Next, clean the cylinder head with solvent and dry it thoroughly. Compressed air will speed the drying process and ensure that all holes and recessed areas are clean.
9 Clean all of the valve springs, collets, retainers and spring seats with solvent and dry them thoroughly. Do the parts from one valve at a time so that no mixing of parts between valves occurs.
10 Scrape off any deposits that may have formed on the valve, then use a motorised wire brush to remove deposits from the valve heads and stems. Again, make sure the valves do not get mixed up.

Inspection

11 Inspect the head very carefully for cracks and other damage. If cracks are found, a new head will be required. Check the cam bearing surfaces for wear and evidence of seizure. Check the camshafts for wear as well (see Section 9).
12 Inspect the outer surfaces of the cam followers for evidence of scoring or other damage. If a follower is in poor condition, it is probable that the bore in which it works is also damaged. Check for clearance between the followers and their bores. If the bores are seriously out-of-round or tapered, the cylinder head and the followers must be renewed.
13 Using a precision straight-edge and a feeler gauge set to the warpage limit listed in the specifications at the beginning of the Chapter, check the head gasket mating surface for warpage. Refer to Section 3 of *Tools and Workshop Tips* in the *Reference* section for details of how to use the straight-edge (see illustration).
14 Examine the valve seats in the combustion chamber. If they are pitted, cracked or burned, the head will require work beyond the scope of the home mechanic. Measure the valve seat width and compare it to this Chapter's Specifications. If it exceeds the service limit, or if it varies around its circumference, valve overhaul is required.
15 Measure the valve stem diameter (see illustration). Clean the valve guides to remove any carbon build-up, then measure the inside diameters of the guides (at both ends and the centre of the guide) with a small-bore gauge and micrometer (see

12.13 Checking for warpage

12.15a Measure the valve stem diameter

12.15b Insert a small hole gauge into the valve guide and expand it so there's a slight drag when it's pulled out

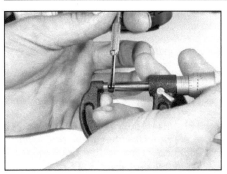

12.15c Measure the small hole gauge with a micrometer

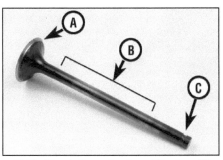

12.16 Check the valve face (A), stem (B) and collet groove (C) for signs of wear and damage

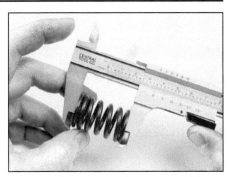

12.17a Measure the free length of the valve springs

illustrations). The guides are measured at the ends and at the centre to determine if they are worn in a bell-mouth pattern (more wear at the ends). If the valve stem or guide is worn beyond its limit, or if the guide is worn unevenly, it must be renewed.

16 Carefully inspect each valve face for cracks, pits and burned spots. Check the valve stem and the collet groove area for cracks. Rotate the valve and check for any obvious indication that it is bent. Check the end of the stem for pitting and excessive wear **(see illustration)**. The presence of any of the above conditions indicates the need for valve servicing. The stem end can be ground down, provided that the amount of stem above the collet groove after grinding is sufficient.

17 Check the end of each valve spring for wear and pitting. Measure the spring free length and compare it to that listed in the

specifications **(see illustration)**. If any spring is shorter than specified it has sagged and must be renewed. Also place the spring upright on a flat surface and check it for bend by placing a ruler against it **(see illustration)**. If the bend in any spring is excessive, it must be renewed.

18 Check the spring retainers and collets for obvious wear and cracks. Any questionable parts should not be reused, as extensive damage will occur in the event of failure during engine operation.

19 If the inspection indicates that no overhaul work is required, the valve components can be reinstalled in the head.

Reassembly

20 Unless a valve service has been performed, before installing the valves in the

head they should be ground in (lapped) to ensure a positive seal between the valves and seats. This procedure requires coarse and fine valve grinding compound and a valve grinding tool. If a grinding tool is not available, a piece of rubber or plastic hose can be slipped over the valve stem (after the valve has been installed in the guide) and used to turn the valve.

21 Apply a small amount of coarse grinding compound to the valve face, then slip the valve into the guide **(see illustration)**. Note: *Make sure each valve is installed in its correct guide and be careful not to get any grinding compound on the valve stem.*

22 Attach the grinding tool (or hose) to the valve and rotate the tool between the palms of your hands. Use a back-and-forth motion (as though rubbing your hands together) rather than a circular motion (ie so that the valve rotates alternately clockwise and anti-clockwise rather than in one direction only) **(see illustration)**. Lift the valve off the seat and turn it at regular intervals to distribute the grinding compound properly. Continue the grinding procedure until the valve face and seat contact area is of uniform width and unbroken around the entire circumference of the valve face and seat **(see illustrations)**.

23 Carefully remove the valve from the guide and wipe off all traces of grinding compound. Use solvent to clean the valve and wipe the seat area thoroughly with a solvent soaked cloth.

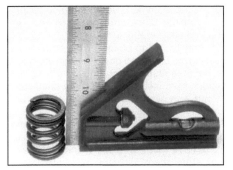

12.17b Check the valve springs for squareness

12.21 Apply the lapping compound very sparingly, in dabs, to the valve face only

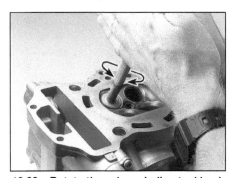

12.22a Rotate the valve grinding tool back and forth between the palms of your hands

12.22b The valve face and seat should show a uniform unbroken ring . . .

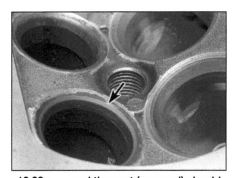

12.22c . . . and the seat (arrowed) should be the specified width all the way round

12.25a Fit the spring seat . . .

12.25b . . . and fit the valve stem seal

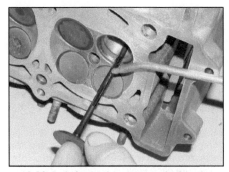

12.26 Lubricate the stem and slide the valve into its correct location

12.27a Fit the inner spring . . .

the valves can't contact the workbench top, then very gently tap each of the valve stems with a soft-faced hammer. This will help seat the collets in their grooves.

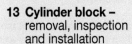 *Check for proper sealing of the valves by pouring a small amount of solvent into each of the valve ports. If the solvent leaks past any valve into the combustion chamber area the valve grinding operation on that valve should be repeated.*

13 Cylinder block –
removal, inspection and installation

Note: *It will be necessary to remove the engine from the frame to enable the cylinder block to be removed.*

Removal

1 Remove the engine from the frame (see Section 5).
2 Remove the cylinder head (see Section 10).
3 Remove the camchain rear guide (see Section 8).
4 Slacken the retaining clips and detach the hoses from the coolant outlet union on the rear of the cylinder block. Undo the retaining bolts and remove the coolant outlet and seal; discard the seal a new one should be used on installation.
5 Free the cylinder block from the crankcase. If it's stuck, tap around its perimeter with a soft-faced hammer. Don't attempt to pry between the block and the crankcase, as you'll ruin the sealing surfaces.
6 Carefully lift the block off the crankcase, passing the camchain down through the block tunnel (see illustration). Prior to freeing the pistons from their bores, stuff the crankcase mouth with clean. lint-free cloth to prevent any debris from falling into the crankcase.
7 Remove the cylinder block base gasket and discard it. If the locating dowels are a loose-fit, remove them from the block/crankcase and store them with the block for safe-keeping.

24 Repeat the procedure with fine valve grinding compound, then repeat the entire procedure for the remaining valves.
25 Fit the spring seat for the first valve in place in the cylinder head then install new valve stem seal onto the guide (**see illustrations**). Use an appropriate size deep socket to push the seal over the end of the valve guide until it is felt to clip into place. Don't twist or cock it, or it will not seal properly against the valve stem. Also, don't remove it again or it will be damaged.
26 Coat the valve stem with engine oil, then install it into its guide, rotating it slowly to avoid damaging the seal (**see illustration**). Check that the valve moves up and down freely in the guide.
27 Install the inner and outer springs, ensuring both springs are fitted with their closer-wound coils facing down into the

cylinder head (**see illustrations**). Ensure both springs are correctly located on the seat then fit the spring retainer, with its shouldered side facing down so that it fits into the top of the springs (**see illustration**).
28 Apply a small amount of grease to the collets to help hold them in place. Compress the springs with the valve spring compressor and install the collets (**see illustration**). When compressing the springs, depress only as far as is absolutely necessary to slip the collets into place. Make certain that the collets are securely locked in the retaining groove then carefully release the spring compressor.
29 Repeat the procedure for the remaining valves. Remember to keep the parts for each valve together and separate from the other valves so they can be reinstalled in the same location.
30 Support the cylinder head on blocks so

12.27b . . . the outer spring . . .

12.27c . . . and the retainer

12.28 Install the collets

Inspection

8 Check the cylinder bores carefully for scratches and score marks.

9 Using the appropriate precision measuring tools, check each cylinder bore diameter. Measure 10 mm down from the top of the bore and 60 mm down from the top of the bore, parallel to the crankshaft axis. Next, measure each cylinder's diameter at the same two locations across the crankshaft axis. Compare the results to this Chapter's Specifications. If the cylinder bores are tapered, out-of-round, worn beyond the specified limits, or badly scuffed or scored, new pistons and cylinder liners (C models) or a new cylinder block (E and F models) will have to be fitted (Kawasaki do not manufacture oversize pistons). **Note:** *On C models, cylinder liner renewal should be entrusted to a Kawasaki dealer or suitable equipped workshop with the necessary tools and facilities.*

10 As an alternative, if the precision measuring tools are not available, a dealer service department or motorcycle repair shop will make the measurements and offer advice concerning servicing of the cylinder bores.

11 If the cylinder bores are in reasonably good condition and not worn to the outside of the limits, and if the piston-to-cylinder clearances can be maintained properly (see Section 14), then the cylinder liners/block (as applicable) will not have to be renewed; hone the bores and fit new piston rings.

12 To perform the honing operation you will need the proper size flexible hone with fine stones, or a 'bottle brush'-type hone, plenty of light oil or honing oil, some shop towels and an electric drill motor. Hold the cylinder block in a vice (cushioned with soft jaws or wood blocks) when performing the honing operation. Mount the hone in the drill motor, compress the stones and slip the hone into the cylinder. Lubricate the cylinder thoroughly, turn on the drill and move the hone up and down in the cylinder bore at a pace which will produce a fine crosshatch pattern on the cylinder wall with the crosshatch lines intersecting at approximately a 60° angle **(see illustration)**. Be sure to use plenty of lubricant and do not take off any more material than is absolutely necessary to produce the desired effect. Do not withdraw the hone from the cylinder while it is running. Instead, shut off the drill and continue moving the hone up and down in the cylinder until it comes to a complete stop, then compress the stones and withdraw the hone. Wipe the oil out of the cylinder and repeat the procedure on the remaining cylinder. Remember, do not remove too much material from the cylinder bore. If you do not have the tools, or do not desire to perform the honing operation, a dealer service department or motorcycle repair shop will generally do it for a reasonable fee.

13 Next, the cylinder bores must be thoroughly washed with warm soapy water to

13.6 Lift off the cylinder block

remove all traces of the abrasive grit produced during the honing operation. Be sure to run a brush through the bolt holes and flush them with running water. After rinsing, dry the cylinder bores thoroughly and apply a coat of light, rust-preventative oil to all machined surfaces.

Installation

Note: *Cylinder block installation will be considerably easier if access to a set of piston ring compressors can be gained.*

14 Obtain two lengths of 10 mm threaded rod, approximately 200 mm in length or alternatively obtain two cylinder head bolts and cut their heads off. These can be used to ensure the cylinder block is lowered squarely onto the pistons.

15 Ensure the crankcase and cylinder block mating surfaces are clean and dry then install the locating dowels in the crankcase.

16 Manoeuvre the new base gasket over the pistons and seat it on the locating dowels, ensuring it is fitted the correct way up **(see illustration)**.

17 Screw the two 10 mm rods/bolts into the diagonally-opposite outer cylinder head bolt threads to form the guides for the cylinder block.

18 Ensure the piston ring end gaps are all correctly spaced (see Section 15) then lubricate the rings with clean engine oil **(see illustration)**. If a set of piston ring compressors are available, fit the compressors to the pistons and clamp the rings in position.

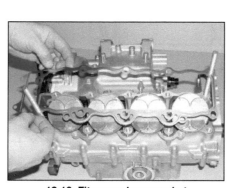

13.16 Fit a new base gasket

13.12 Honing the cylinders with a bottle-brush type hone

19 Position the crankshaft so all pistons are level then lubricate the cylinder bores with plenty of clean engine oil.

20 With the aid of an assistant, carefully lower the cylinder block down over the guide rods/bolts and seat the piston crowns in the base of the liners. Ensure all four pistons remain square then gently ease the cylinder block onto the pistons until the bottom of the cylinder liners slides down past the piston rings.

Caution: If piston ring compressors are not being used, ensure the piston rings do not snag and break as the pistons enter the cylinder liners. The base of each cylinder liner is chamfered to ease installation but great care is still needed.

21 Once all four sets of pistons are correctly located in their bores, remove the piston ring compressors (where fitted) and pass the camchain up through the cylinder block tunnel. Slide the block fully down the pistons, seating it on the locating dowels, and wire the camchain up or pass an object through it to prevent it falling down into the crankcase.

22 Fit a new seal to the coolant outlet groove and fit the outlet to the front of the block. Ensure the seal is correctly fitted then securely tighten the coolant outlet union bolts. Reconnect the hoses to the outlet and securely tighten the retaining clips.

23 Fit the camchain rear guide (Section 8).

24 Remove the guide bolts and install the cylinder head (Section 10).

25 Fit the engine to the frame (Section 5).

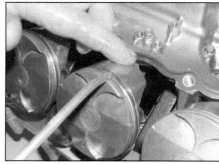

13.18 Lubricate the piston rings with oil

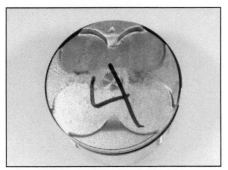

14.4a Mark the top of each piston with its cylinder number

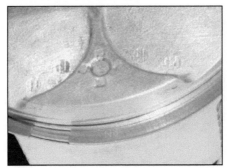

14.4b The circular mark cast into the front of the piston

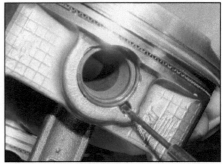

14.5 Prise out the circlip

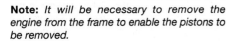

14 Pistons –
removal, inspection and installation

Note: *It will be necessary to remove the engine from the frame to enable the pistons to be removed.*

Removal

1 Remove the engine from the frame (see Section 5).
2 Remove the cylinder head and block (see Sections 10 and 13).
3 Before removing the pistons from the rods, stuff a clean, lint-free cloth into each

14.6a Push out the piston pin

crankcase hole, around the connecting rods. This will prevent the circlips from falling into the crankcase if they are inadvertently dropped.
4 Using a sharp scriber (or a marker pen if the piston is clean enough), mark the number of each piston on its crown **(see illustration)**. Each piston should also have a circular mark cast into the front of its crown **(see illustration)**. If not, scribe an arrow into the piston crown before removal.
5 Support the piston and prise one of the circlips out with a small, flat-bladed screwdriver **(see illustration)** and discard it; circlips must never be re-used.
6 Push the piston pin out from the opposite end to free the piston from the rod **(see illustration)**. You may have to deburr the area around the groove to enable the pin to slide out. If the pin won't come out, you can fabricate a piston pin removal tool from a long bolt, a nut, a piece of tubing and washers **(see illustration)**. Repeat the procedure for the remaining pistons.

Inspection

7 Before the inspection process can be carried out, the pistons must be cleaned and the old piston rings removed.
8 Using a piston ring removal and installation tool, carefully remove the rings from the

pistons **(see illustration)**. Do not nick or gouge the pistons in the process.
9 Scrape all traces of carbon from the tops of the pistons. A hand-held wire brush or a piece of fine emery cloth can be used once most of the deposits have been scraped away. Do not, under any circumstances, use a wire brush mounted in a drill motor to remove deposits from the pistons; the piston material is soft and will be eroded away by the wire brush.
10 Use a piston ring groove cleaning tool to remove any carbon deposits from the ring grooves. If a tool is not available, a piece broken off an old ring will do the job. Be very careful to remove only the carbon deposits. Do not remove any metal and do not nick or gouge the sides of the ring grooves.
11 Once the deposits have been removed, clean the pistons with solvent and dry them thoroughly. Make sure the oil return holes below the oil ring grooves are clear.
12 If the pistons are not damaged or worn excessively and if the cylinders liners/block (as applicable) are not to be renewed, new pistons will not be necessary. Normal piston wear appears as even, vertical wear on the thrust surfaces of the piston and slight looseness of the top ring in its groove. New piston rings, on the other hand, should always be used when an engine is rebuilt and the bores should be honed (see Section 13).
13 Carefully inspect each piston for cracks around the skirt, at the pin bosses and at the ring lands.
14 Look for scoring and scuffing on the thrust faces of the skirt, holes in the piston

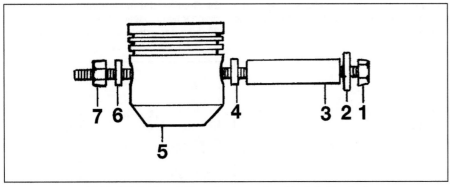

14.6b Fabricate a piston pin removal and installation tool

1	*Bolt*	*3*	*Pipe (A)*	*5*	*Piston*	*7*	*Nut (B)*
2	*Washer*	*4*	*Padding (A)*	*6*	*Washer (B)*		

A Large enough for piston pin to fit inside   *B Small enough to fit through piston pin bore*

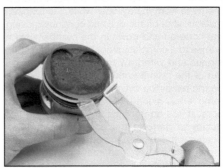

14.8 Removing the piston rings using a ring removal/installation tool

14.15 Measure the piston ring-to-groove clearance using a feeler gauge

14.16 Measure the piston diameter at the specified distance from the bottom of the skirt using a micrometer

crown and burned areas at the edge of the crown. If the skirt is scored or scuffed, the engine may have been suffering from overheating and/or abnormal combustion, which caused excessively high operating temperatures. The oil pump and oil cooler should be checked thoroughly. A hole in the piston crown, an extreme to be sure, is an indication that abnormal combustion (pre-ignition) was occurring. Burned areas at the edge of the piston crown are usually evidence of spark knock (detonation). If any of the above problems exist, the causes must be corrected or the damage will occur again.

15 Measure the piston ring-to-groove clearance by fitting a new piston ring in the ring groove and slipping a feeler gauge in beside it **(see illustration)**. Check the clearance at three or four locations around the groove. Be sure to use the correct ring for each groove; they are different (see Section 15). If the clearance is greater than the service limit, new pistons will have to be used when the engine is reassembled.

16 Calculate the piston-to-bore clearance by measuring the bore (see Section 13) and the piston diameter. Make sure that the pistons and cylinders are correctly matched. Measure the piston across the skirt on the thrust faces at a 90° angle to the piston pin, 5 mm up from the bottom of the skirt **(see illustration)**. Subtract the piston diameter from the bore diameter to obtain the clearance. If it is greater than specified in the Specifications at the beginning of this Chapter, new pistons and cylinder liners (C models) or a new

cylinder block (E and F models) will have to be fitted (Kawasaki do not manufacture oversize pistons).

17 Apply clean engine oil to the pin, insert it into the piston and check for freeplay by rocking the pin back-and-forth. If the pin is loose, new pistons and pins must be installed.

18 Install the rings on the pistons as described in Section 15.

Installation

19 Check that each piston has one new circlip fitted to it and that it is correctly seated in the piston groove with its end gap away from the removal notch in the piston. Insert the piston pin from the opposite side. If it is a tight fit, the piston should be warmed first. If the original pistons are being installed, use the marks made on disassembly to ensure each piston is fitted in its correct location.

20 Lubricate the piston pin and connecting rod small-end bores with clean engine oil.

21 Stuff a clean, lint-free cloth into each crankcase hole, around the connecting rods. This will prevent the circlips from falling into the crankcase if they are inadvertently dropped.

22 Fit the piston to its respective connecting rod making sure that the circular mark cast into the crown of the piston is at the front.

23 Push the piston pin through both piston bosses and the connecting rod bore. If necessary the pin can be tapped carefully into position, using a hammer and suitable drift, whilst supporting the connecting rod and piston. Secure the piston pin in position with a

second new circlip, making sure it is correctly seated in the piston groove with its end gap away from the removal notch in the piston.

24 Once all pistons are correctly installed, fit the cylinder block and head (Sections 13 and 10).

25 Install the engine in the frame (Section 5).

15 Piston rings – installation

1 Before installing new piston rings, their end gaps must be checked.

2 Lay out the new ring sets so the rings will be matched with the same piston and cylinder during the end gap measurement procedure and engine assembly.

3 Insert the top ring into the bottom of the first cylinder and square it up with the cylinder walls by pushing it in with the top of the piston. The ring should be about 25 mm up from the bottom of the cylinder. To measure the end gap, slip a feeler gauge between the ends of the ring and compare the measurement to that given in the Specifications at the beginning of this Chapter **(see illustration)**.

4 If the gap is larger or smaller than specified, double check to make sure that you have the correct rings before proceeding.

5 Repeat the procedure for each ring that will be installed in the first cylinder and for each ring in the remaining cylinders. Remember to keep the rings, pistons and cylinders matched up.

6 Once the ring end gaps have been checked/corrected, the rings can be installed on the pistons.

7 The oil control ring (lowest on the piston) is installed first. It is composed of three separate components. Slip the expander into the groove, then install the lower side rail **(see illustrations)**. Do not use a piston ring installation tool on the oil ring side rails as they may be damaged. Instead, place one end of the side rail into the groove between the expander and the ring land. Hold it firmly in place and slide a finger around the piston while pushing the rail into the groove. Next, install the upper side rail in the same manner.

15.3 Check the piston ring end gap with a feeler gauge

15.7a Installing the oil ring expander – make sure the ends don't overlap

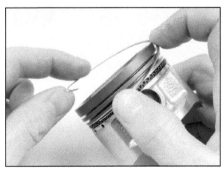

15.7b Installing an oil ring side rail – don't use a ring installation tool to do this

15.9 Fit the second (middle) ring into the middle groove in the piston

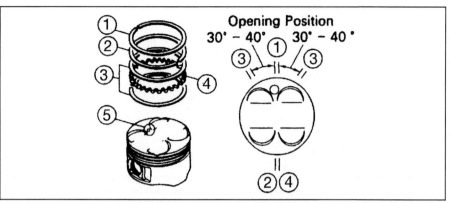

15.11 Ring gap positioning details

1 Top ring
2 Second ring
3 Oil ring side rails

4 Oil ring expander
5 Cast mark (points to the front of the engine)

8 After the three oil ring components have been installed, check to make sure that both the upper and lower side rails can be turned smoothly in the ring groove.

9 Install the second (middle) ring next **(see illustration)**. **Note:** *The second ring and top ring are different and cannot be interchanged. The second ring is easily identified by its* tapered outer edge. To avoid breaking the ring, use a piston ring installation tool and make sure that the ring is fitted the correct way up with its widest point at the bottom and its identification mark (RN) facing up. Fit the ring into the middle groove on the piston. Do not expand the ring any more than is necessary to slide it into place.

10 Finally, install the top ring in the same manner. Make sure the identification mark (R) is facing up.

11 With the piston rings correctly installed, check that each ring is free to rotate easily in its groove. Check the ring-to-groove clearance of each ring using feeler gauges and check that the clearance is within the specified range then position the ring end gaps as shown **(see illustration)**.

12 Repeat the procedure for the remaining pistons and rings.

16.4 Clutch details

1 Clutch cover
2 Gasket
3 Damper
4 Damper cover
5 Washer
6 Needle bearing
7 Lifter
8 Friction plate
9 Plain plate
10 Anti-judder spring
11 Spring seat
12 Clutch centre
13 Spacer
14 Clutch drum
15 Bush
16 Needle bearing
17 Spacer
18 Pressure plate bolt
19 Spring seat
20 Spring
21 Clutch centre nut
22 Washer
23 Pressure plate

16 Clutch – removal, inspection and installation

Note: *The clutch assembly can be removed with the engine in the frame. If the engine has been removed, a clutch centre holding tool will be required to enable the centre nut to be slackened (see Step 12).*

Removal

1 Remove the lower fairing and the right middle fairing panel (see Chapter 8).

2 Drain the engine oil (see Chapter 1). Once the oil has drained, fit a new sealing washer to the drain plug and tighten it to the specified torque.

3 Slacken the clutch cable locknut and adjuster nut then free the lower end of the cable from its mounting bracket and detach the inner cable from the release arm **(see illustrations 17.2a, b, c)**.

4 Working in a criss-cross pattern, evenly slacken and remove the clutch cover retaining bolts along with the cable bracket **(see illustration)**.

5 Pivot the release arm approximately 90° anti-clockwise, to free it from the clutch lifter,

16.5 Remove the clutch cover

16.7 Remove the clutch spring retaining bolts

16.9a Remove the thrust washer . . .

16.9b . . . the needle bearing . . .

16.9c . . . and the clutch lifter

16.10a Remove the friction plates . . .

16.10b . . . and plain plates

and remove the clutch cover from the engine **(see illustration)**. Be prepared to catch any residual oil which may be released as the cover is removed.

6 Remove the clutch cover gasket and discard it. Note the two locating dowels fitted to the crankcase; remove these for safe-keeping if they are loose.

7 Working in a criss-cross pattern, gradually slacken the clutch spring retaining bolts until spring pressure is released. Unscrew the bolts and remove them along with the collars and springs **(see illustration)**.

8 Remove the pressure plate from the clutch.

9 Withdraw the thrust washer, needle bearing

and clutch lifter from the centre of the input shaft **(see illustrations)**.

10 Withdraw the clutch friction plates and plain plates **(see illustrations)**.

11 Remove the anti-judder spring and spring seat from the clutch centre, noting which way around the spring is fitted **(see illustrations)**.

12 To slacken the clutch centre nut the input shaft/clutch centre must be locked in one of the following ways.

a) If the engine is in the frame, lock the clutch through the transmission, by selecting top gear and applying the rear brake hard whilst the nut is slackened.

b) Retain the clutch centre with Kawasaki

16.11a Remove the anti-judder spring . . .

16.11b . . . and the anti-judder spring seat

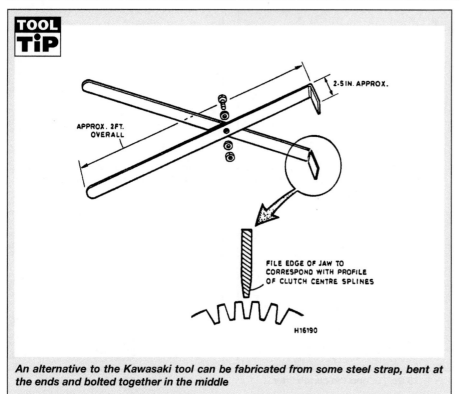

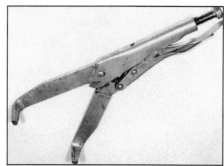

16.12a Special tool used to keep the clutch hub from turning

16.12b Removing the centre nut while using the special holding tool

An alternative to the Kawasaki tool can be fabricated from some steel strap, bent at the ends and bolted together in the middle

service tool (57001-1243) or a universal clutch centre holding tool (available from most good motorcycle accessory dealers). Alternatively, a clutch centre

holding tool can be fabricated from some steel strap, bent at the ends and bolted together in the middle (see Tool Tip and illustrations).

13 Remove the centre nut and discard it; a new one must be used on installation (see illustration).
14 Remove the dished washer, noting which way around it is fitted (see illustration).
15 Remove the clutch centre (see illustration).
16 Slide the large washer off from the input shaft (see illustration).
17 Support the clutch drum then withdraw the centre bush and needle roller bearing. The bush has two threaded holes to ease installation, screw a 4 mm bolt into each of the holes and use the bolts to draw out the bush (see illustrations).
18 Manoeuvre the clutch drum out of position. Remove the oil pump drive gear from the rear of the clutch drum, noting which way around it is fitted (see illustrations).

16.13 Remove the centre nut

16.14 Remove the dished washer

16.15 Remove the clutch centre

16.16 Remove the washer from the input shaft

16.17a Screw in two 4 mm bolts into the bush . . .

16.17b . . . and withdraw the needle roller bearing

16.18a Manoeuvre the clutch drum out of position

16.18b Remove the oil pump drive gear

19 Slide the spacer off the input shaft, noting which way around it is fitted (see illustration).

Inspection

20 After an extended period of service the clutch friction plates will wear and promote clutch slip. Measure the thickness of each friction plate using a vernier caliper and check for warpage using a flat surface and feeler gauges (see illustration). If any plate has worn to or beyond the service limit or exceeds the maximum permissible amount of warpage, all the friction plates should be renewed as a set.

21 The plain plates should not show any signs of excess heating (bluing). Check for warpage using a flat surface and feeler gauges (see illustration). If any plate exceeds the maximum permissible amount of warpage, or shows signs of bluing, all plain plates must be renewed as a set. Note: Plain plates are available in three different thicknesses (2.0, 2.3 and 2.6 mm) to enable the clutch plate assembly thickness to be correctly set (see Step 40). Ensure that the new plates ordered are the same thickness as those being renewed.

22 Inspect the clutch assembly for burrs and indentations on the edges of the protruding tangs of the friction plates and/or slots in the edge of the clutch drum with which they engage. Similarly check for wear between the inner tangs of the plain plates and the slots in the clutch centre. Wear of this nature will cause clutch drag and slow disengagement during gear shifting, since the plates will snag when the pressure plate is lifted. With care, a small amount of wear can be corrected by dressing with a fine file, but if this is excessive the worn components must be renewed.

23 Also inspect the anti-judder spring and seat for signs of wear or distortion and renew if necessary.

24 Inspect the input shaft, centre bush and clutch drum bearing surfaces, along with the needle bearing, for signs of wear and damage. If any component shows signs of wear or damage, it must be renewed.

25 Check the clutch lifter, needle bearing and thrust washer for signs of wear or damage and renew any worn component.

26 Measure the free length of each clutch spring (see illustration). If any one has settled to less than the service limit, the clutch

16.19 Slide the spacer off the input shaft

springs must be renewed as a set.

27 Check that the clutch release arm pivots smoothly in the cover and the oil seal shows no sign of leakage. If necessary, withdraw the arm from the cover noting the correct fitted location of the return spring, then carefully lever the oil seal out from the cover. Check all components for signs of wear or damage, paying particular attention to the arm and needle bearings. Renew the oil seal, regardless of its apparent condition, and renew any other worn component. Note that bearing renewal is a delicate operation and is best entrusted to a Kawasaki dealer or a suitably equipped engineering shop. Lubricate the bearings with molybdenum disulphide grease then press a new oil seal into the top of the cover, ensuring its sealing lip is facing inwards. Lubricate the oil seal lip with a smear of multi-purpose grease then ease the release arm and return spring into

16.21 Check the plain plates for warpage

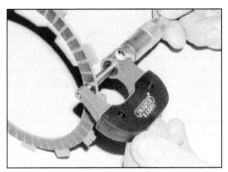

16.20 Check the friction plates for wear

position. Ensure the return spring is correctly engaged with the arm then check the arm pivots freely in the cover.

Installation

28 Remove all traces of gasket from the crankcase and cover sealing surfaces.

29 Slide the spacer onto the input shaft making sure its stepped surface is facing inwards (flat surface facing outwards).

30 Fit the oil pump drive gear to the rear of the clutch drum ensuring the gear flange is facing the drum.

31 Lubricate the centre bush and needle roller bearing with clean engine oil then manoeuvre the clutch drum into position. Ensure the drum is correctly engaged with the primary drive gear and oil pump gear then slide the centre bush and needle roller bearing into position. Ensure the centre bush is fitted with its threaded holes facing outwards.

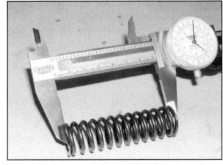

16.26 Measure the spring free length

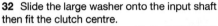
16.36 Engage the tangs with the cutouts

16.41 Apply sealant to the crankcase half joints

32 Slide the large washer onto the input shaft then fit the clutch centre.

33 Fit the dished washer with its 'OUTSIDE' marking facing outwards.

34 Fit the new clutch centre nut and tighten it to the specified torque setting whilst holding the clutch centre using the method employed on removal.

35 Fit the spring seat to the clutch centre followed by the anti-judder spring. **Note:** *The anti-judder spring must be fitted with its convex side facing the spring seat.*

36 Install the first friction plate, aligning its tangs with the slots in the clutch drum, then slide on one of the plain plates, engaging its inner tangs with the slots in the clutch centre. Alternately install all the remaining friction and plain plates, noting that the outer friction plate must be fitted so that its tangs are engaged with the cutouts in the drum housing, not the slots **(see illustration)**. **Note:** *If new clutch plates are being fitted, apply a coating of engine oil to their surfaces to prevent seizure.*

37 Lubricate the clutch lifter, needle bearing and thrust washer bearing surfaces with a smear of molybdenum disulphide grease. Insert the clutch lifter in the input shaft end and fit the bearing and thrust washer.

38 Fit the pressure plate ensuring its inner tangs are correctly engaged with the clutch centre.

39 Fit the clutch springs and install the collars and retaining bolts. Gradually tighten the bolts evenly in a criss-cross pattern until they are all tightened to the specified torque.

40 Once the clutch is correctly assembled, it is necessary to check the clutch plate

assembly thickness. Measure the thickness of the friction and plain plates (distance from the clutch centre outer face to the pressure plate inner face) and compare this to the thickness given in the Specifications. If the thickness is not within the specified range, the clutch assembly will need to be dismantled and the thickness of each of the plain plates measured (see Step 21). Calculate the thickness of the new plain plate(s) required to bring the clutch plate assembly within the specified limits. **Note:** *Standard plain plates are 2.3 mm thick with 2.0 mm and 2.6 mm thick plates produced to facilitate adjustment. When adjusting the thickness note that Kawasaki state that 2.0 mm and 2.6 mm thick plates should not be fitted in the same assembly.* Obtain the necessary plain plate(s) required and reassemble the clutch.

Caution: If the clutch plate assembly thickness is not correctly set, the clutch operation will be adversely affected.

41 Once the clutch plate assembly thickness is correctly set, ensure the mating surfaces are clean and dry then apply a smear of sealant (Kawasaki recommend the use of Kawasaki Bond 56019-120) to the area of the cover mating surface on each side of the crankcase half joints **(see illustration)**. Fit both locating dowels to the crankcase and locate the new gasket on the dowels.

42 Hold the release lever outwards then manoeuvre the clutch cover into position and locate it on the dowels. Pivot the release lever in a clockwise direction to engage it with the clutch lifter then install the cover retaining bolts, not forgetting the clutch cable bracket.

Tighten all bolts by hand then go around and tighten them evenly and progressively to the specified torque setting.

43 Connect the clutch cable to the release arm and seat the outer cable in its bracket. Adjust the clutch cable as described in Chapter 1.

44 Fill the engine with the correct type and amount of oil as described in Chapter 1.

45 Fit the middle and lower fairing (see Chapter 8).

17 Clutch cable – removal and installation

Removal

1 Remove the lower fairing and the right middle fairing panel (see Chapter 8).

2 Free the rubber gaiter then slacken the clutch cable locknut and adjuster nut. Free the lower end of the cable from its mounting bracket and detach the inner cable from the clutch release arm **(see illustrations)**.

3 Slacken the locknut (where necessary) and screw the upper adjuster fully into the clutch lever mounting bracket, aligning the adjuster and locknut slots with the mounting bracket slot.

4 Free the outer cable from the lever mounting bracket and detach the inner cable from the lever.

5 Note the correct routing of the cable then free it from its retaining clamps and guides and remove it from the bike.

6 Examine the cable, looking for worn end fittings or a damaged outer casing, and for signs of fraying of the inner cable. Check the cable's operation; the inner cable should move smoothly and easily through the outer casing. Remember that a cable that appears serviceable when tested off the bike may well be much heavier in operation when in its working position. If necessary, lubricate the cable as described in Chapter 1.

Installation

7 Manoeuvre the cable into position, ensuring it is correctly routed around the fairing mounting bracket and headstock and through

17.2a Slacken the locknut and adjuster nut . . .

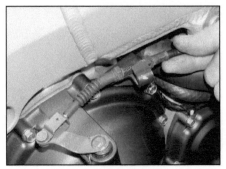
17.2b . . . free the cable from it's mounting bracket . . .

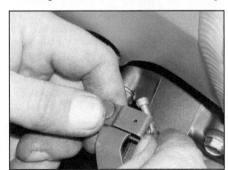
17.2c . . . and detach the cable from the release arm

18.1 Separate the rotor and the driven gear

18.3 Check that the starter clutch won't turn anticlockwise (A),
but turns freely clockwise (B)

the guide on the top of the radiator. Ensure the cable is correctly routed before proceeding.

8 Apply a smear of multi-purpose grease to the cable upper end fitting. Engage the inner cable with the clutch lever and seat the outer cable in the upper adjuster.

9 Engage the lower end of the inner cable with the clutch release lever then seat the outer cable in its mounting bracket.

10 Ensure the upper adjuster is screwed fully into the lever mounting bracket then adjust the cable as described in Chapter 1.

11 Once the cable is correctly adjusted, ensure the locknuts are securely tightened and the rubber gaiter is correctly seated on the lower end of the outer cable.

12 Install the fairing panels (see Chapter 8).

18 Starter motor clutch and idler gear – removal, inspection and installation

Note: *The starter motor clutch and idler gear can be removed with the engine in the frame, noting that a puller will be required to remove the alternator rotor (see Chapter 9).*

Removal

1 The starter motor clutch is fitted to the rear

of the alternator rotor. Remove the rotor assembly as described in Chapter 9 then separate the rotor and driven gear **(see illustration)**.

Inspection

2 Inspect the starter clutch driven gear and idler gear teeth and renew them as a set if any teeth are chipped or missing. Check the idler gear shaft and bearing surfaces for signs of wear or damage, and renew if necessary.

3 Fit the driven gear to the rear of the alternator rotor and attempt to turn it back and forth **(see illustration)**. It should rotate freely in one direction and not at all in the other. If the driven gear turns freely in both directions, or is locked solid, dismantle the starter clutch and inspect the components as follows.

4 Retain the alternator rotor then slacken and remove the six starter clutch holder retaining bolts **(see illustration)**. Separate the holder, one-way clutch and rotor, noting each components correct fitted location **(see illustrations)**.

5 Inspect the one-way clutch rollers and driven gear contact surfaces for signs of wear and scoring. The one-way clutch rollers should be unmarked with no signs of wear such as pitting or flat spots and the driven

gear surface unmarked. Renew worn components as necessary.

6 On reassembly, remove all traces of locking compound from the threads of the holder bolts then lubricate all components with clean engine oil. Fit the one-way clutch to the holder, ensuring its flange is correctly seated in the holder recess, then assemble the holder and clutch with the rotor. Apply locking compound to the holder bolt threads then fit them and tighten to the specified torque.

Installation

7 Assemble the alternator rotor and driven gear and install the alternator rotor as described in Chapter 9.

19 Oil pan – removal and installation

Note: *The oil pan can be removed with the engine in the frame.*

Removal

1 Remove the exhaust system as described in Chapter 4.

2 Drain the engine oil (see Chapter 1). Once the oil has drained, fit a new sealing washer to the drain plug and tighten it to the specified torque.

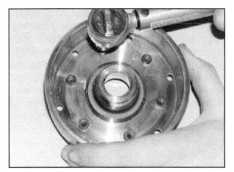

18.4a Remove the retaining bolts . . .

18.4b . . . separate the rotor . . .

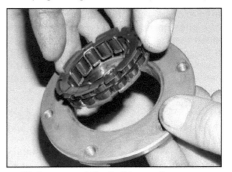

18.4c . . . and the holder and one way clutch

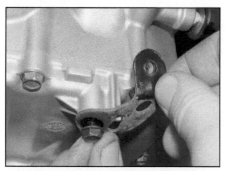

19.3 Remove the fairing mounting bracket

19.6a Remove the oil strainer . . .

19.6b . . . and remove the seal

19.7a Remove the oil pipe . . .

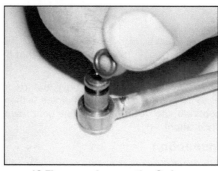

19.7b . . . and renew the O-rings

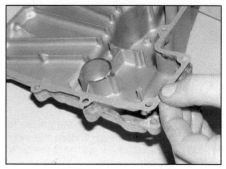

19.12 Fit a new gasket

3 Unscrew the retaining bolt and remove the lower fairing right mounting bracket from the oil pan **(see illustration)**.

4 Working in a criss-cross pattern, gradually loosen the oil pan retaining bolts.

5 Remove all the bolts and lower the oil pan away from the crankcase. If the engine is in the frame, note that as the oil pan is removed, the oil pump pick-up strainer may fall out of position. Recover the oil pan gasket and discard it; a new one must be used on installation.

6 If it was not released when the oil pan was removed, remove the oil pump pick-up strainer from the base of the engine **(see illustration)**. Remove the seal from the pick-up; a new one will be needed for installation **(see illustration)**.

7 Ease the oil pipe carefully out from the base of the crankcase, taking great care not to bend it **(see illustration)**. Remove the O-ring from each oil pipe fitting and discard them; new ones must be used on installation **(see illustration)**.

8 Clean the pick-up strainer mesh in solvent. Check it for clogging or splitting and renew if necessary. Ensure the oil pipe is undamaged and unblocked.

Installation

9 Ensure all mating surfaces are clean and dry.

10 Fit a new O-ring to each oil pipe fitting groove. Lubricate the O-rings with clean engine oil then ease the pipe into position in the crankcase.

11 Fit a new oil pump pick-up strainer seal to the crankcase, making sure its flange is facing the strainer. Fit the strainer, ensuring its locating lugs are positioned on each side of the crankcase oilway.

12 Locate the new gasket on top of the oil pan then fit the oil pan **(see illustration)**. Insert all the retaining bolts and tighten them by hand.

13 Working in a criss-cross pattern, tighten all the oil pan retaining bolts to the specified torque setting.

14 Fit the lower fairing mounting bracket, engaging its slot with the oil pan lug, and securely tighten its retaining bolt.

15 Install the exhaust system as described in Chapter 4.

16 Fill the engine with the correct type and quantity of oil as described in '*Daily (pre-ride) checks*'. Start the engine and check for leaks.

20.6 Fit a new seal on the water pump cover

20 Oil pump and drive gear – removal, inspection and installation

Note: *The oil pump and drive gear can both be removed with the engine in the frame.*

Oil pump

Removal

1 Remove the lower fairing (see Chapter 8).

2 Drain the engine oil (see Chapter 1). Once the oil has drained, fit a new sealing washer to the drain plug and tighten it to the specified torque.

3 Drain the cooling system (see Chapter 1).

4 Release the wiring/hoses from the clamp on the water pump and position them clear of the pump.

5 Release the retaining clips and disconnect the coolant hoses from the water pump cover.

6 Slacken and remove the three retaining bolts, along with the wiring/hose clamp, and remove the water pump cover. Discard the cover seal; a new one will be needed on installation **(see illustration)**. If the cover locating pins are a loose-fit, remove them and store them with the cover for safe-keeping.

7 Unscrew the retaining bolt and remove water pump impeller **(see illustration)**.

8 Screw one of the water pump cover bolts into the end of the pump shaft then use the bolt to pull the shaft out of position; the water pump housing, oil pump cover and oil pump inner rotor will come out with the shaft **(see**

20.7 Undo the retaining bolt and remove the impeller

20.8a Remove the shaft, water pump housing, oil pump cover and inner rotor

20.8b Fit a new O-ring

illustration). Take care not to lose the oil pump cover and water pump housing locating dowels and discard the water pump housing O-ring; a new one will be needed on installation **(see illustration)**.

9 Unscrew the bolt then slide the water pump housing and oil pump cover off the shaft.

10 Slide the oil pump inner rotor off the shaft and recover the drive pin.

11 Remove the oil pump outer rotor from the crankcase, noting which way around it is fitted **(see illustration)**.

Inspection

12 Check the pump cover and inner and outer rotors for scoring and wear and renew all worn components (all parts are available individually). If any component is badly worn or damaged, it's a good idea to renew both rotors and the cover as an assembly. If the pump housing is badly scored, seek the advice of a Kawasaki dealer or motorcycle engineering shop on the best course of action (the housing is an integral part of the crankcase). Refer to Chapter 3 for information of the water pump.

Installation

13 Lubricate the oil pump rotors with clean engine oil.

14 Install the pump outer rotor in the oil pump housing in the crankcase.

15 Fit the drive pin to the pump shaft then slide the oil pump inner rotor along the shaft and engage it with the pin **(see illustration)**. Ensure the pin remains correctly seated in the

rotor slot then fit the assembly to the crankcase, engaging the shaft slot with the drive gear shaft dog and aligning the inner rotor with the outer rotor.

16 Ensure the locating dowel is in position then slide the oil pump cover along the shaft. Align the locating dowel with the crankcase/cover hole and push the cover fully into position.

17 Ensure both locating dowels are in position then fit a new O-ring to the groove in the rear of the water pump housing. Carefully slide the housing along the pump shaft and locate it on the dowels, ensuring the O-ring remains correctly seated in the groove.

18 Fit the water pump impeller to the shaft and install its retaining bolt and washer, tightening it to the specified torque.

19 Ensure both locating pins are in position then fit a new seal to the groove in the rear of the water pump cover. Fit the cover and install the retaining bolts, not forgetting the wiring/hose clamp, and tighten them to the specified torque.

20 Reconnect the coolant hoses to the pump, securing them in position with the retaining clips.

21 Securing the wiring/hose in position with the clamp on the pump.

22 Fill the engine with the correct type and quantity of oil as described in 'Daily (pre-ride) checks'.

23 Refill the cooling system as described in Chapter 1.

24 Start the engine and check for leaks before installing the lower fairing (see Chapter 8).

Oil pump drive gear

Removal

25 Remove the oil pan (see Section 19).

26 Remove the clutch (see Section 16).

27 Using circlip pliers, expand the circlip located on the inside of the crankcase then slide the drive gear out of position. Recover the circlip and inner thrust washer from inside the crankcase and slide the outer thrust washer off from the drive gear shaft.

Inspection

28 Inspect the drive gear teeth and shaft for signs of wear or damage and renew if necessary. If the gear teeth are damaged, be sure to check the oil pump gear on the rear of the clutch drum carefully for signs of wear (see Section 16).

Installation

29 Fit the outer thrust washer onto the drive gear shaft and slide the gear into the crankcase.

30 Locate the inner thrust washer and the circlip on the inner end of the drive gear shaft then push the gear fully into position, engaging its dog with the slot in the pump shaft. Secure the drive gear in position by sliding the inner thrust washer and circlip up tight against the crankcase, making sure the circlip is correctly located in the shaft groove.

31 Install the clutch and oil pan (see Sections 16 and 19).

21 Oil pressure relief valve – removal, inspection and installation

Note: *The oil pressure relief valve can be removed with the engine in the frame.*

Removal

1 Remove the oil pan (see Section 19).

2 Unscrew the oil pressure relief valve from the base of the crankcase **(see illustration)**.

Inspection

3 Clean each valve with solvent and dry it, using compressed air if available.

4 Using a wood or plastic tool, depress the steel ball inside the valve and see if it moves

20.11 Remove the outer rotor from the crankcase

20.15 Engage the inner rotor with the drive pin

21.2 Remove the oil pressure relief valve

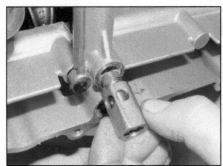

21.6 Fit the oil pressure relief valve

22.5 Remove the centre bolt

smoothly. Make sure it returns to its seat completely. If it doesn't, renew the valve a new one (don't attempt to disassemble and repair it).

Installation

5 Remove all traces of locking compound from the relief valve threads.
6 Apply a drop of locking compound to the valve threads then fit the valve to the crankcase and tighten it to the specified torque **(see illustration)**.
Caution: Ensure no locking compound is allowed to enter the valve bore as this will cause the valve to stick and prevent it functioning correctly.
7 Install the oil pan (see Section 19).

22 Oil cooler –
removal and installation

Removal

1 Remove the lower, right middle panel and inner fairing panel (see Chapter 8).
2 Drain the engine oil (see Chapter 1). Once the oil has drained, fit a new sealing washer to the drain plug and tighten it to the specified torque.
3 Drain the cooling system (see Chapter 1).
4 Slacken the retaining clips and disconnect the coolant hoses from the oil cooler unions.

Note: *If access to the clips is poor, they can be slackened and disconnected once the centre bolt has been removed.*
5 Unscrew the centre bolt and remove the oil cooler from the front of the crankcase **(see illustration)**. Recover the sealing washer from the bolt and the O-ring fitted between cooler and crankcase and discard them both; new ones must be used on installation.

Installation

6 Ensure the oil cooler and crankcase mating surfaces are clean and dry and fit a new O-ring to the groove in the rear of the oil cooler. Smear the O-ring with multi-purpose grease.
7 Manoeuvre the oil cooler into position, ensuring the O-ring remains correctly positioned. Seat the cooler on the crankcase engaging its locating lug with the peg on the crankcase.
8 Apply clean engine oil to the underside of the head and threads of the centre bolt then fit the new sealing washer. Screw the bolt into the oil cooler and tighten it to the specified torque setting.
9 Reconnect the coolant hoses to the oil cooler and securely tighten the retaining clips.
10 Fill the engine with the correct type and quantity of oil (see Chapter 1).
11 Refill the cooling system (see Chapter 1).
12 Start the engine and check for leaks. If all is well, check the oil and coolant levels then install the fairing panels as described in Chapter 8.

23 Gearchange mechanism –
removal, inspection and installation

Note: *The gearchange mechanism components can be removed with the engine in the frame.*

Removal

1 Note the correct fitted position of the gearchange lever linkage on the shaft (make alignment marks if necessary). Ensure the transmission is in neutral then unscrew the clamp bolt and free the linkage from the engine.
2 Remove the clutch (see Section 16).
3 Unscrew the retaining bolts and remove the crankcase oil pipe retaining plates **(see illustration)**. Ease the oil pipe out of position, taking care not to bend it, and remove it from the engine. Remove the O-rings from the oil pipe fittings and discard them; new ones must be used on refitting **(see illustration)**.
4 Remove all traces of dirt from the left end of the gearchange shaft then slide the shaft out of the right side of the engine. Take care not to lose the spacer which is fitted inside the centring spring.
5 Unscrew the shouldered pivot bolt and remove the selector drum stopper arm, spacer and spring, noting each components correct fitted location **(see illustration)**.

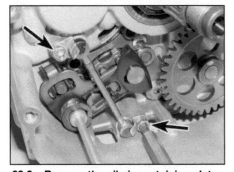

23.3a Remove the oil pipe retaining plates

23.3b Fit new O-rings

23.5 Removing the stopper arm

Inspection

6 Check the gearchange shaft for straight-ness and damage to the splines. If the shaft is bent or the splines are damaged the shaft must be renewed. Inspect the shaft centralising spring and the change lever return springs for signs of damage and renew as necessary. Also check that the centralising spring locating pin in the casing is securely tightened. If it is loose, remove it and apply a suitable thread-locking compound before installing and tightening it to the specified torque.

7 Inspect the stopper arm components **(see illustration)**, paying particular attention to the arm spring, and renew any defective item.

8 Check the condition of the gearchange shaft oil seal and needle roller bearing in the crankcase. To renew an oil seal, lever the old seal carefully out of position with a flat-bladed screwdriver then press the new one into position **(see illustration)**, ensuring its sealing lip is facing inwards. If the needle roller bearing requires renewal, remove the oil seal and note the correct fitted location of the bearing before pressing/drifting it out of position. The new bearing should be pressed or drawn into its bore rather than driven into position to prevent possible damage. A suitable drawbolt arrangement can be made up as described in Section 5 of *Tools and Workshop Tips* in the *Reference* section. Ensure the bearing is correctly positioned in its bore then press the new oil seal into position.

Installation

9 Remove all traces of locking compound from the threads of the stopper arm pivot bolt and the oil pipe retaining plate bolts.

10 Apply a drop of locking compound to the threads of the stopper arm pivot bolt then locate the stopper arm on the bolt shoulder, ensuring it is the correct way around. Fit the spacer and spring then manoeuvre the assembly into position and screw in the pivot bolt a few turns. Locate the stopper arm correctly on the selector drum cam and pivot bolt shoulder then tighten the bolt to the specified torque. Ensure the stopper arm pivots smoothly and is securely held against the selector drum cam by its spring before proceeding.

11 Apply a smear of grease to the gear-change shaft oil seal lip.

12 Ensure the spacer is correctly located inside the centring spring then locate the gearchange shaft in its crankcase bore. Align the shaft centralising spring with its locating pin and push the shaft fully into position, engaging its fork with the selector drum cam.

13 Fit a new O-ring to each oil pipe fitting groove. Lubricate the O-rings with clean engine oil then ease the pipe into position in the crankcase. Apply a drop of locking compound to the threads of each pipe retaining plate bolt then install the plates and bolts, tightening them to the specified torque.

14 Engage the gearchange lever linkage with

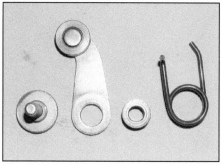

23.7 Stopper arm components

the shaft splines so the lever is correctly positioned. Fit the clamp bolt to the linkage and tighten it securely.

15 Install the clutch (see Section 16).

24 Selector drum and forks – removal, inspection and installation

Note: *The selector drum and forks can in theory be removed with the engine in the frame but it is a very awkward operation. The operation is much easier if the engine is removed and turned upside-down.*

Removal

1 Remove the engine from the frame (if necessary) as described in Section 5.
2 Remove the oil pan (see Section 19).
3 Remove the gearchange mechanism (see Section 23).

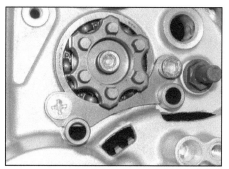

24.4 Remove the selector drum bearing retaining plate

24.8b . . . the bearing . . .

23.8 Removing the oil seal

4 Slacken and remove the retaining screw and bolt and remove the selector drum bearing retaining plate from the right side of the crankcase **(see illustration)**.

5 Withdraw the selector fork front shaft and pivot the centre selector fork clear of the drum.

6 Withdraw the selector fork rear shaft from the crankcase and pivot the left and right selector forks clear of the drum. **Note:** *The left and right selector forks are identical but differ from the (smaller) centre fork. Both fork shafts are also identical.*

7 Withdraw the selector drum and bearing from the crankcase. The selector forks can then be removed from the transmission shafts and lifted out.

8 If necessary, clamp the selector drum in a vice equipped with soft jaws then slacken and remove the cam centre bolt. Remove the cam and bearing from the drum and recover the locating pin **(see illustrations)**.

24.8a Remove the cam . . .

24.8c . . . and recover the locating pin

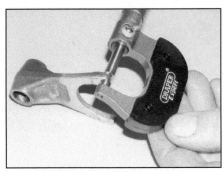

24.10 Measure the fork ends with a micrometer

Inspection

9 The selector forks and shaft should be closely inspected to ensure that they are not badly damaged or worn.

10 Measure the width of both fork ends and the internal diameter of the shaft bore **(see illustration)**. If either fork end or the shaft bore has worn beyond its service limit the selector fork(s) must be renewed.

11 The selector fork shafts can be checked for trueness by rolling them along a flat surface. A bent shaft will cause difficulty in selecting gears and make the gearshift action heavy. If the shaft is bent it must be renewed.

12 Inspect the selector drum grooves and selector fork guide pins for signs of wear or damage. If either component shows signs of damage or has worn beyond the specified limits, the selector fork(s) and drum must be renewed.

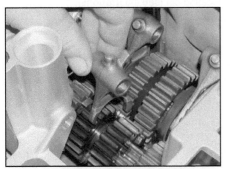

24.18 Install the centre fork on to the input shaft

24.21 Engage the centre fork pin into it's groove on the drum and slide the shaft into position

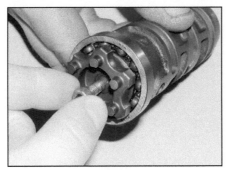

24.14 Fit the centre bolt to the selector drum

13 Check that the selector drum bearing rotates freely and has no sign of freeplay between its inner and outer race. Renew the bearing if it is worn.

Installation

14 Where necessary, remove all traces of locking compound from the threads of the cam centre bolt threads. Fit the bearing to the drum then insert the locating pin into the drum hole and fit the cam, aligning its cutout with the pin. Apply a drop of locking compound to the centre bolt then fit it and tighten to the specified torque **(see illustration)**.

15 Remove all traces of locking compound from the selector drum bearing plate bolt and screw threads.

16 Lubricate the transmission shaft gear selector fork grooves with clean engine oil.

17 Engage the left and right selector forks

24.19 Install the selector drum

24.22 Engage the left and right fork pins into their grooves on the drum and slide the shaft into position

24.17 Install the left and right selector forks on to the output shaft

(both forks are the same) with the output shaft gears ensuring their guide pins are facing towards the drum **(see illustration)**.

18 Engage the (smaller) centre selector fork with the input shaft gear so that its guide pin is facing towards the drum **(see illustration)**.

19 Pivot the selector forks outwards then lubricate the selector drum bearing and grooves with clean engine oil and manoeuvre the selector drum assembly into position **(see illustration)**.

20 Apply a smear of engine oil to the selector fork shafts and slide them partially into the crankcase (both shafts are the same). Ensure each shaft is fitted with the retaining plate groove at its right end.

21 Locate the centre fork pin in its groove in the selector drum then slide the front shaft in through the fork and fully into position **(see illustration)**.

22 Locate the left and right fork pins in their grooves in the selector drum then slide the selector fork rear shaft through both forks and fully into position **(see illustration)**.

23 Manoeuvre the selector drum bearing retaining plate into position and engage it with the slots in the selector fork shafts **(see illustration)**. Apply locking compound to the threads of the retaining plate bolt and screw then fit the bolt and screw and tighten them to their specified torque settings.

24 Install the gearchange mechanism (Section 23) and the oil pan (Section 19).

25 Fit the engine in the frame as described in Section 5.

24.23 Install the bearing retaining plate

25 Crankcase –
separation and reassembly

Separation

1 To examine and repair or renew the crankshaft, connecting rods and bearings and transmission shafts, the crankcase must be split into two parts.

2 To enable the crankcases to be split the engine must be removed from the frame (see Section 5) and the following components first removed with reference to the relevant Sections.

   a) Camshafts.*
   b) Cylinder head.*
   c) Cylinder block.*
   d) Pistons.*
   e) Clutch.
   f) Oil pan.
   g) Oil cooler.
   h) Alternator (Chapter 9).
   i) Starter motor (Chapter 9).
   j) Ignition system pick-up coil and rotor (Chapter 5).

*If no work is to be carried out on the crankshaft, the cylinder head and camshafts can remain in situ.

3 With all the relevant components removed proceed as follows.

4 With the crankcase the right way up, on C and E models remove the engine mounting rubbers from the rear upper mounting (see illustration). If either mounting rubber show signs of wear or damage, renew both as a pair.

5 Slacken and remove the seven 6 mm bolts from the top of the upper crankcase half (see illustration). As each bolt is removed, store it in its relative position in a cardboard template of the crankcase halves. This will ensure that each bolt is returned to its original location on reassembly (there are three different lengths of 6 mm bolt).

6 Next slacken and remove the four 7 mm bolts and the two 8 mm bolts from the top of the upper crankcase half (see Note in Step 5) (see illustration 25.5).

7 Turn the crankcase upside down and slacken and remove the seven 6 mm bolts located along the front edge of the lower crankcase, noting the correct fitted location of the hose guide (the bolts are all the same length) (see illustration).

8 Working in the reverse of the tightening sequence (numbers cast on lower crankcase – see Step 20), gradually slacken the ten 9 mm (main bearing) bolts (see illustration 25.7). Once all the bolts are loose, unscrew them and remove (see Note in Step 5). On later C2 models and all E models, recover the washers fitted to the four longer bolts (7 to 10 in tightening sequence).

9 Carefully lift the lower crankcase half off, leaving the crankshaft and transmission shafts in the upper half of the crankcase. As the lower half is lifted away take care not to

25.4 Remove the engine mounting rubbers – C and E models

dislodge or lose any main bearing inserts.
Note: If it won't come away easily, make sure all fasteners have been removed. Don't pry against the crankcase mating surfaces or they will leak; initial separation can be achieved by tapping gently with a soft-faced mallet.

10 Remove the three locating dowels from the upper/lower crankcase half.

Reassembly

11 Check that the transmission shafts, crankshaft and camchain are correctly installed in the upper crankcase half as described in Sections 28 to 31.

12 Remove all traces of sealant from the crankcase mating surfaces, being careful not to let any fall into the case as this is done.

13 Check that all components are installed and that they can rotate smoothly and easily.

14 Lubricate the transmission shafts and crankshaft with clean engine oil then use a rag soaked in high flash-point solvent to wipe over the gasket surfaces of both halves to remove all traces of oil.

15 Ensure the crankcase half mating surfaces are clean and dry then fit the three locating dowels to the upper half.

16 Apply a thin smear of suitable sealant (Kawasaki recommend the use of Kawasaki Bond 92104-002 on C models and 92104-1063 on E models) to the areas of the lower crankcase half mating surface (see illustration).
Caution: Do not use an excessive amount of sealant, as it will ooze out when the case halves are assembled and may obstruct oil passages and prevent the bearings from seating.

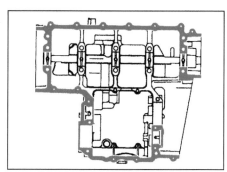

25.16 Apply sealant to the shaded areas

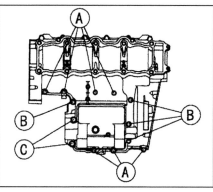

25.5 Upper crankcase bolts arrangement

  A 6 mm bolts   C 8 mm bolts
  B 7 mm bolts

25.7 Lower crankcase bolts arrangement

  A 6 mm bolts   B 9 mm bolts

17 Check the position of the selector drum cam and selector forks (where fitted) and transmission shafts – make sure they're in the neutral position.

18 Make sure that the main bearing inserts are in position and carefully install the lower crankcase half on the upper half. The selector forks (where fitted) must engage with their respective slots in the transmission gears as the halves are joined.

19 Check that the lower crankcase half is correctly seated and that all shafts are free to rotate. Ensure the breather hose is correctly routed through its guide on the lower crankcase half (see illustration).

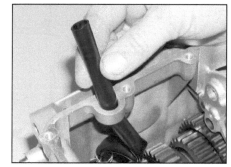

25.19 Ensure that the breather hose is correctly routed

26.2 Unbolt the breather plate

Caution: If the casings are not correctly seated, remove the lower crankcase half and investigate the problem. Do not attempt to pull them together using the crankcase bolts as the casing will crack and be ruined.

20 Lubricate the underside of the head of each of the ten 9 mm (main bearing) bolts with a smear of molybdenum disulphide grease. Note the number cast next to each 9 mm (main bearing) bolt on the lower crankcase (these numbers are the tightening sequence) and install the six shorter bolts in locations 1 to 6 and the four longer bolts in locations 7 to 10. On later C2 models and all E models ensure that a washer is fitted to each of the four longer bolts. Tighten all the 9 mm (main bearing) bolts by hand.

21 Working in the correct sequence, go around and tighten each of the 9 mm bolts to approximately half its specified torque setting, then go around again in the specified sequence and tighten them to the full specified torque setting. Note that the shorter bolts have a slightly different torque setting to the longer bolts (see Specifications).

22 Fit the seven 6 mm bolts along the front of the lower crankcase, ensuring the hose guide is correctly positioned, and tighten them to the specified torque.

23 Turn the crankcase over so that it is upright.

24 Fit the two 8 mm upper crankcase bolts and the four 7 mm bolts (the longer 7 mm bolt is fitted on the left). Tighten the 8 mm bolts to their specified torque then tighten the 7mm bolts to their specified torque.

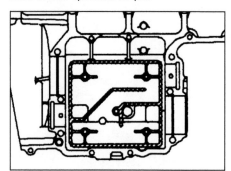

26.9 Apply sealant to the shades areas

25 Install the seven 6 mm bolts in their original locations in the upper crankcase half **(see illustration 25.5)** and tighten them all to the specified torque.

26 With all crankcase fasteners tightened, check that the crankshaft and transmission shafts rotate smoothly and easily. If there are any signs of undue stiffness or of any other problem, the fault must be rectified before proceeding further.

27 Fit the rear upper rubber mountings to the upper crankcase half then install all other removed assemblies in the reverse of the sequence given in Step 2.

26 Crankcase components – inspection and servicing

1 After the crankcases have been separated and the crankshaft and transmission components have been removed, the crankcases should be cleaned thoroughly with new solvent and dried with compressed air.

 Warning: Wear eye protection when using compressed air!

2 Unbolt the breather plate from the inside of the upper crankcase half. Thoroughly clean the breather aperture and the inside of the cover and remove all traces of locking compound from the bolt threads **(see illustration)**.

3 Remove any oil passage plugs that haven't already been removed. All oil passages should be blown out with compressed air.

4 All traces of old gasket sealant should be removed from the mating surfaces. Minor damage to the surfaces can be cleaned up with a fine sharpening stone or grindstone.

Caution: Be very careful not to nick or gouge the crankcase mating surfaces or leaks will result. Check both crankcase halves very carefully for cracks and other damage.

5 All threaded holes must be clean, to ensure accurate torque readings during reassembly. To clean the threads, run the correct-size tap into each of the holes to remove rust, corrosion, thread locking compound or sealant, and to restore damaged threads. If possible, use compressed air to clear the holes of debris produced by this operation. A good alternative is to inject aerosol-applied water-dispersant lubricant into each hole, using the long spout usually supplied.

Warning: Wear eye protection when cleaning out these holes in this way!

6 Small cracks or holes in aluminium castings may be repaired with an epoxy resin adhesive as a temporary measure. Permanent repairs can only be effected by argon-arc welding, and only a specialist in this process is in a position to advise on the economy or practical aspect of such a repair. If any damage is found that can't be repaired, renew the crankcase halves as a set.

7 Damaged threads can be economically reclaimed by using a diamond section wire insert, of the Helicoil type, which is easily fitted after drilling and re-tapping the affected thread. Sheared studs or screws can usually be removed with screw extractors, which consist of a tapered, left thread screw of very hard steel. These are inserted into a pre-drilled hole in the stud, and usually succeed in dislodging the most stubborn stud or screw.

 Refer to Section 2 of Tools and Workshop Tips in the Reference section for details of thread repair methods and using screw extractors.

8 Apply silicone sealant to the threads of the oil passage plugs then fit them to the cases, tightening them securely.

9 Apply a bead of silicone sealant 1 to 1.5 mm thick to the breather plate mating surfaces of the upper crankcase half (Kawasaki recommend the use of Kawasaki Bond 56019-120 – allow the sealant to dry before installing the plate) **(see illustration)**. Apply a drop of locking compound to each retaining bolt then fit the breather plate and install the bolts, tightening them to the specified torque.

27 Main and connecting rod bearings – general note

1 Even though main and connecting rod bearings are generally renewed with new ones during the engine overhaul, the old bearings should be retained for close examination as they may reveal valuable information about the condition of the engine.

2 Bearing failure occurs mainly because of lack of lubrication, the presence of dirt or other foreign particles, overloading the engine and/or corrosion. Regardless of the cause of bearing failure, it must be corrected before the engine is reassembled to prevent it from happening again.

3 When examining the bearings, remove the main bearings from the case halves and the rod bearings from the connecting rods and caps and lay them out on a clean surface in the same general position as their location on the crankshaft journals. This will enable you to match any noted bearing problems with the corresponding crankshaft journal.

4 Dirt and other foreign particles get into the engine in a variety of ways. It may be left in the engine during assembly or it may pass through filters or breathers. It may get into the oil and from there into the bearings. Metal chips from machining operations and normal engine wear are often present. Abrasives are sometimes left in engine components after reconditioning operations such as cylinder honing, especially when parts are not thoroughly cleaned using the proper cleaning methods. Whatever the source, these foreign objects often end up imbedded in the soft bearing material and are easily recognised. Large particles will not imbed in the bearing and will score or gouge the bearing and journal. The best prevention for this cause of bearing failure is to clean all parts thoroughly and keep everything spotlessly clean during engine reassembly. Frequent and regular oil and filter changes are also recommended.

5 Lack of lubrication or lubrication breakdown has a number of interrelated causes. Excessive heat (which thins the oil), overloading (which squeezes the oil from the bearing face) and oil leakage or throw off from excessive bearing clearances, worn oil pump or high engine speeds all contribute to lubrication breakdown. Blocked oil passages will also starve a bearing and destroy it. When lack of lubrication is the cause of bearing failure, the bearing material is wiped or extruded from the steel backing of the bearing. Temperatures may increase to the point where the steel backing and the journal turn blue from overheating.

6 Riding habits can have a definite effect on bearing life. Full throttle low speed operation, or lugging (labouring) the engine, puts very high loads on bearings, which tend to squeeze out the oil film. These loads cause the bearings to flex, which produces fine cracks in the bearing face (fatigue failure). Eventually the bearing material will loosen in pieces and tear away from the steel backing. Short trip riding leads to corrosion of bearings, as insufficient engine heat is produced to drive off the condensed water and corrosive gases produced. These products collect in the engine oil, forming acid and sludge. As the oil is carried to the engine bearings, the acid attacks and corrodes the bearing material.

7 Incorrect bearing installation during engine assembly will lead to bearing failure as well. Tight fitting bearings which leave insufficient bearing oil clearances result in oil starvation. Dirt or foreign particles trapped behind a bearing insert result in high spots on the bearing which lead to failure.

8 To avoid bearing problems, clean all parts thoroughly before reassembly, double check

28.3 To remove a main bearing insert, push it sideways and lift it out

all bearing clearance measurements and lubricate the new bearings with clean engine oil during installation.

28 Crankshaft and main bearings – removal, inspection and installation

Removal

1 Separate the crankcase halves as described in Section 25.

2 Lift the crankshaft out of the upper crankcase half, taking care not to dislodge the bearing inserts, and remove the camchain from the crankshaft.

3 The main bearing inserts can be removed from the crankcase halves by pushing their centres to the side, then lifting them out **(see illustration)**. Keep the bearing inserts in order.

Inspection

General information

4 Remove the connecting rods from the crankshaft (see Section 29).

5 Clean the crankshaft with solvent, using a small cleaning brush to scrub out the oil passages. If available, blow the crank dry with compressed air.

6 Refer to Section 27 and examine the main bearing inserts. If they are scored, badly scuffed or appear to have been seized, new bearings must be installed. Always renew the main bearings as a set. If they are badly

damaged, check the corresponding crankshaft journal. Evidence of extreme heat, such as discoloration, indicates that lubrication failure has occurred. Be sure to thoroughly check the oil pump and pressure relief valve as well as all oil holes and passages before reassembling the engine.

7 The crankshaft journals should be given a close visual examination, paying particular attention where damaged bearing inserts have been discovered. If the journals are scored or pitted in any way a new crankshaft will be required. Note that undersizes are not available, precluding the option of re-grinding the crankshaft.

8 Set the crankshaft on V-blocks and check the runout with a dial indicator touching the centre main bearing journal, comparing your findings with this Chapter's Specifications. If the runout exceeds the limit, renew the crankshaft.

Bearing selection

9 The main bearing running clearance is controlled in production by selecting one of three grades of bearing insert. The grades are indicated by a colour-coding marked on the edge of each insert (this colour-code may no longer be visible on the original bearings). In order, from the thickest to the thinnest, the insert grades are: Blue, Black and Brown. New bearing inserts are selected as follows using the crankshaft journal and crankcase main bearing bore size group markings.

10 The standard crankshaft (main bearing) journal diameter is divided into two size groups to allow for manufacturing tolerances. The size group of each journal can be determined by examining the crankshaft web next to each journal in the locations shown **(see illustration)**. There will either be a No. 1 marking or no marking at all. **Note:** *Ignore the 0 markings (where present) as these refer to the crankpin journals (see Section 29).* If the equipment is available, the size group can be checked by direct measurement **(see illustration)**.

11 The crankcase main bearing bore diameters are also divided into two size groups to allow for manufacturing tolerances. The size group of each main bearing bore can be determined by checking the tab on the

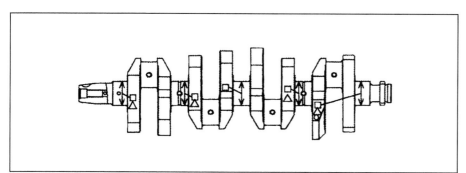

28.10a Crankshaft main journal size marking locations

28.10b Measure the diameter of each crankshaft journal

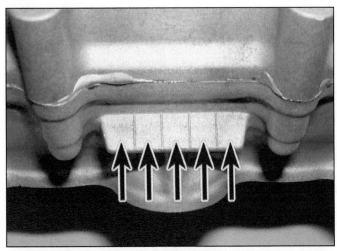

28.11a The main bearing bore size group can be located on the tab on the front of the upper crankcase . . .

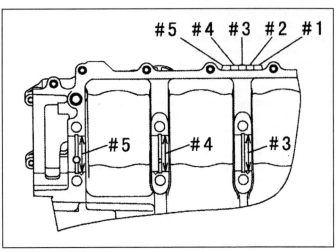

28.11b . . . and applies to the corresponding bore of the crankcase

front of the upper crankcase half (see illustrations). There will either be a 0 marking or no marking at all for each of the main bearing bores. If the equipment is available, the size group can be checked by direct measurement.

12 Match the relevant crankshaft code with its crankcase code and select a new set of bearing inserts using the relevant following table.

Journal size	Bore size	Bearing insert
1	0	Brown
1	None	Black
None	0	Black
None	None	Blue

Oil clearance check

13 Whether new bearing inserts are being fitted or the original ones are being re-used, the main bearing oil clearance should be checked prior to reassembly.

14 Clean the backs of the bearing inserts and the bearing locations in both crankcase halves.

15 Press the bearing inserts into their locations, ensuring that the tab on each insert engages in the notch in the crankcase. Make

sure the bearings are fitted in the correct locations and take care not to touch any insert's bearing surface with your fingers. Note the Nos. 2 and 4 bearing inserts have oil grooves whereas Nos. 1, 3 and 5 bearings are plain.

16 There are two possible ways of checking the oil clearance. The first method is by direct measurement (see Steps 17 and 23) and the second by the use of a product known as Plastigauge (see Steps 18 to 23).

17 If the first method is to be used, with the main bearing inserts in position, carefully lower the lower crankcase half onto the upper half. Make sure that the selector forks (if fitted) engage with their respective slots in the transmission gears as the halves are joined. Check that the lower crankcase half is correctly seated then install the ten 9 mm (main bearing) bolts in their original locations. Note: Do not tighten the crankcase bolts if the casing is not correctly seated. Working in the sequence marked on the crankcase, tighten all the bolts to approximately half the specified torque setting then go around and tighten them to the full specified torque (see Steps 20 and 21 of Section 25). Measure the internal diameter of each assembled pair of bearing inserts. If the diameter of each

corresponding crankshaft journal is measured and then subtracted from the bearing internal diameter, the result will be the main bearing oil clearance.

18 If the second method is to be used, ensure the main bearing inserts are correctly fitted and that the inserts and crankshaft are clean and dry. Lay the crankshaft in position in the upper crankcase.

19 Cut several lengths of the appropriate size Plastigauge (they should be slightly shorter than the width of the crankshaft journal). Place a strand of Plastigauge on each (cleaned) crankshaft journal (see illustration).

20 Carefully lower the lower crankcase half onto the upper half. Make sure that the selector forks (if fitted) engage with their respective slots in the transmission gears as the halves are joined. Check that the lower crankcase half is correctly seated then install the ten 9 mm (main bearing) bolts in their original locations. Note: Do not tighten the crankcase bolts if the casing is not correctly seated. Working in the sequence marked on the crankcase, tighten all the bolts to approximately half the specified torque setting then go around and tighten them to the full specified torque (see Steps 20 and 21 of Section 25). Make sure that the crankshaft is not rotated as the bolts are tightened.

21 Slacken and remove the crankcase bolts, working in the reverse of the sequence marked on the crankcase, then carefully lift off the lower crankcase half, making sure the Plastigauge is not disturbed.

22 Compare the width of the crushed Plastigauge on each crankshaft journal to the scale printed on the Plastigauge envelope to obtain the main bearing oil clearance (see illustration).

23 If the clearance is not within the specified limits, the bearing inserts may be the wrong grade (or excessively worn if the original inserts are being re-used). Before deciding that different grade inserts are needed, make sure that no dirt or oil was trapped between

28.19 Lay the Plastigauge stripes (arrowed) on the journals, parallel to the crankshaft centreline

28.22 Measure the width of the crushed Plastigauge

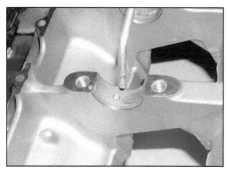

28.27 Lubricate the bearing inserts

the bearing inserts and the crankcase halves when the clearance was measured. If the clearance is excessive, even with new inserts (of the correct size), the crankshaft journal is worn and the crankshaft should be renewed.
24 On completion carefully scrape away all traces of the Plastigauge material from the crankshaft journal and bearing inserts; use a fingernail or other object which is unlikely to score the inserts.

Installation

25 Clean the backs of the bearing inserts and the bearing recesses in both crankcase halves. If new inserts are being fitted, ensure that all traces of the protective grease are cleaned off. Wipe dry the inserts and crankcase halves with a lint-free cloth.
26 Press the bearing inserts into their locations. Make sure the tab on each insert engages in the notch in the casing. Make sure the bearings are fitted in the correct locations and take care not to touch any insert's bearing surface with your fingers. Note that the Nos. 2 and 4 bearing inserts have oil grooves whereas Nos. 1, 3 and 5 bearings are plain.
27 Lubricate the bearing inserts in the upper crankcase with clean engine oil **(see illustration)**.
28 Ensure the connecting rods are correctly fitted to the crankshaft (see Section 29).
29 Locate the camchain on the crankshaft sprocket then lower the crankshaft into position in the upper crankcase.
30 Reassemble the crankcase halves as described in Section 25.

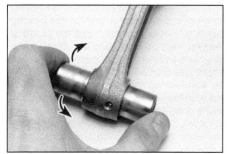

29.6 Check the piston pin and connecting rod small end for excessive wear by rocking the pin back and forth

29 Connecting rods and bearings – removal, inspection and installation

Note: *New connecting rod bearing cap bolts will be need on installation. The nuts can be re-used but we recommend that they are also renewed.*

Removal

1 Remove the crankshaft (see Section 28).
2 Before removing the connecting rods from the crankshaft measure the side clearance of each rod with a feeler gauge **(see illustration)**. If the clearance is greater than the service limit listed in this Chapter's Specifications, the rod will have to be renewed with a new one.
3 Using paint or a suitable marker pen, mark the relevant cylinder number on each connecting rod and bearing cap.
4 Unscrew the bearing cap nuts and remove the first connecting rod and bearing cap, complete with the bearing inserts, from the crankshaft. Immediately install the bearing cap and nuts on the connecting rod so that they are kept together as a matched set.
5 Remove the remaining three connecting rods in the same way.

Inspection

General information

6 Check the connecting rods for cracks and other obvious damage. Lubricate the piston pin for each rod, install it in its original rod and check for play. If it wobbles, renew the connecting rod and/or the pin **(see illustration)**.
7 Refer to Section 27 and examine the connecting rod bearing inserts. If they are scored, badly scuffed or appear to have been seized, new bearings must be installed. Always renew the bearings in the connecting rods as a set. If they are badly damaged, check the corresponding crankpin. Evidence of extreme heat, such as discoloration, indicates that lubrication failure has occurred. Be sure to thoroughly check the oil pump and pressure relief valve as well as all oil holes and passages before reassembling the engine.

29.9 Weight group identification mark

29.2 Measure the side clearance with a feeler gauge

8 Have the rods checked for twist and bending at a dealer service department or other motorcycle repair shop.
9 If a connecting rod is to renewed, be sure to state what weight group it is when ordering. Each connecting rod is marked with a weight code (in the form of a letter) which is stamped across the connecting rod/bearing cap joint **(see illustration)**. To minimise vibration, Kawasaki recommend that all rods should be of the same weight group.

Bearing selection

10 The connecting rod bearing running clearance is controlled in production by selecting one of three grades of bearing insert. The grades are indicated by a colour-coding marked on the edge of each insert (this colour-code may no longer be visible on the original bearings) **(see illustration)**. In order, from the thickest to the thinnest, the insert grades are: Blue, Black or unmarked and Brown. New bearing inserts are selected as follows using the crankpin and connecting rod size group markings.
11 The standard crankpin journal diameter is divided into two size groups to allow for manufacturing tolerances. The size group of each journal can be determined by examining the crankshaft web next to each journal in the locations shown **(see illustration)**. There will either be a 0 marking or no marking at all.
Note: *Ignore the No. 1 markings (where present) as these refer to the main bearing journals (see Section 28).* If the equipment is available, the size group can be checked by direct measurement.

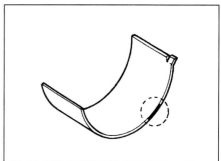

29.10 Location of the bearing colour code

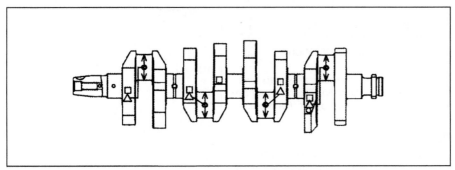

29.11 Crankpin diameter marks

29.16 Engage the tab with the notch

12 The connecting rod bore diameters are also divided into two size groups to allow for manufacturing tolerances. The size group of each main bearing bore can be determined by inspecting the weight group letter which is stamped across the connecting rod/bearing cap joint **(see illustration 29.9)**. If the letter is on its own (not surrounded by a circle), the rod has no marking and if the letter is surrounded by a circle the rod is in size group 0. If the equipment is available, the size group can be checked by direct measurement.

13 Match the relevant connecting rod code with its crankshaft code and select a new set of bearing inserts using the relevant following table.

Connecting rod size	Crankpin size	Bearing insert
None	0	Brown
None	None	Black\unmarked
0	0	Black\unmarked
0	None	Blue

Oil clearance check

14 Whether new bearing inserts are being fitted or the original ones are being re-used, the connecting rod bearing oil clearance should be checked prior to reassembly.
15 Clean the backs of the bearing inserts and the bearing locations in both the connecting rod and bearing cap.
16 Press the bearing inserts into their locations, ensuring that the tab on each insert engages the notch in the connecting rod/bearing cap **(see illustration)**. Make sure

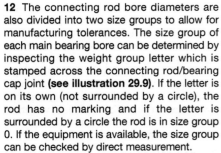

29.18 Measure the internal diameter

the bearings are fitted in the correct locations and take care not to touch any insert's bearing surface with your fingers.
17 There are two possible ways of checking the oil clearance. The first method is by direct measurement (see Steps 18 and 21) and the second by the use of a product known as Plastigauge (see Steps 19 to 21).
18 If the first method is to be used, fit the bearing cap to the connecting rod, with the bearing inserts in place. Make sure the cap is fitted the correct way around so the connecting rod and bearing cap weight/size markings are correctly aligned. Tighten the cap retaining nuts to the specified Stage 1 torque setting and then through the specified Stage 2 angle (see Steps 35 and 36) (use the original bearing cap bolts and nuts for the check, not the new ones) and measure the internal diameter of each assembled pair of bearing inserts **(see illustration)**. If the diameter of each corresponding crankpin journal is measured and then subtracted from the bearing internal diameter, the result will be the connecting rod bearing oil clearance.
19 If the second method is to be used, cut lengths of the appropriate size Plastigauge (they should be slightly shorter than the width of the crankpin) **(see illustration 28.19)**. Place a strand of Plastigauge on each (cleaned) crankpin journal and fit the (clean) piston/connecting rod assemblies, inserts and bearing caps. Make sure the cap is fitted the correct way around so the connecting rod and bearing cap weight/size markings are correctly aligned. Fit the cap retaining nuts (use the original bearing cap bolts and nuts for

29.24 Carefully tap out the original bearing cap bolts

the check, not the new ones) and tighten them first to the specified Stage 1 torque setting and then through the specified Stage 2 angle (see Steps 35 and 36) whilst ensuring that the connecting rod does not rotate. Take care not to disturb the Plastigauge. Slacken the bearing cap nuts and remove the connecting rod assemblies, again taking great care not to rotate the connecting rod.
20 Compare the width of the crushed Plastigauge on each crankpin to the scale printed on the Plastigauge envelope to obtain the connecting rod bearing oil clearance **(see illustration 28.22)**.
21 If the clearance is not within the specified limits, the bearing inserts may be the wrong grade (or excessively worn if the original inserts are being re-used). Before deciding that different grade inserts are needed, make sure that no dirt or oil was trapped between the bearing inserts and the connecting rod or bearing cap when the clearance was measured. If the clearance is excessive, even with new inserts (of the correct size), the crankpin is worn and the crankshaft should be renewed.
22 On completion, carefully scrape away all traces of the Plastigauge material from the crankpin and bearing inserts using a fingernail or other object which is unlikely to score the inserts.

Installation

23 Thoroughly clean the new bearing cap bolts and nuts in a high-flash point solvent to remove all traces of the protective anti-rust compound from their threads. Allow the bolts to dry completely (use compressed air if available). **Note:** *If the bolt length measuring method is to be used to tighten the bearing cap nuts, carefully centre-punch the centre of the each new bolt head and end at this stage to ensure accuracy when measuring the bolt length (see Step 30).*
24 Carefully tap the original bearing cap bolts out from the connecting rod **(see illustration)**, taking great care not damage the connecting rod itself. **Note:** *This is not necessary if new connecting rods are being fitted as they are supplied complete with new bolts and nuts.*
25 Insert the new bolts into the connecting rod, aligning their heads with the connecting rod cutouts, and tap them fully into position.

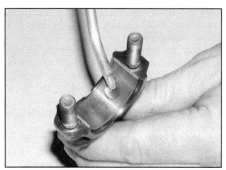

29.28 Lubricate them with engine oil

29.30 Lubricate the seats of the nuts

29.36a Use a angle-measuring gauge

26 Clean the backs of the bearing inserts and the bearing bores in both the connecting rod and bearing cap. If new inserts are being fitted, ensure that all traces of the protective grease are cleaned off using paraffin (kerosene). Wipe dry the inserts and connecting rods with a lint-free cloth.

27 Apply a thin smear of molybdenum disulphide grease to the top of the connecting rod bearing bore then press the bearing inserts into their locations. Make sure the tab on each insert engages the notch in the connecting rod or bearing cap **(see illustration 29.16)**. Make sure the bearings are fitted in the correct locations.

28 Ensure the bearing inserts and crankpin are clean then liberally lubricate them with clean engine oil **(see illustration)**.

29 Ensure the connecting rod and bearing cap mating surfaces are clean and dry. Fit the connecting rod to the crankshaft and install the bearing cap, making sure the cap is fitted the correct way around so the connecting rod and bearing cap weight/size markings are correctly aligned **(see illustration 29.9)**. If the original connecting rod is being reused, use the identification marks made to ensure it is fitted to its original crankpin and is the same way around as was noted prior to removal.

30 Lubricate the threads of the new bearing cap bolts and the seating surface of the nuts with clean engine oil **(see illustration)**. Screw the nuts onto the bolts, tightening them by hand only. Kawasaki give two possible tightening methods for the bearing cap bolts; the bolt length measuring method and the torque tightening method. They state that the bolt length measuring method is the more accurate of the two (and also the most complicated) but either method can be used.

Bolt length measuring tightening method

31 Accurately measure the length of each bearing cap bolt with a point micrometer, locating the point tips in the centre-punched indents. Note the exact length of each bolt.

32 Tighten both nuts to the specified Stage 1 torque and recheck each bolts' length. From this point, evenly tighten both nuts a little at a time, regularly checking the length of each bolt after each tightening. Continue this procedure until both bolts have stretched by

the specified amount (aim to get the stretch in the middle of specified limits), the bearing cap nuts are now correctly tightened.

Caution: If either of the nuts are overtightened and a bolt is stretched beyond the specified limit, the connecting rod must be removed and the bearing cap bolts discarded. Fit two more new bolts and repeat the installation procedure. Never use a bearing cap bolt which has been overstretched as it could break in use, leading to serious engine damage.

33 Check the connecting rod pivots freely on its crankpin and check the side clearance before proceeding (see Step 2).

34 Install the three remaining assemblies in the same way. Where new connecting rods are being installed, ensuring that the connecting rod weight/size markings are all facing the same way.

Torque tightening method

35 Ensure both nuts are hand tight then tighten each one to the specified Stage 1 torque setting.

36 Once both nuts have been tightened to the specified stage, tighten each nut through the specified Stage 2 angle. To ensure accuracy, either of the following methods can be used.

a) *Use an angle-measuring gauge to ensure each nut is tightened through the specified angle (see illustration).*

b) *Use the corners of the nut to measure the tightening angle (the corners are spaced 60° apart). Using paint or a suitable marker pen, make a dot on one of the corners of each nut and a corresponding dot on the connecting rod itself. Rotate the nut accurately through the specified angle so that the second corner back from the mark on the nut is aligned with the mark made on the connecting rod (see illustration).*

37 Check the connecting rod pivots freely on its crankpin and check the side clearance before proceeding (see Step 2).

38 Install the three remaining assemblies in the same way. Where new connecting rods are being installed, ensuring that the connecting rod weight/size markings are all facing the same way.

29.36b Use paint or a marker pen to make alignment marks

30 Camchain – removal, inspection and installation

Removal

1 Remove the engine from the frame (see Section 5).

2 Separate the crankcase halves as described in Section 25. **Note:** *If no work is being carried out on the crankshaft, the cylinder head does not need to be removed (just remove the camshafts).*

3 Disengage the camchain from the crankshaft sprocket and manoeuvre it out of position.

Inspection

4 Check the camchain for wear or damage, such as tight or loose link pins, and renew it if there is any doubt about its condition. The amount of chain wear can be assessed by pulling it tight and measuring a twenty-link length (distance between 21 link pins) section **(see illustration)**. Repeat this check along

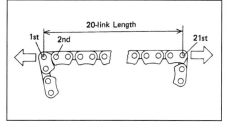

30.4 Camchain stretch measurement

31.6a Insert the half-rings . . .

31.6b . . . and the dowel pins

31.8a Align the bearing groove with the half-ring . . .

31.8b . . . and the dowel pin with the needle roller bearing race hole

several different sections of the chain and compare the results to those given in the specifications. If any section exceeds the specified limit, the camchain must be renewed.

Installation

5 Manoeuvre the camchain in position and engage it correctly with the crankshaft sprocket.
6 Reassemble the crankcase halves (Section 25) and install the engine (Section 5).

31 Transmission shafts – removal and installation

Removal

1 Remove the engine from the frame (see Section 5).

2 Separate the crankcase halves as described in Section 25. **Note:** *If no work is being carried out on the crankshaft, the camshafts and cylinder head do not need to be removed.*
3 Lift the input shaft and output shaft out of the crankcase.
4 Recover the bearing half-rings and dowel pins (one each for both input and output shafts) and store them with the transmission shafts for safe-keeping.
5 If necessary, the transmission shafts can be disassembled and inspected for wear or damage as described in Section 31.

Installation

6 Install the input and output shaft bearing half-rings and dowel pins in the upper crankcase **(see illustrations)**.
7 Lower the output shaft into position in the crankcase half. As the shaft is fitted, align the

bearing groove with the half-ring and engage the needle roller bearing race hole with the dowel pin.
8 Lower the input shaft into position in the upper crankcase, aligning its bearing groove with the half-ring and the needle roller bearing race hole with the dowel pin **(see illustrations)**.
9 Make sure both transmission shafts are correctly seated.
Caution: *If either of the half-rings or dowel pins are not correctly located, the crankcase halves will not seat correctly.*
10 Position the gears in the neutral position and check that the shafts are free to rotate freely before proceeding further.

32 Transmission shafts – disassembly, inspection and reassembly

> **HAYNES HiNT** *When disassembling the transmission shafts, place the parts on a long rod, or thread a wire through them to keep them in order and facing the proper direction (see illustration in Haynes Hint in Section 35 of Chapter 2A).*

1 Remove the shafts from the casing as described in Section 31.

Input shaft

Disassembly

Note: *Discard all circlips; new ones must be used on reassembly.*

2 Using circlip pliers, remove the circlip from the left end of the shaft then slide off the needle roller bearing outer race, bearing and thrust washer **(see illustrations)**.
3 Slide off the 2nd gear, noting which way around it is fitted **(see illustration)**.
4 On E and F models, remove the next circlip and slide off the splined thrust washer.
5 On all models, remove the 6th gear followed by its splined bushing and thrust washer **(see illustrations)**.
6 Remove the next circlip and slide off the

32.2a Remove the outer race . . .

32.2b . . . the needle roller bearing . . .

32.2c . . . and the thrust washer

32.3 Slide off 2nd gear

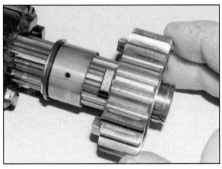

32.5a Slide off 6th gear followed by . . .

32.5b . . . the splined bushing . . .

32.5c . . . and the thrust washer

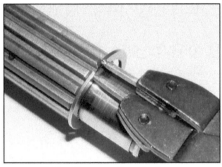

32.6a Remove the circlip . . .

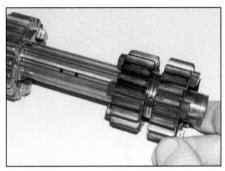

32.6b . . . and remove 3rd/4th gear

3rd/4th gear, noting which way around it is fitted **(see illustrations)**.

7 Remove the next circlip using a suitable pair of circlip pliers **(see illustration)**.

8 Slide off the splined thrust washer followed by the 5th gear, 5th gear bushing and thrust washer **(see illustrations)**.

Inspection

9 Wash all of the components in clean solvent and dry them off.

10 Check the gear teeth for cracking and other obvious damage. Check the gear bushings and the surface in the inner diameter of each gear for scoring or heat discoloration. If the gear or bushing is damaged, renew it.

11 Inspect the dogs and the dog holes in the gears for excessive wear. Renew the paired gears as a set if necessary.

12 The shaft is unlikely to sustain damage unless the engine has seized, placing an

unusually high loading on the transmission, or the machine has covered a very high mileage. Check the surface of the shaft, especially where a pinion turns on it, and renew the shaft if it has scored or picked up. Inspect the

threads of the shafts and check them for trueness by setting them up in V-blocks and measuring any runout with a dial gauge. Damage of any kind can only be cured by renewal.

32.7 Remove the circlip

32.8a Remove the splined thrust washer . . .

32.8b . . . 5th gear . . .

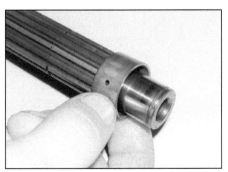

32.8c . . . 5th gear bushing . . .

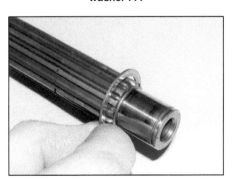

32.8d . . . and the thrust washer

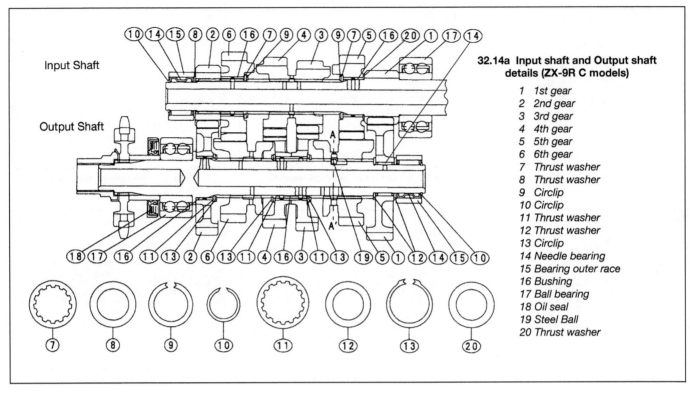

Input Shaft

Output Shaft

32.14a Input shaft and Output shaft details (ZX-9R C models)

1 1st gear
2 2nd gear
3 3rd gear
4 4th gear
5 5th gear
6 6th gear
7 Thrust washer
8 Thrust washer
9 Circlip
10 Circlip
11 Thrust washer
12 Thrust washer
13 Circlip
14 Needle bearing
15 Bearing outer race
16 Bushing
17 Ball bearing
18 Oil seal
19 Steel Ball
20 Thrust washer

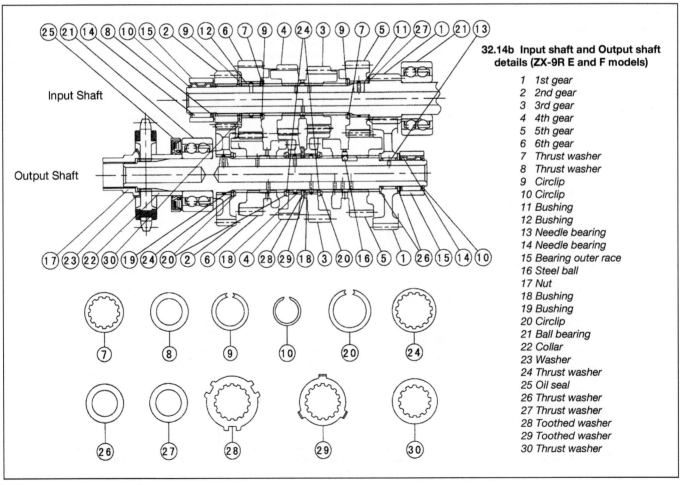

Input Shaft

Output Shaft

32.14b Input shaft and Output shaft details (ZX-9R E and F models)

1 1st gear
2 2nd gear
3 3rd gear
4 4th gear
5 5th gear
6 6th gear
7 Thrust washer
8 Thrust washer
9 Circlip
10 Circlip
11 Bushing
12 Bushing
13 Needle bearing
14 Needle bearing
15 Bearing outer race
16 Steel ball
17 Nut
18 Bushing
19 Bushing
20 Circlip
21 Ball bearing
22 Collar
23 Washer
24 Thrust washer
25 Oil seal
26 Thrust washer
27 Thrust washer
28 Toothed washer
29 Toothed washer
30 Thrust washer

32.22a Slide off the bearing outer race, followed by . . .

32.22b . . . the needle roller bearing . . .

32.22c . . . and the thrust washer

32.23a Remove the 1st gear followed by . . .

32.23b . . . the 1st gear needle roller bearing . . .

32.23c . . . and the thrust washer

13 Check that the outer race of the bearing fitted to the shaft rotates freely and has no sign of freeplay between its inner and outer races. If the bearing requires renewal, a bearing puller will be required to pull the bearing off. Note which way around the bearing is fitted then remove it from the shaft. Ensure the new bearing is fitted the right way around then press/drift it fully onto the shaft using a tubular spacer which bears only on the inner race of the bearing.

Reassembly

14 During reassembly, lubricate all components with engine oil before assembling them **(see illustrations)**. Note: *Always use new circlips on reassembly and ensure each circlip is fitted so its ends are positioned in one of the shaft grooves* (see *Tool and Workshop Tips* in the *Reference* chapter). *When fitting splined bushes/gears, always align one of the components oil holes with one of the shaft oilways.*

15 Slide on the thrust washer and 5th gear bushing then fit the 5th gear with its dogs facing away from the 1st gear. Fit the splined thrust washer and secure the 5th gear components in position with a new circlip, ensuring it is correctly located in the input shaft groove.

16 Install the 3rd/4th gear with its smaller 3rd gear facing the 5th gear. Engage the gear on the shaft splines, aligning its oil hole with the shaft oilway.

17 Fit the another new circlip to the shaft, making sure it is correctly located in the shaft groove.

18 Slide on the splined thrust washer and 6th gear splined bushing, aligning the bushing oil hole with the shaft oilway. Fit the 6th gear so that its dogs are facing the 3rd/4th gear.

19 On E models slide on the splined thrust washer and secure the 6th gear in position with another new circlip, making sure it is correctly located in the shaft groove.

20 On all models, fit the 2nd gear followed by the thrust washer.

21 Liberally oil the needle roller bearing assembly and install the bearing and outer race on the end of the shaft. Secure the bearing in position with a new circlip, making sure it is correctly located in the shaft groove.

Output shaft

Disassembly

Note: *Discard all circlips; new ones must be used on reassembly.*

32.24 Rotate the shaft back and forth to force the balls in to the gear

22 Using circlip pliers, remove the circlip from the right end of the shaft then slide off the needle roller bearing outer race, bearing and thrust washer off the output shaft **(see illustrations)**.

23 Remove the 1st gear, noting which way around it is fitted, followed by the 1st gear needle roller bearing and thrust washer **(see illustrations)**.

24 Hold the output shaft vertically and rotate the shaft rapidly back-and-forth to force the positive neutral finder mechanism steel balls into the 5th gear **(see illustration)**. Once all the balls are in the gear, carefully slide the 5th gear off the shaft, noting which way around it is fitted, and recover the three steel balls.

25 Remove the circlip with a suitable pair of circlip pliers and slide off the splined washer **(see illustrations)**. Continue as described under the relevant sub-heading.

32.25a Remove the circlip . . .

32.25b . . . and then the splined washer

32.26a Remove the 3rd gear . . .

32.26b . . . and then the 4th gear

C models
26 Slide off the 3rd gear and then the 4th gear, noting which way around each one is fitted **(see illustrations)**.
27 Slide off the 3rd/4th gear bushing

followed by the splined thrust washer **(see illustrations)**.
28 Remove the next circlip then slide off the 6th gear, noting which way around it is fitted **(see illustrations)**.

29 Remove the next circlip and slide off splined thrust washer **(see illustrations)**.
30 Remove the 2nd gear, noting which way around it is fitted, and slide off the 2nd gear bushing **(see illustrations)**.
E and F models
31 Slide off the 3rd gear, noting which way around it is fitted, and the 3rd gear bushing.
32 Disengage the lock washer from the special splined washer and slide both off the output shaft.
33 Slide off the 4th gear, noting which way around it is fitted, followed by the 4th gear bushing and splined washer.
34 Remove the next circlip then slide off the 6th gear, noting which way around it is fitted.
35 Remove the next circlip and slide off splined thrust washer.
36 Remove the 2nd gear, noting which way around it is fitted, and slide off the 2nd gear bushing.

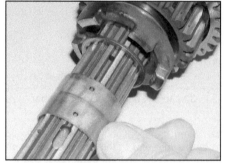

32.27a Remove the 3rd/4th gear bushing from the shaft . . .

32.27b . . . along with the splined thrust washer

32.28a Remove the circlip . . .

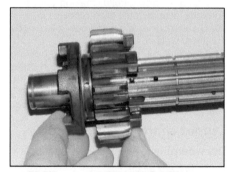

32.28b . . . and slide off the 6th gear

32.29a Remove the circlip . . .

32.29b . . . and the splined thrust washer

32.30a Remove the 2nd gear . . .

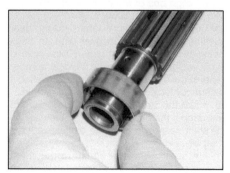

32.30b . . . and the 2nd gear bushing

Inspection

37 Refer to Steps 9 to 13. If the bearing is being removed (see Step 13) from the left end of the shaft, note that the collar will be drawn off at the same time. If the collar surface is marked it must be renewed; the collar runs in the oil seal lip and any damage could lead to oil leakage. Fit the bearing as described (Step 13) then press/drift the collar fully onto the shaft.

Reassembly

38 During reassembly, lubricate all components with engine oil before assembling them **(see illustrations 32.14a or 32.14b). Note:** *Always use new circlips on reassembly and ensure each circlip is fitted so its ends are positioned in one of the shaft grooves (see Tool and Workshop Tips in the Reference chapter). When fitting splined bushes/gears, always align one of the components oil holes with one of the shaft oilways.*

C models

39 Slide on the 2nd gear bushing and install the 2nd gear so that its side on which the gear hub protrudes the most is facing the output shaft bearing. Fit the splined thrust washer and secure the 2nd gear components with a new circlip, making sure it is correctly located in the output shaft groove.
40 Fit the 6th gear to the shaft so that its selector fork groove is facing away from the 2nd gear. Align the gear oil hole with the shaft oilway and slide the gear onto the shaft.
41 Fit another new circlip ensuring it is correctly located in the shaft groove.
42 Slide on the splined thrust washer then align the 3rd/4th gear splined bushing oil holes with the shaft oilways and slide it along the shaft.
43 Fit the 4th gear so that its side on which the gear hub protrudes the most is facing away from the 6th gear.
44 Fit the 3rd gear so that its side on which the gear hub protrudes the most is facing the 4th gear.
45 Slide on the splined thrust washer and secure the 3rd/4th gear components in position with another new circlip, ensuring it is correctly located in the output shaft groove.
46 Position the shaft assembly vertically in a vice with its right end uppermost.
47 Hold the 5th gear vertically so that its selector fork groove is facing downwards (towards the 3rd gear) then insert the three positive neutral finder steel balls into the three smaller holes in the 5th gear (the larger holes are oil holes) **(see illustration)**. Ensure all three balls are in position in the gear then align the balls with the cutouts on the output shaft and lower the gear onto the shaft. Shake the gear/shaft to release the balls and gently pull on the 5th gear to check that the positive neutral finder balls are correctly located in the shaft grooves.

⚠ *Warning: Do not be tempted to use grease to hold the steel balls in the gear as this will prevent the*

positive neutral finder mechanism from functioning correctly.
48 Fit the thrust washer and 1st gear needle roller bearing. Lubricate the bearing then fit the 1st gear so that its side on which the gear hub protrudes the most is facing away from the 5th gear.
49 Fit the next thrust washer and slide on the needle roller bearing. Secure the bearing in position with another new circlip, making sure it is correctly located in the output shaft groove, then lubricate the bearing and fit the outer race.

E and F models

50 Slide on the 2nd gear bushing and install the 2nd gear so that its side on which the gear hub protrudes the most is facing the output shaft bearing. Fit the splined thrust washer and secure the 2nd gear components with a new circlip, making sure it is correctly located in the output shaft groove.
51 Fit the 6th gear to the shaft so that its selector fork groove is facing away from the 2nd gear. Align the gear oil hole with the shaft oilway and slide the gear onto the shaft.
52 Fit another new circlip ensuring it is correctly located in the shaft groove.
53 Slide on the splined thrust washer then align the 4th gear splined bushing oil holes with the shaft oilways and slide it along the shaft.
54 Fit the 4th gear so that its side on which the gear teeth protrude is facing the 6th gear.
55 Fit the special splined washer and slide it along the shaft until it abuts the 4th gear. Fit the lock washer then rotate the splined washer until its cutouts align with the lock washer tabs. Engage the lock washer with the splined washer to lock it in position.
56 Fit the 3rd gear so that its side on which the gear teeth protrude is facing away from the 4th gear.
57 Slide on the splined thrust washer and secure the 3rd gear components in position with another new circlip, ensuring it is correctly located in the output shaft groove.
58 Fit the 5th gear and steel balls as described in Steps 46 and 47.
59 Fit the thrust washer and 1st gear needle roller bearing. Lubricate the bearing then fit the 1st gear so that its side on which the gear

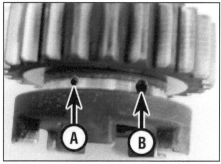

32.47 The small holes (A) in the 5th gear are for the steel balls, whereas the larger holes (B) are oil holes

teeth protrude the most is facing towards the 5th gear.
60 Fit the next thrust washer and slide on the needle roller bearing. Secure the bearing in position with another new circlip, making sure it is correctly located in the output shaft groove, then lubricate the bearing and fit the outer race.

33 Initial start-up after overhaul

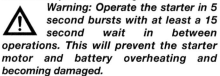

Note: *Do not install the inner and lower fairing panels until after the engine has been run.*
1 Make sure the engine oil and coolant levels are correct (see 'Daily (pre-ride) checks').
2 Turn on the ignition switch and crank the engine over with the starter to prime the lubrication system of the engine.

⚠ *Warning: Operate the starter in 5 second bursts with at least a 15 second wait in between operations. This will prevent the starter motor and battery overheating and becoming damaged.*

3 Make sure there is fuel in the tank then start the engine and allow it idle slowly.

⚠ *Warning: If the oil pressure warning light doesn't go off immediately or soon after the engine starts (a delay of a few seconds is usual), or it comes on while the engine is running, stop the engine immediately and investigate the cause.*

4 Once the oil pressure warning light goes out, bleed the air from the cooling system (see Chapter 1) and top-up the radiator and coolant reservoir fluid levels.
5 Warm the engine up to normal operating temperature whilst checking carefully for oil and coolant leaks. Check the operation of the clutch and transmission then switch off the engine.
6 Make sure the transmission and controls, especially the brakes, function properly before road testing the machine. Refer to Section 34 for the recommended break-in procedure.
7 Upon completion of the road test, and after the engine has cooled down completely, check the engine oil and the coolant level in both the radiator and reservoir before installing the fairing panels.

34 Recommended running-in procedure

1 Any rebuilt engine needs time to break-in, even if parts have been installed in their original locations. For this reason, treat the machine gently for the first few miles to make sure oil has circulated throughout the engine and any new parts installed have started to seat.

2 Even greater care is necessary if the engine has been fitted with a new cylinder block/liners and pistons or a new crankshaft. In the case of new cylinder block/liners and pistons, the engine will have to be broken in as if the machine were new. This means greater use of the transmission and a restraining hand on the throttle until at least 500 miles (800 km) have been covered. There's no point in keeping to any set speed limit – the main idea is to keep from labouring (lugging) the engine and to gradually increase performance until the 500 mile (800 km) mark is reached. These recommendations can be lessened to an extent when only a new crankshaft is installed. Experience is the best guide, since it's easy to tell when an engine is running freely.

3 If a lubrication failure is suspected, stop the engine immediately and try to find the cause. If an engine is run without oil, even for a short period of time, irreparable damage will occur.

Chapter 3
Cooling system

Contents

Degrees of difficulty

| **Easy,** suitable for novice with little experience | **Fairly easy,** suitable for beginner with some experience | **Fairly difficult,** suitable for competent DIY mechanic | **Difficult,** suitable for experienced DIY mechanic | **Very difficult,** suitable for expert DIY or professional ||

Specifications

Coolant
Mixture type and capacity .... see Chapter 1

Pressure cap
Cap valve opening pressure .... 14 to 18 psi (0.95 to 1.25 bar)

Cooling fan switch

	ZX-7R and ZX-9R B models	**ZX-9R C, E and F models**
Switches on (fan cut-in temperature)	93 to 103°C	96 to 100°C
Switches off (cooling fan cut-out temperature)	91 to 95°C	91°C (approximately)

Coolant temperature sensor
Temperature gauge circuit resistance
ZX-7R and ZX-9R B models
   At 80°C .... 47 to 57 ohms
   At 100°C .... 25 to 30 ohms
ZX-9R C, E and F models
   At 50°C .... 9.18 to 9.94 K ohms
   At 80°C .... 2.50 to 3.06 K ohms
   At 120°C .... 650 to 730 ohms

Thermostat
Opening temperature
ZX-7R models
   P1 models .... 58 to 62°C
   All other models .... 80 to 84°C
ZX-9R B models .... 80 to 84°C
ZX-9R C, E and F models .... 58 to 62°C
Valve lift .... 8 mm (minimum) at 95°C

Torque wrench settings
Cooling fan thermostatic switch .... 18 Nm
Coolant temperature gauge sensor
ZX-7R models .... 15 Nm
ZX-9R models .... 8 Nm
Thermostat housing cover bolts – ZX-9R C, E and F models .... 11 Nm
Water pump
ZX-7R and ZX-9R B models
   Mounting and cover bolts .... 10 Nm
   Pipe bolt .... 10 Nm
ZX-9R C, E and F models
   Mounting and cover bolts .... 11 Nm
   Impeller bolt .... 10 Nm

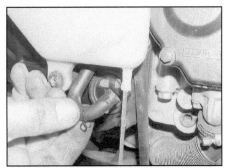

3.2 On ZX-7R and ZX-9R B models, disconnect the overflow hose and allow the reservoir contents to drain into a container

1 General information

The cooling system uses a water/antifreeze coolant to carry away excess energy in the form of heat. The cylinders are surrounded by a water jacket, from which the heated coolant is circulated by thermo-syphonic action in conjunction with a water pump which is driven off the rear of the clutch via the oil pump. The hot coolant passes through the thermostat to the radiator. The coolant then flows down through the radiator core, where it is cooled by the passing air, to the water pump and back to the engine, where the cycle is repeated. The coolant is also circulated around the oil cooler (fitted to the front of the crankcase) to keep the engine oil temperature constant under extreme operating conditions.

A thermostat is fitted in the system to prevent the coolant flowing through the radiator when the engine is cold, therefore accelerating the speed at which the engine reaches normal operating temperature.

The complete cooling system is partially sealed and pressurised, the pressure being controlled by a valve contained in the spring-loaded pressure cap. By pressurising the coolant, the boiling point is raised – preventing premature boiling in adverse conditions. The overflow pipe from the system is connected to a reservoir into which excess coolant is expelled under pressure. The

discharged coolant automatically returns to the radiator when the engine cools.

An electrically-operated cooling fan is fitted to aid cooling in extreme conditions. The fan is fitted to the rear of the radiator and is controlled by a thermostatic switch, which is screwed into the left side of the radiator. The coolant temperature gauge is controlled by the temperature sensor, which is screwed into the thermostat housing (ZX-7R and ZX-9R B models) or the rear of the cylinder head (ZX-9R C, E and F models).

⚠️ *Warning: Do not remove the pressure cap when the engine is hot. Scalding hot coolant and steam may be blown out under pressure, which could cause serious injury. When the engine has cooled, place a thick rag such as a towel over the pressure cap; slowly rotate the cap anti-clockwise to the first stop. This procedure allows any residual pressure to escape. When the steam has stopped escaping, press down on the cap while turning it anti-clockwise, and remove it.*

⚠️ *Warning: Do not allow antifreeze to come into contact with your skin or with the painted surfaces of the motorcycle. Rinse off any spills immediately with plenty of water. Antifreeze is highly toxic if ingested. Never leave antifreeze lying around in an open container or in puddles on the floor; children and pets are attracted by its sweet smell and may drink it. Check with the local authorities about disposing of used antifreeze. Many communities will have collection centres which will see that antifreeze is disposed of safely.*
Caution: At all times use the specified type of antifreeze, and always mix it with distilled water in the correct proportion. The antifreeze contains corrosion inhibitors which are essential to avoid damage to the cooling system. A lack of these inhibitors could lead to a build-up of corrosion which would block the coolant passages, resulting in overheating and severe engine damage. Distilled water must be used as opposed to tap water to avoid a build-up of scale which would also block the passages.

2 Radiator pressure cap – check

1 If problems such as overheating or loss of coolant occur, check the entire system as described in Chapter 1. The pressure cap opening pressure should be checked by a dealer with the special tester required to do the job. If the cap is defective renew it.

3 Coolant reservoir – removal and installation

Removal

ZX-7R and ZX-9R B models

1 Remove the right side lower fairing panel (see Chapter 8).
2 Place a suitable container underneath the reservoir. Release the clip, then detach the radiator overflow hose from the base of the reservoir and allow the coolant to drain into the container (see illustration).
3 Slacken and remove the mounting screws and remove the reservoir, complete with its cover and breather hose (see illustration). On ZX-9R B models, recover the spacers which are fitted between the reservoir and engine (see illustration).

ZX-9R C, E and F models

4 Remove the lower fairing and left middle fairing panel (see Chapter 8).
5 Place a suitable container underneath the reservoir. Release the clip, then detach the radiator overflow hose from the base of the reservoir and allow the coolant to drain into the container (see illustration).
6 Slacken and remove the mounting screws and recover the spacers which are fitted between the reservoir and frame (see illustration).
7 Remove the coolant reservoir, complete with its breather hose (see illustration).

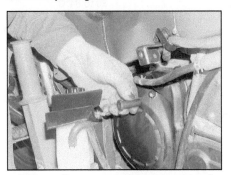

3.3a On ZX-9R B models, undo the retaining screws (arrowed) . . .

3.3b . . . then remove the reservoir and recover the spacers

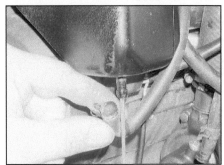

3.5 On ZX-9R C, E and F models, disconnect the overflow hose and allow the reservoir contents to drain into a container

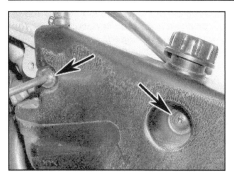

3.6 Undo the retaining screws (arrowed) . . .

Installation

8 Installation is the reverse of removal, noting the following.

  a) *Remove all traces of locking compound from the mounting screws and apply fresh locking compound to each screw prior to installing it.*

  b) *Make sure the hoses are correctly routed and secured with their clips.*

  c) *On completion top-up the reservoir as described in 'Daily (pre-ride) checks'.*

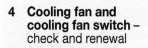

4 Cooling fan and cooling fan switch – check and renewal

Cooling fan

Check

1 If the engine is overheating and the cooling fan is not coming on, first check the cooling fan circuit fuse (see Chapter 9) and then the fan switch, as described in Steps 9 to 14.

2 If the fuse and the fan switch are good and the fan still does not come on, the fault lies either in the cooling fan motor or in the relevant wiring. Test all the wiring and connections as described in Chapter 9.

3 To test the cooling fan motor, it is necessary to locate the motor wiring connector as follows.

  ZX-9R B models – undo the four retaining screws and washers and remove the right side air filter housing intake duct cover. The fan

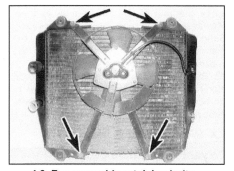

4.6 Fan assembly retaining bolts – ZX-9R B model

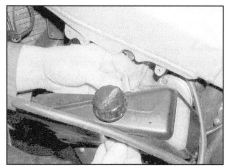

3.7 . . . then remove the reservoir and spacers from the bike

motor connector is located in between the radiator filler neck and the frame; it may be necessary to remove the intake duct to gain access.

  All other models – remove the air filter housing (see Chapter 4). The fan motor connector is located above the cylinder head cover.

4 Disconnect the wiring connector and, using a 12 volt battery and two jumper wires, connect the battery across the terminals of the motor connector. Once connected the fan should operate. If it does not, and the wiring is all good, then the fan motor is faulty.

Renewal

 Warning: The engine must be completely cool before carrying out this procedure.

5 Remove the radiator (see Section 7).

6 Unscrew the mounting bolts and remove the fan assembly from the rear of the radiator **(see illustration)**. There is no point in attempting to dismantle the fan assembly to remove the motor; no spare parts are available, so it must be treated as a sealed unit.

7 Fit the fan assembly to the rear of the radiator and securely tighten its retaining bolts.

8 Install the radiator (see Section 7).

Cooling fan switch

Check

9 If the engine is overheating and the cooling fan is not coming on, first check the cooling

4.10 Cooling fan switch is accessible through the left fairing panel

fan circuit fuse (see Chapter 9). If the fuse is blown, check the fan circuit for a short to earth (see the wiring diagrams at the end of this book).

10 If the fuse is good, disconnect the wiring connector(s) from the fan switch which is accessible through the left fairing panel **(see illustration)**. Switch on the ignition and check that battery voltage is present at the fan switch blue/black terminal; if not, check the wiring and connectors as described in Chapter 9. If battery voltage is present, using a jumper wire if necessary, connect the fan switch connector terminals together. The fan should come on. If it does, the fan switch is proven defective and must be renewed. If it does not come on, the fan motor should be tested (see Steps 3 and 4).

11 If the fan is on all the time, disconnect the switch wiring connector(s). The fan should stop. If it does, the switch is proven defective and must be renewed. If it does not, check the wiring between the switch and the fan for a short, and the fan motor (see Steps 3 and 4).

12 If the fan works but is suspected of cutting in at the wrong temperature, a more comprehensive test of the switch can be made as follows.

13 Remove the switch (see Steps 15 to 17). Fill a small, heatproof, container with oil and place it on a stove. Connect an ohmmeter across the terminals of the switch and, using some wire or other support, suspend the switch in the oil so that just the sensing portion and the threads are submerged **(see illustration)**. Also place a thermometer capable of reading temperatures up to 110°C in the oil so that its bulb is close to the switch. **Note:** *None of the components should be allowed to directly touch the container.*

14 Initially, the ohmmeter reading should show an open circuit (infinite resistance), indicating that the switch is open. Heat the oil, stirring it gently. When the oil reaches the

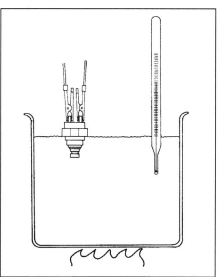

4.13 Cooling fan switch test set-up

4.16 Disconnect the wiring connector(s) from the cooling fan switch (ZX-9R B model shown)

specified temperature, the switch contacts should close and the meter should show continuity (zero resistance). Now turn the heat off. As the oil temperature falls, the switch contacts should open again at the specified temperature and the meter reading should show an open circuit again (infinite resistance). If the meter readings obtained are different, or they are obtained at different temperatures, then the fan switch is faulty and must be renewed.

 Warning: This must be done very carefully to avoid the risk of personal injury.

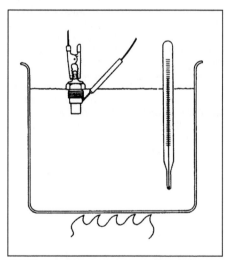

5.6 Temperature gauge sensor test set-up

5.10a On ZX-7R models, the temperature gauge sensor is screwed into the base of the thermostat housing

Renewal

 Warning: The engine must be completely cool before carrying out this procedure.

15 Drain the cooling system (see Chapter 1).
16 Disconnect the wiring connector(s) from the fan switch on the left-hand side of the radiator **(see illustration)**.
17 Unscrew the switch and remove it from the radiator.
18 Apply a suitable sealant to the switch threads (Kawasaki recommend the use of Kawasaki Bond 56019-120), then fit the switch to the radiator and tighten it to the specified torque setting. Take care not to overtighten the switch, as the radiator could be damaged.
19 Reconnect the switch wiring connector(s) and refill the cooling system (see Chapter 1).

5 Coolant temperature gauge and sensor – check and renewal

ZX-7R and ZX-9R B models

Coolant temperature gauge

Check

1 The coolant temperature gauge is located in the instrument cluster and is operated by the coolant temperature sensor on the thermostat housing. If the system malfunctions, check first that the battery is fully charged and that the fuses are all good (see Chapter 9).
2 If the gauge is not working, ensure the ignition is switched off, then disconnect the wiring connector from the coolant temperature sensor, which is fitted to the thermostat housing. On ZX-9R B models, remove the right lower fairing panel (see Chapter 8) to gain access to the sensor; on ZX-7R models, the sensor can be reached through the panel aperture. Turn the ignition switch on; the gauge needle should be at the C (Cold) end of the scale. Turn the ignition switch off again, then earth the sensor wiring connector. Turn the ignition switch on again; the gauge needle should swing towards the H (Hot) end of the scale. If the gauge performs as described, the coolant temperature sensor is proven defective and should be renewed.

5.10b On ZX-9R B models, the temperature gauge sensor is screwed into the front of the thermostat housing

Caution: Do not leave the ignition switched on for any longer than is necessary, or the gauge may be damaged.

3 If the temperature gauge does not perform as expected, the fault lies in the wiring or the gauge itself. Check all the relevant wiring and wiring connectors (see Chapter 9). If all appears to be well, the gauge is defective and must be renewed.
Renewal
4 Refer to Chapter 9.

Temperature gauge sensor

Check
5 If the temperature gauge sensor is suspected of being faulty, it should be removed (see Steps 8 to 10) and checked as follows.
6 Fill a small, heatproof, container with oil and place it on a stove. Connect the positive (+) probe of an ohmmeter to the terminal of the sensor and the negative (–) probe to the sensor body and, using some wire or other support, suspend the sensor in the oil so that just the sensing portion and the threads are submerged **(see illustration)**. Also place a thermometer capable of reading temperatures up to 120°C in the oil, so that its bulb is close to the switch. **Note:** *None of the components should be allowed to directly touch the container.*
7 Heat the oil, stirring it gently. Check that the correct resistance is obtained at the specified temperatures (see Specifications). If the meter readings obtained are significantly different, or they are obtained at different temperatures, then the sensor is faulty and must be renewed. **Note:** *Keep the temperature of the oil constant for a couple of minutes before taking each resistance reading to ensure accurate readings are obtained.*

 Warning: This must be done very carefully to avoid the risk of personal injury.
Renewal
8 On ZX-9R B models, remove the right lower fairing panel (see Chapter 8) to gain access to the sensor. On ZX-7R models, the sensor can be accessed through the lower fairing panel aperture.
9 Drain the cooling system (see Chapter 1).
10 Disconnect the wiring connector from the sensor then unscrew the sensor from the thermostat housing **(see illustrations)**.
11 Ensure the threads are clean and dry, then apply a smear of suitable sealant to them (Kawasaki recommend the use of Kawasaki Bond 56019-120). Fit the sensor to the thermostat housing and tighten it to the specified torque setting.
12 Reconnect the sensor wiring connector, then refill the cooling system (see Chapter 1). On completion, install the fairing panel, where removed (see Chapter 8).

ZX-9R C, E and F models

Coolant temperature gauge

Check
13 The coolant temperature gauge is part of the instrument cluster and is operated by the

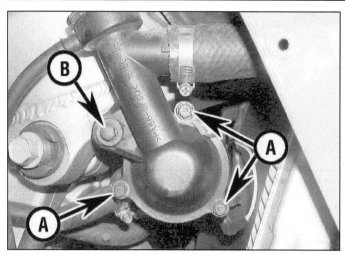

6.4 Thermostat housing bolts (A) and mounting bolt (B) – ZX-7R model

6.9 On ZX-9R B models, slacken the retaining clip and disconnect the overflow hose from the thermostat housing

temperature sensor on the rear of the cylinder head. If the system malfunctions, first check that the battery is fully charged and that the fuses are all good.

14 If the gauge is not working, remove the fuel tank (see Chapter 4). Ensure the ignition is switched off, then disconnect the wiring connector from the coolant temperature sensor (located beneath No. 1 cylinder carburettor). Turn the ignition switch on; none of the gauge segments should be visible. Turn the ignition switch off again, then earth (ground) the terminal of the sensor wiring connector. Turn the ignition switch on again; on C models, all eight segments of the gauge should be visible and the LED warning light should flash and, on E models, the display should read 'HI' and the LED warning light should flash. If the gauge performs as described, the coolant temperature sensor is proven defective and must be renewed.

Caution: Do not leave the ignition switched on for any longer than is necessary to take the reading, or the gauge may be damaged.

15 If the temperature gauge display does not perform as expected, the fault lies in the wiring or the gauge itself. Check all the relevant wiring and wiring connectors (see Chapter 9). If all appears to be well, the instrument cluster is defective and must be renewed. If the necessary equipment is available, a more conclusive test of the gauge can be carried out as described in Chapter 9.

Renewal

16 The temperature gauge is part of the instrument cluster unit (see Chapter 9).

Temperature gauge sensor

Check

17 If the temperature gauge sensor is suspected of being faulty, it should be removed (see Steps 18 to 20) and checked as described in Steps 6 and 7.

Renewal

18 Remove the fuel tank (see Chapter 4).

19 Drain the cooling system (see Chapter 1).

20 Disconnect the wiring connector from the sensor, then unscrew it from the rear of the cylinder head.

21 Ensure the threads are clean and dry, then apply a smear of suitable sealant to them (Kawasaki recommend the use of Kawasaki Bond 56019-120). Fit the sensor to the cylinder head and tighten it to the specified torque setting.

22 Reconnect the sensor wiring connector and install the fuel tank (see Chapter 4).

23 Refill the cooling system (see Chapter 1).

6 Thermostat – removal, check and installation

Removal

⚠ *Warning: The engine must be completely cool before carrying out this procedure.*

1 The thermostat is automatic in operation and should give many years of service without requiring attention. In the event of a failure, the valve will probably jam open, in which case the engine will take much longer than normal to warm up. Conversely, if the valve jams shut, the coolant will be unable to circulate and the engine will overheat. Neither

6.10a Unscrew the housing bolts . . .

condition is acceptable, and the fault must be investigated promptly.

ZX-7R models

2 Remove the left and right lower fairing panels (see Chapter 8).

3 Drain the cooling system (see Chapter 1).

4 Slacken the three bolts securing the two halves of the thermostat housing together **(see illustration)**.

5 Unscrew the bolt securing the thermostat housing to the frame and recover the collar and mounting rubber positioned on either side of the housing.

6 Remove the three bolts, noting the correct location of the earth lead, then separate the two halves of the housing. Lift out the thermostat and discard the housing O-ring; a new one must be used on installation.

ZX-9R B models

7 Remove the left and right lower fairing panels (see Chapter 8).

8 Drain the cooling system (see Chapter 1).

9 Release the retaining clip and disconnect the overflow hose from the thermostat housing cover **(see illustration)**.

10 Unscrew the retaining bolts and lift the cover off the thermostat housing **(see illustration)**. Discard the housing O-ring; a new one must be used on installation **(see illustration)**.

6.10b . . . and remove the O-ring . . .

6.11 . . . then lift out the thermostat

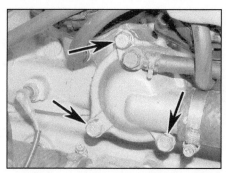

6.14a Unscrew the three retaining bolts (arrowed – shown with carburettors removed) . . .

6.14b . . . then free the thermostat cover and O-ring from the cylinder head . . .

11 Lift out the thermostat and remove it from the bike **(see illustration)**.

ZX-9R C, E and F models

12 Drain the cooling system (see Chapter 1).
13 Remove the fuel tank (see Chapter 4).
14 Unscrew the three bolts and free the thermostat cover from the rear of the cylinder head **(see illustration)**. Discard the cover O-ring; a new one must be used on installation **(see illustration)**.
15 Remove the thermostat from the cylinder head **(see illustration)**.

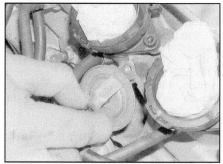

6.15 . . . and remove the thermostat

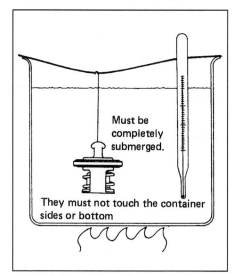

6.17 Thermostat test set-up

Must be completely submerged.

They must not touch the container sides or bottom

Check

16 Examine the thermostat visually before carrying out the test. If it remains in the open position at room temperature, it should be renewed.
17 Suspend the thermostat by a piece of wire in a container of cold water. Place a thermometer in the water so that the bulb is close to the thermostat **(see illustration)**. Heat the water, noting the temperature when the thermostat opens, and compare the result with the specifications given at the beginning of the Chapter. Also check the amount the valve opens after it has been heated at 95°C for a few minutes and compare the measurement to the specifications. If the readings obtained differ from those given, the thermostat is faulty and must be renewed.

 Warning: This must be done very carefully to avoid the risk of personal injury.

Installation

ZX-7R models

18 Locate the thermostat in the inner half of the housing, positioning it so its air bleed-hole is uppermost.
19 Fit the new O-ring to the recess in the outer half, then assemble the thermostat housing. Install the housing bolts, not forgetting the earth lead, and tighten them securely.
20 Position a collar and mounting rubber on either side of the housing, then fit the mounting bolt and tighten it securely.
21 Refill the cooling system, then install the fairing panels (see Chapters 1 and 8).

ZX-9R B models

22 Locate the thermostat correctly in the housing.
23 Fit the new O-ring to the recess in the cover. Fit the cover to the housing and securely tighten its retaining bolts.
24 Securely reconnect the overflow hose, then refill the cooling system (see Chapter 1).
25 On completion, install the fairing panels (see Chapter 8).

ZX-9R C, E and F models

26 Locate the thermostat correctly in the cylinder head.

27 Fit the new O-ring to the recess in the cover and locate the cover on the head. Install the cover retaining bolts and tighten them to the specified torque.
28 Install the fuel tank, then refill the cooling system (see Chapter 1).

7 Radiator – removal and installation

Removal

 Warning: The engine must be completely cool before carrying out this procedure.

ZX-7R and ZX-9R B models

1 Remove the complete fairing (see Chapter 8).
2 Drain the cooling system (see Chapter 1).
3 On ZX-7R models, remove the fuel tank and air cleaner housing (see Chapter 4). Disconnect the cooling fan motor wiring connector, located above the cylinder head cover, then free the wiring harness so that it can be removed with the radiator.
4 On ZX-9R B models, disconnect the cooling fan motor wiring connector located between the thermostat housing and frame, and free the wiring harness so that it can be removed with the radiator **(see illustration)**.
5 On all models, slacken the retaining clips and disconnect the coolant hoses from the

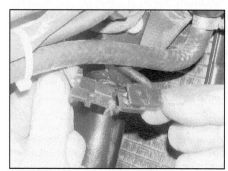

7.4 On ZX-9R B models, disconnect the cooling fan motor wiring connector, which is located near the thermostat housing

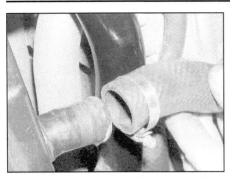

7.5 Slacken the retaining clips and disconnect the coolant hoses from the left- and right-hand sides of the radiator

7.7 Unscrew the mounting bolts and remove the radiator from the bike

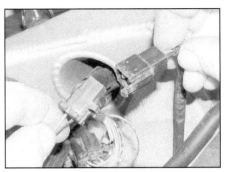

7.11 On ZX-9R C, E and F models, disconnect the cooling fan wiring connector, which is located above the cylinder head . . .

left- and right-hand sides of the radiator, noting their correct fitted locations **(see illustration)**.

6 Disconnect the wiring connectors from the cooling fan switch, fitted to the left side of the radiator.

7 Slacken and remove the two upper and two lower mounting bolts and manoeuvre the radiator assembly out of position (on ZX-9R B models, note the correct fitted location of the horn) **(see illustration)**. Recover the collar from each radiator mounting rubber and inspect the rubbers for signs of damage or deterioration, renewing them as a set if necessary.

ZX-9R C, E and F models

8 Remove the lower fairing and both middle panels (see Chapter 8).
9 Drain the cooling system (see Chapter 1).

10 Remove the fuel tank and air cleaner housing (see Chapter 4).
11 Disconnect the cooling fan motor wiring connector, located above the cylinder head cover, then free the wiring harness so that it can be removed with the radiator **(see illustration)**.
12 Disconnect the wiring connector from the cooling fan switch, fitted to the left-hand side of the radiator **(see illustration)**.
13 Slacken the retaining clips and disconnect the coolant hoses from the left- and right-hand sides of the radiator, noting their correct fitted locations **(see illustrations)**. Free the clutch cable from its guide on the right-hand side of the radiator.
14 Slacken and remove the two upper bolts, noting the correct fitted position of the horn bracket, and lower mounting bolt **(see illustrations)**. Manoeuvre the radiator assembly out of position **(see illustration)**.

Recover the collar from each radiator mounting rubber and inspect the rubbers for signs of damage or deterioration, renewing them as a set if necessary.

Installation

15 Ensure the mounting rubbers and collars are correctly fitted to the radiator, then manoeuvre the radiator into position. Fit the mounting bolts, not forgetting the horn mounting bracket (ZX-9R models), and tighten them securely.
16 Ensure the cooling fan motor wiring is correctly routed and reconnect it to the main wiring harness.
17 Reconnect all the coolant hoses, securing them in position with the retaining clips. Pass the clutch cable back through its guide.
18 Reconnect the cooling fan switch wiring connector(s).

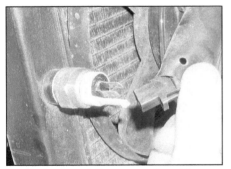

7.12 . . . and disconnect the wiring connector from the cooling fan switch

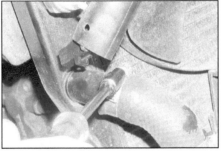

7.13a Slacken the retaining clips and disconnect the coolant hoses from the left- . . .

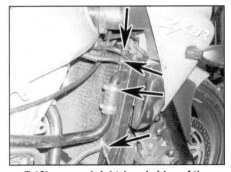

7.13b . . . and right-hand sides of the radiator

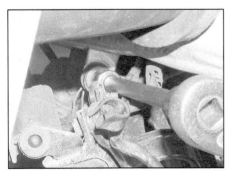

7.14a Slacken and remove the upper . . .

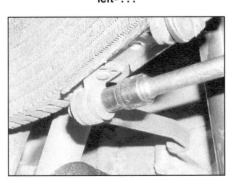

7.14b . . . and lower mounting bolts . . .

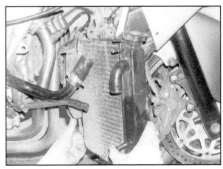

7.14c . . . then manoeuvre the radiator out of position

8.5a On ZX-7R and ZX-9R B models, unscrew the bolt . . .

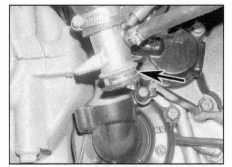

8.5b . . . then free the pipe from the water pump cover and recover the O-ring (arrowed)

8.6 Slacken the retaining clip and disconnect the cylinder block hose from the pump

19 Install the air cleaner housing and fuel tank (where necessary) as described in Chapter 4.
20 Refill the cooling system (see Chapter 1).
21 On completion install the fairing panels (see Chapter 8).

8 Water pump –
check, removal and installation

Check

1 The water pump is located on the lower, left-hand side of the engine. Visually check the area around the pump for signs of leakage.
2 To prevent leakage of water from the cooling system to the lubrication system and vice versa, two seals are fitted on the pump shaft. On the underside of the pump body there is also a drainage hole. If either seal fails, this hole should allow the coolant or oil to escape and prevent the oil and coolant mixing.
3 The seal on the water pump side is of the mechanical type which bears on the rear face

of the impeller. The second seal, which is mounted behind the mechanical seal, is of the normal feathered lip type. On ZX-7R and ZX-9R B models, the pump must be treated as a sealed unit; neither seal is available separately. On ZX-9R C, E and F models, the seals can be renewed if leakage has occurred.

Removal
ZX-7R and ZX-9R B models

4 Drain the coolant (see Chapter 1). Place a suitable container below the water pump to catch any residual oil as the water pump is removed.
5 Unscrew the retaining bolt and free the radiator lower hose pipe from the water pump cover **(see illustration)**. Recover the pipe O-ring and discard it; a new one should be used on installation **(see illustration)**.
6 Slacken the retaining clip and disconnect the cylinder block hose from the water pump **(see illustration)**.
7 Slacken and remove the two bolts securing the pump to the crankcase (there is no need to remove the other two bolts, they secure the cover to the pump) **(see illustration)**.
8 Withdraw the pump from the crankcase **(see illustration)**. Remove the O-ring from the

rear of the pump body and discard it, as a new one must be used.
9 If necessary, unscrew the two bolts and remove the cover from the pump. Discard the cover seal; a new one should be used on installation.
10 If the drainage hole shows signs of leakage, or the pump impeller is badly corroded, the pump assembly must be renewed.

ZX-9R C, E and F models

11 Drain the coolant (see Chapter 1). Place a suitable container below the water pump to catch any residual oil as the water pump housing is removed.
12 Release the wiring/hoses from the clamp on the water pump and position them clear of the pump **(see illustration)**.
13 Release the retaining clips and disconnect the coolant hoses from the pump cover **(see illustrations)**.
14 Slacken and remove the three retaining bolts, along with the wiring/hose clamp, and remove the pump cover **(see illustration)**. Discard the cover seal; a new one will be needed on installation. If the cover locating pins are loose-fit, remove them and store them with the cover for safe-keeping.

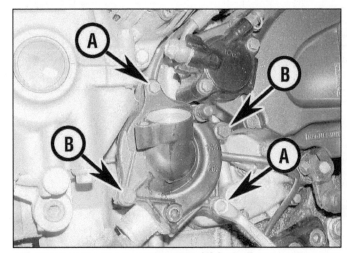

8.7 Unscrew the two mounting bolts (A) (bolts B secure the cover to the pump) . . .

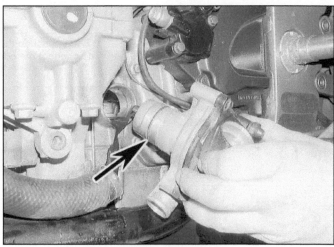

8.8 . . . then remove the pump assembly from the engine and recover its O-ring

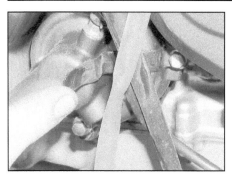

8.12 On ZX-9R C, E and F models, release the wiring and hoses from the pump clamp

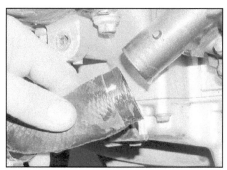

8.13a Slacken the retaining clips and disconnect the radiator hose . . .

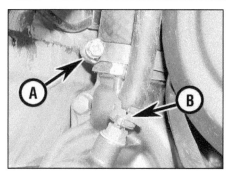

8.13b . . . cylinder block hose (A) and carburettor hose (B – UK models) from the pump cover

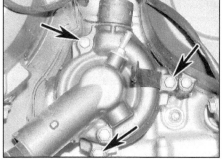
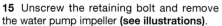

8.14 Unscrew the retaining bolts (arrowed) and remove the pump cover and seal

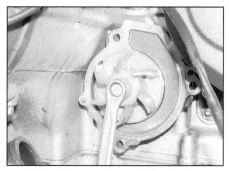

8.15a Unscrew the retaining bolt . . .

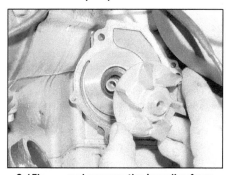

8.15b . . . and remove the impeller from the shaft

15 Unscrew the retaining bolt and remove the water pump impeller **(see illustrations)**.

16 Screw one of the water pump cover bolts into the end of the pump shaft. Push firmly on the bolt to ensure the pump shaft and oil pump components remain in the crankcase, then slide the water pump housing off **(see illustration)**. Recover the pump housing dowels and discard its O-ring; a new one will be needed on installation.

17 If the drainage hole shows signs of leakage, both the housing seals should be renewed. To renew the seals, carefully prise the mechanical seal and oil seal out of

position, noting which way round they are fitted. Carefully press the new oil seal fully into the housing, ensuring its sealing lip is facing the correct way (towards the oil pump), then carefully fit the new mechanical seal. Ensure both seals are correctly located (this is especially important for the mechanical seal), otherwise leakage could occur.

18 Inspect the pump impeller for signs of damage or corrosion and renew if necessary.

19 Also check the pump shaft for signs of damage and renew if necessary (see Chapter 2B).

Installation

ZX-7R and ZX-9R B models

20 Apply a smear of engine oil to the new O-ring and install it onto the rear of the pump body. Install the pump into the crankcase, aligning the slot in the impeller shaft with the tab on the oil pump shaft **(see illustration)**.

21 Where necessary, fit the new seal to the pump cover, then fit the cover to the pump, tightening its retaining bolts to the specified torque.

22 Install the pump mounting bolts and tighten them to the specified torque.

8.16 Screw a cover bolt into the pump shaft, then withdraw the pump housing – whilst pushing the bolt firmly into the engine to ensure the oil pump components remain in position

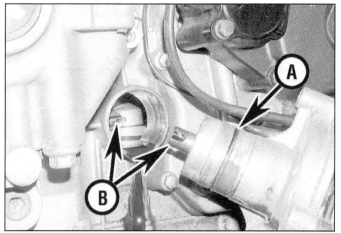

8.20 Ensure the O-ring (A) is correctly fitted, then install the pump – aligning the slot in the impeller shaft with the tab on the oil pump shaft (B)

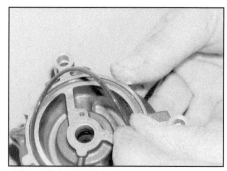

8.28a Fit a new O-ring to the groove in the rear of the pump housing . . .

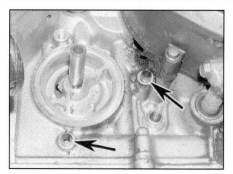

8.28b . . . then ensure the locating dowels (arrowed) are in position . . .

8.28c . . . and slide the housing into position

23 Reconnect the cylinder block hose to the pump and securely tighten its retaining clip.
24 Apply a smear of engine oil to the new O-ring, then fit it to the radiator hose pipe. Ease the pipe into position in the pump cover and tighten its retaining bolt to the specified torque.
25 Refill the cooling system (see Chapter 1).
26 On completion, install the fairing panels (see Chapter 8) and check the engine oil level (see *Daily (pre-ride) checks*).

ZX-9R C, E and F models

27 Ensure the oil pump components are correctly fitted to the crankcase (see Chapter 2B).
28 Ensure both locating dowels are in position, then fit a new O-ring to the groove in the rear of the water pump housing **(see illustrations)**. Carefully slide the housing along the pump shaft and locate it on the dowels, ensuring the O-ring remains correctly seated in the groove **(see illustration)**.
29 Fit the water pump impeller to the shaft and install its retaining bolt and washer, tightening it to the specified torque.
30 Ensure both locating pins are in position, then fit a new seal to the groove in the rear of the water pump cover **(see illustration)**. Fit the cover and install the retaining bolts, not forgetting the wiring/hose clamp, and tighten

them to the specified torque.
31 Reconnect the coolant hoses to the pump, securing them in position with the retaining clips.
32 Securing the wiring/hose in position with the clamp on the pump.
33 Refill the cooling system as described in Chapter 1.
34 Check the engine oil level (see *Daily (pre-ride) checks*), then start the engine and check for leaks before installing the lower fairing (see Chapter 8).

---

9 Coolant hoses – removal and installation

Removal

1 Before removing the hoses, drain the coolant (see Chapter 1).
2 To disconnect a hose, release the retaining clips and move them along the hose, clear of the relevant union. There are two different types of clip – the standard screw-type clip, and the spring clip (fitted to the smaller bore hoses), released by squeezing their ends together with a pair of pliers. Carefully work the hose free.

Caution: The radiator unions are fragile. Do not use excessive force when attempting to remove the hoses.

3 If a hose proves stubborn, release it by rotating it on its union before working it off. If all else fails, cut the hose with a sharp knife, then slit it at each union so that it can be peeled off in two pieces. Whilst this means renewing the hose, it is preferable to buying a new radiator.

Installation

4 Slide the clips onto the hose, and then work it on to its respective union.

HAYNES HINT
If the hose is difficult to push on to its union, it can be softened by soaking it in very hot water, or alternatively a little soapy water can be used as a lubricant.

5 Rotate the hose on its unions to settle it in position before sliding the clips into place and tightening them securely. Some hoses are equipped with alignment marks to ensure they are correctly positioned; align the paint mark on the hose with the raised mark on the union before tightening the clip **(see illustration)**.
6 On completion, refill the cooling system (see Chapter 1).

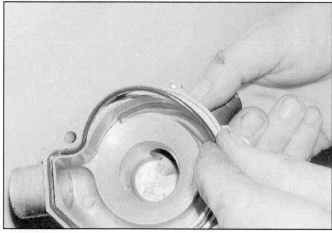

8.30 Ensure the new seal is correctly located in its groove in the pump cover

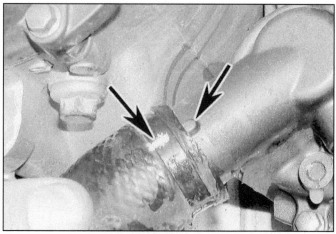

9.5 Some hoses are equipped with alignment marks; align the paint mark with the raised mark on the union, to ensure the hose is correctly positioned

Chapter 4
Fuel and exhaust systems

Contents

Degrees of difficulty

| Easy, suitable for novice with little experience | Fairly easy, suitable for beginner with some experience | Fairly difficult, suitable for competent DIY mechanic | Difficult, suitable for experienced DIY mechanic 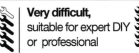 | Very difficult, suitable for expert DIY or professional |

Specifications

General

Fuel tank capacity
| | |
ZX-7R models . . . . 18 lit, inc. 5 lit reserve
ZX-9R B models . . . . 20 lit, inc. 4 lit reserve
ZX-9R C and E models . . . . 19 lit, inc. 4 lit reserve
Fuel grade
UK models . . . . 91 RON unleaded
US models . . . . 87 Antiknock index, unleaded
Carburettor type
ZX-7R models . . . . Keihin CVKD38
ZX-9R B, C and F models . . . . Keihin CVKD40
ZX-9R E models . . . . Keihin CVRD40

Fuel pump

Fuel pump cut-off pressure . . . . 1.6 to 2.3 psi (0.11 to 0.16 bar)
Fuel pump relay internal resistance . . . . see text
Fuel cut-off valve protrusion
Battery connected . . . . 18.6 to 19.1 mm
Battery disconnected . . . . 16.6 mm

Jet sizes – ZX-7R models

Main jet
Cylinders 1 and 4 . . . . 200*
Cylinders 2 and 3 . . . . 210*
Main air jet 60
Jet needle
US models N3HC
All other models N3GF
Pilot jet 42*
Pilot air jet 140
Starter jet 55

*On US models used at high altitude (above 4000 ft), Kawasaki recommend that the main jets are changed to 195 (cylinders 1 and 4) and 200 (cylinders 2 and 3) and the pilot jet to 40.

Jet sizes – ZX-9R B models

Main jet
    US models 190*
    All other models 200
Main air jet 50
Jet needle
    Cylinders 1 and 4 . . . . N67T
    Cylinders 2 and 3 . . . . N67U
Pilot jet 35*
Pilot air jet 120
Starter jet 58
*On US models used at high altitude (above 4000 ft), Kawasaki recommend that the main jets are changed to 185 and the pilot jets to 32.

Jet sizes – ZX-9R C models

Main jet 155*
Main air jet 70
Jet needle N74V
Pilot jet 38*
Pilot air jet 120
Starter jet 48
*On US models (except California models) used at high altitude (above 4000 ft), Kawasaki recommend that the main jets are changed to 152 and the pilot jets to 32. California models require no adjustment.

Jet sizes – ZX-9R E models

Main jet
    Cylinders 1 and 4 . . . . 160*
    Cylinders 2 and 3 . . . . 165*
Main air jet
    California, German and Swiss models 50
    All other models 70
Jet needle N99B
Pilot jet 38*
Pilot air jet 90
Starter jet 48
*On US models (except California models) used at high altitude (above 4000 ft), Kawasaki recommend that the main jets are changed to 152 and the pilot jets to 35.

Jet sizes – ZX-9R F models

Main jet
    Cylinders 1 and 4 165
    Cylinders 2 and 3 160
Main air jet 70
Jet needle
    Cylinders 1 and 4 . . . . N6NF
    Cylinders 2 and 3 . . . . N74W
Pilot jet 38
Pilot air jet 125
Starter jet 48

Carburettor adjustments

Float height
    ZX-9R E models . . . . 4 ± 2 mm
    All other models . . . . 13 ± 2 mm
Fuel level
    ZX-7R models and ZX-9R B models . . . . 5 ± 1 mm below the mark
    ZX-9R C and F models . . . . 4.5 ± 1 mm below the mark
    ZX-9R E models . . . . 18.5 ± 1 mm below the mark
Pilot screw (turns out)
    European models
        ZX-7R models . . . . 1 ¾
        ZX-9R B models . . . . 1 ½ ± ¼
        ZX-9R C models 2
        ZX-9R E models . . . . 1 ⅝
    US models . . . . Not available
Carburettor synchronisation . . . . see Chapter 1
Throttle and choke cable freeplay . . . . see Chapter 1

Torque wrench settings

Air suction valve cover bolts
    ZX-7R models and ZX-9R B models . . . . 10 Nm
    ZX-9R C models . . . . 11 Nm
    ZX-9R E models . . . . 13 Nm
Silencer mounting nuts – ZX-9R C models . . . . 34 Nm

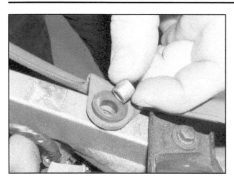

2.3a On ZX-7R models, undo the side cover front retaining screws and recover the spacers from the mounting rubbers . . .

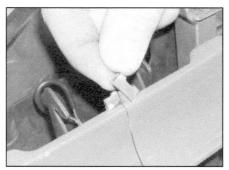

2.3b . . . then release the clips securing the side covers together

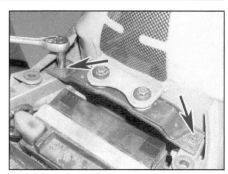

2.4 Undo the two bolts (arrowed) securing the tank rear mounting bracket to the frame . . .

1 General information and precautions

The fuel system consists of the fuel tank, the fuel tap, the fuel filter, the fuel pump and relay, the carburettors and the connecting lines, hoses and control cables. The carburettors used are four constant vacuum Keihin with butterfly-type throttle valves. For cold starting, an enrichment circuit is actuated by a cable from the choke lever mounted on the left handlebar.

Air is drawn into the carburettors via an air filter which is housed under the fuel tank. The air filter housing intakes are located in the upper fairing and use the forward motion of the bike to create a ram-air effect in the airbox.

The exhaust system is a four-into-one design. On ZX-9R C and E California, German and Swiss market models, and on all ZX-9R F models, a full catalytic converter is incorporated in the exhaust system and fuel cut-off valves are fitted (see Section 22). UK ZX-9R E models are equipped with a pre-catalytic converter element in the pipe but not the main element in the silencer or the fuel cut-off valves (see Section 23).

Many of the fuel system service procedures are considered routine maintenance items and for that reason are included in Chapter 1.

Precautions

⚠️ **Warning: Petrol (gasoline) is extremely flammable, so take extra precautions when you work on any part of the fuel system. Don't smoke or allow open flames or bare light bulbs near the work area, and don't work in a garage where a natural gas-type appliance is present. If you spill any fuel on your skin, rinse it off immediately with soap and water. When you perform any kind of work on the fuel system, wear safety glasses and have a fire extinguisher suitable for a class B type fire (flammable liquids) on hand.**

Always perform service procedures in a well-ventilated area to prevent a build-up of fumes.

Never work in a building containing a gas appliance with a pilot light, or any other form of naked flame. Ensure that there are no naked light bulbs or any sources of flame or sparks nearby.

Do not smoke (or allow anyone else to smoke) while in the vicinity of petrol (gasoline) or of components containing it. Remember the possible presence of vapour from these sources and move well clear before smoking.

Check all electrical equipment belonging to the house, garage or workshop where work is being undertaken (see the *Safety first!* section of this manual). Remember that certain electrical appliances such as drills, cutters etc. create sparks in the normal course of operation and must not be used near petrol (gasoline) or any component containing it. Again, remember the possible presence of fumes before using electrical equipment.

Always mop up any spilt fuel and safely dispose of the rag used.

Any stored fuel that is drained off during servicing work must be kept in sealed containers that are suitable for holding petrol (gasoline), and clearly marked as such; the containers themselves should be kept in a safe place. Note that this last point applies equally to the fuel tank if it is removed from the machine; also remember to keep its filler cap closed at all times.

Read the *Safety first!* section of this manual carefully before starting work.

2 Fuel tank – removal and installation

⚠️ **Warning: Refer to the precautions given in Section 1 before starting work.**

ZX-7R models

Removal

1 Turn the fuel tap to the 'OFF' position.
2 Remove the seats (see Chapter 8).
3 Slacken and remove the screw and spacer from the left and right side cover front mounting rubbers and slide off the clips

securing the side covers together **(see illustrations)**.
4 Unscrew the two bolts securing the fuel tank rear mounting bracket to the frame **(see illustration)**.
5 Slacken and remove the two fuel tank front mounting bolts **(see illustration)**.
6 Lift the rear of the tank and disconnect the fuel hose from the tap. On California models, also mark and disconnect the evaporative emission system hoses from the rear of the tank.
Caution: On California models plug the evaporative emission system hoses to prevent the vapour separator canister from being contaminated (see Section 21).
7 Lift the tank away from the machine, taking care not to damage the side covers, disconnecting the tank breather/drain hose as it becomes accessible. Take care not to lose the collars from the front mounting rubbers or the rear mounting rubbers from the underside of the tank. If necessary remove the bolts and collars and separate the rear mounting bracket from the tank.
8 Inspect all mounting rubbers for signs of damage or deterioration and renew them if necessary.

Installation

9 Ensure the mounting rubbers are correctly fitted then insert the collars into the bottom of both tank front mounting rubbers. Where necessary, fit the collars to the top of the rear mounting rubbers then install the mounting bracket, tightening its retaining bolts securely.
10 Manoeuvre the tank into position, taking

2.5 . . . and the two front mounting bolts

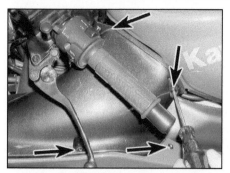

2.16a On ZX-9R B models, undo the screws (arrowed) . . .

2.16b . . . and remove the covers from the air filter housing intake ducts

2.17a Undo the retaining screw . . .

2.17b . . . and remove the control knob from the fuel tap

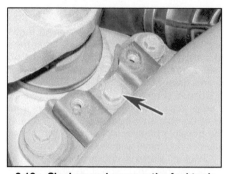

2.18a Slacken and remove the fuel tank front mounting bolt (arrowed) . . .

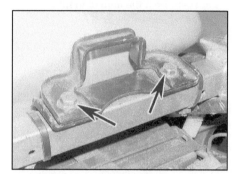

2.18b . . . and rear mounting bolts (arrowed)

care not to damage the side covers, and securely reconnect the fuel and breather/drain hoses. On California models also connect the evaporative emission system hoses.
11 Ensure the tank is correctly seated then fit

the front and rear mounting bolts and tighten them securely.
12 Ensure the side covers are correctly seated then fit the cover spacers, screws and clips.

13 Turn on the fuel tap then start the engine and check that there is no sign of fuel leakage. If all is well, install the seats (see Chapter 8).

ZX-9R B models

Removal

14 Turn the fuel tap to the 'OFF' position.
15 Remove the seats (see Chapter 8).
16 Undo the four retaining screws and washers securing each air filter housing intake duct cover in position and remove both the left and right covers (see illustrations).
17 Undo the screw and remove the control knob from the fuel tap (see illustrations).
18 Slacken and remove the bolts securing the tank front and rear mounting brackets to the frame (see illustration).
19 Disconnect the breather/drain hose from the rear of the tank (see illustration). On California models, also mark and disconnect the evaporative emission hoses from the rear of the tank.
Caution: On California models plug the evaporative emission system hoses to prevent the vapour separator canister from being contaminated (see Section 21).
20 Disconnect the fuel hose from the tap (see illustration).
21 Trace the wiring back from the fuel gauge sender unit and disconnect it at the connector (see illustration).
22 Lift the fuel tank carefully out of position, taking care not to lose the mounting rubbers from the underside of the tank (see illustration). With the tank removed, if

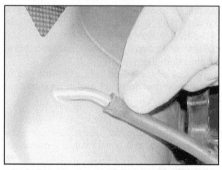

2.19 Disconnect the breather/drain hose from the rear of the tank

2.20 Lift the rear of the tank and disconnect the fuel hose from the tap

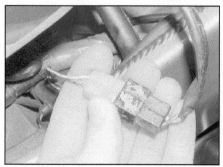

2.21 Disconnect the fuel gauge sender unit wiring connector

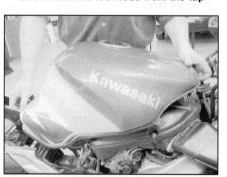

2.22a Removing the fuel tank – ZX-9R B model

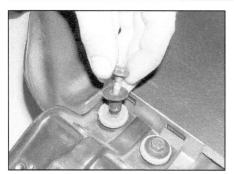

2.22b Slacken and remove the bolts and collars and remove the mounting brackets from the tank

2.22c Inspect the tank mounting rubbers for damage and deterioration and renew if necessary

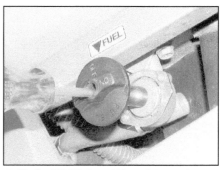

2.30 On ZX-9R C and E models, undo the retaining screw and remove the control knob from the fuel tap

necessary, slacken and remove the bolts and collars and separate the front and rear mounting brackets from the tank **(see illustration)**. Inspect the tank mounting rubbers for damage or deterioration and renew them if necessary **(see illustration)**.

Installation

23 Where necessary, ensure the mounting rubbers are correctly located in the mounting brackets then fit the brackets to the tank. Install the collars in the rubbers then securely tighten the bracket bolts.
24 Ensure the mounting rubbers are correctly fitted then manoeuvre the tank into position. Securely reconnect the fuel hose and the fuel gauge sender wiring connector then seat the tank on the frame.
25 Reconnect the breather/drain hose to the tank. On California models also connect the evaporative emission system hoses. Fit the front and rear mounting bolts and tighten them securely.
26 Install the fuel tap control knob and securely tighten its screw.
27 Turn on the fuel tap then start the engine and check that there is no sign of fuel leakage. If all is well, install the seats (see Chapter 8) then fit the covers to the air filter intake ducts.

ZX-9R C, E and F models

Removal

28 Turn the fuel tap to the 'OFF' position.
29 Remove the seats (see Chapter 8).
30 Undo the screw and remove the control knob from the fuel tap **(see illustration)**.
31 Slacken and remove the bolts securing the tank front and rear mountings to the frame **(see illustration)**. Remove the seat mounting bracket which is fitted to the tank rear mounting bolts **(see illustration)**.
32 Disconnect the breather/drain hose from the rear of the tank **(see illustration)**. On California models, also mark and disconnect the evaporative emission hoses from the rear of the tank.
Caution: On California models plug the evaporative emission system hoses to prevent the vapour separator canister from being contaminated (see Section 21).

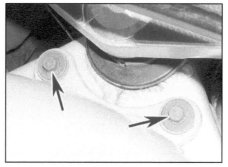

2.31a Slacken and remove the fuel tank front mounting bolts (arrowed) . . .

33 Disconnect the fuel hose from the tap.
34 Lift the fuel tank carefully out of position, taking care not to lose the collars from the underside of the mounting rubbers **(see illustration)**. Inspect the tank mounting rubbers for damage or deterioration and renew them if necessary.

Installation

35 Ensure the mounting rubbers are correctly fitted and fit the mounting collars to the underside of the rubbers.
36 Manoeuvre the tank into position and seat it correctly on the frame.
37 Securely reconnect the fuel hose and the breather/drain hose to the tank. On California models also connect the evaporative emission system hoses.
38 Fit the seat mounting bracket collars to the rear of the tank then fit the front and rear mounting bolts and tighten them securely.

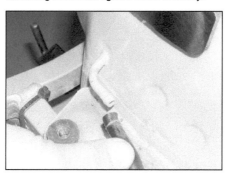

2.32 Disconnect the breather/drain hose from the rear of the tank

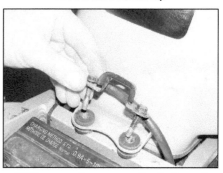

2.31b . . . and rear mounting bolts and remove the seat mounting bracket

39 Install the fuel tap control knob and securely tighten its screw.
40 Turn on the fuel tap then start the engine and check that there is no sign of fuel leakage. If all is well, install the seats (see Chapter 8).

3 Fuel tank – cleaning and repair

1 All repairs to the fuel tank should be carried out by a professional who has experience in this critical and potentially dangerous work. Even after cleaning and flushing of the fuel system, explosive fumes can remain and ignite during repair of the tank.
2 If the fuel tank is removed from the bike, it should not be placed in an area where sparks or open flames could ignite the fumes coming out of the tank. Be especially careful inside

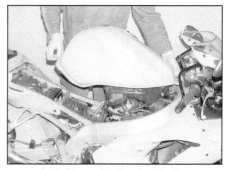

2.34 Removing the fuel tank – ZX-9R C model

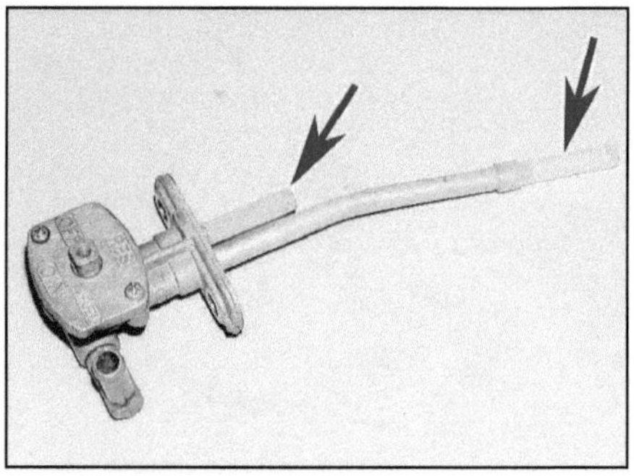

4.4 Check the fuel tap filters for signs of damage or blockage

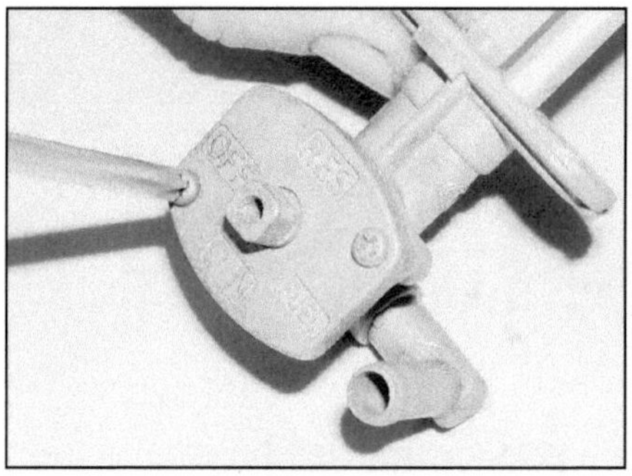

4.11a Undo the retaining screws and remove the retaining plate from the tap . . .

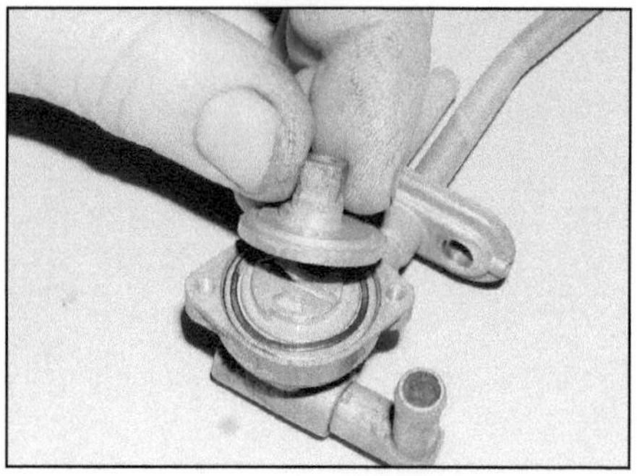

4.11b . . . followed by the adapter . . .

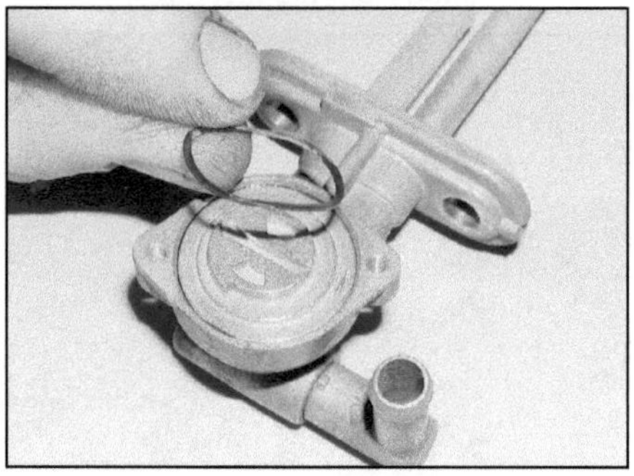

4.11c . . . and washer

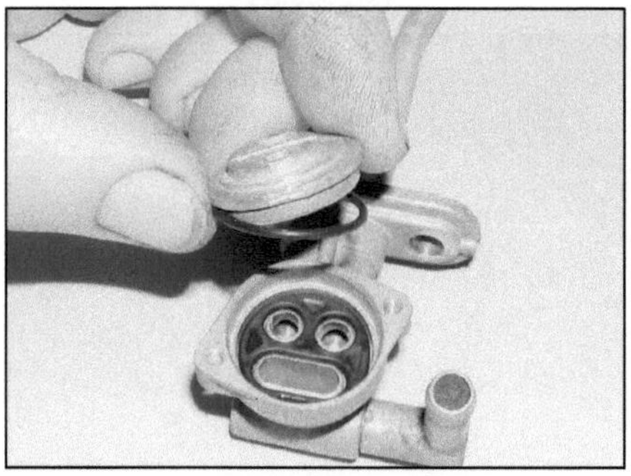

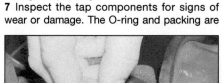

4.11d Lift out the valve and O-ring from the tap and recover the packing

garages where a natural gas-type appliance is located, because the pilot light could cause an explosion.

4 Fuel tap – removal, overhaul and installation

Warning: Refer to the precautions given in Section 1 before starting work.

Removal

1 Remove the fuel tank (see Section 2) and drain its contents into a suitable container.

2 Place the tank upside down on some soft cloth to prevent damage to the paintwork.

3 Slacken and remove the retaining bolts and sealing washers and remove the fuel tap assembly from the tank. Recover the tap rubber seal. The tap seal and retaining bolt sealing washers must be renewed if they show signs of wear or damage.

4 Check the fuel tap filters for signs damage or deterioration **(see illustration)**. If the filters are damaged they should be renewed (the filters are not available separately – the complete tap assembly will have to be renewed), if they are dirty clean them in fresh fuel.

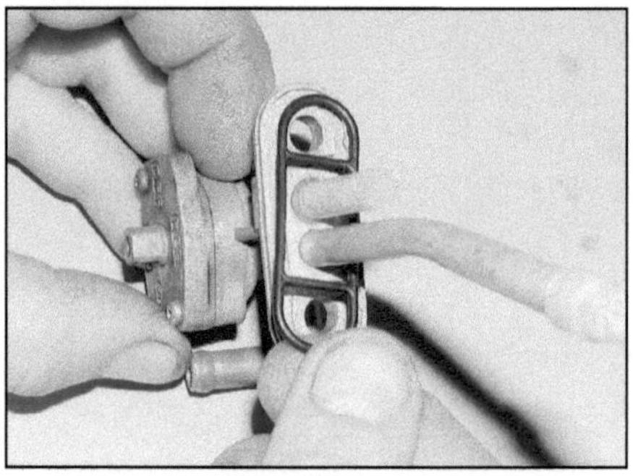

4.14 Fit the rubber seal to the tap groove then install the tap

Overhaul

ZX-7R models

5 Remove the tap (see Steps 1 to 4) then undo the screw and remove the control knob from the tap.

6 Slacken and remove the two screws and lift off the retaining plate from the tap. Remove the valve from the tap body and recover the O-ring and packing.

7 Inspect the tap components for signs of wear or damage. The O-ring and packing are the only components available separately; if any other components are worn the complete tap assembly will have to be renewed.

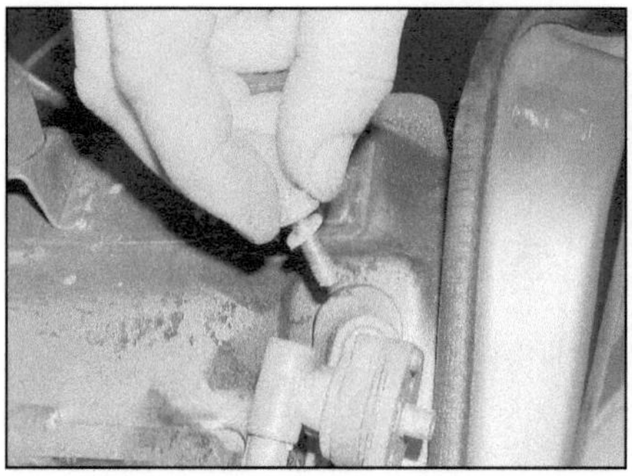

4.15 Ensure the sealing washers are in position before installing the tap bolts

8 Fit the packing and new O-ring to the tap then install the valve and fit the retaining plate. Fit the retaining plate screws and screw them in evenly until both are securely tightened.

9 Fit the control knob, tightening its retaining screw securely, and check the operation of the tap before fitting the tap to the tank.

ZX-9R models

10 Remove the tap (see Steps 1 to 4).

11 Slacken and remove the two screws and remove the retaining plate, adapter, washer and valve from the tap body followed by the O-ring and packing **(see illustrations)**.

12 Inspect the tap components for signs of wear or damage. The O-ring and packing are the only components available separately; if any other components are worn the complete tap assembly will have to be renewed.

13 Fit the packing and new O-ring to the tap then install the valve, washer and retaining plate. Fit the screws and screw them in evenly until both are securely tightened. Check the operation of the tap before fitting it to the tank.

Installation

14 Ensure the tap filters are clean and securely fitted then fit the rubber seal to the tap **(see illustration)**.

15 Fit the tap to the tank, ensuring the seal remains correctly seated, then fit the sealing washers and retaining bolts **(see illustration)**. Tighten the bolts evenly and progressively until both are secure.

16 Fit the fuel tank (see Section 2).

5 Fuel pump and relay – check

1 The fuel pump operates when the starter button is depressed and when the engine is running. The fuel pump supplies fuel to the carburettors when the fuel level in the float chambers is low; when the fuel reaches the predetermined level, the fuel pressure rises and the fuel pump automatically shuts off. The fuel pressure sensor is integral with the pump.

If the fuel pump is thought to be faulty, carry out the following checks.

Fuel pump check

Note: *A suitable automotive-type fuel pressure gauge will be required to check the fuel pump cut-off pressure.*

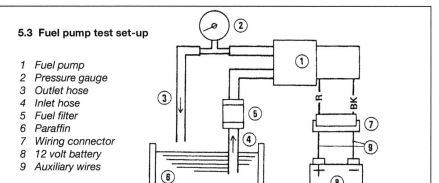

5.3 Fuel pump test set-up

1 Fuel pump
2 Pressure gauge
3 Outlet hose
4 Inlet hose
5 Fuel filter
6 Paraffin
7 Wiring connector
8 12 volt battery
9 Auxiliary wires

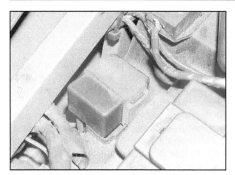

5.5a Fuel pump relay location – ZX-7R model

5.5b Fuel pump relay location – ZX-9R B model

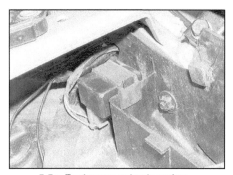

5.5c Fuel pump relay location – ZX-9R C and E models

5.5d Fuel pump relay location (arrowed) – ZX-9R F models

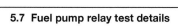

Fuel Pump Relay Internal Resistance

Range	Tester (+) Lead Connection			
x 1 kΩ	1	2	3	4
* 1	–	∞	∞	∞
2	∞	–	∞	∞
3	∞	10-100	–	∞
4	∞	20-200	1 - 5	–

*: Tester (–) Lead Connection

5.7 Fuel pump relay test details

2 Remove the fuel pump complete with the fuel filter (see Sections 6 and 7).

3 Fill a container with paraffin (kerosene) and hook up the fuel pump, hoses and filter as shown **(see illustration)**. Connect a fuel pressure gauge to the high pressure side with a T-fitting as shown.

Warning: Do NOT use petrol (gasoline) for this test! It is unnecessary and dangerous.

4 Hook up the pump wiring connector to a 12-volt battery as shown **(see illustration 5.3)** and note whether the pump comes on:

a) If the pump operates, check the pump relay.
b) If the pump does not operate, it's defective – renew it.
c) If the pump operates AND the fuel relay is also okay, close the outlet hose momentarily while the pump is running – when the pump stops, note the indicated pressure on the fuel pressure gauge and compare this reading to the fuel pressure listed in this Chapter's Specifications. If the gauge reading is outside of that specified, the pump is defective – renew it.

Fuel pump relay check

5 The fuel pump relay is located under the seat. Remove the seats (see Chapter 8) to gain access to the relay which is positioned as follows.

a) ZX-7R models – the relay is located on the right of the junction box **(see illustration)**.
b) ZX-9R B models – the relay is located just in front of the junction box **(see illustration)**.
c) ZX-9R C and E models – the relay is located to the rear of the toolkit **(see illustration)**.
d) ZX-9R F models – the relay is located to the rear of the junction box **(see illustration)**.

6 Ensure the ignition is switched off, then free the relay from its mounting and disconnect it from the wiring connector.

7 Using the Kawasaki tester, Pt. No. 57001-1394, set the ohmmeter scale to the 1 x K ohms range and measure the resistance at the indicated terminals **(see illustration)**. If your readings are not as specified in the table, renew the fuel pump relay. If your readings are okay, check the fuel pump itself.

Caution: Using a meter other than that specified may produce inaccurate results and could damage the fuel pump relay. If the meter is not available, have the relay checked by a Kawasaki dealer.

6 Fuel pump – removal and installation

Warning: Refer to the precautions given in Section 1 before starting work.

ZX-7R models

Removal

1 Remove the fuel tank (see Section 2).
2 Trace the wiring back from the fuel pump and disconnect it at the connector.
3 Trace the wiring back from the brake light switch to its wiring connectors and disconnect the switch from the main wiring harness.
4 Unscrew the bolts securing the rider's right-hand footrest bracket to the frame and

6.12 Release the retaining clip and disconnect the fuel pump hose from the T-piece

position the bracket clear of the frame to give access to the pump.

5 Release the retaining clips and disconnect the fuel hoses from their pump unions.

6 Slide the pump to the rear to free its mounting rubber from the bracket and manoeuvre the pump out of position. If necessary, separate the pump and mounting rubber.

Installation

7 Ensure the pump is correctly located in the mounting rubber then manoeuvre it into position, ensuring the mounting rubber slots are correctly located on the bracket lugs.

8 Connect the fuel hoses to the pump ensuring the fuel filter (inlet) hose is connected to the pump front union and the carburettor (outlet) hose to the rear. Secure both hoses in position with the retaining clips.

9 Reconnect the pump wiring connector then seat the footrest bracket on the frame and

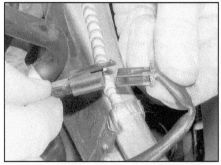

6.13 Trace the wiring back from the pump and disconnect it at the wiring connector

securely tighten its mounting bolts. Reconnect the brake light switch wiring connectors.

10 Install the fuel tank (see Section 2).

ZX-9R B models

Removal

11 Remove the fuel tank (see Section 2).

12 Release the retaining clip and detach the fuel pump (outlet) hose from the carburettor fuel hose T-piece **(see illustration)**.

13 Trace the wiring back from the fuel pump and disconnect it at the wiring connector **(see illustration)**.

14 Free the wiring from the retaining clips then unscrew the two bolts securing the fuel pump/filter mounting bracket to the frame, noting the correct fitted location of the earth (ground) lead, then manoeuvre the fuel pump/filter assembly out of position **(see illustrations)**.

6.14a Free the wiring then undo the bolts, noting the earth lead location (arrowed) . . .

15 Free the fuel pump mounting rubber from the bracket and free the fuel filter from its mounting rubber **(see illustrations)**. Release the retaining clip and disconnect the pump from the filter hose **(see illustration)**. If necessary, separate the carburettor (outlet) hose and mounting rubber from the pump.

Installation

16 Ensure the mounting rubber is correctly fitted to the pump then fit the carburettor (outlet) hose to the pump rear union and secure it in position with the retaining clip.

17 Connect the fuel filter hose to the pump front union and secure it in position with the retaining clip, then fit the pump and filter assembly to its mounting bracket.

18 Manoeuvre the assembly into position and securely tighten the bracket mounting bolts, remembering to fit the wiring clip to each bolt and the earth (ground) lead to the right side bolt.

19 Reconnect the pump wiring connector.

20 Reconnect the pump hose to the carburettor T-piece and secure it in position with the retaining clip.

21 Install the fuel tank (see Section 2).

ZX-9R C, E and F models

Removal

22 Remove the fuel tank (see Section 2).

23 Release the retaining clip and detach the fuel pump (outlet) hose from the carburettor fuel hose T-piece.

24 Trace the wiring back from the fuel pump and disconnect it at the wiring connector **(see illustration)**.

6.14b . . . then remove the fuel pump and filter assembly

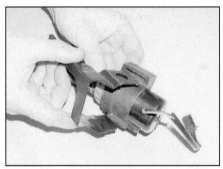

6.15a Free the fuel pump mounting rubber from the bracket . . .

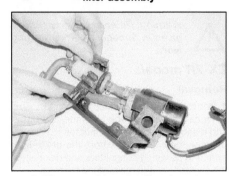

6.15b . . . and free the filter from its mounting rubber

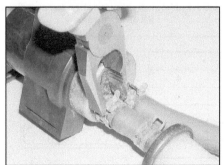

6.15c Release the retaining clip and disconnect the filter hose from the pump

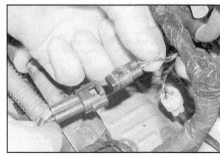

6.24 On ZX-9R C, E and F models, disconnect the fuel pump wiring connector . . .

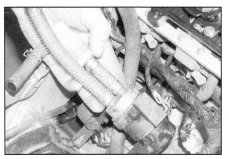

6.25 . . . then free the fuel pump and filter mounting rubbers from the bracket and remove the assembly from the bike

25 Free the fuel pump and filter mounting rubbers from the bracket and manoeuvre the fuel pump/filter assembly out of position (see illustration).
26 Release the retaining clip and disconnect the pump from the filter hose. If necessary, separate the carburettor (outlet) hose and mounting rubber from the pump.

Installation

27 Ensure the mounting rubber is correctly fitted to the pump then fit the carburettor (outlet) hose to the pump rear union and secure it in position with the retaining clip. Connect the fuel filter hose to the pump front union and secure it in position with the retaining clip.
28 Manoeuvre the assembly into position and locate the pump and filter mounting rubbers correctly on the bracket.
29 Reconnect the pump wiring connector.
30 Reconnect the pump hose to the carburettor T-piece and secure it in position with the retaining clip.
31 Install the fuel tank (see Section 2).

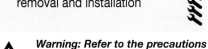

7 Fuel filter –

   removal and installation

> **Warning: Refer to the precautions given in Section 1 before starting work.**

ZX-7R models

Removal

1 Remove the fuel tank (see Section 2).

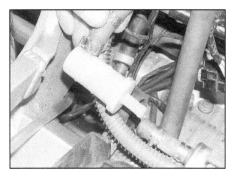

7.12 Removing the fuel filter – ZX-9R C, E and F models

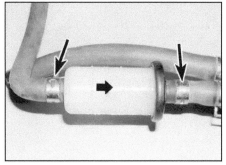

7.7 Release the clips (arrowed) and detach the filter from its hoses

2 Release the retaining clip and detach the fuel filter (inlet) hose from the fuel pump.
3 Slacken and remove the fuel filter bracket mounting bolt and remove the bracket complete with the filter and hoses.
4 Note the correct fitted location of the filter and hoses then disconnect both hoses from the filter and free the filter from its mounting rubber.

Installation

5 Installation is the reverse of removal, noting that the arrow on the filter must point in the direction of fuel flow (towards the pump). Ensure the fuel hoses are correctly reconnected and securely held in position by the retaining clips.

ZX-9R B models

Removal

6 Remove the fuel pump and filter assembly as described in Steps 11 to 14 of Section 6.
7 Free the fuel pump mounting rubber from the bracket and free the fuel filter from its mounting rubber. Release the retaining clips and disconnect the filter from the pump hose and the fuel tank hose from the filter, noting which way around it is fitted (see illustration).

Installation

8 Ensure that the arrow on the filter is pointing in the direction of fuel flow (towards the fuel pump), then connect the filter to the fuel pump hose and secure it in position with the retaining clip (see illustration).
9 Reconnect the fuel tank hose to the filter, securing it in position with the retaining clip, then fit the pump and filter assembly on the

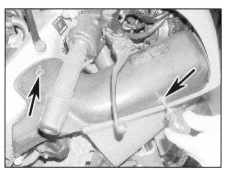

8.2a On ZX-7R models, undo the screws (arrowed) . . .

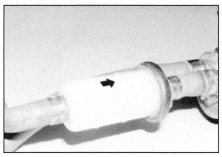

7.8 Ensure that the new filter is installed with its arrow pointing in the direction of fuel flow

mounting bracket.
10 Install the pump and filter assembly as described in Steps 18 to 21 of Section 6.

ZX-9R C, E and F models

Removal

11 Remove the fuel tank (see Section 2).
12 Free the fuel filter mounting rubber from its bracket then release the retaining clip and disconnect the filter from the pump hose (see illustration).
13 With the filter removed, release the retaining clip and disconnect the fuel tank hose.

Installation

14 Installation is the reverse of removal, noting that the arrow on the filter must point in the direction of fuel flow (towards the pump). Ensure the fuel hoses are correctly reconnected and securely held in position by the retaining clips.

8 Air filter housing –

   removal and installation

ZX-7R models

Removal

1 Remove the fuel tank (see Section 2).
2 Undo the retaining screws securing each air filter housing intake duct cover in position and remove both the left and right covers (see illustrations).

8.2b . . . and remove the air filter housing intake duct covers

8.3a Remove the rubber intake duct section . . .

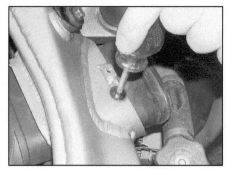

8.3b . . . then undo the screw . . .

8.3c . . . and remove the duct section which passes through the frame

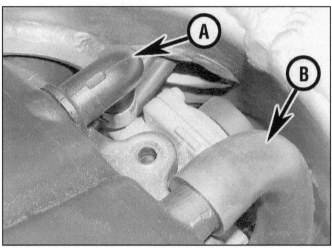

8.4 Disconnect the vent valve hose (A) and vacuum control valve hose (B) from the front of the housing . . .

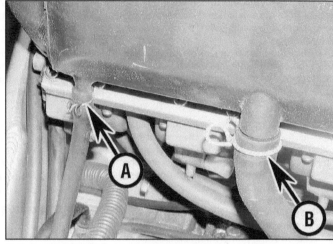

8.5 . . . and the drain hose (A) and breather hose (B) from the rear of the housing

3 Working on the right side, unclip the intake duct rubber section then undo the screw and remove the intake duct section by passing it through the frame (see illustrations). Remove the left side rubber section and intake duct in the same way.

4 Disconnect the vacuum control valve and vent valve hoses from the front of the housing (see illustration).

5 Release the retaining clips and detach the breather hose and drain hose from the rear of the housing (see illustration).

6 Prise out the rubber plugs from the air filter housing cover to gain access to the housing bolts (see illustration).

7 Slacken and remove the three mounting bolts and lift off the air filter housing (see illustration). Recover the rubber seal from the carburettor mounting plate and the seal from each intake duct aperture; renew any seal which shows signs of damage or deterioration (see illustration).

Installation

8 Installation is the reverse of removal, noting the following points.

a) Ensure the air filter housing and intake duct rubber seals are in good condition.

b) Ensure all hoses are correctly and securely reconnected.

c) Ensure the intake ducts and rubbers are correctly installed with the arrow marked on each component pointing forwards.

ZX-9R B models

Removal

9 Remove the fuel tank (see Section 2).

10 Slacken the retaining clips securing the air filter housing intake ducts to the upper fairing ducts (see illustration).

11 Release the retaining clips and disconnect the vacuum control valve hose and the drain hoses from the left side of the housing (see illustrations).

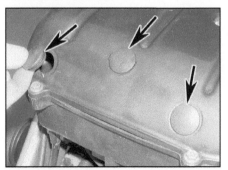

8.6 Remove the rubber plugs (arrowed) to gain access to the housing bolts

8.7a Removing the air filter housing – ZX-7R model

8.7b Check the housing seal for signs of damage and renew if necessary

8.10 On ZX-9R B models, slacken the clips securing the intake ducts to the filter housing

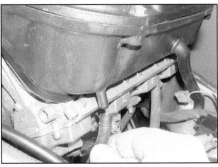

8.11a Disconnect the drain hose from the rear of the housing . . .

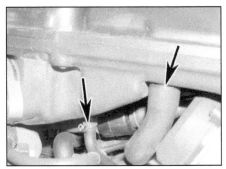

8.11b . . . and the drain hose and vacuum control valve hose from the left side of the housing

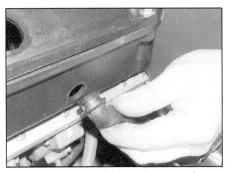

8.12 Disconnect the breather hose from the rear of the housing

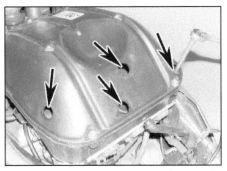

8.13 Remove the rubber plugs (arrowed) then slacken and remove the mounting bolts . . .

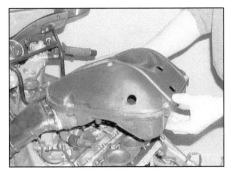

8.14 . . . and lift off the air filter housing

12 Detach the breather hose from the rear of the housing **(see illustration)**.
13 Prise out the rubber plugs from the air filter housing cover to gain access to the housing bolts **(see illustration)**.
14 Slacken and remove the four mounting bolts and lift off the air filter housing **(see illustration)**. Recover the rubber seal from the carburettor mounting plate; the seal must be renewed if it shows signs of damage or deterioration.

Installation

15 Installation is the reverse of removal, noting the following points.
  a) *Ensure the air filter housing rubber seal is in good condition.*
  b) *Ensure all hoses and the intake ducts are correctly and securely reconnected.*

ZX-9R C, E and F models

Removal

16 Remove the fuel tank (see Section 2).
17 Release the retaining clips and detach the breather hose and drain hose from the rear of the housing **(see illustration)**.
18 Release the retaining clip and disconnect the vacuum control valve hose from the right side of the housing **(see illustration)**.
19 Free the wiring harness from its clips on each side of the housing then slacken the retaining clips securing the air filter housing intakes to the ducts **(see illustrations)**.

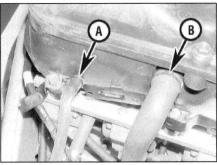

8.17 On ZX-9R C, E and F models, disconnect the drain hose (A) and breather hose (B) from the rear of the housing . . .

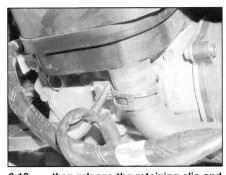

8.18 . . . then release the retaining clip and disconnect the vacuum control valve hose from the right side of the housing

8.19a Release the wiring from its retaining clips . . .

8.19b . . . then slacken the retaining clip securing the intake ducts to the housing

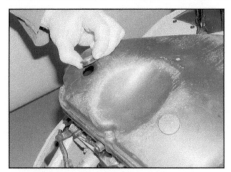

8.20 Remove the rubber plugs . . .

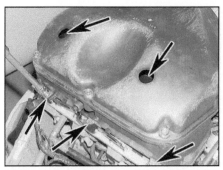

8.21a . . . then slacken and remove the five mounting bolts (arrowed) . . .

8.21b . . . and remove the bracket from the rear of the housing

8.21c Removing the air filter housing

20 Prise out the two rubber plugs from the air filter housing cover to gain access to the housing bolts **(see illustration)**.
21 Slacken and remove the five mounting bolts (two accessed through the lid and three located along the back of the housing) and remove the bracket **(see illustrations)**. Lift off the air filter housing and recover the rubber seal from the carburettor mounting plate; the seal must be renewed if it shows signs of damage or deterioration **(see illustration)**.

Installation

22 Installation is the reverse of removal, noting the following points.
 a) Ensure the air filter housing rubber seal is in good condition.
 b) Ensure all hoses and the intake ducts are correctly and securely reconnected.

9 Carburettors – removal and installation

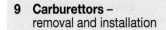

 Warning: Refer to the precautions given in Section 1 before starting work.

Removal

Note: On UK models (and certain other European models) hot coolant is diverted to the carburettors through a system of hoses to prevent carburettor icing. The hoses are referred to as part of the cooling system – see Chapter 1, Section 18 for details of the system filter.
1 Remove the fuel tank (Section 2).
2 Remove the air filter housing (Section 8).
3 Release the retaining clip and detach the fuel pump hose from the carburettor fuel hose

T-piece **(see illustration)**. Continue as described under the sub-heading appropriate to your model.

ZX-7R models

4 Release the retaining clip and disconnect the vent hose from the carburettor vent tube **(see illustration)**.
5 On UK models (and most other European models) locate the carburettor coolant hoses on the left and right sides of the carburettors. Clamp the hoses to minimise coolant loss then release the retaining clips and detach both hoses. **Note:** Access to the hoses is difficult with the carburettors in position; if necessary disconnect the hoses once the carburettors are freed from their intake rubbers.
6 Back off the throttle and choke cable adjusters to obtain maximum freeplay in the cables (see Chapter 1).
7 Slacken the four retaining clips securing the intake rubbers to the carburettors then ease the carburettors out of position, freeing the idle speed adjuster from its bracket.
8 Free the choke outer cable from its bracket then detach the inner cable from the carburettor linkage.
9 Free the throttle outer cables from their bracket then detach the inner cables from the throttle cam. The carburettors can then be removed from the bike. **Note:** If there is insufficient freeplay to enable the throttle cables to be disconnected, separate the switch assembly and detach the cables from the twistgrip first (see Section 15).
10 Tape over/plug the intake rubbers to prevent dirt/debris from entering the intake ports exposed by the removal of the carburettors. If the intake rubbers show signs of damage or deterioration they must be renewed.

ZX-9R B models

11 On all except California models, release the retaining clips and detach the air vent filters from the carburettor vent tubes **(see illustration)**. Also disconnect the vacuum hose from the air injection system vacuum control valve and free it from the carburettors.
12 On California models release the retaining clip and disconnect the vent hose from the carburettor vent tube.

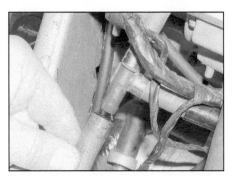

9.3 Release the retaining clip and disconnect the fuel pump hose from the carburettor T-piece

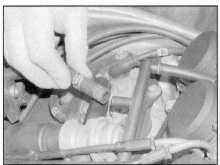

9.4 On ZX-7R models, release the retaining clip and disconnect the vent hose from the carburettor tube

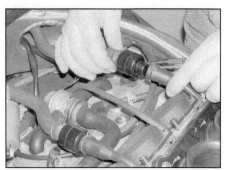

9.11 On ZX-9R B models, release the clips and detach the air vent filters from the carburettor vent tubes

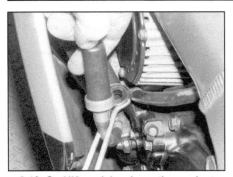

9.13 On UK models, clamp the coolant hoses on each side of the carburettors to minimise coolant loss

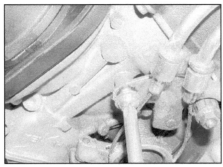

9.15a Undo the throttle cable bracket screw . . .

9.15b . . . then free the cables from the bracket and detach them from the throttle cam

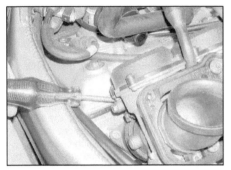

9.16a Slacken the retaining clips . . .

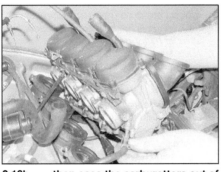

9.16b . . . then ease the carburettors out of their intake rubbers

9.18 On ZX-9R C, E and F models, release the retaining clip and disconnect the vent hose from the carburettor vent tube

13 On UK models (and most other European models), locate the carburettor coolant hoses on the left and right sides of the carburettors. Clamp the hoses to minimise coolant loss then release the retaining clips and detach both hoses **(see illustration)**. **Note:** *Access to the hoses is difficult with the carburettors in position; if necessary disconnect the hoses once the carburettors are freed from their intake rubbers.*

14 On all models, back off the adjusters to obtain maximum freeplay in the throttle and choke cables (see Chapter 1).

15 Undo the retaining screw securing the throttle cable bracket to the right end of the carburettors, noting the correct fitted location of the choke linkage return spring **(see illustration)**. Free the outer cables from the

bracket and detach the inner cables from the throttle cam **(see illustration)**.

16 Slacken the four retaining clips securing the intake rubbers to the carburettors then ease the carburettors out of position, freeing the idle speed adjuster from its bracket **(see illustrations)**.

17 Free the choke outer cable from its bracket then detach the inner cable from the carburettor linkage and remove the carburettors from the bike. Tape over/plug the intake rubbers to prevent dirt/debris from entering the intake ports exposed by the removal of the carburettors. If the intake rubbers show signs of damage or deterioration they must be renewed.

ZX-9R C, E and F models

18 Release the retaining clip and disconnect

the vent hose from the carburettor vent tube **(see illustration)**.

19 On UK models (and most other European models), locate the carburettor coolant hoses on the left and right sides of the carburettors. Clamp the hoses to minimise coolant loss then release the retaining clips and detach both hoses **(see illustrations)**. **Note:** *If access to the hoses is difficult with the carburettors in position, disconnect them once the carburettors are freed from their intake rubbers.*

20 Trace the wiring back from the throttle sensor (on the right end of the carburettors) and disconnect its wiring connector **(see illustration)**. On California, German and Swiss models, also disconnect the wiring connectors from the carburettor fuel cut-off valves.

21 Back off the throttle and choke cable

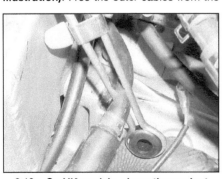

9.19a On UK models, clamp the coolant hoses on the left side of the carburettors . . .

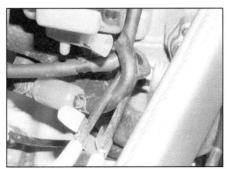

9.19b . . . and the right side of the carburettors to minimise coolant loss

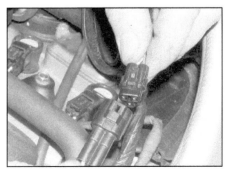

9.20 Disconnect the throttle position sensor wiring connector

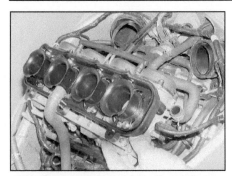

9.22 Slacken the retaining clips and ease the carburettors out from the intake rubbers

adjusters to obtain maximum freeplay in the cables (see Chapter 1).

22 Slacken the four retaining clips securing the intake rubbers to the carburettors then ease the carburettors out of position, freeing the idle speed adjuster from its bracket **(see illustration)**.

23 Free the choke outer cable from its bracket then detach the inner cable from the carburettor linkage.

24 Free the throttle outer cables from their bracket then detach the inner cables from the throttle cam. The carburettors can then be

removed from the bike. **Note:** *If there is insufficient freeplay to enable the throttle cables to be disconnected, separate the switch assembly and detach the cables from the twistgrip first (see Section 15).*

25 Tape over/plug the intake rubbers to prevent dirt/debris from entering the intake ports exposed by the removal of the carburettors. If the intake rubbers show signs of damage or deterioration they must be renewed.

Installation

26 Installation is the reverse of removal, noting the following.

a) *Check for cracks or splits in the cylinder head intake manifold rubbers, and renew them if necessary. If the intake manifold rubbers are to be renewed, also renew the O-rings (fitted between the rubber and cylinder head).*

b) *Make sure the carburettors are fully engaged with the intake rubbers and the clamps are securely tightened.*

c) *Make sure all hoses are correctly routed and secured and not trapped or kinked.*

d) *Refer to Section 15 for installation of the throttle cables and to Section 16 for the choke cable. Check the operation of the cables and adjust them as necessary (see Chapter 1).*

e) *Check idle speed and carburettor synchronisation and adjust as necessary (see Chapter 1).*

f) *Check the entire fuel system for leaks.*

10 Carburettor overhaul – general information

1 Poor engine performance, hesitation, hard starting, stalling, flooding and backfiring are all signs that major carburettor maintenance may be required.

2 Keep in mind, however, that many so-called carburettor problems are really not carburettor problems at all, but mechanical problems within the engine or ignition system malfunctions. Before assuming that a carburettor is in need of maintenance and beginning a major overhaul, the following checks should be made.

3 Check the fuel tap, fuel pump, the filters, the fuel lines, the tank filler cap vent, the intake manifold hose clamps, the hoses, the air filter element, the cylinder compression, the spark plugs, and the carburettor synchronisation.

4 Most carburettor problems are caused by dirt particles, varnish and other deposits

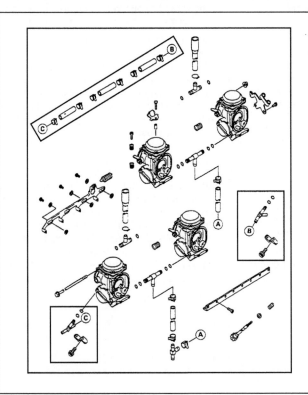
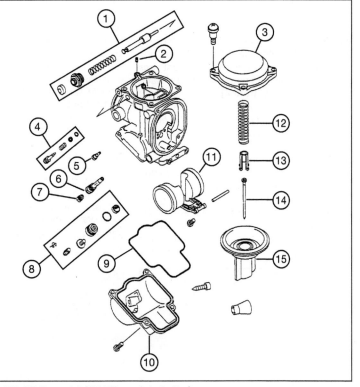

11.1a Carburettor components – ZX-9R B model (ZX-7R model similar)

1 Choke plunger components	6 Air bleed pipe	10 Float chamber	15 Vacuum piston
2 Air leak jet	7 Main jet	11 Float	A Fuel hose fittings
3 Vacuum chamber cover	8 Needle valve and seat	12 Spring	B and C Coolant hose fittings
4 Pilot screw components	assembly	13 Spring seat	(UK models)
5 Pilot jet	9 Float chamber gasket	14 Needle	

which build up in and block the fuel and air passages. Also, in time, gaskets and O-rings shrink or deteriorate and cause fuel and air leaks which lead to poor performance.

5 When a carburettor is overhauled, it is generally disassembled completely and the parts are cleaned thoroughly with a carburettor cleaning solvent and dried with filtered, unlubricated compressed air. The fuel and air passages are also blown through with compressed air to force out any dirt that may have been loosened but not removed by the solvent. Once the cleaning process is complete, the carburettor is reassembled using new gaskets, O-rings and, generally, a new inlet needle valve and seat.

6 Before disassembling the carburettors, make sure you have a carburettor rebuild kit (which will include all necessary O-rings and other parts), some carburettor cleaner, a supply or rags, some means of blowing out the carburettor passages and a clean place to work.

> **HAYNES HiNT** *It is recommended that only one carburettor be overhauled at a time to avoid mixing up parts.*

11 Carburettors –
disassembly, cleaning and inspection

> ⚠ **Warning: Refer to the warning in Section 1 concerning contact with fuel.**

Disassembly

Note: *Do not separate the carburettors unless the O-rings on the fuel and vent fittings* between the carburettors are leaking or the choke plungers require attention. Each carburettor can be dismantled sufficiently for all normal cleaning and adjustments while in place on the mounting brackets. On ZX-9R C and E models, note it will be necessary to separate the carburettors to enable the air cut-off valve diaphragms (where fitted – not all E models have them) to be inspected.

Caution: On ZX-9R C, E and F models, do not disturb the throttle position sensor. Refer to Chapter 5 for checking and adjusting the sensor.

1 Remove the carburettors from the machine as described in Section 9. Set the assembly on a clean working surface. Dismantle each carburettor separately, to avoid interchanging any of the parts, as follows **(see illustrations)**.

2 Remove the four screws securing the vacuum chamber cover to the carburettor body;

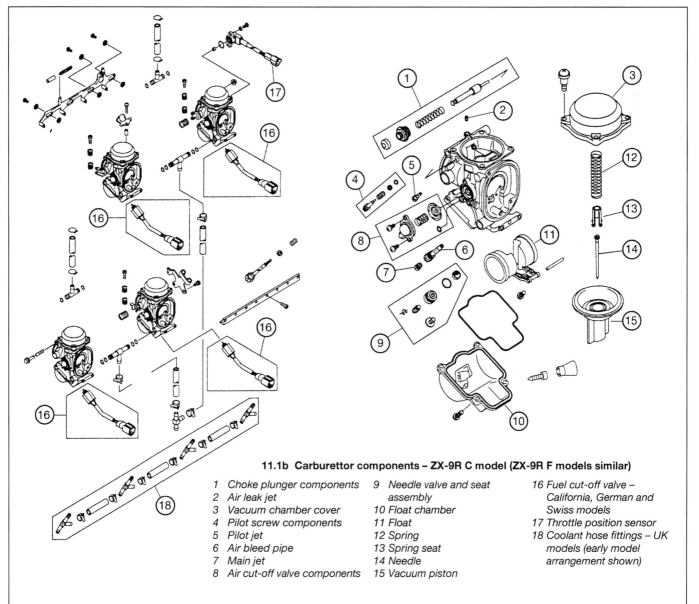

11.1b Carburettor components – ZX-9R C model (ZX-9R F models similar)

1 Choke plunger components	9 Needle valve and seat assembly	16 Fuel cut-off valve – California, German and Swiss models
2 Air leak jet	10 Float chamber	
3 Vacuum chamber cover	11 Float	
4 Pilot screw components	12 Spring	17 Throttle position sensor
5 Pilot jet	13 Spring seat	18 Coolant hose fittings – UK models (early model arrangement shown)
6 Air bleed pipe	14 Needle	
7 Main jet	15 Vacuum piston	
8 Air cut-off valve components		

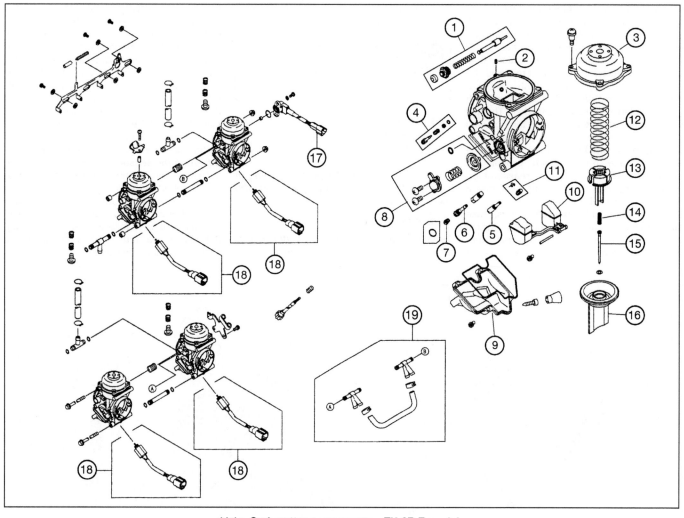

11.1c Carburettor components – ZX-9R E models

Note: *The air vent and coolant hose fittings shown are for the ZX-9R E1 models. The fittings differ on E2 models – note their arrangement when removing the carburettor assembly (Section 9) and when separating the carburettors (Section 13).*

1 Choke plunger components	6 Air bleed pipe	12 Spring
2 Air leak jet	7 Main jet	13 Spring seat
3 Vacuum chamber cover	8 Air cut-off valve components	14 Spring
4 Pilot screw components	9 Float chamber	15 Needle
5 Pilot jet	10 Float	16 Vacuum piston
	11 Needle valve and clip	17 Throttle position sensor

18 Fuel cut-off valve –
  California, German and
  Swiss models
19 Coolant hose fittings –
  UK models

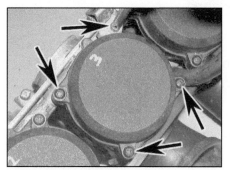

11.2a Remove the four screws (arrowed) securing the vacuum chamber cover to the carburettor

11.2b On No. 3 carburettor remove the choke cable bracket and dowel which is retained by the front screw

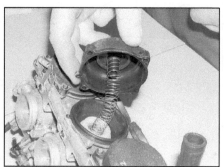

11.2c Lift off the cover and remove the piston spring . . .

11.2d . . . then carefully remove the diaphragm/piston assembly

11.4b . . . then ease the coolant hose fittings out from the base of each carburettor and remove the fittings and hoses as an assembly

if No. 3 carburettor is being dismantled, recover the choke cable bracket and dowel from the front screw **(see illustrations)**. Lift the cover off and remove the piston spring **(see illustration)**.

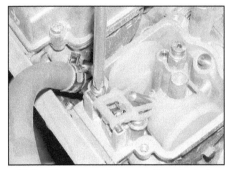

11.6a Slacken and remove the pivot pin screw . . .

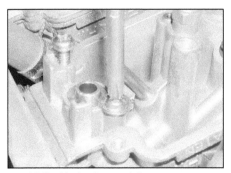

11.7a Undo the retaining screw . . .

11.3 Remove the spring seat and needle from the piston

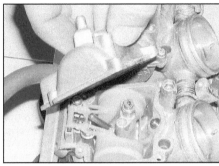

11.5 Undo the screws and remove the float chamber

Peel the diaphragm away from its groove in the carburettor body, being careful not to tear it. Lift out the diaphragm/ piston assembly taking care not to lose the air leak jet from the carburettor/diaphragm **(see illustration)**.

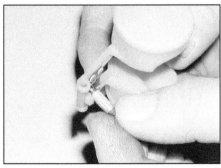

11.6b . . . then lift out the float and needle valve assembly

11.7b . . . and remove the needle valve seat complete with its O-ring and filter

11.4a On UK models, slacken the retaining screws and plates . . .

3 Remove the piston spring seat (if it wasn't in the end of the spring). On ZX-7R and ZX-9R B, C and F models, withdraw the needle from the piston and recover the washer(s) (where fitted) from the top of the needle **(see illustration)**. On ZX-9R E models recover the small spring fitted between the spring seat and needle then withdraw the needle and washer from the piston.
4 On UK (and most European) ZX-7R and ZX-9R B, C and F models, undo the retaining screws and remove the coolant hose fitting retaining plate from the base of the float chamber **(see illustration)**. Ease each coolant hose fitting out of position and remove the four fittings and associated hoses as an assembly **(see illustration)**.
5 Remove the four screws securing the float chamber to the carburettor body. Remove the float chamber and seal **(see illustration)**. On later UK (and most European) ZX-7R P5 and ZX-9R C2 models, note the correct fitted location of the coolant hose fitting retaining plate fitted to the float chamber rear outer screw (Nos. 1 and 4 carburettors).
6 Slacken the float pivot pin retaining screw then remove the float and needle valve from the carburettor body **(see illustration)**. Detach the needle valve from the float and pull out the pivot pin **(see illustration)**.
7 On all except ZX-9R E models, remove the retaining screw and remove the needle valve seat along with its O-ring and filter **(see illustrations)**.
8 Unscrew the main jet from the air bleed pipe **(see illustration)**. On ZX-9R E California, German and Swiss models, recover the O-ring

11.8 Unscrew the main jet from the air bleed pipe . . .

11.9 . . . then unscrew the air bleed pipe from the carburettor

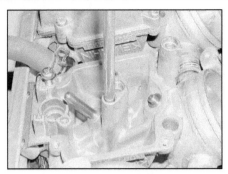

11.10 Unscrew the pilot jet from the carburettor

which is fitted between the main jet and air bleed pipe.

9 Unscrew the air bleed pipe from the carburettor body **(see illustration)**.

10 Using a small, flat-bladed screwdriver, remove the pilot jet from the carburettor body **(see illustration)**.

11 The pilot (idle mixture) screw is located in the bottom of the carburettor body. On US models (and some European models), the pilot screw is hidden behind a blanking plug which will have to be removed if the screw is to be taken out **(see illustration)**. To do this, punch a hole in the plug then prise it out. On all models, turn the pilot screw in, counting the number of turns until it bottoms lightly.

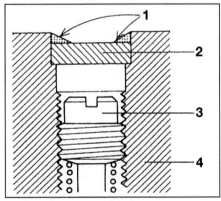

11.11a Pilot screw arrangement – US models

1 Bonding agent
2 Blanking plug
3 Pilot screw
4 Carburettor body

11.11c . . . then remove the screw complete with its O-ring, washer and spring

Record that number for use when installing the screw. Now remove the pilot screw along with its spring, washer and O-ring **(see illustrations)**.

12 If the carburettors have been separated, unscrew the choke plunger nut and withdraw the plunger, spring, nut and cap assembly from the carburettor.

13 On ZX-9R C, E and F models, if the carburettors have been separated, undo the two screws and remove the air cut-off valve cover (where fitted) from the left side of the carburettor body **(see illustration)**. Remove the spring, O-ring and diaphragm, taking great care not to tear it **(see illustration)**.

Cleaning

Caution: Use only a carburettor cleaning solution that is safe for use with plastic parts (be sure to read the label on the container).

11.11b Record the correct fitted position of the pilot screw . . .

11.13a On ZX-9R C, E and F models, undo the two screws . . .

14 Submerge the metal components in the carburettor cleaner for approximately thirty minutes (or as the directions recommend).

15 After the carburettor has soaked long enough for the cleaner to loosen and dissolve most of the varnish and other deposits, use a brush to remove the stubborn deposits. Rinse it again, then dry it with compressed air. Blow out all of the fuel and air passages in the main and upper body.

16 On UK (and most European) models, remove the coolant filter from its plastic housing (located in the hose linking the carburettor coolant hoses to the thermostat housing/engine) and blow compressed air through it (see Chapter 1).

Caution: Never clean the jets or passages with a piece of wire or a drill bit, as they will be enlarged, causing the fuel and air metering rates to be upset.

Inspection

17 Check the operation of the choke plunger (where removed). If it doesn't move smoothly, renew it, along with the return spring.

18 Check the tapered portion of the pilot screw for wear or damage. Renew the pilot screw assembly if necessary.

19 Check the carburettor body, float chamber and vacuum chamber cover for cracks, distorted sealing surfaces and other damage. If any defects are found, renew the faulty component, although renewal of the entire carburettor will probably be necessary (check with your parts supplier for the availability of separate components).

20 Check the jet needle for straightness by rolling it on a flat surface (such as a piece of glass). Renew it if it's bent or if the tip is worn.

21 Check the needle jet and renew it if it's worn or damaged.

22 Check the tip of the fuel inlet needle valve **(see illustration)**. If it has grooves or scratches in it, it must be renewed. Push in on the spring-loaded rod in the base of the needle valve, then release it – if it doesn't spring back, renew the needle valve and seat as an assembly.

23 Check the O-rings on the float chamber, the pilot screw and the needle valve seat. Renew them if they're damaged **(see illustration)**.

11.13b . . . and remove the air cut-off valve cover, spring, diaphragm and O-ring from the carburettor

24 Operate the throttle shaft to make sure the throttle butterfly valve opens and closes smoothly. If it doesn't, and this is not due to dirt or any other obstruction, renew the carburettor.
25 Check the floats for damage. This will usually be apparent by the presence of fuel inside one of the floats. If the floats are damaged, they must be renewed.
26 Check the diaphragm for splits, holes and general deterioration and renew it if any are found. Holding it up to a light will help to reveal problems of this nature.
27 Insert the vacuum piston in the carburettor body and see that it moves up and down smoothly. Check the surface of the piston for wear. If it's worn excessively or doesn't move smoothly in the bore, renew the carburettor.
28 On UK (and most European) models, remove the coolant valve from the hose linking the water pump to the carburettors. Blow through the valve and check that it is open – if no air passes through the valve, replace it with a new one.

12 Carburettors – reassembly and float height adjustment

Caution: When installing the jets, be careful not to over-tighten them – they're made of soft material and can distort, strip or shear easily.

1 If the choke plunger was removed, install it in its bore, followed by its spring and nut. Tighten the nut securely and install the cap.
2 On ZX-9R C, E and F models if the air cut-off valve diaphragm has been removed, fit the diaphragm to the carburettor making sure the pin is correctly located in its bore and the diaphragm bead seats correctly in its recess. Fit the spring to the diaphragm and the O-ring to the carburettor then install the cover, tightening its retaining screws securely.
3 On all models, install the pilot screw (if removed) along with its spring, washer and O-ring, turning it in until it seats lightly **(see illustration)**. Now, turn the screw out the number of turns that was previously recorded (see Section 11, Step 11). If a blanking plug

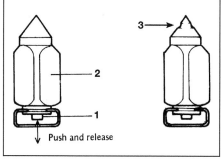
11.22 Check the needle valve (2) and spring-loaded rod (1). Inspect the valve tip (3) for grooves or scratches

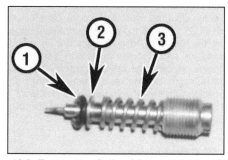
12.3 Ensure the O-ring (1), washer (2) and spring (3) are correctly fitted to the pilot screw

was fitted (all US and some European models), install a new plug in the hole over the screw. Ensure the plug is correctly seated then secure it in position with a little bonding agent around its circumference. **Note:** *If installing a new pilot screw, set it to the number of turns out given in the Specifications at the beginning of this Chapter.*
4 Install the pilot jet, tightening it securely **(see illustration)**.
5 Install the air bleed pipe, tightening it securely **(see illustration)**. On ZX-9R E California, German and Swiss models install the O-ring on the end of the air bleed pipe.
6 Install the main jet into the air bleed pipe, tightening it securely.
7 On ZX-7R and ZX-9R B, C and F models, fit the washer(s) (where fitted) to the top of the needle then drop the jet needle down into its hole in the vacuum piston. On ZX-9R E models

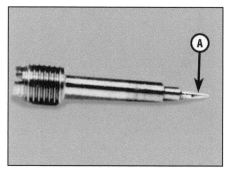
11.23 Check the tapered portion (A) of the pilot screw for wear or damage

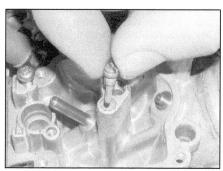
12.4 Fit the pilot jet to the carburettor

fit the washer to the needle then drop the needle down into the vacuum piston and fit the small spring. On all models, install the spring seat over the needle, making sure it is positioned so that it doesn't cover the hole in the bottom of the vacuum piston **(see illustration)**.
8 Ensure the air leak jet is in position then install the diaphragm/vacuum piston assembly into the carburettor body **(see illustration)**. Fit the spring into the piston, making sure it locates correctly over the spring seat. Seat the bead of the diaphragm into the groove in the top of the carburettor body, making sure the diaphragm isn't distorted or kinked.

> **HAYNES HiNT** *Seating the diaphragm bead is not always an easy task. If the diaphragm seems too large in diameter and*

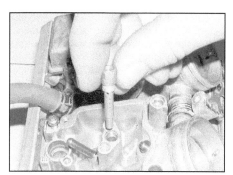
12.5 Screw the air bleed pipe securely into the carburettor

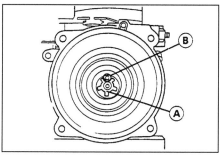
12.7 Ensure the spring seat (A) is positioned so that it does not cover the hole (B) in the vacuum piston

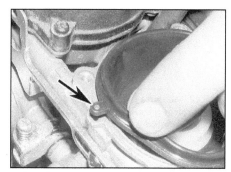
12.8 Ensure the air leak jet is in position

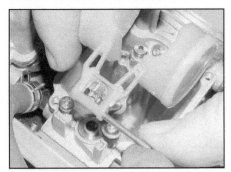

12.11 Manoeuvre the float and needle valve into position and insert the pivot pin

doesn't want to seat in the groove, place the vacuum chamber cover over the carburettor diaphragm, insert your finger into the throat of the carburettor and push up on the vacuum piston. Push down gently on the vacuum chamber cover – it should drop into place, indicating the diaphragm has seated in its groove.

9 Install the vacuum chamber cover, tightening the screws securely. If you're working on the No. 3 carburettor, don't forget to install the dowel and choke cable bracket.
10 Invert the carburettor and install the fuel inlet filter, O-ring and needle valve seat (where removed) and secure it with the screw.
11 Ensure the spring clip is correctly fitted to the needle valve then fit the needle valve to the tab on the float. Manoeuvre the assembly into position in the carburettor, making sure the needle valve is correctly located in its seat **(see illustration)**. Insert the float pivot pin and secure it in position with the retaining screw.
12 To check the float height, hold the carburettor so the float hangs down, then tilt it back until the needle valve is just seated but not so far that its spring-loaded rod is

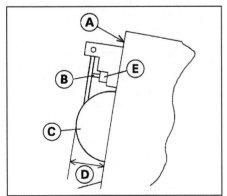

12.12 Measure the float height with the carburettor tilted so that the needle valve is just seated but not compressing its spring-loaded rod

A Carburettor mating surface	C Float
	D Float height measurement
B Needle valve spring-loaded rod	E Needle valve

compressed at all. Measure the distance from the float chamber gasket surface to the base of the float and compare your measurement to the float height listed in this Chapter's Specifications **(see illustration)**. If it isn't as specified, carefully bend the tang that contacts the valve needle up or down until the float height is correct.
13 Install the seal in the groove in the float chamber then fit the float chamber to the carburettor **(see illustration)**. Install the float chamber screws, tightening them securely; on later UK (and most European) ZX-7R P5 and ZX-9R C2 models, ensure the coolant hose fitting retaining plate is correctly fitted to the relevant rear retaining screw (Nos. 1 and 4 carburettors).
14 On UK (and most European) ZX-7R and ZX-9R B, C and F models, ensure the O-rings on the coolant hose fittings are in good condition and lubricate them with a smear of engine oil. Ease the fittings carefully into the carburettor bodies and secure them in position with the retaining plates and screws.
15 Install the carburettors as described in Section 9.

13 Carburettors – separation and reassembly

Separation

Note: *The carburettors do not need to be separated for normal overhaul unless the choke plungers require attention (see Section 11). On ZX-9R C, E and F models it will also be necessary to separate the carburettors to enable the air cut-off valve diaphragms (where fitted – not all E models have them) to be inspected.*

1 Remove the carburettors from the machine as described in Section 9. Mark the body of each carburettor with its cylinder number to ensure that it is positioned correctly on reassembly.
2 Unscrew the mounting bolts and remove the air filter housing mounting plate and intake ducts from the carburettors. On ZX-7R and ZX-9R B, C and F models recover the O-ring from the rear of each carburettor.

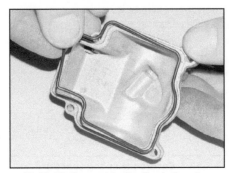

12.13 Fit the seal to the float chamber groove

3 On UK (and most European) ZX-7R and ZX-9R B, C and F models, undo the retaining screws and remove the coolant hose fitting retaining plate from the base of each float chamber. Ease each coolant hose fitting out of position and remove the four fittings and associated hoses as an assembly. On later ZX-7R P5 and ZX-9R C2 models, release the retaining clips and remove the hoses linking the additional coolant fittings on the sides of each carburettor.
4 On all models, unhook the choke linkage return spring and remove it from the carburettors.
5 Slacken and remove the three screws and remove the choke linkage from the carburettors. Recover the six plastic washers which are fitted (one on each side of the linkage) to the retaining screws.
6 Before proceeding further note the correct fitted locations on the throttle linkage springs and the air vent, fuel and (where fitted) coolant fittings. Using a pair of pointed-nose pliers, remove the spring from each of the throttle linkage adjusters to remove the risk of the springs being lost during separation of the carburettors.
7 On ZX-7R and ZX-9R B, C and F models, unscrew the nut on the end of the long through-bolt and withdraw the bolt, then remove the screws securing the mounting bar to the rear of the carburettors and remove the bar, noting how it fits. On ZX-9R E models unscrew the nut on the end of each long through-bolt and withdraw them both.
8 Carefully separate the carburettors, taking care not to damage the connecting fittings, and recover the springs fitted in between the carburettors.

Reassembly

9 Inspect the O-rings on all the air vent, fuel and (where fitted) coolant fittings and renew any which show signs of damage or deterioration. Lubricate the O-rings on the fittings with a light film of oil and install them into their respective holes, making sure they are pressed fully home.
10 Position the coil springs between the carburettors then gently push the carburettors together whilst aligning the throttle linkages and the connecting fittings to make sure they engage properly.
11 Once all the carburettors are correctly joined, fit the mounting bar and its screws, and/or the long through-bolt(s) and nut(s), tighten them lightly only. Set the carburettors on a surface plate or sheet of glass, then align them with a straight-edge placed along the edges of the bores. When the centrelines of the carburettors are all in horizontal and vertical alignment, tighten the screws and/or through-bolt nut(s) securely.
12 Fit the spring to each of the throttle linkage adjusters. Visually synchronise the throttle butterfly valves, turning the adjusting screws on the throttle linkage, if necessary, to equalise the clearance between the butterfly valve and

throttle bore of each carburettor. Check to ensure the throttle operates smoothly.

13 Fit a plastic washer to the choke linkage mountings on Nos. 1, 3 and 4 carburettors (no washers or screw is fitted to No. 2 carburettor). Install the choke linkage, making sure it engages correctly with all the choke plungers. Fit the outer plastic washers and install the screws, tightening them securely. Install the choke linkage return spring, then check that the choke mechanism operates smoothly and closes fully under spring pressure.

14 On ZX-7R and ZX-9R B, C and F models, fit a new O-ring to the rear of each carburettor and on ZX-9R E models ensure the intake rubbers are securely fitted to the rear of each carburettor.

15 Install the air filter housing mounting plate and intake ducts, and tighten the retaining bolts securely.

16 On UK (and most European) ZX-7R and ZX-9R B, C and F models, ensure the O-rings on the coolant hose fittings are in good condition and lubricate them with a smear of engine oil. Ease the fittings carefully into the carburettor bodies and secure them in position with the retaining plates and screws. On later ZX-7R P5 and ZX-9R C2 models, refit the hoses connecting the additional coolant hose fittings and secure them in position with the retaining clips.

17 Install the carburettors as described in Section 9.

14 Carburettors – fuel level adjustment

> ⚠ **Warning: Refer to the warning in Section 1 concerning contact with fuel.**

1 Remove the fuel tank (see Section 2).

2 Disconnect the fuel pump hose from the carburettor fuel hose T-piece and connect an auxiliary fuel tank to the carburettors with a suitable length of hose.

3 Support the motorcycle in an upright position using an auxiliary stand and attach Kawasaki service tool No. 57001-1017 (a clear plastic tube graduated in millimetres) to the drain fitting on the bottom of the carburettor float chambers (all four will need to be checked). An alternative to this tool is a length of clear plastic tubing and an accurate ruler. Hold the graduated tube (or the free end of the clear plastic tube) against the carburettor body, as shown **(see illustrations)**. If the Kawasaki tool is being used, raise the zero mark to a point several millimetres above the index mark on the carburettor main body. If a piece of clear plastic tubing is being used, make a mark on the tubing at a point several millimetres above the index mark.

4 Unscrew the drain screw at the bottom of the float chamber a couple of turns, then let fuel flow into the tube. Wait for the fuel level to stabilise, then slowly lower the tube until the

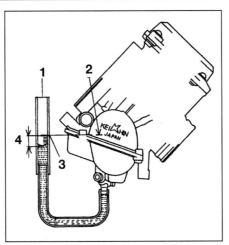

14.3a Fuel level checking details – ZX-7R and ZX-9R B, C and F models

1 Fuel level gauge
2 Index mark
3 Zero mark
4 Fuel level measurement

zero mark is level with the index mark on the carburettor body. **Note:** *Don't lower the zero mark below the index mark on the carburettor then bring it back up – the reading will be inaccurate. If this happens, drain the fuel from the tube and start again.*

5 Measure the distance between the mark and the top of the fuel level in the tube or gauge. This distance is the fuel level – write it down on a piece of paper, screw in the drain screw, shut off the fuel flow, then move on to the next carburettor and check it in the same way. Compare your fuel level readings to the value listed in this Chapter's Specifications.

6 If the fuel level in each carburettor is correct, ensure all the drain screws are tight then reconnect the fuel pump hose and install the fuel tank.

7 If the fuel level in any carburettor is not as specified, the float height is incorrect and in need of adjustment. Remove the carburettors (see Section 9) then remove the float chambers and adjust the float height as described in Section 12. **Note:** *Bending the tang up increases the float height and lowers the fuel level – bending it down decreases the float height and raises the fuel level.* Once the float heights are all correctly set, fit the float

15.6a On ZX-9R B models, undo the two screws . . .

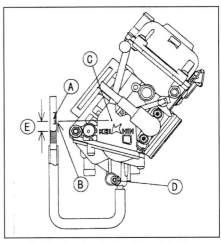

14.3b Fuel level checking details – ZX-9R E models

A Fuel level gauge
B Zero mark
C Index mark
D Drain screw
E Fuel level measurement

chambers and reinstall the carburettors. Check the fuel level again before installing the fuel tank (see Section 2).

15 Throttle cables – removal and installation

Removal

1 Remove the fuel tank (Section 2) and air filter housing (Section 8).

2 Slacken the locknuts and back off the adjusters to obtain maximum freeplay in both throttle cables. Proceed as follows under the sub-heading appropriate to your model.

ZX-7R models

3 Undo the two retaining screws and separate the two halves of the right handlebar switch assembly. Note how the outer cables locate in the switch assembly then free them and detach the inner cables from the throttle twistgrip. **Note:** *If necessary, undo the clamp bolts and free the front brake master cylinder from the handlebar to improve access to the switch/cables.*

4 Once the cables are free from the twistgrip, free the lower end of each cable from its mounting bracket on the carburettors and detach the inner cables from the throttle cam. **Note:** *If necessary, slacken the retaining clips and ease the carburettors out from the intake rubbers to improve access to the cables. Note that there is no need to disconnect any hoses from the carburettors.*

5 Note the correct routing of each cable then release any retaining clamps and remove both cables from the bike.

ZX-9R B models

6 Undo the two retaining screws and separate the two halves of the right handlebar switch assembly **(see illustration)**. Note how

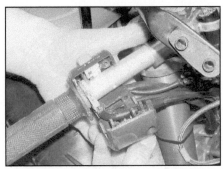

15.6b ... then separate the switch assembly and detach the cables from the twistgrip

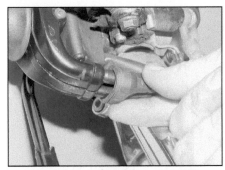

15.9 On ZX-9R C, E and F models, release the rubber gaiter from the twistgrip housing

the cables locate in the switch assembly then free them and detach the inner cables from the throttle twistgrip **(see illustration)**. Note: *If necessary, undo the clamp bolts and free the front brake master cylinder from the handlebar to improve access to the switch/cables. Ensure the master cylinder is kept upright to prevent possible fluid spillage from its reservoir.*

7 Once the cables are free from the twistgrip, free the lower end of each cable from its mounting bracket on the right end of the carburettors and detach the inner cables from the throttle cam.

8 Note the correct routing of each cable then release any retaining clamps and remove both cables from the bike.

ZX-9R C, E and F models

9 Fold back the throttle cable rubber gaiter to free it from the twistgrip housing **(see illustration)**.

10 Undo the two retaining screws and separate the two halves of the twistgrip housing **(see illustration)**. Note how the cables locate in the housing then detach the inner cables from the throttle twistgrip **(see illustration)**.

11 Once the cables are free from the throttle twistgrip, free the lower end of each cable from its mounting bracket on the carburettors and detach the inner cables from the throttle cam. **Note:** *If necessary, slacken the retaining clips and ease the carburettors out from the intake rubbers to improve access to the*

cables. Note that there is no need to disconnect any hoses from the carburettors.

12 Note the correct routing of each cable then release any retaining clamps and remove the cables from the bike.

Installation

ZX-7R models

13 Ensure the opening and closing cables are correctly positioned then attach the lower end of each inner cable to the throttle cam and locate the outer cables correctly in the carburettor bracket. Where necessary, seat the carburettors correctly in the intake rubbers and securely tighten their retaining clips

14 Pass both cables through the frame cutout, around the headstock and between the forks, making sure they are correctly routed, and secure them in position with the necessary clamps. The cables must not interfere with any other component and should not be kinked or sharply bent.

15 Lubricate the upper end of each cable with multi-purpose grease and attach the cables correctly to the throttle grip. Locate the outer cables correctly in the switch halves then assemble the switch on the handlebar, locating the rear half locating peg in the handlebar hole. Ensure the switch and cables are correctly assembled then securely tighten the switch screws. Where necessary, refit the master cylinder to the handlebar (see Chapter 7).

16 Adjust the cables as described in Chapter 1. Turn the handlebars from side to side to make sure the cables don't cause the steering to bind.

17 Install the air filter housing and fuel tank (see Sections 8 and 2).

18 On completion, start the engine and turn the handlebars from side to side to make sure the idle speed doesn't rise as the bars are turned. If it does, the cables are incorrectly routed and the problem must be sorted before the motorcycle is ridden.

ZX-9R B models

19 Install the cables as described in Steps 13 to 18.

ZX-9R C, E and F models

20 Ensure the opening and closing cables are correctly positioned then attach the lower end of each inner cable to the throttle cam and locate the outer cables correctly in the carburettor bracket. Where necessary, seat the carburettors correctly in the intake rubbers and securely tighten their retaining clips

21 Pass both cables through the frame cutout, around the headstock and between the forks, making sure they are correctly routed, and secure them in position with the necessary clamps. The cables must not interfere with any other component and should not be kinked or sharply bent.

22 Lubricate the upper end of each cable with multi-purpose grease and attach the cables correctly to the throttle grip. Locate the outer cables correctly in the twistgrip housing then assemble the housing on the handlebar, ensuring the locating peg is correctly seated in the handlebar hole. Ensure the twistgrip housing and cables are correctly assembled then securely tighten the retaining screws before seating the cable gaiter correctly on the housing.

23 Adjust the cables as described in Chapter 1. Turn the handlebars from side to side to make sure the cables don't cause the steering to bind.

24 Install the air filter housing and fuel tank (see Sections 8 and 2).

25 On completion, start the engine and turn the handlebars back and forth to make sure the idle speed doesn't rise as the bars are turned. If it does, the cables are incorrectly routed and the problem must be sorted before the motorcycle is ridden.

15.10a Undo the two screws ...

15.10b ... then separate the housing halves and detach the cables from the twistgrip

16 Choke cable – removal and installation

Removal

1 Remove the fuel tank (Section 2) and air filter housing (Section 8).

2 Slacken the locknut and back off the adjuster to obtain maximum freeplay in the choke cable.

3 Undo the two retaining screws and separate the two halves of the left handlebar switch assembly. Note how the choke cable locates in the switch assembly then free the outer cable from the switch and detach the inner cable from the choke lever (see illustration). **Note:** *On ZX-7R and ZX-9R B models, undo the clamp bolts and free the clutch master cylinder from the handlebar to improve access to the switch/cable. On ZX-9R B models keep the master cylinder upright to prevent fluid spillage from its reservoir.*

4 Once the cable is free from the switch, free the lower end of the cable from its mounting bracket on the carburettors and detach the inner cables from the choke linkage (see illustration).

5 Note the correct routing of the choke cable then release any retaining clamps and remove it from the bike.

Installation

6 Attach the lower end of the choke cable to the linkage and locate the outer cable correctly in the carburettor bracket.

7 Pass the cable through the frame cutout and between the forks, making sure it is correctly routed, and secure it in position with the necessary clamps. The cable must not interfere with any other component and should not be kinked or sharply bent.

8 Lubricate the upper end of the cable with multi-purpose grease and attach it correctly to the choke lever. Locate the lever and outer cable correctly in the switch halves then assemble the switch on the handlebar, locating the rear half locating peg in the handlebar hole. Ensure the switch, lever and cable are correctly assembled then securely tighten the switch screws. Where necessary, refit the master cylinder to the handlebar (see Chapter 2A).

9 Adjust the cable as described in Chapter 1. Turn the handlebars from side to side to make sure the cable doesn't cause the steering to bind.

10 Install the air filter housing and fuel tank (see Sections 8 and 2).

17 Air/fuel mixture adjustment – general information

Caution: Incorrect adjustment of the air/fuel mixture can affect the efficiency of the catalytic converter (where fitted).

Adjustment – UK

1 If the engine runs extremely rough at idle or continually stalls, and if a carburettor overhaul does not cure the problem, the pilot screws probably require adjustment to achieve a smooth idle and restore low speed performance. It is worth noting at this point that unless you have the skill to carry this out on a multi-cylinder machine it is best to entrust the task to a motorcycle dealer, tuner or fuel

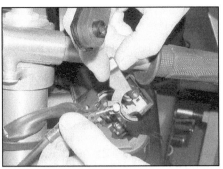

16.3 Separate the left handlebar switch assembly then free the choke cable from the lever

systems specialist. Note that you will need a long thin screwdriver with an angled end to access the pilot screws. Remove the lower fairing panels on ZX-7R and ZX-9R B models or the lower fairing and middle fairing panels on ZX-9R C, E and F models (see Chapter 8).

2 Before adjusting the pilot screws, the engine must be warmed up to normal working temperature. Stop the engine and screw in all four pilot screws until they seat lightly, then back them out to the number of turns specified (see this Chapter's Specifications). This is the base position for adjustment.

3 Start the engine and reset the idle speed to the correct level (see Chapter 1). Working on one carburettor at a time, turn the pilot screw by a small amount either side of this position to find the point at which the highest consistent idle speed is obtained. When you've reached this position, reset the idle speed to the specified amount (see Chapter 1). Repeat on the other three carburettors in turn.

Other markets

4 Due to the increased emphasis on controlling exhaust emissions in certain world markets, regulations have been formulated which prevent adjustment of the air/fuel mixture. On such models the pilot screw positions are pre-set at the factory and in some cases have a limiter cap fitted to prevent tampering. Where adjustment is possible, it can only be made in conjunction with an exhaust gas analyser to ensure that the machine does not exceed the emissions regulations.

18.6 Silencer mounting bolt – ZX-9R B model

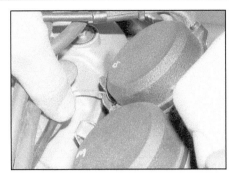

16.4 Free the outer cable from its bracket and detach the inner cable from the carburettor choke linkage

18 Exhaust system – removal and installation

> **Warning: If the engine has been running the exhaust system will be very hot. Allow the system to cool before carrying out any work.**

Removal

Silencer – ZX-7R models

1 Undo the screws and remove the C-shaped cover from the front of the silencer.

2 Unscrew the three nuts securing the silencer to the front pipe assembly.

3 Slacken and remove the silencer mounting nut, bolt and washer then free the silencer from the front pipe assembly and remove it from the motorcycle. Remove the silencer gasket and discard it.

4 Take care not to lose the collars from the silencer mounting rubber. Inspect the mounting rubber for signs of damage or deterioration and renew if necessary.

Silencer – ZX-9R B models

5 Loosen the bolt of the clamp securing the silencer to the front pipe assembly.

6 Slacken and remove the silencer mounting nut, bolt and washer then free the silencer from the front pipe assembly and remove it from the motorcycle (see illustration). Remove the silencer gasket and discard it.

7 Check both the silencer mounting bushes for signs of damage or deterioration and renew if necessary.

Silencer – ZX-9R C and F models

8 Undo the screws and remove the C-shaped cover from the front of the silencer.

9 Unscrew the three nuts securing the silencer to the front pipe assembly.

10 Slacken and remove the silencer mounting nut, bolt and washer then free the silencer from the front pipe assembly and remove it from the motorcycle. Remove the silencer gasket and discard it.

11 Recover the dished washer fitted between the silencer and outer mounting bush and check both the bushes for signs of damage or

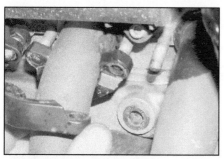

18.20 Unscrew the nuts and free the front pipe collar halves from the cylinder head studs

deterioration. Renew the mounting bushes if necessary.

Silencer – ZX-9R E models

12 Loosen the bolt of the clamp securing the silencer to the front pipe assembly.
13 Slacken and remove the silencer mounting nuts, bolts and washers then free the silencer from the front pipe assembly and remove it from the motorcycle. Remove the silencer gasket and discard it.
14 Check all the silencer mounting bushes for signs of damage or deterioration and renew if necessary.

Complete system – ZX-7R models

15 Remove the radiator (see Chapter 3).
16 Slacken and remove the nuts securing the front pipes to the cylinder head and free the collars from their studs.
17 Slacken and remove the silencer mounting nut, bolt and washer then free the front pipes from the cylinder head and remove the complete exhaust system from the bike. Remove the front pipe gaskets and discard them.
18 Take care not to lose the collars from the silencer mounting rubber. Inspect the mounting rubber for signs of damage or deterioration and renew if necessary.

Complete system – ZX-9R B models

19 Remove the radiator (see Chapter 3).
20 Slacken and remove the nuts securing the front pipes to the cylinder head. Free the front pipe collar halves from their studs and remove them from the bike **(see illustration)**.
21 Unscrew the nut securing the front pipe

bracket to its mounting on the underside of the oil pan **(see illustration)**.
22 Slacken and remove the silencer mounting nut, bolt and washer. Free the front pipes from the cylinder head and mounting point, then remove the complete exhaust system from the bike. Remove the front pipe gaskets and discard them.
23 Check both the silencer and front pipe mounting bushes for signs of damage or deterioration and renew if necessary.

Complete system – ZX-9R C and F models

24 Remove the lower and middle fairing fairing panels and inner panel as described in Chapter 8.
25 Referring to Chapter 3, unbolt the radiator lower mounting bracket and remove it from the engine. Slacken the radiator upper mounting bolts then pivot the radiator fully forwards and hold it in position by retightening the upper bolts.
26 Slacken and remove the nuts securing the front pipes to the cylinder head and free the collars from their studs. On ZX-9R F models, also slacken and remove the nut, bolt and washer securing the exhaust pipe mid-section to the bracket on the underside of the frame **(see illustration)**.
27 Slacken and remove the silencer mounting nut, bolt and washer. Free the front pipes from the cylinder head and remove the complete exhaust system, taking great care not to damage the radiator. Remove the front pipe gaskets and discard them. On ZX-9R F models, if required, slacken the clamp securing the exhaust pipe mid-section to the front pipes and separate the assembly, noting the location of the pipe gasket.
28 Recover the dished washer fitted between the silencer and outer mounting bush and check both bushes for signs of damage or deterioration. Renew the mounting bushes if necessary. On ZX-9R F models, check the condition of the mounting bushes in the bracket on the underside of the frame.

Complete system – ZX-9R E models

29 Carry out the operations described in Steps 24 to 26.
30 Slacken and remove the silencer mounting nuts, bolts and washers. Free the

front pipes from the cylinder head and remove the complete exhaust system, taking great care not to damage the radiator. Remove the front pipe gaskets and discard them **(see illustration)**.

Installation

31 Installation is the reverse of removal, noting the following.
a) Discard any removed gasket and fit a new one.
b) Where the silencer is being installed, tighten the silencer nuts/clamp bolt (as applicable) first before tightening the mounting bolt.
c) Where the complete system is being installed, tighten the front pipe to cylinder head nuts first before tightening the mounting bolt(s).

19 Secondary air injection system components

General information

1 To reduce the amount of unburned hydrocarbons released in the exhaust gases, a secondary air injection system is fitted to all models. The system is very simple in operation, consisting of the vacuum control valve located directly above the cylinder head cover, and the air suction valves which are actually inside the cover **(see illustration)**.
2 When there is a negative pulse in the exhaust gases, filtered air is drawn through the vacuum control valve, air suction valves and cylinder head passages and into the exhaust ports. This air then mixes with the exhaust gases, causing any unburned particles of the fuel in the mixture to be burnt in the exhaust port/pipes. This process changes a considerable amount of hydrocarbons and carbon monoxide into relatively harmless carbon dioxide and water. The air suction valves in the cylinder head cover act as check valves and prevent the flow of exhaust gases back up the cylinder head passages and into the air filter housing.

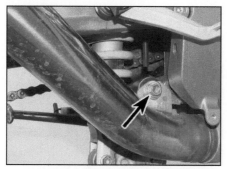

18.21 Unscrew the nut securing the front pipe bracket to the mounting on the oil pan

18.26 Bolt (arrowed) secures exhaust mid-section to frame – ZX-9R F models

18.30 Discard all exhaust gaskets. New ones must be used on installation

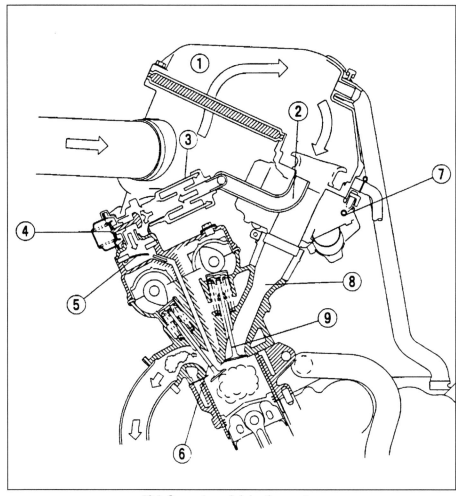

19.1 Secondary air injection system

1 *Air filter housing*	4 *Vacuum switching valve*	7 *Carburettors*
2 *Hose*	5 *Air suction valve*	8 *Inlet manifold*
3 *Vacuum valve*	6 *Exhaust valve*	9 *Inlet valve*

Checking

4 The air suction valves are regularly checked as part of the maintenance schedule (see Chapter 1) but if at any time it is noted that the engine is idling erratically then suspect a problem with the air suction valves. Remove the valves and check for obvious signs of damage and renew if necessary.

5 If it is noted that the engine backfires and pops on the overrun, then it is likely that the vacuum control valve is faulty. Remove the valve and check it as follows.

6 With the vacuum control valve removed, blow through the valve from the air filter housing hose and check that air flows freely through the valve. Apply a vacuum to the control valve diaphragm then repeat the check; the valve should now be closed and no longer allow air to flow through it. If a vacuum pump and gauge are available, the exact closing pressure of the valve can be checked; this should require 430 to 490 mmHg of vacuum. If the vacuum control valve is faulty it must be renewed.

Removal and installation

Vacuum control valve

7 Remove the fuel tank (Section 2) and air filter housing (Section 8) to gain access to the vacuum control valve which is located on the top of the cylinder head cover.

8 Note the correct routing of all the valve hoses then disconnect the vacuum hose from the control valve (**see illustration**).

9 Ease the valve hoses out from the air suction valve covers and remove the control valve and hose assembly from the bike (**see illustration**). If necessary, separate the hoses and intake silencer (where fitted) from the valve.

10 Installation is the reverse of removal ensuring that the valve is fitted with its air hole facing downwards.

Air suction valves

11 Remove the vacuum control valve as described in Steps 7 to 9. Each suction valve assembly can then be removed as follows.

12 Unscrew the two bolts and lift off the valve cover from the cylinder head cover (**see illustration**).

3 The vacuum control valve is fitted to prevent the flow of air through the suction valves when the engine is on overrun (motorcycle moving with the throttle closed). Whilst the engine is on the overrun, the excess air flowing into the exhaust ports could cause the unburnt fuel particles to explode (heard as backfiring or popping noises) resulting in damage to the air suction valves. The vacuum control valve is connected to one of the inlet tracts. When the engine is on the overrun, a high vacuum (low pressure) is present in the inlet tract. This vacuum acts on the control valve diaphragm and closes off the air supply to the suction valves.

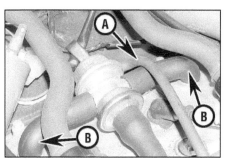

19.8 Disconnect the vacuum hose (A) from the control valve then free the valve hoses (B) from the suction valve covers . . .

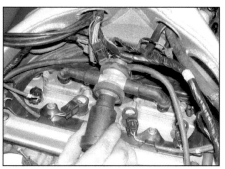

19.9 . . . and remove the valve assembly from the bike

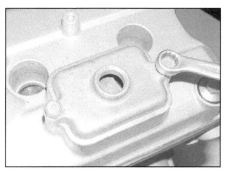

19.12 Unscrew the bolts and remove the suction valve cover . . .

13 Lift out the suction valve assembly, noting which way around it is fitted, and recover the valve gasket **(see illustrations)**. Discard the gasket.

14 Installation is the reverse of removal, using a new gasket. Ensure the valve assembly is installed correctly and tighten the cover bolts to the specified torque.

20 Carburettor vent valve (ZX-7R models except California)

General information

1 On all ZX-7R models (except California) a carburettor vent valve is fitted **(see illustration)**. **Note:** *On California models the same vacuum valve is fitted but it controls the evaporative emission system (see Section 21).*
2 When the engine is stopped, fuel vapour from the carburettor float chambers is allowed to flow through the valve and vent to atmosphere. When the engine is started, inlet manifold depression opens the switches controlling the vacuum valve which then allows the float chamber vapours to be drawn into the air filter housing to be burned during the normal combustion process.

Checking

3 If ever the valve is suspected of being faulty, it should be removed and tested as follows. Prior to testing remove the drain screw from the base of the vent valve and drain off any fuel. Ensure the O-ring is in good condition then securely refit the screw to the valve.
4 With the vent valve removed, blow through the valve from the carburettor hose union and check that air flows freely through the valve and out of the vent union. Apply a vacuum (approximately 1.5 cmHg) to the vent valve diaphragm then blow down the carburettor hose union again; the vent valve should now have switched and the air should flow through the valve and out of the air filter housing hose union. If the vent valve is faulty it must be renewed.

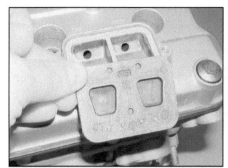

19.13a . . . then lift out the valve assembly . . .

Removal and installation

5 Remove the fuel tank (Section 2) and air filter housing (Section 8) to gain access to the vent valve which is located just behind the headstock of the frame.
6 Ease the valve out from its mounting rubber **(see illustration)**.
7 Note the correct routing of the valve hoses then disconnect both the carburettor and vacuum hoses **(see illustration)**. Remove the valve from the bike, complete with the air filter hose.
8 Installation is the reverse of removal.

21 Evaporative emission control system (California models only)

1 On all California models, an evaporative emission control system is fitted to prevent the escape of fuel vapours into the atmosphere. The fuel tank is sealed and the tank filler cap has a one-way valve which allows air into the tank as the volume of fuel decreases but prevents any fuel vapour from escaping.
2 When the engine is stopped, fuel vapour from the tank and the carburettor float chambers is allowed to flow into a charcoal canister (located under the seat) where it is absorbed and stored whilst the motorcycle is standing. A separator is fitted to the hose between the fuel tank and canister to prevent

19.13b . . . and gasket from the cylinder head cover

the canister being saturated with fuel.
3 When the engine is started, inlet manifold depression opens the evaporative emission control system vacuum valve which then allows the stored vapours to be drawn into the inlet tracts to be burned during the normal combustion process.
4 The system is not adjustable and can be tested only by a Kawasaki dealer. Checks which can be performed by the owner are given in Chapter 1.

22 Catalytic converter and fuel cut-off valves - ZX-9R C and E (not UK) and F models

General information

Note: *German and Swiss market versions of the ZX-9R C are known as the ZX-9R D.*
1 The ZX-9R C and E models available in California, Germany and Switzerland, and all ZX-9R F models, are fitted with a catalytic converter in the exhaust system. To protect the catalytic converter and help it operate efficiently, a fuel cut-off valve is fitted to each carburettor **(see illustration)**.
2 The exhaust system uses two converter elements, one located in the exhaust pipe just ahead of the silencer, and the other located in the front section of the silencer. The catalytic converter reduces the harmful elements of the exhaust gases to acceptable levels by converting carbon monoxide (CO), hydrocarbons (HC) and nitrogen oxides (NO_x)

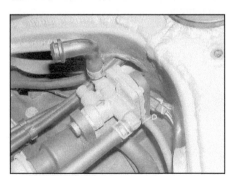

20.1 Carburettor vent valve location – ZX-7R model

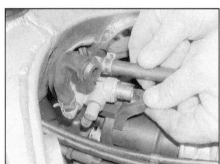

20.6 Ease the vent valve out from its mounting rubber . . .

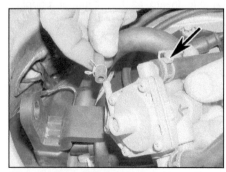

20.7 . . . then disconnect the vacuum hose and carburettor hose (arrowed) and remove the valve from the bike

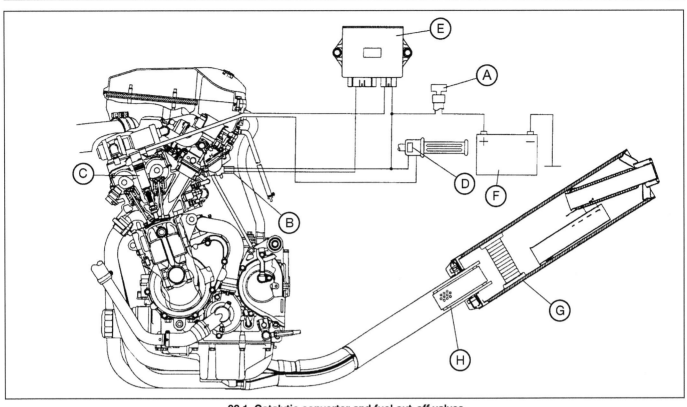

22.1 Catalytic converter and fuel cut-off valves

A Ignition (main) switch
B Throttle position sensor
C Ignition coil

D Engine stop switch
E IC igniter unit
F Battery

G Main catalytic converter element
H Pre-catalytic converter element

into carbon dioxide (CO_2), water (H_2O) and nitrogen (N_2).

3 The fuel cut-off valves installed on the carburettor float chambers provide protection for the catalytic converters by preventing excess fuel being passed into the exhaust system. If a high level of unburnt fuel enters the exhaust system the catalysts will overheat and may eventually meltdown. The cut-off valves are controlled by the IC igniter and function if the ignition is cut because of the speed limiter, if the engine kill switch is turned OFF when the engine is running, or if a misfire or interruption in the ignition coil primary circuit occurs. Since the fuel cut-off valves are unlikely to operate under normal running conditions, the IC igniter is programmed to operate the valves for an instant every time the engine is started; in this way the valves are less likely to become gummed up with fuel deposits.

4 The following precautions should be noted:

a) Always use unleaded fuel only. Leaded fuel will poison the catalytic converter and reduce its efficiency.

b) Always use the specified engine oil. Do not use engine oil which has phosphorus (P), lead (Pb) or sulphur (S) ingredients.

c) Do not coast the motorcycle at any time with the ignition main switch OFF or engine kill switch OFF. With the switches OFF, the fuel cut-off valves are disabled and will allow unburnt fuel to pass into the exhaust system leading to overheating of the catalytic converters and their eventual failure due to meltdown.

d) In the case of a flat battery, do not push-start the engine. Recharge the battery or connect up an auxiliary battery using jumper leads.

e) Do not continue to use the motorcycle if it develops a misfire or ignition system fault. Correct the fault at the earliest opportunity.

f) Keep the fuel and ignition systems in good order – if the fuel/air mixture is suspected of being incorrect have it checked by a dealer equipped with an exhaust gas analyser.

g) Take care to avoid burns when handling the silencer and exhaust pipe; these components can become extremely hot.

h) Check the secondary air injection system suction valves at the specified interval (see Chapter 1).

Checking

5 The catalytic converter can only be checked using a good-quality exhaust gas analyser and therefore testing will have to be left to a Kawasaki dealer. If a fuel cut-off valve

is thought to be faulty it can be tested as follows.

6 Remove the valve (see below) from the carburettor and measure the protrusion of the plunger from the valve body **(see illustration)**.

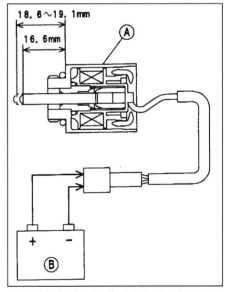

22.6 Fuel cut-off valve test set-up

A Fuel cut-off valve   B 12 volt battery

Connect a 12 volt battery to the terminals of the valve wiring connector as shown and measure the plunger protrusion again. If the plunger does not move when the battery is connected, or if the plunger protrusion differs from that specified the valve is faulty and should be renewed.

Removal and installation

Catalytic converter

7 The catalytic converter is an integral part of the exhaust system. Refer to Section 18 for removal and installation details.

Fuel-cut-off valve

Warning: Refer to the warning in Section 1 concerning contact with fuel.

8 Remove the fuel tank (see Section 2). Each valve can then be removed as follows.
9 Connect a hose to the union on the base of the float chamber then slacken the drain screw and drain the contents of the carburettor in a suitable container. Once the carburettor is empty, securely tighten the drain screw and disconnect the hose.
10 Trace the wiring back from the cut-off valve and disconnect it at the connector. **Note:** *If more than one cut-off valve is to be removed, number each valve (1 to 4) to ensure it is refitted to the correct carburettor. The valves fitted to carburettors 1 and 4 (wiring connector coloured grey) differ from those fitted to carburettors 2 and 3 (wiring connector coloured brown) and must not be interchanged.*
11 Unscrew the valve and remove it from the float chamber.
12 Installation is the reverse of removal. Ensure each valve is fitted to its original carburettor.

23 Catalytic converter - ZX-9R E UK models

General information

1 The ZX-9R E model available in the UK is fitted with a pre-catalytic converter in the exhaust system. The converter element is located in the exhaust pipe, just ahead of the silencer. The catalytic converter reduces the harmful elements of the exhaust gases to acceptable levels by converting carbon monoxide (CO), hydrocarbons (HC) and nitrogen oxides (NO_x) into carbon dioxide (CO_2), water (H_2O) and nitrogen (N_2).
2 The following precautions should be noted:
a) *Always use unleaded fuel only. Leaded fuel will poison the catalytic converter and reduce its efficiency.*
b) *Always use the specified engine oil. Do not use engine oil which has phosphorus (P), lead (Pb) or sulphur (S) ingredients.*
c) *In the case of a flat battery, do not push-start the engine. Recharge the battery or connect up an auxiliary battery using jumper leads.*
d) *Do not continue to use the motorcycle if it develops a misfire or ignition system fault. Correct the fault at the earliest opportunity.*
e) *Keep the fuel and ignition systems in good order – if the fuel/air mixture is suspected of being incorrect have it checked by a dealer equipped with an exhaust gas analyser.*
f) *Take care to avoid burns when handling the silencer and exhaust pipe; these components can become extremely hot.*
g) *Check the secondary air injection system suction valves at the specified interval (see Chapter 1).*

Checking

3 The catalytic converter can only be checked using a good-quality exhaust gas analyser and therefore testing will have to be left to a Kawasaki dealer.

Removal and installation

4 The catalytic converter is an integral part of the silencer. Refer to Section 18 for removal and installation details.

Chapter 5
Ignition system

Contents

Degrees of difficulty

Easy, suitable for novice with little experience 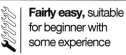	Fairly easy, suitable for beginner with some experience	Fairly difficult, suitable for competent DIY mechanic 	Difficult, suitable for experienced DIY mechanic	Very difficult, suitable for expert DIY or professional

Specifications

General

Cylinder identification	1 to 4 from left to right
Firing order	1-2-4-3

Spark plugs

Plug type and gap	see Chapter 1

Ignition timing

ZX-7R models
  UK and US (except California) models

At 1100 rpm	10° BTDC
At 5000 rpm	45° BTDC

  California models

At 1300 rpm	5° BTDC
At 5000 rpm	40° BTDC

ZX-9R B models
  UK and US (except California) models

At 1100 rpm	10° BTDC
At 5800 rpm	45° BTDC

  California models

At 1300 rpm	5° BTDC
At 5800 rpm	40° BTDC

ZX-9R C models

At 1100 rpm	10° BTDC
At 5000 rpm	32.5° BTDC

ZX-9R E and F models

At 1100 rpm	10° BTDC
At 5000 rpm	37.5° BTDC

Test data

Ignition coil
    ZX-7R and ZX-9R B models
        Primary resistance . . . . 2.3 to 3.5 ohms
        Secondary resistance . . . . 12 to 18 K ohms
        Arcing distance (minimum) . . . . 7 mm
    ZX-9R C, E and F models
        Primary resistance . . . . 0.85 to 1.15 ohms
        Secondary resistance . . . . 9.6 to 14.4 K ohms
        Arcing distance (minimum) . . . . Not available
Pick-up coil resistance . . . . 375 to 565 ohms
Camshaft sensor resistance – ZX-9R C models . . . . 400 to 460 ohms
Throttle position sensor output voltage – ZX-9R C, E and F models
    Engine idling . . . . 0.9 to 1.1 volts
    Throttle held fully open (engine stopped) . . . . 4.06 to 4.26 volts

Torque wrench settings

Pick-up coil cover bolts
    ZX-9R C models . . . . 11 Nm
    All other models . . . . 10 Nm
Pick-up coil mounting bolts
    ZX-7R and ZX-9R B models . . . . 8 Nm
    ZX-9R C, E and F models . . . . 6 Nm
Timing rotor bolt
    ZX-7R and ZX-9R B models . . . . 25 Nm
    ZX-9R C, E and F models . . . . 39 Nm

1 General information

ZX-7R and ZX-9R B models

ZX-7R and ZX-9R B models are equipped with a fully transistorised electronic ignition system consisting of a pick-up coil, an IC igniter unit, the ignition coils, the spark plugs along with the associated switches and wiring linking the components.

The ignition triggers on the timing rotor, fitted to the right-hand end of the crankshaft, magnetically operate the pick-up coil as the crankshaft rotates. The pick-up coil sends a signal to the IC (ignition control) igniter unit which then supplies the ignition HT coils with the power necessary to produce a spark at the plugs.

The system uses two coils, one supplying Nos. 1 and 4 cylinder spark plugs and the other supplying Nos.2 and 3 cylinder plugs. Each ignition coil operates on the `wasted spark' principle with each spark plug sparking twice for every cycle of the engine; once on the compression stroke and once on the exhaust stroke. The IC igniter incorporates an electronic advance system and has no provision for ignition timing adjustment.

ZX-9R C, E and F models

These models are equipped with a fully transistorised electronic ignition system which is far more sophisticated than that fitted to the ZX-7R and ZX-9R B models. The ignition system components consist of the pick-up coil, the throttle position sensor, the IC igniter unit, the ignition coils and the spark plugs along with the associated switches and wiring linking the components. On C models a camshaft sensor is also incorporated in the system.

The IC (ignition control) igniter unit receives signals from the following components.

a) *Pick-up coil (operated by the timing rotor on the right-hand end of the crankshaft) – informs the IC igniter of crankshaft speed and position.*

b) *The throttle position sensor (fitted to No. 4 carburettor) – informs the IC igniter of the throttle valve opening.*

c) *Camshaft sensor – C models only (operated by the trigger on the left-hand end of the exhaust camshaft) – informs the IC igniter of camshaft speed and position.*

The IC igniter unit uses the signals from the pick-up coil and (where fitted) camshaft sensor to determine the engine speed and piston position and the signal from the throttle position sensor to determine the load on the engine. The IC igniter then determines the required ignition advance setting and ignition HT coil charging time and supplies the HT coils with the power necessary to produce a spark at the plugs. There is no provision for ignition timing adjustment.

The system uses four ignition HT coils, one for each spark plug. Each coil is connected directly to the spark plug which obviates the need for any HT leads.

All models

The ignition system incorporates a safety interlock circuit which will cut the ignition if the sidestand is put down whilst the engine is running and in gear, or if a gear is selected whilst the engine is running and the sidestand is down. It also prevents the engine from being started if the sidestand is down and the engine is in gear unless the clutch lever is pulled in.

Because of their nature, the individual ignition system components can be checked but not repaired. If ignition system troubles occur, and the faulty component can be isolated, the only cure for the problem is to replace the part with a new one. Keep in mind that most electrical parts, once purchased, cannot be returned. To avoid unnecessary expense, make very sure the faulty component has been positively identified before buying a replacement part.

2 Ignition system – check

⚠️ *Warning: The energy levels in electronic systems can be very high. On no account should the ignition be switched on whilst the plugs or plug caps are being held. Shocks from the HT circuit can be most unpleasant. Secondly, it is vital that the engine is not turned over or run with any of the plug caps removed, and that the plugs are soundly earthed (grounded) when the system is checked for sparking. The ignition system components can be seriously damaged if the HT circuit becomes isolated. Ensure the ignition is switched off before any ignition system wiring connector is disconnected or reconnected.*

1 As no means of adjustment is available, any failure of the system can be traced to failure of a system component or a simple wiring fault.

Of the two possibilities, the latter is by far the most likely. In the event of failure, check the system in a logical fashion, as described below.

2 Remove the fuel tank and air filter housing (see Chapter 4) to gain access to the ignition coils/spark plugs.

3 Ensure the ignition is switched off then disconnect the fuel pump wiring connector (see Chapter 4).

4 Disconnect the plug caps (ZX-7R and ZX-9R B models) or ignition coils (ZX-9R C, E and F models) from the spark plugs. Connect each cap/coil to a spare spark plug and lay each plug on the engine with the threads contacting the engine. If necessary, hold each spark plug with an insulated tool.

⚠️ *Warning: Do not remove any of the spark plugs from the engine to perform this check – atomised fuel being pumped out of the open spark plug hole could ignite, causing severe injury!*

5 Having observed the above precautions, check that the kill switch is in the 'RUN' position and the transmission is in neutral, then turn the ignition switch ON and turn the engine over on the starter motor. If the system is in good condition a regular, fat blue spark should be evident at each plug electrode. If the spark appears thin or yellowish, or is non-existent, further investigation will be necessary. Before proceeding further, turn the ignition OFF and remove the key as a safety measure.

6 The ignition system must be able to produce a spark which is capable of jumping a particular size gap. Kawasaki state that the system should produce a spark capable of jumping at least 7 mm on ZX-7R and ZX-9R B models; no specification is given for the ZX-9R C, E and F models but 7 mm should be regarded as a minimum. A simple testing tool can be made to test the minimum gap across which the spark will jump (see **Tool Tip**) or alternatively it is possible to buy an ignition spark gap tester tool and some of these tools are adjustable to alter the spark gap **(see illustration)**.

7 Connect No. 1 plug cap/coil to the protruding electrode on the test tool, and clip the tool to a good earth (ground) on the engine or frame. Ensure the other three plugs are still earthed and check the transmission is in neutral and the kill switch is in the 'RUN' position. Turn the ignition switch ON and turn the engine over on the starter motor. If the system is in good condition a regular, fat blue spark should be seen to jump the gap between the nail ends. Repeat the test for the Nos. 2 to 4 caps/coils. If the test results are good the entire ignition system can be considered good. If the spark appears thin or yellowish, or is non-existent, further investigation is required.

8 Ignition faults can be divided into two categories, namely those where the ignition system has failed completely, and those

A simple spark gap testing tool can be made from a block of wood, a large alligator clip and two nails, one of which should protrude so that a spark plug cap or bare HT lead end can be connected to its base. Make sure the gap between the tips of the two nails is the same as specified.

which are due to a partial failure. The likely faults are listed below, starting with the most probable source of failure. Work through the list systematically, referring to the subsequent sections for full details of the necessary checks and tests. **Note:** *Before checking the following items ensure that the battery is fully charged and that all fuses are in good condition.*

a) *Loose, corroded or damaged wiring connections, broken or shorted wiring between any of the component parts of the ignition system.*

b) *Faulty spark plug, dirty, worn or corroded plug electrodes, or incorrect gap between electrodes.*

c) *Faulty HT lead or spark plug cap (ZX-7R and ZX-9R B models only).*

d) *Faulty ignition (main) switch or engine kill switch (see Chapter 9).*

e) *Faulty neutral, clutch or sidestand switch (see Chapter 9).*

f) *Faulty pick-up coil or damaged rotor.*

g) *Faulty ignition HT coil(s).*

h) *Faulty camshaft sensor or rotor (ZX-9R C models only).*

i) *Faulty throttle position sensor (ZX-9R C, E and F models only).*

j) *Faulty IC igniter unit.*

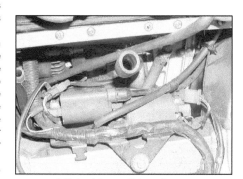

3.2 Ignition coil locations – ZX-7R model

2.6 Typical spark gap tester in use

9 If the above checks don't reveal the cause of the problem, have the ignition system tested by a Kawasaki dealer equipped with the special diagnostic tester.

10 On completion, securely reconnect the plug caps/coils to the plugs. Reconnect the fuel pump wiring connector and install the air filter housing and fuel tank (see Chapter 4).

3   Ignition coils –
check, removal and installation

ZX-7R models

Check

1 In order to determine conclusively that the ignition coils are defective they should be tested by a Kawasaki dealer. However, the coils can be checked visually (for cracks and other damage) and the primary and secondary coil resistances can be measured with an ohmmeter. If the coils are undamaged, and if the resistances are as specified, they are probably capable of proper operation.

2 To gain access to the coils, HT leads and plug caps remove the fuel tank and air filter housing (see Chapter 4) **(see illustration)**.

3 Unplug the primary circuit electrical connectors from the coil(s) and pull the spark plug caps off the plugs that are connected to the coil being checked. Mark the locations of all wires before disconnecting them.

4 Place the ohmmeter selector switch in the ohms x 1 position and check the coil primary resistance by attaching one ohmmeter lead to one of the primary terminals and the other ohmmeter lead to the other primary terminal. Compare the measured resistance to the value listed in this Chapter's Specifications. If required, check the primary resistance of the other coil.

5 Place the ohmmeter selector switch in the K ohms position. To check the coil secondary resistance, unscrew the spark plug caps from the leads, then insert the ohmmeter leads into the ends of the spark plug leads. Compare the measured resistance to the values listed in this Chapter's Specifications. If required, check the secondary resistance of the other coil.

3.13a Checking ignition coil primary resistance – ZX-9R B model

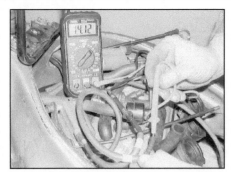

3.13b Checking ignition coil secondary resistance – ZX-9R B model

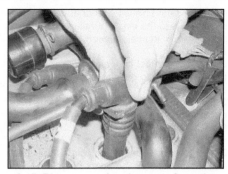

3.15 Disconnect the plug caps from the plugs

6 If the resistances are not as specified, unscrew the spark plug lead retainers from the coil, detach the leads and check the resistance again. If it is now within specifications, one or both of the leads is bad. If it's still not as specified, the coil is probably defective and should be replaced with a new one.

Removal and installation

7 Remove the fuel tank and air filter housing (see Chapter 4).
8 Disconnect the plug caps from the plugs.
9 Unscrew the bolt and free the coil mounting bracket from the frame. Take care not to lose the collar from the underside of the bracket mounting rubber.
10 Make a note of which colour wire fits on which terminal (label them with tape, if necessary, to aid installation) then disconnect the primary circuit electrical connectors from the coils and remove the coil and bracket assembly from the bike.
11 With the assembly removed, unscrew the retaining nuts then free both coils from the bracket, noting the spacer which is fitted between the coils. Recover the spacers from the mounting bracket studs.

> **HAYNES HINT** *If you're removing both coils and the HT leads are not numbered, it's a good idea to label the coils with the cylinder numbers to which they're connected.*

12 Installation is the reverse of removal. Make sure the wiring connectors and

HT leads are securely connected. Make sure the primary circuit electrical connectors are attached to the proper terminals – the red and black wires connect to Nos. 1 and 4 ignition coil (red to positive, black to negative) and the red and green wires attach to Nos. 2 and 3 coil (red to positive, green to negative).

ZX-9R B models

Check

13 Check the coils as described in Steps 1 to 6 **(see illustrations)**.

Removal and installation

14 Remove the fuel tank and air filter housing (see Chapter 4). Each coil can be removed as follows.
15 Disconnect the plug caps from the plugs **(see illustration)**.
16 Make a note of which colour wire fits on which terminal, then disconnect the primary circuit electrical connectors **(see illustration)**. If necessary, label the wires with tape to aid installation.
17 Unscrew the two retaining bolts and remove the coil along with the flanged spacers fitted between the coil and frame **(see illustration)**.

> **HAYNES HINT** *If you're removing both coils and the HT leads are not numbered, it's a good idea to label the coils with the cylinder numbers to which they're connected.*

18 Installation is the reverse of removal. Make sure the wiring connectors and HT leads are securely connected. Make sure the primary circuit electrical connectors are attached to the proper terminals – the red and black wires connect to Nos. 1 and 4 ignition coil (red to positive, black to negative) and the red and green wires attach to Nos. 2 and 3 coil (red to positive, green to negative).

ZX-9R C, E and F models

Check

19 In order to determine conclusively that the ignition coils are defective they should be tested by a Kawasaki dealer. However, the coils can be checked visually (for cracks and other damage) and the primary and secondary coil resistances can be measured with an ohmmeter. If the coils are undamaged, and if the resistances are as specified, they are probably capable of proper operation.
20 Remove the coils (see below) and check each one as follows.
21 Place the ohmmeter selector switch in the ohms x 1 position. To check the coil primary resistance, measure the resistance between the coil (primary) wiring terminals **(see illustration)**. Compare the measured resistance to the value listed in this Chapter's Specifications.
22 Place the ohmmeter selector switch in the K ohms position. To check the coil secondary resistance, connect one of the meter leads to the coil negative (–) wiring terminal and the other to the spark plug terminal **(see illustration)**. Compare the measured

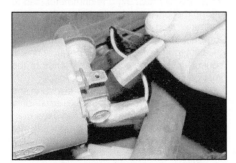

3.16 Disconnect the primary circuit electrical connectors from the coil terminals

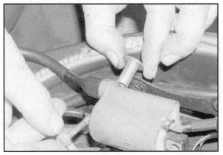

3.17 Unscrew the retaining bolts and recover the flanged spacers fitted between the coil and frame

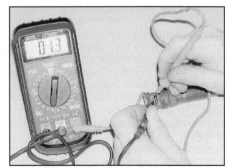

3.21 Checking ignition coil primary resistance – ZX-9R C, E and F models

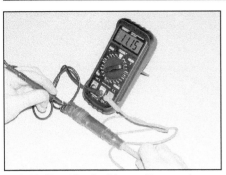

3.22 Checking ignition coil secondary resistance – ZX-9R C, E and F models

resistance to the values listed in this Chapter's Specifications.

23 If the resistances are not as specified, the coil is probably defective and should be replaced with a new one.

Removal and installation

24 Remove the fuel tank and air filter housing (see Chapter 4).

25 Disconnect the wiring connector from the coil then pull the coil out of position **(see illustrations)**. If more than one coil is being removed, note the correct fitted location of each wiring connector to ensure they are correctly reconnected.

26 Installation is the reverse of removal ensuring the wiring connectors are connected to the correct coils. The correct locations are as follows.

No. 1 coil – white/red and red wires
No. 2 coil – white/blue and red wires

4.3 Checking pick-up coil resistance

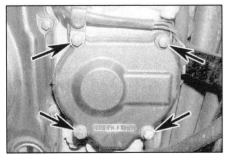

4.10a On ZX-7R and ZX-9R B models, the pick-up coil cover is retained by four bolts (arrowed)

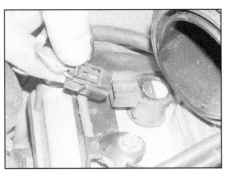

3.25a Disconnect the wiring connector . . .

No. 3 coil – white/green and red wires
No. 4 coil – white/yellow and red wires

4 Pick-up coil – check, removal and installation

Check

1 Remove the fuel tank (see Chapter 4).
2 Trace the pick-up coil wiring back from the cover on the right-hand end of the crankshaft and disconnect it at the three-pin connector (containing yellow, black, and blue/red wires).
3 Connect the probes of an ohmmeter between the yellow wire terminal and the black wire terminal on the pick-up coil side of the wiring connector and compare the reading with the resistance range listed in this Chapter's Specifications **(see illustration)**.

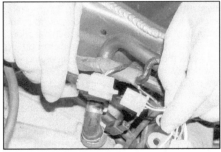

4.9 Trace the pick-up coil wiring back and disconnect its connector from the main harness

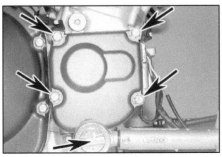

4.10b On ZX-9R C, E and F models, the pick-up coil cover is retained by five bolts (arrowed)

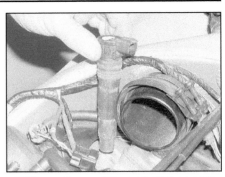

3.25b . . . then pull the coil off the spark plug

4 Set the ohmmeter on the highest resistance range. Measure the resistance between a good earth (ground) and the yellow and black terminals in the connector. The meter should indicate infinite resistance.
5 If the pick-up coil fails either of the above tests it is probably faulty, and should be replaced with a new one.

Removal

6 Remove the fuel tank (see Chapter 4).
7 On ZX-7R and ZX-9R B models remove the right-hand lower fairing panel (Chapter 8) then remove the coolant reservoir (Chapter 3).
8 On ZX-9R C, E and F models remove the lower fairing and right-hand middle fairing panel (see Chapter 8).
9 On all models, trace the pick-up coil wiring from the cover on the right-hand side of the engine and disconnect it at the three-pin connector **(see illustration)**. Peel back the rubber cover then slacken the screw and detach the wiring connector from the oil pressure switch (the switch wiring is located in the same connector as the pick-up coil). Release the pick-up coil/oil pressure switch wiring from its retaining clamp(s).
10 Unscrew the retaining bolts, noting the correct fitted location of the wiring clamp(s), and remove the pick-up coil cover from the right-hand end of the crankshaft **(see illustrations)**. Discard the cover seal – a new one should be used on installation.
11 Free the wiring grommet from its recess, then unscrew the mounting bolts and remove the pick-up coil from the bike, noting the routing of its wiring **(see illustration)**.

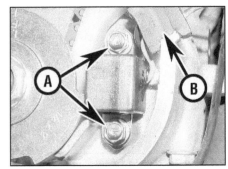

4.11 Pick-up coil bolts (A) and wiring grommet (B)

4.13 Apply sealant to the wiring grommet before seating it in the crankcase cutout

4.14 Apply sealant to the crankcase mating surface on each side of the joint and also to the wiring grommet

4.15a Fit a new seal to the pick-up cover groove . . .

4.15b . . . then fit the cover to the engine . . .

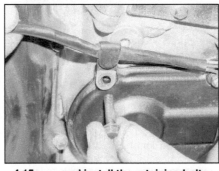
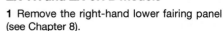

4.15c . . . and install the retaining bolts, ensuring the wiring clamp(s) are correctly positioned (ZX-9R B shown)

Installation

12 Ensure the crankcase and cover mating surfaces are clean and dry and the pick-up coil grommet is clean. On all except ZX-9R C models, remove all traces of locking compound from the cover bolt threads.

13 Locate the pick-up coil correctly on the crankcase and tighten its retaining bolts to the specified torque. Apply silicone sealant (Kawasaki recommend the use of Kawasaki Bond 56019-120) to the wiring grommet and seat the grommet correctly in its notch in the crankcase **(see illustration)**.

14 Apply a smear of silicone sealant to the area of the crankcase mating surface on each side of the crankcase half joints and also to the pick-up coil wiring grommet **(see illustration)**.

15 Locate the new seal correctly in the pick-up coil cover groove, then fit the cover to the crankcase **(see illustrations)**. Screw in the bolts, complete with the wiring clamp(s), and tighten them to the specified torque **(see illustration)**. On all except ZX-9R C models, apply a few drops of locking compound to the threads of the cover bolts prior to installation.

16 Route the wiring harness correctly up between the engine and frame, securing it is position with the clamp(s), and reconnect it to the main harness. Reconnect the oil pressure switch wiring connector, tightening its retaining screw securely, and seat the rubber cover back over the switch.

17 On ZX-7R and ZX-9R B models install the coolant reservoir (Chapter 3).

18 On all models, fit the fuel tank and fairing panel(s) (Chapters 4 and 8).

5 Timing rotor – removal and installation

Removal

ZX-7R and ZX-9R B models

1 Remove the right-hand lower fairing panel (see Chapter 8).

2 Remove the coolant reservoir (see Chapter 3).

3 Unscrew the retaining bolts, noting the correct fitted location of the wiring clamp(s), and remove the pick-up coil cover from the right-hand end of the crankshaft. Discard the cover seal, a new one should be used on installation.

4 Retain the rotor with a ring spanner on the rotor hex then slacken the rotor retaining bolt **(see illustration)**. Unscrew the bolt and remove the rotor from the crankshaft end. If the rotor locating pin is a loose-fit, remove it from the crankshaft and store it with the rotor for safe-keeping **(see illustration)**.

ZX-9R C, E and F models

5 Remove the lower fairing and right middle fairing panel (see Chapter 8).

6 Unscrew the retaining bolts, noting the correct fitted location of the wiring clamps, and remove the pick-up coil cover from the right-hand end of the crankshaft. Discard the cover seal – a new one should be used on installation.

7 Select 1st gear and have an assistant apply the rear brake firmly to prevent rotation whilst you slacken the timing rotor bolt. Unscrew the bolt and remove the timing rotor from the crankshaft end. **Note:** *If the engine has been removed from the frame, remove the cover from the left-hand end of the crankshaft and prevent crankshaft rotation by holding either the alternator rotor with a strap wrench or the rotor bolt with a socket/spanner (see Chapter 9). Alternatively, if the timing rotor has two holes it can be retained with a suitable peg spanner.*

5.4a On ZX-7R and ZX-9R B models, retain the rotor with a ring spanner then slacken the rotor bolt

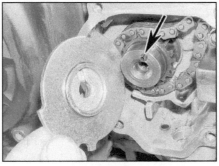

5.4b Remove the rotor from the crankshaft noting the locating pin (arrowed)

Installation

ZX-7R and ZX-9R B models

8 Ensure the locating pin is in position then fit the timing rotor, aligning its cutout with the pin. Ensure the timing rotor is correctly engaged with the pin and screw the retaining bolt fully in. Retain the rotor with a spanner and tighten the rotor bolt to the specified torque.

9 Ensure the crankcase and cover mating surfaces are clean and dry and remove all traces of locking compound from the threads of the cover retaining bolts.

10 Apply a smear of silicone sealant (Kawasaki recommend the use of Kawasaki Bond 56019-120) to the area of the crankcase mating surface on each side of the crankcase half joints and also to the pick-up coil wiring grommet.

11 Locate the new seal correctly in the pick-up coil cover groove then fit the cover to the crankcase. Apply a few drops of locking compound to each cover retaining bolt then screw in the bolts, complete with the wiring clamp(s). Ensure the clamp(s) are correctly positioned then tighten the bolts to the specified torque.

12 Fit the coolant reservoir (Chapter 3).

13 Install the fairing panel as described in Chapter 8.

ZX-9R C, E and F models

14 Position the timing rotor with its markings facing outwards, then align its wide (master) spline with that of the crankshaft and slide it into position **(see illustration)**. Fit the retaining bolt and tighten it to the specified torque, preventing rotation by using the method employed on removal **(see illustration)**.

15 Ensure the crankcase and cover mating surfaces are clean and dry. On E models, remove all traces of locking compound from the threads of the cover retaining bolts.

16 Apply a smear of silicone sealant (Kawasaki recommend the use of Kawasaki Bond 56019-120) to the area of the crankcase mating surface on each side of the crankcase half joints and also to the pick-up coil wiring grommet.

17 Locate the new seal correctly in the pick-up

5.14a On ZX-9R C and E models, align the wide (master) spline (arrowed) of the rotor with that of the crankshaft . . .

coil cover groove, then fit the cover to the crankcase. Screw in the bolts, complete with the wiring clamps, and tighten them to the specified torque. On E models, apply a few drops of locking compound to each cover retaining bolt prior to refitting.

18 Install the fairing panels as described in Chapter 8.

6 IC igniter unit – removal, check and installation

Removal

1 On ZX-7R and ZX-9R B models, remove the side covers (see Chapter 8) to gain access to the IC igniter unit which is mounted on the right-hand side of the subframe **(see illustrations)**.

2 On ZX-9R C and E models, remove the rider's seat to gain access to the IC igniter unit which is fixed to the mudguard **(see illustration)**.

3 On ZX-9R F models, remove the seat cowling (see Chapter 8) to gain access to the IC igniter unit which is mounted on the left-hand side of the sub-frame.

4 On all models, unscrew the retaining bolts then, ensuring the ignition is switched off, disconnect the wiring connector(s) and remove the IC igniter unit from the bike.

Check

5 The IC igniter unit is a delicate and expensive component requiring the use of a

5.14b . . . then slide on the rotor and fit the retaining bolt

specific tester to check its condition. Take the machine to a Kawasaki dealer if the unit is suspected of being faulty.

Installation

6 Ensure the ignition is switched off then reconnect the wiring connector(s) to the unit. Seat the unit correctly in position and securely tighten its retaining bolts.

7 Install the side covers/seats (as applicable) as described in Chapter 8.

7 Throttle position sensor (ZX-9R C, E and F models) – check, adjustment and renewal

Note: On ZX-9R C models, the Kawasaki auxiliary wiring harness (Pt. No. 57001-1400) will be needed to enable the throttle position sensor to be checked and accurately adjusted. If access to this wiring harness cannot be gained, do no disturb the sensor. If the sensor is thought to be faulty take the bike to a Kawasaki dealer for testing. On ZX-9R E and F models, if the sensor is thought to be faulty, have the sensor and IC igniter unit tested by a Kawasaki dealer.

Check and adjustment – ZX-9R C models

1 Before checking the sensor itself, ensure the carburettors are correctly synchronised and the idle speed is correctly set (see Chapter 1).

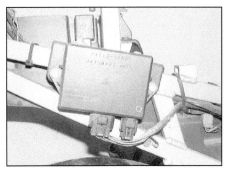

6.1a IC igniter unit location – ZX-7R model

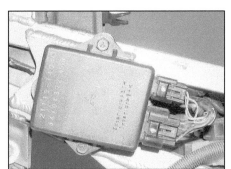

6.1b IC igniter unit location – ZX-9R B model

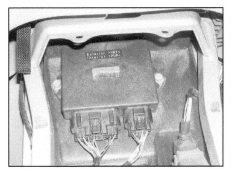

6.2 IC igniter unit location – ZX-9R C and E model

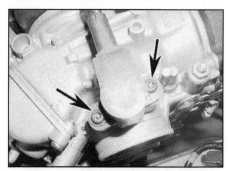

7.8 On ZX-9R C and E models, never slacken the throttle position sensor screws (arrowed) unless the sensor is to be renewed or adjusted

2 Remove the fuel tank (see Chapter 4). Arrange a temporary fuel supply, either by positioning the tank on a suitable base on the motorcyle (taking care not to scratch any paintwork and ensuring that the tank is safely and securely supported), by using extra long fuel pipes to the now-remote fuel tank, or by using a small temporary tank.

3 The throttle position sensor is mounted on the outside of the right-hand carburettor. Ensure the ignition is switched off, then disconnect the sensor wiring connector from the main harness. Connect one end of the Kawasaki auxiliary wiring harness (Pt. No. 57001-1400) to the throttle sensor connector and the other to the main harness. **Caution: Do not allow the auxiliary wiring harness terminals to contact each other or any other part of the motorcycle.**

4 Connect the positive (+) lead of a voltmeter to the yellow lead of the auxiliary harness and the negative (–) lead to the black terminal of the harness. Start the engine and note the voltage reading obtained with the engine idling. Compare this to the reading given in this Chapter's Specifications. If the recorded

voltage differs from that specified, slacken the sensor mounting screws and rotate the sensor until the output is within the specified range, then securely retighten the screws.

5 Once the sensor is correctly adjusted, stop the engine. Turn the ignition back on again and note the voltage reading obtained with the throttle held fully open. Compare this to the reading given in the Specifications.

6 If the throttle sensor fails either of the above tests, it is probably faulty and should be replaced with a new one.

Renewal

7 Remove the fuel tank (see Chapter 4).

8 The throttle position sensor is mounted on the outside of the right-hand carburettor **(see illustration)**. Disconnect the wiring connector, then unscrew the sensor mounting screws and remove the sensor, noting how it fits.

9 Install the sensor, ensuring it engages correctly with the throttle valve spindle, and lightly tighten its retaining screws.

10 Check and adjust the sensor as described in Steps 2 to 5.

11 Once the sensor is correctly adjusted, remove the auxiliary wiring harness and connect the sensor wiring connector securely to the main harness. Install the fuel tank (Chapter 4).

8 Camshaft sensor (ZX-9R C models) – check, removal and installation

Check

1 Remove the fuel tank (see Chapter 4).

2 Trace the wiring back from the sensor on the front, left-hand end of the cylinder head to its connector on the left-hand side of the air filter housing. Ensure the ignition is switched off, then disconnect the connector.

3 Connect the probes of an ohmmeter between the terminals on the sensor side of the wiring connector and compare the reading with the range of resistance listed in this Chapter's Specifications.

4 Set the ohmmeter on the highest resistance range. Measure the resistance between a good earth (ground) and each terminal in the sensor connector. The meter should indicate infinite resistance.

5 If the sensor fails either of the above tests, it is probably faulty and should be replaced with a new one.

Removal

6 Remove the fuel tank (see Chapter 4). The sensor is fitted to the front of the cylinder head and is accessible through the cutout in the left-hand middle panel.

7 Trace the wiring back from the sensor and disconnect its connector from the main wiring harness. Free the sensor wiring from its retaining clips and pull the connector through to the front of the engine. If necessary, remove the air filter housing (see Chapter 4) to improve access to the wiring.

8 Unscrew the retaining bolt and ease the camshaft sensor out from the front of the cylinder head.

Installation

9 Ensure the sensor sealing ring is in good condition then lubricate it with a smear of engine oil to aid installation.

10 Ease the sensor into position in the cylinder head and fit its retaining bolt, tightening it securely.

11 Route the sensor wiring correctly up over the cylinder head and securely connect it to the main wiring harness.

12 Install the air filter housing (where removed) and fuel tank as described in Chapter 4.

Chapter 6
Frame, suspension and final drive

Contents

Degrees of difficulty

Easy, suitable for novice with little experience	Fairly easy, suitable for beginner with some experience	Fairly difficult, suitable for competent DIY mechanic	Difficult, suitable for experienced DIY mechanic	Very difficult, suitable for expert DIY or professional

Specifications

Front forks

Fork oil type
   ZX-7R and ZX-9R B and F models .... Kayaba 01 (SAE 5W)
   ZX-9R C and E models .... Kayaba G10 (SAE 10W)
Fork oil capacity
   Dry (after stripdown)
      ZX-7R models .... 431 ± 4 ml
      ZX-9R B models
         B1, B2 and US B3 models .... 463 ± 4 ml
         B4 and UK B3 models .... 457 ± 4 ml
      ZX-9R C models .... 565 ± 4 ml
      ZX-9R E models .... 535 ± 4 ml
      ZX-9R F models .... 533 ± 4 ml
   At oil change (approximate)
      ZX-7R models .... 365 ml
      ZX-9R B models
         B1, B2 and US B3 models .... 395 ml
         B4 and UK B3 models .... 390 ml
      ZX-9R C models .... 479 ml
      ZX-9R E models .... 455 ml
      ZX-9R F models .... 453 ml
Fork oil level*
   ZX-7R models .... 110 ± 2 mm
   ZX-9R B models
      B1, B2 and US B3 models .... 86 ± 2 mm
      B4 and UK B3 models .... 90 ± 2 mm
   ZX-9R C models .... 123 ± 2 mm
   ZX-9R E and F models .... 118 ± 2 mm

Front forks (continued)

Fork spring free length
    ZX-7R models
        Standard . . . . 328.9 mm
        Service limit . . . . 322 mm
    ZX-9R B models
        B1, B2 and US B3 models
            Standard . . . . 304.6 mm
            Service limit . . . . 300 mm
        B4 and UK B3 models
            Standard . . . . 387.4 mm
            Service limit . . . . 380 mm
    ZX-9R C models
        Standard . . . . 289.1 mm
        Service limit . . . . 280 mm
    ZX-9R E and F models
        Standard . . . . 234.6 mm
        Service limit . . . . 230 mm

Oil level is measured from the top of the tube with the fork spring removed, the leg fully compressed and the damper rod fully inserted.

Final drive

Chain type
    ZX-7R models . . . . RK525ROZ2 (110 links)
    ZX-9R B models . . . . EK50UV-X (112 links)
    ZX-9R C and E models . . . . EK525UVX (110 links)
    ZX-9R F model . . . . EK525UVXL2 (110 links)

Torque wrench settings

Bottom yoke fork clamp bolt
    ZX-7R and ZX-9R B models . . . . 28 Nm
    ZX-9R C, E and F models . . . . 20 Nm
Clutch master cylinder mounting clamp bolts . . . . 11 Nm
Fork damper assembly bolt . . . . 39 Nm
Fork top cap . . . . 23 Nm
Fork top cap damper rod locknut
    ZX-7R and ZX-9R B models . . . . 15 Nm
    ZX-9R C, E and F models . . . . 27 Nm
Front brake master cylinder mounting clamp bolts
    ZX-7R models . . . . 11 Nm
    ZX-9R models . . . . 9 Nm
Front sprocket cover bolts . . . . 10 Nm
Front sprocket nut . . . . 125 Nm
Handlebar holder clamp bolt
    ZX-7R and ZX-9R B and C models . . . . 23 Nm
    ZX-9R E and F models . . . . 25 Nm
Handlebar mounting bolt . . . . 34 Nm
Handlebar holder-to-top yoke bolt . . . . 10 Nm
Rear brake master cylinder bolts
    ZX-7R and ZX-9R B and C models . . . . 23 Nm
    ZX-9R E and F models . . . . 25 Nm
Rear shock absorber mounting bolt nuts
    ZX-7R and ZX-9R B models . . . . 59 Nm
    ZX-9R C, E and F models . . . . 34 Nm
Rear sprocket nuts
    ZX-7R and ZX-9R B and C models . . . . 74 Nm
    ZX-9R E and F models . . . . 59 Nm
Rider's footrest bolt . . . . 34 Nm
Sidestand bracket bolts . . . . 49 Nm
Speed sensor bolt – ZX-9R C, E and F models . . . . 7 Nm
Steering head bearing adjuster nut*
    ZX-7R models
        Initial torque . . . . 54 Nm (apply a force of 30.5 kg/300N)
        Final torque . . . . 5 Nm (apply a force of 2.8 kg/28N)
    ZX-9R B and C models
        Initial torque . . . . 39 Nm (apply a force of 22.2 kg/220N)
        Final torque . . . . 5 Nm (apply a force of 2.8 kg/28N)
    ZX-9R E and F models
        Adjuster nut . . . . 20 Nm (apply a force of 11.3 kg/111N)
        Locknut . . . . 10 Nm (apply a force of 5.6 kg/55N)

Figure given in brackets is the necessary force to apply to the special Kawasaki tool 57001-1100 to obtain the specified torque – see Section 8 text

Torque wrench settings (continued)

Steering stem nut
ZX-7R models . . . . 54 Nm
ZX-9R B and C models . . . . 39 Nm
ZX-9R E and F models . . . . 49 Nm
Suspension linkage pivot bolt nuts
Rocker arm bolt nut
ZX-7R and ZX-9R B models . . . . 59 Nm
ZX-9R C, E and F models . . . . 34 Nm
Tie rod bolt nuts . . . . 59 Nm
Swingarm
Pivot shaft . . . . 20 Nm
Pivot nut
ZX-7R and ZX-9R B models . . . . 98 Nm
ZX-9R C models . . . . 110 Nm
ZX-9R E and F models . . . . 125 Nm
Pivot shaft locknut . . . . 98 Nm
Top yoke fork clamp bolt
ZX-7R and ZX-9R B models . . . . 21 Nm
ZX-9R C, E and F models . . . . 20 Nm

1 General information

Front suspension is by a pair of oil-damped telescopic forks which have a conventional damper system and are adjustable for spring pre-load and compression and rebound damping.

At the rear, an alloy swingarm acts on a single shock absorber via a three-way linkage. The shock absorber is adjustable for spring pre-load and compression and rebound damping. The swingarm is mounted onto the frame.

The drive to the rear wheel is by chain.

2 Frame – inspection and repair

1 The frame should not require attention unless accident damage has occurred. In most cases, frame renewal is the only satisfactory remedy for such damage. A few frame specialists have the jigs and other equipment necessary for straightening the frame to the required standard of accuracy, but even then there is no simple way of assessing to what extent the frame may have been over-stressed.
2 After the machine has accumulated a lot of miles, the frame should be examined closely for signs of cracking or splitting at the welded joints. Loose engine mount bolts can cause ovaling or fracturing of the mounting tabs. Minor damage can often be repaired by specialist welding, depending on the extent and nature of the damage.
3 Remember that a frame which is out of alignment will cause handling problems. If misalignment is suspected as the result of an accident, it will be necessary to strip the machine completely so the frame can be thoroughly checked.

3 Footrests and brackets – removal and installation

Rider's footrest
Removal
1 Remove the retaining clip from the footrest pivot pin, then withdraw the pivot pin and remove the footrest, noting the fitting of the return spring.
Installation
2 Installation is the reverse of removal.

Passenger footrests
Removal
3 Remove the retaining clip from the footrest pivot pin.
4 On ZX-9R E and F models, withdraw the pivot pin and carefully remove the footrest from the bracket, noting the correct fitted position of the detent plate, ball and spring.
5 On all other models, withdraw the pivot pin and carefully remove the footrest from the bracket, noting the correct fitted position of the stepped washer, collar and spring.
Installation
6 Installation is the reverse of removal. Check that the detent mechanism functions correctly before securing the pivot pin in position with the retaining clip.

Rider's right side footrest bracket assembly
Removal
7 Remove the side covers/seat cowling to gain access to the rear brake light switch connector (see Chapter 8).
8 Trace the wiring back from the rear brake light switch and disconnect it at the wiring connectors. Free the switch wiring from any relevant clips or ties so the switch is free to be removed with the bracket.

9 Loosen the rear brake master cylinder mounting bolts.
10 Slacken and remove the mounting bolts and free the bracket from the frame.
11 Remove the split pin and withdraw the clevis pin securing the rear brake master cylinder pushrod to the brake pedal.
12 Remove the mounting bolts and free the master cylinder and heel plate from the footrest bracket then remove the bracket assembly from the bike. **Note:** *There is no need to disconnect the hydraulic hoses from the cylinder.*
13 If necessary, unhook the brake light switch spring from the pedal then unscrew the footrest bolt and separate the footrest, brake pedal and mounting bracket. Check the pedal pivot bush for signs of wear or damage and renew if necessary.
Installation
14 If the brake pedal was removed, remove all traces of locking compound from the footrest bolt threads. Apply a smear of multi-purpose grease to the pivot bush then reassemble the footrest, brake pedal and bracket. Apply a drop of locking compound to the threads of the footrest retaining bolt then fit the bolt and tighten it to the specified torque. Hook the brake light switch spring back onto the pedal pin.
15 Locate the master cylinder and heel plate on the bracket and fit its mounting bolts, tightening them to the specified torque. Align the pushrod with the pedal then fit the clevis pin and secure it in position with a new split pin.
16 Locate the bracket on the frame and securely tighten its mounting bolts.
17 Ensure the rear brake light switch wiring is correctly routed and retained by all the necessary clips then reconnect it to the main wiring harness.
18 Refit the side covers/seat cowling (see Chapter 8). Check the operation of the rear brake and brake light before riding the bike on the road.

Rider's left side footrest bracket assembly

Removal

19 Note the correct fitted position of the gearchange lever on its shaft (make alignment marks if necessary) then unscrew the clamp bolt and free the gearchange lever from the engine.

20 Slacken and remove the mounting bolts and free the bracket from the frame.

21 If necessary, unscrew the footrest bolt and separate the footrest, gearchange linkage and mounting bracket. Check components for signs of wear or damage and renew if necessary. On ZX-9R C, E and F models the gearchange lever grease seals should be renewed if they show signs of deterioration.

Installation

22 If the gearchange linkage was removed, remove all traces of locking compound from the footrest bolt threads. Apply a smear of multi-purpose grease to the footrest and linkage pivots then reassemble the footrest, gearchange linkage and bracket. Apply a drop of locking compound to the threads of the footrest retaining bolt then fit the bolt and tighten it to the specified torque.

23 Locate the bracket on the frame and securely tighten its mounting bolts.

24 Engage the gearchange lever linkage with the shaft splines so the lever is correctly positioned. Fit the clamp bolt to the linkage and tighten it securely.

Passenger right side footrest bracket assembly

Removal

25 On ZX-9R B models remove the side covers (see Chapter 8).

26 On all models, slacken and remove the silencer mounting bolt nut then withdraw the bolt, noting the correct fitted location of the washer(s).

27 Unscrew the two mounting bolts and (where fitted) nuts and remove the footrest bracket from the rear subframe.

Installation

28 Installation is the reverse of removal.

Passenger left side footrest bracket assembly

Removal

29 On ZX-9R B models remove the seat cowling (see Chapter 8).

30 On all models, unscrew the two mounting bolts and (where fitted) nuts and remove the footrest bracket from the subframe.

Installation

31 Installation is the reverse of removal.

---

4 Sidestand –
removal and installation

ZX-7R and ZX-9R B models

Removal

1 Support the bike on an auxiliary stand then carefully unhook and remove the stand spring.

2 Unscrew the nut from the sidestand pivot bolt then remove the pivot bolt and stand from the mounting bracket.

3 To remove the mounting bracket, undo the retaining screws and free the sidestand switch from the bracket (see Chapter 9). **Note:** *There is no need to disconnect the switch wiring connector.* Undo the mounting bolts then remove the bracket from the frame.

Installation

4 If the mounting bracket was removed, first remove all traces of locking compound from the sidestand switch screw threads. Fit the bracket to the frame and tighten its mounting bolts to the specified torque. Apply a drop of locking compound to the switch retaining screw threads then locate the switch on the bracket and securely tighten its retaining bolts.

5 Lubricate the pivot bolt with clean engine oil then fit the stand and bolt to the bracket. Securely tighten the bolt then fit the nut to the bolt and tighten securely.

6 Reconnect the sidestand spring and check that it holds the stand securely up when not in use – an accident is almost certain to occur if the stand extends while the machine is in motion. Also check the operation of the sidestand switch (see Chapter 1).

ZX-9R C, E and F models

Removal

7 Unscrew the mounting bolt and free the sidestand switch from the stand bracket (see Chapter 9). **Note:** *There is no need to disconnect the switch wiring connector.*

8 Support the bike on an auxiliary stand then carefully unhook and remove the stand spring.

9 Unscrew the nut from the sidestand pivot bolt then remove the pivot bolt and stand from the mounting bracket.

10 If necessary, unscrew the mounting bolts and remove the sidestand bracket from the frame.

Installation

11 If the mounting bracket was removed, fit the bracket to the frame and tighten its mounting bolts to the specified torque.

12 Apply multi-purpose grease to the pivot bolt shank then fit the sidestand to its bracket and insert the pivot bolt. Securely tighten the pivot bolt then fit the nut to the bolt and tighten it securely.

---

13 Reconnect the sidestand spring and check that it holds the stand securely up when not in use – an accident is almost certain to occur if the stand extends while the machine is in motion.

14 Locate the switch onto the sidestand bracket, making sure the switch lever is correctly engaged with the sidestand pin. Fit the switch mounting bolt and tighten it securely. Check the operation of the sidestand switch (see Chapter 1).

5 Handlebars –
removal and installation

Right handlebar – ZX-7R models

Removal

1 Undo the retaining screw and remove the end cap/weight from the handlebar.

2 Undo the bolts and free the front brake and clutch master cylinder reservoir brackets from the top yoke. Position both reservoirs clear of the yoke, keeping them upright to prevent possible fluid leakage.

3 Unscrew the bolts securing the left and right handlebars to the underside of the top yoke.

4 Slacken and remove the steering stem nut and washer.

5 Loosen the top yoke clamp bolts then lift off the yoke and position it clear of the steering stem/forks.

6 Disconnect the wiring from the brake light switch on the master cylinder assembly.

7 Unscrew the two front brake master cylinder assembly clamp bolts and position the master cylinder clear of the handlebar, making sure no strain is placed on the hydraulic hose.

8 Unscrew the two handlebar switch screws then free the switch from the handlebar.

9 If the handlebar is to be removed from its holder, loosen its mounting bolt now.

10 Slacken the holder clamp bolt then free the handlebar from the top of the fork tube and the throttle twistgrip and remove it from the bike. If necessary, unscrew the mounting bolt and separate the handlebar and holder.

Installation

11 Remove all traces of locking compound from the threads of the handlebar mounting bolt, holder-to-top yoke bolt and the end cap screw.

12 Where necessary, fit the handlebar to its holder ensuring the locating pin is correctly located in the cutout. Apply a drop of locking compound to the mounting bolt threads then fit it and tighten to the specified torque (this will be easier once the holder is fitted to the fork tube).

13 Lubricate the handlebar and throttle twistgrip bearing surfaces with a smear of multi-purpose grease. Slide the twistgrip onto the handlebar and locate the holder on the fork tube.

14 Locate the top yoke back in position and fit the washer and steering stem nut. Tighten the steering stem nut to the specified torque then tighten both the top yoke clamp bolts to their specified torque setting.

15 Apply locking compound to the threads of the handlebar holder-to-top yoke bolts then fit both bolts and tighten them to the specified torque.

16 Tighten the right handlebar holder clamp bolt to its specified torque setting.

17 Ensure the throttle cables are correctly attached to the grip then lubricate their upper ends with multi-purpose grease. Locate the outer cables correctly in the switch halves then assemble the switch on the handlebar, placing the rear half locating peg in the handlebar hole. Ensure the switch and cables are correctly assembled then securely tighten the switch screws.

18 Locate the master cylinder on the handlebar and fit the mounting clamp with its arrow mark facing upwards. Align the master cylinder mounting clamp split with the punch mark on the top of the handlebar then tighten the mounting clamp upper bolt to the specified torque followed by the lower bolt.

19 Reconnect the wiring connector to the brake light switch.

20 Locate the brake and clutch fluid reservoir brackets correctly on the top yoke and tighten their retaining bolts securely.

21 Apply a drop of locking compound to the threads of the end cap/weight screw. Fit the end cap/weight to the handlebar and securely tighten its retaining screw.

22 On completion, check the throttle cable adjustment and the brake light switch operation (see Chapter 1) and the clutch and brake fluid levels (see *Daily (pre-ride) checks*) before riding the machine on the road.

Left handlebar – ZX-7R models

Removal

23 Remove the top yoke as described in Steps 1 to 5.

24 Disconnect the wiring connector from the clutch switch then unscrew the two clutch master cylinder assembly clamp bolts and position the master cylinder clear of the handlebar, making sure no strain is placed on the hydraulic hose.

25 Unscrew the two handlebar switch screws then free the switch from the handlebar.

26 If the handlebar is to be removed from its holder, loosen its mounting bolt now.

27 Slacken the holder clamp bolt then free the handlebar from the top of the fork tube and remove it from the bike. If necessary, unscrew the mounting bolt and separate the handlebar and holder.

Installation

28 Carry out the operations described in Steps 11 and 12.

29 Locate the handlebar holder on the fork tube then fit the top yoke back in position. Install the washer and steering stem nut,

tightening it to the specified torque, then tighten both the top yoke clamp bolts to their specified torque setting.

30 Apply locking compound to the threads of the handlebar holder-to-top yoke bolts then fit both bolts and tighten them to their specified torque.

31 Tighten the left handlebar holder clamp bolt to its specified torque setting.

32 Lubricate the upper end of the choke cable with multi-purpose grease and attach it correctly to the choke lever. Locate the lever and outer cable correctly in the switch halves then assemble the switch on the handlebar, locating the rear half locating peg in the handlebar hole. Ensure the switch, lever and cable are correctly assembled then securely tighten the switch screws.

33 Locate the master cylinder on the handlebar and fit the mounting clamp with its arrow mark facing upwards. Align the master cylinder mounting clamp split with the punch mark on the top of the handlebar then tighten the mounting clamp upper bolt to the specified torque followed by the lower bolt.

34 Reconnect the wiring connector to the clutch switch.

35 Locate the brake and clutch fluid reservoir brackets correctly on the top yoke and tighten their retaining bolts securely.

36 If a new handlebar grip needs to be installed ensure the handlebar surface is clean and dry. Apply a suitable adhesive to the inside of the new grip then slide the grip onto the bar until it butts up against the switch.

37 Apply a drop of locking compound to the threads of the end cap/weight screw. Fit the end cap/weight to the handlebar and securely tighten its retaining screw.

38 On completion, check the choke cable operation (see Chapter 1) and the clutch and brake fluid levels (see *Daily (pre-ride) checks*) before riding the machine on the road.

Right handlebar – ZX-9R B models

Removal

39 Undo the retaining screw and remove the end cap and weight from the handlebar.

40 Disconnect the wiring from the brake light switch on the master cylinder assembly.

41 Unscrew the two front brake master cylinder assembly clamp bolts and position the master cylinder clear of the handlebar, making sure no strain is placed on the hydraulic hose. Keep the master cylinder reservoir upright to prevent possible fluid leakage.

42 If the handlebar is to be removed from its holder, loosen its mounting bolt now.

43 Unscrew the two handlebar switch screws then free the switch from the handlebar.

44 Unscrew the bolt securing the handlebar to the top yoke.

45 Slacken the holder clamp bolt then free the handlebar from the top of the fork tube and the throttle twistgrip and remove it from the bike. If necessary, unscrew the mounting bolt and separate the handlebar and holder.

Installation

46 Remove all traces of locking compound from the threads of the handlebar mounting bolt, holder-to-top yoke bolt and the end cap screw.

47 Where necessary, fit the handlebar to its holder ensuring the locating pin is correctly located in the cutout. Apply a drop of locking compound to the mounting bolt threads then fit it and tighten to the specified torque (this will be easier once the holder is fitted to the fork tube).

48 Lubricate the handlebar and throttle twistgrip bearing surfaces with a smear of multi-purpose grease. Slide the twistgrip onto the handlebar and locate the holder on the fork tube.

49 Apply locking compound to the threads of the handlebar holder-to-top yoke bolt then fit the bolt, tightening it to the specified torque.

50 Tighten the right handlebar holder clamp bolt to its specified torque setting.

51 Ensure the throttle cables are correctly attached to the grip then lubricate their upper ends with multi-purpose grease. Locate the outer cables correctly in the switch halves then assemble the switch on the handlebar, placing the rear half locating peg in the handlebar hole. Ensure the switch and cables are correctly assembled then securely tighten the switch screws.

52 Locate the master cylinder on the handlebar and fit the mounting clamp with its arrow mark facing upwards. Align the master cylinder mounting clamp split with the handlebar switch split then tighten the mounting clamp upper bolt to the specified torque followed by the lower bolt.

53 Reconnect the wiring connector to the brake light switch.

54 Apply a drop of locking compound to the threads of the end cap/weight screw. Fit the end cap/weight to the handlebar and securely tighten its retaining screw.

55 On completion, check the throttle cable adjustment and the brake light switch operation (see Chapter 1) and the brake fluid level (see *Daily (pre-ride) checks*) before riding the machine on the road.

Left handlebar – ZX-9R B models

Removal

56 Carry out the operations described in Steps 39 to 44 substituting clutch master cylinder for all references to brake master cylinder.

57 Slacken the holder clamp bolt then free the handlebar from the top of the fork tube and remove it from the bike. If necessary, unscrew the mounting bolt and separate the handlebar and holder.

Installation

58 Carry out the operations described in Steps 46 and 47 then locate the handlebar holder on the fork tube.

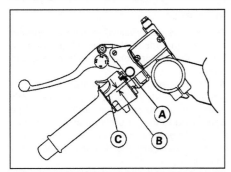

5.62 On ZX-9R B models, position the clutch master cylinder clamp upper split (A) 5mm (B) to the rear of the handlebar switch split (C)

59 Apply locking compound to the threads of the handlebar holder-to-top yoke bolt then fit the bolt, tightening it to the specified torque.
60 Tighten the left handlebar holder clamp bolt to its specified torque setting.
61 Lubricate the upper end of the choke cable with multi-purpose grease and attach it correctly to the choke lever. Locate the lever and outer cable correctly in the switch halves then assemble the switch on the handlebar, placing the rear half locating peg in the handlebar hole. Ensure the switch, lever and cable are correctly assembled then securely tighten the switch screws.
62 Locate the master cylinder on the handlebar and fit the mounting clamp with its arrow mark facing upwards. Position the master cylinder so that its clamp upper split is located 5 mm to the rear of the handlebar switch split **(see illustration)** then tighten the mounting clamp upper bolt to the specified torque followed by the lower bolt.
63 Reconnect the wiring connector to the clutch switch.
64 If a new handlebar grip needs to be installed ensure the handlebar surface is clean and dry. Apply a suitable adhesive to the inside of the new grip then slide the grip onto the bar until it butts up against the switch.
65 Apply a drop of locking compound to the threads of the end cap/weight screw. Fit the end cap/weight to the handlebar and securely tighten its retaining screw.
66 On completion, check the choke cable operation (see Chapter 1) and the clutch fluid level (see *Daily (pre-ride) checks*) before riding the machine on the road.

Right handlebar – ZX-9R C models

Removal

67 Undo the retaining screw and remove the end cap and weight from the handlebar.
68 Disconnect the wiring from the brake light switch on the master cylinder assembly.
69 Unscrew the two front brake master cylinder assembly clamp bolts and position the master cylinder clear of the handlebar, making sure no strain is placed on the hydraulic hose.
70 Fold back the throttle cable rubber gaiter

to free it from the twistgrip housing. Undo the two retaining screws and separate the two halves of the twistgrip housing. Note how the cables locate in the housing then detach the inner cables from the twistgrip.
71 Unscrew the two handlebar switch screws then free the switch from the handlebar.
72 If the handlebar is to be removed from its holder, loosen its mounting bolt now.
73 Unscrew the bolt securing the handlebar to the top yoke.
74 Slacken the holder clamp bolt then free the handlebar from the top of the fork tube and the throttle twistgrip and remove it from the bike. If necessary, unscrew the mounting bolt and separate the handlebar and holder.

Installation

75 Install the handlebar as described in Steps 46 to 50.
76 Assemble the two halves of the switch on the handlebar, ensuring the switch peg is correctly located in the handlebar hole, and securely tighten its retaining screws.
77 Lubricate the upper end of each throttle cable with multi-purpose grease and attach the cables correctly to the throttle grip. Locate the outer cables correctly in the twistgrip housing then assemble the housing on the handlebar, ensuring the locating peg is correctly seated in the handlebar hole. Ensure the twistgrip housing and cables are correctly assembled then securely tighten the retaining screws before seating the cable gaiter correctly on the housing.
78 Locate the master cylinder on the handlebar and fit the mounting clamp with its arrow mark facing upwards. Position the master cylinder so that its clamp upper split is aligned with the throttle housing split then tighten the mounting clamp upper bolt to the specified torque followed by the lower bolt.
79 Reconnect the wiring connector to the brake light switch.
80 Apply a drop of locking compound to the threads of the end cap/weight screw. Fit the end cap/weight to the handlebar and securely tighten its retaining screw.
81 On completion, check the throttle cable adjustment and brake light switch operation (see Chapter 1) and the brake fluid level (see *Daily (pre-ride) checks*) before riding the machine on the road.

Left handlebar – ZX-9R C models

Removal

82 Undo the retaining screw and remove the end cap and weight from the handlebar.
83 Disconnect the wiring from the switch on the clutch lever bracket.
84 Unscrew the clutch lever bracket clamp bolts and position the lever clear of the handlebar.
85 Unscrew the two handlebar switch screws then free the switch from the handlebar.
86 If the handlebar is to be removed from its holder, loosen its mounting bolt now.

87 Unscrew the bolt securing the handlebar to the top yoke.
88 Slacken the holder clamp bolt then free the handlebar from the top of the fork tube and remove it from the bike. If necessary, unscrew the mounting bolt and separate the handlebar and holder.

Installation

89 Install the handlebar as described in Steps 58 to 61.
90 Locate the clutch lever bracket on the handlebar and fit the mounting clamp with its arrow mark facing upwards. Position the lever so that its clamp upper split is aligned with the handlebar switch split then securely tighten the mounting clamp upper bolt followed by the lower bolt.
91 Reconnect the wiring connector to the clutch switch.
92 If a new handlebar grip needs to be installed ensure the handlebar surface is clean and dry. Apply a suitable adhesive to the inside of the new grip then slide the grip onto the bar until it butts up against the switch.
93 Apply a drop of locking compound to the threads of the end cap/weight screw. Fit the end cap/weight to the handlebar and securely tighten its retaining screw.
94 On completion, check the choke cable and clutch operation (see Chapter 1) before riding the machine on the road.

Right handlebar – ZX-9R E and F models

Removal

95 Undo the retaining screw and remove the end cap and weight from the handlebar.
96 Undo the screw and free the front brake master cylinder reservoir from its bracket on the top yoke. Position the reservoir clear of the yoke, keeping it upright to prevent possible fluid leakage.
97 Unscrew the bolts securing the left and right handlebars to the underside of the top yoke.
98 Slacken and remove the steering stem nut and washer.
99 Loosen the top yoke clamp bolts then lift off the yoke and position it clear of the steering stem/forks.
100 Disconnect the wiring from the brake light switch on the master cylinder assembly.
101 Unscrew the two front brake master cylinder assembly clamp bolts and position the master cylinder clear of the handlebar, making sure no strain is placed on the hydraulic hose.
102 Fold back the throttle cable rubber gaiter to free it from the twistgrip housing. Undo the two retaining screws and separate the two halves of the twistgrip housing. Note how the cables locate in the housing then detach the inner cables from the twistgrip.
103 Unscrew the two handlebar switch screws then free the switch from the handlebar.
104 If the handlebar is to be removed from its holder, loosen its mounting bolt now.

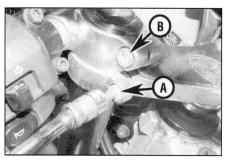

6.4 Slacken the top yoke clamp bolt (A) and the handlebar holder clamp bolt (B) (ZX-9R C model shown)

105 Slacken the holder clamp bolt then free the handlebar from the top of the fork tube and the throttle twistgrip and remove it from the bike. If necessary, unscrew the mounting bolt and separate the handlebar and holder.

Installation

106 Install the handlebar as described in Steps 11 to 16.
107 Install all other components as described in Steps 76 to 81.

Left handlebar – ZX-9R E and F models

Removal

108 Carry out the operations described in Steps 95, 97, 98 and 99.
109 Disconnect the wiring from the switch on the clutch lever bracket.
110 Unscrew the clutch lever bracket clamp bolts and position the lever clear of the handlebar.
111 Unscrew the two handlebar switch screws then free the switch from the handlebar.
112 If the handlebar is to be removed from its holder, loosen its mounting bolt now.
113 Slacken the holder clamp bolt then free the handlebar from the top of the fork tube and remove it from the bike. If necessary, unscrew the mounting bolt and separate the handlebar and holder.

Installation

114 Install the handlebar as described in Steps 28 to 32.
115 Install all other components as described in Steps 90 to 94.

6 Forks – removal and installation

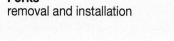

Removal

1 Remove the complete fairing (see Chapter 8).
2 Remove the front wheel (see Chapter 7).
3 Remove the front mudguard (see Chapter 8). Each fork can then be removed as follows.
4 Slacken the top yoke and handlebar holder clamp bolts **(see illustration)**. Where necessary, release the tie securing the cables/wiring to the fork tube.

6.5 If the fork is to be dismantled slacken the top cap whilst the fork is still clamped in the bottom yoke

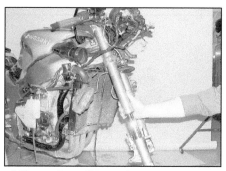

6.6b ... then slide the fork leg out of the yokes (ZX-9R B model shown)

5 If the fork is to be dismantled, unscrew the top cap from the fork by a few turns **(see illustration)**.
6 Slacken the bottom yoke clamp bolt(s) and remove the fork by twisting it and pulling it downwards **(see illustrations)**.

 HAYNES HiNT *If the fork leg is seized in the yokes, spray the area with penetrating oil and allow time for it to soak in before trying again.*

Installation

7 Remove all traces of corrosion from the fork tube and the yokes.
8 Slide the fork up through the bottom and top yokes and handlebar holder. Lightly tighten the bottom yoke clamp bolt to hold the fork in position.
9 On ZX-7R models position the fork in the

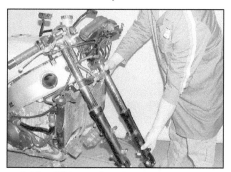

6.11a Slide the fork into the yokes ...

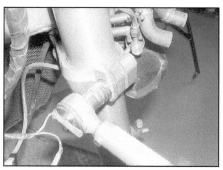

6.6a Slacken the bottom yoke clamp bolt ...

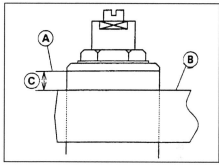

6.9 On ZX-7R models, position the fork in the yokes so that the top of the outer tube (A) protrudes from the top yoke upper surface (B) by 2 mm (C)

yokes so that the top of the outer tube is exactly 2 mm above the upper surface of the top yoke **(see illustration)**. Once the fork tube is correctly positioned tighten the bottom yoke clamp bolt to the specified torque setting.
10 On ZX-9R B models position the fork in the yokes so that the top of the outer tube is level with the upper surface of the handlebar. Once the fork tube is correctly positioned tighten the bottom yoke clamp bolt to the specified torque setting.
11 On ZX-9R C, E and F models position the fork in the yokes so that the top of the inner tube is level with the upper surface of the top yoke **(see illustration)**. Once the fork tube is correctly positioned tighten the bottom yoke clamp bolt(s) to the specified torque setting **(see illustration)**.

6.11b ... then position it as described in the text before tightening the bottom yoke clamp bolt to the specified torque

6.12a Tighten the top cap to the specified torque . . .

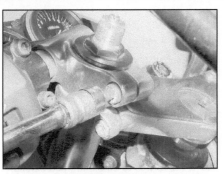

6.12b . . . then tighten the top yoke and handlebar holder clamp bolts to the specified torque

12 Ensure the top cap is tightened to the specified torque then tighten the top yoke and handlebar holder clamp bolts to their specified torque settings **(see illustrations)**.
13 Fit the front mudguard and wheel, then install the fairing (see Chapters 7 and 8).
14 Ensure the front forks are correctly adjusted (see Section 12) and check the operation of the front forks and brakes before taking the machine out on the road.

7 Forks –
disassembly, inspection and reassembly

ZX-7R and ZX-9R B models

Note: *A thick 10 mm washer will be required to hold the fork spring in position (see Steps 4 and 5). Reassembly will also be made easier if a long M10 x 1.0 bolt and nut can be obtained (see Step 36).*

Disassembly

1 Always dismantle the fork legs separately to avoid interchanging any of the parts and thus causing an accelerated rate of wear. Store all components in separate, clearly marked containers **(see illustration)**.
2 If the damper assembly is to be removed from the inner tube, it is advisable to slacken the damper bolt before dismantling begins. Remove the front wheel axle clamp bolts from the base of the inner tube and the axle nut (if the left fork is being stripped) to allow access to the damper bolt. If necessary, to prevent the damper rotating, compress the fork so that the spring exerts maximum pressure on the damper, then have an assistant slacken the bolt. If the damper assembly rotates, preventing the bolt from being slackened, then a damper holding tool will be required (see Step 14). **Note:** *The fork seals and bushes can be renewed without removing the damper assembly from the inner tube.*
3 Support the fork in an upright position then back off the spring preload adjuster and fully unscrew the top cap from the outer tube **(see illustration)**.
4 In order to remove the top cap, it is necessary to compress the fork spring slightly and hold it in position by sliding a holder between the top cap locknut and spring seat.

7.1 Front fork components – ZX-9R B model (ZX-7R model similar)

1	Top cap	9	Bottom bush
2	O-ring	10	Washer
3	Spacer and spring seat – early models	11	Oil seal
		12	Retaining clip
		13	Dust seal
4	Spring seat – later models	14	Top bush
		15	Inner tube
5	Spring	16	Sealing washer
6	Locknut	17	Damper bolt
7	Damper assembly	18	Compression damper adjuster
8	Outer tube		

7.3 On ZX-7R and ZX-9R B models, unscrew the top cap from the outer tube

7.5 Compress the fork spring then slide the slotted washer in between the spring seat and locknut

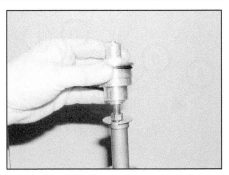

7.6a Unscrew the top cap assembly . . .

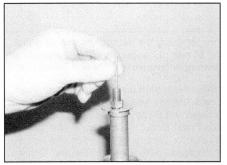

7.6b . . . then withdraw the adjuster rod

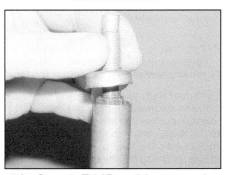

7.8a On early ZX-9R models, remove the spring seat . . .

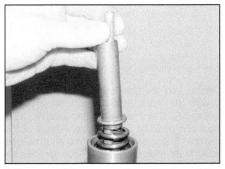

7.8b . . . and the spacer from the top of the spring

In the absence of the Kawasaki special tool and holder (57001-1338 and 57001-1374), obtain a thick washer with a 10 mm inside diameter and cut a slot in it to allow it to pass around the piston rod.

5 With the aid of an assistant, compress the fork spring until it is possible to slide the slotted washer in between the top of the spring seat and the base of the top cap locknut **(see illustration)**. Once the washer is in position gently release the fork spring; the top cap locknut should now be clearly visible. *Caution: Ensure the fork spring is securely held by the washer before proceeding.*

6 Retain the top cap then slacken the locknut. Unscrew the top cap assembly from the damper rod then withdraw the rebound damping adjuster rod **(see illustrations)**.

7 Compress the fork spring again until it is

possible to remove the slotted washer, then carefully release the fork spring.

8 Lift off the spring seat and/or spacer (as applicable) and withdraw the fork spring, noting which way up it is fitted **(see illustrations)**.

9 Invert the fork outer tube over a suitable container and pump both the fork outer tube and damper rod to expel as much fork oil as possible.

10 Carefully prise out the dust seal from the base of the outer tube to gain access to the oil seal retaining clip **(see illustration)**.

11 Slide the inner tube out of the outer tube then ease the retaining clip out of position, taking care not to scratch the surface of the tube **(see illustration)**.

12 To separate the outer tube from the inner tube it is necessary to displace the bottom

bush and oil seal. The top bush should not pass through the bottom bush. Push the inner tube gently inwards then pull it sharply outwards until the top bush strikes the bottom bush **(see illustration)**. Repeat this operation until the bottom bush and seal are tapped out of the outer tube.

13 With the outer tube removed, slide the bottom bush, washer, oil seal, retaining clip and dust seal off the inner tube, noting which way up they fit **(see illustration overleaf)**. Discard the dust seal and oil seal as new ones must be used. Kawasaki also recommend that both the top and bottom bushes are renewed as well, regardless of their apparent condition. *Caution: Do not remove the top bush from the inner tube unless it is to be renewed.*

14 If necessary, remove the previously slackened damper bolt and its copper sealing

7.10 Prise out the dust seal from the base of the outer tube . . .

7.11 . . . then ease the retaining clip out of position

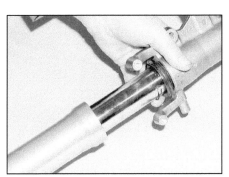

7.12 Separate the inner and outer tubes as described in the text

7.13 Separate the fork tubes and remove the components from the inner tube

A *Dust seal*	C *Oil seal*
B *Retaining*	D *Washer*
clip	E *Bottom bush*

F *Top bush –*
remove only if it
is being renewed

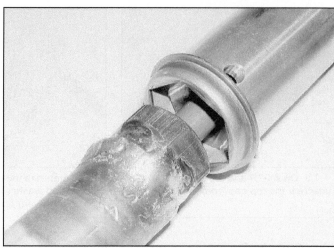

7.14 Home-made tool for retaining the damper assembly whilst the bolt is slackened. The 24 mm nut engages with the hexagonal cutout in the top of the damper (shown with damper removed)

washer from the bottom of the inner tube then invert the tube and tip out the damper assembly. Discard the sealing washer, as a new one must be used on reassembly. If the damper assembly spins around and the bolt cannot be unscrewed, a special tool will be required to retain the damper. In the absence of the special Kawasaki holding tool (57001-1297), a suitable alternative can be made by fixing a nut (24 mm in width) to the end of a piece of tubing and drilling a hole in the other end of the tube. Pass the tube down over the damper rod and locate the nut in the top of the damper body **(see illustration)**. Retain the tool with a screwdriver passed through the hole then slacken and remove the bolt.

15 Unscrew the compression damping adjuster from the base of the inner tube and recover its O-ring **(see illustration)**.

Inspection

16 Clean all parts in solvent and blow them dry with compressed air, if available. Check the fork inner tube for score marks, scratches, flaking of the chrome finish and excessive or abnormal wear. Look for dents in the tube and renew the tube in both forks if any are found. Check the fork seal area of the tube for nicks, gouges and scratches. If damage is evident, leaks will occur. Also check the oil seal washer for damage or distortion and renew it, if necessary. Renew all seals and O-rings, regardless of their condition.

17 Check the fork inner tube for runout using V-blocks and a dial gauge, or have it done by a dealer. If any discernible amount of runout is measured (Kawasaki do not specify a limit), the inner tube should be renewed.

⚠️ *Warning: If the inner tube is bent, it should not be straightened; renew it.*

18 Check the spring for cracks and other damage. Measure the spring free length and compare the measurement to the specifications at the beginning of the Chapter. If it is defective or sagged below the service limit, renew the springs in both forks. Never renew only one spring.

19 Examine the working surfaces of the two bushes and the washer fitted between the bottom bush and oil seal; if worn or scuffed they must be renewed (Kawasaki recommend that both bushes are renewed every time the fork is stripped). To remove the top bush from the inner tube, prise it apart at the slit using a flat-bladed screwdriver and slide it off. Make sure the new one seats properly **(see illustration)**.

20 Check the damper assembly for damage and wear, and renew the assembly if necessary.

Reassembly

21 Insert the damper assembly (where removed) into the inner tube **(see illustration)**. Fit a new copper sealing washer to the damper bolt then apply a few drops of thread locking compound to the bolt threads. Install the bolt into the bottom of the slider and tighten it to the specified torque setting **(see illustration)**. **Note:** *If the damper assembly rotates inside the tube, use the holding tool (Step 14).*

7.15 Unscrew the compression damper adjuster and O-ring from the base of the inner tube

7.19 Only remove the top bush from the inner tube if it is being renewed

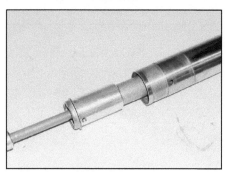

7.21a Insert the damper assembly into the inner tube . . .

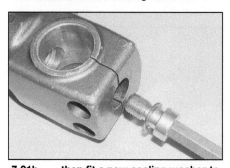

7.21b . . . then fit a new sealing washer to the damper bolt, apply locking compound to its threads, then fit the bolt and tighten to the specified torque

7.24 Carefully slide the dust seal onto the inner tube

7.26 Ensure the oil seal is the correct way up then slide it onto the inner tube

7.27a Fit the washer . . .

7.27b . . . and slide the bottom bush onto the inner tube

7.28 Ensure all components are correctly fitted then insert the inner tube into the outer tube

7.29 Tap the bottom bush fully into position, taking care not to scratch the inner tube

Alternatively temporarily install the fork spring, spring seat and/or spacer (as applicable) in the inner tube and fit the top cap to the outer tube. Fit the outer tube to the inner tube and compress the fork to hold the damper.

22 Fit a new O-ring to the compression damper adjuster then fit the adjuster to the inner tube and tighten it securely.

23 Oil the fork inner tube and top bush with the specified fork oil.

24 Lubricate the lips of the new dust seal then slide it down the inner tube, ensuring it is the right way around **(see illustration)**.

 HAYNES HiNT *Place a small plastic bag over the upper end of the inner tube and lubricate the bag with fork oil – this will help prevent damage to the seal lips as they pass over the tube end and top bush.*

25 Fit the oil seal retaining clip to the inner tube.

26 Lubricate the new oil seal with fork oil then carefully slide the seal onto the inner tube, making sure its marked surface is facing downwards (main sealing lip upwards) **(see illustration)**.

27 Fit the washer then slide the bottom bush onto the inner tube having lubricated it with fork oil **(see illustrations)**.

28 Ensure all components are correctly installed then insert the inner tube into the outer tube **(see illustration)**.

29 Press the bottom bush squarely into its recess in the outer tube as far as possible. Tap the bush squarely into position using a hammer and punch, taking great care not to scratch the fork tube **(see illustration)**. Ensure the bush is correctly seated before continuing.

HAYNES HiNT *Ensure the inner tube remains fully extended from the outer tube whilst the bush is being tapped into position. Any accidental damage will then be confined to the area of the inner tube which remains above the oil seal and bottom bush during normal use.*

30 Slide the washer up against the bottom bush then press the oil seal into the outer tube. Carefully tap the seal into place as described in Step 29 until the retaining clip groove is visible.

31 Once the seal is correctly seated, secure it in position with the retaining clip ensuring it is correctly located in its groove **(see illustration)**.

32 Slide the dust seal along the inner tube and press it fully into the outer tube **(see illustration)**.

33 Support the fork in an upright position then fully insert the rod into the damper assembly and slide the outer tube fully down the inner tube.

34 Measure out the correct amount of the specified fork oil (see Specifications at the

7.31 Secure the oil seal in position with the retaining clip . . .

7.32 . . . then press the dust seal into the outer tube

7.34a Fill the fork with the specified type and amount of oil

beginning of the Chapter for fork oil type, capacity and level). Slowly pour in the oil whilst pushing the damper assembly rod up and down **(see illustration)**. Fill the fork with oil then slowly pump the outer tube up and down a few times to purge the air from between the inner and outer tubes. **Note:** *Ensure the fork oil level is kept above the oil holes in the inner tube whilst doing this* **(see illustration)**. Add the remaining fork oil whilst pumping the damper rod. Once all the oil has been added, fully insert the rod into the damper and slide the outer tube fully down the inner tube then leave the fork to stand for at least five minutes to allow any trapped air to surface. Check the fork oil level from the top of the tube **(see illustration)**. Add or subtract fork oil until it is at the specified level.

35 Fully extend the damper rod. Ensure the top cap locknut is fitted with its flat surface uppermost and screw the nut onto the rod so

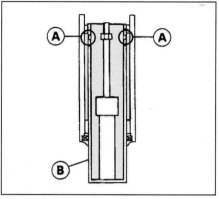

7.34b Keep the oil level above the bleed holes (A) in the inner tube (B) to ensure all air is purged from between the inner and outer tubes

that there is at least 12 mm of thread exposed above the nut.

36 Reassembly will be much easier if a damper rod holder is available. In the absence of the special Kawasaki tool (57001-1298), an M10 x 1.0 nut and bolt can be used to hold the rod in the extended position. Screw the nut onto the end of the damper rod threads then screw the bolt into the nut **(see illustration)**.

37 Install the fork spring, ensuring that its smaller diameter end is at the top **(see illustration)**.

38 Fit the spacer and/or spring seat (as applicable) to the upper end of the fork spring **(see illustration)**.

7.34c Once all the oil has been added, check the oil level as described in text

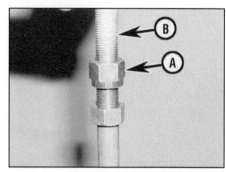

7.36 Screw an M10 x 1.0 nut (A) onto the end of the damper rod and screw a bolt (B) into the nut. The bolt can then be used to hold the rod in the extended position.

39 With the aid of an assistant, hold the damper rod in the fully extended position then compress the fork spring until it is possible to slide the slotted washer in between the base of the top cap locknut and the top of the spring seat **(see illustration)**. Ensure the washer is correctly positioned then gently release the fork spring. Ensure the fork spring is securely held by the washer then unscrew the nut and bolt from the end of the damper rod.

40 Remove the original O-ring from the top cap and install a new one, lubricating it with a smear of fork oil **(see illustration)**. Position the rebound damping adjuster so the distance from the bottom of the adjuster to the bottom of the spring preload adjuster is 25 mm **(see illustration)**.

7.37 Install the fork spring so that its smaller diameter end is at the top

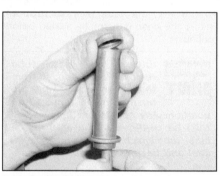

7.38 On ZX-9R B early models, fit the spacer and spring seat to the top of the spring

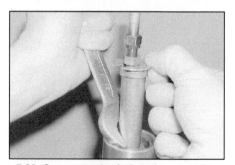

7.39 Compress the fork spring and slide the slotted washer in between the spring seat and locknut

7.40a Fit a new O-ring to the top cap

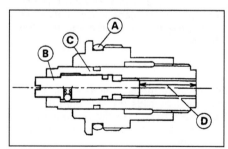

7.40b Position the rebound damper adjuster (B) in the top cap (C) so that the distance from the base of the damper adjuster to the base of the spring preload adjuster (D) is 25 mm. Ensure the O-ring (A) is correctly located in its groove

41 Insert the rebound damping adjuster rod into the centre of the damper rod then screw the top cap fully onto the rod. Hold the top cap stationary and tighten its locknut to the specified torque.

42 Compress the fork spring again until it is possible to remove the slotted washer, then carefully release the fork spring, making sure the spring seat passes over the locknut and seats correctly against the preload adjuster.

43 Check that all components are correctly seated, then carefully screw the top cap into the outer tube, making sure it is not cross-threaded. **Note:** *The top cap can be tightened to its specified torque setting at this stage if the tube can be held firmly enough, but do not risk distorting the outer tube by overtightening it. A better method is to tighten the top cap when the fork has been reinstalled and is securely held in the yokes.*

44 Install the forks and set the fork adjustments as required (see Sections 6 and 12).

ZX-9R C, E and F models

Disassembly

45 Always dismantle the fork legs separately to avoid interchanging any of the parts and thus causing an accelerated rate of wear. Store all components in separate, clearly marked containers **(see illustration)**.

46 Before dismantling the fork, it is advisable to slacken the damper bolt in the base of the outer tube. Remove the front wheel axle clamp bolts from the base of the inner tube and the axle nut (if the left fork is being stripped) to allow access to the damper bolt **(see illustration)**. If necessary, to prevent the damper rotating, compress the inner tube in the outer tube so that the spring exerts maximum pressure on the damper, then have an assistant slacken the bolt. If the damper assembly rotates, preventing the bolt from being slackened, then a damper holding tool will be required (see Step 53).

47 Support the fork in an upright position then back off the spring preload adjuster and fully unscrew the top cap from the inner tube.

48 Retain the top cap then slacken the top cap locknut **(see illustration)**. The top cap assembly can then be unscrewed from the damper rod.

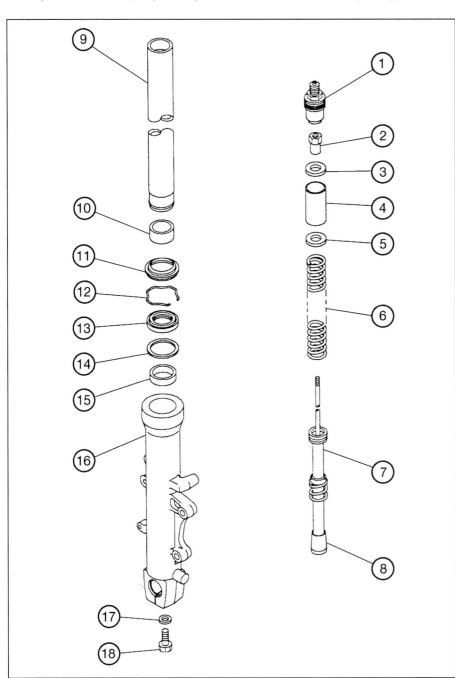

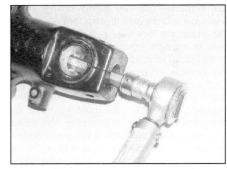

7.46 Slacken the damper bolt before removing the top cap from the inner tube

7.48 Retain the top cap and slacken the locknut

7.45 Front fork components – ZX-9R C, E and F models

1 Top cap	6 Spring	10 Bottom bush	15 Top bush
2 Locknut	7 Damper	11 Dust seal	16 Outer tube
3 Upper washer	assembly	12 Retaining clip	17 Sealing washer
4 Spacer	8 Damper seat	13 Oil seal	18 Damper bolt
5 Lower washer	9 Inner tube	14 Washer	

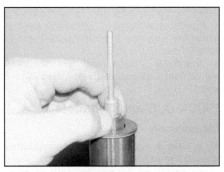

7.49 Unscrew the top cap then withdraw the adjuster rod from the damper rod

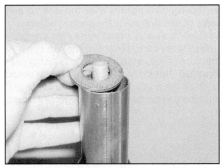

7.50a Remove the upper washer and spacer . . .

7.50b . . . then lift off the lower washer . . .

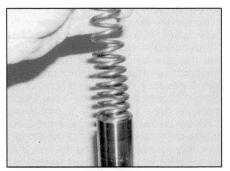

7.51 . . . and withdraw the spring

7.55 Ease the dust seal out from the top of the outer tube . . .

49 Remove the rebound damping adjuster rod from the centre of the damper rod **(see illustration)**.
50 Slide the inner tube down into the outer tube and lift off the upper washer, spacer and lower washer **(see illustrations)**.
51 Withdraw the fork spring, noting which way up it is fitted **(see illustration)**.
52 Invert the fork over a suitable container and pump both the inner tube and damper rod to expel as much fork oil as possible.
53 Remove the previously slackened damper bolt and its copper sealing washer from the bottom of the slider. Discard the sealing washer, as a new one must be used on reassembly. If the damper assembly spins around and the bolt cannot be unscrewed, a holding tool will be required to retain it. In the absence of the special Kawasaki tool (57001-1406), a suitable alternative can be made from a length of square-section metal tubing, 20 mm in width, with a hole drilled in one end. Pass the

tubing down over the damper rod and locate it in the top of the damper body. Retain the tubing with a screwdriver passed through the hole then slacken and remove the bolt.
54 Invert the fork and tip out the damper assembly from the inner tube.
55 Carefully prise out the dust seal from the top of the slider to gain access to the oil seal retaining clip **(see illustration)**. Discard the dust seal, as a new one must be used. **Note:** *On ZX-9R F models, if required, remove the stoneguard from the top of the outer tube to gain access to the dust seal.*
56 Slide the inner tube into the outer tube then carefully remove the retaining clip, taking care not to scratch the surface of the tube **(see illustration)**. **Note:** *Do not force the inner tube fully into the outer tube as this could damage the damper assembly seat.*
57 To separate the inner tube from the outer tube it is necessary to displace the top bush and oil seal. The bottom bush should not pass

through the top bush. Push the inner tube gently inwards then pull the tube sharply outwards until the bottom bush strikes the top bush. Repeat this operation until the top bush and seal are tapped out of the outer tube.
58 With the tube removed, slide off the oil seal and its washer, noting which way up they fit. Discard the oil seal, as a new one must be used. The top bush can then also be slid off its upper end. Kawasaki also recommend that both the top and bottom bushes are renewed as well, regardless of their apparent condition. *Caution: Do not remove the bottom bush from the inner tube unless it is to be renewed.*
59 Tip the damper assembly seat out from the outer tube.

Inspection

60 Inspect all components as described in Steps 16 to 18.
61 Examine the working surfaces of the two bushes and the washer fitted between the top bush and oil seal; if worn or scuffed they must be renewed (Kawasaki recommend that both bushes are renewed every time the fork is stripped). To remove the bottom bush from the inner tube, prise it apart at the slit using a flat-bladed screwdriver and slide it off. Make sure the new one seats properly.
62 Check the damper assembly and its rebound spring for damage and wear, and renew the assembly if necessary. The rebound spring is not available separately.

Reassembly

63 Insert the damper assembly into the inner tube then fit the damper seat **(see illustration)**.
64 Oil the inner tube and lower bush with the specified fork oil then carefully insert the assembly into the outer tube, making sure the seat remains correctly fitted to the end of the damper assembly.
65 Fit a new copper sealing washer to the damper bolt then apply a few drops of locking compound to the bolt threads. Install the bolt into the bottom of the outer tube and tighten it to the specified torque setting **(see illustration)**. **Note:** *If the damper assembly rotates inside the tube, use the holding tool (Step 53) or temporarily install the fork spring, washers and spacer and the top cap and compress the fork to hold the damper.*

7.56 . . . then carefully prise out the retaining clip

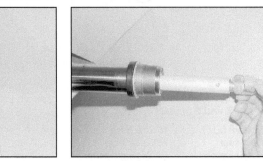

7.63 Insert the damper assembly into the inner tube then fit the damper seat

7.65 Fit a new sealing washer then apply locking compound to the damper bolt threads and tighten the bolt to the specified torque

66 Oil the top bush and slide it down over the inner tube **(see illustration)**. Press the bush squarely into its recess in the outer tube, then install the oil seal washer **(see illustration)**. Tap the bush squarely into position, taking great care not to scratch the inner tube surface. In the absence of the Kawasaki service tool, a suitable piece of tubing slightly larger in diameter than the inner tube and slightly smaller in diameter than the oil seal recess in the outer tube can be used as a slide-hammer. Ensure the bush is correctly seated before continuing.

Ensure the inner tube remains fully pushed into the outer tube during assembly. Any accidental damage should then be confined to the area of the inner tube which remains above the oil seal during normal use. If a new top bush has been installed, use the original bush as a spacer to prevent possible damage to the new bush.

67 Lubricate the new oil seal with fork oil then carefully slide the seal onto the inner tube, making sure its marked surface is facing upwards (main seal downwards) **(see illustration)**. Drive the seal into place as described in Step 66 until the retaining clip groove is visible above the seal.
68 Once the seal is correctly seated, fit the retaining clip, making sure it is correctly located in its groove.

7.66a Slide the top bush down the inner tube . . .

69 Lubricate the lips of the new dust seal then slide it down the inner tube and press it fully into position. On ZX-9R F models, if removed, install the stoneguard on the top of the outer tube.
70 Support the fork in an upright position then fully insert the rod into the damper assembly and slide the inner tube fully into the outer tube.
71 Measure out the correct amount of the specified fork oil (see Specifications at the beginning of this Chapter for fork oil type, capacity and level). Slowly pour in the oil whilst pushing the damper assembly rod up and down **(see illustration)**. Fill the fork with oil then slowly pump the inner tube up and down a few times. Add the remaining fork oil whilst pumping the damper rod. Once all the oil has been added, fully insert the rod into the damper and slide the inner tube fully into the outer tube then leave the fork to stand for at least five minutes to allow any trapped air to surface. Check the fork oil level from the top of the tube **(see illustration)**. Add or subtract fork oil until it is at the specified level.
72 Check the top cap O-ring for signs of damage or deterioration and renew if necessary. Position the rebound damping adjuster so that the distance from the bottom of the adjuster to the bottom of the spring preload adjuster is 25 mm **(see illustration 7.40b)**.
73 Fully extend the damper rod. Ensure the top cap locknut is fitted with its flat surface uppermost and screw the nut onto the rod so that there is at least 12 mm of thread exposed above the nut.
74 Insert the fork spring, ensuring that its

7.66b . . . followed by the washer

7.67 Ensure the oil seal is fitted the correct way up

tighter-pitched coils are at the bottom **(see illustration)**.
75 Keep the damper rod fully extended and fit the lower washer, spacer and upper washer to the top of the fork spring.
76 Insert the rebound damping adjuster rod into the centre of the damper rod then screw the top cap fully onto the rod. Hold the top cap stationary and tighten its locknut to the specified torque.
77 Check that all components are correctly seated then carefully screw the top cap into the outer tube, making sure it is not cross-threaded. **Note:** *The top cap can be tightened to its specified torque setting at this stage if the tube can be held firmly enough, but do not risk distorting the inner tube by overtightening it. A better method is to tighten the top cap when the fork has been reinstalled and is securely held in the yokes.*
78 Install the forks and set the fork adjustments as required (see Sections 6 and 12).

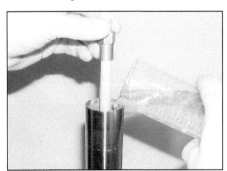

7.71a Fill the fork with the specified type and amount of oil . . .

7.71b . . . then check the oil level as described in text

7.74 Fit the fork spring with its tighter-pitched coils at the bottom

8 Steering stem –
removal and installation

Caution: *Although not strictly necessary, before removing the steering stem it is recommended that the fuel tank is removed. This will prevent accidental damage to the paintwork and improve access slightly.*

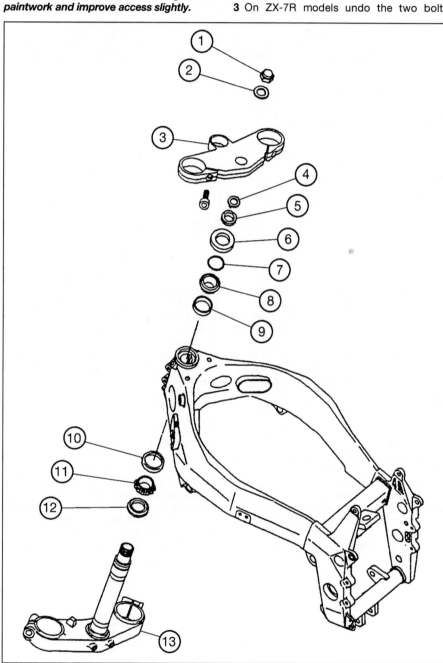

8.6a Steering stem components – ZX-7R model (ZX-9R B and C similar)

1 Nut	5 Adjuster nut	10 Outer race
2 Washer	6 Dust seal	11 Lower bearing
3 Top yoke	7 O-ring	12 Dust seal
4 Lockwasher	8 Upper bearing	13 Steering stem
	9 Outer race	

ZX-7R and ZX-9R B and C models

Removal

1 Remove the front forks (see Section 6).

2 To improve access, unbolt the upper fairing/rear view mirror bracket from the frame and remove it from the bike, taking care not to lose the collars from the bracket mounting rubbers.

3 On ZX-7R models undo the two bolts securing the front brake hose joint to the bottom yoke and disconnect the wiring connectors from the horn.

4 On ZX-9R B models undo the bolts securing the front brake hose joint to the bottom yoke and remove the yoke cover and mounting bracket assembly.

5 On ZX-9R C models undo the two bolts securing the front brake hose joint to the bottom yoke.

6 On all models, slacken and remove the steering stem nut and washer **(see illustrations)**.

7 Carefully lift the top yoke/handlebar assembly off the steering stem and position it clear, making sure no strain is placed on the wiring/cables. Use a rag to protect other components and try to ensure the brake fluid and (where fitted) clutch fluid reservoirs are kept upright to prevent fluid spillage.

8 Lift off the lockwasher from the steering stem **(see illustration)**.

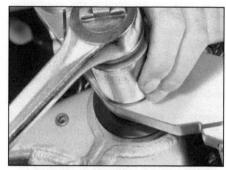

8.6b Slacken and remove the steering stem nut . . .

8.6c . . . and washer

8.8 Lift off the lockwasher from the steering stem

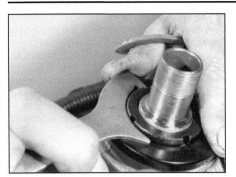

8.9 Using a C-spanner to unscrew the adjuster nut

8.10 Removing the upper bearing from the steering head

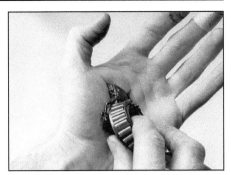

8.13 Work grease well into the bearing rollers

8.14a Slide the upper bearing down the steering stem . . .

8.14b . . . then fit the O-ring and dust seal . . .

8.14c . . . and screw on the adjuster nut

9 Support the bottom yoke then slacken the adjuster nut using either a C-spanner, a peg-spanner or a drift located in one of the notches **(see illustration)**. Unscrew and remove the adjuster nut, noting which way up it is fitted, then gently lower the steering stem/bottom yoke out of the frame.

10 Remove the dust seal, O-ring and the upper bearing from the top of the steering head **(see illustration)**.

11 Remove all traces of old grease from the bearings and races and check them for wear or damage as described in Section 9. **Note:** *Do not attempt to remove the lower bearing from the steering stem or the outer races from the frame unless the bearings are to be renewed. If the O-ring and upper dust seal show any sign of damage or deterioration they should be renewed.*

Installation

12 Ensure the lower bearing and dust seal are correctly installed on the steering stem. On ZX-7R models, also ensure the horn mounting bracket is bolted securely to the rear of the bottom yoke.

13 Smear a liberal quantity of multi-purpose grease on the bearing races in the frame and work the grease well into both the upper and lower bearings **(see illustration)**. Also apply a smear of grease to the O-ring and upper dust seal surfaces and the steering stem.

14 Carefully lift the steering stem/bottom yoke up through the frame and locate the lower bearing in its outer race. Slide the upper bearing down the steering stem and locate it in the upper race, then fit the O-ring and dust seal **(see illustrations)**. Screw the adjuster nut onto the steering stem, ensuring its shoulder is facing downwards, and tighten it by hand **(see illustration)**.

15 Locate the top yoke back on the steering stem, then fit the washer and steering stem nut, tightening it lightly.

16 To preload the bearings to the torque specified by the manufacturer (see Specifications) it will be necessary to use the Kawasaki service tool (57001-1100), which is a C-spanner with a hole for a spring balance to be attached. Using the service tool and a spring balance, apply the specified **initial** force to the service tool at a right-angle (90°) to the centre of the steering stem axis, to tighten the adjuster nut to the specified torque **(see illustration)**. Turn the steering stem from lock-to-lock approximately 5 times to settle the bearings and races in position. After pre-loading the bearings, fully slacken the adjuster nut then apply the specified **final** force to the service tool to correctly set the bearing adjustment. **Note:** *It is important to check the feel of the steering afterwards as described below; if it is too tight readjust the bearings as described below.*

17 If the service tool is not available, tighten the adjuster nut hard using a conventional C-wrench to preload the bearings. Rotate the steering stem lock-to-lock a few times then adjust as follows.

18 Slacken the adjuster nut slightly until pressure is just released, then turn it slowly clockwise until resistance is just evident. The object is to set the adjuster nut so that the bearings are under a very light loading, just enough to remove any freeplay.

Caution: Take great care not to apply excessive pressure because this will cause premature failure of the bearings.

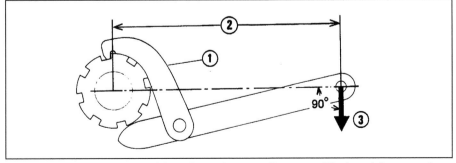

8.16 Kawasaki service tool (1) for tightening the adjuster nut. The length between the tool hole and steering stem centre (2) is 180 mm and when the specified force is applied at a right-angle (3) the correct torque will be applied to the adjuster nut

8.20 Engage the lockwasher with the adjuster nut cutouts then seat the top yoke back on the steering stem

19 With the bearings correctly adjusted, remove the steering stem nut and washer again and lift off the top yoke.

20 Fit the lockwasher, ensuring it is correctly engaged with the adjuster nut cutouts, then seat the top yoke back on the steering stem **(see illustration)**. Fit the washer and steering stem nut, tightening it lightly only at this stage.

21 On ZX-7R models reconnect the wiring to the horn and secure the front brake hose joint to the bottom yoke.

22 On ZX-9R B models locate the cover assembly and brake hose joint on the bottom yoke and securely tighten the retaining bolts.

23 On ZX-9R C models locate the front brake hose joint on the bottom yoke and securely tighten the retaining bolts.

24 Where necessary, ensure the mounting rubbers and collars are correctly positioned then fit the fairing/rear view mirror bracket to the frame.

25 Install the front forks as described in Section 6 noting that the clamp bolts and the steering stem nut must be tightened to their specified torque settings in the following order.

 a) Top yoke clamp bolts.
 b) Steering stem nut.
 c) Bottom yoke clamp bolts.
 d) Handlebar holder clamp bolts.

26 On completion, check the steering stem bearing adjustment as described in Chapter 1.

ZX-9R E and F models

Removal

27 Remove the front forks (see Section 6). If necessary, to improve access unbolt the upper fairing/rear view mirror bracket from the frame and remove it from the bike. Remove the air filter intake duct cover brackets from the bracket mounting rubbers noting that the left and right brackets are different.

28 Undo the two bolts and remove the cover and spacer bracket from the front of the bottom yoke (the longer bolt also secures the brake hose joint to the yoke). Unscrew the radiator mounting bolt which retains the horn bracket and position the horn clear of the bottom yoke.

29 Slacken and remove the steering stem nut and washer **(see illustration)**. Carefully lift the top yoke assembly off the steering stem and position it clear making sure no strain is placed on the wiring/cables. Use a rag to protect other components and try to ensure the brake fluid reservoir is kept upright to prevent fluid spillage.

30 Using either a C-spanner, a peg spanner or a suitable drift located in one of the notches, unscrew and remove the locknut from the steering stem.

31 Support the bottom yoke then remove the adjuster nut and gently lower the steering stem/bottom yoke out of the frame. Remove the lower bearing from the steering stem.

32 Remove the dust seal, inner race and upper bearing from the top of the steering head.

33 Remove all traces of old grease from the bearings and races and check them for wear or damage as described in Section 9. **Note:** *Do not attempt to remove the lower bearing inner race from the steering stem or the outer races from the frame unless the bearings are to be renewed.* If the upper dust seal shows any sign of damage or deterioration it should be renewed.

Installation

34 Ensure the lower bearing inner race and dust seal are correctly installed on the steering stem.

35 Smear a liberal quantity of multi-purpose grease on the bearing races and work the

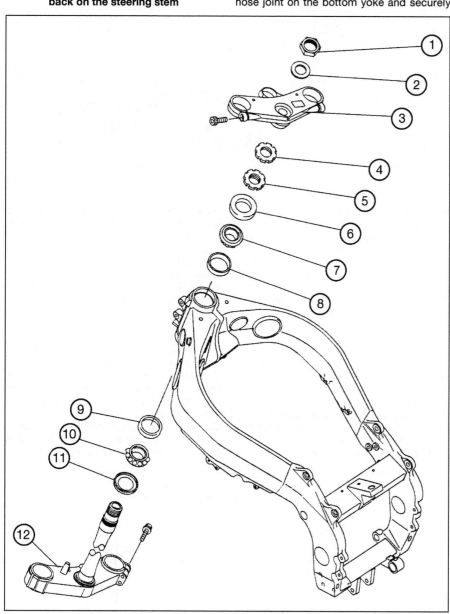

8.28 Steering stem components – ZX-9R E and F model

1 Nut	4 Locknut	7 Upper bearing	10 Lower bearing
2 Washer	5 Adjuster nut	8 Outer race	11 Dust seal
3 Top yoke	6 Dust seal	9 Outer race	12 Steering stem

grease well into both the upper and lower bearings. Also apply a smear of grease to the upper dust seal surface and the steering stem.

36 Locate the lower bearing on its inner race then carefully lift the steering stem/bottom yoke up through the frame. Locate the lower bearing in its outer race then slide the upper bearing down the steering stem. Locate the upper bearing correctly in the outer race then fit the bearing inner race and dust seal and screw on the adjuster nut, tightening it by hand.

37 Fit the locknut then locate the top yoke back on the steering stem. Fit the washer and steering stem nut, tightening it lightly.

38 To preload the bearings to the torque specified by the manufacturer (see Specifications) it will be necessary to use the Kawasaki service tool (57001-1100), which is a C-spanner with a hole for a spring balance to be attached. Using the service tool and a spring balance, apply the specified force to the service tool at a right-angle (90°) to the centre of the steering stem axis, to tighten the adjuster nut to the specified torque **(see illustration 8.16)**. Turn the steering stem from lock-to-lock a few times to settle the bearings and races in position. Slacken the adjuster nut slightly then retighten to the specified torque again then secure it in position by tightening the locknut to the specified torque. **Note:** *It is important to check the feel of the steering afterwards as described below; if it is too tight readjust the bearings as described below.*

39 If the service tool is not available, tighten the adjuster nut hard using a conventional C-wrench to preload the bearings. Rotate the steering stem lock-to-lock a few times then adjust as follows.

40 Slacken the adjuster nut slightly until pressure is just released, then turn it slowly clockwise until resistance is just evident. The object is to set the adjuster nut so that the bearings are under a very light loading, just enough to remove any freeplay. Once the adjuster nut is correctly set, secure it in position by tightening the locknut. Check the feel of the bearings again once the locknut is tight, to ensure the bearing adjustment has been correctly set. If necessary, slacken the locknut again and adjust as necessary.

Caution: Take great care not to apply excessive pressure because this will cause premature failure of the bearings.

41 With the bearings correctly adjusted, locate the brake hose joint on the bottom yoke then fit the spacer bracket and cover and securely tighten the retaining bolts.

42 Where necessary, ensure the mounting rubbers and air filter duct cover brackets are correctly positioned then fit the fairing/rear view mirror bracket to the frame.

43 Locate the horn bracket on the radiator upper mounting and securely tighten the mounting bolt.

44 Install the front forks as described in Section 6 noting that the clamp bolts and the

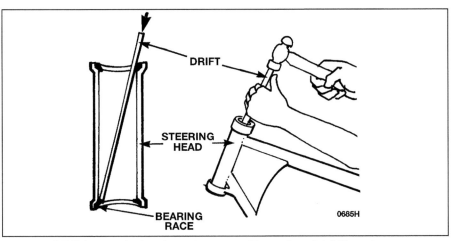

9.5 **Drive out the bearing outer races with a soft-metal drift as shown**

steering stem nut must be tightened to their specified torque settings in the following order.

a) *Top yoke clamp bolts.*
b) *Steering stem nut.*
c) *Bottom yoke clamp bolts.*
d) *Handlebar holder clamp bolts.*

45 On completion, check the steering stem bearing adjustment as described in Chapter 1.

9 Steering head bearings – inspection and renewal

Inspection

1 Remove the steering stem (see Section 8).

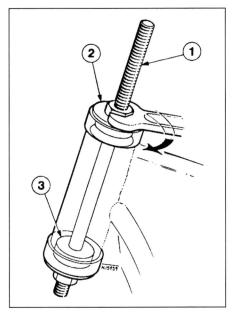

9.7 **Drawbolt arrangement for fitting steering stem bearing outer races**

1 *Long bolt or threaded rod*
2 *Thick washer*
3 *Guide for outer race*

2 Remove all traces of old grease from the bearings and races and check them for wear or damage.

3 On ZX-7R and ZX-9R B and C models, the outer races should be polished and free from indentations. Inspect the bearing rollers for signs of wear, damage or discoloration, and examine the bearing roller retainer cage for signs of cracks or splits. Spin the bearings by hand. They should spin freely and smoothly. If there are any signs of wear on any of the above components, both upper and lower bearing assemblies must be renewed as a set. Only remove the outer races and the lower bearing if they need to be renewed – do not re-use them once they have been removed.

4 On ZX-9R E and F models, the inner and outer races should be polished and free from indentations. Inspect the bearing balls for signs of wear, damage or discoloration, and examine the bearing ball retainer cage for signs of cracks or splits. If there are any signs of wear on any of the above components, both upper and lower bearing assemblies must be renewed as a set. Only remove the outer races and the lower bearing inner race if they need to be renewed – do not re-use them once they have been removed.

Renewal

Note: *Obtain new bearings and new dust seals before proceeding.*

5 The outer races are an interference fit in the frame headstock and can be tapped from position with a suitable drift **(see illustration)**. Tap firmly and evenly around each race to ensure that it is driven out squarely. It may prove advantageous to curve the end of the drift slightly to improve access. **Note:** *The upper and lower bearings are different.*

6 Alternatively, the races can be removed using a slide-hammer type bearing extractor; these can often be hired from tool shops.

7 The new outer races can be pressed into the head using a drawbolt arrangement, or by using a large diameter tubular drift **(see illustration)**. Ensure that the drawbolt washer or drift (as applicable) bears only on the outer

9.8a Do not remove the lower bearing and dust seal from the steering stem unless they are to be renewed

edge of the race and does not contact the race bearing surface.

 HAYNES HiNT *Installation of new bearing outer races is made much easier if the races are left overnight in the freezer. This causes them to contract slightly making them a looser fit.*

8 To remove the lower bearing or inner race (as applicable) from the steering stem, use two screwdrivers placed on opposite sides of the race to work it free. If the bearing/race is firmly in place it will be necessary to use a bearing puller **(see illustrations)**. With the bearing/inner race removed, lift off the dust seal and discard it.
9 Fit the new dust seal to the steering stem, then slide on the new bearing/inner race. A length of tubing with an internal diameter slightly larger than the steering stem will be needed to tap the new race into position **(see illustration)**. Ensure that the drift bears only

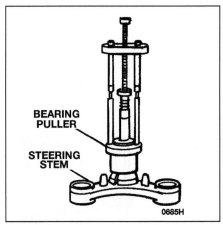

9.8b A bearing puller will probably be needed to remove the lower bearing from the steering stem

on the inner edge of the race and does not contact the bearing surface.
10 Ensure the lower bearing/inner race (as applicable) and both outer races are correctly seated, then install the steering stem as described in Section 8.

10 Rear suspension linkage – removal, inspection and installation

Removal

Tie rods

1 On ZX-7R and ZX-9R B models remove the complete exhaust system (see Chapter 4). **Note:** *If a non-standard exhaust system is fitted, removal may not be necessary.*

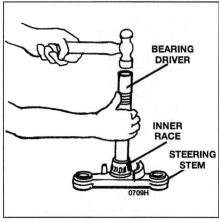

9.9 Fit the dust seal and drive the new lower bearing on using a length of tubing which bears only on the bearing inner race

2 On all models, support the motorcycle on an auxiliary stand so the rear wheel is raised clear of the ground with no weight on the rear suspension linkage. This can be done either by using an auxiliary stand which engages with the swingarm pivot or by supporting the bike on an auxiliary stand(s) positioned underneath the base of the frame (this is where the Kawasaki jack (57001-1238) locates once the sidestand/fairing bracket have been removed) or the footrest brackets. Once the bike is securely supported, position a block of wood in between the tyre and the ground; this will prevent the swingarm dropping as the suspension linkage bolts are withdrawn **(see illustration)**.
Caution: Ensure the bike is securely supported before proceeding.
3 Unscrew the nuts and remove the bolts securing the tie rods to the swingarm and rocker arm. Remove both tie rods from the bike, noting each one's correct fitted location **(see illustration)**.

Rocker arm

4 On ZX-9R E models, remove the silencer; on ZX-9R F models, remove the silencer and exhaust pipe mid-section; on all other models, remove the complete exhaust system (see Chapter 4). **Note:** *If a non-standard exhaust system is fitted, removal may not be necessary.*
5 Support the bike as described in Step 2.

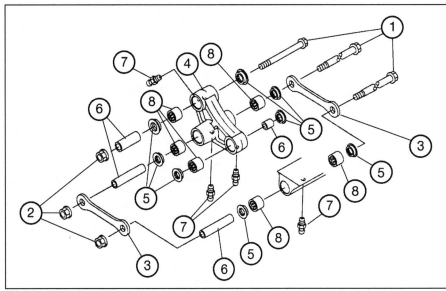

10.2 Suspension linkage components

1 Bolt	4 Rocker arm	7 Grease nipple
2 Nut	5 Dust seal	(ZX-9R E and F models)
3 Tie rod	6 Inner sleeve	8 Bearing

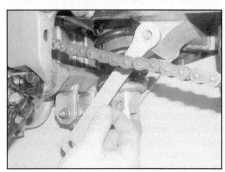

10.3 Removing a tie rod

6 Unscrew the nut and remove the shock absorber lower mounting bolt **(see illustration)**.

7 Unscrew the nut and remove the bolt securing the tie rods to the rocker arm, then pivot the rods clear.

8 Slacken and remove the nut and bolt securing the rocker arm to the frame and remove the arm from the bike **(see illustration)**.

Inspection

9 Withdraw the inner sleeve from each bearing and thoroughly clean all components, removing all traces of dirt, corrosion and grease **(see illustration)**.

10 Inspect all components closely, looking for obvious wear such as heavy scoring, or for damage such as cracks or distortion. Renew as necessary.

11 If any of the dust seals are damaged they should be renewed. Carefully lever the old seal out of position, using a flat-bladed screwdriver, and press the new seal squarely into position ensuring its sealing lip is facing inwards.

12 If any of the bearings are damaged, it will be necessary to renew the bearings, inner sleeve and dust seals. Remove the dust seals and note the correct fitted location of each bearing before pressing/drifting them out of position. The new bearings should be pressed or drawn into their bores rather than driven into position, to prevent possible damage. In the absence of a press, a suitable drawbolt arrangement can be made up as described in Section 5 of *Tools and Workshop Tips* in the *Reference* section. Ensure both bearings are fitted with their marked surfaces facing outwards and are centrally positioned before pressing the new dust seals into position.

13 Lubricate the needle roller bearings, the inner sleeves and the dust seal lips with molybdenum disulphide grease and slide each inner sleeve carefully into position.

Installation

Tie rods

14 If not already done, lubricate the seals, needle roller bearings, inner sleeves and the pivot bolts. Kawasaki recommend the use of molybdenum disulphide grease on ZX-7R and ZX-9R B models and multi-purpose grease on ZX-9R C, E and F models.

15 Offer up the tie rods, ensuring they are fitted in their original locations, and insert both the pivot bolts. On ZX-9R C, E and F models ensure the tie rods are fitted with their chamfered surfaces facing outwards. If new tie rods are being installed they can be fitted on either side (they are identical).

16 Fit the nuts to the pivot bolts and tighten them to the specified torque setting **(see illustration)**.

17 Remove the wood from underneath the rear wheel then take the bike off its auxiliary stand.

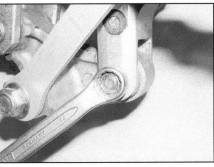

10.6 Unscrew the nut and withdraw the shock absorber lower mounting bolt

18 On ZX-7R and ZX-9R B models install the exhaust system (see Chapter 4).

19 On ZX-9R E and F models ensure all linkage bearings are fully lubricated by using a grease gun on the grease nipples (see Chapter 1).

20 On all models, check the operation of the rear suspension before taking the machine on the road.

Rocker arm

21 If not already done, lubricate the seals, needle roller bearings, inner sleeves and the pivot bolts. Kawasaki recommend the use of molybdenum disulphide grease on ZX-7R and ZX-9R B models and multi-purpose grease on ZX-9R C, E and F models.

22 Align the rocker arm with the frame and insert the pivot bolt.

23 Align both tie rods with the rocker arm and insert the pivot bolt.

24 Align the shock absorber lower mounting with the rocker arm and insert the bolt.

25 Fit the nuts to the rocker arm, tie rod and shock absorber bolts and tighten them to their specified torque settings.

26 Remove the wood from underneath the rear wheel, then take the bike off its auxiliary stand.

27 Install the silencer/exhaust system (as applicable – see Chapter 4).

28 On ZX-9R E and F models ensure all linkage bearings are fully lubricated by using a grease gun on the grease nipples (see Chapter 1).

29 On all models, check the operation of the rear suspension before taking the machine on the road.

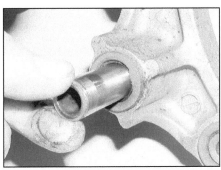

10.9 Withdraw each inner sleeve and check the bearings and seals for wear or damage

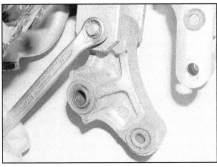

10.8 Slacken and remove the nut and bolt securing the rocker arm to the frame

11 Rear shock absorber – removal, inspection and installation

Removal

ZX-7R models

1 Remove the fuel tank (see Chapter 4).

2 Remove the seats, side covers and lower fairing panels (see Chapter 8).

3 Unclip the turn signal relay from the rear mudguard and disconnect the wiring connectors from the turn signal lights and number plate light.

4 Unscrew the rear mudguard mounting bolts (two on each side), noting the correct fitted location of the earth lead, then manoeuvre the mudguard out of position. Recover the collars which are fitted in between the rear mountings and subframe and the caged nuts from the front mountings. **Note:** *On California models it will also be necessary to free the evaporative emission system charcoal canister and hoses from the mudguard.*

5 Remove the battery (see Chapter 9) and free the fuel pump relay, junction box and starter relay from the battery case.

6 Unscrew the bolt securing the rear brake fluid reservoir to the battery case. Keep the reservoir upright to prevent fluid loss.

7 Unscrew the mounting bolts (one on each side) and manoeuvre the battery case out of position.

8 Support the motorcycle on an auxiliary

10.16 Tighten all pivot bolt nuts to the specified torque

stand so the rear wheel is raised clear of the ground with no weight on the rear suspension linkage. This can be done either by using an auxiliary stand which engages with the swingarm pivot or by supporting the bike on an auxiliary stand(s) positioned underneath the base of the frame (this is where the Kawasaki jack (57001-1238) locates once the sidestand/fairing bracket have been removed) or the footrest brackets. Once the bike is securely supported, position a block of wood in between the tyre and the ground; this will prevent the swingarm dropping as the shock absorber bolts are withdrawn.

Caution: Ensure the bike is securely supported before proceeding.

9 Unscrew the nut and withdraw the shock absorber lower mounting bolt.

10 Unscrew the nut from the shock absorber upper mounting bolt. Withdraw the bolt and manoeuvre the shock absorber upwards and out of position.

ZX-9R B models

Caution: Do not attempt to separate the shock absorber and reservoir. The reservoir and shock absorber contain pressurised nitrogen. If this gas is not released in a controlled manner, personal injury will result. Also note that once the gas has been released the shock absorber must be renewed or recharged by a suspension specialist.

11 Remove the seats, side covers and lower fairing panels (see Chapter 8).

12 Remove the fuel tank and silencer (see Chapter 4).

13 Remove the battery (see Chapter 9).

14 Unscrew the bolt securing the rear brake fluid reservoir to the rear mudguard. Keep the reservoir upright to prevent fluid loss.

15 Slacken the retaining clamps and free the shock absorber reservoir from its bracket on the right side of the subframe.

16 Support the bike as described in Step 8.

17 Unscrew the nut and withdraw the bolt securing the tie rods to the swingarm.

18 Unscrew the nut and withdraw the shock absorber lower mounting bolt then pivot the tie rods and rocker arm clear of the shock absorber.

19 Slacken and remove the upper mounting bolt and nut then lower the shock absorber and reservoir assembly out of position.

ZX-9R C, E and F models

20 Support the bike as described in Step 8.

21 Unscrew the nuts from the shock absorber upper and lower mounting bolts **(see illustrations)**. Withdraw both bolts then manoeuvre the shock absorber upwards and out of position **(see illustration)**. On ZX-9R F models, lower the rear wheel onto the ground to provide clearance to lift the shock absorber out **(see illustration)**.

Inspection

22 Inspect the shock absorber for obvious physical damage and oil leakage, and the coil spring for looseness, cracks or signs of fatigue.

11.21a On ZX-9R C and E models, slacken and remove the lower mounting nut and bolt . . .

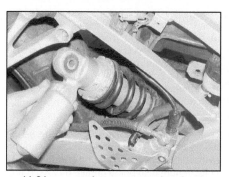
11.21c . . . and manoeuvre the shock absorber out of position

The shock absorber is a sealed unit and cannot be dismantled. **Note:** *The shock absorber contains pressurised nitrogen. If a new shock absorber is being fitted, the gas charge should be released from the old unit before it is discarded. To do this, wearing thick gloves and eye protection, remove the cap from the end of the shock absorber reservoir. Using a long screwdriver, depress the valve core to safely release the nitrogen whilst keeping well away from the valve. Once all the pressure has been released the unit can be safely discarded.*

23 On ZX-9R models, the shock absorber upper mounting bush can be renewed if it shows signs of damage or deterioration. Note the correct fitted location of the bush before pressing/drifting it out of position. The new bush should be pressed/tapped into position using a suitable tubular spacer which bears only on the hard outer edge of the bush. Alternatively, a suitable drawbolt arrangement can be made up as described in Section 5 of *Tools and Workshop Tips* in the *Reference* section.

24 Check the shock absorber lower mounting bearing as described in Section 10.

Installation

ZX-7R models

25 If not already done, lubricate the shock absorber lower mounting bearings, inner sleeve and the pivot bolt with molybdenum disulphide grease.

26 Manoeuvre the shock absorber into position and insert the upper and lower mounting bolts. Fit the nuts to the mounting bolts and tighten them to the specified torque.

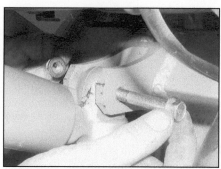
11.21b . . . and the upper mounting nut and bolt . . .

11.21d Lifting the rear shock out – ZX-9R F model

27 Install the battery case and lightly tighten its mounting bolts.

28 Install the rear mudguard, ensuring it is correctly engaged with the battery case. Ensure the caged nuts and mounting collars are correctly positioned then insert the mounting bolts, not forgetting the earth lead which should be fitted to the front, right side bolt. Securely tighten both the mudguard and battery case bolts.

29 Refit the rear brake reservoir bolt, clip the relays and junction box back onto the battery case/mudguard and reconnect the wiring to the turn signals and number plate light. Install the battery (see Chapter 9).

30 Install the fuel tank (see Chapter 4) then fit the fairing panels, side covers and seats (see Chapter 8).

31 Check the adjustment settings and operation of the rear suspension before taking the machine on the road.

ZX-9R B models

32 If not already done, lubricate the shock absorber lower mounting and the tie rod bearings, inner sleeves and the pivot bolts with molybdenum disulphide grease.

33 Manoeuvre the shock absorber upwards and into position ensuring that the rebound damping adjuster and reservoir hose union are facing towards the rear. Ensure that the reservoir is correctly routed through the subframe, then insert the upper and lower mounting bolts. Fit the nuts to the bolts, tightening them lightly only at this stage.

34 Align the tie rods with the swingarm and fit the pivot bolt and nut.

12.1 Adjusting the front fork spring pre-load setting

12.2 Adjusting the front fork rebound damping setting

12.3 Adjusting the front fork compression damping setting

35 Tighten the tie rod pivot bolt nut to the specified torque then tighten the shock absorber upper and lower mounting bolts to the specified torque.
36 Locate the reservoir on the subframe bracket and secure it in position with the retaining clamps.
37 Refit the rear brake fluid reservoir bolt and install the battery (see Chapter 9).
38 Install the fuel tank and silencer (see Chapter 4).
39 Fit the fairing panels, side covers and seats (see Chapter 8).
40 Check the adjustment settings and operation of the rear suspension before taking the machine on the road.

ZX-9R C, E and F models

41 If not already done, lubricate the shock absorber lower mounting bearings, inner sleeve and the pivot bolt with multi-purpose grease.
42 Manoeuvre the shock absorber into position and insert the upper and lower mounting bolts. Fit the nuts to the mounting bolts and tighten them to the specified torque.
43 Check the adjustment settings and operation of the rear suspension before taking the machine on the road.

12 Suspension – adjustments

Note: *All standard recommended settings given by Kawasaki are for a solo rider weighing approximately 68 kg.*

Front forks

Caution: Always make sure both left and right fork leg adjustments are equally set, to ensure the motorcycle handles predictably.

Spring pre-load adjustment

1 The spring pre-load is set using the adjuster fitted to the centre of each fork top cap. The standard setting recommended by Kawasaki is set by measuring the distance from the top of the adjuster to the upper surface of the top cap (it can also be set using the marks on the side of the adjuster body). Turn the adjuster clockwise to increase the pre-load and anti-clockwise to

decrease it **(see illustration)**. The adjuster has a range of between 5 and 20 mm, the standard recommended setting is as follows.

Model	Standard preload setting
ZX-7R models	16 mm (between the 6th and 7th marks)
ZX-9R B models	15 mm (6th mark)
ZX-9R C models	17 mm (7th mark)
ZX-9R E models	13 mm
ZX-9R F models	15 mm

Rebound damping adjustment

2 The fork rebound damping is set using the adjuster located in the top of the pre-load adjuster **(see illustration)**. To establish the standard setting (see standard settings and adjustment range below), rotate the adjuster fully clockwise until it stops; do not force it. From this point, rotate the adjuster anti-clockwise whilst counting the number of clicks or turns. To soften the damping, rotate the adjuster further anti-clockwise and to stiffen the damping rotate the adjuster further clockwise.

Model	Standard rebound damping setting
ZX-7R models	7th click out from the max (usable range 1 to 12-13 clicks)
ZX-9R B models	6th click out from the max (usable range 1 to 12-13 clicks)
ZX-9R C models	5th click out from the max (usable range 1 to 12-14 clicks)
ZX-9R E models	8th click out from the max (usable range 1 to 12 clicks)
ZX-9R F models	1 1/4 turns out from the max (usable range 0 to 3 turns)

Compression damping adjustment

3 The fork compression damping is set using the adjuster on the bottom of the fork tube **(see illustration)**. To establish the standard setting (see standard settings and adjustment range below), rotate the adjuster fully clockwise until it stops; do not force it. From this point, rotate the adjuster anti-clockwise whilst counting the

number of clicks or turns. To further soften the damping, rotate the adjuster further anti-clockwise and to stiffen the damping rotate the adjuster further clockwise.

Model	Standard compression damping setting
ZX-7R models	6th click out from the max (usable range 1 to 8 clicks)
ZX-9R B models	5th click out from the max (usable range 1 to 7-9 clicks)
ZX-9R C models	7th click out from the max (usable range 1 to 10-12 clicks)
ZX-9R E models	8th click out from the max (usable range 1 to 12 clicks)
ZX-9R F models	1 1/4 turns out from the max (usable range 0 to 3 turns)

Rear shock absorber
Spring pre-load adjustment

4 Spring pre-load adjustment on the rear shock absorber is made by repositioning the large locknut and adjuster nut, which form the spring upper seat, on the shock absorber body **(see illustration)**. Using a large C-spanner, slacken the locknut, then turn the adjuster nut clockwise to increase pre-load and anti-clockwise to decrease it. Once the pre-load is correctly set, secure the adjuster nut in position with the locknut.
5 On ZX-7R and ZX-9R B models, in order to

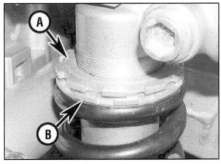
12.4 Rear shock absorber spring preload is adjusted by slackening the locknut (A) and repositioning the adjuster nut (B)

establish the standard pre-load setting, it is necessary to allow the spring to extend to its natural free length. The easiest way to do this is to remove the shock absorber from the bike (see Section 11) then fully slacken the locknut and back off the adjuster nut until the spring tension is fully relieved. Measure the shock absorber spring free length and note it down in a safe place. Use the adjuster nut to compress the spring by the specified amount, then securely tighten the locknut. The standard setting and recommended adjustment range are as follows.

Model	Standard preload setting
ZX-7R models	Compress the spring by 13 mm (usable range 0 to 28 mm)
ZX-9R B models	Compress the spring by 12 mm (usable range 12 to 22 mm)

6 On ZX-9R C, E and F models, the standard pre-load setting can be established by measuring the length of the shock absorber spring either with the shock absorber removed from the bike (see Section 11) or with the bike supported so there is no load on the rear suspension. The standard setting and recommended adjustment range are as follows.

Model	Standard preload setting
ZX-9R C models	Spring length 192.5 mm (usable range 182.5 to 202.5 mm)
ZX-9R E models	Spring length 178.5 mm (usable range 168 to 188 mm)
ZX-9R F models	Spring length 177.5 mm (usable range 171.5 to 191.5 mm)

Rebound damping adjustment

7 On ZX-7R and ZX-9R B models, rebound damping adjustment is set using the adjuster on the bottom of the shock absorber (see illustration). The amount of damping is indicated by a number on the adjuster. There are four positions. The standard position is No. 2., the weakest is No. 1 and the strongest No. 4. Turn the adjuster until the desired setting, indicated by the number, aligns with the index mark on the shock body and a click is felt.

12.7 On ZX-7R and ZX-9R B models, the rebound damping adjuster (arrowed) is located at the bottom of the shock absorber

8 On ZX-9R C, E and F models, rebound damping adjustment is set using the adjuster on the left-hand side of the shock absorber lower end (see illustration). To establish the standard setting (see standard settings and adjustment range below), rotate the adjuster fully clockwise (in the direction of the 'H' arrow) until it stops; do not force it. From this point, rotate the adjuster anti-clockwise whilst counting the number of clicks or turns. To further soften the damping, rotate the adjuster further anti-clockwise (in the direction of the 'S' arrow) and to stiffen the damping rotate the adjuster further clockwise (in the direction of the 'H' arrow).

Model	Standard rebound damping setting
ZX-9R C models	5th click out from the max (usable range 1 to 20-22 clicks)
ZX-9R E models	8th click out from the max (usable range 1 to 18 clicks)
ZX-9R F models	3 1/2 turns out from the max (usable range 0 to 4 1/2 turns)

Compression damping adjuster

9 Compression damping is set using the adjuster on the shock absorber reservoir. On ZX-9R B models the reservoir is located on the right side of the bike, just behind the passenger footrest, and is linked to the shock absorber by a hose (see illustration). On all other models the reservoir is built into the

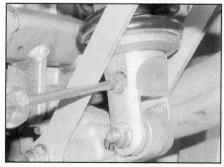

12.8 On ZX-9R C and E models, the rebound damping adjuster is on the left side of the shock absorber lower end

shock absorber and the adjuster is located on the left side of the shock absorber upper end (see illustrations).

10 To establish the standard setting (see standard settings and adjustment range below), rotate the adjuster fully clockwise (in the direction of the 'H' arrow) until it stops; do not force it. From this point, rotate the adjuster anti-clockwise whilst counting the number of clicks or turns. To further soften the damping, rotate the adjuster further anti-clockwise (in the direction of the 'S' arrow) and to stiffen the damping rotate the adjuster further clockwise (in the direction of the 'H' arrow)

Model	Standard compression damping setting
ZX-7R models	15th click out from the max (usable range 1 to 16-22 clicks)
All ZX-9R B1 and B2 models and US B3 models	10th click out from the max (usable range 1 to 16-22 clicks)
All ZX-9R B4 models and UK B3 models	12th click out from the max (usable range 1 to 16-22 clicks)
ZX-9R C models	12th click out from the max (usable range 1 to 20-22 clicks)
ZX-9R E models	10th click out from the max (usable range 1 to 20 clicks)
ZX-9R F models	3 3/4 turns out from the max (usable range 0 to 5 turns)

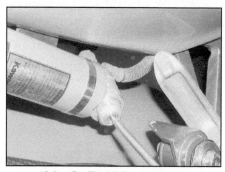

12.9a On ZX-9R B models, the compression damper adjuster is located on the shock absorber remote reservoir

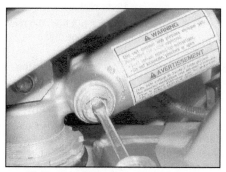

12.9b Location of the compression damping adjuster on ZX-7R and ZX-9R C and E models

12.9c Location of the compression damping adjuster on ZX-9R F models

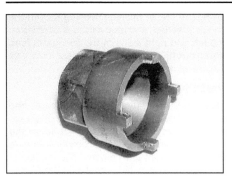

13.0 Special socket for slackening/
tightening the swingarm locknut

13 Swingarm –
removal and installation

Note: *A special socket will be needed to slacken/tighten the pivot bolt locknut. If the Kawasaki service tool (57001-1370 for ZX-7R and ZX-9R B and F models and 57001-1354 for ZX-9R C and E models) or a pattern equivalent is not available, a suitable alternative can be made by cutting a spare socket as shown* **(see illustration)**.

Removal

1 Remove the lower fairing panel(s) (see Chapter 8).
2 Support the motorcycle on an auxiliary stand so that the rear wheel is raised clear of the ground with no weight on the rear suspension linkage. This can be done by

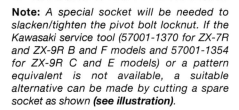

13.11a Unscrew the locknut from the pivot shaft

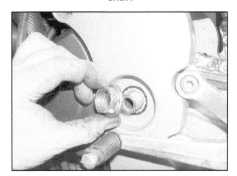

13.12 Unscrew the nut from the opposite end of the pivot shaft . . .

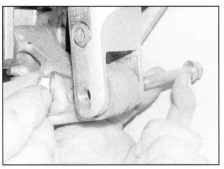

13.9 Unscrew the nut and withdraw the shock absorber lower mounting bolt

supporting the bike on an auxiliary stand(s) positioned underneath the base of the frame (this is where the Kawasaki jack (57001-1238) locates once the sidestand/fairing bracket has been removed) or the footrest brackets.
Caution: Ensure the bike is securely supported before proceeding.
3 Remove the rear wheel (see Chapter 7).
4 On ZX-7R models, remove the left side rider's footrest bracket (see Section 3).
5 On ZX-9R B models remove the silencer (see Chapter 4).
6 Undo the retaining screws and remove the drive chain cover from the swingarm. Note that on ZX-9R F models, the cover is a two-piece item; the upper edge of the front half is secured by a trim clip – undo the centre screw and pull the clip out.
7 Undo the retaining screw(s) or bolt(s) and free the brake hose guide(s) from the swingarm. On ZX-9R F models, follow the procedure in

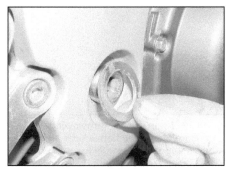

13.11b On **ZX-9R C** also remove the washer

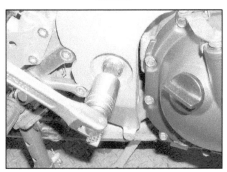

13.13 . . . then unscrew the pivot shaft from the frame

13.10 Unscrew the nut and withdraw the bolt securing the tie rods to the swingarm

Chapter 7, Section 7, and disconnect the rear brake hose from the brake caliper. Feed the hose through the fixed guide on the swingarm and secure it clear of the swingarm.
8 On ZX-9R F models, the drive chain passes through the swingarm. If required, follow the procedure in Section 16 and remove the front sprocket, then slip the chain over the output shaft and remove it with the swingarm. Alternatively, follow the procedure in Section 15 and split the chain to allow the swingarm to be removed. Kawasaki list a joining link as a replacement part for their original equipment chain.
9 Slacken the shock absorber upper mounting bolt nut. Slacken and remove the shock absorber lower mounting nut and bolt **(see illustration)**.
10 Slacken and remove the nut and bolt securing the tie rods to the swingarm, then pivot the suspension linkage clear of the shock absorber **(see illustration)**.
11 Using the special socket or a suitable home-made alternative (see Note at start of Section), slacken and remove the locknut from the end of the swingarm pivot bolt (the locknut is fitted to the left end of the shaft on ZX-7R and ZX-9R B models and the right end on ZX-9R C, E and F models) **(see illustration)**. On ZX-9R C models remove the washer from the pivot shaft **(see illustration)**.
12 Unscrew the pivot nut from the opposite end of the swingarm pivot shaft **(see illustration)**.
13 Unscrew the swingarm pivot shaft from the frame **(see illustration)**.
14 Support the swingarm then withdraw the pivot shaft **(see illustration)**. Manoeuvre the

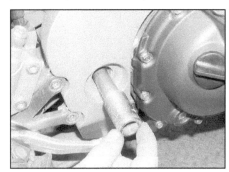

13.14a Withdraw the pivot shaft . . .

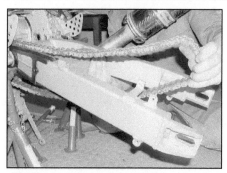

13.14b ... then manoeuvre the swingarm out of position

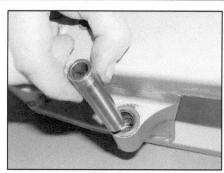

13.15 Lubricate the inner sleeves, bearings and dust seals

swingarm out of position, freeing it from the shock absorber, and recover the spacers from the left and right sides of the swingarm **(see illustration)**. Inspect the assembly as described in Section 14.

Installation

15 If not already done, lubricate the swingarm pivot seals, bearings, inner sleeve and the pivot shaft, and also lubricate the suspension linkage bearing components **(see illustration)**. Kawasaki recommend the use of molybdenum disulphide grease on ZX-7R and ZX-9R B models and multi-purpose grease on ZX-9R C, E and F models.

16 Fit the left and right spacers to the swingarm. On ZX-7R and ZX-9R B models ensure the spacer with the circular flange is fitted to the right side of the swingarm and the spacer with the square flange is fitted to the left. On ZX-9R C, E and F models fit the spacer with the square flange to the right side of the swingarm and the spacer with the circular flange to the left side **(see illustrations)**.

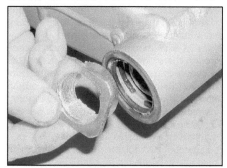

13.16a On ZX-9R C, E and F models, ensure the spacer with the square flange is fitted to the right of the swingarm ...

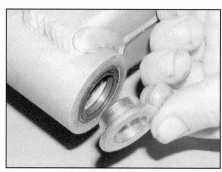

13.16b ... and the spacer with the circular flange to the left

17 Manoeuvre the swingarm into position, engaging it correctly with the shock absorber and drive chain. On ZX-9R F models, if the chain is in place on the swingarm, ensure it is correctly located over the front sprocket.

18 On ZX-7R and ZX-9R B models, ensure one of the flats on the swingarm left side spacer square flange is correctly located against the lug cast of the inside of the frame, then align the swingarm pivot with the frame and insert the pivot shaft from the left side **(see illustration)**.

19 On ZX-9R C, E and F models, ensure one of the flats on the swingarm right side spacer square flange is correctly located against the lug cast of the inside of the frame, then align the swingarm pivot with the frame and insert the pivot shaft from the right side **(see illustration)**.

20 On all models tighten the swingarm pivot shaft to its specified torque **(see illustration)**. **Note:** *On ZX-9R E and F models, there should be no clearance between the square flanged spacer and the frame.*

21 Fit the pivot nut to the shaft and tighten it to the specified torque **(see illustration)**.

22 Fit the washer (ZX-9R C models only) and screw the locknut onto the pivot shaft and

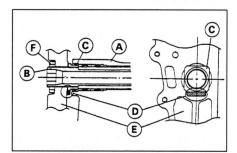

13.18 Swingarm fixing details (ZX-7R shown – others similar)

A Swingarm	D Frame lug
B Pivot shaft	E Frame
C Dust seal	F Locknut

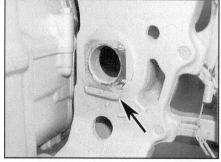

13.19 When installing the swingarm, ensure one of the flats on the spacer square flange is correctly located against the lug (arrowed) on the frame

13.20 Tighten the pivot shaft to the specified torque ...

13.21 ... then fit the pivot nut to the shaft and tighten it to the specified torque

13.22 Tighten the pivot shaft locknut to the specified torque then check that the swingarm pivots smoothly

tighten it to the specified torque (see illustration). Check the swingarm pivots smoothly on its bearings before proceeding.

23 Align the swingarm with the tie rods and insert the pivot bolt and the shock absorber lower mounting bolt. Fit the nuts to the bolts, then tighten the shock absorber upper and lower mounting bolts and the tie rod bolt to their specified torque settings.

24 Fit the brake hose guide(s) and the drive chain cover to the swingarm. On ZX-9R F models, install the rear brake hose and bleed the rear brake (see Chapter 7, Section 11).

25 On ZX-7R models, install the footrest bracket (see Section 3) and fit the battery case/rear mudguard (see Steps 27 to 29 of Section 11).

26 On ZX-9R B models, install the silencer (see Chapter 4).

27 On all models, fit the rear wheel (see Chapter 7). On ZX-9R F models, if the drive chain has been split, follow the procedure in Section 15 and install a new joining link.

28 Adjust the drive chain slack as described in Chapter 1.

29 Check the operation of the rear brake and suspension before taking the machine on the road. On ZX-9R E and F models ensure that the swingarm pivot bearings are fully lubricated by using a grease gun on the grease nipples (see Chapter 1).

14 Swingarm –
inspection and bearing renewal

Inspection

1 Remove the left and right spacers from the swingarm then withdraw the needle roller bearing inner sleeve from the left side of the swingarm pivot (see illustration).

2 Inspect all components closely, looking for obvious wear such as heavy scoring, or for damage such as cracks or distortion. The left side pivot bearing consists of two needle roller bearings and the right side bearing of a ball bearing and needle roller bearing. If any bearing shows signs of wear or damage it is recommended that all four bearings and the inner sleeve are renewed as a set.

3 If the dust seals are damaged, the old seals can be levered out of position using a flat-bladed screwdriver. Ensure the sealing lip of the new seal is facing inwards then press the seal squarely into position until it is flush with the swingarm.

4 Whilst the swingarm is removed, also inspect the drive chain slider for signs of wear or damage along its complete length and renew if necessary.

Bearing renewal

5 To renew the bearings, remove the dust seals from the swingarm pivot then, using circlip pliers, remove the circlip from the right side of the swingarm pivot. Note the correct fitted location of each bearing before pressing/drifting it out of position.

6 The new bearings should be pressed or drawn into position rather than driven into position to prevent possible damage. In the absence of a press, a suitable drawbolt arrangement can be made up as described in Section 5 of *Tools and Workshop Tips* in the *Reference* section. Ensure all bearings are fitted with their manufacturers markings facing outwards and ensure the inner bearing is firmly located against its stop before installing the outer bearing. Secure the right side bearings in position with the circlip, making sure it is correctly located in its groove, then press the new dust seals into position.

7 Lubricate all the bearings and seals with grease (Kawasaki recommend the use of molybdenum disulphide grease on ZX-7R and ZX-9R B models and multi-purpose grease on ZX-9R C, E and F models) then insert the inner sleeve into the needle roller bearings.

15 Drive chain –
removal, cleaning and installation

Removal

Endless chain

Note: *An endless chain has no riveted (joining) link – all links and pins are the same. The chain fitted as original equipment and supplied as a spare part from Kawasaki dealers is of the endless type.*

1 Remove the front sprocket cover as described in Section 16.

2 Remove the swingarm (see Section 13).

3 Slip the chain off the front sprocket and remove it from the bike.

Rivet link chain

Note: *Most replacement chains are supplied with a riveted (joining) link, which can be recognised by the identification marks on its side plate (which is usually a different colour), as well as by the staked ends of the link's two pins, which look as if they have been deeply centre-punched – instead of peened over as with all the other pins.*

⚠️ **Warning: NEVER install a drive chain which uses a clip-type master (split) link. Use ONLY the correct service tools to secure the staked-type master link – if you do not have access to such tools, have the chain renewed by a dealer to be sure of having it securely installed.**

4 Support the bike on an auxiliary stand so that the rear wheel is off the ground.

5 Locate the joining link in a suitable position to work on by rotating the back wheel.

6 Slacken the drive chain as described in Chapter 1.

7 Split the chain at the joining link using the chain cutter, following the manufacturer's

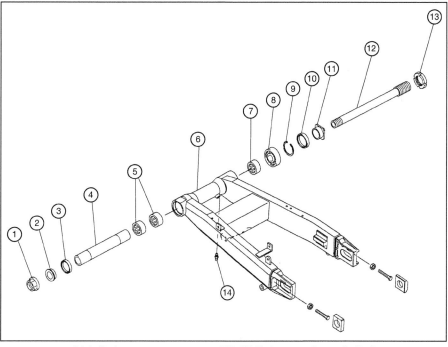

14.1 Swingarm components (ZX-9R E shown, others similar)

1 *Pivot nut*	5 *Needle roller*	8 *Ball bearing*	12 *Pivot shaft*
2 *Circular flanged*	*bearings*	9 *Circlip*	13 *Locknut*
spacer	6 *Swingarm*	10 *Dust seal*	14 *Grease nipple*
3 *Dust seal*	7 *Needle roller*	11 *Square flanged*	*(ZX-9R E only)*
4 *Inner sleeve*	*bearing*	*spacer*	

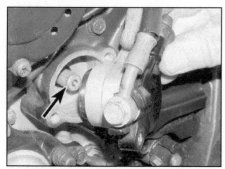

16.6 Remove the clutch slave cylinder from the sprocket cover taking care not to lose the end piece (arrowed) from the pushrod

operating instructions carefully (see also Section 8 in *Tools and Workshop Tips* in the *Reference* section). Free the chain from the rear sprocket then, with the transmission in neutral, pull it off the front sprocket. Discard the rivet link components, a new one must be used on installation.

>
> *If a spare length of chain is available, hook this onto one end of the fitted chain before pulling the chain off the front sprocket. Pull the fitted chain off the front sprocket and detach it, leaving the spare chain in position. The spare chain can then be used to draw the fitted chain back on with the sprocket cover in position.*

Cleaning

8 Soak the chain in paraffin (kerosene) for approximately five or six minutes. If the chain is very dirty, use a soft-bristled brush to removed caked-on deposits.
Caution: Don't use petrol (gasoline), solvent or other cleaning fluids which might damage its internal sealing properties. Don't use high-pressure water. Remove the chain, wipe it off, then blow-dry it with compressed air immediately. The entire process shouldn't take longer than ten minutes – if it does, the O-rings in the chain rollers could be damaged.

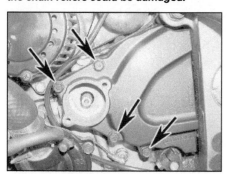

16.8a On ZX-9R B models, unscrew the bolts (arrowed) . . .

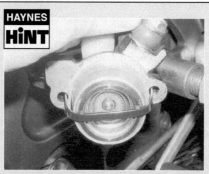

To prevent the piston being accidentally expelled, retain it with a cable tie passed through the cylinder mounting bolts holes and tightened securely around the cylinder

Installation

Endless chain

9 Hook the chain onto the front sprocket then install the swingarm (see Section 13).
10 Install the front sprocket cover (see Section 16) then adjust and lubricate the drive chain (as described in Chapter 1).

Rivet link chain

> ⚠️ *Warning: If you do not have access to a chain riveting tool, have the chain fitted by a dealer. NEVER install a drive chain which uses a clip-type master (split) link.*

11 If necessary, remove the front sprocket cover from the engine as described in Section 16.
12 Install the drive chain around the front and rear sprockets and leave the two ends in a convenient position to work on.
13 Fit an O-ring to each of the new rivet link pins then join the ends of the chain with the link, ensuring the link is fitted from the inside. Fit another O-ring to each of the link pins then fit the side plate with its identification marks facing out; use the chain tool to press the side plate into position.
14 Stake the new link pins using the chain riveting tool, following the instructions of both the chain manufacturer and the tool manufacturer carefully. Refer to Section 8 of

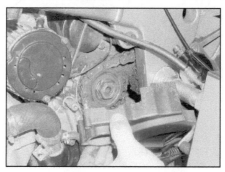

16.8b . . . then remove the sprocket cover

Tools and Workshop Tips in the *Reference* section for chain riveting details using a typical commercially available tool.
15 After riveting, check the rivet link pin ends for any signs of cracking. If there is any evidence of cracking, the rivet link, O-rings and side plate must be removed and the procedure repeated with a new link assembly.
16 Install the sprocket cover (where removed) as described in Section 16.
17 Adjust and lubricate the chain following the procedures described in Chapter 1.

16 Sprockets – check and renewal

Check

1 To gain access to the front sprocket, drive chain guide plate and swingarm drive chain slider, remove the sprocket cover (ZX-7R and ZX-9R B models, see Steps 5 to 8; ZX-9R C, E and F models, see Steps 21 and 22).
2 Check the wear pattern on both sprockets (see Chapter 1). If the sprocket teeth are worn excessively, renew the chain and both sprockets as a set. Whenever the sprockets are inspected, the drive chain should also be inspected (see Chapter 1). If you are renewing the chain, renew the sprockets as well.
3 Also check the drive chain guide plate and the drive chain slider on the swingarm for signs of wear or damage and renew if necessary (see Chapter 1).
4 Install the sprocket cover (ZX-7R and ZX-9R B models, see Steps 17 to 20; ZX-9R C, E and F models, see Steps 24 and 25) then adjust and lubricate the chain following the procedures described in Chapter 1.

Renewal

Front sprocket – ZX-7R and ZX-9R B models

5 Remove the left side fairing lower panel (see Chapter 8).
6 Unscrew the clutch slave cylinder bolts and free the cylinder from the sprocket cover, taking care not to lose the end piece from the pushrod **(see illustration)**. **Note:** *There is no need to disconnect the hydraulic hose from the cylinder.*
Caution: Do not operate the clutch lever whilst the cylinder is detached.
7 On ZX-7R models undo the three retaining bolts and remove the rear section of the sprocket cover from the front section. Slacken and remove the three bolts securing the front section of the cover to the crankcase and remove the cover. Recover the locating dowels and store them with the cover for safe-keeping.
8 On ZX-9R B models undo the four retaining bolts and remove the sprocket cover from the engine **(see illustrations)**. Recover the

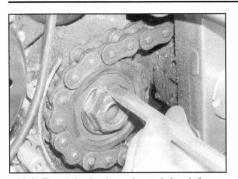

16.9 Bend the lockwasher tab back from the sprocket nut

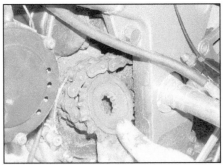

16.12 Free the sprocket from the drive chain and slide it off the output shaft

16.14 Fit a new lockwasher, ensuring it engages correctly with the output shaft splines . . .

16.15 . . . then screw on the sprocket nut

16.16 Tighten the sprocket nut to the specified torque and secure it in position by bending the lockwasher up against one of its flats

locating dowels and store them with the cover for safe-keeping.

9 On all models, bend the lockwasher tab back clear of the front sprocket nut, using a hammer and suitable chisel/punch **(see illustration)**.

10 Have an assistant apply the rear brake hard to prevent rotation, then slacken the sprocket nut. Remove the nut and discard the lockwasher; a new one should be used on installation.

11 Release the drive chain tension (see Chapter 1).

12 Free the sprocket from the drive chain and slide it off the output shaft **(see illustration). Note:** *If the sprocket is to be fitted again mark it in some way to ensure it is installed the correct way round.*

13 Slide the sprocket onto the output shaft and engage it with the drive chain. A new

sprocket can be fitted either way round but if the original sprocket is being refitted, ensure it is installed the same way round as was noted on removal.

14 Ensure the output shaft and sprocket nut threads are clean and dry then fit the new lockwasher, ensuring it is correctly engaged with the output shaft splines **(see illustration)**.

15 Lubricate the threads and face of the sprocket nut with clean engine oil then screw the nut onto the output shaft **(see illustration)**. Tighten the nut to the specified torque, using the method employed on removal to prevent the sprocket from turning (see Step 10).

16 Secure the nut in position by bending the

lockwasher up against one of the nut flats **(see illustration)**.

17 On ZX-7R models, ensure the locating dowels are in position then fit the front section of the sprocket cover. Tighten the bolts to the specified torque then install the rear section of the cover and tighten its bolts also to the specified torque.

18 On ZX-9R B models, ensure the locating dowels are in position then fit the sprocket cover to the engine. Install the cover retaining bolts and tighten them to the specified torque.

19 On all models, ensure the cover and clutch slave cylinder surfaces are clean and dry. Ensure the end piece is correctly fitted to the pushrod, then remove the cable tie (where fitted) and fit the slave cylinder, tightening its retaining bolts securely.

20 Install the lower fairing panel (see Chapter 8) then adjust and lubricate the chain following the procedures described in Chapter 1.

Front sprocket – ZX-9R C, E and F models

21 Unscrew the bolt and free the speed sensor from the sprocket cover **(see illustrations)**.

22 Slacken and remove the four retaining bolts, noting the correct fitted location of the clamp and idle speed adjuster bracket, and remove the sprocket cover from the engine **(see illustrations)**. Recover the locating dowels and store them with the cover for safe-keeping.

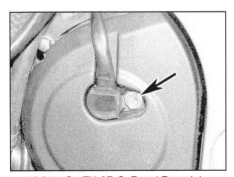

16.21a On ZX-9R C, E and F models, unscrew the bolt (arrowed) . . .

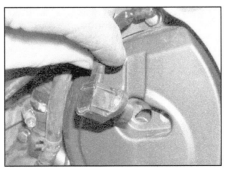

16.21b . . . and free the speed sensor from the sprocket cover

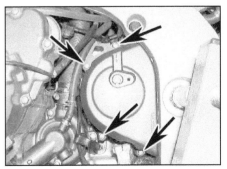

16.22a Unscrew the retaining bolts (arrowed) . . .

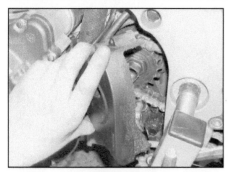

16.22b . . . and remove the sprocket cover from the engine

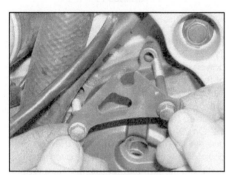

16.24 Remember to fit the idle speed adjuster bracket with the cover upper bolts

23 Renew the sprocket as described in Steps 9 to 16 **(see illustration)**.
24 Ensure the locating dowels are in position then fit the sprocket cover to the engine. Install the cover retaining bolts, ensuring the idle speed adjuster bracket and clamp are

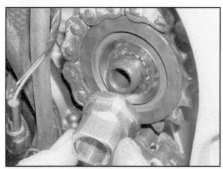

16.23 Ensure the lockwasher is correctly engaged with the output shaft splines then fit the nut

correctly positioned, and tighten them to the specified torque **(see illustration)**.
25 Remove all traces of locking compound from the threads of the speed sensor bolt and apply a drop of fresh locking compound to the bolt. Fit the speed sensor to the sprocket cover then fit the retaining bolt, tightening it to the specified torque.
26 Adjust and lubricate the chain following the procedures described in Chapter 1.

Rear sprocket

27 Remove the rear wheel (see Chapter 7).
28 Unscrew the nuts securing the sprocket to the coupling and remove the sprocket, noting which way round it is fitted.
29 Check that the sprocket studs are secure in the coupling. If any are loose, remove them all and clean their threads, then apply a suitable non-permanent thread locking compound and tighten them securely. To ease removal and tightening of the studs,

thread two nuts onto the stud and use one as a locknut and the other to unscrew and tighten the studs (see Section 2 of *Tools and Workshop Tips* in the *Reference* section).
30 Install the sprocket onto the coupling with the stamped tooth number facing out, then fit the nuts, tightening them evenly and progressively to the specified torque.
31 Install the rear wheel (see Chapter 7), then adjust and lubricate the chain following the procedures described in Chapter 1.

17 Rear sprocket coupling/rubber damper – inspection and renewal

1 Remove the rear wheel (see Chapter 7).
2 Lift the sprocket coupling from the wheel, taking care not to lose the spacer which is fitted to the inside of the coupling bearing. Check the coupling for cracks and damage, and replace it with a new one if necessary.
3 Remove the rubber damper segments from the sprocket coupling or wheel (as applicable) and check each one for cracks, hardening and general deterioration **(see illustration)**. If any segment shows signs of wear or damage, renew all the rubber dampers as a complete set.
4 Checking and renewal procedures for the coupling bearing are in Chapter 7.
5 Ensure all the rubber dampers are correctly fitted and that the spacer is in position in the coupling bearing then fit the sprocket coupling to the rear wheel **(see illustrations)**.
6 Install the rear wheel (see Chapter 7).

17.3 Check the rubber damper segments for damage and deterioration

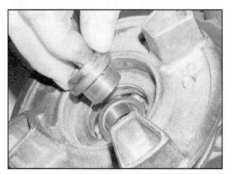

17.5a Ensure the spacer is correctly fitted to the bearing . . .

17.5b . . . before fitting the sprocket coupling to the rear wheel

Chapter 7
Brakes, wheels and tyres

Contents

Degrees of difficulty

Easy, suitable for novice with little experience	Fairly easy, suitable for beginner with some experience	Fairly difficult, suitable for competent DIY mechanic	Difficult, suitable for experienced DIY mechanic	Very difficult, suitable for expert DIY or professional

Specifications

Brakes

Brake fluid type . . . . DOT 4
Front disc thickness
  ZX-7R and ZX-9R B models
    Standard . . . . . . 4.8 to 5.2 mm
    Service limit . . . . 4.5 mm
  ZX-9R C models
    Standard . . . . . . 4.4 to 4.6 mm
    Service limit . . . . 4.0 mm
  ZX-9R E and F models
    Standard . . . . . . 4.8 to 5.1 mm
    Service limit . . . . 4.5 mm
Front disc maximum runout . . . . . . 0.3 mm
Rear disc minimum thickness
  ZX-7R and ZX-9R B models
    Standard . . . . . . 5.8 to 6.1 mm
    Service limit . . . . 5.5 mm
  ZX-9R C, E and F models
    Standard . . . . . . 4.8 to 5.1 mm
    Service limit . . . . 4.5 mm
Rear disc maximum runout . . . . . . 0.3 mm

Wheels

Maximum wheel runout (front and rear)
  Axial (side-to-side) . . . . . . 0.5 mm
  Radial (out-of-round) . . . . . . 0.8 mm
Maximum axle runout (front and rear) . . . . . . 0.2 mm

Tyres

Tyre pressures . . . . see *Daily (pre-ride)* checks
Tyre sizes
  Front 120/70 ZR17
  Rear
    ZX-7R models 190/50 ZR17
    ZX-9R B and C models . . . . . . 180/55 ZR 17 73W
    ZX-9R E and F models . . . . . . 190/50 ZR 17 73W

Torque wrench settings

Bleed valve	8 Nm
Brake hose banjo bolts	25 Nm
Front brake caliper mounting bolts	34 Nm
Front brake caliper half joining bolts	21 Nm
Front brake disc bolts	
ZX-7R and ZX-9R B and C models	23 Nm
ZX-9R E and F models	27 Nm
Front brake pad pin – ZX-9R F models	3 Nm
Front brake master cylinder	
Mounting clamp bolt	
ZX-7R models	11 Nm
ZX-9R models	9 Nm
Brake lever pivot bolt nut	6 Nm
Front wheel	
Axle	
ZX-7R and ZX-9R B models	145 Nm
ZX-9R C models	110 Nm
ZX-9R E models	125 Nm
ZX-9R F models	127 Nm
Axle clamp bolts	20 Nm
Rear brake caliper	
Mounting bolts	25 Nm
Caliper half joining bolts – ZX-7R models	29 Nm
Rear brake disc bolts	
ZX-7R and ZX-9R B and C models	23 Nm
ZX-9R E and F models	27 Nm
Rear brake master cylinder	
ZX-7R and ZX-9R B and C models	23 Nm
ZX-9R E and F models	25 Nm
Pushrod clevis locknut – all models	18 Nm
Rear wheel axle	
ZX-7R and ZX-9R B models	145 Nm
ZX-9R C models	110 Nm
ZX-9R E models	125 Nm
ZX-9R F models	127 Nm

1 General information

All models covered in this manual are fitted with cast alloy wheels designed for tubeless tyres only. Both front and rear brakes are hydraulically operated disc brakes.
Caution: Disc brake components rarely require disassembly. Do not disassemble components unless absolutely necessary. If a hydraulic brake line is loosened, the entire system must be disassembled, drained, cleaned and then properly filled and bled upon reassembly. Do not use solvents on internal brake components. Solvents will cause the seals to swell and distort. Use only clean brake fluid or denatured alcohol for cleaning. Use care when working with brake fluid as it can injure your eyes and it will damage painted surfaces and plastic parts.

2 Front brake pads – renewal

⚠ *Warning: Renew both sets of front brake pads at the same time – never renew the pads on only one*

disc, as uneven braking may result. Note that the dust created by wear of the pads may contain asbestos, which is a health hazard. Never blow it out with compressed air, and don't inhale any of it. An approved filtering mask should be worn when working on the brakes. DO NOT use petrol or petroleum-based solvents to clean brake parts; use brake cleaner or denatured alcohol only.

1 On ZX-7R and ZX-9R B, C and E models, undo the two screws and lift the pad spring off the caliper, noting which way round it fits **(see illustrations)**. Remove the R-clip from the pad retaining pin, then withdraw the pin and lift the pads out of the caliper **(see illustrations)**.

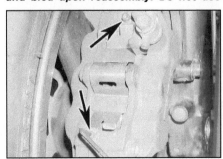

2.1a Undo the two screws (arrowed) . . .

2.1b . . . and lift the pad spring off the caliper

2.1c Remove the R-clip from the pad retaining pin

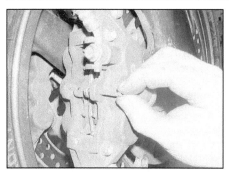

2.1d Withdraw the retaining pin . . .

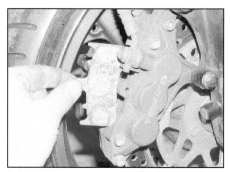

2.1e . . . and remove both brake pads from the caliper

2.2a Undo the pad pin . . .

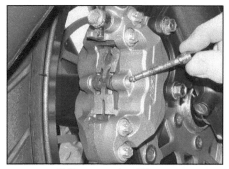

2.2b . . . and pull it out

2.2c Lift off the pad spring . . .

2.2d . . . and remove the pads from the caliper

2 On ZX-9R F models, undo the pad pin and remove it; lift off the pad spring, noting how it fits, then lift the pads out of the caliper **(see illustrations)**.

3 Inspect the surface of each pad for contamination and check that the friction material has not worn down level with or beyond the wear limit grooves or cut-outs **(see illustration)**. If either pad is worn down to, or beyond, the wear limit, is fouled with oil or grease, or heavily scored or damaged by dirt and debris, all pads must be renewed as a set. Note that it is not possible to degrease the friction material; if the pads are contaminated in any way they must be renewed.

4 Check that each pad has worn evenly at each end, and that each has the same amount of wear as the other. If uneven wear is noticed, one or more of the pistons are probably sticking in the caliper, in which case

the calipers must be overhauled (see Section 3).

5 If the pads are in good condition, clean them carefully to remove all traces of road dirt and corrosion, using a fine wire brush which is completely free of oil and grease. Using a pointed instrument, clean out the grooves in the friction material and dig out any embedded particles of foreign matter. Any areas of glazing may be removed using an emery cloth.

6 Check the condition of the brake disc (see Section 4).

7 Remove all traces of corrosion from the pad retaining pin. Inspect the pin for signs of damage and renew it if necessary.

8 If new pads are being installed, push the pistons as far back into the caliper as possible by hand or by using a piece of wood as a lever. Due to the increased friction material thickness of new pads, it may be necessary to

remove the master cylinder reservoir cover and diaphragm and extract some fluid. On early ZX-9R B models with four-piston front brake calipers, ensure all the insulators are correctly inserted in the pistons.

9 Smear the backs of the pads and the shank of the pad retaining pin with copper-based grease, making sure that none gets on the front or sides of the pads.

10 Insert each pad into the caliper, making sure its friction material is facing the brake disc **(see illustration)**.

11 On ZX-7R and ZX-9R B, C and E models, slide the pad retaining pin into position – ensure that the pin goes through the hole in both pads and that the R-clip hole is towards the outer end of the pin. Fit the R-clip in the pin between the outer pad and the caliper body. Fit the pad spring and secure it with the screws.

12 On ZX-9R F models, install the pad spring, then install the pad pin and tighten it to the specified torque.

13 If removed, slide the caliper back into position making sure the pads pass on each side of the disc, and tighten the caliper mounting bolts to the specified torque. Operate the brake lever several times to bring the pads back into contact with the disc.

14 Repeat the above procedure and renew the pads on the opposite caliper.

15 With both sets of pads renewed, operate the brake lever several times to ensure the pads are in firm contact with the discs, then check the master cylinder reservoir fluid level (see *Daily (pre-ride) checks*). Once the fluid

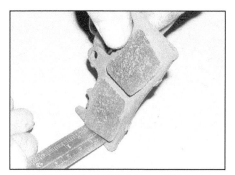

2.3 Measure the thickness of the pad friction material

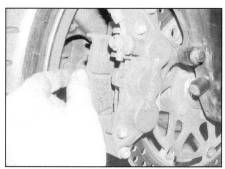

2.10 Ensure both pads are fitted with their friction material facing the brake disc

level is correct, check the operation of the brake before riding the motorcycle.

⚠️ *Warning: New pads will not give full braking efficiency until they have bedded in. Be prepared for this, and avoid hard braking as far as possible for the first few miles or so after pad renewal.*

3 Front brake calipers –
removal, overhaul and installation 🔧

⚠️ *Warning: If a caliper requires overhaul (usually indicated by leaking fluid or sticky operation), all old brake fluid should be flushed from the system. Note also that the dust created by the brake system may contain asbestos, which is harmful to your health. Never blow it out with compressed air and don't inhale any of it. An approved filtering mask should be worn when working on the brakes. Do not, under any circumstances, use petroleum-based solvents to clean brake parts. Use clean brake fluid, brake cleaner or denatured alcohol only.*

Removal

1 Remove the brake pads from the caliper (see Section 2).
2 If the caliper is to be overhauled, loosen the four bolts securing the caliper body halves together. **Note:** On ZX-9R F models, a Torx socket will be required to undo the caliper body bolts.

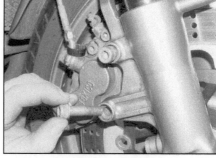

3.4 Unscrew the mounting bolts and slide the brake caliper off the disc

3 Note the correct fitted locations of the brake hose end fitting, then unscrew the banjo bolt and separate the hose from the caliper. Plug the hose end or wrap a plastic bag tightly around the hose to minimise fluid loss and prevent dirt from entering the system. Discard the sealing washers, as new ones must be used on installation. **Note:** *If you are planning to overhaul the caliper and don't have a source of compressed air to blow out the pistons, just loosen the banjo bolt at this stage and retighten it lightly. The bike's hydraulic system can then be used to force the pistons out of the body once the caliper has been freed from the fork tube. Disconnect the hose when the pistons have been sufficiently displaced.*
4 Slacken and remove the caliper mounting bolts, then remove the assembly from the fork tube **(see illustration)**.

Overhaul

5 Clean the exterior of the caliper with denatured alcohol or brake system cleaner **(see illustrations)**.
6 Unscrew the four bolts and separate the inner and outer halves of the caliper body **(see illustration)**. Recover the two O-rings which are fitted to the brake fluid passages and discard them; new ones should be used on reassembly.
7 Overhaul each half of the caliper body separately to avoid interchanging any of the components. Before removing the pistons from their bores, make identification markings to ensure each one is reinstalled in its original bore. On early ZX-9R B models with four-piston front brake calipers, take care not to lose the insulator from each piston.
8 Withdraw the partially ejected pistons from the caliper body **(see illustration)**. **Note:** *On six-piston calipers, the lower pistons differ from the centre and upper pistons.*

HAYNES HiNT *If the pistons cannot be withdrawn by hand, they can be pushed out using compressed air (see illustration 3.8b). Block one of the caliper half fluid passages using the old O-ring and a piece of wood then apply the air pressure to the other passage; on the outer half it will also be necessary to block the brake hose union. Only low pressure should be required, such as is generated by a foot pump.*

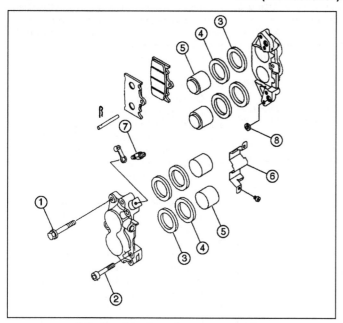

**3.5a Front brake caliper components –
four-piston caliper (ZX-9R B1/B2 shown)**

1 *Mounting bolt*	5 *Piston*
2 *Joining bolt*	6 *Pad spring*
3 *Piston seal*	7 *Bleed valve*
4 *Dust seal*	8 *O-ring*

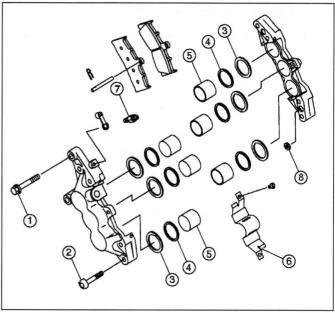

**3.5b Front brake caliper components –
six-piston caliper**

1 *Mounting bolt*	5 *Piston*
2 *Joining bolt*	6 *Pad spring*
3 *Piston seal*	7 *Bleed valve*
4 *Dust seal*	8 *O-ring*

3.6 Remove the four bolts (arrowed) and separate the inner and outer halves of the caliper

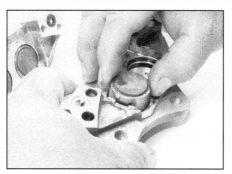

3.8a Withdraw the partially-ejected pistons from the caliper body

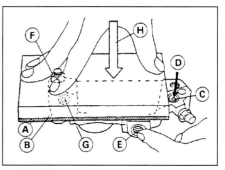

3.8b If the pistons prove stubborn to move, push them out using compressed air – see Haynes Hint

A Cloth
B Piece of wood
C Fluid passage
D Compressed air
E Banjo bolt hole
F Nut and bolt
G O-ring to seal fluid passage
H Push down firmly on wood to ensure an air-tight seal

9 Using a wooden or plastic tool, remove the dust seals from the caliper bores. Discard them, as new ones must be used on installation. If a metal tool is being used, take great care not to damage the caliper bores.
10 Remove and discard the piston seals in the same way.
11 Clean the pistons and bores with denatured alcohol, clean brake fluid or brake system cleaner. If compressed air is available, use it to dry the parts thoroughly (make sure it's filtered and unlubricated).
Caution: Do not, under any circumstances, use a petroleum-based solvent to clean brake parts.
12 Inspect the caliper bores and pistons for signs of corrosion, nicks and burrs and loss of plating. If surface defects are present, the caliper assembly must be renewed (Kawasaki do not specify any service limits for the caliper components). If the caliper is in bad shape the master cylinder should also be checked.
13 Lubricate the new piston seals with clean brake fluid and install them in their grooves in the caliper bores **(see illustration)**.

⚠ *Warning: On six-piston calipers ensure all seals are fitted only to their relevant caliper bore; the lower seals differ from those fitted to the centre and upper bores. As a precaution, when you purchase the seals have the dealer mark each one with its correct fitted location. This will avoid confusion on reassembly; the seals are only marginally different, but failure to install them*

correctly could lead to faulty operation/brake failure.
14 Lubricate the new dust seals with clean brake fluid and install them in their grooves in the caliper bores.
15 Lubricate the pistons with clean brake fluid and install them closed-end first into their original caliper bores. Using your thumbs, push the pistons all the way in, making sure they enter the bore squarely. On early ZX-9R B models with four-piston front brake calipers, ensure the insulators are correctly inserted in the pistons.
16 Once both halves have been overhauled and all the pistons are correctly fitted, ensure the mating surfaces are clean and dry, then fit a new O-ring to each of the caliper fluid passages.
17 Assemble both halves of the caliper, ensuring the O-rings remain correctly positioned, and fit the four bolts, tightening them to the specified torque. **Note:** *The caliper bolts can be tightened to the specified torque setting at this stage if the caliper can be held firmly enough, but do not risk damaging it. A better method is to tighten the bolts when the caliper has been reinstalled and is securely bolted to the fork tube.*

Installation

18 Locate the caliper assembly on the fork slider and fit the mounting bolts, tightening them to the specified torque **(see illustration)**.
19 Position a new sealing washer on each side of the brake hose union and screw in the banjo bolt. Ensure the end fitting is correctly positioned then tighten the banjo bolt to the specified torque.

20 Install the brake pads as described in Section 2.
21 Bleed the front brake as described in Section 11.
22 Check that there are no fluid leaks and thoroughly test the operation of the brake before riding the motorcycle.

4 Front brake discs – inspection, removal and installation

Inspection

1 Visually inspect the surface of the disc for score marks and other damage. Light scratches are normal after use and won't affect brake operation, but deep grooves and heavy score marks will reduce braking efficiency and accelerate pad wear. If a disc is badly grooved it must be machined or renewed.
2 To check disc runout, position the bike on an auxiliary stand so that the wheel is raised off the ground. Mount a dial gauge on a fork leg, with the plunger on the gauge touching the surface of the disc about 10 mm from the outer edge **(see illustration)**. Rotate the

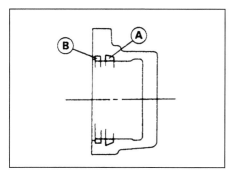

3.13 Correct piston seal (A) and dust seal (B) orientation

3.18 Ensure the pads pass on either side of the disc then tighten the caliper mounting bolts to the specified torque

4.2 Using a dial gauge to check brake disc runout

4.3a The minimum disc thickness is stamped into the disc

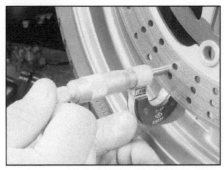

4.3b Using a micrometer to measure disc thickness

4.5 Unscrew the bolts (arrowed) and remove the disc

wheel and watch the gauge needle, comparing the reading with the limit listed in the Specifications at the beginning of the Chapter. If the runout is greater than the service limit, check the wheel bearings for play (see Chapter 1). If the bearings are worn, renew them (see Section 16) and repeat this check. If the runout is still excessive, the disc will have to be renewed, although machining by an engineer may be possible.

3 The disc must not be machined or allowed to wear down to a thickness less than the service limit listed in this Chapter's Specifications and as marked on the disc itself **(see illustration)**. The thickness of the disc can be checked with a micrometer **(see illustration)**. If the thickness of the disc is less than the service limit, it must be renewed.

Removal

4 Remove the front wheel (see Section 14).
Caution: Do not lay the wheel down and allow it to rest on either disc – this could warp the disc. Set the wheel on wood blocks so that the disc doesn't support the weight of the wheel.

5 Mark the relationship of the disc to the wheel, so it can be installed in the same position. Unscrew the disc retaining bolts, loosening them a little at a time in a criss-cross pattern to avoid distorting the disc, then remove the disc from the wheel **(see illustration)**.

6 If both discs are to be removed, note that the left and right discs are different and must not be swapped. Make identification marks on removal to avoid confusion on installation.

Installation

7 Install the disc on the wheel, making sure the marks made are on the outside and the arrow stamped on the disc is pointing in the direction of normal rotation. If the original disc is being installed, align the previously applied matchmarks.

8 Fit the disc retaining bolts and tighten them in a criss-cross pattern evenly and progressively to the specified torque.

9 Clean all grease off the brake disc(s) using acetone or brake system cleaner. If a new brake disc has been installed, remove any protective coating from its working surfaces.

10 Install the wheel (see Section 14).

11 Operate the brake lever several times to

bring the pads into contact with the disc. Check the operation of the brake carefully before riding the bike.

---

5 Front brake master cylinder – removal, overhaul and installation

1 If the master cylinder is leaking fluid, or if the lever does not produce a firm feel when the brake is applied, and bleeding the brakes does not help (see Section 11), and the hydraulic hoses are all in good condition, then master cylinder overhaul is recommended.

2 Before disassembling the master cylinder, read through the entire procedure and make sure that you obtain all parts required. You will also need some new brake fluid, some clean rags and internal circlip pliers. **Note:** *To prevent damage to the paint from spilled brake fluid, always cover the surrounding components when working on the master cylinder.*
Caution: Disassembly, overhaul and reassembly of the brake master cylinder must be done in a spotlessly clean work area to avoid contamination and possible failure of the brake hydraulic system components.

Removal

3 Disconnect the wiring connector(s) from the

brake light switch on the base of the master cylinder.

4 Note the correct fitted locations of the brake hose end fitting, then unscrew the banjo bolt and separate the hose from the master cylinder. Plug the hose end or wrap a plastic bag tightly around it to minimise fluid loss and prevent dirt entering the system. Discard the sealing washers, as new ones must be used on installation.

5 On ZX-9R B models, unscrew the mounting clamp bolts and remove the master cylinder from the handlebar. Remove the reservoir cover retaining screws and lift off the cover, the diaphragm plate and the rubber diaphragm and empty the reservoir contents into a suitable container.

6 On ZX-7R and ZX-9R C, E and F models, unscrew the bolts and remove the master cylinder mounting clamp, then undo the fluid reservoir mounting bolt and remove the master cylinder and reservoir assembly from the bike. Unscrew the reservoir cap then lift out the diaphragm plate and the rubber diaphragm and empty the reservoir contents into a suitable container.

Overhaul

7 Undo the screw and remove the brake light switch from the base of the master cylinder **(see illustrations)**.

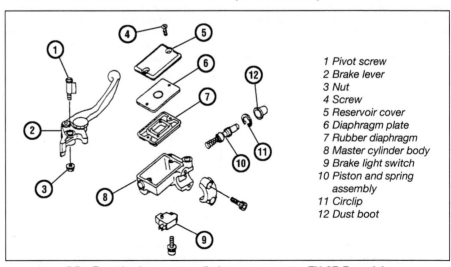

1 Pivot screw
2 Brake lever
3 Nut
4 Screw
5 Reservoir cover
6 Diaphragm plate
7 Rubber diaphragm
8 Master cylinder body
9 Brake light switch
10 Piston and spring assembly
11 Circlip
12 Dust boot

5.7a Front brake master cylinder components – ZX-9R B models

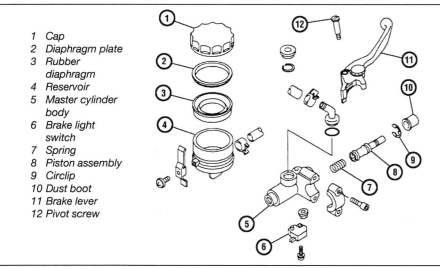

1 Cap
2 Diaphragm plate
3 Rubber diaphragm
4 Reservoir
5 Master cylinder body
6 Brake light switch
7 Spring
8 Piston assembly
9 Circlip
10 Dust boot
11 Brake lever
12 Pivot screw

5.7b Front brake master cylinder components –
ZX-9R C model (ZX-7R and ZX-9R E and F similar)

5.9 Remove the rubber dust boot . . .

8 Unscrew the nut from the brake lever pivot screw, then remove the screw and lever from the master cylinder.
9 Carefully remove the dust boot from the end of the piston **(see illustration)**.
10 Using circlip pliers, remove the circlip and slide out the piston assembly and spring, noting how they fit **(see illustration)**. Lay the parts out in the correct fitted order to prevent confusion during reassembly **(see illustration)**.
11 On ZX-7R and ZX-9R C, E and F models ease the dust cap out from the master cylinder fluid reservoir union port. Remove the circlip, then separate the reservoir union and master cylinder and recover the O-ring.
12 Clean all parts with clean brake fluid or denatured alcohol. If compressed air is available, use it to dry the parts thoroughly (make sure it's filtered and unlubricated).
Caution: Do not, under any circumstances, use a petroleum-based solvent to clean brake parts.
13 Check the master cylinder bore for corrosion, scratches, nicks and score marks. If damage or wear is evident, the master cylinder must be renewed. If the master cylinder is in poor condition, then the brake calipers should be checked as well. Check that the fluid inlet and outlet ports in the master cylinder are clear. Inspect the reservoir cover rubber diaphragm and renew it if it is damaged or has deteriorated.
14 The piston assembly and spring are supplied together as an assembly, all other components can be ordered individually **(see illustration)**. Renew all rubber components regardless of their apparent condition.
15 Insert the new spring into the master cylinder, ensuring its tapered end is facing towards the piston.
16 Lubricate the new piston and seal assembly with clean brake fluid and apply a smear of silicone grease to the seal lips.

Ensure the assembly is the correct way round, then carefully ease it into the master cylinder, making sure the seal lips do not turn inside out as they slip into the bore. Depress the piston and install the circlip, making sure that it locates in the master cylinder groove.
17 Lubricate the new rubber dust boot with a smear of silicone grease, then fit it to the piston. Ensure the inner lip of the boot is correctly located in the piston groove and the outer lip in the master cylinder bore.
18 Fit the lever and install the pivot screw. Securely tighten the pivot screw, then fit the nut and tighten to the specified torque.
19 Fit the brake light switch to the master

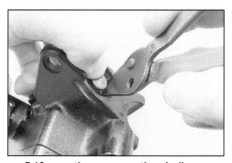

5.10a . . . then remove the circlip . . .

5.14 Renew the piston spring assembly if there is any doubt about its condition

cylinder and securely tighten its retaining screw.
20 On ZX-7R and ZX-9R C, E and F models, fit the new O-ring to the master cylinder and seat the reservoir fluid union in position. Secure the union in position with the circlip then slide the dust cap into position.

Installation

21 On ZX-7R models, locate the master cylinder on the handlebar and fit the mounting clamp with its arrow mark facing upwards. Align the master cylinder mounting clamp upper split with the punch mark on the top of the handlebar, then tighten the mounting clamp upper bolt to the specified torque followed by the lower bolt. Fit the fluid reservoir to its mounting bracket and securely tighten its retaining bolt.
22 On ZX-9R B models, locate the master cylinder on the handlebar and fit the mounting clamp with its arrow mark facing upwards **(see illustration)**. Position the master cylinder so that its clamp upper split is aligned with the

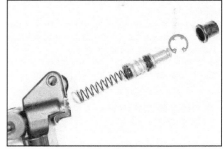

5.10b . . . and extract the piston assembly and spring from the master cylinder

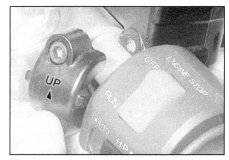

5.22 Ensure the master cylinder clamp is fitted with its arrow mark facing upwards

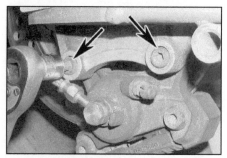

6.1 On ZX-7R models, unscrew the mounting bolts and slide the caliper off the disc . . .

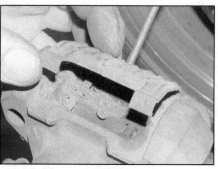

6.2 . . . then unclip the plastic cover from the caliper

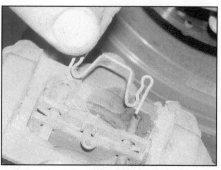

6.3 Remove the retaining pin clip from the pins

handlebar switch split, then tighten the mounting clamp upper bolt to the specified torque followed by the lower bolt.

23 On ZX-9R C, E and F models, locate the master cylinder on the handlebar and fit the mounting clamp with its arrow mark facing upwards. Align the master cylinder mounting clamp upper split with the throttle grip housing split, then tighten the mounting clamp upper bolt to the specified torque followed by the lower bolt. Fit the fluid reservoir to its mounting bracket and securely tighten its retaining bolt.

24 On all models, position a new sealing washer on each side of the brake hose end fitting, then connect the hose to the master cylinder. Ensure the hose end fitting is correctly positioned, then tighten the banjo bolt to the specified torque.

25 Connect the wiring connector(s) to the brake light switch wiring.

26 Fill the fluid reservoir with specified fluid (see *Daily (pre-ride) checks*), then bleed the air from the front brake as described in Section 11.

27 Ensure the fluid level is correct then fit the reservoir rubber diaphragm, diaphragm plate and cap/cover (as applicable).

28 Thoroughly check the operation of the front brake before riding the motorcycle.

6 Rear brake pads – renewal

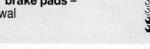

⚠️ **Warning: The dust created by the brake system may contain asbestos, which is harmful to your health. Never blow it out with compressed air and don't inhale any of it. An approved filtering mask should be worn when working on the brakes.**

ZX-7R models

1 Unscrew the caliper mounting bolts and slide the caliper off the disc **(see illustration)**.

2 Carefully unclip the plastic cover from the caliper to gain access to the pads **(see illustration)**. Note the correct fitted locations of the pad retaining pin clip and pad anti-rattle springs before proceeding.

3 Remove the pad retaining pin clip, then slide one of the retaining pins out of position **(see illustration)**. Remove the anti-rattle springs, then slide out the second retaining pin and withdraw the brake pads from the caliper. Take care not to lose the insulators from the caliper pistons.

4 Inspect the surface of each pad for contamination and check that the friction material has not worn down level with or beyond the wear limit grooves in the pad edge. If either pad is worn down to, or beyond, the wear limit, is fouled with oil or grease, or heavily scored or damaged by dirt and debris, both pads must be renewed as a set. Note that it is not possible to degrease the friction material; if the pads are contaminated in any way they must be renewed. Also check that each pad has worn evenly at each end, and that each has the same amount of wear as the other. If uneven wear is noticed, one or more of the pistons are probably sticking in the caliper, in which case the caliper must be overhauled (see Section 7).

5 If the pads are in good condition, clean them carefully to remove all traces of road dirt and corrosion using a fine wire brush which is completely free of oil and grease. Using a pointed instrument, clean out the grooves in the friction material and dig out any embedded particles of foreign matter. Any areas of glazing may be removed using emery cloth.

6 Check the condition of the brake disc (see Section 8).

7 Remove all traces of corrosion from the pad retaining pins. Inspect each pin for signs of damage and renew it if necessary.

8 If new pads are being installed, push the pistons as far back into the caliper as possible by hand or by using a piece of wood as a lever. Due to the increased friction material thickness of new pads, it may be necessary to remove the master cylinder reservoir cover and diaphragm and to extract some fluid.

9 Smear the backs of the pads and the shank of each pad retaining pin with copper-based grease, making sure that none gets on the front or sides of the pads.

10 Ensure the insulators are fitted to the pistons, then insert each pad into the caliper making sure that its friction material is facing the brake disc. Ensuring that its retaining clip hole is towards the outer end of the pin, slide one of the pad retaining pins into position and through the hole in each pad.

11 Fit an anti-rattle spring to each pad, ensuring the spring ends are correctly located under the installed pad retaining pin and each spring is hooked correctly over the pad backing plate (both anti-rattle springs must be in between the pads so they are facing towards each other) **(see illustration)**.

12 Locate the second pad retaining pin in the caliper body, ensuring its retaining clip hole is outermost. Slide the pin fully into position whilst depressing the anti-rattle springs; the pin must go through both pad holes and over the top of both spring ends **(see illustration)**.

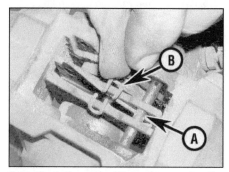

6.11 Hook the anti-rattle springs under the installed pin (A) and over the pad backing plate (B) . . .

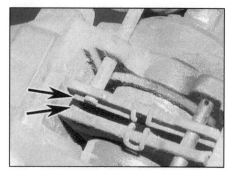

6.12 . . . then install the second retaining pin ensuring it passes through the pad holes and over the anti-rattle springs (arrowed)

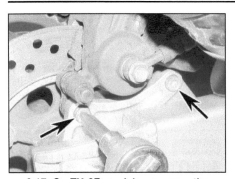

6.17 On ZX-9R models, unscrew the mounting bolts (arrowed) and slide the brake caliper off the disc

6.18a Remove the R-clip . . .

6.18b . . . then slide out the retaining pin . . .

13 Ensure the pads and anti-rattle springs are correctly fitted, then secure the retaining pins in position with the retaining clip. Ensure the clip is securely located in both retaining pin holes, then clip the plastic cover back onto the caliper.
14 Slide the caliper back into position, making sure the pads pass on each side of the disc, and tighten the caliper mounting bolts to the specified torque.
15 Operate the brake pedal several times to bring the pads into firm contact with the disc.
16 Check the master cylinder reservoir fluid level (see *Daily (pre-ride) checks*) and check the operation of the brake before riding the motorcycle.

 New pads will not give full braking efficiency until they have bedded in. Be prepared for this, and avoid hard braking as far as possible for the first few miles or so after pad renewal.

ZX-9R models

17 Unscrew the caliper mounting bolts and slide the caliper off the disc (see illustration).
18 Remove the R-clip, then slide the pad retaining pin out of position and withdraw the brake pads from the caliper (see illustrations). Remove the pad anti-rattle spring from the caliper body and the pad retainer from the mounting bracket. Take care not to lose the insulator from the caliper piston.

19 Inspect the surface of each pad for contamination and check that the friction material has not worn down level with or beyond the wear limit grooves in the pad edge. If either pad is worn down to, or beyond, the wear limit, is fouled with oil or grease, or heavily scored or damaged by dirt and debris, both pads must be renewed as a set. Note that it is not possible to degrease the friction material; if the pads are contaminated in any way they must be renewed. Also check that each pad has worn evenly at each end, and that each has the same amount of wear as the other. If uneven wear is noticed, the caliper is probably sticking on the mounting bracket – in which case the caliper must be overhauled (see Section 7).
20 If the pads are in good condition, clean them carefully to remove all traces of road dirt and corrosion using a fine wire brush which is completely free of oil and grease. Using a pointed instrument, clean out the grooves in the friction material and dig out any embedded particles of foreign matter. Any areas of glazing may be removed using emery cloth.
21 Check the condition of the brake disc (see Section 8).
22 Remove all traces of corrosion from the pad retaining pin. Inspect the pin for signs of damage and renew it if necessary. Renew the anti-rattle spring if it shows signs of damage.
23 If new pads are being installed, push the piston as far back into the caliper as possible

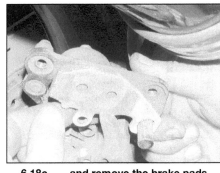

6.18c . . . and remove the brake pads

by hand or by using a piece of wood as a lever. Due to the increased friction material thickness of new pads, it may be necessary to remove the master cylinder reservoir cover and diaphragm and to extract some fluid.
24 Smear the backs of the pads and the shank of each pad retaining pin with copper-based grease, making sure that none gets on the front or sides of the pads.
25 Ensure the insulator is correctly fitted to the piston, then clip the anti-rattle spring into the caliper body (see illustrations).
26 Ensure the pad retainer is correctly fitted to the mounting bracket, then fit the outer pad with its friction material facing away from the piston (towards the disc) (see illustration). Ensure the pad and retainer are correctly located in the mounting bracket.

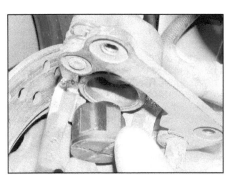

6.25a Ensure the insulator is in position in the piston . . .

6.25b . . . and the anti-rattle spring (arrowed) is clipped securely onto the caliper body

6.26 Ensure the pad retainer (arrowed) is correctly fitted then install the outer pad

27 Locate the inner pad on the mounting bracket pin and seat it correctly in the caliper, ensuring its friction material is facing towards the piston.

28 Slide the pad retaining pin into position, ensuring its R-clip hole is towards the outer end of the pin, and through the hole in each pad. Secure the retaining pin in position with the R-clip, ensuring the clip is positioned between the inner pad and the caliper body.

29 Slide the caliper onto the disc, ensuring the pads pass on each side of the disc, then tighten the mounting bolts to the specified torque **(see illustration)**.

30 Operate the brake pedal several times to bring the pads into firm contact with the disc.

31 Check the master cylinder reservoir fluid level (see *Daily (pre-ride) checks*) and check the operation of the brake before riding the motorcycle.

> **HAYNES HiNT** *New pads will not give full braking efficiency until they have bedded in. Be prepared for this, and avoid hard braking as far as possible for the first few miles or so after pad renewal.*

7 Rear brake caliper – removal, overhaul and installation

> ⚠ **Warning: If a caliper requires overhaul (usually indicated by leaking fluid or sticky operation), all old brake fluid should be flushed from the system. Note that the dust created by the brake system may contain asbestos, which is harmful to your health. Never blow it out with compressed air and don't inhale any of it. An approved filtering mask should be worn when working on the brakes. Do not, under any circumstances, use petroleum-based solvents to clean brake parts. Use clean brake fluid, brake cleaner or denatured alcohol only.**

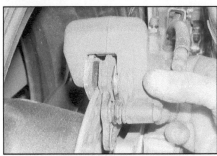

6.29 Slide the caliper into position ensuring the pads pass on either side of the disc

Removal

1 Note the correct fitted locations of the brake hose end fitting, then unscrew the banjo bolt and separate the hose from the caliper. Plug the hose end or wrap a plastic bag tightly around the hose to minimise fluid loss and prevent dirt entering the system. Discard the sealing washers, as new ones must be used on installation. **Note:** *If you are planning to overhaul the caliper and don't have a source of compressed air to blow out the pistons, just loosen the banjo bolt at this stage and retighten it lightly. The bike's hydraulic system can then be used to force the pistons out of the body once the caliper has been removed from the disc. Disconnect the hose once the pistons have been sufficiently displaced.*

2 On ZX-7R models, if the caliper is to be overhauled loosen the two bolts securing the caliper body halves together.

3 Slacken and remove the caliper mounting bolts, then remove the assembly from the disc.

4 If necessary, remove the brake pads as described in Section 6.

Overhaul

ZX-7R models

5 Clean the exterior of the caliper with denatured alcohol or brake system cleaner **(see illustration)**.

6 Unscrew the two bolts and separate the

inner and outer halves of the caliper body. Recover the O-ring which is fitted to the brake fluid passage and discard it; a new one should be used on reassembly.

7 Overhaul each half of the caliper body separately to avoid interchanging any of the components.

8 Withdraw the partially ejected piston from the caliper body.

> **HAYNES HiNT** *If the piston cannot be withdrawn by hand, it can be pushed out using compressed air. Block the caliper half fluid passages using the old O-ring and a piece of wood, then apply the air pressure to the banjo bolt hole (outer half) or the bleed nipple hole (inner half). Only low pressure should be required, such as is generated by a foot pump.*

9 Using a wooden or plastic tool, remove the dust seal from the caliper bore. Discard the seal, as a new one must be used on installation. If a metal tool is being used, take great care not to damage the caliper bores.

10 Remove and discard the piston seal in the same way.

11 Clean the piston and bore with denatured alcohol, clean brake fluid or brake system cleaner. If compressed air is available, use it to dry the parts thoroughly (make sure it's filtered and unlubricated).

Caution: Do not, under any circumstances, use a petroleum-based solvent to clean brake parts.

12 Inspect the caliper bore and piston for signs of corrosion, nicks and burrs and loss of plating. If surface defects are present, the caliper assembly must be renewed (Kawasaki do not specify any service limits for the caliper components). If the caliper is in bad shape the master cylinder should also be checked.

13 Lubricate the new piston seal with clean brake fluid and install it in its groove in the caliper bore **(see illustration 3.13)**.

14 Lubricate the new dust seal with clean brake fluid and install it in its groove in the caliper bore.

15 Lubricate the piston with clean brake fluid and install it closed-end first into the caliper bore. Using your thumbs, push the piston all the way in, making sure it enters the bore squarely.

16 Once both halves have been overhauled and both pistons are correctly fitted, ensure the mating surfaces are clean and dry, then fit a new O-ring to the caliper fluid passage.

17 Assemble both halves of the caliper, ensuring the O-ring remains correctly positioned, and fit the two bolts, tightening them to the specified torque. **Note:** *The caliper bolts can be tightened to the specified torque setting at this stage if the caliper can be held firmly enough, but do not risk damaging it. A better method is to tighten the bolts when the caliper has been reinstalled and is securely bolted to the fork tube.*

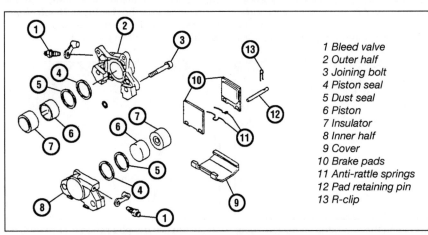

1 Bleed valve
2 Outer half
3 Joining bolt
4 Piston seal
5 Dust seal
6 Piston
7 Insulator
8 Inner half
9 Cover
10 Brake pads
11 Anti-rattle springs
12 Pad retaining pin
13 R-clip

7.5 Rear brake caliper components – ZX-7R models

ZX-9R models

18 Clean the exterior of the caliper with denatured alcohol or brake system cleaner, then separate the caliper and mounting bracket **(see illustrations)**.

19 Withdraw the partially ejected piston from the caliper body.

HAYNES HiNT *If the piston cannot be withdrawn by hand, it can be pushed out using compressed air applied to the banjo bolt hole. Only low pressure should be required, such as is generated by a foot pump. Wrap the caliper in rag to prevent the piston being forcibly expelled.*

20 Using a wooden or plastic tool, remove the dust seal from the caliper bore. Discard the seal, as a new one must be used on installation. If a metal tool is being used, take great care not to damage the caliper bores.

21 Remove and discard the piston seal in the same way.

22 Clean the piston and bore with denatured alcohol, clean brake fluid or brake system cleaner. If compressed air is available, use it to dry the parts thoroughly (make sure it's filtered and unlubricated).

Caution: Do not, under any circumstances, use a petroleum-based solvent to clean brake parts.

23 Inspect the caliper bore and piston for signs of corrosion, nicks and burrs and loss of plating. If surface defects are present, the caliper assembly must be renewed (Kawasaki

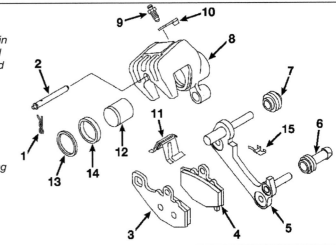

1 R-clip
2 Pad retaining pin
3 Inner brake pad
4 Outer brake pad
5 Mounting bracket
6 Dust boot
7 Dust boot
8 Caliper body
9 Bleed valve
10 Dust cap
11 Anti-rattle spring
12 Piston
13 Dust seal
14 Piston seal
15 Pad retainer

7.18a Rear brake caliper components – ZX-9R models

do not specify any service limits for the caliper components). If the caliper is in bad shape the master cylinder should also be checked.

24 Inspect the mounting bracket pins for signs of wear or damage and renew the bracket if worn. Renew the bracket pin dust boots regardless of their apparent condition **(see illustration)**.

25 Lubricate the new piston seal with clean brake fluid and install it in its groove in the caliper bore **(see illustration 3.13)**.

26 Lubricate the new dust seal with clean brake fluid and install it in its groove in the caliper bore.

27 Lubricate the piston with clean brake fluid and install it closed-end first into the caliper

bore. Using your thumbs, push the piston all the way in, making sure it enters the bore squarely **(see illustration)**.

28 Ensure both the dust boots are correctly fitted to the caliper body then lubricate the mounting bracket pins with silicone grease **(see illustration)**. Slide the mounting bracket into the caliper making sure the dust boots are both correctly seated on the bracket.

Installation

29 Install the brake pads (where removed) as described in Section 6.

30 Slide the caliper into position, ensuring the pads pass on either side of the disc, and tighten the mounting bolts to the specified torque.

31 Position a new sealing washer on each side of the hose union and screw in the banjo bolt. Ensure the hose end fitting is correctly positioned then tighten the banjo bolt to the specified torque.

32 Bleed the rear brake as described in Section 11.

33 Check that there are no fluid leaks and thoroughly test the operation of the brake before riding the motorcycle.

8 Rear brake disc – inspection, removal and installation

Inspection

1 Visually inspect the surface of the disc for score marks and other damage. Light scratches are normal after use and won't affect brake operation, but deep grooves and heavy score marks will reduce braking efficiency and accelerate pad wear. If a disc is badly grooved it must be machined or renewed.

2 To check disc runout, position the bike on an auxiliary stand so that the wheel is raised off the ground. Mount a dial gauge on the swingarm, with the plunger on the gauge touching the surface of the disc about 10 mm

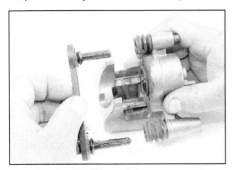

7.18b On ZX-9R models, separate the caliper and mounting bracket

7.24 Fit new dust boots to the caliper assembly

7.27 Push the piston squarely into the caliper bore

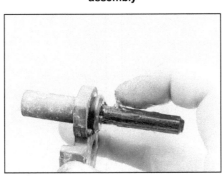

7.28 Lubricate the mounting bracket pins with silicone grease

from the outer edge. Rotate the wheel and watch the gauge needle, comparing the reading with the limit listed in the Specifications at the beginning of the Chapter. If the runout is greater than the service limit, check the wheel bearings for play (see Chapter 1). If the bearings are worn, renew them (see Section 16) and repeat this check. If the runout is still excessive, the disc will have to be renewed, although machining by an engineer may be possible.

3 The disc must not be machined or allowed to wear down to a thickness less than the service limit listed in this Chapter's Specifications and as marked on the disc itself. The thickness of the disc can be checked with a micrometer **(see illustration)**. If the thickness of the disc is less than the service limit, it must be renewed.

Removal

4 Remove the rear wheel (see Section 15).

5 Mark the relationship of the disc to the wheel, so it can be installed in the same position. Unscrew the disc retaining bolts, loosening them a little at a time in a criss-cross pattern to avoid distorting the disc, then remove the disc from the wheel **(see illustration)**.

Installation

6 Install the disc on the wheel, making sure the marked side is on the outside and the arrow stamped on the disc is pointing in the direction of normal rotation. If the original disc is being installed, align the previously applied matchmarks.

7 On ZX-9R C, E and F models, remove all traces of locking compound from the disc retaining bolt threads and apply a drop of fresh locking compound to each bolt.

8 On all models, fit the disc retaining bolts and tighten them in a criss-cross pattern evenly and progressively to the specified torque.

9 Clean all grease off the brake disc using acetone or brake system cleaner. If a new brake disc has been installed, remove any protective coating from its working surfaces.

10 Install the wheel (see Section 15).

11 Operate the brake pedal several times to bring the pads into contact with the disc. Check the operation of the brake carefully before riding the bike.

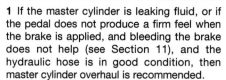

9 Rear brake master cylinder – removal, overhaul and installation

1 If the master cylinder is leaking fluid, or if the pedal does not produce a firm feel when the brake is applied, and bleeding the brake does not help (see Section 11), and the hydraulic hose is in good condition, then master cylinder overhaul is recommended.

2 Before disassembling the master cylinder, read through the entire procedure and make sure that you obtain all parts required. You will also need some new brake fluid, some clean rags and internal circlip pliers. **Note:** *To prevent damage to the paint from spilled brake fluid, always cover the surrounding components when working on the master cylinder.*

Caution: Disassembly, overhaul and reassembly of the brake master cylinder must be done in a spotlessly clean work area to avoid contamination and possible failure of the brake hydraulic system components.

Removal

3 Note the correct fitted location of the brake hose end fitting, then unscrew the banjo bolt and separate the hose from the top of the master cylinder. Plug the hose end fitting or wrap a plastic bag tightly around the hose to minimise fluid loss and prevent dirt entering the system. Discard the sealing washers, as new ones must be used on installation.

4 Loosen the master cylinder mounting bolts, then unscrew the bolts securing the footrest bracket assembly to the frame.

5 Release the retaining clip and disconnect the brake fluid reservoir hose from its union on the master cylinder body. Allow the fluid reservoir contents to drain into a container.

6 Remove the split pin from the clevis pin securing the brake pedal to the master cylinder pushrod and withdraw the clevis pin. Discard the split pin, as a new one must be used.

7 Unscrew the retaining bolts and remove the master cylinder and heel plate from the footrest bracket.

Overhaul

8 Remove the circlip, then separate the fluid reservoir union and master cylinder and recover the O-ring **(see illustration)**.

9 Dislodge the rubber dust boot from the base of the master cylinder to reveal the pushrod retaining circlip.

10 Depress the pushrod and, using circlip pliers, remove the circlip. Withdraw the pushrod assembly from the master cylinder then, noting each component's correct fitted location, remove the piston assembly and spring. If they are difficult to remove, apply low pressure compressed air to the fluid outlet. Lay the parts out in the correct fitted order to prevent confusion during reassembly.

11 Clean all parts with clean brake fluid or denatured alcohol.

Caution: Do not, under any circumstances, use a petroleum-based solvent to clean brake parts. If compressed air is available, use it to dry the parts thoroughly (make sure it's filtered and unlubricated).

12 Check the master cylinder bore for corrosion, scratches, nicks and score marks. If damage or wear is evident, the master cylinder must be renewed. If the master cylinder is in poor condition, then the brake caliper should be checked as well. Check that the fluid inlet and outlet ports in the master

8.3 Using a micrometer to measure brake disc thickness

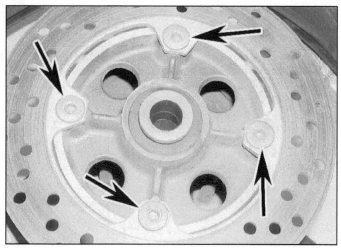

8.5 Unscrew the mounting bolts (arrowed) and remove the rear brake disc

cylinder are clear. Inspect the fluid reservoir, rubber diaphragm cover and its joining hose for cracks or splits and renew it if necessary. Renew the pushrod assembly if the dust boot is damaged.

13 The piston assembly and spring are supplied together as an assembly, all other components can be ordered individually. Renew all rubber components regardless of their apparent condition.

14 Insert the new spring into the master cylinder, ensuring its tapered end is facing towards the piston.

15 Lubricate the new piston and seal assembly with clean brake fluid and apply a smear of silicone grease to the seal lips. Ensure the assembly is the correct way round, then carefully ease it into the master cylinder, making sure the seal lips do not turn inside out as they slip into the bore.

16 Insert the pushrod assembly and secure it in position with the circlip. Ensure the circlip is correctly located in the master cylinder groove, then seat the dust boot back in the cylinder bore.

17 Fit a new O-ring and install the fluid reservoir union in the master cylinder body. Secure the union in position with the circlip making sure it is correctly located in its groove.

18 Check that the master cylinder pushrod length is correctly set (the length of the pushrod affects the height of the brake pedal). Kawasaki recommend that the distance between the centres of the master cylinder lower mounting bolt hole and the clevis pin hole should be 67 ± 1 mm on ZX-7R and ZX-9R B, C and E models, and 73 ± 1 mm on ZX-9R F models. However, the pedal height can be altered to suit individual tastes. This is best done after the assembly is installed – by slackening the clevis locknut, then turning the pushrod itself, using a spanner on the flats on the top of the rod, until the desired pedal height is obtained. Tighten the clevis locknut to the specified torque on completion.

Installation

19 Locate the master cylinder and heel plate on the bracket and fit its mounting bolts. Align the pushrod with the pedal, then fit the clevis pin and secure it in position with a new split pin.

20 Reconnect the fluid reservoir hose to the master cylinder union and secure it in position with the retaining clip.

21 Locate the footrest bracket on the frame and securely tighten its mounting bolts.

22 Tighten the master cylinder mounting bolts to the specified torque.

23 Position a new sealing washer on each side of the brake hose end fitting and insert the banjo bolt. Ensure the end fitting is correctly positioned, then tighten the banjo bolt to the specified torque.

24 Fill the fluid reservoir with the specified brake fluid (see *Daily (pre-ride) checks*) and

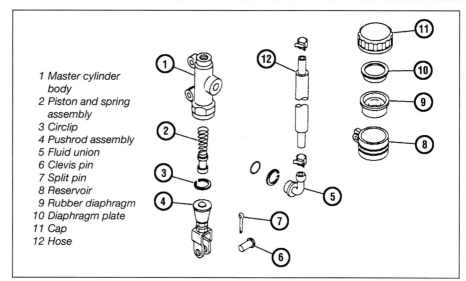

1 Master cylinder body
2 Piston and spring assembly
3 Circlip
4 Pushrod assembly
5 Fluid union
6 Clevis pin
7 Split pin
8 Reservoir
9 Rubber diaphragm
10 Diaphragm plate
11 Cap
12 Hose

9.8 Rear brake master cylinder assembly (ZX-9R C models shown, others similar)

bleed the rear brake as described in Section 11.

25 Check the operation of the brake carefully before riding the motorcycle.

10 Brake hoses and unions – inspection and renewal

Inspection

1 The brake hoses and their associated fittings should be checked regularly (see Chapter 1).

2 Twist and flex the rubber hoses while looking for cracks, bulges and seeping fluid **(see illustration)**. Check extra carefully around the areas where the hoses connect with the end fittings, as these are common areas for hose failure.

3 Inspect the banjo fittings connected to the brake hoses. If the fittings are rusted, scratched or cracked, renew them.

Renewal

4 The brake hoses are all secured in position

by banjo union fittings. Before disconnecting a hose union remove all traces of dirt, then cover the surrounding area with plenty of rags to catch all spilt fluid.

5 Note the correct positioning of the hose end fittings, then unscrew the banjo bolt from each end of the hose. Note the correct routing of the hose, then free it from its retaining clips and guides and remove it from the bike. Discard the sealing washers fitted to the hose end fittings **(see illustration)**.

6 Fit the new hose, making sure it is correctly routed and isn't twisted or otherwise strained, and secure it in position with the necessary clips and guides.

7 Position a new sealing washer on each side of the hose end fittings, then screw in the banjo bolts. Ensure each end fitting is correctly positioned either against its stop or in between the lugs (as applicable), then tighten the banjo bolts to the specified torque setting.

8 Fill the brake system with new fluid of the specified type (see *Daily (pre-ride) checks*) and bleed the air from the relevant brake (see Section 11). Check the operation of the brakes carefully before riding the motorcycle.

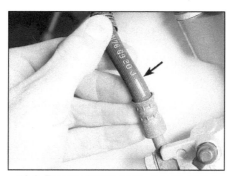

10.2 Flex the brake hose and check for signs of cracks, bulges or fluid leakage

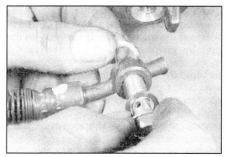

10.5 Unscrew the banjo bolt and recover the sealing washer fitted on each side of the hose union

11 Brake system bleeding

1 Bleeding the brakes is simply the process of removing all the air bubbles from the brake fluid reservoirs, the hoses and the brake calipers. Bleeding is necessary whenever a brake system hydraulic connection is loosened, when a component or hose is renewed, or when the master cylinder or caliper is overhauled. Leaks in the system may also allow air to enter, but leaking brake fluid will reveal their presence and warn you of the need for repair.

2 To bleed the brakes, you will need some new DOT 4 brake fluid, a length of clear vinyl or plastic tubing, a small container partially filled with clean brake fluid, some rags and a spanner to fit the brake caliper bleed valves.

Front brake

3 Cover the fuel tank and other painted components to prevent damage in the event that brake fluid is spilled.

4 Remove the master cylinder reservoir cap/cover (see *Daily (pre-ride) checks*) and lift out the diaphragm plate and diaphragm. Slowly pump the brake lever a few times, until no air bubbles can be seen floating up from the holes in the bottom of the reservoir; this bleeds the air from the master cylinder end of the line. Loosely refit the reservoir cap/cover.

5 Pull the dust cap off the bleed valve. Attach one end of the clear vinyl or plastic tubing to the bleed valve on one of the front calipers and submerge the other end in the brake fluid in the container.

6 Check the fluid level. Do not allow this to drop below the lower mark during the bleeding process.

7 Carefully pump the brake lever three or four times and hold it in while opening the caliper bleed valve **(see illustration)**. When the valve is opened, brake fluid will flow out of the caliper into the clear tubing and the lever will move towards the handlebar.

8 Retighten the bleed valve, then release the brake lever gradually. Repeat the process until no air bubbles are visible in the brake fluid leaving the valve, and the lever is firm when applied. Disconnect the bleeding equipment, then tighten the bleed valve to the specified torque and install the dust cap.

9 Attach the tubing to the bleed valve on the opposite caliper (see Step 5) and repeat the procedure described in Steps 6 to 8, until all air is removed from the system and the brake lever feels firm again.

10 Top the fluid level up to the upper level mark (see *Daily (pre-ride) checks*) then install the diaphragm and diaphragm plate, and securely refit the reservoir cap/cover (as applicable). Wipe up any spilled brake fluid and check the entire system for leaks. Thoroughly test the operation of the brake before riding the motorcycle.

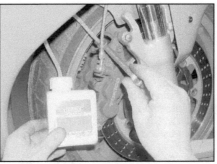

11.7 Bleeding a front brake caliper

Rear brake

11 Cover the area around the rear brake fluid reservoir to prevent damage in the event that brake fluid is spilled.

12 Remove the master cylinder reservoir cap (see *Daily (pre-ride) checks*) and lift out the diaphragm plate and diaphragm. Slowly pump the brake pedal a few times, until no air bubbles can be seen floating up from the holes in the bottom of the reservoir. This bleeds the air from the master cylinder end of the line. Loosely refit the reservoir cover.

13 Pull the dust cap off the bleed valve. Attach one end of the clear vinyl or plastic tubing to the bleed valve on the rear caliper and submerge the other end in the brake fluid in the container. On ZX-7R models start on the inner (rear) bleed valve.

14 Check the fluid level. Do not allow this to drop below the lower mark during the bleeding process.

15 Carefully pump the brake pedal three or four times and hold it down while opening the caliper bleed valve. When the valve is opened, brake fluid will flow out of the caliper into the clear tubing and the pedal will move further downwards.

16 Retighten the bleed valve, then release the brake lever gradually. Repeat the process until no air bubbles are visible in the brake fluid leaving the valve, and the lever is firm when applied. Disconnect the bleeding equipment, then tighten the bleed valve to the specified torque and install the dust cap.

17 On ZX-7R models, attach the tubing to the outer (front) bleed valve on the caliper (see

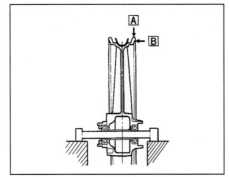

12.2 Check the wheel for radial (out-of-round) runout (A) and axial (side-to-side) runout (B)

Step 13) and repeat the procedure described in Steps 14 to 16, until all air is removed from the system and the brake lever feels firm again.

18 Top the fluid level up to the upper level mark (see *Daily (pre-ride) checks*) then install the diaphragm and diaphragm plate, and securely refit the reservoir cap. Wipe up any spilled brake fluid and check the entire system for leaks. Thoroughly test the operation of the brake before riding the motorcycle.

> **HAYNES HINT** *If it's not possible to produce a firm feel to the lever or pedal, the fluid my be aerated. Let the brake fluid in the system stabilise for a few hours and, when the tiny bubbles in the system have settled out, repeat the procedure. Failure to bleed satisfactorily, after a reasonable repetition of the procedure, may be due to worn master cylinder seals.*

12 Wheels – inspection and repair

1 In order to carry out a proper inspection of the wheels, place the bike on an auxiliary stand and support it so that the wheel being inspected is raised off the ground. Clean the wheels thoroughly to remove mud and dirt that may interfere with the inspection procedure or mask defects. Make a general check of the wheels (see Chapter 1) and tyres (see *Daily (pre-ride) checks*).

2 Attach a dial gauge to the fork tube or the swingarm and position its stem against the side of the rim. Spin the wheel slowly and check the axial (side-to-side) runout of the rim. In order to check radial (out of round) runout accurately with the dial gauge, the wheel would have to be removed from the machine, and the tyre from the wheel. With the axle clamped in a vice and the dial gauge positioned on the top of the rim, the wheel can be rotated to check the runout **(see illustration)**.

3 An easier, though slightly less accurate, method is to attach a stiff wire pointer to the fork tube or the swingarm and position the end a fraction of an inch from the wheel (where the wheel and tyre join). If the wheel is true, the distance from the pointer to the rim will be constant as the wheel is rotated. **Note:** *If wheel runout is excessive, check the wheel bearings very carefully before renewing the wheel.*

4 The wheels should also be visually inspected for cracks, flat spots on the rim and other damage. Look very closely for dents in the area where the tyre bead contacts the rim. Dents in this area may prevent complete sealing of the tyre against the rim, which leads to deflation of the tyre over a period of time. If damage is evident, or if runout in either direction is excessive, the wheel will have to be renewed. Never attempt to repair a damaged cast alloy wheel.

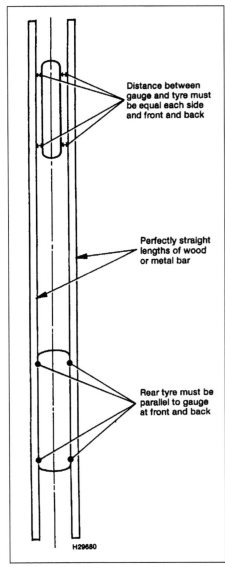

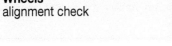

13.7 Wheel alignment check using a
straight-edge

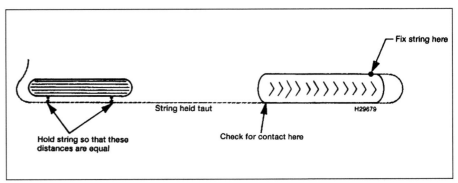

13.5 Wheel alignment check using string

13 Wheels – alignment check

1 Misalignment of the wheels, which may be due to a cocked rear wheel or a bent frame, swingarm or fork yokes can cause strange and possibly serious handling problems. If the frame, swingarm or yokes are at fault, repair by a frame specialist or renewal are the only options.
2 To check the alignment you will need an assistant and a length of string or a perfectly straight piece of wood, and a ruler. A plumb bob or other suitable weight will also be required.
3 In order to make a proper check of the wheels it is necessary to support the bike in an upright position, using an auxiliary stand. Measure the width of both tyres at their

widest points. Subtract the smaller measurement from the larger measurement, then divide the difference by two. The result is the amount of offset that should exist between the front and rear tyres on both sides.
4 If a string is used, have your assistant hold one end of it about halfway between the floor and the rear axle, touching the rear sidewall of the tyre.
5 Run the other end of the string forward and pull it tight so that it is roughly parallel to the floor. Slowly bring the string into contact with the front sidewall of the rear tyre, then turn the front wheel until it is parallel with the string (see illustration). Measure the distance from the front tyre sidewall to the string.
6 Repeat the procedure on the other side of the motorcycle. The distance from the front tyre sidewall to the string should be equal on both sides.
7 As was previously pointed out, a perfectly straight length of wood or metal bar may be substituted for the string (see illustration). The procedure is the same.
8 If the distance between the string and the tyre is greater on one side, or if the rear wheel appears to be cocked, refer to Section 2 of Chapter 1 and check that the chain adjuster markings on each side of the swingarm coincide.
9 If the front-to-back alignment is correct, the wheels still may be out of alignment vertically.
10 Using the plumb bob, or other suitable weight, and a length of string, check the rear

wheel to make sure it is vertical. To do this, hold the string against the tyre upper sidewall and allow the weight to settle just off the floor. When the string touches both the upper and lower tyre sidewalls and is perfectly straight, the wheel is vertical. If it is not, place thin spacers under one leg of the stand.
11 Once the rear wheel is vertical, check the front wheel in the same manner. If both wheels are not perfectly vertical, the frame and/or major suspension components are bent.

14 Front wheel – removal and installation

Removal

1 Slacken the right side axle clamp bolts, then loosen the axle a few turns (see illustration).
2 Position the motorcycle on an auxiliary stand and tie down the rear of the motorcycle to raise the front wheel off the ground. Alternatively, remove the lower fairing panel(s) (see Chapter 8) and support the bike under the engine to raise the front wheel.
3 On ZX-7R and ZX-9R B models, unscrew the knurled retaining ring and disconnect the speedometer cable from its drive on the left side of the front wheel (see illustration).
4 On ZX-9R B models, remove the front mudguard (see Chapter 8).

14.1 Slacken the right side axle clamp
bolts a few turns

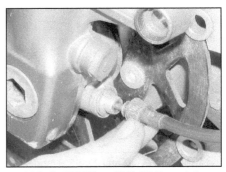

14.3 On ZX-7R and ZX-9R B models,
unscrew the retaining ring and detach the
speedometer cable from its drive

14.5 Unscrew the mounting bolts and slide both calipers off the discs and position them clear of the wheel

14.7a Withdraw the axle from the right side of the wheel . . .

14.7b . . . then manoeuvre the front wheel out of position

5 On all models, slacken and remove the mounting bolts securing the brake calipers to the fork tubes. Slide both caliper assemblies off the discs and position them clear of the wheel **(see illustration)**. Support each caliper with a piece of wire or a bungee cord so that no strain is placed on its hydraulic hose. **Note:** *There is no need to disconnect the hoses from the calipers.*
Caution: Do not operate the brake lever with the calipers removed.
6 Unscrew the axle until it is free from the axle nut.
7 Support the wheel, then withdraw the axle from the right side and carefully lower the wheel and manoeuvre it out of position **(see illustrations)**. If necessary, slacken the left side axle clamp bolts and remove the axle nut from the left fork.
8 On ZX-7R and ZX-9R B models, remove the speedometer drive from the left side of the wheel and the spacer from the right side.
9 On ZX-9R C, E and F models, remove the spacer from the left and right side of the wheel (both spacers are the same).
Caution: Don't lay the wheel down and allow it to rest on a disc – the disc could become warped. Set the wheel on wood blocks so the disc doesn't support the weight of the wheel.
10 On all models, check the axle for straightness by rolling it on a flat surface such as a piece of plate glass (first wipe off all old grease

and remove any corrosion using fine emery cloth). If the equipment is available, place the axle in V-blocks and measure the runout using a dial gauge. If the axle is bent or the runout exceeds the limit specified, renew it.
11 Refer to Section 16 if wheel bearing renewal is required.

Installation
ZX-7R and ZX-9R B models
12 Where necessary, insert the axle nut into the left fork tube. Ensure the nut is pushed fully into position, so that its flange is tight against the fork, then tighten the clamp bolts to the specified torque.
13 Apply a smear of grease to the inside of the spacer and speedometer drive and also to the dust seal lips. Fit the speedometer drive to the left side of the wheel, ensuring the drive gear dogs are correctly aligned with the cutouts in the drive collar **(see illustration)**. Fit the spacer to the right side of the wheel **(see illustration)**.
14 Manoeuvre the wheel into position, making sure the directional arrow on the wheel/tyre is pointing in the normal direction of rotation. Apply a thin coat of grease to the axle.
15 Lift the wheel into position and place the lug on the speedometer drive housing in between the stops on the left fork tube. Ensure the spacer is still correctly fitted to the right side of the wheel, then slide in the axle

from the right side. Screw the axle in, tightening it lightly only at this stage.
16 Slide the brake calipers into position, making sure the pads pass on each side of the discs, then fit the mounting bolts and tighten them to the specified torque.
17 Reconnect the speedometer cable to its drive and securely tighten its retaining ring.
18 Apply the front brake a few times to bring the pads back into contact with the discs, then remove the bike from its stand. Tighten the axle to the specified torque, then tighten the right side axle clamp bolts to the specified torque.
19 Install the lower fairing panels (see Chapter 8) and check the operation of the front brake before riding the motorcycle. On ZX-9R B models, also fit the front mudguard.

ZX-9R C, E and F models
20 Where necessary, insert the axle nut into the left fork tube. Ensure the nut is pushed fully into position, so that its flange is tight against the fork, then tighten the clamp bolts to the specified torque.
21 Apply a smear of grease to the inside of each wheel spacer and the dust seal lips, then fit the spacers to the left and right sides of the wheel (both spacers are the same) **(see illustration)**.
22 Manoeuvre the wheel into position, making sure the directional arrow on the wheel/tyre is pointing in the normal direction of rotation. Apply a thin coat of grease to the axle.

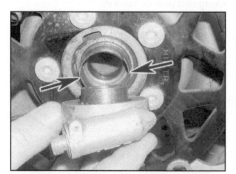

14.13a On ZX-7R and ZX-9R B models, ensure the speedometer drive dogs engage correctly with the drive collar cutouts (arrowed) . . .

14.13b . . . and fit the spacer to the right side of the wheel

14.21 On ZX-9R C and E models, fit the spacers to the left and right sides of the wheel

14.23 Manoeuvre the front wheel into position then insert the axle from the right side

23 Lift the wheel into position, making sure the spacers remain correctly fitted, then slide in the axle from the right side **(see illustration)**. Screw the axle in, tightening it lightly only at this stage.
24 Slide the brake calipers into position, making sure the pads pass on each side of the discs, then fit the mounting bolts and tighten them to the specified torque **(see illustration)**.
25 Apply the front brake a few times to bring the pads back into contact with the discs, then remove the bike from its stand. Tighten the axle to the specified torque, then tighten the right side axle clamp bolt to the specified torque.

14.24 Slide on the brake calipers, ensuring the pads pass on either side of the disc, and tighten the mounting bolts to the specified torque

26 Install the lower fairing panel (see Chapter 8) and check the operation of the front brake before riding the motorcycle.

15 Rear wheel – removal and installation

Removal

1 Remove the split pin and slacken the axle nut a few turns. On ZX-9R F models, remove the brake caliper mounting bolts, then slide

the caliper off the disc and secure it with a cable tie or string to avoid straining the brake hose **(see illustration 6.17)**.
2 Position the motorcycle on an auxiliary stand so that the rear wheel is clear of the ground.
3 Unscrew the axle nut and remove the washer and the adjuster position marker **(see illustration)**.
4 Support the wheel, then withdraw the axle from the right and lower the wheel to the ground **(see illustration)**. On ZX-7R and ZX-9R B, C and E models, retrieve the adjuster position marker from the right side of the swingarm and store it with the axle; note how the caliper bracket locates against the swingarm and support it so that it will not fall off its lug. On ZX-9R F models, note how the flats on the axle head locate against the right-hand adjuster marker and remove the marker with the axle, then withdraw the caliper bracket **(see illustrations)**.
5 Disengage the chain from the sprocket and hang it over the swingarm end. The wheel can then be manoeuvred out of position.
Caution: Do not lay the wheel down and allow it to rest on the disc or the sprocket – they could become warped. Set the wheel on wood blocks so the disc or the sprocket doesn't support the weight of the wheel. Do not operate the brake pedal with the wheel removed.

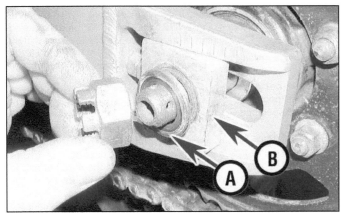

15.3 Unscrew the nut from the rear axle and remove the washer (A) and adjuster position marker (B)

15.4a Withdraw the rear axle and recover the adjuster position marker (arrowed) then lower the wheel to the ground

15.4b On ZX-9R F models, note how the flats (arrowed) align . . .

15.4c . . . then withdraw the axle with the adjuster marker

15.4d Remove the caliper bracket

15.10a On ZX-9R C, E and F models, fit the flanged spacer to the right side of the rear wheel . . .

15.10b . . . and the plain spacer to the left side

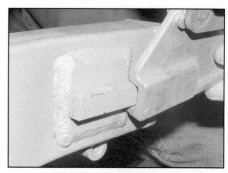

15.11 Ensure the brake caliper bracket slot is correctly engaged with the swingarm lug

6 Check the axle for straightness by rolling it on a flat surface such as a piece of plate glass (first wipe off all old grease and any corrosion with fine emery cloth). If the equipment is available, place the axle in V-blocks and check the runout using a dial gauge. If the axle is bent or the runout exceeds the limit specified at the beginning of the Chapter, replace it with a new one.

7 Remove the spacer from each side of the wheel, noting each one's correct fitted location. Check the condition of the dust seals and wheel bearings (see Section 16).

Installation

8 Apply a thin coat of grease to the lips of each dust seal, and also to the spacers and the axle. Slide the right side adjuster position marker onto the axle, making sure its marking is visible from the right side.

9 On ZX-7R and ZX-9R B models, install the shorter spacer into the left-hand side of the wheel and the longer spacer into the right-hand side.

10 On ZX-9R C, E and F models, install the flanged spacer into the right side of the wheel and the plain spacer into the left side (see illustrations).

11 On all models, manoeuvre the wheel so that it is between the ends of the swingarm and apply a thin coat of grease to the axle. Position the brake caliper bracket against the swingarm so that the lug on the swingarm fits into the slot in the bracket (see illustration).

To ease installation, lever the brake pads further apart to increase clearance for the brake disc.

12 Engage the drive chain with the sprocket and lift the wheel into position. As the wheel is lifted, ensure both spacers and caliper bracket remain in position. On the ZX-9R C and E models, make sure the brake disc passes in between the rear brake pads.

13 Insert the axle and right adjuster marker from the right side of the bike, making sure it passes through the caliper bracket. Push the axle fully into position and seat the adjuster marker correctly in the swingarm with its index marks at the top and bottom.

14 Fit the left side adjuster marker to the axle and locate it in the swingarm so that its index marks are facing outwards and are at the top and bottom. Fit the washer and screw on the axle nut, which should be tightened only lightly at this stage. On the ZX-9R F models, install the caliper on the brake disc, ensuring the disc passes in between the brake pads, then fit the caliper mounting bolts and tighten them to the specified torque.

15 Operate the brake pedal several times to bring the pads back into contact with the disc, then remove the bike from its stand.

16 Adjust the drive chain tension (see Chapter 1), then tighten the axle nut to the specified torque and secure it in position with a new split pin. Check the operation of the rear brake carefully before riding the bike.

16 Wheel bearings – renewal

Note: *Always renew the wheel bearings as a set. Never renew the bearings individually. Avoid using a high pressure cleaner on the wheel bearing area.*

Front wheel bearings

1 Remove the wheel (see Section 14).

2 Set the wheel on blocks so as not to allow the weight of the wheel to rest on either of the brake discs.

3 Using a flat-bladed screwdriver, carefully prise out the dust seal(s) from the hub. Discard the seal(s); new ones should be fitted.

4 On ZX-7R and ZX-9R B models, using circlip pliers, remove the circlips from the left and right sides of the wheel hub and lift out the speedometer drive collar from the left side of the hub (see illustrations).

5 On ZX-9R C, E and F models, using circlip pliers, remove the circlip from the right side of the hub.

6 On all models, using a metal rod (preferably a brass drift punch) inserted through the centre of the left side bearing, tap evenly around the inner race of the right bearing to drive it from the hub (see illustration). The bearing spacer will also come out.

7 Lay the wheel on its other side so that the left bearing faces down. Drive the bearing out of the wheel using the same technique as above.

16.4a On ZX-7R and ZX-9R B models, remove the circlip . . .

16.4b . . . and lift out the speedometer drive collar from the left side of the front wheel

16.6 Tap the bearing out using a hammer and metal rod inserted through the centre of the opposite bearing

16.11 Tap each bearing into position using a socket which contacts only the bearing outer race

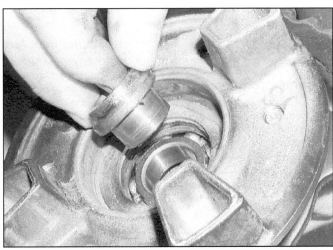

16.25a Ensure the spacer is correctly fitted to the coupling bearing . . .

8 If the bearings are of the unsealed type or are only sealed on one side, clean them with a high flash-point solvent (one which won't leave any residue) and blow them dry with compressed air (don't let the bearings spin as you dry them). Apply a few drops of oil to the bearing. **Note:** *If the bearing is sealed on both sides don't attempt to clean it.*

9 Hold the outer race of the bearing and rotate the inner race – if the bearing doesn't turn smoothly, has rough spots or is noisy, renew it.

 HAYNES HiNT *Refer to Tools and Workshop Tips (Section 5) for more information about bearings.*

10 If the bearing is good and can be re-used and isn't sealed on both sides, wash it in solvent once again and dry it, then pack the bearing with grease.

11 Thoroughly clean the hub area of the wheel. First install the left side bearing into its recess in the hub, with the marked or sealed side facing outwards. Using the old bearing, a bearing driver or a socket large enough to contact the outer race of the bearing, drive the bearing in until it's completely seated **(see illustration)**.

12 Turn the wheel over and install the bearing spacer. Drive the right side bearing into position using the same method.

13 On ZX-7R and ZX-9R B models, fit the speedometer drive collar to the left side of the hub, aligning its tangs with the wheel cutouts, and secure it in position with the circlip. Fit the other circlip to the right side of the hub. Ensure both circlips are correctly located in their grooves.

14 On ZX-9R C, E and F models, fit the circlip to the right side of the hub, making sure it is correctly located in its groove.

15 On all models, apply a smear of grease to the lips of the dust seals, then press them into the wheel. Gently drive them into position using a seal or bearing driver which contacts only the hard outer edge of the seal.

16 Clean off all grease from the brake discs using acetone or brake system cleaner then install the wheel (see Section 14).

Rear wheel bearings

17 Remove the rear wheel (see Section 15).

18 Lift the sprocket coupling from the wheel, taking care not to lose the spacer which is fitted to the inside of the coupling bearing.

19 Set the wheel on blocks so as not to allow the weight of the wheel to rest on the brake disc.

20 Using a flat-bladed screwdriver, carefully prise out the dust seal from the right side of the hub. Discard the seal; a new one should be fitted.

21 Using circlip pliers, remove the circlip from the right side of the hub.

22 Renew the bearings as described in Steps 6 to 12.

23 Install the circlip in the right side of the hub, making sure it is correctly located in its groove.

24 Apply a smear of grease to the lips of the dust seal, then press it into the right side of the hub. Gently drive the seal into position using a seal or bearing driver which contacts only the hard outer edge of the seal.

25 Ensure all the rubber dampers are correctly fitted and that the spacer is in position in the coupling bearing, then fit the sprocket coupling to the rear wheel **(see illustrations)**.

26 Clean off all grease from the brake disc using acetone or brake system cleaner, then install the wheel (see Section 15).

Sprocket coupling bearing

27 Remove the rear wheel (see Section 15).

28 Lift the sprocket coupling from the wheel and remove the spacer which is fitted to the inside of the coupling bearing.

29 Using a flat-bladed screwdriver, carefully prise out the dust seal from the coupling hub. Discard the seal; a new one should be fitted.

30 Using circlip pliers, remove the circlip from the coupling hub.

31 Support the sprocket coupling on blocks of wood so the sprocket faces downwards. Using a metal rod (preferably a brass drift punch), tap evenly around the inner race of the bearing to drive it out from the inside.

32 Check the bearing as described in Steps 8 to 10.

33 Thoroughly clean the hub area of the sprocket coupling, then install the bearing into its recess in the hub, with the marked or sealed side facing outwards. Using the old bearing, a bearing driver or a socket large enough to contact the outer race of the bearing, drive the bearing in until it is completely seated.

34 Secure the bearing in position with the circlip, making sure it is correctly located in its groove.

35 Apply a smear of grease to the lips of the dust seal, then press the seal into the coupling. Gently drive it into position, using a seal or bearing driver which contacts only the hard outer edge of the seal.

36 Fit the spacer to the inside of the coupling bearing then, ensuring all the rubber dampers are correctly installed, fit the sprocket coupling to the rear wheel **(see illustrations 16.25a and 16.25b)**.

37 Install the wheel (see Section 15).

16.25b . . . then fit the sprocket coupling to the wheel

17 Tyres –
general information and fitting

General information

1 The wheels fitted to all models are designed to take tubeless tyres only. Tyre sizes are given in the Specifications at the beginning of this Chapter.

2 Refer to *Daily (pre-ride) checks* at the beginning of this manual for tyre maintenance.

Fitting new tyres

3 When selecting new tyres, ensure they are the correct size and speed rating and that front and rear tyre types are compatible; if necessary seek advice from a tyre fitting specialist **(see illustration overleaf)**.

4 It is recommended that tyre fitting is carried out by a motorcycle tyre specialist rather than attempted in the home workshop. This is particularly relevant in the case of tubeless tyres because the force required to break the seal between the wheel rim and tyre bead is substantial, and is usually beyond the capabilities of an individual working with normal tyre levers. Additionally, the specialist will be able to balance the wheels after tyre fitting.

5 Note that punctured tubeless tyres can in some cases be repaired, but such repairs must be carried out by a tyre fitting specialist.

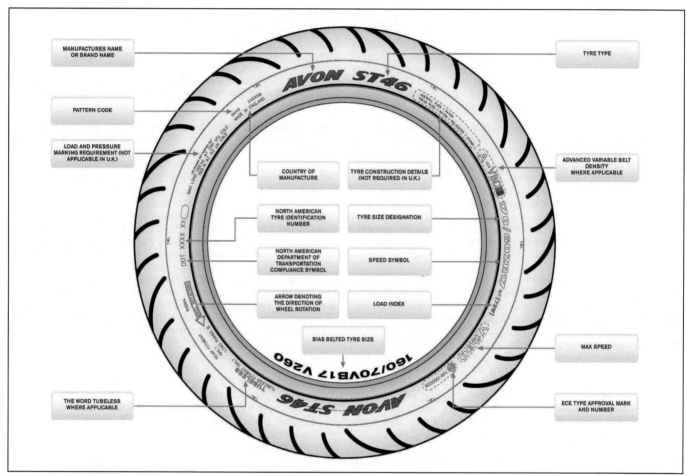

17.3 Common tyre sidewall markings

Chapter 8
Bodywork

Contents

Degrees of difficulty

Easy, suitable for novice with little experience | **Fairly easy,** suitable for beginner with some experience | **Fairly difficult,** suitable for competent DIY mechanic | **Difficult,** suitable for experienced DIY mechanic | **Very difficult,** suitable for expert DIY or professional

1 General information

This Chapter covers the procedures necessary to remove and install the body parts. Since many service and repair operations on these motorcycles require the removal of the body parts, the procedures are grouped here and referred to from other Chapters.

In the case of damage to the body parts, it is usually necessary to remove the broken component and renew it. The material the body panels are composed of does not lend itself to conventional repair techniques. Note that there are, however, some companies that specialise in 'plastic welding', and there are a number of bodywork repair kits now available for motorcycles.

When attempting to remove any body panel, first study it closely, noting any fasteners and associated fittings, to be sure of returning everything to its correct place on installation. In some cases, the aid of an assistant will be required when removing panels, to help avoid the risk of damage to paintwork. If, after its fasteners have been removed, a panel will not release, DO NOT FORCE IT. Check that all fasteners have been removed and try again. Where a panel engages another by means of tabs, be careful not to break the tab or its mating slot, or to damage the paintwork. Remember that a few moments of patience at this stage will save you a lot of money in replacing broken fairing panels!

Before attempting to install a body panel, study its fasteners and associated fittings. Check that these are in good condition, including all trim nuts or clips and damping/rubber mounts; renew any faulty ones. Check also that all mounting brackets are straight and repair or renew them, if necessary. Where assistance was required to remove a panel, make sure your assistant is on hand to install it.

Tighten the fasteners securely but be careful not to overtighten any of them or the panel may break (not always immediately), due to the uneven stress. Where quick-release fasteners are fitted, turn them 90° anti-clockwise to release them, and 90° clockwise to secure them.

2 Seat – removal and installation

Passenger seat
Removal

1 Insert the ignition key into the seat lock, and turn it anti-clockwise to release the seat. Pull up on the rear of the passenger seat and release it from the subframe.

Installation

2 Engage the lugs on the front of the seat with the hooks on the subframe, then push down on the rear of the seat until it locks firmly into position.

Rider's seat – ZX-7R models
Removal

3 Remove the passenger seat (Step 1).
4 Pull up on the seat release latch, then lift the rear of the rider's seat and slide it backwards and away from the motorcycle.

Installation

5 Slide the seat into position, making sure its tab engages correctly with the fuel tank, then push down on the rear of the seat until it locks firmly into position.
6 Install the passenger seat (Step 2).

Rider's seat – ZX-9R models
Removal

7 Remove the passenger seat (Step 1).
8 Slacken and remove the retaining bolt(s) and remove the seat bracket **(see illustrations)**. Lift the rear of the rider's seat

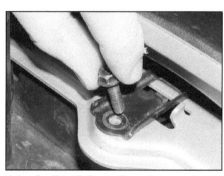
2.8a On ZX-9R C and E models, bracket is secured by single bolt

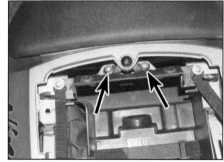
2.8b On ZX-9R F models, unscrew two bolts . . .

2.8c . . . and remove the bracket . . .

2.8d . . . then lift off the rider's seat. Note the tab (arrowed)

ZX-7R models

Removal

1 Remove the seats (see Section 2).
2 Slacken and remove the four bolts securing the pillion grab-handle bracket to the subframe **(see illustration)**.
3 Undo the seat lock screws and free the lock from the grab-handle bracket **(see illustration)**.
4 Slacken and remove the screws (two on each side) securing the side covers to the sub-frame **(see illustration)**. Recover the spacer from each mounting rubber and the luggage tie-down hook brackets **(see illustrations)**.
5 Slide off the clips securing the left and right side covers together **(see illustration)**.
6 Disconnect the wiring connector from the tail light **(see illustration)**.
7 Free the side cover assembly (complete with grab-handles and tail light) from the subframe and manoeuvre it away from the bike **(see illustration)**. To separate the side covers, proceed as follows.
8 Remove the single screw from underneath the tail light unit and the screws securing the centre cover to the top of the left and right side covers **(see illustration)**. Carefully lift the front of the centre cover and move it

and slide it backwards and away from the motorcycle **(see illustration)**.

Installation

9 Slide the seat into position, making sure its

tab engages correctly with the front bracket. Fit the rear mounting bracket, ensuring the seat rear pegs are correctly located in their holes, and securely tighten the seat retaining bolt(s).
10 Install the passenger seat (Step 2).

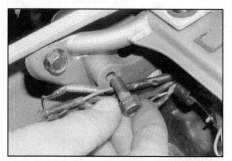

3.2 On ZX-7R models, unscrew the bolts securing the grab-handle bracket to the subframe

3.3 Undo the screws securing the seat lock to the grab-handle bracket

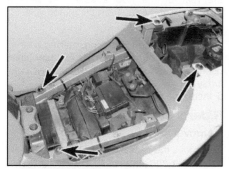

3.4a Undo the screws (arrowed) securing the side covers to the subframe . . .

3.4b . . . and recover the spacer from each mounting rubber

3.4c Also remove the luggage tie-down hook brackets from between the side covers and subframe

3.5 Remove the clips securing the side covers together

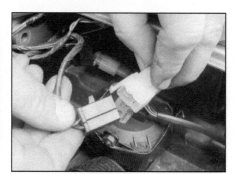

3.6 Disconnect the tail light wiring connector . . .

3.7 . . . then free the side cover assembly from the subframe

backwards to free its locating tabs from the side covers **(see illustration)**.

9 Undo the bolts and remove the grab-handles, noting the rubber spacers which are fitted between the handles and covers **(see illustrations)**.

10 Slacken and remove the screw and spacer securing each side cover to the grab-handle bracket, then separate the side covers from the bracket **(see illustrations)**.

Installation

11 Installation is the reverse of removal, noting the following.

a) Inspect the side cover and grab-handle mounting rubbers for damage or deterioration, and renew if necessary.
b) Ensure the centre cover is correctly engaged with the side cover before fitting its screws.
c) Ensure a spacer is fitted to each of the side cover mounting rubbers.
d) Check the operation of the tail light and seat lock before installing the seats.

ZX-9R B models

Removal

12 Remove the seats (see Section 2).

13 On later models, undo the bolts and remove the pillion grab-handles, noting the rubber spacers which are fitted between the handles and side covers.

14 On all models, slide off the clips securing the left and right side covers together **(see illustration)**.

15 Slacken and remove the screws (three on each side) securing both side covers to the subframe, and recover the spacer from the front and rear mounting rubbers **(see illustration)**.

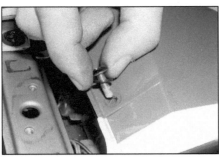

3.8a To separate the side covers, undo the lower screw and two upper screws (one shown) . . .

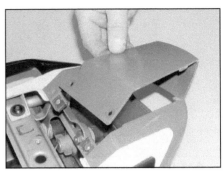

3.8b . . . then remove the centre cover from between the side covers

3.9a Unscrew the retaining bolts (arrowed) . . .

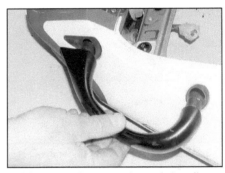

3.9b . . . and remove the grab-handles

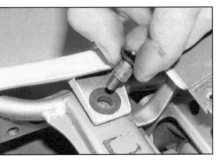

3.10a Slacken and remove the screw and spacer securing the side cover to the grab-handle bracket . . .

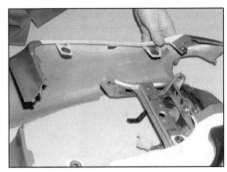

3.10b . . . and remove the side cover

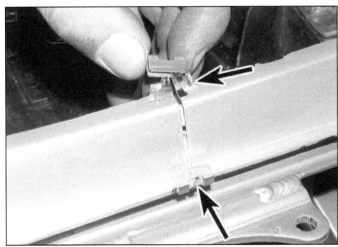

3.14 On ZX-9R B models, slide off the clips securing the left and right side covers together . . .

3.15 . . . then slacken and remove the screws securing the covers to the subframe

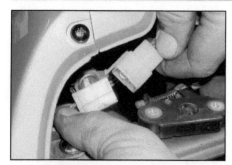

3.16 Disconnect the tail light wiring connector . . .

3.17 . . . then free the side cover assembly from the subframe

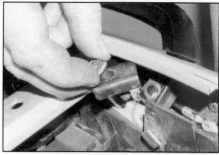

3.21a On ZX-9R C and E models, unscrew the grab-handle retaining bolts . . .

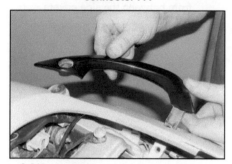

3.21b . . . and remove both handles . . .

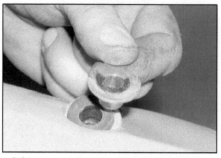

3.21c . . . and recover the spacers from the rear mounting rubbers

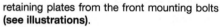

3.22 Undo the screws (arrowed) securing the seat cowling to the subframe

16 Disconnect the wiring connector from the tail light **(see illustration)**.

17 Free the side cover assembly (complete with tail light) from the subframe and manoeuvre it away from the bike **(see illustration)**.

18 To separate the side covers, remove the tail light (see Chapter 9) then undo the three retaining screws and separate the side covers and centre cover.

3.23 Undo the seat lock retaining screws . . .

Installation

19 Installation is the reverse of removal, noting the following.

a) *Inspect the side cover and (where fitted) grab-handle mounting rubbers for damage or deterioration, and renew if necessary.*

b) *Ensure the centre cover is correctly engaged with the side cover before fitting its screws.*

c) *Ensure a spacer is fitted to each of the front and rear side cover mounting rubbers.*

d) *Check the operation of the tail light and seat lock before installing the seats.*

ZX-9R C and E models

Removal

20 Remove the seats (see Section 2).

21 Undo the bolts and remove the pillion grab-handles. Recover the spacers from the grab-rail rear mounting rubbers and the

retaining plates from the front mounting bolts **(see illustrations)**.

22 Slacken and remove the screws and washers (two on each side) securing the seat cowling to the subframe **(see illustration)**.

23 Slacken and remove the two screws securing the seat lock to the subframe **(see illustration)**.

24 Slide the seat cowling backwards to free it from the subframe and remove the cowling from the bike, complete with the seat lock and cable **(see illustration)**.

Installation

25 Installation is the reverse of removal.

ZX-9R F models

Removal

26 Remove the seats (see Section 2).

27 Remove the bolts securing the top of the seat cowling to the frame, noting the location of the washers, luggage straps and spacers **(see illustrations)**.

3.24 . . . then manoeuvre the seat cowling away from the subframe

3.27a Seat cowling is secured by three bolts (arrowed)

3.27b Note the location of the washers . . .

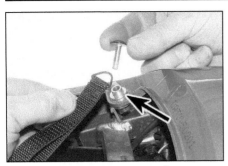

3.27c . . . luggage straps and spacers (arrowed)

3.28 Remove the trim clips as described

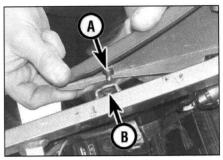

3.29 Ease the peg (A) out of the grommet (B)

3.30a Disconnect the tail light wiring connector . . .

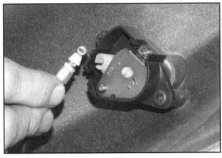

3.30b . . . and detach the seat lock cable

3.31 Lift off the seat cowling

28 Remove the two trim clips securing the underside of the cowling to the frame **(see illustration)**. **Note:** *To remove the trim clips, first undo the centre screw, then pull the clip out.*

29 Pull the front corners of the cowling outwards to release the pegs from the grommets on the frame **(see illustration)**. Carefully ease the right-hand side of the cowling up over the regulator/rectifier, then ease the left-hand side of the cowling up over the IC igniter.

30 Disconnect the tail light assembly wiring connector and detach the actuating cable from the passenger seat lock, noting how it fits **(see illustrations)**.

31 Lift off the seat cowling **(see illustration)**.

Installation

32 Installation is the reverse of removal. Check the operation of the passenger seat lock mechanism before installing the seat.

4 Rear view mirrors – removal and installation

Removal

1 Unscrew the retaining nuts and remove the mirror from the bike, complete with its rubber spacer **(see illustrations)**.

Installation

2 Fit the rubber spacer and install the mirror, tightening its mounting nuts securely.

4.1a Unscrew the retaining nuts . . .

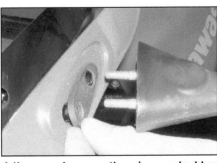

4.1b . . . and remove the mirror and rubber spacer from the fairing

5 Fairing panels – removal and installation

ZX-7R models

Lower panels

Removal

1 Each lower panel can be removed as follows.

2 Slide off the clip securing the rear of the left and right side lower panels together **(see illustration)**.

3 Unscrew the bolt securing the base of the lower panel to the inner panel **(see illustration)**.

5.2 On ZX-7R models, slide off the clip securing the rear of the left and right lower panels together

5.3 Undo the screw securing the lower panel to the inner panel

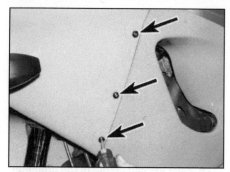

5.4 Undo the three screws securing the lower panel to the upper fairing . . .

4 Unscrew the three screws and washers securing the lower fairing panel to the upper fairing **(see illustration)**.

5 Slacken and remove the three panel mounting bolts, then disengage the panel from the upper and inner fairing panels and remove it from the bike **(see illustration)**. Recover the collars from the panel mounting rubbers and check the rubbers for damage or deterioration.

6 If both lower panels are being removed, remove the remaining panel (complete with inner fairing panel) as described in Steps 4 and 5.

Installation

7 Installation is the reverse of removal, noting the following.

a) *Inspect the lower and inner panel and mounting rubbers for damage or deterioration, and renew if necessary.*

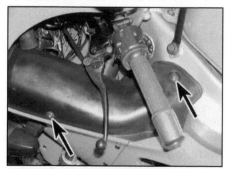

5.11a Undo the retaining screws (arrowed) . . .

5.14 Disconnect the upper fairing wiring harness connectors

5.5 . . . then unscrew the mounting bolts and remove the lower panel from the bike

b) *Ensure the inner panel mounting rubbers are correctly fitted before installing the lower fairing.*

c) *Ensure the lower panel is correctly engaged with the inner panel and upper fairing before fitting its screws.*

d) *Ensure the collars are correctly fitted to the three lower panel mounting rubbers.*

Inner panel

Removal

8 Remove one of the fairing lower panels (see Steps 1 to 5).

9 Unscrew the bolt securing the inner panel to the other lower panel, then remove the inner panel, taking care not to lose its mounting rubbers.

Installation

10 Installation is the reverse of removal. Make sure the mounting rubbers are correctly fitted to the lower panel brackets and ensure

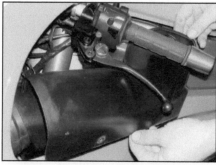

5.15a Unscrew the nuts securing the upper fairing to its mounting bracket . . .

the all inner panel locating pegs seat correctly in the rubbers.

Upper fairing

Removal

11 Undo the retaining screws securing each air filter housing intake duct cover in position, and remove both the left and right covers **(see illustrations)**.

12 Remove both rear view mirrors (see Section 4).

13 Slacken and remove the screws and washers (3 on either side) securing the upper fairing to each lower fairing panel **(see illustration 5.4)**.

14 Disconnect the upper fairing wiring harness connectors which are located on the left of the headlight **(see illustration)**.

15 Unscrew the nuts securing the upper fairing to its mounting bracket; on UK models, the left side nut retains the headlight relay bracket **(see illustration)**. Manoeuvre the upper fairing assembly forwards, freeing its intake chambers from the intake duct rubbers, and away from the bike **(see illustration)**. Recover the rubber spacers which are fitted between the fairing and mirror mounting points on the bracket.

Installation

16 Installation is the reverse of removal, noting the following points.

a) *Ensure the rubber spacers are correctly fitted to the mirror mounting points on the fairing bracket before installing the fairing.*

b) *Ensure the air filter intake duct rubbers are correctly engaged with the upper fairing chambers before fitting the mounting nuts.*

c) *Ensure the wiring is correctly routed and securely reconnected. Check the operation of the lights and turn signals before taking the bike on the road.*

ZX-9R B models

Lower fairing

Removal

17 Each lower panel can be removed as follows.

18 Slide off the clip securing the rear of the left and right side lower panels together.

19 Unscrew the bolt securing the base of the

5.11b . . . and remove the intake duct covers

5.15b . . . then remove the upper fairing from the bike

lower panel to the inner panel.

20 Unscrew the four screws and washers securing the lower fairing panel to the upper fairing and the single screw securing it to the air filter intake duct cover.

21 Slacken and remove the three panel mounting bolts, then disengage the panel from the upper and inner fairing panels and remove it from the bike. Recover the collars from the panel mounting rubbers and check the rubbers for damage or deterioration.

22 If both lower panels are being removed, remove the inner panel (see Step 25) then remove the remaining panel as described in Steps 20 and 21.

Installation

23 Installation is the reverse of removal, noting the following.

   a) Inspect the lower and inner panel and mounting rubbers for damage or deterioration, and renew if necessary.
   b) Ensure the inner panel mounting rubbers are correctly fitted before installing the lower panel.
   c) Ensure the lower panel is correctly engaged with the inner panel and upper fairing before fitting its screws.
   d) Ensure the collars are correctly fitted to the three lower panel mounting rubbers.

Inner panel

Removal

24 Remove one of the fairing lower panels (see Steps 17 to 21).

25 Unscrew the bolt securing the inner panel to the other lower panel, then remove the inner panel, taking care not to lose its mounting rubbers.

Installation

26 Installation is the reverse of removal. Make sure the mounting rubbers are correctly fitted to the lower panel brackets and ensure all the inner panel locating pegs seat correctly in the rubbers.

Upper fairing

Removal

27 Undo the retaining screws and washers securing each air filter housing intake duct cover in position and remove both the left and right covers **(see illustrations)**.

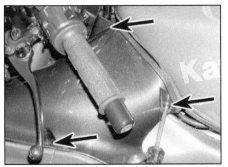
5.27a On ZX-9R B models, undo the retaining screws (arrowed) . . .

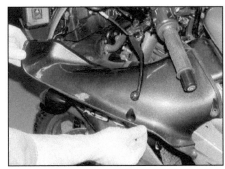
5.27b . . . and remove the intake duct covers

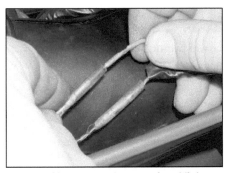
5.30 Disconnect the turn signal light wiring connectors

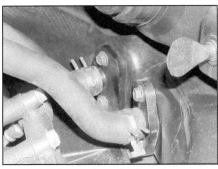
5.31 Release the retaining clips and disconnect the air vent filter hoses from the upper fairing intake ducts

28 Remove both rear view mirrors (see Section 4).

29 Slacken and remove the screws and washers (4 on either side) securing the upper fairing to each lower fairing panel.

30 Disconnect the wiring connectors from the headlight unit and turn signal lights **(see illustration)**.

31 Release the retaining clips and disconnect the air vent filter hoses from the fairing intakes **(see illustration)**. Also, slacken the retaining clips securing the air filter housing intakes to the fairing intake ducts.

32 Unscrew the nuts securing the upper fairing to its mounting bracket, then manoeuvre the upper fairing assembly forwards and away from the bike; on UK models, free the sidelight bulbholder from the

light as the fairing is removed **(see illustrations)**. Recover the rubber spacers which are fitted between the fairing and mirror mounting points on the bracket **(see illustration)**.

Installation

33 Installation is the reverse of removal, noting the following points.

   a) Ensure the rubber spacers are correctly fitted to the mirror mounting points on the fairing bracket before installing the fairing.
   b) Ensure the air filter intake ducts are correctly engaged with the upper fairing before fitting the mounting nuts.
   c) Ensure all wiring is correctly routed and securely reconnected. Check the operation of the lights and turn signals before taking the bike on the road.

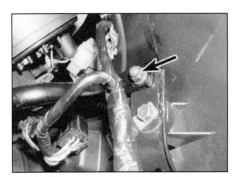
5.32a Unscrew the nut (arrowed) on each side . . .

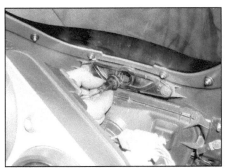
5.32b . . . then free the upper fairing from its mounting bracket and free the sidelight bulbholder (UK models only) from the light

5.32c Recover the rubber spacers, which are fitted between the fairing and mirror mounting points on the bracket

5.34 On ZX-9R C and E models, undo the screws (A) securing the lower fairing to middle panel and the mounting bolts (B) . . .

5.35 . . . then remove the lower fairing from the bike

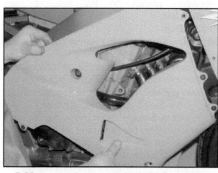

5.38 Remove all the retaining screws (arrowed) . . .

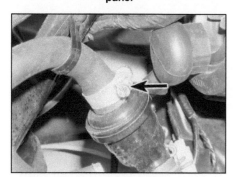

5.39 . . . and remove the middle fairing panel

ZX-9R C, E and F models

Lower fairing

Removal

34 Slacken and remove the upper screws and washers (two on either side) securing the lower fairing to the inner and middle fairing panels (see illustration).

35 Slacken and remove the three mounting bolts (one on the left, two on the right), then pull the front of the lower fairing downwards to disengage it from the inner panel and remove it from the bike (see illustration). Recover the collars from the panel mounting rubbers and check the rubbers for damage or deterioration.

Installation

36 Installation is the reverse of removal, noting the following.

a) Inspect the lower fairing mounting rubbers for damage or deterioration, and renew if necessary.

b) Ensure the lower fairing is correctly engaged with the inner and middle panels before fitting its screws.

c) Ensure the collars are correctly fitted to the three lower fairing mounting rubbers.

Middle fairing panel

Removal

37 Remove the lower fairing (see Steps 34 and 35). Each middle fairing panel can then be removed as follows.

38 Undo the five screws and washers securing the middle fairing panel to the upper

fairing and the single screw and washer securing it to the base of the radiator (see illustration).

39 Slacken and remove the middle panel mounting bolt (see illustration 5.38) then pull the front of the panel outwards to disengage it from the inner panel and remove it from the bike (see illustration). Recover the collar from the panel mounting rubber and check the rubber for damage or deterioration.

Installation

40 Installation is the reverse of removal, noting the following.

a) Inspect the mounting rubbers for damage or deterioration, and renew if necessary.

b) Ensure the middle fairing panel is correctly engaged with the inner panel before fitting its screws.

c) Ensure the collar is correctly fitted to the panel mounting rubber.

Inner panel

Removal

41 Remove the lower fairing and one of the middle panels (see above).

42 Pull the inner panel out from the remaining middle panel and remove it from the bike.

Installation

43 Installation is the reverse of removal.

Upper fairing

Removal

44 Remove the lower fairing, both middle fairing panels and the inner panel (see above).

45 Remove both rear view mirrors (Section 4) and the windshield (Section 7).

46 On E and F models, remove the retaining screws and clips securing each air filter housing intake duct cover in position, and remove both the left and right covers.

47 On all models, release the retaining clip and disconnect the vent hose from the air vent filter (located just in front of the headstock) (see illustration).

48 Disconnect the upper fairing wiring harness connector, which is located in front of the instrument cluster (see illustration).

49 Slacken the retaining clips securing the air filter housing left and right intake ducts to the fairing intakes (see illustration).

50 On C models, pull out the R-clips and

5.47 Slacken the retaining clip (arrowed) and detach the air vent filter hose

5.48 Locate the upper fairing wiring harness connector and disconnect it from the main wiring harness

5.49 Slacken the retaining clips and detach the air filter housing intake ducts from the fairing

5.50a On C models, remove the R-clips ...

remove the washers securing the upper fairing to its mounting bracket **(see illustrations)**.

51 On E and F models, slacken and remove the nuts and washers securing the headlight unit to the fairing mounting bracket. Also remove the screw securing each air filter housing intake duct cover to the bracket on the frame.

52 On all models, release the upper fairing from its mountings and remove it from the bike. Recover the rubber spacers which are fitted between the fairing and mirror mounting points on the bracket. Inspect the spacers and upper fairing mounting rubbers for signs of damage or deterioration, and renew if necessary.

Installation

53 Installation is the reverse of removal, noting the following points.

a) Ensure the rubber spacers are correctly fitted to the mirror mounting points on the

5.50b ... and washers securing the upper fairing to its mounting bracket

fairing bracket before installing the fairing.
b) Ensure the air filter intake ducts are correctly engaged with the upper fairing before securing the fairing in position.
c) Ensure all wiring is correctly routed and securely reconnected. Check the operation of the lights and turn signals before taking the bike on the road.

6 Front mudguard – removal and installation

ZX-7R and ZX-9R B models

Removal

Front section

1 Unscrew the two screws and washers securing the front section of the mudguard to

the rear section, then undo the screw and washer securing it to each fork tube and remove the mudguard front section in a forwards direction **(see illustrations)**.

Rear section

2 Remove the mudguard front section (Step 1).

3 Free the brake hose guides and speedometer cable guide from the mudguard rear section **(see illustration)**. Release each guide by squeezing together its retaining clips with a pair of pointed-nose pliers.

4 Slacken and remove the bolts securing the mudguard rear section to each fork tube and recover the collar and rubber washer from each mounting. The rear section can then be manoeuvred out of position

Installation

5 Installation is the reverse of removal. Do not overtighten the screws.

ZX-9R C and E models

Removal

6 Free the brake hose guides from the mudguard **(see illustration)**. Release each guide by squeezing together its retaining clips with a pair of pointed-nose pliers.

7 Slacken and remove the screw, washer and spacer securing the mudguard left and right side covers to the fork tubes **(see illustration)**.

8 Slacken and remove the bolts (two on each side) securing the mudguard to each fork tube and recover the collar and rubber washer from

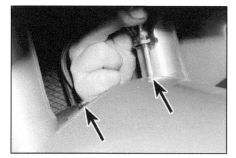

6.1a On ZX-7R and ZX-9R B models, undo the two screws (arrowed) securing the front section to the rear section ...

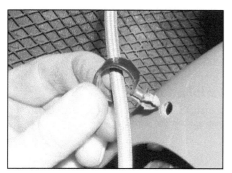

6.3 Release the brake hose and speedometer cable guides from the rear section of the mudguard

6.1b ... and the screw securing the mudguard to each fork tube ...

6.6 On ZX-9R C and E models, release the brake hose guides from the mudguard

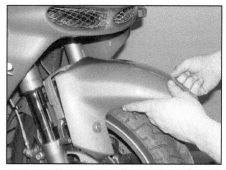

6.1c ... then remove the front section of the mudguard

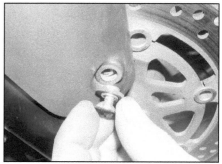

6.7 Remove the screw, washer and spacer securing each mudguard side cover to the fork tube

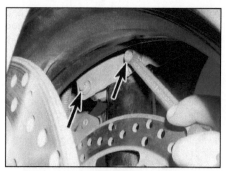

6.8a Slacken and remove the bolts (arrowed) securing the mudguard to the fork tubes . . .

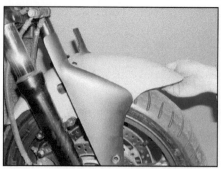

6.8b . . . then manoeuvre the mudguard assembly out of position

6.9 If necessary, undo the screws and separate the mudguard and side covers

6.12a Remove the bolts (A) on the front edge of the fork tube. Note bolts (B) on the rear edge of the tube

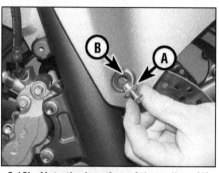

6.12b Note the location of the collars (A) and rubber washers (B)

6.13 Lift off the front mudguard

each mounting **(see illustration)**. The mudguard assembly can then be manoeuvred out of position **(see illustration)**.

9 If necessary, the mudguard side covers can be removed once their retaining screws have been undone **(see illustration)**.

Installation

10 Installation is the reverse of removal. Do not overtighten the screws.

ZX-9R F models

Removal

11 Free the brake hose guides from the mudguard **(see illustration 6.3)**.

12 Remove the bolts (two on each side) securing the mudguard to the front edge of each fork tube, noting the location of the collars and rubber washers **(see illustrations)**.

13 Remove the bolts (one on each side) securing the mudguard to the rear edge of each fork tube **(see illustration 6.12a)**. Lift off the mudguard **(see illustration)**.

Installation

14 Installation is the reverse of removal. Do not overtighten the screws.

7 Windshield – removal and installation

Removal

1 Remove the screws and washers securing the windshield to the fairing, and remove the windshield, noting how it fits **(see illustrations)**. On ZX-9R B models, recover the spacer which is fitted between the windshield and the fairing.

Installation

2 Installation is the reverse of removal. Do not overtighten the screws.

7.1a Undo the retaining screws . . .

7.1b . . . and remove the windshield from the upper fairing

Chapter 9
Electrical system

Contents

Degrees of difficulty

Easy, suitable for novice with little experience	Fairly easy, suitable for beginner with some experience	Fairly difficult, suitable for competent DIY mechanic	Difficult, suitable for experienced DIY mechanic	Very difficult, suitable for expert DIY or professional

Specifications

Battery

Capacity
  ZX-7R and ZX-9R B models 12V 10Ah
  ZX-9R C, E and F models 12V 8Ah
Voltage
  Fully charged
    ZX-7R and ZX-9R B models . . . . 12.6V or more
    ZX-9R C, E and F models . . . . 12.8V or more
  Discharged . . . . below 12.3V
Charging rate
  Normal
    ZX-7R and ZX-9R B models . . . . 1.2A for 5 to 10 hours
    ZX-9R C, E and F models . . . . 0.9A for 5 to 10 hours
  Quick
    ZX-7R and ZX-9R B models . . . . 5.0A for 1 hr
    ZX-9R C, E and F models . . . . 4.0A for 1 hr

Charging system

Current leakage . . . . 1mA (max)
Regulated voltage output
  ZX-7R and ZX-9R B models . . . . 14.2 to 14.8V @ 4000 rpm
  ZX-9R C, E and F models . . . . 14.7 ± 0.5V @ 4000 rpm
Unregulated voltage output
  ZX-7R and ZX-9R B models . . . . Not applicable
  ZX-9R C, E and F models . . . . 45V or more @ 4000 rpm
Alternator stator coil resistance
  ZX-7R and ZX-9R B models . . . . Not applicable
  ZX-9R C models . . . . 0.2 to 0.6 ohms
  ZX-9R E and F models . . . . 0.05 to 0.60 ohms

Starter motor

Brush length
    Standard . . . . 12.0 mm
    Service limit (min) . . . . 8.5 mm
Commutator diameter
    Standard . . . . 28 mm
    Service limit (min) . . . . 27 mm

Fuses

Main 30A
Horn 10A
Ignition 10A
Tail light 10A
Headlight 10A
Additional headlight fuse – ZX-9R E and F models 20A
Fan 10A
Accessories 10A
Turn signal 10A

Bulbs

Headlights
    ZX-7R models
        UK and US models . . . . 45/45W H4 halogen
        Europe models
            Left bulb . . . . 55W H3 halogen
            Right bulb . . . . 55W H1 halogen
    ZX-9R B models
        UK and US models . . . . 60/55W H4 halogen
        Europe models
            Left bulb . . . . 55W H1 halogen
            Right bulb . . . . 55W H3 halogen
    ZX-9R C, E and F models . . . . 60/55W H4 halogen
Sidelight (UK and Europe models) 5W
Brake/tail lights
    UK and Europe models 21/5W
    US models 27/8W
Turn signal lights
    UK and Europe models 21W
    US models 23W
Instrument cluster
    ZX-7R and ZX-9R B models
        Warning light bulbs 3.4W
        Illumination bulbs 1.7W
    ZX-9R C models 2.0W
    ZX-9R E and F models
        Warning light bulbs 1.1W
        Illumination bulbs 0.7W

Torque wrench settings

Alternator mounting bolts – ZX-7R and ZX-9R B models . . . . 25 Nm
Alternator fixings – ZX-9R C, E and F models
    Cover bolts
        C models . . . . 11 Nm
        E and F models . . . . 10 Nm
    Rotor bolt . . . . 110 Nm
    Stator coil bolts . . . . 12 Nm
    Stator coil wiring harness plate bolts . . . . 8 Nm
Clutch master cylinder mounting bolts – ZX-7R and ZX-9R B models . 11 Nm
Front brake master cylinder mounting clamp bolt
    ZX-7R models . . . . 11 Nm
    ZX-9R models . . . . 9 Nm
Neutral switch
    ZX-7R models . . . . 4 Nm
    ZX-9R models . . . . 15 Nm
Oil pressure switch . . . . 15 Nm
Starter motor mounting bolts . . . . 10 Nm

1 General information

All models have a 12-volt electrical system charged by a three-phase alternator with a separate regulator/rectifier.

The regulator maintains the charging system output within the specified range to prevent overcharging, and the rectifier converts the AC (Alternating Current) output of the alternator to DC (Direct Current) to power the lights and other components and to charge the battery. On ZX-7R and ZX-9R B models, the alternator is mounted on the top of the crankcase and is chain-driven off the rear of the clutch via a driveshaft and rubber damper arrangement. On ZX-9R C, E and F models, the alternator rotor is mounted on the left end of the crankshaft and the stator is fixed to the inside of the crankcase cover.

The starter motor is on the top of the crankcase. The starting system includes the motor, the battery, the relay and the various wires and switches. If the engine kill switch is in the 'RUN' position and the ignition (main) switch is ON, the starter relay allows the starter motor to operate only if the transmission is in neutral (neutral switch on). If the transmission is in gear, the clutch lever must also be pulled into the handlebar and the sidestand must be up.

Note: *Keep in mind that electrical parts, once purchased, cannot be returned. To avoid unnecessary expense, make sure that the faulty component has been positively identified before buying a new part.*

2 Electrical system – fault finding

⚠ **Warning: To prevent the risk of short circuits, the ignition (main) switch must always be OFF and the battery negative (–) terminal should be disconnected before any of the bike's other electrical components are disturbed. Don't forget to reconnect the terminal securely once work is finished or if battery power is needed for circuit testing.**

1 A typical electrical circuit consists of an electrical component, the switches, relays, etc. related to that component, and the wiring and connectors that hook the component to both the battery and the frame.

2 Electrical problems often stem from simple causes, such as loose or corroded connections, or a blown fuse. So, before tackling any troublesome electrical circuit, take the following simple steps. Firstly, study the *Wiring Diagrams* at the end of this Chapter thoroughly to get a complete picture of what makes up that individual circuit – trouble spots can often be pinpointed by finding out whether other components related to that

circuit are operating properly. If several components or circuits fail at one time, it is likely that the fault lies in the fuse or earth (ground) connection, since it is not unusual for several circuits to be routed through the same fuse and earth (ground) connections.

3 Secondly, visually check the condition of the fuse, wires and connections in the problem circuit. Intermittent failures can be especially frustrating, since it is not always possible to duplicate the failure when it is convenient to test. Dirty or loose connections or wires can cause intermittent failures, so clean all connections in the affected circuit, whether or not they appear to be good, and wiggle all connections and wires to check for looseness.

4 If further investigation is needed, utilising testing instruments, use the wiring diagram to plan where you will make the necessary connections in order to pinpoint the trouble spot accurately.

5 The basic instruments and tools needed for electrical fault finding include a battery and bulb test circuit, a continuity tester, a test light, and a jumper wire. A multimeter capable of reading volts, ohms and amps is also very useful as an alternative to the above, and is necessary for performing more extensive tests and checks.

HAYNES HINT *Refer to Fault Finding Equipment in the Reference section for details of how to use electrical test equipment.*

3 Battery – removal, installation, inspection and maintenance

Caution: Be extremely careful when handling or working around the battery. The electrolyte is very caustic and an explosive gas (hydrogen) is given off when the battery is charging.

Removal and installation

1 Remove the seats (see Chapter 8).

2 Unscrew the negative (–) terminal bolt first and disconnect the lead from the battery **(see illustration)**. Lift up the red insulating cover to access the positive (+) terminal, then unscrew the bolt and disconnect the lead. Unhook the rubber band (ZX-7R and ZX-9R B models only) and lift the battery from the bike.

3 On installation, clean the battery terminals and lead ends with a wire brush or knife and emery paper. Reconnect the leads, connecting the positive (+) terminal first.

HAYNES HINT *Battery corrosion can be kept to a minimum by applying a layer of petroleum jelly to the terminals after the cables have been connected.*

4 Ensure the insulating cover is correctly

fitted then, on ZX-7R and ZX-9R B models, secure the battery in position with the rubber strap. On all models install the seats (see Chapter 8).

Inspection and maintenance

5 The battery fitted to the models covered in this manual is of the maintenance-free (sealed) type, it therefore does not require topping up. However, the following checks should still be regularly performed.

6 Check the battery terminals and leads for tightness and corrosion. If corrosion is evident, unscrew the terminal screws and disconnect the leads from the battery, disconnecting the negative (–) terminal first, and clean the terminals and lead ends with a wire brush or knife and emery paper. Reconnect the leads, connecting the negative (–) terminal last, and apply a thin coat of petroleum jelly to the connections to deter further corrosion.

7 The battery case should be kept clean to prevent current leakage, which can discharge the battery over a period of time (especially when it sits unused). Wash the outside of the case with a solution of baking soda and water. Rinse the battery thoroughly, then dry it.

8 Look for cracks in the case and renew the battery if any are found. If acid has been spilled on the frame or the battery box, neutralise it with a baking soda and water solution, dry it thoroughly, then touch up any damaged paint.

9 If the motorcycle sits unused for long periods of time, disconnect the cables from the battery terminals, negative (–) terminal first. Refer to Section 4 and charge the battery once every month to six weeks.

10 The condition of the battery can be assessed by measuring the voltage present at the battery terminals. Connect the voltmeter positive (+) probe to the battery positive (+) terminal, and the voltmeter negative (–) probe to the battery negative (–) terminal. When fully charged, there should be more than 12.6 volts present on ZX-7R and ZX-9R B models, and 12.8 volts on ZX-9R C, E and F models. If the voltage falls much below this the battery must be removed, disconnecting the negative (–) terminal first, and recharged as described below in Section 4.

3.2 Always disconnect the negative lead from the battery first

5.2a Unclip the cover from the junction box to gain access to most fuses . . .

5.2b . . . and disconnect the starter relay wiring connector to access the main fuse

4 Battery – charging

Caution: Be extremely careful when handling or working around the battery. The electrolyte is very caustic and an explosive gas (hydrogen) is given off when the battery is charging.

1 Remove the battery (see Section 3). Connect the charger to the battery, making sure that the positive (+) lead on the charger is connected to the positive (+) terminal on the battery, and the negative (–) lead is connected to the negative (–) terminal.

2 Kawasaki recommend that the battery is charged for 5 to 10 hours at a maximum rate of 1.2 amps on ZX-7R and ZX-9R B models, and 0.9 amps on ZX-9R C, E and F models. Exceeding these recommendations can cause the battery to overheat, buckling the plates and rendering it useless. Few owners will have access to an expensive current-controlled charger, so if a normal domestic charger is used check that, after a possible initial peak, the charge rate falls to a safe level. If the battery becomes hot during charging, **stop**. Further charging will cause damage. **Note:** *In emergencies the battery can be charged at a*

5.3 Pull out the relevant fuse

higher rate of around 4.0 amps for a period of 1 hour. However, this is not recommended and the low amp charge is by far the safer method of charging the battery.

3 If the recharged battery discharges rapidly when left disconnected, it is likely that an internal short caused by physical damage or sulphation has occurred, and a new battery will be required. (A battery in good order will tend to lose its charge at about 1% per day.)

4 Install the battery (see Section 3).

5 If the motorcycle sits unused for long periods of time, charge the battery once every month to six weeks and leave it disconnected.

5 Fuses – check and renewal

1 The electrical system is protected by fuses of different ratings which are all located under the seat. All fuses, except the main fuse, are housed in the junction box, which is directly behind the battery. The main fuse is integral with the starter relay, which is just in front of, and to the left, of the fusebox. On ZX-9R E and F models, an additional headlight fuse is also fitted to its own holder, located behind the junction box.

2 To access the fuses, remove the seats (see Chapter 8) then unclip the junction box cover **(see illustration)**. To gain access to the main fuse, ensure the ignition is switched off, then disconnect the starter relay wiring connector **(see illustration)**.

3 To remove a fuse, first switch off the ignition, then pull the fuse out of its terminals **(see illustration)**. If you can't pull the fuse out with your fingertips, use a pair of suitable pliers. A blown fuse is easily identified by a break in the element. Each fuse is clearly marked with its rating and must only be replaced by a fuse of the correct rating; the fuses are also colour-coded for easy

recognition. A spare fuse of each rating is housed in the junction box. If a spare fuse is used, always renew it so that a spare of each rating is carried on the bike at all times.

⚠️ *Warning: Never put in a fuse of a higher rating, or bridge the terminals with any other substitute – however temporary it may be. Serious damage may be done to the circuit, or a fire may start.*

4 If a new fuse blows immediately, find the cause before renewing it again; a short to earth (ground) as a result of faulty insulation is most likely. Look for bare wires and chafed, melted or burned insulation.

5 Occasionally a fuse will blow or cause an open-circuit for no obvious reason. Corrosion of the fuse ends and fusebox terminals may occur and cause poor fuse contact. If this happens, remove the corrosion with a wire brush or emery paper, then spray the fuse end and terminals with electrical contact cleaner.

6 Lighting system – check

1 Power for operation of the headlight, tail light, brake light and instrument cluster lights is provided by the battery. If none of the lights operate, always check battery voltage before proceeding. Low battery voltage indicates either a faulty battery or a defective charging system. Refer to Section 3 for battery checks and Sections 29 and 30 for charging system tests. Also, check the condition of the fuses.

Headlight

2 If the headlight fails to work, first check the fuse with the key ON (see Section 5), and then the bulb (see Section 7). If they are both good, use jumper wires to connect the bulb directly to the battery terminals. If the light comes on, the problem lies either in the wiring, in one of the switches in the circuit, or in the headlight

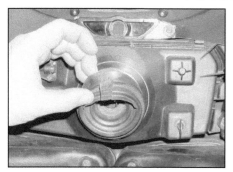

7.1 Remove the rubber dust cover from the rear of the light unit . . .

7.2a . . . then release the retaining clip . . .

7.2b . . . and remove the bulb (shown with fairing removed for clarity)

relay(s) (where fitted). Refer to Section 20 for the switch testing procedures, Section 34 for the junction box, and also the *Wiring Diagrams* at the end of this Chapter. Headlight relay locations are as follows.

a) *UK ZX-7R models – mounted on the left-hand side of the upper fairing bracket.*

b) *UK (and Europe) ZX-9R C models – located in front of the battery (remove the seats for access).*

c) *All ZX-9R E and F models – both HI and LO beam relays are mounted on the front of the upper fairing bracket.; on E models remove the upper fairing for access and on F models remove the windshield.*

d) *All US models – a relay is incorporated in the junction box (see Section 34).*

Tail light

3 If the tail light fails to work, check the bulbs and the bulb terminals first, then the fuse, then check for battery voltage at the red terminal on the supply side of the tail light wiring connector. If voltage is present, check the earth (ground) circuit for an open or poor connection.

4 If no voltage is indicated, check the wiring between the tail light and the ignition switch, then check the switch. Also check the lighting switch (UK and Europe models only).

Brake light

5 If the brake light fails to work, check the bulbs and the bulb terminals first, then the fuse, then check for battery voltage at the blue/red terminal on the supply side of the tail

light wiring connector, with the brake lever pulled in or the pedal depressed. If voltage is present, check the earth (ground) circuit for an open or poor connection.

6 If no voltage is indicated, check the brake light switches, then the wiring between the tail light and the switches.

7 See Section 14 for brake light switch checks and Section 9 for brake/tail light bulb renewal.

Instrument and warning lights

8 See Section 17 for instrument and warning light bulb renewal.

Turn signal lights

9 See Section 11 for turn signal circuit check.

---

7 Headlight bulbs and sidelight (Europe models only) bulbs – renewal

Headlight

⚠ *Warning: Allow the bulbs time to cool before removing them if the headlight has just been on.*

Note: *The headlight bulb(s) are of the quartz-halogen type. Do not touch the bulb glass, as skin acids will shorten the bulb's service life. If the bulb is accidentally touched, it should be wiped carefully, when cold, with a rag soaked in methylated spirit, and dried before fitting.*

1 Disconnect the relevant wiring connector from the back of the headlight assembly and

remove the rubber dust cover, noting how it fits **(see illustration)**.

2 Unhook the bulb retaining clip, then remove the bulb **(see illustrations)**.

3 Fit the new bulb, bearing in mind the information in the **Note** above. Make sure the tabs on the bulb fit correctly in the slots in the bulb housing, and secure it in position with the retaining clip.

4 Install the dust cover, making sure it is correctly seated and with the 'TOP' mark at the top, and connect the wiring connector **(see illustration)**.

5 Check the operation of the headlight.

> **HAYNES HINT** *Always use a paper towel or dry cloth when handling new bulbs to prevent injury if the bulb should break, and to prolong bulb life.*

Sidelight – Europe models only

ZX-7R and ZX-9R B, E and F models

6 Remove the windshield (see Chapter 8).

7 Free the bulbholder from the rear of the sidelight/headlight (as applicable), then carefully pull the bulb out of the holder **(see illustrations)**.

8 Install the new bulb in the bulbholder, then securely fit the bulbholder. Make sure the bulbholder is correctly seated, then check the operation of the sidelight before installing the windshield (see Chapter 8).

7.4 Ensure the dust cover is correctly installed with its 'TOP' mark uppermost

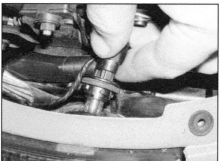

7.7a Free the bulbholder from the rear of the sidelight . . .

7.7b . . . then pull the bulb out of its holder (ZX-9R B shown)

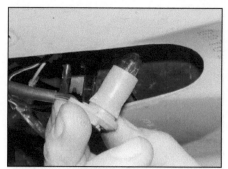

7.9 On ZX-9R C models, undo the retaining screws (arrowed) and remove the access cover from the upper fairing

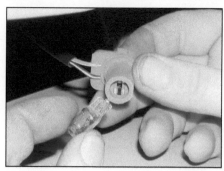

7.10a Release the bulbholder from the base of the headlight . . .

7.10b . . . then pull the bulb out of the holder

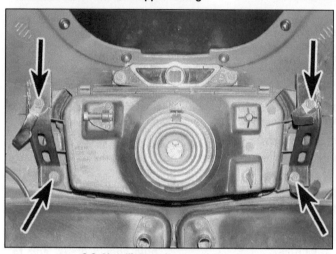

8.2 Headlight unit mounting bolts – ZX-9R B model

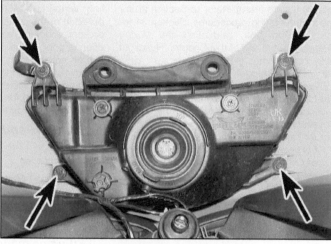
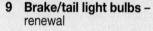

8.3 Headlight unit mounting bolts – ZX-9R C model

ZX-9R C models

9 Undo the retaining screws and remove the access cover from beneath the headlight unit **(see illustration)**.
10 Pull the bulbholder out of its socket in the base of the headlight, then carefully pull the bulb out of the holder **(see illustrations)**.
11 Install the new bulb in the bulbholder, then install the bulbholder by pressing it in. Make sure the bulbholder is correctly seated, then securely fit the access cover to the fairing.
12 Check the operation of the sidelight.

8 Headlight assembly – removal and installation

Removal

1 Remove the upper fairing (see Chapter 8).
2 On ZX-7R and ZX-9R B models, slacken and remove the headlight unit mounting bolts and remove the fairing mounting brackets (which differ from each other), noting their correct fitted locations **(see illustration)**. Remove the headlight unit from the fairing, taking care not to lose the collar from each mounting rubber. Inspect the headlight mounting rubbers for signs of damage or deterioration, and renew if necessary.

3 On ZX-9R C models, unscrew the mounting bolts and remove the headlight unit from the fairing **(see illustration)**.
4 On ZX-9R E and F models, slacken and remove the upper mounting nuts and lower mounting bolts and remove the washers and rubber spacers from the upper mounting studs. Remove the headlight unit from the fairing.

Installation

5 Installation is the reverse of removal. Install the fairing (see Chapter 8) then check the operation of the headlight unit and the headlight aim (see Chapter 1).

9 Brake/tail light bulbs – renewal

1 Remove the passenger seat (see Chapter 8).
2 Rotate the relevant bulbholder anti-clockwise and withdraw it from the tail light **(see illustration)**.
3 Push the bulb into the holder and twist it anti-clockwise to remove it **(see illustration)**. Check the socket terminals for corrosion and clean them if necessary. Line up the pins of the new bulb with the slots in the socket, then

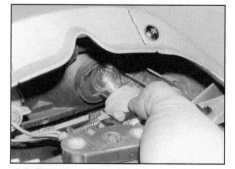

9.2 Free the bulbholder from the tail light unit . . .

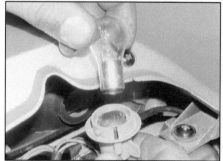

9.3 . . . then push the bulb in and turn it anti-clockwise to release it from the holder

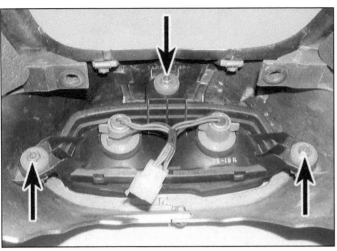

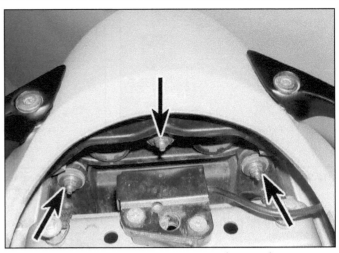

**10.4 Tail light unit retaining bolts (arrowed) –
ZX-9R B model**

**10.7 Tail light unit retaining nuts (arrowed) –
ZX-9R C, E and F models**

push the bulb in and turn it clockwise until it locks into place. **Note:** *The pins on the bulb are offset so it can only be installed one way. It is a good idea to use a paper towel or dry cloth when handling the new bulb to prevent injury if the bulb should break, and to prolong bulb life.*
4 Install the bulbholder into the tail light and turn it clockwise to secure it.
5 Check the operation of the brake/tail light, then fit the seat.

10 Tail light assembly – removal and installation

Removal

ZX-7R models

1 Remove the side cover assembly from the bike and separate the covers (see Chapter 8).
2 Slacken and remove the retaining nuts and washers, then remove the tail light unit from the bracket. Recover the collar from each mounting rubber. Inspect the mounting rubbers for signs of damage or deterioration, and renew if necessary.

ZX-9R B models

3 Remove the side cover assembly from the bike (see Chapter 8).
4 Unscrew the bolts and remove the tail light from the side cover assembly **(see illustration)**. Recover the collars from the mounting rubbers and check the rubbers for signs of damage or deterioration.

ZX-9R C, E and F models

5 Remove the seat cowling (see Chapter 8).
6 Rotate the bulbholders anti-clockwise and free them from the tail light.
7 Slacken and remove the retaining nuts and washers and remove the tail light from the bike **(see illustration)**. Recover the collars

from the mounting rubbers and check the rubbers for signs of damage or deterioration.

Installation

8 Installation is the reverse of removal. Check the operation of the brake/tail lights before using the motorcycle on the road.

11 Turn signal circuit – check

1 Power for operation of the turn signal lights is provided by the battery. So, if the lights do not operate, always check the battery voltage first. Low battery voltage indicates either a faulty battery or a defective charging system. Refer to Section 3 for battery checks and Sections 29 and 30 for charging system tests. Also, check the fuse (see Section 5) and the switch (see Section 20).
2 Most turn signal problems are the result of a burned-out bulb or corroded socket. This is especially true when the turn signals function properly in one direction but fail to flash in the other direction. Check the bulbs and the sockets (see Section 12).
3 If the bulbs and sockets are good, check for

power at the turn signal relay as follows. On ZX-9R E and F models, the relay is located either under the air filter housing or the rider's seat – remove the housing (see Chapter 4) or the seat (see Chapter 8) for access. On all other models, the relay is located under the rider's seat **(see illustrations)**. On ZX-7R models, also remove the side cover assembly to improve access to the relay (see Chapter 8). Disconnect the relay wiring connector and check for power at the brown/red (ZX-7R and ZX-9R B models) or brown/yellow (ZX-9R C, E and F models) wire terminal in the connector with the ignition ON. Turn the ignition OFF when the check is complete.
4 If no power was present at the relay, check the wiring from the relay to the ignition (main) switch for continuity.
5 If power was present at the relay, using the appropriate wiring diagram at the end of this Chapter, check the wiring between the relay, turn signal switch and turn signal lights for continuity. If the wiring and switch are sound, renew the relay.
6 If the turn signals work, but either too fast or too slowly, and the bulbs, wiring and switches are all good, count the number of flashes in one minute – there should be between 75 and 95. If not, renew the relay.

**11.3a Turn signal relay location –
ZX-7R model**

**11.3b Turn signal relay location –
ZX-9R B model**

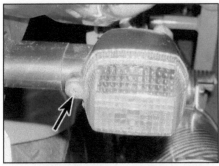

12.1 Undo the retaining screw (arrowed) and remove the lens . . .

12 Turn signal bulbs – renewal

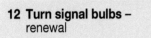

1 Undo the retaining screw and remove the lens from the turn signal light unit **(see illustration)**. Take care not to lose the lens seal.

2 Push the bulb into the holder and twist it anti-clockwise to remove it **(see illustration)**. Check the socket terminals for corrosion and clean them if necessary. Line up the pins of the new bulb with the slots in the socket, then push the bulb in and turn it clockwise until it locks into place.

3 Ensure the seal is correctly fitted to the light unit then fit the lens, securing it in position with the retaining screw **(see illustration)**. Do not overtighten the screw; the lens is easily cracked.

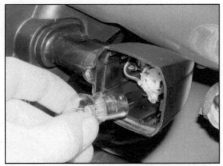

12.2 . . . then remove the bulb by pushing it in and turning it anti-clockwise

13 Turn signal assemblies – removal and installation

Removal

Front turn signal light

1 Remove the upper fairing (see Chapter 8).

2 On ZX-7R and ZX-9R C, E and F models, undo the retaining screw(s), then free the resonator chamber from the base of the air filter intake duct and remove it from the fairing **(see illustration)**.

3 On all models, undo the retaining screw(s) and remove the relevant air filter intake duct assembly from the fairing to gain access to the rear of the turn signal light **(see illustration)**.

4 Undo the retaining screw and remove the

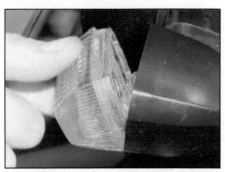

12.3 Ensure the seal is in position before installing the lens

outer plate from the turn signal **(see illustrations)**.

5 Lever the inner plate out of position and remove the turn signal light from the fairing **(see illustrations)**.

6 If necessary, slacken and remove the nut and retaining plate, then separate the light unit from its stalk.

Rear turn signal light

7 Remove the passenger seat (see Chapter 8) and locate the turn signal wiring connectors. Disconnect the wiring connectors and release the wiring so it is free to be removed with the light. If necessary, remove the side covers/ seat cowling (as applicable) to improve access to the turn signal light wiring.

8 Slacken and remove the retaining nut and plate then free the turn signal from the rear mudguard and remove it from the bike. Check the mounting rubber for signs of damage or

13.2 Undo the screw(s) and remove the resonator chamber (ZX-9R C shown)

13.3 Undo the screw(s) and remove the air filter intake duct from the upper fairing (ZX-9R B shown)

13.4a Remove the retaining screw . . .

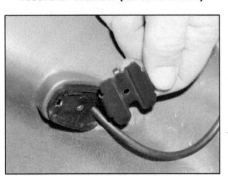

13.4b . . . and lift off the outer plate

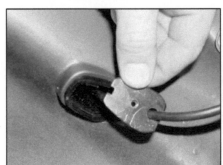

13.5a Lever the inner plate out of position . . .

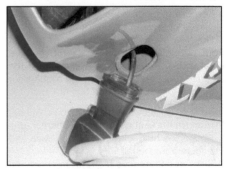

13.5b . . . then remove the turn signal from the fairing

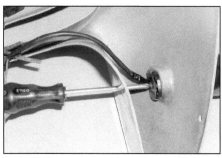

13.10 Ensure the turn signal is correctly installed, then securely tighten its retaining screw

deterioration, and renew if damaged. If necessary, separate the light unit from its stalk.

Installation

Front turn signal light

9 Where necessary, assemble the light unit and stalk and fit the retaining plate and nut, tightening it securely.
10 Fit the turn signal light unit to the upper fairing, ensuring the stalk rubber is correctly seated. Locate the inner plate correctly in the rubber, ensuring the wiring passes through the plate cutout, then fit the outer plate and securely tighten the retaining screw **(see illustration)**.
11 Fit the air filter intake duct and (where necessary) resonator chamber and securely tighten the retaining screws.
12 Fit the upper fairing (see Chapter 8) and check the operation of the turn signals before using the bike on the road.

Rear turn signal light

13 Where necessary, assemble the light unit and stalk.
14 Ensure the mounting rubber is in position, then fit the turn signal, passing the wiring through the rubber and retaining plate. Seat the turn signal in the mudguard, then fit the retaining plate and securely tighten the retaining nut.
15 Ensure the wiring is correctly routed and securely reconnected then check the operation of the turn signals.
16 Install the side covers/seat cowling (where removed) and the seat (see Chapter 8).

14 Brake light switches – check and renewal

Circuit check

1 Before checking any electrical circuit, check the bulb (see Section 9) and fuse (see Section 5). If the front brake switch is being checked, carry out the check at the switch terminals. If the rear brake light switch is being checked, remove the seats and (where necessary) the side covers/seat cowling (see Chapter 8) to gain access to the switch wiring connector(s).

14.5 Disconnect the wiring connector(s) from the front brake light switch

2 Using a multimeter or test light connected to a good earth (ground), with the ignition ON check for voltage at terminals of the brake light switch wiring connector(s) – there will be battery voltage on one terminal (the red/white or red/blue wire terminal) and zero on the other with the lever/pedal at rest. If there's no voltage present at either, check the wiring between the switch and the fuse (see the *Wiring Diagrams* at the end of this Chapter).
3 If voltage is available, touch the probe of the test light to the other terminal of the switch, then pull the brake lever in or depress the brake pedal. If no reading is obtained or the test light doesn't light up, renew the switch.
4 If a reading is obtained or the test light does light up, yet the bulbs still do not come on, check the wiring between the switch and the brake light bulbs (see the *Wiring Diagrams* at the end of this Chapter).

Switch renewal

Front brake lever switch

5 The switch is mounted on the underside of the brake master cylinder. Disconnect the wiring connectors from the switch **(see illustration)**.
6 Remove the single screw securing the switch to the bottom of the master cylinder, and remove the switch.
7 Installation is the reverse of removal. The switch is not adjustable.

Rear brake pedal switch

8 The switch is mounted on the inside of the right-hand footrest bracket. Remove the seats

15.2 On ZX-7R and ZX-9R B models, unscrew the retaining ring and detach the cable from the instrument cluster

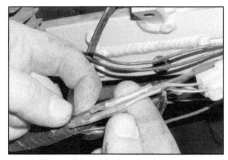

14.8 Trace the wiring back from the rear brake light switch and disconnect it from the main wiring harness

and (where necessary) the side covers/seat cowling for access to the connector(s) (see Chapter 8). Trace the wiring from the switch and disconnect it at the connectors **(see illustration)**.
9 Detach the lower end of the switch spring from the brake pedal, then unscrew and remove the switch. If necessary, improve access to the switch by unbolting the footrest bracket from the frame.
10 Installation is the reverse of removal. Make sure the brake light is activated just before the rear brake pedal takes effect. If adjustment is necessary, hold the switch and turn the adjusting ring on the switch body.

15 Instrument cluster and speedometer cable/speed sensor – removal and installation

Instrument cluster

Note: *Ensure the instrument cluster is kept the right way up when removed. If it is left face down for any length of time its gauges could become damaged.*

Removal

ZX-7R and ZX-9R B models

1 Remove the upper fairing (see Chapter 8).
2 Unscrew the knurled retaining ring and disconnect the speedometer cable from the instrument cluster **(see illustration)**.
3 Disconnect the instrument cluster wiring connectors and free the wiring from its retaining clips **(see illustration)**.

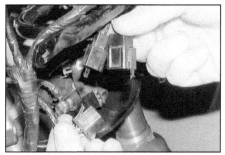

15.3 Disconnect the cluster wiring connectors and free the wiring from its clips

15.4a Slacken and remove the retaining nuts and washers (arrowed) . . .

15.4b . . . and remove the instrument cluster

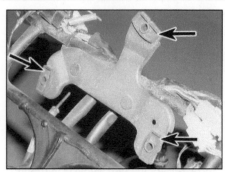

15.4c Inspect the cluster mounting rubbers (arrowed) for damage, and renew as a set if worn

4 Slacken and remove the three retaining nuts and washers and remove the instrument cluster from its bracket (see illustrations). Inspect the rubber mountings and renew them if they are damaged (see illustration).

ZX-9R C, E and F models
5 Remove the windshield (see Chapter 8). If necessary, access can be further improved by removing the upper fairing.
6 Peel back the rubber dust cover, then disconnect the wiring connector from the instrument cluster (see illustration).
7 Slacken and remove the three retaining nuts and washers and remove the instrument cluster from its bracket. Inspect the rubber mountings and renew them if they are damaged.

Installation

ZX-7R and ZX-9R B models
8 Ensure the rubber mountings are in position, then install the instrument cluster. Fit the washers and retaining nuts and tighten them securely.
9 Reconnect the instrument cluster wiring connectors and secure the wiring in position with the retaining clips.
10 Reconnect the speedometer cable and securely tighten its retaining ring.
11 Install the upper fairing (see Chapter 8).

ZX-9R C, E and F models
12 Ensure the rubber mountings are in position, then install the instrument cluster. Fit the washers and retaining nuts and tighten them securely.
13 Reconnect the wiring connector securely, then seat the dust cover correctly in position.

14 Install the windshield (see Chapter 8).

Speedometer cable – ZX-7R and ZX-9R B models

Removal

15 Remove the upper fairing (see Chapter 8).
16 Unscrew the speedometer cable retaining ring from the rear of the instrument cluster and detach the cable (see illustration 15.2).
17 Unscrew the retaining ring securing the lower end of the cable to the drive unit on the wheel and detach the cable (see illustration).
18 Free the cable from its retaining guides and clips and remove it from the bike, noting its correct routing.

Installation

19 Route the cable correctly and pass it through its relevant guides and clips.
20 Align the inner cable lower end with the drive gear and connect the cable to the drive unit, tightening its retaining ring securely.
21 Connect the cable upper end to the instrument cluster and securely tighten the retaining ring.
22 Check that the cable doesn't restrict steering movement or interfere with any other components, then install the upper fairing (see Chapter 8).

Speed sensor – ZX-9R C, E and F models

Removal

23 Remove the fuel tank as described in Chapter 4.

24 Trace the wiring back from the sensor to its connector on the right-hand side of the frame. Disconnect the wiring connector and release the wiring, noting its correct routing, so it is free to be removed with the sensor.
25 Unscrew the mounting bolt and remove the sensor from the front sprocket cover (see illustration).

Installation

26 Ensure the sensor and sprocket cover are clean and dry, then seat the sensor in position. Ensure the sensor is correctly seated, then securely tighten its retaining bolt.
27 Route the wiring correctly and reconnect the wiring connector securely.
28 Refit the fuel tank (see Chapter 4).

16 Instruments and sensors – check and renewal

ZX-7R and ZX-9R B models

Speedometer

Check
1 Remove the cable as described in Section 15 and check its condition.
2 If the cable is in good condition, support the bike using an auxiliary stand so that the front wheel is off the ground. With the cable disconnected from the drive unit, spin the wheel and check that the drive unit gear spins. If not, remove the front wheel and

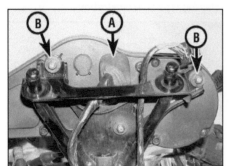

15.6 Instrument cluster wiring connector (A) and retaining nuts (B) – ZX-9R C model

15.17 On ZX-7R and ZX-9R B models, unscrew the retaining ring and detach the speedometer cable from its drive

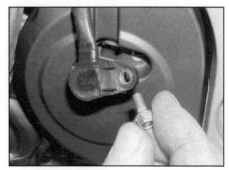

15.25 On ZX-9R C, E and F models, unscrew the bolt and free the speed sensor from the sprocket cover

16.4a Unscrew the retaining screws (arrowed – ZX-9R B shown) . . .

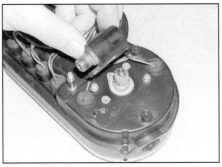

16.4b . . . and remove the speedometer drive unit from the cluster

16.5a Undo the retaining screw . . .

16.5b . . . and remove the reset knob

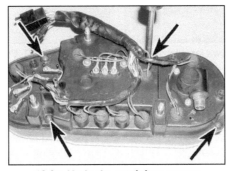

16.6a Undo the retaining screws (arrowed) . . .

16.6b . . . and lift off the instrument cluster front cover

check the drive unit and drive collar (see Chapter 7, Section 14).

3 If both the cable and drive unit are in good condition then the speedometer itself must be faulty (either the speedometer head or the drive gearbox).

Renewal

4 Remove the instrument cluster as described in Section 15 then undo the two screws and remove the speedometer drive unit from the rear of the cluster **(see illustrations)**

5 Undo the retaining screw and remove the trip meter reset knob from the instrument cluster **(see illustrations)**.

6 Unscrew the retaining screws and lift off the front cover from the instrument cluster **(see illustrations)**.

7 Unscrew the retaining screws from the rear of the cluster then carefully remove the speedometer head from the case **(see illustration)**.

8 Install the speedometer by reversing the removal sequence. Take care not to overtighten any retaining screws as the components are fragile and can easily be damaged.

Speedometer cable – renewal

9 See Section 15.

Tachometer

Check

10 If the system malfunctions, first check that the battery is fully charged, and that the terminals are clean, and that the wiring and fuses are in good condition.

11 Remove the upper fairing (see Chapter 8), then unscrew the retaining nuts and washers and free the instrument cluster from the mounting bracket (see Section 15 – leaving the wiring connectors connected) to gain access to the tachometer wiring terminals.

12 Undo the retaining screw and detach the black wire from its tachometer terminal. Refit the screw to the terminal, minus the black wire, and tighten securely. Turn the ignition switch on then, using an auxiliary wire, repeatedly connect and disconnect the tachometer brown wire terminal to the black terminal screw whilst observing the gauge needle. As the brown terminal is connected/disconnected the tachometer needle should be seen to flicker. If the needle does not move, the tachometer is faulty and must be renewed.

Renewal

13 Carry out the operations described in Steps 4 to 6.

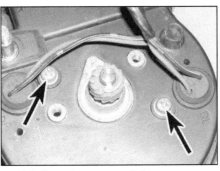

16.7 Speedometer retaining screws – ZX-9R B model

14 Note the correct fitted locations of the tachometer wires, then undo the retaining screws and carefully remove the tachometer from the case **(see illustration)**.

15 Install the tachometer by reversing the removal sequence, ensuring that the wires are correctly reconnected. Take care not to overtighten any retaining screws, as the components are fragile and can easily be damaged.

Temperature gauge

Check

16 The temperature gauge check is described in Chapter 3.

Renewal

Note: *On ZX-9R B models, the temperature gauge is combined with the fuel gauge.*

17 Carry out the operations described in Steps 4 to 6.

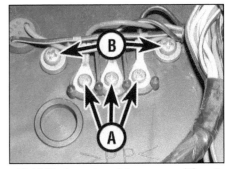

16.14 Tachometer wiring screws (A) and retaining screws (B) – ZX-9R B model

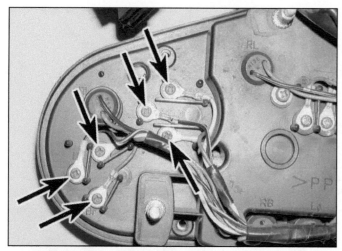

16.18 Fuel/temperature gauge wiring screws (arrowed) –
ZX-9R B model

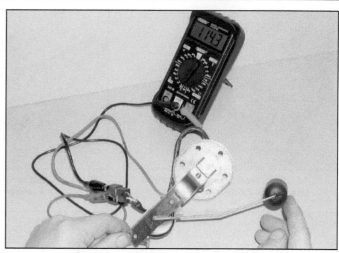

16.23 Checking the fuel gauge sender unit

18 Note the correct fitted locations of the gauge wires, then undo the retaining screws and carefully remove the gauge from the case **(see illustration)**.
19 Install the gauge by reversing the removal sequence, ensuring that the wires are correctly reconnected. Take care not to overtighten any retaining screws, as the components are fragile and can easily be damaged.

Fuel gauge and sender unit – ZX-9R B models

Check
20 If the fuel gauge malfunctions, check first that the battery is fully charged (see Section 4) and that the fuses are all good (see Section 5).
21 If the gauge is not working, remove the fuel tank (see Chapter 4). Ensure that the ignition is switched off, then locate the fuel gauge wiring connector. Turn the ignition switch on; the gauge needle should be at the 'E' (Empty) end of the scale. Turn the ignition switch off again then, using an auxiliary wire, connect the terminals of the wiring connector together. Turn the ignition switch on again; the gauge needle should swing towards the 'F' (Full) end of the scale. If the gauge performs as described, the fuel gauge sender unit is proven defective; the sender unit can be tested as described in Step 23.

Caution: Do not leave the ignition switched on for any longer than is necessary or the gauge may be damaged.
22 If the temperature gauge does not perform as expected, the fault lies in the wiring or the gauge itself. Check all relevant wiring and wiring connectors. If all appears to be well, the gauge is defective and must be renewed.
23 To test the fuel gauge sender unit, first remove it from the fuel tank (see below). Connect an ohmmeter across the sender unit terminals then check the resistance reading whilst moving the float arm slowly from the full to empty position and back again **(see illustration)**. Compare the readings obtained to those given in the Specifications, not only should the full and empty readings be as specified but the value should change evenly and progressively as the float arm is moved. If not the sender unit is faulty and should be renewed.

Renewal
24 The fuel gauge is combined with the temperature gauge. Renewal is as described in Steps 17 to 19.
25 To renew the fuel gauge sender, remove the fuel tank (see Chapter 4) and drain the fuel tank into a suitable container.
26 Unscrew the retaining bolts then manoeuvre the sender unit out of position,

taking care not to bend the float arm **(see illustrations)**. Remove the rubber seal from the sender and discard it; a new one must be used.
27 Installation is the reverse of the removal sequence using a new seal **(see illustration)**. Check for fuel leaks before starting the engine.

ZX-9R C, E and F models

28 On these models the instrument cluster assembly is a sealed unit, with all instruments being operated off the same printed circuit board. If the instrument cluster malfunctions, first check that the battery is fully charged and that the terminals are clean, and that the wiring and fuses are in good condition. Each of the display functions can be checked as follows but if any one is faulty the complete instrument cluster must be renewed. **Note:** *Before condemning the instrument cluster, take the assembly to an electronics engineer for testing. They maybe able to repair the assembly for a fraction of the cost of a new component.*
Caution: Whilst testing the instrument cluster, great care must be taken not to connect the test equipment in any other way than that specified. If the test equipment is incorrectly connected, the instrument cluster is likely to be damaged.

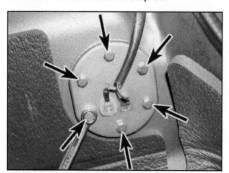

16.26a On ZX-9R B models, unscrew the retaining bolts (arrowed) . . .

16.26b . . . then carefully remove the sender unit from the fuel tank

16.27 Fit a new seal to the fuel gauge sender unit to prevent leaks

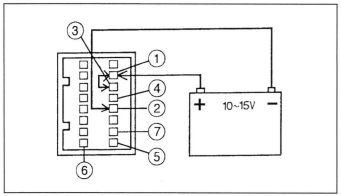

**16.29a LCD display check details –
ZX-9R C model**

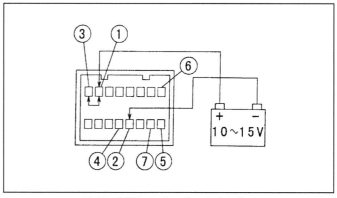

**16.29b LCD display check details –
ZX-9R E and F models**

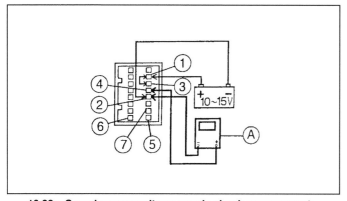

**16.33a Speed sensor voltage supply check arrangement –
ZX-9R C model**

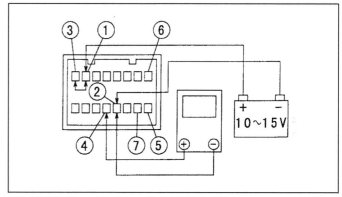

**16.33b Speed sensor voltage supply check arrangement –
ZX-9R E and F models**

LCD display check

29 With the instrument cluster removed (see Section 15), use auxiliary wires to connect the positive (+) terminal of a 12 volt battery to the No. 1 and 3 terminals of the cluster wiring connector, and its negative (–) terminal to the No. 2 terminal **(see illustrations)**.

30 With the battery connected, all the LCD display segments and the coolant temperature warning LED should be illuminated. While the segments are illuminated, press and hold the mode switch and check the display cycles through its three modes (odometer, trip meter and clock) and also check the operation of the reset button in each mode.

31 If the LCD displays do not function as described, then the instrument cluster assembly is faulty and must be renewed.

Speedometer check

32 A full check of the speedometer function requires the use of an oscillator and should, therefore, be entrusted to a Kawasaki dealer. Without an oscillator, the speedometer function can be checked as follows, but have your findings confirmed by a Kawasaki dealer before condemning the instrument cluster.

33 With the instrument cluster removed (see Section 15), use auxiliary wires to connect the positive (+) terminal of a 12 volt battery to the No. 1 and 3 terminals of the cluster wiring

connector, and its negative (–) terminal to the No. 2 terminal. Connect the positive (+) lead of a voltmeter to terminal No. 4 of the connector and the negative (–) lead to terminal No. 2 and check the voltage reading (this checks the supply to the speed sensor) **(see illustrations)**. If the voltage reading is less than 7 volts, the instrument cluster is faulty and should be renewed.

34 If the speed sensor supply voltage is correct, remove the speed sensor (see Section 15) and check it as follows. Connect a 12 volt battery, a 10 k ohm resistor and a voltmeter (set to the DC volt scale – an analogue gauge is best for this test) to the speed sensor wiring connector as shown **(see illustration)**. With all components correctly connected, wave a flat-bladed screwdriver closely past each side of the speed sensor while observing the gauge. If the sensor is functioning correctly, the voltmeter will register a reading every time the screwdriver passes the sensor. If the sensor is faulty, it must be renewed.

Tachometer check

35 A full check of the tachometer function requires the use of an oscillator and should therefore be entrusted to a Kawasaki dealer. Without an oscillator, the tachometer function can be checked as follows, but have your findings confirmed by a Kawasaki dealer

before condemning the instrument cluster.

36 With the instrument cluster removed (see Section 15), use auxiliary wires to connect a 12 volt battery to the cluster wiring connector as shown in **illustrations 16.29a or 16.29b** (as applicable). With the battery correctly connected, use an auxiliary wire to repeatedly connect and disconnect the No. 1 terminal to the No. 6 terminal while observing the tachometer gauge needle. As the terminals are connected/disconnected the tachometer needle should be seen to flicker. If the needle does not move, the tachometer is faulty.

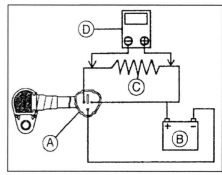

**16.34 Speed sensor check arrangement –
ZX-9R C, E and F models**

*A Wire connecter   C 10 K ohm resistor
B 12V battery   D Voltmeter*

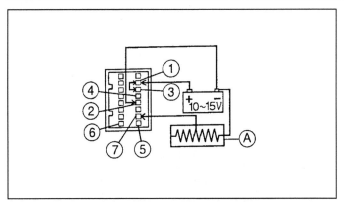

16.37 Coolant temperature gauge check arrangement using a 0 to 25 K ohm variable resistor (A) – ZX-9R C model

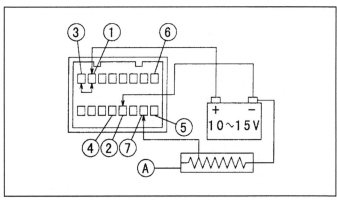

16.38 Coolant temperature gauge check arrangement using a 0 to 10 K ohm variable resistor (A) – ZX-9R E and F models

Coolant temperature gauge check

37 On C models, with the instrument cluster removed (see Section 15), use auxiliary wires to connect the positive (+) terminal of a 12 volt battery to the No. 1 and 3 terminals of the cluster wiring connector, and its negative (–) terminal to the No. 2 terminal **(see illustration)**. Connect a variable resistor (operating range zero to 25 K ohm) between the No. 7 terminal of the connector and the battery negative (–) terminal as shown. Starting with the resistor at the 25 K ohm setting, slowly reduce the resistance to zero. As the resistance drops, the display segments of the temperature gauge should illuminate at the resistances specified in the following table. If the segments do not illuminate, or if they do so at resistances different to those specified, the gauge is faulty and must be renewed.

Resistance value	Number of display segments illuminated
24400	1
9560	2
6180	3
2780	4
1340	5
950	6
810	7
690	8
690 or less	All segments and the warning light should flash continuously

38 On E models, with the instrument cluster removed (see Section 15), use auxiliary wires to connect the positive (+) terminal of a 12 volt battery to the No. 1 and 3 terminals of the cluster wiring connector, and its negative (–) terminal to the No. 2 terminal **(see illustration)**. Connect a variable resistor (operating range zero to 10 K ohm) between the No. 7 terminal of the connector and the battery negative (–) terminal as shown. Starting with the resistor at the 10 K ohm setting, slowly reduce the resistance to zero. As the resistance drops, the display reading should increase as specified according to the following table. If the display reading does not perform correctly, then it is faulty and must be renewed.

Resistance value	Temperature displayed	Warning light
9560	50°C (122°F)	Off
2780	80°C (176°F)	Off
950	110°C (230°F)	Off
810	115°C (239°F)	On
690 or less	HI	Flash continuously

Instrument cluster renewal

39 Remove the instrument cluster (see Section 15).
40 Unscrew the retaining screws and lift the case off the instrument cluster **(see illustrations)**. The instrument cluster can then be lifted out of the front cover **(see illustration)**.

41 Install the instrument cluster by reversing the removal sequence. Take care not to overtighten any retaining screws, as the components are fragile and can easily be damaged.

17 Instrument and warning light bulbs – renewal

ZX-7R and ZX-9R B models

1 Remove the upper fairing (see Chapter 8).
2 Some of the bulbs are accessible with the instrument cluster in place, but access to others is quite restricted. If it is too restricted for the bulb you are changing, displace the instrument cluster from its mounting bracket (see Section 15) to improve access.
3 Ease the bulbholder out from the instrument case, then pull the bulb from its holder **(see illustrations)**.
4 If the socket contacts are dirty or corroded, scrape them clean and spray them with electrical contact cleaner before a new bulb is installed.
5 Push the new bulb carefully into the holder, then fit the bulbholder securely into the case.
6 Refit the instrument cluster to the mounting bracket (where necessary), then install the upper fairing (see Chapter 8).

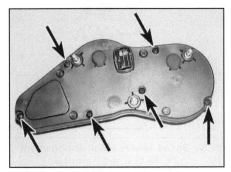

16.40a On ZX-9R C and E models, undo the screws (arrowed) . . .

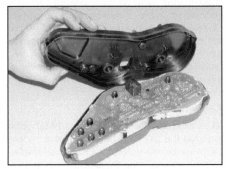

16.40b . . . and lift off the case . . .

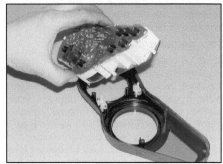

16.40c . . . then remove the instrument cluster assembly from the front cover

ZX-9R C models

7 Remove the instrument cluster (see Section 15).

8 To renew the speedometer or tachometer illumination bulb, remove the rubber access plug from the rear of the case then rotate the bulbholder anti-clockwise and remove it from the cluster circuit board. Pull the bulb out of its holder.

9 To renew a warning light bulb, unscrew the retaining screws and lift the case off the rear of the instrument cluster. Rotate the relevant bulbholder anti-clockwise and remove it from the circuit board, then pull the bulb out of its holder **(see illustrations)**.

10 If the socket contacts are dirty or corroded, scrape them clean and spray them with electrical contact cleaner before a new bulb is installed.

11 Push the new bulb carefully into the holder, then fit the bulbholder securely into the case. Fit the access plug securely to the case or fit the case and securely tighten its retaining screws.

12 Install the instrument cluster (see Section 15).

ZX-9R E and F models

13 Remove the instrument cluster (see Section 15).

14 Unscrew the retaining screws and lift the case off the rear of the instrument cluster. Rotate the relevant bulbholder anti-clockwise and remove it from the circuit board (the bulbs are integral with the holders).

15 Fit the new bulbholder securely to the printed circuit board, then fit the case and securely tighten its retaining screws.

16 Install the instrument cluster (see Section 15).

18 Oil pressure switch – check, removal and installation

Check

1 The oil pressure warning light should come on when the ignition (main) switch is turned ON and extinguish a few seconds after the engine is started. If the oil pressure warning light comes on whilst the engine is running, stop the engine immediately and carry out an oil level check (see *Daily (pre-ride) checks*), and if the level is correct, an oil pressure check (see Chapter 1).

2 If the oil pressure warning light does not come on when the ignition is turned on, check the bulb (see Section 17) and fuse (see Section 5).

3 The oil pressure switch is screwed into the right-hand side of the front of the crankcase, below the pick-up coil cover. Remove the lower fairing panel to gain access to the switch (see Chapter 8).

4 Pull the rubber cover off the switch and remove the screw securing the wiring

17.3a On ZX-7R and ZX-9R B models, ease the bulbholder out from the instrument cluster . . .

connector. With the ignition switched ON, earth (ground) the wire on the crankcase and check that the warning light comes on. If the light comes on, the switch is proven defective and must be renewed.

5 If the light still does not come on, check for voltage at the wire terminal. If there is no voltage present, check the wire between the switch, the instrument cluster and fuse for continuity (see the *Wiring Diagrams* at the end of this Chapter).

6 If the warning light comes on whilst the engine is running, yet the oil pressure is satisfactory, remove the wire from the oil pressure switch. With the wire detached and the ignition switched ON, the light should be out. If it is illuminated, the wire between the switch and instrument cluster must be earthed (grounded) at some point. If the wiring is good, the switch must be assumed faulty and renewed.

Removal

7 Remove the lower fairing panel (see Chapter 8) then drain the engine oil (see Chapter 1).

8 Pull the rubber cover off the switch and remove the screw securing the wiring connector.

9 Unscrew the oil pressure switch and withdraw it from the crankcase.

Installation

10 Apply silicone sealant (Kawasaki recommend the use of Kawasaki Bond 56019-120) to the switch threads, then fit the

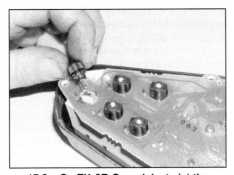

17.9a On ZX-9R C models, twist the warning light bulbholder anti-clockwise to free it from the circuit board . . .

17.3b . . . and pull the bulb out from the holder

switch to the crankcase and tighten it to the torque setting specified at the beginning of the Chapter.

11 Attach the wiring connector to the switch, tightening its retaining screw securely, then fit the rubber cover.

12 Refill the engine using the specified grade and quantity of oil (see Chapter 1). Run the engine and check that the switch operates correctly before installing the fairing panel (see Chapter 8).

19 Ignition (main) switch – check, removal and installation

⚠️ *Warning: To prevent the risk of short circuits, disconnect the battery negative (–) lead before making any ignition (main) switch checks.*

Check

1 Remove the air filter housing (see Chapter 4). Trace the ignition (main) switch wiring back from the base of the switch and disconnect it at the connector located above the engine.

2 Using an ohmmeter or a continuity tester, check the continuity of the connector terminal pairs on the switch side of the connector (see the *Wiring Diagrams* at the end of this Chapter). Continuity should exist between the terminals connected by a solid line on the diagram when the switch is in the indicated position.

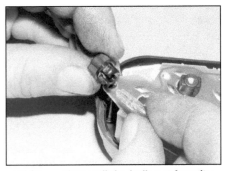

17.9b . . . then pull the bulb out from its holder

19.4 The ignition (main) switch wiring connector is located above the engine

3 If the switch fails any of the tests, replace it with a new one.

Removal

4 Remove the upper fairing (see Chapter 8) and the air filter housing (see Chapter 4). Trace the ignition (main) switch wiring back from the base of the switch and disconnect it at the connector located directly above the engine **(see illustration)**. Draw the wiring through to the switch, noting its routing.

5 Special shear-head security Torx bolts are used to mount the ignition switch. Remove the two special Torx bolts, using a centre punch and hammer to initially slacken them. Alternatively, drill the bolt heads off. New bolts must be used on installation. Access to the bolts is best obtained by displacing the instrument cluster bracket from the steering head – it is secured by two bolts. If required, first remove the instrument cluster (see Section 15) – though, with care, the bracket can be displaced with the cluster still mounted.

Installation

6 Installation is the reverse of removal. Using new shear-head Torx bolts, tighten them until the tool slips round on the bolt head, or the bolt head sheers off. Make sure wiring is securely connected and correctly routed.

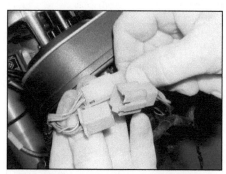

21.2 Trace the handlebar switch wiring back and disconnect its wiring connectors from the main wiring harness (ZX-9R B shown)

20 Handlebar switches – check

1 Generally speaking, the switches are reliable and trouble-free. Most troubles, when they do occur, are caused by dirty or corroded contacts, but wear and breakage of internal parts is a possibility that should not be overlooked. If breakage does occur, the entire switch and related wiring harness will have to be renewed, as individual parts are not available.

2 The switches can be checked for continuity using an ohmmeter or a continuity test light. Always disconnect the battery negative (–) lead, which will prevent the possibility of a short circuit, before making the checks.

3 On ZX-9R C models, remove the air filter housing to gain access to the switch wiring connectors, which are located above the engine unit. On all other models, remove the upper fairing (see Chapter 8) to gain access to the wiring connectors. Trace the wiring harness of the switch in question back to its connector(s) and disconnect it/them.

4 Check for continuity between the terminals of the switch harness with the switch in the various positions (ie switch off – no continuity, switch on – continuity) – see the *Wiring Diagrams* at the end of this Chapter.

5 If the continuity check indicates the existence of a problem, refer to Section 21, remove the switch and spray the switch contacts with electrical contact cleaner. If they are accessible, the contacts can be scraped clean with a knife or polished lightly with fine abrasive paper. If switch components are damaged or broken, it will be obvious when the switch is disassembled.

21 Handlebar switches – removal and installation

Right-hand switch – ZX-7R and ZX-9R B models

Removal

1 Remove the upper fairing (see Chapter 8) to gain access to the switch wiring connectors.

2 Trace the wiring harness of the switch back to its connectors and disconnect them **(see illustration)**. Work back along the harness, freeing it from all the relevant clips and ties, noting its correct routing.

3 Disconnect the wiring from the front brake light switch.

4 Unscrew the two front brake master cylinder assembly clamp bolts and position the master cylinder clear of the handlebar, making sure no strain is placed on the hydraulic hose. On ZX-9R B models, ensure the master cylinder is kept upright to prevent possible fluid spillage from its reservoir.

5 Undo the two retaining screws and separate the two halves of the handlebar switch assembly. Note how the throttle cables locate in the switch assembly, then free them and remove the switch from the handlebar.

Installation

6 Lubricate the upper end of each throttle cable with multi-purpose grease. Locate the cables correctly in the switch halves, then assemble the switch on the handlebar, seating the rear half locating peg in the handlebar hole. Ensure the switch and cables are correctly assembled then securely tighten the switch screws.

7 Locate the master cylinder on the handlebar and fit the mounting clamp with its arrow mark facing upwards. On ZX-7R models, align the master cylinder mounting clamp upper split with the punch mark on the top of the handlebar and, on ZX-9R B models, align the mounting clamp upper split with the handlebar switch split. Once the master cylinder is correctly positioned, tighten the mounting clamp upper bolt to the specified torque, followed by the lower one.

8 Ensure the switch wiring is correctly routed and retained by all the relevant clips and ties, then securely reconnect its wiring connectors and the brake light switch wiring.

9 Install the upper fairing (see Chapter 8). On completion, check the operation of the switch and front brake light before using the bike on the road. Also check the action of the throttle cables (see Chapter 1).

Right-hand switch – ZX-9R C, E and F models

Removal

10 On C models, remove the fuel tank and air filter housing to gain access to the switch wiring connector(s) (see Chapter 4) **(see illustration)**.

11 On E and F models, remove the upper fairing (see Chapter 8) to gain access to the switch wiring connector(s).

12 On all models, trace the wiring harness of the switch back to its connector(s) and disconnect the switch. Work back along the harness, freeing it from all the relevant clips and ties, noting its correct routing.

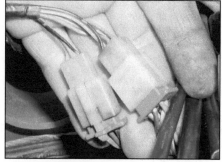

21.10 On ZX-9R C models, the handlebar switch wiring connectors are located underneath the air filter housing

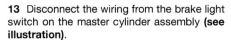

21.13 Disconnect the wiring connector(s) from the front brake light switch

21.14a Release the rubber gaiter from the throttle twistgrip housing . . .

21.14b . . . then remove the retaining screws and separate the housing

13 Disconnect the wiring from the brake light switch on the master cylinder assembly **(see illustration)**.
14 Fold back the throttle cable rubber gaiter to free it from the twistgrip housing **(see illustration)**. Undo the two retaining screws and separate the two halves of the twistgrip housing, noting how the cables locate in the housing **(see illustration)**.
15 To improve access, unscrew the two front brake master cylinder assembly clamp bolts and position the master cylinder clear of the handlebar, making sure no strain is placed on the hydraulic hose.
16 Unscrew the two handlebar switch screws, then free the switch from the handlebar.

Installation

17 Assemble the two halves of the switch on the handlebar, ensuring the switch peg is correctly located in the handlebar hole, and tighten the retaining screws securely.
18 Lubricate the upper end of each throttle cable with multi-purpose grease. Locate the outer cables correctly in the twistgrip housing, then assemble the housing on the handlebar, ensuring the locating peg is correctly seated in the handlebar hole. Ensure the twistgrip housing and cables are correctly assembled, then tighten the retaining screws securely before seating the cable gaiter correctly on the housing.
19 Locate the master cylinder on the handlebar and fit the mounting clamp with its arrow mark facing upwards. Position the master cylinder so that its clamp upper split is

aligned with the throttle housing split, then tighten the mounting clamp upper bolt to the specified torque, followed by the lower one.
20 Ensure the switch wiring is correctly routed and retained by all the relevant clips and ties, then securely reconnect its wiring connector(s) and the brake light switch wiring.
21 Install the air filter housing and fuel tank (see Chapter 4) on C models, or the upper fairing (Chapter 8) on E and F models. On completion, check the operation of the switch and front brake light before using the bike on the road. Also check the action of the throttle cables (see Chapter 1).

Left handlebar switch – all models

Removal

22 On ZX-9R C models, remove the fuel tank and air filter housing to gain access to the switch wiring connector(s) (see Chapter 4) **(see illustrations)**.
23 On all other models, remove the upper fairing (see Chapter 8) to gain access to the switch wiring connector(s).
24 On all models, trace the wiring harness of the switch back to its connector(s) and disconnect the switch. Work back along the harness, freeing it from all the relevant clips and ties, noting its correct routing.
25 Disconnect the wiring from the clutch switch.
26 On ZX-7R and ZX-9R B models, unscrew the two clutch master cylinder assembly clamp bolts and position the master cylinder

clear of the handlebar, making sure no strain is placed on the hydraulic hose. On ZX-9R B models, keep the master cylinder reservoir upright to prevent possible fluid leakage.
27 On ZX-9R C, E and F models, unscrew the two clutch lever mounting clamp bolts and position the lever clear of the handlebar, making sure no strain is placed on the cable.
28 On all models, unscrew the two handlebar switch screws, then free the switch from the handlebar and choke lever and remove it from the bike **(see illustration)**.

Installation

29 Lubricate the upper end of the choke cable with multi-purpose grease. Locate the lever and outer cable correctly in the switch halves, then assemble the switch on the handlebar, locating the rear half locating peg in the handlebar hole. Ensure the switch, lever and cable are correctly assembled, then securely tighten the switch screws.
30 On ZX-7R and ZX-9R B models, locate the master cylinder on the handlebar and fit the mounting clamp with its arrow mark facing upwards. On ZX-7R models, align the master cylinder mounting clamp split with the punch mark on the top of the handlebar and, on ZX-9R B models, position the master cylinder so its clamp upper split is located 5 mm to the rear of the handlebar switch split. Once the master cylinder is correctly positioned, tighten the mounting clamp upper bolt, followed by the lower, to the specified torque.
31 On ZX-9R C, E and F models, locate the clutch lever bracket on the handlebar and fit

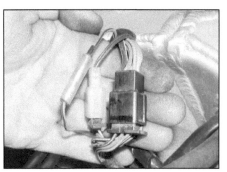

21.22a On ZX-9R C models, the left handlebar switch wiring connectors are located under the air filter housing . . .

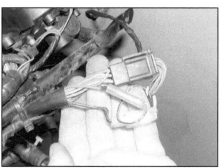

21.22b . . . on all other models, they can be found behind the upper fairing (ZX-9R B shown)

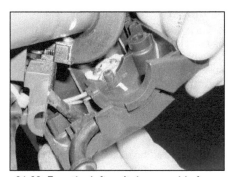

21.28 Free the left switch assembly from the handlebar and choke lever

the mounting clamp with its arrow mark facing upwards. Position the lever so that its clamp upper split is aligned with the handlebar switch split, then securely tighten the mounting clamp upper bolt, followed by the lower one.

32 Ensure the switch wiring is correctly routed and retained by all the relevant clips and ties, then securely reconnect all its wiring connectors.

33 Install the air filter housing and fuel tank on ZX-9R C models (see Chapter 4), or the upper fairing on all other models (see Chapter 8). On completion, check the operation of the handlebar switches and clutch switch before using the bike on the road. Also check the action of the choke cable (see Chapter 1).

22 Neutral switch – check, removal and installation

Check

1 Before checking the electrical circuit, check the bulb (see Section 17) and fuse (see Section 5).

2 The switch is located on the left-hand side of the engine, directly below the front sprocket cover. Make sure the transmission is in neutral, then disconnect the wiring connector from the switch; on ZX-7R models, trace the wire back from the switch and disconnect it at the wiring connector.

3 With the connector disconnected and the ignition switched ON, the neutral light should be out. If not, the wire between the connector and instrument cluster must be earthed (grounded) at some point.

4 Check for continuity between the switch terminal and the crankcase. With the transmission in neutral, there should be continuity. With the transmission in gear, there should be no continuity. If the tests prove otherwise, then the switch is faulty.

5 If the continuity tests prove the switch is good, check for voltage at the wire terminal using a test light. If there is no voltage present, check the wiring between the switch, junction box and instrument cluster (see the *Wiring Diagrams* at the end of this Chapter).

Removal

6 Drain the engine oil (see Chapter 1). The neutral switch is fitted to the left-hand side of the engine, just below the front sprocket cover. Removal is as follows.

ZX-7R models

7 Trace the wiring back from the switch and disconnect it from the main wiring harness.

8 Undo the two screws and free the neutral switch from the gearchange mechanism cover. Recover the switch O-ring and discard it; a new one should be used on installation. Remove the neutral switch contact and spring from the end of the selector drum for safe-keeping.

ZX-9R models

10 Disconnect the wiring connector from the switch, then unscrew the switch and remove it from the crankcase **(see illustration)**. Discard the sealing washer; a new one should be used on installation.

Installation

ZX-7R models

11 Ensure the spring and contact are correctly installed in the selector drum.

12 Fit a new O-ring to the switch, fit the switch to the gearchange mechanism cover and tighten its retaining screws securely.

13 Ensure the wire is correctly routed, then reconnect it to the main wiring harness.

14 Refill the engine using the specified grade and quantity of oil (see Chapter 1), then check the operation of the switch.

ZX-9R models

15 Ensure the switch threads are clean and dry then fit a new sealing washer.

16 Apply silicone sealant (Kawasaki recommend the use of Kawasaki Bond 56019-120) to the switch threads then fit the switch to the crankcase and tighten it to the torque setting specified at the beginning of the Chapter. Securely reconnect the wiring connector.

17 Refill the engine using the specified grade and quantity of oil (see Chapter 1 Specifications) then check the operation of the switch.

23 Sidestand switch – check and renewal

Check

1 The sidestand switch is mounted on the sidestand bracket and is part of the bike's safety circuit. It prevents the engine from being started whilst in gear unless the clutch lever is pulled in and the sidestand is up; and it stops the engine running whilst in gear if the sidestand is down. Before checking the electrical circuit, check the fuse (see Section 5).

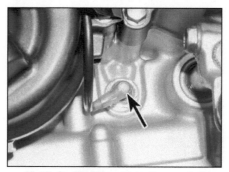

22.10 On ZX-9R models, the neutral switch (arrowed) is screwed into the left side of the crankcase

2 Support the bike on an auxiliary stand, then trace the wiring back from the switch to its connector(s) and disconnect the switch. If necessary, remove the fuel tank (see Chapter 4) to gain access to the wiring connector(s).

3 Connect an ohmmeter across the switch terminals and check the operation of the switch. With the sidestand up there should be continuity (zero resistance) between the terminals, and with the sidestand down there should be no continuity (infinite resistance).

4 If the switch does not perform as expected, it is defective and must be renewed. If the switch is good, check the wiring between the various components in the starter safety circuit (see the *Wiring Diagrams* at the end of this Chapter).

Renewal

5 The sidestand switch is mounted on the sidestand bracket. If necessary, remove the lower fairing panel (see Chapter 8) for improved access.

6 Trace the wiring back from the switch to its connector(s) and disconnect the switch. If necessary, remove the fuel tank (see Chapter 4) to gain access to the connector(s).

7 Work back along the switch wiring, freeing it from any relevant retaining clips and ties, and noting its correct routing.

8 On ZX-7R and ZX-9R B models, undo the retaining screws and remove the sidestand switch from the bike. Remove all traces of locking compound from the sidestand switch screw threads. Apply a drop of fresh locking compound to each screw, then locate the new switch on the bracket and tighten its retaining screws securely.

9 On ZX-9R C, E and F models, unscrew the mounting bolt then free the switch from the sidestand and bracket and remove it from the bike. Locate the new switch onto the sidestand bracket, making sure the switch lever is correctly engaged with the sidestand pin. Fit the switch mounting bolt and tighten it securely.

10 On all models, make sure the wiring is correctly routed and retained by all the necessary clips, then reconnect the connector(s) and check the operation of the sidestand switch.

11 Where necessary, install the fairing lower panel (see Chapter 8) and fuel tank (see Chapter 4).

24 Clutch switch – check and renewal

Check

1 The clutch switch is mounted onto the underside of the clutch master cylinder/lever bracket (as applicable) and is part of the bike's safety circuit. It prevents the engine from being started whilst in gear unless the clutch lever is pulled in and the sidestand is up.

25.1a On ZX-7R models, the horn is mounted on the rear of the bottom yoke

25.1b On ZX-9R models, the horn is mounted on one of the radiator upper mounting bolts (ZX-9R B shown)

25.8 Unscrew the mounting bolt, then disconnect the wiring connectors and remove the horn (ZX-9R B shown with fairing removed)

2 To check the switch, disconnect the wiring connector. Connect the positive probe of an ohmmeter or a continuity test light to the central switch terminal, and the negative probe to one of the outer terminals, then note the meter reading – first with the clutch lever out, and then with the lever pulled in. Now connect the negative probe to the other outer switch terminal and, again, note the readings with the lever out and in. With the probes connected one way, there should be continuity with the clutch lever released and no continuity with the lever pulled in. With the probes connected the other way, there should be no continuity with the lever released and continuity with the lever pulled in.

3 If the switch is good, check the other components in the starter circuit, as described in the relevant sections of this Chapter. If all components are good, check the wiring between the various components (see the *Wiring Diagrams* at the end of this Chapter).

Renewal

4 Disconnect the wiring connector(s) from the clutch switch.

5 Undo the retaining screw and remove the switch from the master cylinder/lever bracket (as applicable).

6 Installation is the reverse of removal. Check the operation of the switch before using the bike on the road.

25 Horn –
check and renewal

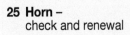

Check

1 On ZX-7R models, the horn is mounted on the rear of the bottom yoke and, on ZX-9R models, it is mounted onto a bracket attached to one of the radiator upper mounting bolts **(see illustrations)**.

2 Disconnect the wiring connectors from the horn. Using two jumper wires, apply battery voltage directly to the terminals on the horn. If the horn sounds, check the switch (see

Section 21) and the wiring between the switch and the horn (see the *Wiring Diagrams* at the end of this Chapter).

3 If the horn does not sound, renew it.

Renewal

ZX-7R models

4 The horn is mounted on the rear of the bottom yoke.

5 Disconnect the wiring connectors from the horn, then unscrew the mounting bracket bolts and remove the horn from the bike.

6 Install the horn and tighten its retaining bolts securely. Connect the wiring connectors and check the horn operation.

ZX-9R models

7 On B models, the horn bracket is attached to the radiator left upper mounting bolt and, on C, E and F models, it is fitted to the right upper mounting bolt.

8 Unscrew the mounting bolt and free the horn bracket from the radiator. Disconnect the wiring connectors and remove the horn from the bike **(see illustration)**.

9 Reconnect the wiring connectors securely, then locate the horn bracket on the radiator mounting and tighten the mounting bolt securely. Check the horn operation before using the bike.

26.2 The starter relay is located under the seats

26 Starter relay –
check and renewal

Check

1 If the starter circuit is faulty, first check the fuse (see Section 5).

2 The starter relay is located under the rider's seat. Remove the seats for access (see Chapter 8). Lift the rubber terminal cover and unscrew the bolt securing the starter motor lead **(see illustration)**; position the lead away from the relay terminal. With the ignition switch ON, the engine kill switch in the 'RUN' position and the transmission in neutral, press the starter switch. The relay should be heard to click.

3 If the relay does not click, switch off the ignition and remove the relay as described below; test it as follows.

4 Set a multimeter to the ohms x 1 scale and connect it across the relay's starter motor and battery lead terminals **(see illustration)**. Using a fully-charged 12 volt battery and two insulated jumper wires, connect the positive (+ve) terminal of the battery to the yellow/red wire terminal of the relay, and the negative (–ve) terminal to the black/yellow wire terminal of the relay. At this point the relay should be heard to click and the multimeter should read

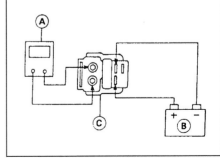

26.4 Starter relay test arrangement

A Ohmmeter   *C Starter relay*
B 12 volt battery

26.8 Disconnect the wiring connector from the starter relay . . .

0 ohms (continuity). If this is the case, the relay is proved good. If the relay does not click when battery voltage is applied and indicates no continuity (infinite resistance) across its terminals, it is faulty and must be replaced.

5 If the relay is good, check for battery voltage between the yellow/red wire and the black/yellow wire when the starter button is pressed. Check the other components in the starter circuit, as described in the relevant sections of this Chapter. If all components are good, check the wiring between the various components (see the *Wiring Diagrams* at the end of this Chapter).

Renewal

6 The starter relay is located underneath the rider's seat, on the left-hand side of the junction box. To gain access to the relay, remove the seats (see Chapter 8).

7 Disconnect the battery negative (–) terminal.

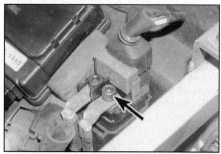

27.4 On ZX-7R models, unscrew the bolt and detach the starter motor lead from the relay

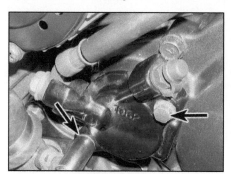

27.15a On ZX-9R B models, unscrew the retaining bolts . . .

26.9 . . . then unscrew the bolts (arrowed) and detach the battery and starter motor leads

8 Disconnect the wiring connector from the starter relay **(see illustration)**.

9 Lift the insulating cover, then unscrew the two bolts securing the starter motor and battery leads to the relay and detach both leads **(see illustration)**.

10 Free the relay from its mounting and remove it from the bike.

11 Installation is the reverse of removal, making sure that the battery and starter motor leads are fitted the correct way round and that their bolts are securely tightened. Ensure the rubber insulation cover is correctly fitted to the relay, then reconnect the battery negative lead.

27 Starter motor – removal and installation

ZX-7R models

Removal

1 Remove the seats (see Chapter 8) and disconnect the battery negative (–) lead.

2 Remove the fuel tank (see Chapter 4).

3 Remove the alternator as described in Section 31.

4 Lift the insulation cover, then unscrew the bolt and detach the starter motor lead from the starter relay **(see illustration)**. Note the correct routing of the lead, then free it from any relevant clips and ties so it can be removed with the motor.

5 Unscrew the two bolts securing the starter motor to the crankcase, then slide the starter

27.15b . . . and free the slave cylinder from the sprocket cover (pushrod end piece arrowed)

motor out of position and remove it from the bike.

6 Remove the O-ring on the end of the starter motor and discard it, as a new one must be used. If necessary, peel back the rubber terminal cover, then remove the nut securing the starter lead to the motor and detach the lead.

Installation

7 Where necessary, connect the starter lead to the motor and secure it with the nut. Make sure the rubber cover is correctly seated over the terminal.

8 Install a new O-ring on the end of the starter motor and ensure it is seated in its groove. Apply a smear of engine oil to the O-ring to aid installation.

9 Ensure the crankcase and starter motor mating surfaces are clean and dry, then manoeuvre the motor into position and slide it into the crankcase. Ensure that the starter motor teeth mesh correctly with those of the idler gear, then fit the mounting bolts and tighten to the specified torque.

10 Route the starter motor lead correctly up to the relay, securing it in position with the relevant clips and ties. Securely tighten the lead retaining bolt and seat the insulation cover correctly on the relay.

11 Install the alternator (see Section 31), then reconnect the battery negative (–) lead. Check the operation of the starter motor before installing the fuel tank and fairing panel (see Chapters 4 and 8).

ZX-9R B models

Removal

12 Remove the seats (see Chapter 8) and disconnect the battery negative (–) lead.

13 Remove the fuel tank and fuel pump assembly (see Chapter 4).

14 Remove the left side fairing lower panel (see Chapter 8).

15 Unscrew the clutch slave cylinder bolts and free the cylinder from the sprocket cover, taking care not to lose the end piece from the pushrod **(see illustrations) (see Haynes Hint)**

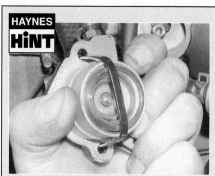

To prevent the piston being accidentally expelled, retain it with a cable tie passed through the cylinder mounting bolts holes and securely tightened around the cylinder.

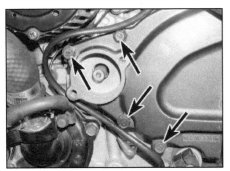

27.16 Unscrew the retaining bolts (arrowed) and remove the sprocket cover

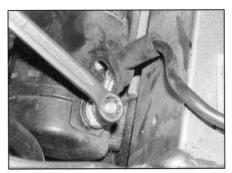

27.17 Unscrew the nut and detach the lead from the starter motor

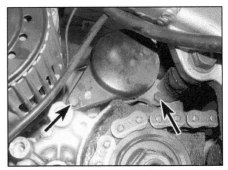

27.18a Unscrew the bolts (arrowed) . . .

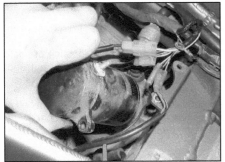

27.18b . . . then manoeuvre the starter motor out of position

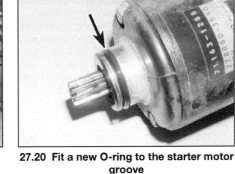

27.20 Fit a new O-ring to the starter motor groove

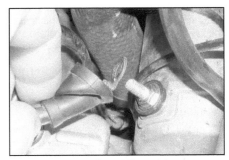

27.29 On ZX-9R C and E models, unscrew the nut and detach the lead from the starter motor

Note: *There is no need to disconnect the hydraulic hose from the cylinder.*
Caution: Do not operate the clutch lever whilst the cylinder is detached.

16 Undo the four retaining bolts and remove the sprocket cover from the engine **(see illustration)**. Recover the locating dowels and store them with the cover for safe-keeping.

17 Peel back the rubber terminal cover, then remove the nut securing the starter lead to the motor and detach the lead **(see illustration)**.

18 Unscrew the two bolts securing the starter motor to the crankcase, then slide the starter motor out of position and remove it from the machine **(see illustrations)**.

19 Remove the O-ring on the end of the starter motor and discard it, as a new one must be used.

Installation

20 Install a new O-ring on the end of the

starter motor and ensure it is seated in its groove **(see illustration)**. Apply a smear of engine oil to the O-ring to aid installation.

21 Ensure the crankcase and starter motor mating surfaces are clean and dry, then manoeuvre the motor into position and slide it into the crankcase. Ensure that the starter motor teeth mesh correctly with those of the idler gear, then fit the mounting bolts and tighten them to the specified torque.

22 Connect the starter lead to the motor and secure it with the nut. Make sure the rubber cover is correctly seated over the terminal.

23 Install the fuel pump and tank (see Chapter 4), then reconnect the battery and check the operation of the starter motor.

24 Ensure the locating dowels are in position then fit the sprocket cover to the engine. Install the cover retaining bolts and tighten them to the specified torque.

25 Ensure the cover and clutch slave cylinder

surfaces are clean and dry. Ensure the end piece is correctly fitted to the pushrod, then remove the cable tie (where fitted) and fit the slave cylinder, tightening its retaining bolts securely.

26 Install the lower fairing panel (see Chapter 8).

ZX-9R C, E and F models

Removal

27 Remove the seats (see Chapter 8) and disconnect the battery negative (–) lead.

28 Remove the fuel tank (see Chapter 4).

29 Peel back the rubber terminal cover, then remove the nut securing the starter lead to the motor and detach the lead **(see illustration)**.

30 On C models, unscrew the four bolts and remove the cover and sound-deadening insulation from the top of the crankcase **(see illustrations)**.

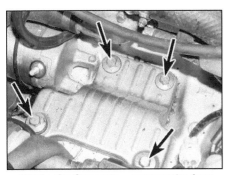

27.30a On C models, unscrew the four bolts (arrowed) . . .

27.30b . . . and lift off the cover . . .

27.30c . . . and sound-deadening insulation from the top of the crankcase

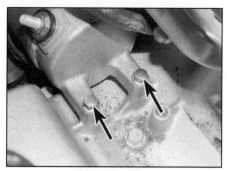

27.31a Unscrew the two bolts
(arrowed) . . .

27.31b . . . then manoeuvre the starter
motor out of position

27.33 Fit a new O-ring to the starter motor
prior to installation

31 On all models, unscrew the two bolts securing the starter motor to the crankcase, then slide the starter motor out of position and remove it from the machine **(see illustrations)**.

32 Remove the O-ring on the end of the starter motor and discard it, as a new one must be used.

Installation

33 Install a new O-ring on the end of the starter motor and ensure it is seated in its groove **(see illustration)**. Apply a smear of engine oil to the O-ring to aid installation.

34 Ensure the crankcase and starter motor mating surfaces are clean and dry, then manoeuvre the motor into position and slide it into the crankcase. Ensure that the starter motor teeth mesh correctly with those of the idler gear, then fit the mounting bolts and tighten them to the specified torque.

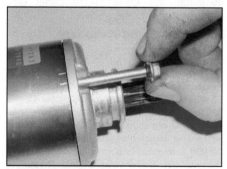

28.3 Unscrew the long bolts from the
starter motor, complete with their O-rings

35 Connect the starter lead to the motor and secure it with the nut. Make sure the rubber cover is correctly seated over the terminal.

36 On C models, fit the sound deadening insulation and cover to the crankcase and securely tighten its retaining bolts.

37 On all models, install the fuel tank (see Chapter 4), then reconnect the battery and check the operation of the starter motor.

---

28 Starter motor –
disassembly, inspection
and reassembly

Disassembly

1 Remove the starter motor (see Section 27).

2 Note the alignment marks between the main housing and the front and rear covers, or make your own if they aren't clear.

3 Unscrew the two long bolts and withdraw them from the starter motor **(see illustration)**. Remove the O-ring from each bolt and discard it; new ones should be used on reassembly.

4 Wrap some insulating tape around the teeth on the end of the starter motor shaft – this will protect the oil seal from damage as the front cover is removed. Remove the front cover from the motor **(see illustration)**. Remove the front cover O-ring from the main housing and discard it; a new one should be used on reassembly.

5 Remove the rear cover and brushplate assembly from the motor. Remove the cover

O-ring from the main housing and discard it, as a new one must be used.

6 Withdraw the armature from the main housing.

7 Noting the correct fitted location of each component, unscrew the terminal nut and remove it along with its insulating washer. Withdraw the terminal bolt and brushplate assembly from the rear cover and recover the O-ring and insulating pad from the bolt.

8 Lift the brush springs and slide the brushes from their holders.

Inspection

9 The parts of the starter motor that are most likely to require attention are the brushes. Measure the length of the brushes and compare the results to the brush length listed in this Chapter's Specifications **(see illustration)**. If any of the brushes are worn beyond the service limit, renew the brush plate and terminal bolt assemblies. If the brushes are not worn excessively, or cracked, chipped, or otherwise damaged, they may be re-used.

10 Inspect the commutator bars on the armature for scoring, scratches and discoloration. The commutator can be cleaned and polished with crocus cloth, but do not use sandpaper or emery paper. After cleaning, wipe away any residue with a cloth soaked in electrical system cleaner or denatured alcohol. Check for commutator wear by measuring its diameter and comparing it to the specified diameter (see this Chapter's Specifications) **(see illustration)**.

28.4 Slide the front cover off the motor

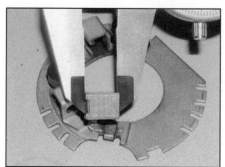

28.9 Measure the length of each starter
motor brush to check the amount of wear

28.10 Measuring armature commutator
diameter to check for wear

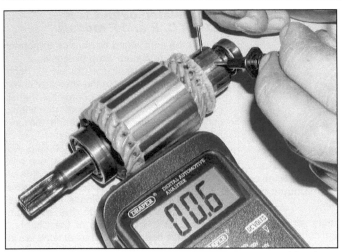

28.11a Using an ohmmeter, test the armature by checking for continuity between each bar of the commutator . . .

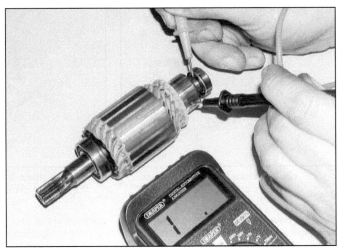

28.11b . . . and between each bar and the armature shaft

28.15a Ensure the insulator pad (arrowed) is correctly fitted, then insert the terminal bolt

28.15b Fit the O-ring to the terminal bolt . . .

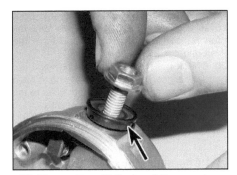

28.15c . . . then fit the insulating washer (arrowed) and nut, tightening it securely

11 Using an ohmmeter or a continuity test light, check for continuity between the commutator bars (see illustration). Continuity should exist between each bar and all of the others. Also, check for continuity between the commutator bars and the armature shaft (see illustration). There should be no continuity (infinite resistance) between the commutator and the shaft. If the checks indicate otherwise, the armature is defective.

12 With the rear cover, terminal bolt and brushplate components correctly assembled, check for continuity between the terminal bolt and the cover/brush plate. There should be continuity (infinite resistance), if not there is a short circuit; check the terminal bolt insulating pad, O-ring and washer for signs of damage.

13 Check the front end of the armature shaft for worn, cracked, chipped and broken teeth. If the shaft is damaged or worn, renew the armature.

14 Inspect the end covers for signs of cracks or wear. Inspect the magnets in the main housing, and the housing itself, for cracks.

Reassembly

15 Ensure that the insulator pad is in place in the rear cover, then insert the terminal bolt

(see illustration). Fit the O-ring and the insulating washer to the bolt and fit the nut (see illustrations). Ensure all components are correctly located, then tighten the nut securely. Check for continuity between the terminal bolt and cover before proceeding (see Step 12).

16 Slide the brushes back into position in their holders and place the brush spring ends onto the brushes. Locate the brushplate

assembly in the rear cover, making sure its tab is correctly located in the slot in the cover (see illustration).

17 Insert the armature into the rear cover, locating the brushes on the commutator bars as you do, taking care not to damage them (see illustration). Check that each brush is securely pressed against the commutator by its spring and is free to move easily in its holder.

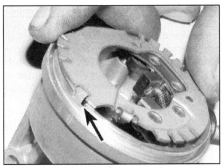

28.16 Locate the brushes in their holders and locate the brushplate assembly in the rear cover, aligning its tab (arrowed) in the cover slot

28.17 Insert the armature into the rear cover, ensuring the brushes are correctly located on the commutator

28.18a Fit a new O-ring to the rear cover . . .

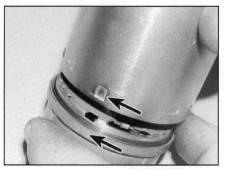

28.18b . . . then fit the housing, aligning the marks (arrowed) made/noted on removal

18 Fit a new rear cover O-ring, then fit the housing over the armature and onto the rear cover, aligning the marks noted/made on removal **(see illustrations)**.
19 Apply a smear of grease to the lips of the front cover oil seal and fit a new front cover O-ring **(see illustration)**. Install the front cover, aligning the marks made on removal, then remove the protective tape from the shaft end.
20 Check the marks made on removal are correctly aligned, then fit a new O-ring to each of the starter motor bolts. Fit both bolts to the starter motor and tighten them securely.
21 Install the starter motor (see Section 27).

29 Charging system testing – general information and precautions

1 If the performance of the charging system is suspect, the system as a whole should be checked first, before testing the individual components. **Note:** *Before beginning the checks, make sure the battery is fully charged and that all system connections are clean and tight.*
2 Checking the output of the charging system and the performance of the various components within the charging system requires the use of a multimeter (with voltage, current and resistance checking facilities).
3 When making the checks, follow the procedures carefully to prevent incorrect

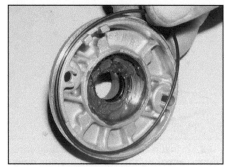

28.19 Fit a new O-ring, then fit the front cover to the motor

connections or short circuits, as irreparable damage to electrical system components may result if short circuits occur.
4 If a multimeter is not available, the job of checking the charging system should be left to a dealer or automotive electrician.

30 Charging system – output test

1 If the charging system of the machine is thought to be faulty, remove the seats (see Chapter 8) and perform the following checks.

Regulated voltage output test – all models

2 Start the engine and warm it up to normal operating temperature. Stop the engine.
3 To check the voltage output connect a multimeter set to the 0-20 volts DC scale (voltmeter) across the terminals of the battery (positive (+) lead to battery positive (+) terminal, negative (–) lead to battery negative (–) terminal). Start the engine and slowly increase engine speed to approximately 4000 rpm and note the reading obtained. The regulated voltage should be as specified at the beginning of the Chapter.
4 On ZX-7R and ZX-9R B models, if the voltage is outside these limits, have the alternator checked by a Kawasaki dealer or an auto-electrical specialist (see Section 31).
5 On ZX-9R C, E and F models, if the voltage is outside these limits, carry out the unregulated voltage check and stator coil checks (see Steps 6 to 10). **Note:** *If the voltage is below the limit, then it is more likely that the alternator is faulty. If the voltage is above the limit, it is more likely that the regulator is faulty.*

 HAYNES HINT *Clues to a faulty regulator are constantly blowing bulbs, with brightness varying considerably with engine speed, and battery overheating.*

Unregulated output test – ZX-9R C, E and F models

6 Start the engine and warm it up to normal operating temperature. Stop the engine.
7 Remove the fuel tank (see Chapter 4). Trace the alternator wiring from the alternator cover and disconnect it at the connector. Either position the alternator end of the wiring connector so that it is accessible with the tank reinstalled, or rig up a remote fuel tank.
8 Using a multimeter set to 0-250 volts AC range, connect the meter probes to one pair of yellow terminals on the alternator side of the connector. Start the engine and increase its speed to 4000 rpm. Check the voltage output and compare it to the minimum specified at the beginning of the Chapter. Connect the meter to each pair of terminals in turn, taking three readings in all. If any of the readings are below the minimum specified, check the stator coil resistance (see below). If the readings are good, the regulator is probably at fault (see Section 33).

Alternator stator coil test – ZX-9R C, E and F models

9 Remove the fuel tank (see Chapter 4). Trace the alternator wiring from the alternator cover and disconnect it at the connector.
10 Using a multimeter set to the ohms x 1 scale, check the resistance between each of the yellow wires on the alternator side of the connector, taking a total of three readings. Also check for continuity between each yellow terminal and ground (earth). If the stator coil windings are in good condition, resistance between each of the terminals should be as specified at the beginning of this Chapter, with no continuity (infinite resistance) between any of the terminals and ground (earth). If not, the alternator stator coil assembly is at fault and should be replaced. If the resistance readings are as specified but the alternator output is low when tested as above, replace the rotor with a new one. **Note:** *Before condemning the stator coils, check the fault is not due to damaged wiring between the connector and coils.*

31 Alternator – check, removal and installation

ZX-7R and ZX-9R B models

Check

1 The alternator contains both the regulator and rectifier assemblies. If the regulated voltage check shows up an alternator problem, a quick check can be made by removing the end cover from the alternator (this can be done without removing the alternator from the engine). Check the internal wiring for signs of damage. If no obvious signs of damage are present, the alternator should be taken to a Kawasaki dealer or an auto-electrical specialist for further testing.

31.6a On ZX-7R and ZX-9R B models,
unscrew the bolt . . .

31.6b . . . then free the coolant pipe from
the water pump cover and recover the
O-ring (arrowed)

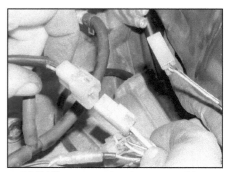

31.7 Disconnect the alternator wiring
connector

Testing of the alternator components requires specialist equipment and if carried out carelessly, could actually damage the regulator and rectifier assemblies.

Removal

2 Remove the fuel tank (see Chapter 4).
3 Remove the left lower fairing panel (see Chapter 8).
4 Unscrew the clutch slave cylinder bolts and free the cylinder from the sprocket cover, taking care not to lose the end piece from the pushrod **(see illustrations 27.15a and 27.15b)**. (see **Haynes Hint** at Step 15 of Section 27)
Note: *There is no need to disconnect the hydraulic hose from the cylinder.*
Caution: Do not operate the clutch lever whilst the cylinder is detached.
5 Drain the cooling system (see Chapter 1).
6 Unscrew the bolt and free the radiator lower hose pipe from the water pump cover **(see illustration)**. Recover the pipe O-ring and discard it; a new one should be used on installation **(see illustration)**.
7 Trace the wiring back from the alternator and disconnect its connector from the main wiring harness **(see illustration)**.
8 Slacken and remove the three mounting bolts and manoeuvre the alternator out of position **(see illustrations)**. Remove the O-ring from the end of the alternator and discard it, as a new one must be used.

9 Remove the rubber damper segments from the drive coupling **(see illustration)**. If any segment shows signs of damage or deterioration renew all the segments as a set.

Installation

10 Install the rubber damper segments correctly in the drive coupling.
11 Install a new O-ring on the end of the alternator. Ensure the O-ring is seated in its groove and apply a smear of engine oil to it to aid installation.
12 Ensure the crankcase and alternator mating surfaces are clean and dry, then manoeuvre the alternator into position. Ensure the alternator flange is correctly engaged with the drive coupling segments, then fit the mounting bolts and tighten them to the specified torque.
13 Ensure the wiring is correctly routed, then reconnect the alternator connector.
14 Fit a new O-ring, then seat the metal pipe back in the water pump cover and securely tighten its retaining bolt.
15 Ensure the cover and clutch slave cylinder surfaces are clean and dry. Ensure the end piece is correctly fitted to the pushrod, then remove the cable tie (where fitted) and fit the slave cylinder, tightening its retaining bolts securely.
16 Install the fuel tank and fairing panel, then refill the cooling system (see Chapter 1).

ZX-9R C, E and F models
Check
17 Carry out the voltage output and stator coil checks described in Section 30.

Alternator cover and stator
Removal
18 Remove the lower fairing and left middle fairing panel (see Chapter 8).
19 Remove the fuel tank (see Chapter 4).
20 Remove the coolant reservoir (see Chapter 3).
21 Disconnect the wiring connectors from the neutral switch and coolant temperature gauge sensor (the connectors are part of the alternator harness), then disconnect the alternator connector from the main wiring harness.
22 Drain the engine oil (see Chapter 1) or be prepared for some oil loss as the alternator cover is removed.
23 Unscrew the alternator cover retaining bolts and withdaw the cover squarely from the engine unit. **Note:** *Due to the magnetic pull of the rotor, the cover may prove difficult to remove. Do not pry the cover away with a screwdriver, as the mating surfaces will be damaged.*
24 Remove the cover locating dowels from the crankcase and discard the gasket.

31.8a Unscrew the mounting bolts
(arrowed) . . .

31.8b . . . then remove the alternator from
the engine, noting its O-ring (arrowed)

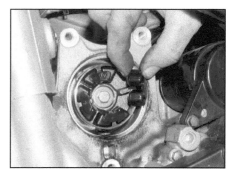

31.9 Remove the rubber damper segments
from the drive coupling and check them
for wear or damage

31.25 Alternator wiring harness plate bolts (A) and stator bolts (B) – ZX-9R C and E models

31.27a Apply sealant to the crankcase mating surface on either side of the joints . . .

25 To remove the stator, unscrew the two bolts and remove the wiring harness plate from inside the cover (see illustration). Unscrew the four stator retaining bolts, then remove the assembly, noting how the rubber wiring grommet fits.

Installation

26 If the stator was removed, get rid of all traces of sealant from the stator wiring grommet and the cover. Apply fresh sealant to the grommet, then install the stator into the cover, ensuring the grommet is correctly located in the cover groove. Tighten the stator

31.27b . . . then fit a new gasket onto the locating dowels (arrowed)

retaining bolts to the specified torque, then fit the wiring harness plate and tighten its bolts to the specified torque.

27 Ensure the mating surfaces are clean and dry, then apply a smear of sealant to the area of the crankcase mating surface on either side of the crankcase half joints (see illustration). Fit both locating dowels to the crankcase and locate the new gasket on the dowels (see illustration).

28 Ensure the starter idler gear is correctly installed, then fit the alternator cover assembly to the engine and locate it on the dowels.

Caution: Take care not to trap your fingers between the cover and the crankcase; the rotor will magnetically attract the stator as the cover is fitted.

29 Install the cover bolts and tighten them evenly to the specified torque.

30 Ensure the wiring is correctly routed and reconnect the connectors to the main harness, coolant temperature sensor and neutral switch.

31 Install the coolant reservoir and top up with coolant (see Chapter 3).

32 Fit the fuel tank (see Chapter 4).

33 Refill the engine with oil (see Chapter 1).

34 Install the fairing panels (see Chapter 8).

Alternator rotor

Removal

Note: *To remove the alternator rotor the special Kawasaki rotor puller and adapter (Tool No. 57001-1216 and Tool No.57001-1405) or a pattern equivalent will be required. Do not attempt to remove the rotor using any other method.*

35 Remove the alternator cover as described in Steps 18 to 24.

36 Withdraw the shaft and remove the starter motor idler gear from the engine (see illustration).

37 Slacken and remove the rotor retaining bolt and washer whilst holding the rotor to prevent it turning. The rotor can be retained using a large strap wrench (see illustration). Alternatively, if the engine is still in the frame, the engine can be locked through the transmission by selecting top gear and applying the rear brake hard.

38 Screw the rotor puller adapter (see Note) onto the rotor and tighten it securely (see illustration). Screw the puller tightly into the centre of the adapter and tap sharply on the end of puller tool to release the rotor's grip on the tapered crankshaft end. Remove the rotor assembly, complete with the starter motor

31.36 Withdraw the shaft and remove the starter motor idler gear

31.37 Retain the rotor with a strap wrench, then unscrew the retaining bolt

31.38a Kawasaki adapter (A) and rotor puller (B) for releasing the alternator rotor from the crankshaft taper

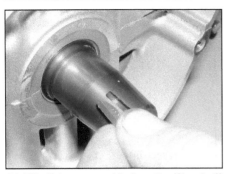

31.38b Take care not to lose the Woodruff key from the crankshaft end

31.40 Lubricate the one-way clutch with oil, then fit the starter clutch driven gear to the rear of the alternator rotor

31.42 Slide the rotor and gear assembly onto the crankshaft, aligning its slot with the Woodruff key

driven gear; the driven gear can then be separated from the rotor. Remove the Woodruff key from the crankshaft end and store it with the rotor for safe-keeping **(see illustration)**. Refer to Chapter 2B for information on the starter clutch components.

Installation

39 Using solvent, remove all traces of oil and grease from the tapered mating surfaces of the crankshaft and rotor. Apply a thin smear of molybdenum disulphide grease to the flat surface of the crankshaft on which the starter clutch driven gear rotates, ensuring no grease gets on the tapered surface.

40 Lubricate the starter one-way clutch with clean engine oil, then fit the driven gear to the rear of the alternator rotor **(see illustration)**.

41 Ensure the Woodruff key is correctly fitted in the crankshaft slot.

42 Make sure that no metal objects have attached themselves to the magnet on the inside of the rotor, then slide on the rotor/driven gear assembly, aligning its slot with the key **(see illustration)**.

43 Install the rotor bolt and washer and tighten it to the specified torque, using the method employed on removal to prevent the rotor from turning **(see illustrations)**.

44 Mesh the idler gear correctly with the starter motor pinion and driven gear then insert its shaft, locating it correctly in the crankcase.

45 Fit the alternator cover as described in Steps 27 to 34.

32 Regulator and rectifier (ZX-7R and ZX-9R B models) – check and renewal

1 The alternator contains both the regulator and rectifier assemblies. If the regulated voltage check shows up an alternator problem, a quick check can be made by removing the end cover from the alternator (this can be done without removing the alternator from the engine). Check the internal wiring for signs of damage. If no obvious signs of damage are present, the alternator should be taken to a Kawasaki dealer or an auto-electrical specialist for further testing. Testing of the alternator components requires

31.43a Fit the washer and retaining bolt . . .

specialist equipment and if carried out carelessly, could actually damage the regulator and rectifier assemblies.

2 Renewal of the regulator and rectifier assemblies requires the use of a soldering iron and carries a high risk of damaging the new components if not carried out correctly. For this reason it is recommended that the job is entrusted to a Kawasaki dealer or auto-electrical specialist.

33 Regulator/rectifier (ZX-9R C, E and F models) – check and renewal

Check

1 If the regulated voltage check shows up a charging system problem but the unregulated voltage check and stator coil checks show the

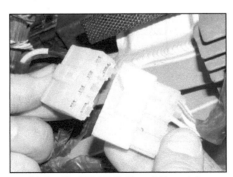

33.3a On ZX-9R C, E and F models, disconnect the wiring connector . . .

31.43b . . . and tighten it to the specified torque whilst retaining the rotor with a strap wrench

alternator to be functioning correctly, then it is likely that the regulator/rectifier unit is faulty. Testing of the regulator/rectifier requires specialist equipment and if carried out carelessly, could actually damage the unit. If a fault is suspected, the unit should be taken to a Kawasaki dealer or an auto-electrical specialist for further testing. The best means of testing is to substitute the regulator/rectifier with a replacement which is known to be in working order.

Renewal

2 Remove the seat cowling (see Chapter 8). The regulator/rectifier is mounted on the left side of the rear subframe.

3 Ensure the ignition is switched off, then disconnect the regulator/rectifier unit wiring connector(s) **(see illustration)**. Unscrew the mounting bolts and remove the unit from the subframe **(see illustration)**.

33.3b . . . then unscrew the mounting bolts (arrowed) and remove the regulator/ rectifier unit from the subframe

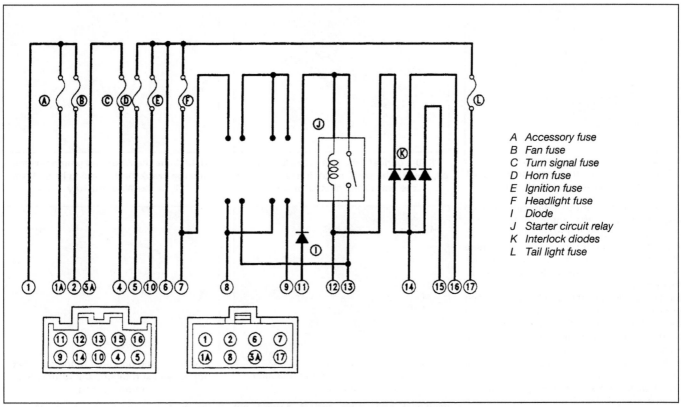

**34.3a Junction box internal circuitry and terminal identification –
UK (and European) models except ZX-9R F2**

A Accessory fuse
B Fan fuse
C Turn signal fuse
D Horn fuse
E Ignition fuse
F Headlight fuse
I Diode
J Starter circuit relay
K Interlock diodes
L Tail light fuse

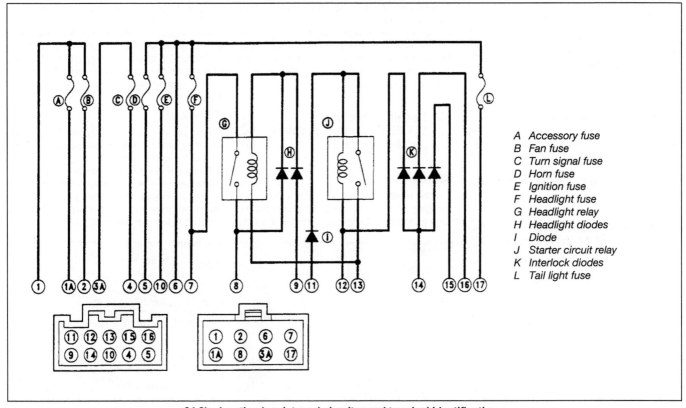

**34.3b Junction box internal circuitry and terminal identification –
US models and all ZX-9R F2 models**

A Accessory fuse
B Fan fuse
C Turn signal fuse
D Horn fuse
E Ignition fuse
F Headlight fuse
G Headlight relay
H Headlight diodes
I Diode
J Starter circuit relay
K Interlock diodes
L Tail light fuse

4 Fit the new regulator/rectifier and securely tighten its mounting bolts. Reconnect the wiring connector(s) then install the seat cowling (see Chapter 8).

34 Junction box – check and renewal

Check

1 Remove the seats (see Chapter 8).
2 The junction box contains the starter circuit relay, the headlight relay (US and all ZX-9R F2 models), and diodes, as well as the fusebox. The starter circuit relay and interlock diodes are part of the safety circuit which prevents the engine from being started whilst in gear unless the clutch lever is pulled in and the sidestand is up; and stops the engine running whilst in gear if the sidestand is down. Slide the junction box out of its holder and disconnect the wiring connectors.
3 Using an ohmmeter or continuity tester and 12 volt battery, connect the meter probes and the battery leads (when specified) to the terminals on the junction box connectors, as indicated in the various tables shown **(see illustrations)**. When testing the diode circuit, test each following terminal pair in one direction, then reverse the probes and test the pair in the other direction.

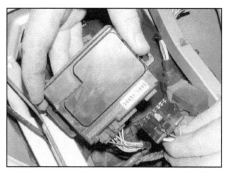

34.7 Free the junction box from its holder and disconnect its wiring connectors

Fuse circuit checks

Connect meter to terminals	Reading obtained
1 and 1A	0 ohms
1 and 2	0 ohms
3A and 4	0 ohms
6 and 5	0 ohms
6 and 10	0 ohms
6 and 7	0 ohms
6 and 17	0 ohms
1A and 8	Open circuit (infinite resistance)
2 and 8	Open circuit (infinite resistance)
3A and 8	Open circuit (infinite resistance)
6 and 2	Open circuit (infinite resistance)
6 and 3A	Open circuit (infinite resistance)
17 and 3A	Open circuit (infinite resistance)

Starter relay circuit inspection (battery disconnected)

Connect meter to terminals	Reading obtained
9 and 11	Open circuit (infinite resistance)
12 and 13	Open circuit (infinite resistance)
13 (positive lead) and 11 (negative lead)	Open circuit (infinite resistance)
12 (positive lead) and 11 (negative lead)	Not an open circuit (the actual reading is not important)

Headlight relay circuit inspection (battery disconnected) – US models and all ZX-9R F2 models

Connect meter to terminals	Reading obtained
7 and 8	Open circuit (infinite resistance)
7 and 13	Open circuit (infinite resistance)
13 (positive lead) and 9 (negative lead)	Not an open circuit (the actual reading is not important)

Starter relay circuit inspection (battery connected)

Connect 12 volt battery to terminals	Connect meter to terminals	Reading obtained
11 (positive lead) and 12 (negative lead)	13 (positive lead) and 11 (negative lead)	Not an open circuit (the actual reading is not important

Headlight relay circuit inspection with battery connected – US models and all ZX-9R F2 models

Connect 12 volt battery to terminals	Connect meter to terminals	Reading obtained
9 (positive lead) and 13 (negative lead)	7 and 8	0 ohms

Diode circuit inspection – UK (and European) models except ZX-9R F2

Connect meter to terminals	Reading obtained
12 and 11, 12 and 14, 15 and 14, 16 and 14	A low resistance reading should be obtained in one direction, a reading at least ten times higher in the opposite direction when the meter leads are swapped

Diode circuit inspection – US models and all ZX-9R F2 models

Connect meter to terminals	Reading obtained
12 and 11, 12 and 14, 15 and 14, 16 and 14, 13 and 8, 13 and 9	A low resistance reading should be obtained in one direction a reading at least ten times higher in the opposite direction when the meter leads are swapped

4 If any of the above checks do not provide the expected reading, the junction box is faulty and must be replaced.
5 If the junction box is good, check the other components in that circuit as described in the relevant sections of this Chapter. If all components are good, check the wiring between the various components (see the *Wiring Diagrams* at the end of this Chapter).

Renewal

6 Remove the seats (see Chapter 8).
7 Slide the junction box out of its holder then, ensuring the ignition is switched off, disconnect the wiring connectors **(see illustration)**. Install the new box and make sure the connectors are secure.

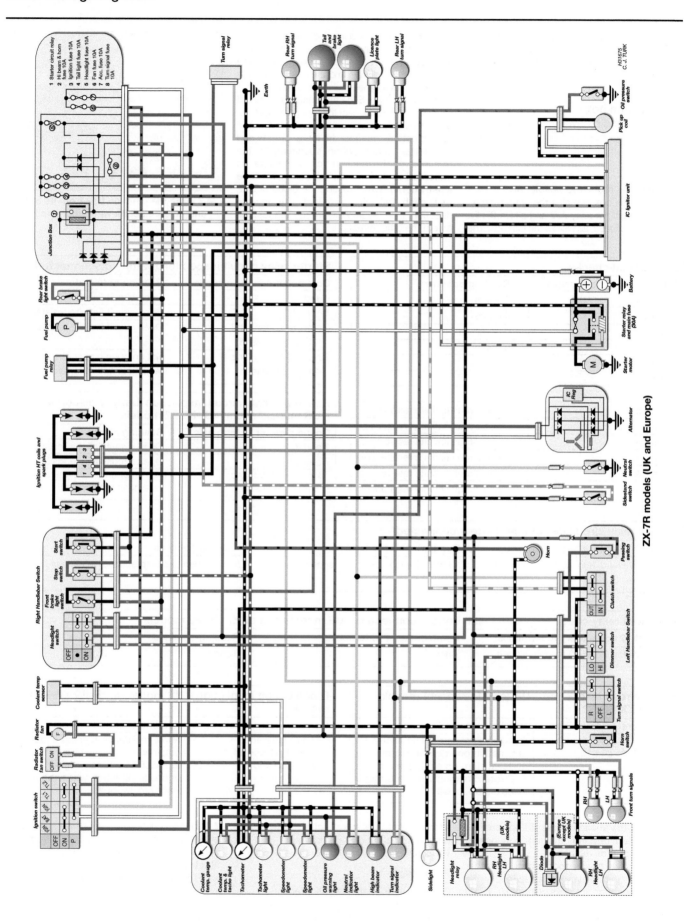

ZX-7R models (UK and Europe)

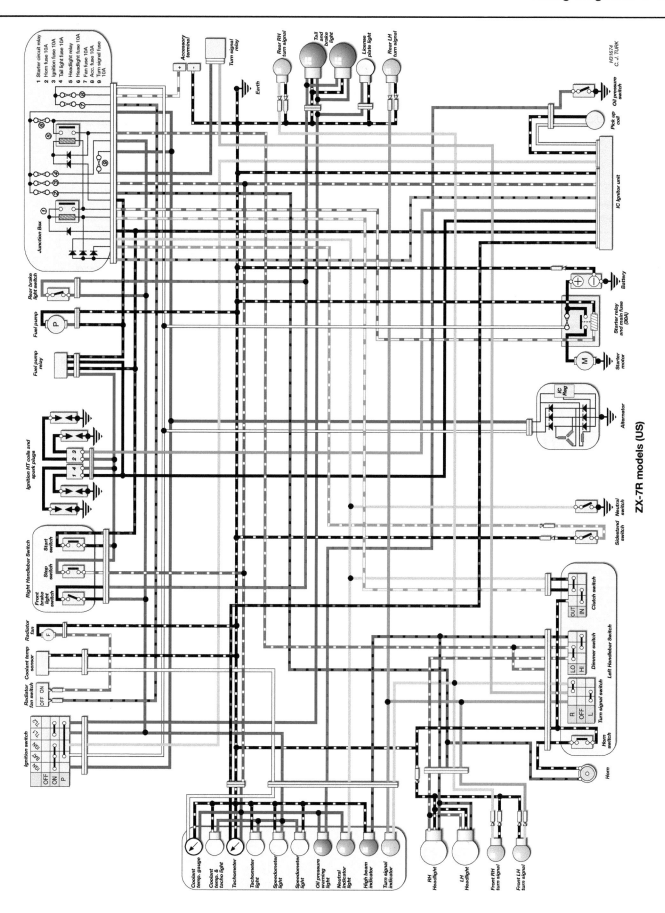

ZX-7R models (US)

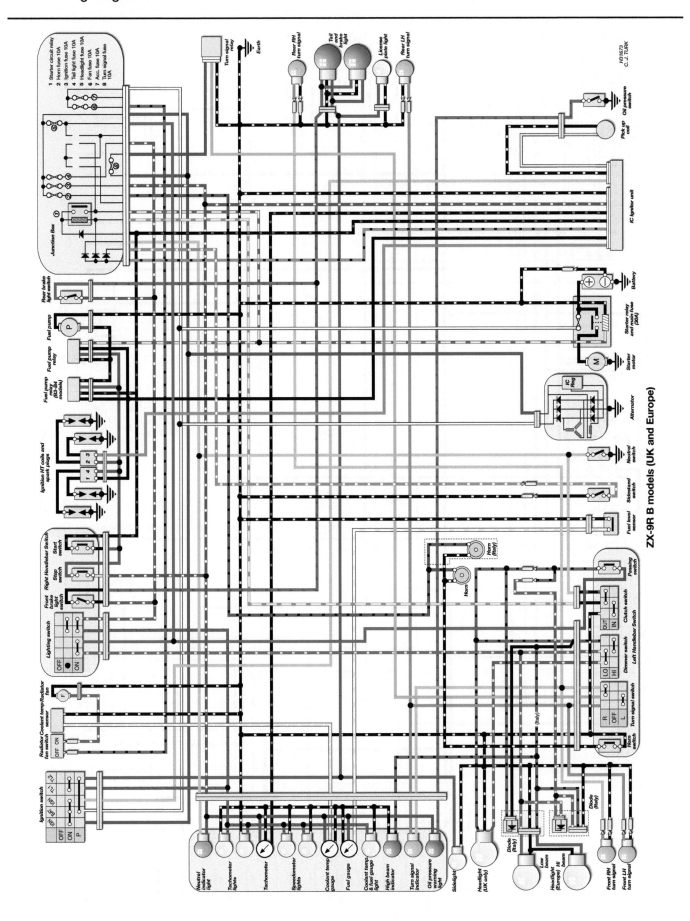

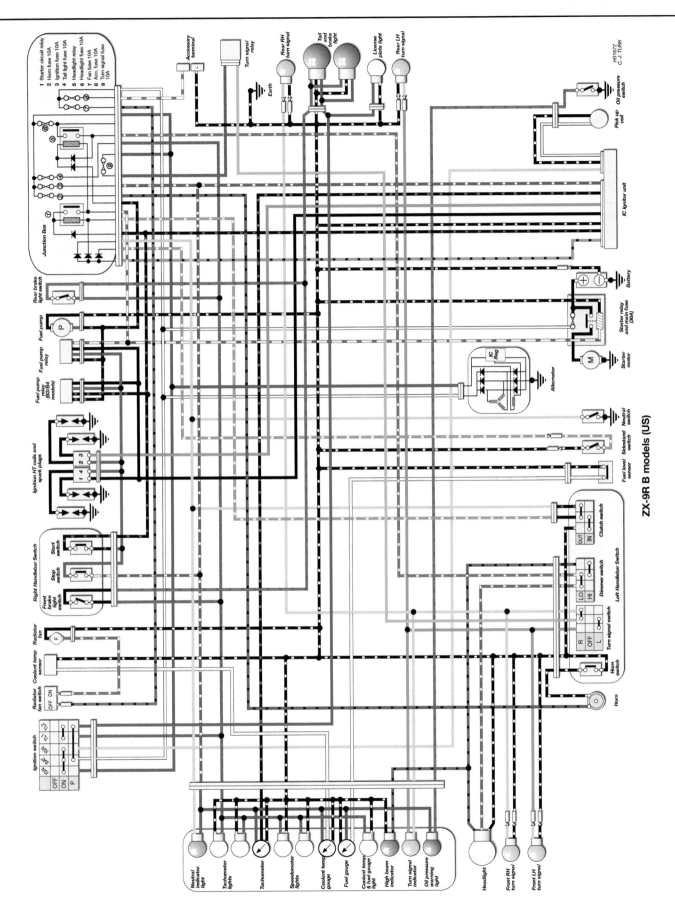

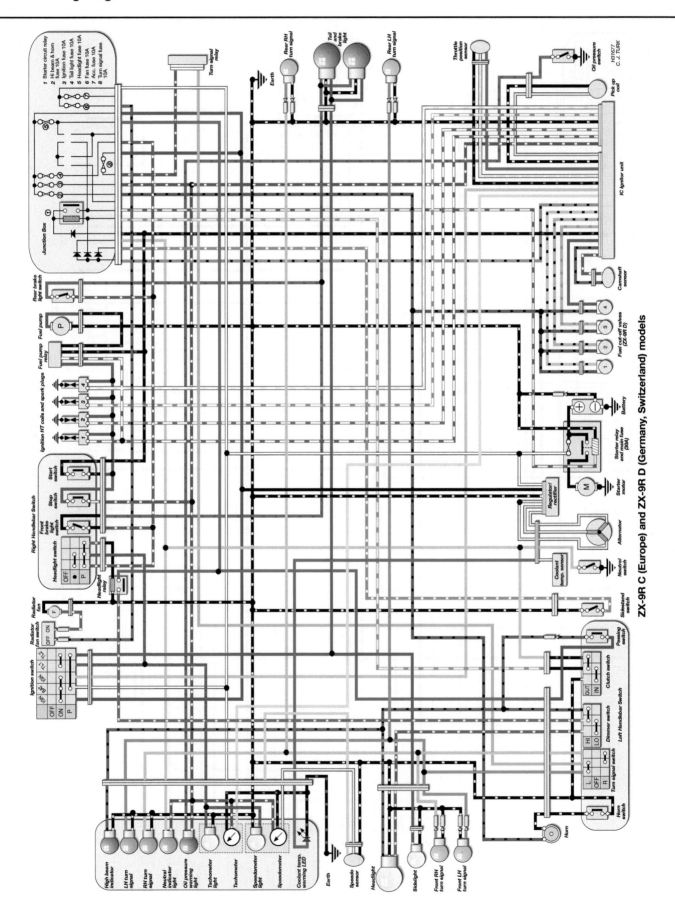

ZX-9R C (Europe) and ZX-9R D (Germany, Switzerland) models

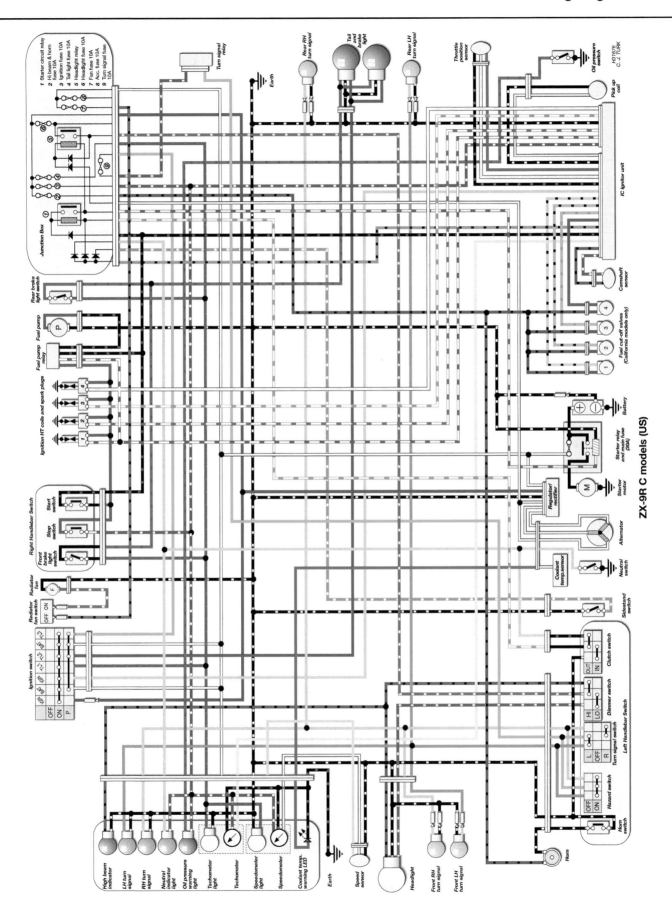

ZX-9R C models (US)

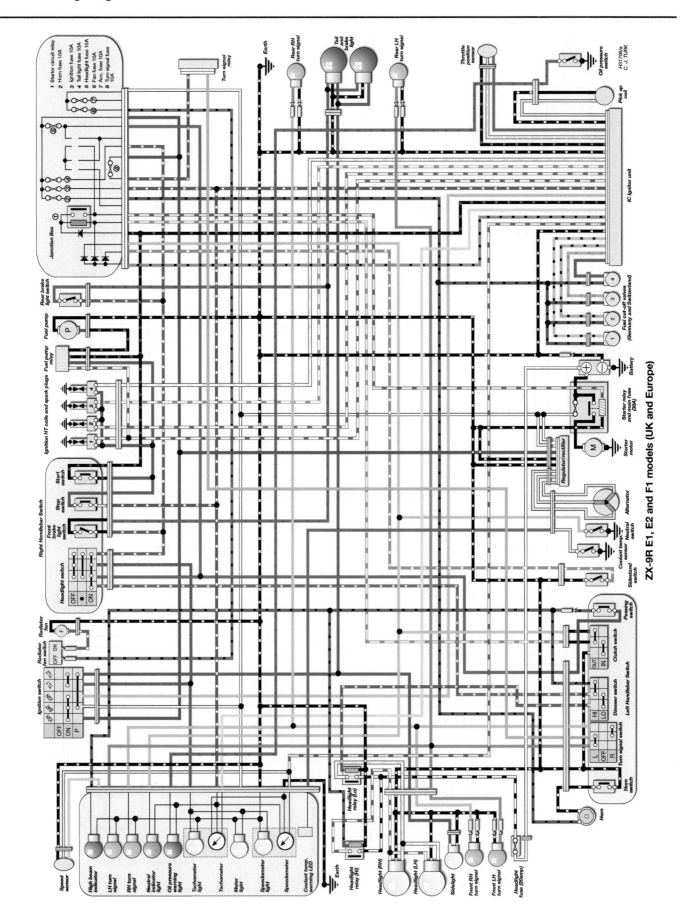

ZX-9R E1, E2 and F1 models (UK and Europe)

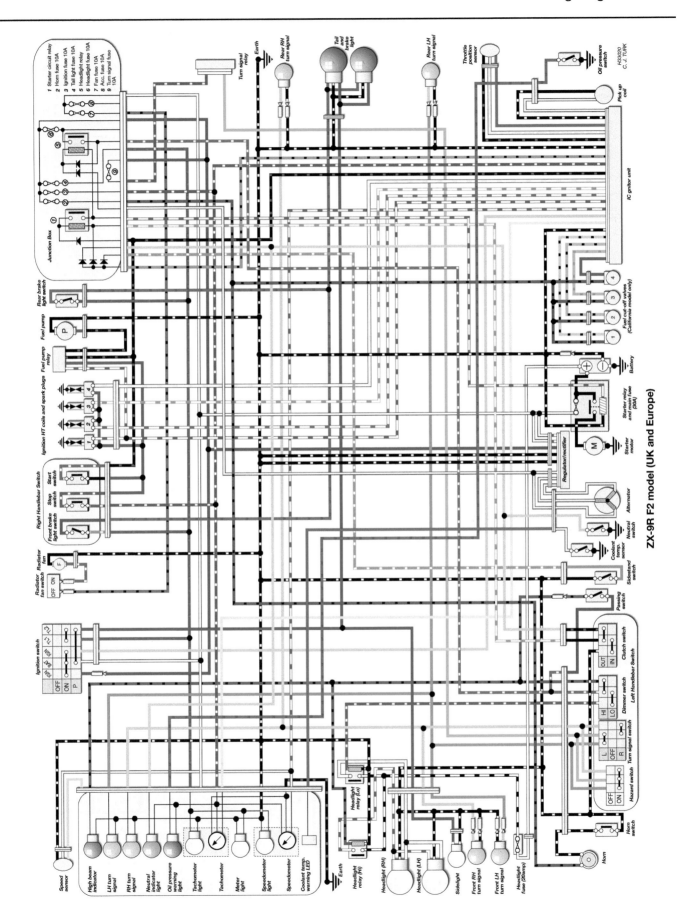

ZX-9R F2 model (UK and Europe)

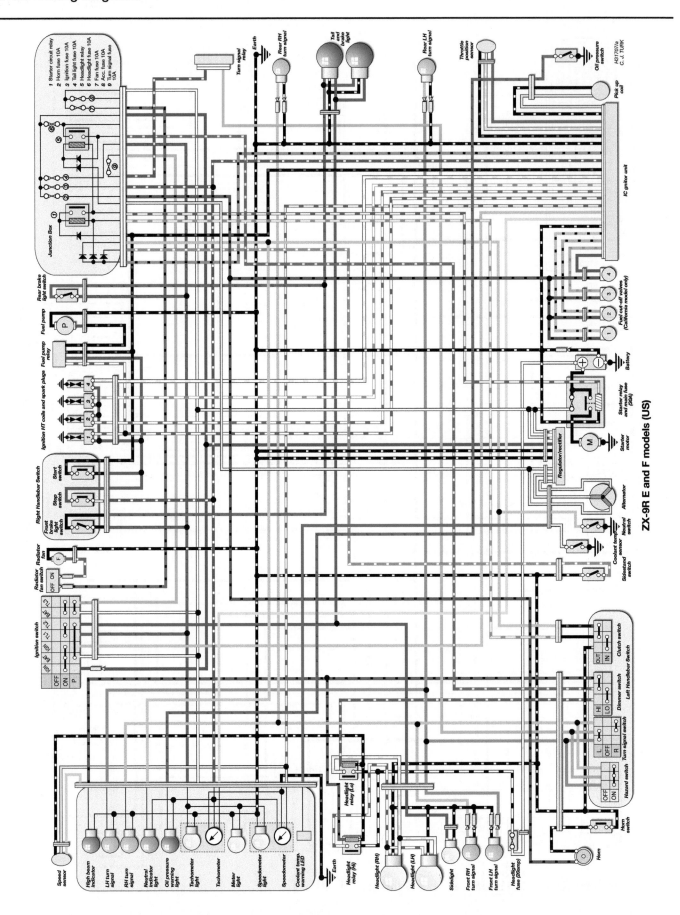

ZX-9R E and F models (US)

Reference

Tools and Workshop Tips

● Building up a tool kit and equipping your workshop ● Using tools ● Understanding bearing, seal, fastener and chain sizes and markings ● Repair techniques

Security

● Locks and chains ● U-locks ● Disc locks ● Alarms and immobilisers ● Security marking systems ● Tips on how to prevent bike theft

Lubricants and fluids

● Engine oils ● Transmission (gear) oils ● Coolant/anti-freeze ● Fork oils and suspension fluids ● Brake/clutch fluids ● Spray lubes, degreasers and solvents

Conversion Factors

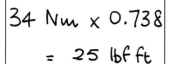

● Formulae for conversion of the metric (SI) units used throughout the manual into Imperial measures

MOT Test Checks

● A guide to the UK MOT test ● Which items are tested ● How to prepare your motorcycle for the test and perform a pre-test check

Storage

● How to prepare your motorcycle for going into storage and protect essential systems ● How to get the motorcycle back on the road

Fault Finding

● Common faults and their likely causes ● How to check engine cylinder compression ● How to make electrical tests and use test meters

Index

Buying tools

A toolkit is a fundamental requirement for servicing and repairing a motorcycle. Although there will be an initial expense in building up enough tools for servicing, this will soon be offset by the savings made by doing the job yourself. As experience and confidence grow, additional tools can be added to enable the repair and overhaul of the motorcycle. Many of the specialist tools are expensive and not often used so it may be preferable to hire them, or for a group of friends or motorcycle club to join in the purchase.

As a rule, it is better to buy more expensive, good quality tools. Cheaper tools are likely to wear out faster and need to be renewed more often, nullifying the original saving.

> **Warning: To avoid the risk of a poor quality tool breaking in use, causing injury or damage to the component being worked on, always aim to purchase tools which meet the relevant national safety standards.**

The following lists of tools do not represent the manufacturer's service tools, but serve as a guide to help the owner decide which tools are needed for this level of work. In addition, items such as an electric drill, hacksaw, files, soldering iron and a workbench equipped with a vice, may be needed. Although not classed as tools, a selection of bolts, screws, nuts, washers and pieces of tubing always come in useful.

For more information about tools, refer to the Haynes *Motorcycle Workshop Practice TechBook* (Bk. No. 3470).

Manufacturer's service tools

Inevitably certain tasks require the use of a service tool. Where possible an alternative tool or method of approach is recommended, but sometimes there is no option if personal injury or damage to the component is to be avoided. Where required, service tools are referred to in the relevant procedure.

Service tools can usually only be purchased from a motorcycle dealer and are identified by a part number. Some of the commonly-used tools, such as rotor pullers, are available in aftermarket form from mail-order motorcycle tool and accessory suppliers.

Maintenance and minor repair tools

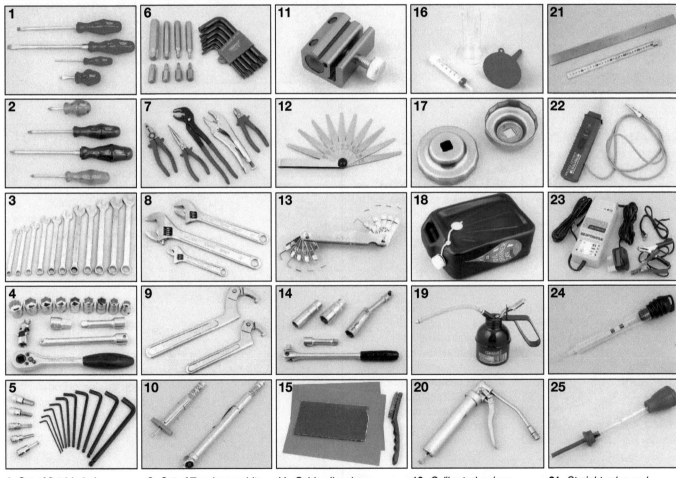

1 Set of flat-bladed screwdrivers
2 Set of Phillips head screwdrivers
3 Combination open-end and ring spanners
4 Socket set (3/8 inch or 1/2 inch drive)
5 Set of Allen keys or bits
6 Set of Torx keys or bits
7 Pliers, cutters and self-locking grips (Mole grips)
8 Adjustable spanners
9 C-spanners
10 Tread depth gauge and tyre pressure gauge
11 Cable oiler clamp
12 Feeler gauges
13 Spark plug gap measuring tool
14 Spark plug spanner or deep plug sockets
15 Wire brush and emery paper
16 Calibrated syringe, measuring vessel and funnel
17 Oil filter adapters
18 Oil drainer can or tray
19 Pump type oil can
20 Grease gun
21 Straight-edge and steel rule
22 Continuity tester
23 Battery charger
24 Hydrometer (for battery specific gravity check)
25 Anti-freeze tester (for liquid-cooled engines)

Repair and overhaul tools

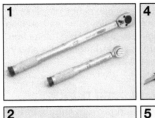

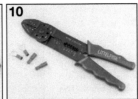

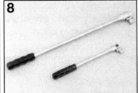

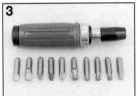
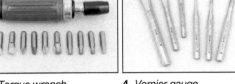
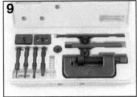

1 Torque wrench
   (small and mid-ranges)
2 Conventional, plastic or
   soft-faced hammers
3 Impact driver set

4 Vernier gauge
5 Circlip pliers (internal and
   external, or combination)
6 Set of cold chisels
   and punches

7 Selection of pullers
8 Breaker bars
9 Chain breaking/
   riveting tool set

10 Wire stripper and
    crimper tool
11 Multimeter (measures
    amps, volts and ohms)
12 Stroboscope (for
    dynamic timing checks)

13 Hose clamp
    (wingnut type shown)
14 Clutch holding tool
15 One-man brake/clutch
    bleeder kit

Specialist tools

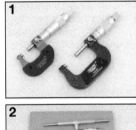
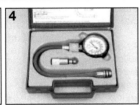

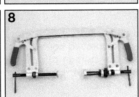
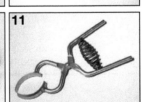

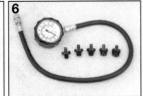

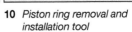
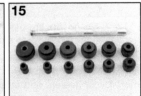

1 Micrometers
   (external type)
2 Telescoping gauges
3 Dial gauge

4 Cylinder
   compression gauge
5 Vacuum gauges (left) or
   manometer (right)
6 Oil pressure gauge

7 Plastigauge kit
8 Valve spring compressor
   (4-stroke engines)
9 Piston pin drawbolt tool

10 Piston ring removal and
    installation tool
11 Piston ring clamp
12 Cylinder bore hone
    (stone type shown)

13 Stud extractor
14 Screw extractor set
15 Bearing driver set

1 Workshop equipment and facilities

The workbench

● Work is made much easier by raising the bike up on a ramp - components are much more accessible if raised to waist level. The hydraulic or pneumatic types seen in the dealer's workshop are a sound investment if you undertake a lot of repairs or overhauls **(see illustration 1.1)**.

1.1 Hydraulic motorcycle ramp

● If raised off ground level, the bike must be supported on the ramp to avoid it falling. Most ramps incorporate a front wheel locating clamp which can be adjusted to suit different diameter wheels. When tightening the clamp, take care not to mark the wheel rim or damage the tyre - use wood blocks on each side to prevent this.
● Secure the bike to the ramp using tie-downs **(see illustration 1.2)**. If the bike has only a sidestand, and hence leans at a dangerous angle when raised, support the bike on an auxiliary stand.

1.2 Tie-downs are used around the passenger footrests to secure the bike

● Auxiliary (paddock) stands are widely available from mail order companies or motorcycle dealers and attach either to the wheel axle or swingarm pivot **(see illustration 1.3)**. If the motorcycle has a centrestand, you can support it under the crankcase to prevent it toppling whilst either wheel is removed **(see illustration 1.4)**.

1.3 This auxiliary stand attaches to the swingarm pivot

1.4 Always use a block of wood between the engine and jack head when supporting the engine in this way

Fumes and fire

● Refer to the Safety first! page at the beginning of the manual for full details. Make sure your workshop is equipped with a fire extinguisher suitable for fuel-related fires (Class B fire - flammable liquids) - it is not sufficient to have a water-filled extinguisher.
● Always ensure adequate ventilation is available. Unless an exhaust gas extraction system is available for use, ensure that the engine is run outside of the workshop.
● If working on the fuel system, make sure the workshop is ventilated to avoid a build-up of fumes. This applies equally to fume build-up when charging a battery. Do not smoke or allow anyone else to smoke in the workshop.

Fluids

● If you need to drain fuel from the tank, store it in an approved container marked as suitable for the storage of petrol (gasoline) **(see illustration 1.5)**. Do not store fuel in glass jars or bottles.

1.5 Use an approved can only for storing petrol (gasoline)

● Use proprietary engine degreasers or solvents which have a high flash-point, such as paraffin (kerosene), for cleaning off oil, grease and dirt - never use petrol (gasoline) for cleaning. Wear rubber gloves when handling solvent and engine degreaser. The fumes from certain solvents can be dangerous - always work in a well-ventilated area.

Dust, eye and hand protection

● Protect your lungs from inhalation of dust particles by wearing a filtering mask over the nose and mouth. Many frictional materials still contain asbestos which is dangerous to your health. Protect your eyes from spouts of liquid and sprung components by wearing a pair of protective goggles **(see illustration 1.6)**.

1.6 A fire extinguisher, goggles, mask and protective gloves should be at hand in the workshop

● Protect your hands from contact with solvents, fuel and oils by wearing rubber gloves. Alternatively apply a barrier cream to your hands before starting work. If handling hot components or fluids, wear suitable gloves to protect your hands from scalding and burns.

What to do with old fluids

● Old cleaning solvent, fuel, coolant and oils should not be poured down domestic drains or onto the ground. Package the fluid up in old oil containers, label it accordingly, and take it to a garage or disposal facility. Contact your local authority for location of such sites or ring the oil care hotline.

OIL CARE
FOLLOW THE CODE
OIL BANK LINE
0800 66 33 66
www.oilbankline.org.uk

Note: It is antisocial and illegal to dump oil down the drain. To find the location of your local oil recycling bank, call this number free.

In the USA, note that any oil supplier must accept used oil for recycling.

2 Fasteners -
screws, bolts and nuts

Fastener types and applications

Bolts and screws

● Fastener head types are either of hexagonal, Torx or splined design, with internal and external versions of each type **(see illustrations 2.1 and 2.2)**; splined head fasteners are not in common use on motorcycles. The conventional slotted or Phillips head design is used for certain screws. Bolt or screw length is always measured from the underside of the head to the end of the item **(see illustration 2.11)**.

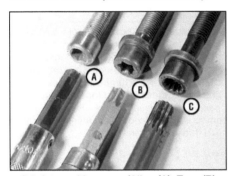

2.1 Internal hexagon/Allen (A), Torx (B) and splined (C) fasteners, with corresponding bits

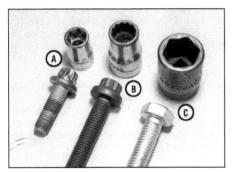

2.2 External Torx (A), splined (B) and hexagon (C) fasteners, with corresponding sockets

● Certain fasteners on the motorcycle have a tensile marking on their heads, the higher the marking the stronger the fastener. High tensile fasteners generally carry a 10 or higher marking. Never replace a high tensile fastener with one of a lower tensile strength.

Washers **(see illustration 2.3)**

● Plain washers are used between a fastener head and a component to prevent damage to the component or to spread the load when torque is applied. Plain washers can also be used as spacers or shims in certain assemblies. Copper or aluminium plain washers are often used as sealing washers on drain plugs.

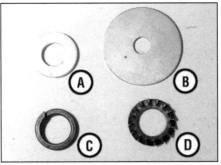

2.3 Plain washer (A), penny washer (B), spring washer (C) and serrated washer (D)

● The split-ring spring washer works by applying axial tension between the fastener head and component. If flattened, it is fatigued and must be renewed. If a plain (flat) washer is used on the fastener, position the spring washer between the fastener and the plain washer.
● Serrated star type washers dig into the fastener and component faces, preventing loosening. They are often used on electrical earth (ground) connections to the frame.
● Cone type washers (sometimes called Belleville) are conical and when tightened apply axial tension between the fastener head and component. They must be installed with the dished side against the component and often carry an OUTSIDE marking on their outer face. If flattened, they are fatigued and must be renewed.
● Tab washers are used to lock plain nuts or bolts on a shaft. A portion of the tab washer is bent up hard against one flat of the nut or bolt to prevent it loosening. Due to the tab washer being deformed in use, a new tab washer should be used every time it is disturbed.
● Wave washers are used to take up endfloat on a shaft. They provide light springing and prevent excessive side-to-side play of a component. Can be found on rocker arm shafts.

Nuts and split pins

● Conventional plain nuts are usually six-sided **(see illustration 2.4)**. They are sized by thread diameter and pitch. High tensile nuts carry a number on one end to denote their tensile strength.

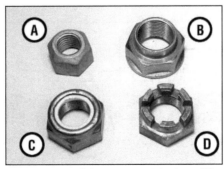

2.4 Plain nut (A), shouldered locknut (B), nylon insert nut (C) and castellated nut (D)

● Self-locking nuts either have a nylon insert, or two spring metal tabs, or a shoulder which is staked into a groove in the shaft - their advantage over conventional plain nuts is a resistance to loosening due to vibration. The nylon insert type can be used a number of times, but must be renewed when the friction of the nylon insert is reduced, ie when the nut spins freely on the shaft. The spring tab type can be reused unless the tabs are damaged. The shouldered type must be renewed every time it is disturbed.
● Split pins (cotter pins) are used to lock a castellated nut to a shaft or to prevent slackening of a plain nut. Common applications are wheel axles and brake torque arms. Because the split pin arms are deformed to lock around the nut a new split pin must always be used on installation - always fit the correct size split pin which will fit snugly in the shaft hole. Make sure the split pin arms are correctly located around the nut **(see illustrations 2.5 and 2.6)**.

2.5 Bend split pin (cotter pin) arms as shown (arrows) to secure a castellated nut

2.6 Bend split pin (cotter pin) arms as shown to secure a plain nut

Caution: If the castellated nut slots do not align with the shaft hole after tightening to the torque setting, tighten the nut until the next slot aligns with the hole - never slacken the nut to align its slot.

● R-pins (shaped like the letter R), or slip pins as they are sometimes called, are sprung and can be reused if they are otherwise in good condition. Always install R-pins with their closed end facing forwards **(see illustration 2.7)**.

2.7 Correct fitting of R-pin. Arrow indicates forward direction

Circlips (see illustration 2.8)

● Circlips (sometimes called snap-rings) are used to retain components on a shaft or in a housing and have corresponding external or internal ears to permit removal. Parallel-sided (machined) circlips can be installed either way round in their groove, whereas stamped circlips (which have a chamfered edge on one face) must be installed with the chamfer facing away from the direction of thrust load **(see illustration 2.9)**.

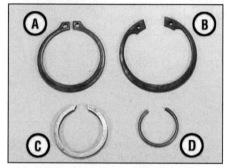

2.8 External stamped circlip (A), internal stamped circlip (B), machined circlip (C) and wire circlip (D)

● Always use circlip pliers to remove and install circlips; expand or compress them just enough to remove them. After installation, rotate the circlip in its groove to ensure it is securely seated. If installing a circlip on a splined shaft, always align its opening with a shaft channel to ensure the circlip ends are well supported and unlikely to catch **(see illustration 2.10)**.

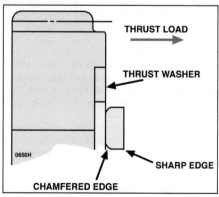

2.9 Correct fitting of a stamped circlip

THRUST LOAD

THRUST WASHER

SHARP EDGE

CHAMFERED EDGE

0650H

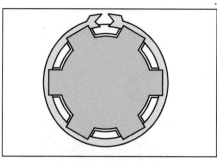

2.10 Align circlip opening with shaft channel

● Circlips can wear due to the thrust of components and become loose in their grooves, with the subsequent danger of becoming dislodged in operation. For this reason, renewal is advised every time a circlip is disturbed.

● Wire circlips are commonly used as piston pin retaining clips. If a removal tang is provided, long-nosed pliers can be used to dislodge them, otherwise careful use of a small flat-bladed screwdriver is necessary. Wire circlips should be renewed every time they are disturbed.

Thread diameter and pitch

● Diameter of a male thread (screw, bolt or stud) is the outside diameter of the threaded portion **(see illustration 2.11)**. Most motorcycle manufacturers use the ISO (International Standards Organisation) metric system expressed in millimetres, eg M6 refers to a 6 mm diameter thread. Sizing is the same for nuts, except that the thread diameter is measured across the valleys of the nut.

● Pitch is the distance between the peaks of the thread **(see illustration 2.11)**. It is expressed in millimetres, thus a common bolt size may be expressed as 6.0 x 1.0 mm (6 mm thread diameter and 1 mm pitch). Generally pitch increases in proportion to thread diameter, although there are always exceptions.

● Thread diameter and pitch are related for conventional fastener applications and the accompanying table can be used as a guide. Additionally, the AF (Across Flats), spanner or socket size dimension of the bolt or nut **(see illustration 2.11)** is linked to thread and pitch specification. Thread pitch can be measured with a thread gauge **(see illustration 2.12)**.

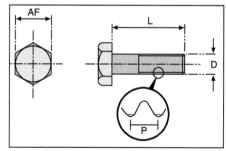

2.11 Fastener length (L), thread diameter (D), thread pitch (P) and head size (AF)

AF

L

D

P

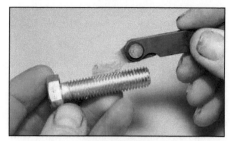

2.12 Using a thread gauge to measure pitch

AF size	Thread diameter x pitch (mm)
8 mm	M5 x 0.8
8 mm	M6 x 1.0
10 mm	M6 x 1.0
12 mm	M8 x 1.25
14 mm	M10 x 1.25
17 mm	M12 x 1.25

● The threads of most fasteners are of the right-hand type, ie they are turned clockwise to tighten and anti-clockwise to loosen. The reverse situation applies to left-hand thread fasteners, which are turned anti-clockwise to tighten and clockwise to loosen. Left-hand threads are used where rotation of a component might loosen a conventional right-hand thread fastener.

Seized fasteners

● Corrosion of external fasteners due to water or reaction between two dissimilar metals can occur over a period of time. It will build up sooner in wet conditions or in countries where salt is used on the roads during the winter. If a fastener is severely corroded it is likely that normal methods of removal will fail and result in its head being ruined. When you attempt removal, the fastener thread should be heard to crack free and unscrew easily - if it doesn't, stop there before damaging something.

● A smart tap on the head of the fastener will often succeed in breaking free corrosion which has occurred in the threads **(see illustration 2.13)**.

● An aerosol penetrating fluid (such as WD-40) applied the night beforehand may work its way down into the thread and ease removal. Depending on the location, you may be able to make up a Plasticine well around the fastener head and fill it with penetrating fluid.

2.13 A sharp tap on the head of a fastener will often break free a corroded thread

● If you are working on an engine internal component, corrosion will most likely not be a problem due to the well lubricated environment. However, components can be very tight and an impact driver is a useful tool in freeing them **(see illustration 2.14)**.

2.14 Using an impact driver to free a fastener

● Where corrosion has occurred between dissimilar metals (eg steel and aluminium alloy), the application of heat to the fastener head will create a disproportionate expansion rate between the two metals and break the seizure caused by the corrosion. Whether heat can be applied depends on the location of the fastener - any surrounding components likely to be damaged must first be removed **(see illustration 2.15)**. Heat can be applied using a paint stripper heat gun or clothes iron, or by immersing the component in boiling water - wear protective gloves to prevent scalding or burns to the hands.

2.15 Using heat to free a seized fastener

● As a last resort, it is possible to use a hammer and cold chisel to work the fastener head unscrewed **(see illustration 2.16)**. This will damage the fastener, but more importantly extreme care must be taken not to damage the surrounding component.

Caution: Remember that the component being secured is generally of more value than the bolt, nut or screw - when the fastener is freed, do not unscrew it with force, instead work the fastener back and forth when resistance is felt to prevent thread damage.

2.16 Using a hammer and chisel to free a seized fastener

Broken fasteners and damaged heads

● If the shank of a broken bolt or screw is accessible you can grip it with self-locking grips. The knurled wheel type stud extractor tool or self-gripping stud puller tool is particularly useful for removing the long studs which screw into the cylinder mouth surface of the crankcase or bolts and screws from which the head has broken off **(see illustration 2.17)**. Studs can also be removed by locking two nuts together on the threaded end of the stud and using a spanner on the lower nut **(see illustration 2.18)**.

2.17 Using a stud extractor tool to remove a broken crankcase stud

2.18 Two nuts can be locked together to unscrew a stud from a component

● A bolt or screw which has broken off below or level with the casing must be extracted using a screw extractor set. Centre punch the fastener to centralise the drill bit, then drill a hole in the fastener **(see illustration 2.19)**. Select a drill bit which is approximately half to three-quarters the

2.19 When using a screw extractor, first drill a hole in the fastener . . .

diameter of the fastener and drill to a depth which will accommodate the extractor. Use the largest size extractor possible, but avoid leaving too small a wall thickness otherwise the extractor will merely force the fastener walls outwards wedging it in the casing thread.

● If a spiral type extractor is used, thread it anti-clockwise into the fastener. As it is screwed in, it will grip the fastener and unscrew it from the casing **(see illustration 2.20)**.

2.20 . . . then thread the extractor anti-clockwise into the fastener

● If a taper type extractor is used, tap it into the fastener so that it is firmly wedged in place. Unscrew the extractor (anti-clockwise) to draw the fastener out.

 Warning: Stud extractors are very hard and may break off in the fastener if care is not taken - ask an engineer about spark erosion if this happens.

● Alternatively, the broken bolt/screw can be drilled out and the hole retapped for an oversize bolt/screw or a diamond-section thread insert. It is essential that the drilling is carried out squarely and to the correct depth, otherwise the casing may be ruined - if in doubt, entrust the work to an engineer.
● Bolts and nuts with rounded corners cause the correct size spanner or socket to slip when force is applied. Of the types of spanner/socket available always use a six-point type rather than an eight or twelve-point type - better grip

2.21 Comparison of surface drive ring spanner (left) with 12-point type (right)

is obtained. Surface drive spanners grip the middle of the hex flats, rather than the corners, and are thus good in cases of damaged heads **(see illustration 2.21)**.

● Slotted-head or Phillips-head screws are often damaged by the use of the wrong size screwdriver. Allen-head and Torx-head screws are much less likely to sustain damage. If enough of the screw head is exposed you can use a hacksaw to cut a slot in its head and then use a conventional flat-bladed screwdriver to remove it. Alternatively use a hammer and cold chisel to tap the head of the fastener around to slacken it. Always replace damaged fasteners with new ones, preferably Torx or Allen-head type.

A dab of valve grinding compound between the screw head and screw-driver tip will often give a good grip.

Thread repair

● Threads (particularly those in aluminium alloy components) can be damaged by overtightening, being assembled with dirt in the threads, or from a component working loose and vibrating. Eventually the thread will fail completely, and it will be impossible to tighten the fastener.

● If a thread is damaged or clogged with old locking compound it can be renovated with a thread repair tool (thread chaser) **(see illustrations 2.22 and 2.23)**; special thread

2.22 A thread repair tool being used to correct an internal thread

2.23 A thread repair tool being used to correct an external thread

chasers are available for spark plug hole threads. The tool will not cut a new thread, but clean and true the original thread. Make sure that you use the correct diameter and pitch tool. Similarly, external threads can be cleaned up with a die or a thread restorer file **(see illustration 2.24)**.

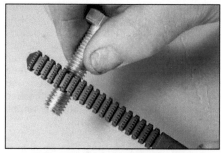

2.24 Using a thread restorer file

● It is possible to drill out the old thread and retap the component to the next thread size. This will work where there is enough surrounding material and a new bolt or screw can be obtained. Sometimes, however, this is not possible - such as where the bolt/screw passes through another component which must also be suitably modified, also in cases where a spark plug or oil drain plug cannot be obtained in a larger diameter thread size.

● The diamond-section thread insert (often known by its popular trade name of Heli-Coil) is a simple and effective method of renewing the thread and retaining the original size. A kit can be purchased which contains the tap, insert and installing tool **(see illustration 2.25)**. Drill out the damaged thread with the size drill specified **(see illustration 2.26)**. Carefully retap the thread **(see illustration 2.27)**. Install the

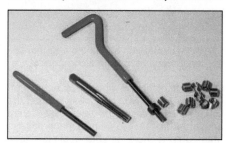

2.25 Obtain a thread insert kit to suit the thread diameter and pitch required

2.26 To install a thread insert, first drill out the original thread . . .

2.27 . . . tap a new thread . . .

2.28 . . . fit insert on the installing tool . . .

2.29 . . . and thread into the component . . .

2.30 . . . break off the tang when complete

insert on the installing tool and thread it slowly into place using a light downward pressure **(see illustrations 2.28 and 2.29)**. When positioned between a 1/4 and 1/2 turn below the surface withdraw the installing tool and use the break-off tool to press down on the tang, breaking it off **(see illustration 2.30)**.

● There are epoxy thread repair kits on the market which can rebuild stripped internal threads, although this repair should not be used on high load-bearing components.

Thread locking and sealing compounds

● Locking compounds are used in locations where the fastener is prone to loosening due to vibration or on important safety-related items which might cause loss of control of the motorcycle if they fail. It is also used where important fasteners cannot be secured by other means such as lockwashers or split pins.

● Before applying locking compound, make sure that the threads (internal and external) are clean and dry with all old compound removed. Select a compound to suit the component being secured - a non-permanent general locking and sealing type is suitable for most applications, but a high strength type is needed for permanent fixing of studs in castings. Apply a drop or two of the compound to the first few threads of the fastener, then thread it into place and tighten to the specified torque. Do not apply excessive thread locking compound otherwise the thread may be damaged on subsequent removal.

● Certain fasteners are impregnated with a dry film type coating of locking compound on their threads. Always renew this type of fastener if disturbed.

● Anti-seize compounds, such as copper-based greases, can be applied to protect threads from seizure due to extreme heat and corrosion. A common instance is spark plug threads and exhaust system fasteners.

3 Measuring tools and gauges

Feeler gauges

● Feeler gauges (or blades) are used for measuring small gaps and clearances (see illustration 3.1). They can also be used to measure endfloat (sideplay) of a component on a shaft where access is not possible with a dial gauge.

● Feeler gauge sets should be treated with care and not bent or damaged. They are etched with their size on one face. Keep them clean and very lightly oiled to prevent corrosion build-up.

3.1 Feeler gauges are used for measuring small gaps and clearances - thickness is marked on one face of gauge

● When measuring a clearance, select a gauge which is a light sliding fit between the two components. You may need to use two gauges together to measure the clearance accurately.

Micrometers

● A micrometer is a precision tool capable of measuring to 0.01 or 0.001 of a millimetre. It should always be stored in its case and not in the general toolbox. It must be kept clean and never dropped, otherwise its frame or measuring anvils could be distorted resulting in inaccurate readings.

● External micrometers are used for measuring outside diameters of components and have many more applications than internal micrometers. Micrometers are available in different size ranges, eg 0 to 25 mm, 25 to 50 mm, and upwards in 25 mm steps; some large micrometers have interchangeable anvils to allow a range of measurements to be taken. Generally the largest precision measurement you are likely to take on a motorcycle is the piston diameter.

● Internal micrometers (or bore micrometers) are used for measuring inside diameters, such as valve guides and cylinder bores. Telescoping gauges and small hole gauges are used in conjunction with an external micrometer, whereas the more expensive internal micrometers have their own measuring device.

External micrometer

Note: *The conventional analogue type instrument is described. Although much easier to read, digital micrometers are considerably more expensive.*

● Always check the calibration of the micrometer before use. With the anvils closed (0 to 25 mm type) or set over a test gauge (for

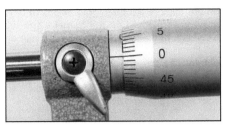

3.2 Check micrometer calibration before use

the larger types) the scale should read zero **(see illustration 3.2)**; make sure that the anvils (and test piece) are clean first. Any discrepancy can be adjusted by referring to the instructions supplied with the tool. Remember that the micrometer is a precision measuring tool - don't force the anvils closed, use the ratchet (4) on the end of the micrometer to close it. In this way, a measured force is always applied.

● To use, first make sure that the item being measured is clean. Place the anvil of the micrometer (1) against the item and use the thimble (2) to bring the spindle (3) lightly into contact with the other side of the item **(see illustration 3.3)**. Don't tighten the thimble down because this will damage the micrometer - instead use the ratchet (4) on the end of the micrometer. The ratchet mechanism applies a measured force preventing damage to the instrument.

● The micrometer is read by referring to the linear scale on the sleeve and the annular scale on the thimble. Read off the sleeve first to obtain the base measurement, then add the fine measurement from the thimble to obtain the overall reading. The linear scale on the sleeve represents the measuring range of the micrometer (eg 0 to 25 mm). The annular scale

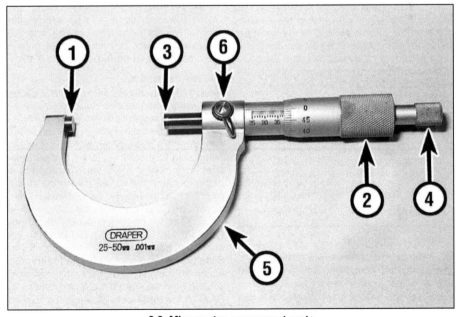

3.3 Micrometer component parts

1 Anvil	3 Spindle	5 Frame
2 Thimble	4 Ratchet	6 Locking lever

on the thimble will be in graduations of 0.01 mm (or as marked on the frame) - one full revolution of the thimble will move 0.5 mm on the linear scale. Take the reading where the datum line on the sleeve intersects the thimble's scale. Always position the eye directly above the scale otherwise an inaccurate reading will result.

In the example shown the item measures 2.95 mm **(see illustration 3.4)**:

Linear scale	2.00 mm
Linear scale	0.50 mm
Annular scale	0.45 mm
Total figure	**2.95 mm**

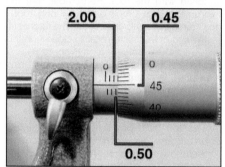

3.4 Micrometer reading of 2.95 mm

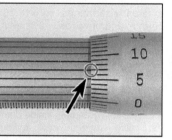

3.5 Micrometer reading of 46.99 mm on linear and annular scales . . .

3.6 . . . and 0.004 mm on vernier scale

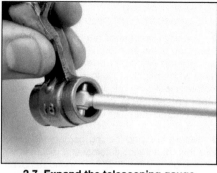

3.7 Expand the telescoping gauge in the bore, lock its position . . .

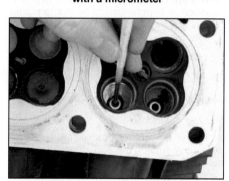

3.8 . . . then measure the gauge with a micrometer

Most micrometers have a locking lever (6) on the frame to hold the setting in place, allowing the item to be removed from the micrometer.
● Some micrometers have a vernier scale on their sleeve, providing an even finer measurement to be taken, in 0.001 increments of a millimetre. Take the sleeve and thimble measurement as described above, then check which graduation on the vernier scale aligns with that of the annular scale on the thimble **Note:** *The eye must be perpendicular to the scale when taking the vernier reading - if necessary rotate the body of the micrometer to ensure this.* Multiply the vernier scale figure by 0.001 and add it to the base and fine measurement figures.

In the example shown the item measures 46.994 mm **(see illustrations 3.5 and 3.6)**:

Linear scale (base)	46.000 mm
Linear scale (base)	00.500 mm
Annular scale (fine)	00.490 mm
Vernier scale	00.004 mm
Total figure	**46.994 mm**

Internal micrometer

● Internal micrometers are available for measuring bore diameters, but are expensive and unlikely to be available for home use. It is suggested that a set of telescoping gauges and small hole gauges, both of which must be used with an external micrometer, will suffice for taking internal measurements on a motorcycle.
● Telescoping gauges can be used to

measure internal diameters of components. Select a gauge with the correct size range, make sure its ends are clean and insert it into the bore. Expand the gauge, then lock its position and withdraw it from the bore **(see illustration 3.7)**. Measure across the gauge ends with a micrometer **(see illustration 3.8)**.
● Very small diameter bores (such as valve guides) are measured with a small hole gauge. Once adjusted to a slip-fit inside the component, its position is locked and the gauge withdrawn for measurement with a micrometer **(see illustrations 3.9 and 3.10)**.

Vernier caliper

Note: *The conventional linear and dial gauge type instruments are described. Digital types are easier to read, but are far more expensive.*
● The vernier caliper does not provide the precision of a micrometer, but is versatile in being able to measure internal and external diameters. Some types also incorporate a depth gauge. It is ideal for measuring clutch plate friction material and spring free lengths.
● To use the conventional linear scale vernier, slacken off the vernier clamp screws (1) and set its jaws over (2), or inside (3), the item to be measured **(see illustration 3.11)**. Slide the jaw into contact, using the thumb-wheel (4) for fine movement of the sliding scale (5) then tighten the clamp screws (1). Read off the main scale (6) where the zero on the sliding scale (5) intersects it, taking the whole number to the left of the zero; this provides the base measurement. View along the sliding scale and select the division which

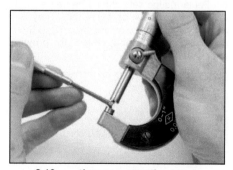

3.9 Expand the small hole gauge in the bore, lock its position . . .

3.10 . . . then measure the gauge with a micrometer

lines up exactly with any of the divisions on the main scale, noting that the divisions usually represents 0.02 of a millimetre. Add this fine measurement to the base measurement to obtain the total reading.

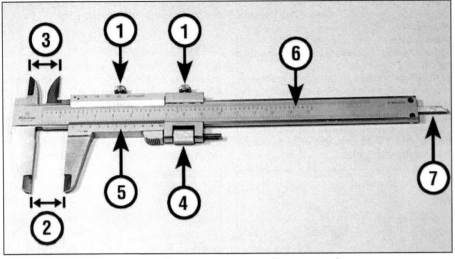

3.11 Vernier component parts (linear gauge)

1 Clamp screws	3 Internal jaws	5 Sliding scale	7 Depth gauge
2 External jaws	4 Thumbwheel	6 Main scale	

In the example shown the item measures 55.92 mm **(see illustration 3.12)**:

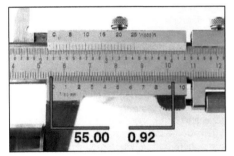

3.12 Vernier gauge reading of 55.92 mm

Base measurement	55.00 mm
Fine measurement	00.92 mm
Total figure	**55.92 mm**

● Some vernier calipers are equipped with a dial gauge for fine measurement. Before use, check that the jaws are clean, then close them fully and check that the dial gauge reads zero. If necessary adjust the gauge ring accordingly. Slacken the vernier clamp screw (1) and set its jaws over (2), or inside (3), the item to be measured **(see illustration 3.13)**. Slide the jaws into contact, using the thumbwheel (4) for fine movement. Read off the main scale (5) where the edge of the sliding scale (6) intersects it, taking the whole number to the left of the zero; this provides the base measurement. Read off the needle position on the dial gauge (7) scale to provide the fine measurement; each division represents 0.05 of a millimetre. Add this fine measurement to the base measurement to obtain the total reading.

In the example shown the item measures 55.95 mm **(see illustration 3.14)**:

Base measurement	55.00 mm
Fine measurement	00.95 mm
Total figure	**55.95 mm**

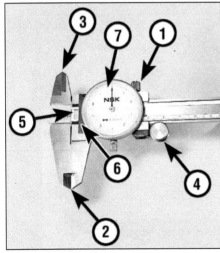

3.13 Vernier component parts (dial gauge)

1 Clamp screw	5 Main scale
2 External jaws	6 Sliding scale
3 Internal jaws	7 Dial gauge
4 Thumbwheel	

3.14 Vernier gauge reading of 55.95 mm

Plastigauge

● Plastigauge is a plastic material which can be compressed between two surfaces to measure the oil clearance between them. The width of the compressed Plastigauge is measured against a calibrated scale to determine the clearance.

● Common uses of Plastigauge are for measuring the clearance between crankshaft journal and main bearing inserts, between crankshaft journal and big-end bearing inserts, and between camshaft and bearing surfaces. The following example describes big-end oil clearance measurement.

● Handle the Plastigauge material carefully to prevent distortion. Using a sharp knife, cut a length which corresponds with the width of the bearing being measured and place it carefully across the journal so that it is parallel with the shaft **(see illustration 3.15)**. Carefully install both bearing shells and the connecting rod. Without rotating the rod on the journal tighten its bolts or nuts (as applicable) to the specified torque. The connecting rod and bearings are then disassembled and the crushed Plastigauge examined.

3.15 Plastigauge placed across shaft journal

● Using the scale provided in the Plastigauge kit, measure the width of the material to determine the oil clearance **(see illustration 3.16)**. Always remove all traces of Plastigauge after use using your fingernails.

Caution: Arriving at the correct clearance demands that the assembly is torqued correctly, according to the settings and sequence (where applicable) provided by the motorcycle manufacturer.

3.16 Measuring the width of the crushed Plastigauge

Dial gauge or DTI (Dial Test Indicator)

● A dial gauge can be used to accurately measure small amounts of movement. Typical uses are measuring shaft runout or shaft endfloat (sideplay) and setting piston position for ignition timing on two-strokes. A dial gauge set usually comes with a range of different probes and adapters and mounting equipment.

● The gauge needle must point to zero when at rest. Rotate the ring around its periphery to zero the gauge.

● Check that the gauge is capable of reading the extent of movement in the work. Most gauges have a small dial set in the face which records whole millimetres of movement as well as the fine scale around the face periphery which is calibrated in 0.01 mm divisions. Read off the small dial first to obtain the base measurement, then add the measurement from the fine scale to obtain the total reading.

In the example shown the gauge reads 1.48 mm **(see illustration 3.17)**:

Base measurement	1.00 mm
Fine measurement	0.48 mm
Total figure	**1.48 mm**

3.17 Dial gauge reading of 1.48 mm

● If measuring shaft runout, the shaft must be supported in vee-blocks and the gauge mounted on a stand perpendicular to the shaft. Rest the tip of the gauge against the centre of the shaft and rotate the shaft slowly whilst watching the gauge reading **(see illustration 3.18)**. Take several measurements along the length of the shaft and record the

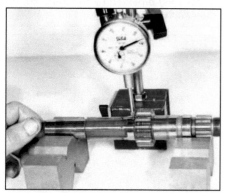

3.18 Using a dial gauge to measure shaft runout

maximum gauge reading as the amount of runout in the shaft. **Note:** *The reading obtained will be total runout at that point - some manufacturers specify that the runout figure is halved to compare with their specified runout limit.*

● Endfloat (sideplay) measurement requires that the gauge is mounted securely to the surrounding component with its probe touching the end of the shaft. Using hand pressure, push and pull on the shaft noting the maximum endfloat recorded on the gauge **(see illustration 3.19)**.

3.19 Using a dial gauge to measure shaft endfloat

● A dial gauge with suitable adapters can be used to determine piston position BTDC on two-stroke engines for the purposes of ignition timing. The gauge, adapter and suitable length probe are installed in the place of the spark plug and the gauge zeroed at TDC. If the piston position is specified as 1.14 mm BTDC, rotate the engine back to 2.00 mm BTDC, then slowly forwards to 1.14 mm BTDC.

Cylinder compression gauges

● A compression gauge is used for measuring cylinder compression. Either the rubber-cone type or the threaded adapter type can be used. The latter is preferred to ensure a perfect seal against the cylinder head. A 0 to 300 psi (0 to 20 Bar) type gauge (for petrol/gasoline engines) will be suitable for motorcycles.

● The spark plug is removed and the gauge either held hard against the cylinder head (cone type) or the gauge adapter screwed into the cylinder head (threaded type) **(see illustration 3.20)**. Cylinder compression is measured with the engine turning over, but not running - carry out the compression test as described in

3.20 Using a rubber-cone type cylinder compression gauge

Fault Finding Equipment. The gauge will hold the reading until manually released.

Oil pressure gauge

● An oil pressure gauge is used for measuring engine oil pressure. Most gauges come with a set of adapters to fit the thread of the take-off point **(see illustration 3.21)**. If the take-off point specified by the motorcycle manufacturer is an external oil pipe union, make sure that the specified replacement union is used to prevent oil starvation.

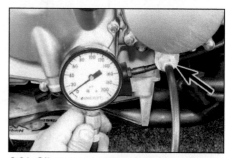

3.21 Oil pressure gauge and take-off point adapter (arrow)

● Oil pressure is measured with the engine running (at a specific rpm) and often the manufacturer will specify pressure limits for a cold and hot engine.

Straight-edge and surface plate

● If checking the gasket face of a component for warpage, place a steel rule or precision straight-edge across the gasket face and measure any gap between the straight-edge and component with feeler gauges **(see illustration 3.22)**. Check diagonally across the component and between mounting holes **(see illustration 3.23)**.

3.22 Use a straight-edge and feeler gauges to check for warpage

3.23 Check for warpage in these directions

● Checking individual components for warpage, such as clutch plain (metal) plates, requires a perfectly flat plate or piece or plate glass and feeler gauges.

4 Torque and leverage

What is torque?

● Torque describes the twisting force about a shaft. The amount of torque applied is determined by the distance from the centre of the shaft to the end of the lever and the amount of force being applied to the end of the lever; distance multiplied by force equals torque.

● The manufacturer applies a measured torque to a bolt or nut to ensure that it will not slacken in use and to hold two components securely together without movement in the joint. The actual torque setting depends on the thread size, bolt or nut material and the composition of the components being held.

● Too little torque may cause the fastener to loosen due to vibration, whereas too much torque will distort the joint faces of the component or cause the fastener to shear off. Always stick to the specified torque setting.

Using a torque wrench

● Check the calibration of the torque wrench and make sure it has a suitable range for the job. Torque wrenches are available in Nm (Newton-metres), kgf m (kilograms-force metre), lbf ft (pounds-feet), lbf in (inch-pounds). Do not confuse lbf ft with lbf in.

● Adjust the tool to the desired torque on the scale (see illustration 4.1). If your torque wrench is not calibrated in the units specified, carefully convert the figure (see *Conversion Factors*). A manufacturer sometimes gives a torque setting as a range (8 to 10 Nm) rather than a single figure - in this case set the tool midway between the two settings. The same torque may be expressed as 9 Nm ± 1 Nm. Some torque wrenches have a method of locking the setting so that it isn't inadvertently altered during use.

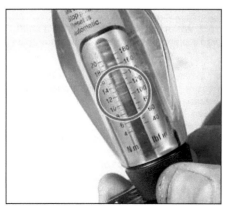

4.1 Set the torque wrench index mark to the setting required, in this case 12 Nm

● Install the bolts/nuts in their correct location and secure them lightly. Their threads must be clean and free of any old locking compound. Unless specified the threads and flange should be dry - oiled threads are necessary in certain circumstances and the manufacturer will take this into account in the specified torque figure. Similarly, the manufacturer may also specify the application of thread-locking compound.

● Tighten the fasteners in the specified sequence until the torque wrench clicks, indicating that the torque setting has been reached. Apply the torque again to double-check the setting. Where different thread diameter fasteners secure the component, as a rule tighten the larger diameter ones first.

● When the torque wrench has been finished with, release the lock (where applicable) and fully back off its setting to zero - do not leave the torque wrench tensioned. Also, do not use a torque wrench for slackening a fastener.

Angle-tightening

● Manufacturers often specify a figure in degrees for final tightening of a fastener. This usually follows tightening to a specific torque setting.

● A degree disc can be set and attached to the socket (see illustration 4.2) or a protractor can be used to mark the angle of movement on the bolt/nut head and the surrounding casting (see illustration 4.3).

4.2 Angle tightening can be accomplished with a torque-angle gauge . . .

4.3 . . . or by marking the angle on the surrounding component

Loosening sequences

● Where more than one bolt/nut secures a component, loosen each fastener evenly a little at a time. In this way, not all the stress of the joint is held by one fastener and the components are not likely to distort.

● If a tightening sequence is provided, work in the REVERSE of this, but if not, work from the outside in, in a criss-cross sequence (see illustration 4.4).

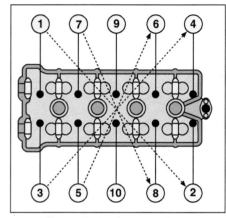

4.4 When slackening, work from the outside inwards

Tightening sequences

● If a component is held by more than one fastener it is important that the retaining bolts/nuts are tightened evenly to prevent uneven stress build-up and distortion of sealing faces. This is especially important on high-compression joints such as the cylinder head.

● A sequence is usually provided by the manufacturer, either in a diagram or actually marked in the casting. If not, always start in the centre and work outwards in a criss-cross pattern (see illustration 4.5). Start off by securing all bolts/nuts finger-tight, then set the torque wrench and tighten each fastener by a small amount in sequence until the final torque is reached. By following this practice,

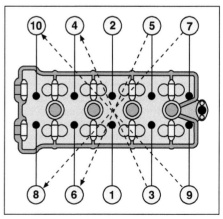

4.5 When tightening, work from the inside outwards

the joint will be held evenly and will not be distorted. Important joints, such as the cylinder head and big-end fasteners often have two- or three-stage torque settings.

Applying leverage

● Use tools at the correct angle. Position a socket wrench or spanner on the bolt/nut so that you pull it towards you when loosening. If this can't be done, push the spanner without curling your fingers around it **(see illustration 4.6)** - the spanner may slip or the fastener loosen suddenly, resulting in your fingers being crushed against a component.

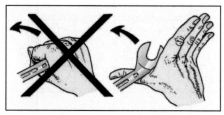

4.6 If you can't pull on the spanner to loosen a fastener, push with your hand open

● Additional leverage is gained by extending the length of the lever. The best way to do this is to use a breaker bar instead of the regular length tool, or to slip a length of tubing over the end of the spanner or socket wrench.
● If additional leverage will not work, the fastener head is either damaged or firmly corroded in place (see *Fasteners*).

---

5 Bearings

Bearing removal and installation

Drivers and sockets

● Before removing a bearing, always inspect the casing to see which way it must be driven out - some casings will have retaining plates or a cast step. Also check for any identifying markings on the bearing and if installed to a certain depth, measure this at this stage. Some roller bearings are sealed on one side - take note of the original fitted position.
● Bearings can be driven out of a casing using a bearing driver tool (with the correct size head) or a socket of the correct diameter. Select the driver head or socket so that it contacts the outer race of the bearing, not the balls/rollers or inner race. Always support the casing around the bearing housing with wood blocks, otherwise there is a risk of fracture. The bearing is driven out with a few blows on the driver or socket from a heavy mallet. Unless access is severely restricted (as with wheel bearings), a pin-punch is not recommended unless it is moved around the bearing to keep it square in its housing.

● The same equipment can be used to install bearings. Make sure the bearing housing is supported on wood blocks and line up the bearing in its housing. Fit the bearing as noted on removal - generally they are installed with their marked side facing outwards. Tap the bearing squarely into its housing using a driver or socket which bears only on the bearing's outer race - contact with the bearing balls/rollers or inner race will destroy it **(see illustrations 5.1 and 5.2)**.
● Check that the bearing inner race and balls/rollers rotate freely.

5.1 Using a bearing driver against the bearing's outer race

5.2 Using a large socket against the bearing's outer race

Pullers and slide-hammers

● Where a bearing is pressed on a shaft a puller will be required to extract it **(see illustration 5.3)**. Make sure that the puller clamp or legs fit securely behind the bearing and are unlikely to slip out. If pulling a bearing

5.3 This bearing puller clamps behind the bearing and pressure is applied to the shaft end to draw the bearing off

off a gear shaft for example, you may have to locate the puller behind a gear pinion if there is no access to the race and draw the gear pinion off the shaft as well **(see illustration 5.4)**.

> *Caution: Ensure that the puller's centre bolt locates securely against the end of the shaft and will not slip when pressure is applied. Also ensure that puller does not damage the shaft end.*

5.4 Where no access is available to the rear of the bearing, it is sometimes possible to draw off the adjacent component

● Operate the puller so that its centre bolt exerts pressure on the shaft end and draws the bearing off the shaft.
● When installing the bearing on the shaft, tap only on the bearing's inner race - contact with the balls/rollers or outer race with destroy the bearing. Use a socket or length of tubing as a drift which fits over the shaft end **(see illustration 5.5)**.

5.5 When installing a bearing on a shaft use a piece of tubing which bears only on the bearing's inner race

● Where a bearing locates in a blind hole in a casing, it cannot be driven or pulled out as described above. A slide-hammer with knife-edged bearing puller attachment will be required. The puller attachment passes through the bearing and when tightened expands to fit firmly behind the bearing **(see illustration 5.6)**. By operating the slide-hammer part of the tool the bearing is jarred out of its housing **(see illustration 5.7)**.
● It is possible, if the bearing is of reasonable weight, for it to drop out of its housing if the casing is heated as described opposite. If this

5.6 Expand the bearing puller so that it locks behind the bearing . . .

5.7 . . . attach the slide hammer to the bearing puller

method is attempted, first prepare a work surface which will enable the casing to be tapped face down to help dislodge the bearing - a wood surface is ideal since it will not damage the casing's gasket surface. Wearing protective gloves, tap the heated casing several times against the work surface to dislodge the bearing under its own weight **(see illustration 5.8)**.

5.8 Tapping a casing face down on wood blocks can often dislodge a bearing

● Bearings can be installed in blind holes using the driver or socket method described above.

Drawbolts

● Where a bearing or bush is set in the eye of a component, such as a suspension linkage arm or connecting rod small-end, removal by drift may damage the component. Furthermore, a rubber bushing in a shock absorber eye cannot successfully be driven out of position. If access is available to a engineering press, the task is straightforward. If not, a drawbolt can be fabricated to extract the bearing or bush.

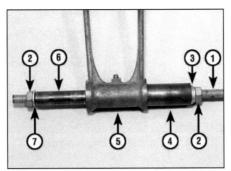

5.9 Drawbolt component parts assembled on a suspension arm

1 Bolt or length of threaded bar
2 Nuts
3 Washer (external diameter greater than tubing internal diameter)
4 Tubing (internal diameter sufficient to accommodate bearing)
5 Suspension arm with bearing
6 Tubing (external diameter slightly smaller than bearing)
7 Washer (external diameter slightly smaller than bearing)

5.10 Drawing the bearing out of the suspension arm

● To extract the bearing/bush you will need a long bolt with nut (or piece of threaded bar with two nuts), a piece of tubing which has an internal diameter larger than the bearing/bush, another piece of tubing which has an external diameter slightly smaller than the bearing/ bush, and a selection of washers **(see illustrations 5.9 and 5.10)**. Note that the pieces of tubing must be of the same length, or longer, than the bearing/bush.
● The same kit (without the pieces of tubing) can be used to draw the new bearing/bush back into place **(see illustration 5.11)**.

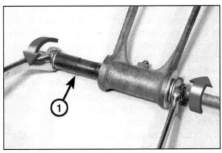

5.11 Installing a new bearing (1) in the suspension arm

Temperature change

● If the bearing's outer race is a tight fit in the casing, the aluminium casing can be heated to release its grip on the bearing. Aluminium will expand at a greater rate than the steel bearing outer race. There are several ways to do this, but avoid any localised extreme heat (such as a blow torch) - aluminium alloy has a low melting point.
● Approved methods of heating a casing are using a domestic oven (heated to 100°C) or immersing the casing in boiling water **(see illustration 5.12)**. Low temperature range localised heat sources such as a paint stripper heat gun or clothes iron can also be used **(see illustration 5.13)**. Alternatively, soak a rag in boiling water, wring it out and wrap it around the bearing housing.

> ⚠ **Warning: All of these methods require care in use to prevent scalding and burns to the hands. Wear protective gloves when handling hot components.**

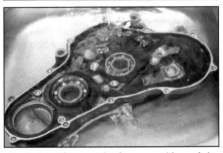

5.12 A casing can be immersed in a sink of boiling water to aid bearing removal

5.13 Using a localised heat source to aid bearing removal

● If heating the whole casing note that plastic components, such as the neutral switch, may suffer - remove them beforehand.
● After heating, remove the bearing as described above. You may find that the expansion is sufficient for the bearing to fall out of the casing under its own weight or with a light tap on the driver or socket.
● If necessary, the casing can be heated to aid bearing installation, and this is sometimes the recommended procedure if the motorcycle manufacturer has designed the housing and bearing fit with this intention.

● Installation of bearings can be eased by placing them in a freezer the night before installation. The steel bearing will contract slightly, allowing easy insertion in its housing. This is often useful when installing steering head outer races in the frame.

Bearing types and markings

● Plain shell bearings, ball bearings, needle roller bearings and tapered roller bearings will all be found on motorcycles (see illustrations 5.14 and 5.15). The ball and roller types are usually caged between an inner and outer race, but uncaged variations may be found.

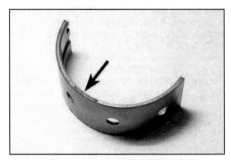

5.14 Shell bearings are either plain or grooved. They are usually identified by colour code (arrow)

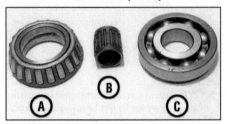

5.15 Tapered roller bearing (A), needle roller bearing (B) and ball journal bearing (C)

● Shell bearings (often called inserts) are usually found at the crankshaft main and connecting rod big-end where they are good at coping with high loads. They are made of a phosphor-bronze material and are impregnated with self-lubricating properties.

● Ball bearings and needle roller bearings consist of a steel inner and outer race with the balls or rollers between the races. They require constant lubrication by oil or grease and are good at coping with axial loads. Taper roller bearings consist of rollers set in a tapered cage set on the inner race; the outer race is separate. They are good at coping with axial loads and prevent movement along the shaft - a typical application is in the steering head.

● Bearing manufacturers produce bearings to ISO size standards and stamp one face of the bearing to indicate its internal and external diameter, load capacity and type (see illustration 5.16).

● Metal bushes are usually of phosphor-bronze material. Rubber bushes are used in suspension mounting eyes. Fibre bushes have also been used in suspension pivots.

5.16 Typical bearing marking

Bearing fault finding

● If a bearing outer race has spun in its housing, the housing material will be damaged. You can use a bearing locking compound to bond the outer race in place if damage is not too severe.

● Shell bearings will fail due to damage of their working surface, as a result of lack of lubrication, corrosion or abrasive particles in the oil (see illustration 5.17). Small particles of dirt in the oil may embed in the bearing material whereas larger particles will score the bearing and shaft journal. If a number of short journeys are made, insufficient heat will be generated to drive off condensation which has built up on the bearings.

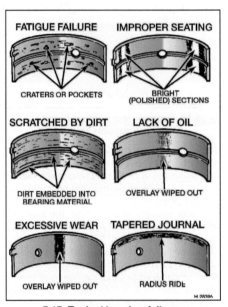

5.17 Typical bearing failures

● Ball and roller bearings will fail due to lack of lubrication or damage to the balls or rollers. Tapered-roller bearings can be damaged by overloading them. Unless the bearing is sealed on both sides, wash it in paraffin (kerosene) to remove all old grease then allow it to dry. Make a visual inspection looking to dented balls or rollers, damaged cages and worn or pitted races (see illustration 5.18).

● A ball bearing can be checked for wear by listening to it when spun. Apply a film of light oil to the bearing and hold it close to the ear - hold the outer race with one hand and spin the inner

5.18 Example of ball journal bearing with damaged balls and cages

5.19 Hold outer race and listen to inner race when spun

race with the other hand (see illustration 5.19). The bearing should be almost silent when spun; if it grates or rattles it is worn.

6 Oil seals

Oil seal removal and installation

● Oil seals should be renewed every time a component is dismantled. This is because the seal lips will become set to the sealing surface and will not necessarily reseal.

● Oil seals can be prised out of position using a large flat-bladed screwdriver (see illustration 6.1). In the case of crankcase seals, check first that the seal is not lipped on the inside, preventing its removal with the crankcases joined.

6.1 Prise out oil seals with a large flat-bladed screwdriver

● New seals are usually installed with their marked face (containing the seal reference code) outwards and the spring side towards the fluid being retained. In certain cases, such as a two-stroke engine crankshaft seal, a double lipped seal may be used due to there being fluid or gas on each side of the joint.

● Use a bearing driver or socket which bears only on the outer hard edge of the seal to install it in the casing - tapping on the inner edge will damage the sealing lip.

Oil seal types and markings

● Oil seals are usually of the single-lipped type. Double-lipped seals are found where a liquid or gas is on both sides of the joint.
● Oil seals can harden and lose their sealing ability if the motorcycle has been in storage for a long period - renewal is the only solution.
● Oil seal manufacturers also conform to the ISO markings for seal size - these are moulded into the outer face of the seal (see illustration 6.2).

6.2 These oil seal markings indicate inside diameter, outside diameter and seal thickness

7 Gaskets and sealants

Types of gasket and sealant

● Gaskets are used to seal the mating surfaces between components and keep lubricants, fluids, vacuum or pressure contained within the assembly. Aluminium gaskets are sometimes found at the cylinder joints, but most gaskets are paper-based. If the mating surfaces of the components being joined are undamaged the gasket can be installed dry, although a dab of sealant or grease will be useful to hold it in place during assembly.
● RTV (Room Temperature Vulcanising) silicone rubber sealants cure when exposed to moisture in the atmosphere. These sealants are good at filling pits or irregular gasket faces, but will tend to be forced out of the joint under very high torque. They can be used to replace a paper gasket, but first make sure that the width of the paper gasket is not essential to the shimming of internal components. RTV sealants should not be used on components containing petrol (gasoline).
● Non-hardening, semi-hardening and hard setting liquid gasket compounds can be used with a gasket or between a metal-to-metal joint. Select the sealant to suit the application: universal non-hardening sealant can be used on virtually all joints; semi-hardening on joint faces which are rough or damaged; hard setting sealant on joints which require a permanent bond and are subjected to high temperature and pressure. **Note:** *Check first if the paper gasket has a bead of sealant*

impregnated in its surface before applying additional sealant.
● When choosing a sealant, make sure it is suitable for the application, particularly if being applied in a high-temperature area or in the vicinity of fuel. Certain manufacturers produce sealants in either clear, silver or black colours to match the finish of the engine. This has a particular application on motorcycles where much of the engine is exposed.
● Do not over-apply sealant. That which is squeezed out on the outside of the joint can be wiped off, whereas an excess of sealant on the inside can break off and clog oilways.

Breaking a sealed joint

● Age, heat, pressure and the use of hard setting sealant can cause two components to stick together so tightly that they are difficult to separate using finger pressure alone. Do not resort to using levers unless there is a pry point provided for this purpose (see illustration 7.1) or else the gasket surfaces will be damaged.
● Use a soft-faced hammer (see illustration 7.2) or a wood block and conventional hammer to strike the component near the mating surface. Avoid hammering against cast extremities since they may break off. If this method fails, try using a wood wedge between the two components.

Caution: If the joint will not separate, double-check that you have removed all the fasteners.

7.1 If a pry point is provided, apply gently pressure with a flat-bladed screwdriver

7.2 Tap around the joint with a soft-faced mallet if necessary - don't strike cooling fins

Removal of old gasket and sealant

● Paper gaskets will most likely come away complete, leaving only a few traces stuck on

Most components have one or two hollow locating dowels between the two gasket faces. If a dowel cannot be removed, do not resort to gripping it with pliers - it will almost certainly be distorted. Install a close-fitting socket or Phillips screwdriver into the dowel and then grip the outer edge of the dowel to free it.

the sealing faces of the components. It is imperative that all traces are removed to ensure correct sealing of the new gasket.
● Very carefully scrape all traces of gasket away making sure that the sealing surfaces are not gouged or scored by the scraper (see illustrations 7.3, 7.4 and 7.5). Stubborn deposits can be removed by spraying with an aerosol gasket remover. Final preparation of

7.3 Paper gaskets can be scraped off with a gasket scraper tool . . .

7.4 . . . a knife blade . . .

7.5 . . . or a household scraper

7.6 Fine abrasive paper is wrapped around a flat file to clean up the gasket face

7.7 A kitchen scourer can be used on stubborn deposits

the gasket surface can be made with very fine abrasive paper or a plastic kitchen scourer **(see illustrations 7.6 and 7.7)**.

● Old sealant can be scraped or peeled off components, depending on the type originally used. Note that gasket removal compounds are available to avoid scraping the components clean; make sure the gasket remover suits the type of sealant used.

8 Chains

Breaking and joining final drive chains

● Drive chains for all but small bikes are continuous and do not have a clip-type connecting link. The chain must be broken using a chain breaker tool and the new chain securely riveted together using a new soft rivet-type link. Never use a clip-type connecting link instead of a rivet-type link, except in an emergency. Various chain breaking and riveting tools are available, either as separate tools or combined as illustrated in the accompanying photographs - read the instructions supplied with the tool carefully.

> ⚠ **Warning: The need to rivet the new link pins correctly cannot be overstressed - loss of control of the motorcycle is very likely to result if the chain breaks in use.**

● Rotate the chain and look for the soft link. The soft link pins look like they have been

8.1 Tighten the chain breaker to push the pin out of the link . . .

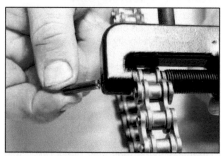

8.2 . . . withdraw the pin, remove the tool . . .

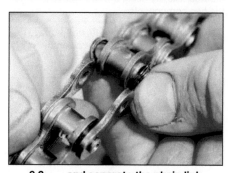

8.3 . . . and separate the chain link

deeply centre-punched instead of peened over like all the other pins **(see illustration 8.9)** and its sideplate may be a different colour. Position the soft link midway between the sprockets and assemble the chain breaker tool over one of the soft link pins **(see illustration 8.1)**. Operate the tool to push the pin out through the chain **(see illustration 8.2)**. On an O-ring chain, remove the O-rings **(see illustration 8.3)**. Carry out the same procedure on the other soft link pin.

> *Caution: Certain soft link pins (particularly on the larger chains) may require their ends to be filed or ground off before they can be pressed out using the tool.*

● Check that you have the correct size and strength (standard or heavy duty) new soft link - do not reuse the old link. Look for the size marking on the chain sideplates **(see illustration 8.10)**.

● Position the chain ends so that they are engaged over the rear sprocket. On an O-ring

8.4 Insert the new soft link, with O-rings, through the chain ends . . .

8.5 . . . install the O-rings over the pin ends . . .

8.6 . . . followed by the sideplate

chain, install a new O-ring over each pin of the link and insert the link through the two chain ends **(see illustration 8.4)**. Install a new O-ring over the end of each pin, followed by the sideplate (with the chain manufacturer's marking facing outwards) **(see illustrations 8.5 and 8.6)**. On an unsealed chain, insert the link through the two chain ends, then install the sideplate with the chain manufacturer's marking facing outwards.

● Note that it may not be possible to install the sideplate using finger pressure alone. If using a joining tool, assemble it so that the plates of the tool clamp the link and press the sideplate over the pins **(see illustration 8.7)**. Otherwise, use two small sockets placed over

8.7 Push the sideplate into position using a clamp

8.8 Assemble the chain riveting tool over one pin at a time and tighten it fully

8.9 Pin end correctly riveted (A), pin end unriveted (B)

the rivet ends and two pieces of the wood between a G-clamp. Operate the clamp to press the sideplate over the pins.

● Assemble the joining tool over one pin (following the maker's instructions) and tighten the tool down to spread the pin end securely **(see illustrations 8.8 and 8.9)**. Do the same on the other pin.

> ⚠ **Warning: Check that the pin ends are secure and that there is no danger of the sideplate coming loose. If the pin ends are cracked the soft link must be renewed.**

Final drive chain sizing

● Chains are sized using a three digit number, followed by a suffix to denote the chain type **(see illustration 8.10)**. Chain type is either standard or heavy duty (thicker sideplates), and also unsealed or O-ring/X-ring type.

● The first digit of the number relates to the pitch of the chain, ie the distance from the centre of one pin to the centre of the next pin **(see illustration 8.11)**. Pitch is expressed in eighths of an inch, as follows:

8.10 Typical chain size and type marking

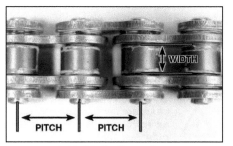

8.11 Chain dimensions

Sizes commencing with a 4 (eg 428) have a pitch of 1/2 inch (12.7 mm)
Sizes commencing with a 5 (eg 520) have a pitch of 5/8 inch (15.9 mm)
Sizes commencing with a 6 (eg 630) have a pitch of 3/4 inch (19.1 mm)

● The second and third digits of the chain size relate to the width of the rollers, again in imperial units, eg the 525 shown has 5/16 inch (7.94 mm) rollers **(see illustration 8.11)**.

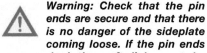

9 Hoses

Clamping to prevent flow

● Small-bore flexible hoses can be clamped to prevent fluid flow whilst a component is worked on. Whichever method is used, ensure that the hose material is not permanently distorted or damaged by the clamp.

a) A brake hose clamp available from auto accessory shops **(see illustration 9.1)**.
b) A wingnut type hose clamp **(see illustration 9.2)**.

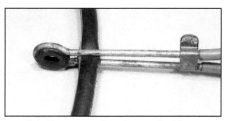

9.1 Hoses can be clamped with an automotive brake hose clamp . . .

9.2 . . . a wingnut type hose clamp . . .

c) Two sockets placed each side of the hose and held with straight-jawed self-locking grips **(see illustration 9.3)**.
d) Thick card each side of the hose held between straight-jawed self-locking grips **(see illustration 9.4)**.

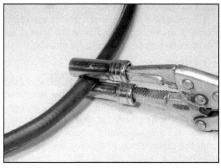

9.3 . . . two sockets and a pair of self-locking grips . . .

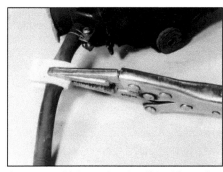

9.4 . . . or thick card and self-locking grips

Freeing and fitting hoses

● Always make sure the hose clamp is moved well clear of the hose end. Grip the hose with your hand and rotate it whilst pulling it off the union. If the hose has hardened due to age and will not move, slit it with a sharp knife and peel its ends off the union **(see illustration 9.5)**.

● Resist the temptation to use grease or soap on the unions to aid installation; although it helps the hose slip over the union it will equally aid the escape of fluid from the joint. It is preferable to soften the hose ends in hot water and wet the inside surface of the hose with water or a fluid which will evaporate.

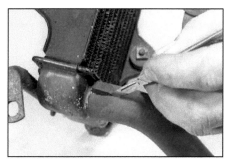

9.5 Cutting a coolant hose free with a sharp knife

Preparing for storage

Before you start

If repairs or an overhaul is needed, see that this is carried out now rather than left until you want to ride the bike again.

Give the bike a good wash and scrub all dirt from its underside. Make sure the bike dries completely before preparing for storage.

Engine

● Remove the spark plug(s) and lubricate the cylinder bores with approximately a teaspoon of motor oil using a spout-type oil can (see illustration 1). Reinstall the spark plug(s). Crank the engine over a couple of times to coat the piston rings and bores with oil. If the bike has a kickstart, use this to turn the engine over. If not, flick the kill switch to the OFF position and crank the engine over on the starter (see illustration 2). If the nature on the ignition system prevents the starter operating with the kill switch in the OFF position,

remove the spark plugs and fit them back in their caps; ensure that the plugs are earthed (grounded) against the cylinder head when the starter is operated (see illustration 3).

⚠️ *Warning: It is important that the plugs are earthed (grounded) away from the spark plug holes otherwise there is a risk of atomised fuel from the cylinders igniting.*

HAYNES HiNT *On a single cylinder four-stroke engine, you can seal the combustion chamber completely by positioning the piston at TDC on the compression stroke.*

● Drain the carburettor(s) otherwise there is a risk of jets becoming blocked by gum deposits from the fuel (see illustration 4).

● If the bike is going into long-term storage, consider adding a fuel stabiliser to the fuel in the tank. If the tank is drained completely, corrosion of its internal surfaces may occur if left unprotected for a long period. The tank can be treated with a rust preventative especially for this purpose. Alternatively, remove the tank and pour half a litre of motor oil into it, install the filler cap and shake the tank to coat its internals with oil before draining off the excess. The same effect can also be achieved by spraying WD40 or a similar water-dispersant around the inside of the tank via its flexible nozzle.

● Make sure the cooling system contains the correct mix of antifreeze. Antifreeze also contains important corrosion inhibitors.

● The air intakes and exhaust can be sealed off by covering or plugging the openings. Ensure that you do not seal in any condensation; run the engine until it is hot,

Squirt a drop of motor oil into each cylinder

Flick the kill switch to OFF . . .

. . . and ensure that the metal bodies of the plugs (arrows) are earthed against the cylinder head

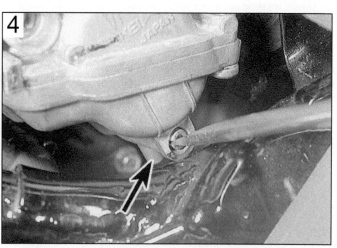

Connect a hose to the carburettor float chamber drain stub (arrow) and unscrew the drain screw

U-locks

Pros: *Highly effective deterrent which can be used to secure the bike to a post or railings. Most U-locks come with a carrier which allows the lock to be easily carried on the bike.*

Cons: *Not as flexible to use as a lock and chain.*

● These are solid locks which are similar in use to a lock and chain. U-locks are lighter than a lock and chain but not so flexible to use. The length and shape of the lock shackle limit the objects to which the bike can be secured **(see illustration 4)**.

Disc locks

Pros: *Small, light and very easy to carry; most can be stored underneath the seat.*

Cons: *Does not prevent the motorcycle being lifted into a van. Can be very embarrassing if you*

U-locks can be used to secure the bike to a solid object – ensure you purchase one which is long enough

forget to remove the lock before attempting to ride off!

● Disc locks are designed to be attached to the front brake disc. The lock passes through one of the holes in the disc and prevents the wheel rotating by jamming against the fork/brake caliper **(see illustration 5)**. Some are equipped with an alarm siren which sounds if the disc lock is moved; this not only acts as a theft deterrent but also as a handy reminder if you try to move the bike with the lock still fitted.

● Combining the disc lock with a length of cable which can be looped around a post or railings provides an additional measure of security **(see illustration 6)**.

Alarms and immobilisers

Pros: *Once installed it is completely hassle-free to use. If the system is 'Thatcham' or 'Sold Secure-approved', insurance companies may give you a discount.*

Cons: *Can be expensive to buy and complex to install. No system will prevent the motorcycle from being lifted into a van and taken away.*

● Electronic alarms and immobilisers are available to suit a variety of budgets. There are three different types of system available: pure alarms, pure immobilisers, and the more expensive systems which are combined alarm/immobilisers **(see illustration 7)**.
● An alarm system is designed to emit an audible warning if the motorcycle is being tampered with.
● An immobiliser prevents the motorcycle being started and ridden away by disabling its electrical systems.
● When purchasing an alarm/immobiliser system, check the cost of installing the system unless you are able to do it yourself. If the motorcycle is not used regularly, another consideration is the current drain of the system. All alarm/immobiliser systems are powered by the motorcycle's battery; purchasing a system with a very low current drain could prevent the battery losing its charge whilst the motorcycle is not being used.

A typical disc lock attached through one of the holes in the disc

A disc lock combined with a security cable provides additional protection

A typical alarm/immobiliser system

Indelible markings can be applied to most areas of the bike – always apply the manufacturer's sticker to warn off thieves

Chemically-etched code numbers can be applied to main body panels . . .

. . . again, always ensure that the kit manufacturer's sticker is applied in a prominent position

Security marking kits

Pros: *Very cheap and effective deterrent. Many insurance companies will give you a discount on your insurance premium if a recognised security marking kit is used on your motorcycle.*

Cons: *Does not prevent the motorcycle being stolen by joyriders.*

● There are many different types of security marking kits available. The idea is to mark as many parts of the motorcycle as possible with a unique security number **(see illustrations 8, 9 and 10)**. A form will be included with the kit to register your personal details and those of the motorcycle with the kit manufacturer. This register is made available to the police to help them trace the rightful owner of any motorcycle or components which they recover should all other forms of identification have been removed. Always apply the warning stickers provided with the kit to deter thieves.

Ground anchors, wheel clamps and security posts

Pros: *An excellent form of security which will deter all but the most determined of thieves.*

Cons: *Awkward to install and can be expensive.*

● Whilst the motorcycle is at home, it is a good idea to attach it securely to the floor or a solid wall, even if it is kept in a securely locked garage. Various types of ground anchors, security posts and wheel clamps are available for this purpose **(see illustration 11)**. These security devices are either bolted to a solid concrete or brick structure or can be cemented into the ground.

Permanent ground anchors provide an excellent level of security when the bike is at home

Security at home

A high percentage of motorcycle thefts are from the owner's home. Here are some things to consider whenever your motorcycle is at home:
✔ Where possible, always keep the motorcycle in a securely locked garage. Never rely solely on the standard lock on the garage door, these are usual hopelessly inadequate. Fit an additional locking mechanism to the door and consider having the garage alarmed. A security light, activated by a movement sensor, is also a good investment.

✔ Always secure the motorcycle to the ground or a wall, even if it is inside a securely locked garage.
✔ Do not regularly leave the motorcycle outside your home, try to keep it out of sight wherever possible. If a garage is not available, fit a motorcycle cover over the bike to disguise its true identity.
✔ It is not uncommon for thieves to follow a motorcyclist home to find out where the bike is kept. They will then return at a later date. Be aware of this whenever you are returning

home on your motorcycle. If you suspect you are being followed, do not return home, instead ride to a garage or shop and stop as a precaution.
✔ When selling a motorcycle, do not provide your home address or the location where the bike is normally kept. Arrange to meet the buyer at a location away from your home. Thieves have been known to pose as potential buyers to find out where motorcycles are kept and then return later to steal them.

Security away from the home

As well as fitting security equipment to your motorcycle here are a few general rules to follow whenever you park your motorcycle.
✔ Park in a busy, public place.
✔ Use car parks which incorporate security features, such as CCTV.

✔ At night, park in a well-lit area, preferably directly underneath a street light.
✔ Engage the steering lock.
✔ Secure the motorcycle to a solid, immovable object such as a post or railings with an additional lock. If this is not possible,

secure the bike to a friend's motorcycle. Some public parking places provide security loops for motorcycles.
✔ Never leave your helmet or luggage attached to the motorcycle. Take them with you at all times.

Lubricants and fluids

A wide range of lubricants, fluids and cleaning agents is available for motor-cycles. This is a guide as to what is available, its applications and properties.

Four-stroke engine oil

● Engine oil is without doubt the most important component of any four-stroke engine. Modern motorcycle engines place a lot of demands on their oil and choosing the right type is essential. Using an unsuitable oil will lead to an increased rate of engine wear and could result in serious engine damage. Before purchasing oil, always check the recommended oil specification given by the manufacturer. The manufacturer will state a recommended 'type or classification' and also a specific 'viscosity' range for engine oil.

● The oil 'type or classification' is identified by its API (American Petroleum Institute) rating. The API rating will be in the form of two letters, e.g. SG. The S identifies the oil as being suitable for use in a petrol (gasoline) engine (S stands for spark ignition) and the second letter, ranging from A to J, identifies the oil's performance rating. The later this letter, the higher the specification of the oil; for example API SG oil exceeds the requirements of API SF oil. **Note:** *On some oils there may also be a second rating consisting of another two letters, the first letter being C, e.g. API SF/CD. This rating indicates the oil is also suitable for use in a diesel engines (the C stands for compression ignition) and is thus of no relevance for motorcycle use.*

● The 'viscosity' of the oil is identified by its SAE (Society of Automotive Engineers) rating. All modern engines require multigrade oils and the SAE rating will consist of two numbers, the first followed by a W, e.g. 10W/40. The first number indicates the viscosity rating of the oil at low temperatures (W stands for winter – tested at –20ºC) and the second number represents the viscosity of the oil at high temperatures (tested at 100ºC). The lower the number, the thinner the oil. For example an oil with an SAE 10W/40 rating will give better cold starting and running than an SAE 15W/40 oil.

● As well as ensuring the 'type' and 'viscosity' of the oil match the recommendations, another consideration to make when buying engine oil is whether to purchase a standard mineral-based oil, a semi-synthetic oil (also known as a synthetic blend or synthetic-based oil) or a fully-synthetic oil. Although all oils will have a similar rating and viscosity, their cost will vary considerably; mineral-based oils are the cheapest, the fully-synthetic oils the most expensive with the semi-synthetic oils falling somewhere in-between. This decision is very much up to the owner, but it should be noted that modern synthetic oils have far better lubricating and cleaning qualities than traditional mineral-based oils and tend to retain these properties for far longer. Bearing in mind the operating conditions inside a modern, high-revving motorcycle engine it is highly recommended that a fully synthetic oil is used. The extra expense at each service could save you money in the long term by preventing premature engine wear.

● As a final note always ensure that the oil is specifically designed for use in motorcycle engines. Engine oils designed primarily for use in car engines sometimes contain additives or friction modifiers which could cause clutch slip on a motorcycle fitted with a wet-clutch.

Two-stroke engine oil

● Modern two-stroke engines, with their high power outputs, place high demands on their oil. If engine seizure is to be avoided it is essential that a high-quality oil is used. Two-stroke oils differ hugely from four-stroke oils. The oil lubricates only the crankshaft and piston(s) (the transmission has its own lubricating oil) and is used on a total-loss basis where it is burnt completely during the combustion process.

● The Japanese have recently introduced a classification system for two-stroke oils, the JASO rating. This rating is in the form of two letters, either FA, FB or FC – FA is the lowest classification and FC the highest. Ensure the oil being used meets or exceeds the recommended rating specified by the manufacturer.

● As well as ensuring the oil rating matches the recommendation, another consideration to make when buying engine oil is whether to purchase a standard mineral-based oil, a semi-synthetic oil (also known as a synthetic blend or synthetic-based oil) or a fully-synthetic oil. The cost of each type of oil varies considerably; mineral-based oils are the cheapest, the fully-synthetic oils the most expensive with the semi-synthetic oils falling somewhere in-between. This decision is very much up to the owner, but it should be noted that modern synthetic oils have far better lubricating properties and burn cleaner than traditional mineral-based oils. It is therefore recommended that a fully synthetic oil is used. The extra expense could save you money in the long term by preventing premature engine wear, engine performance will be improved, carbon deposits and exhaust smoke will be reduced.

● Always ensure that the oil is specifically designed for use in an injector system. Many high quality two-stroke oils are designed for competition use and need to be pre-mixed with fuel. These oils are of a much higher viscosity and are not designed to flow through the injector pumps used on road-going two-stroke motorcycles.

Transmission (gear) oil

● On a two-stroke engine, the transmission and clutch are lubricated by their own separate oil bath which must be changed in accordance with the Maintenance Schedule.
● Although the engine and transmission units of most four-strokes use a common lubrication supply, there are some exceptions where the engine and gearbox have separate oil reservoirs and a dry clutch is used.
● Motorcycle manufacturers will either recommend a monograde transmission oil or a four-stroke multigrade engine oil to lubricate the transmission.
● Transmission oils, or gear oils as they are often called, are designed specifically for use in transmission systems. The viscosity of these oils is represented by an SAE number, but the scale of measurement applied is different to that used to grade engine oils. As a rough guide a SAE90 gear oil will be of the same viscosity as an SAE50 engine oil.

Shaft drive oil

● On models equipped with shaft final drive, the shaft drive gears are will have their own oil supply. The manufacturer will state a recommended 'type or classification' and also a specific 'viscosity' range in the same manner as for four-stroke engine oil.
● Gear oil classification is given by the number which follows the API GL (GL standing for gear lubricant) rating, the higher the number, the higher the specification of the oil, e.g. API GL5 oil is a higher specification than API GL4 oil. Ensure the oil meets or

exceeds the classification specified and is of the correct viscosity. The viscosity of gear oils is also represented by an SAE number but the scale of measurement used is different to that used to grade engine oils. As a rough guide an SAE90 gear oil will be of the same viscosity as an SAE50 engine oil.
● If the use of an EP (Extreme Pressure) gear oil is specified, ensure the oil purchased is suitable.

Fork oil and suspension fluid

● Conventional telescopic front forks are hydraulic and require fork oil to work. To ensure the forks function correctly, the fork oil must be changed in accordance with the Maintenance Schedule.
● Fork oil is available in a variety of viscosities, identified by their SAE rating; fork oil ratings vary from light (SAE 5) to heavy (SAE 30). When purchasing fork oil, ensure the viscosity rating matches that specified by the manufacturer.
● Some lubricant manufacturers also produce a range of high-quality suspension fluids which are very similar to fork oil but are designed mainly for competition use. These fluids may have a different viscosity rating system which is not to be confused with the SAE rating of normal fork oil. Refer to the manufacturer's instructions if in any doubt.

Brake and clutch fluid

● All disc brake systems and some clutch systems are hydraulically operated. To ensure correct operation, the hydraulic fluid must be changed in accordance with the Maintenance Schedule.
● Brake and clutch fluid is classified by its DOT rating with most motorcycle manufacturers specifying DOT 3 or 4 fluid. Both fluid types are glycol-based and can be mixed together without adverse effect; DOT 4 fluid exceeds the requirements of DOT 3

fluid. Although it is safe to use DOT 4 fluid in a system designed for use with DOT 3 fluid, never use DOT 3 fluid in a system which specifies the use of DOT 4 as this will adversely affect the system's performance. The type required for the system will be marked on the fluid reservoir cap.
● Some manufacturers also produce a DOT 5 hydraulic fluid. DOT 5 hydraulic fluid is silicone-based and is not compatible with the glycol-based DOT 3 and 4 fluids. Never mix DOT 5 fluid with DOT 3 or 4 fluid as this will seriously affect the performance of the hydraulic system.

Coolant/antifreeze

● When purchasing coolant/antifreeze, always ensure it is suitable for use in an aluminium engine and contains corrosion inhibitors to prevent possible blockages of the internal coolant passages of the system. As a general rule, most coolants are designed to be used neat and should not be diluted whereas antifreeze can be mixed with distilled water to provide a coolant solution of the required strength. Refer to the manufacturer's instructions on the bottle.
● Ensure the coolant is changed in accordance with the Maintenance Schedule.

Chain lube

● Chain lube is an aerosol-type spray lubricant specifically designed for use on motorcycle final drive chains. Chain lube has two functions, to minimise friction between the final drive chain and sprockets and to prevent corrosion of the chain. Regular use of a good-quality chain lube will extend the life of the drive chain and sprockets and thus maximise the power being transmitted from the transmission to the rear wheel.
● When using chain lube, always allow some time for the solvents in the lube to evaporate before riding the motorcycle. This will minimise the amount of lube which will

'fling' off from the chain when the motorcycle is used. If the motorcycle is equipped with an 'O-ring' chain, ensure the chain lube is labelled as being suitable for use on 'O-ring' chains.

Degreasers and solvents

● There are many different types of solvents and degreasers available to remove the grime and grease which accumulate around the motorcycle during normal use. Degreasers and solvents are usually available as an aerosol-type spray or as a liquid which you apply with a brush. Always closely follow the manufacturer's instructions and wear eye protection during use. Be aware that many solvents are flammable and may give off noxious fumes; take adequate precautions when using them (see Safety First!).

● For general cleaning, use one of the many solvents or degreasers available from most motorcycle accessory shops. These solvents are usually applied then left for a certain time before being washed off with water.

Brake cleaner is a solvent specifically designed to remove all traces of oil, grease and dust from braking system components. Brake cleaner is designed to evaporate quickly and leaves behind no residue.

Carburettor cleaner is an aerosol-type solvent specifically designed to clear carburettor blockages and break down the hard deposits and gum often found inside carburettors during overhaul.

Contact cleaner is an aerosol-type solvent designed for cleaning electrical components. The cleaner will remove all traces of oil and dirt from components such as switch contacts or fouled spark plugs and then dry, leaving behind no residue.

Gasket remover is an aerosol-type solvent designed for removing stubborn gaskets from engine components during overhaul. Gasket remover will minimise the amount of scraping required to remove the gasket and therefore reduce the risk of damage to the mating surface.

Spray lubricants

● Aerosol-based spray lubricants are widely available and are excellent for lubricating lever pivots and exposed cables and switches. Try to use a lubricant which is of the dry-film type as the fluid evaporates, leaving behind a dry-film of lubricant. Lubricants which leave behind an oily residue will attract dust and dirt which will increase the rate of wear of the cable/lever.

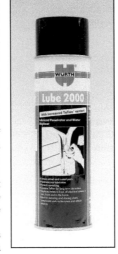

● Most lubricants also act as a moisture dispersant and a penetrating fluid. This means they can also be used to 'dry out' electrical components such as wiring connectors or switches as well as helping to free seized fasteners.

Greases

● Grease is used to lubricate many of the pivot-points. A good-quality multi-purpose grease is suitable for most applications but some manufacturers will specify the use of specialist greases for use on components such as swingarm and suspension linkage bushes. These specialist greases can be purchased from most motorcycle (or car) accessory shops; commonly specified types include molybdenum disulphide grease, lithium-based grease, graphite-based grease, silicone-based grease and high-temperature copper-based grease.

Gasket sealing compounds

● Gasket sealing compounds can be used in conjunction with gaskets, to improve their sealing capabilities, or on their own to seal metal-to-metal joints. Depending on their type, sealing compounds either set hard or stay relatively soft and pliable.

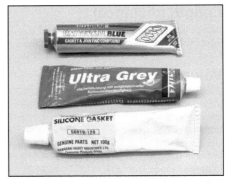

● When purchasing a gasket sealing compound, ensure that it is designed specifically for use on an internal combustion engine. General multi-purpose sealants available from DIY stores may appear visibly similar but they are not designed to withstand the extreme heat or contact with fuel and oil encountered when used on an engine (see 'Tools and Workshop Tips' for further information).

Thread locking compound

● Thread locking compounds are used to secure certain threaded fasteners in position to prevent them from loosening due to vibration. Thread locking compounds can be purchased from most motorcycle (and car) accessory shops. Ensure the threads of the both components are completely clean and dry before sparingly applying the locking compound (see 'Tools and Workshop Tips' for further information).

Fuel additives

● Fuel additives which protect and clean the fuel system components are widely available. These additives are designed to remove all traces of deposits that build up on the carburettors/injectors and prevent wear, helping the fuel system to operate more efficiently. If a fuel additive is being used, check that it is suitable for use with your motorcycle, especially if your motorcycle is equipped with a catalytic converter.

● Octane boosters are also available. These additives are designed to improve the performance of highly-tuned engines being run on normal pump-fuel and are of no real use on standard motorcycles.

Length (distance)

Inches (in)	x 25.4	= Millimetres (mm)	x 0.0394	= Inches (in)
Feet (ft)	x 0.305	= Metres (m)	x 3.281	= Feet (ft)
Miles	x 1.609	= Kilometres (km)	x 0.621	= Miles

Volume (capacity)

Cubic inches (cu in; in³)	x 16.387	= Cubic centimetres (cc; cm³)	x 0.061	= Cubic inches (cu in; in³)
Imperial pints (Imp pt)	x 0.568	= Litres (l)	x 1.76	= Imperial pints (Imp pt)
Imperial quarts (Imp qt)	x 1.137	= Litres (l)	x 0.88	= Imperial quarts (Imp qt)
Imperial quarts (Imp qt)	x 1.201	= US quarts (US qt)	x 0.833	= Imperial quarts (Imp qt)
US quarts (US qt)	x 0.946	= Litres (l)	x 1.057	= US quarts (US qt)
Imperial gallons (Imp gal)	x 4.546	= Litres (l)	x 0.22	= Imperial gallons (Imp gal)
Imperial gallons (Imp gal)	x 1.201	= US gallons (US gal)	x 0.833	= Imperial gallons (Imp gal)
US gallons (US gal)	x 3.785	= Litres (l)	x 0.264	= US gallons (US gal)

Mass (weight)

Ounces (oz)	x 28.35	= Grams (g)	x 0.035	= Ounces (oz)
Pounds (lb)	x 0.454	= Kilograms (kg)	x 2.205	= Pounds (lb)

Force

Ounces-force (ozf; oz)	x 0.278	= Newtons (N)	x 3.6	= Ounces-force (ozf; oz)
Pounds-force (lbf; lb)	x 4.448	= Newtons (N)	x 0.225	= Pounds-force (lbf; lb)
Newtons (N)	x 0.1	= Kilograms-force (kgf; kg)	x 9.81	= Newtons (N)

Pressure

Pounds-force per square inch (psi; lbf/in²; lb/in²)	x 0.070	= Kilograms-force per square centimetre (kgf/cm²; kg/cm²)	x 14.223	= Pounds-force per square inch (psi; lbf/in²; lb/in²)
Pounds-force per square inch (psi; lbf/in²; lb/in²)	x 0.068	= Atmospheres (atm)	x 14.696	= Pounds-force per square inch (psi; lbf/in²; lb/in²)
Pounds-force per square inch (psi; lbf/in²; lb/in²)	x 0.069	= Bars	x 14.5	= Pounds-force per square inch (psi; lbf/in²; lb/in²)
Pounds-force per square inch (psi; lbf/in²; lb/in²)	x 6.895	= Kilopascals (kPa)	x 0.145	= Pounds-force per square inch (psi; lbf/in²; lb/in²)
Kilopascals (kPa)	x 0.01	= Kilograms-force per square centimetre (kgf/cm²; kg/cm²)	x 98.1	= Kilopascals (kPa)
Millibar (mbar)	x 100	= Pascals (Pa)	x 0.01	= Millibar (mbar)
Millibar (mbar)	x 0.0145	= Pounds-force per square inch (psi; lbf/in²; lb/in²)	x 68.947	= Millibar (mbar)
Millibar (mbar)	x 0.75	= Millimetres of mercury (mmHg)	x 1.333	= Millibar (mbar)
Millibar (mbar)	x 0.401	= Inches of water (inH$_2$O)	x 2.491	= Millibar (mbar)
Millimetres of mercury (mmHg)	x 0.535	= Inches of water (inH$_2$O)	x 1.868	= Millimetres of mercury (mmHg)
Inches of water (inH$_2$O)	x 0.036	= Pounds-force per square inch (psi; lbf/in²; lb/in²)	x 27.68	= Inches of water (inH$_2$O)

Torque (moment of force)

Pounds-force inches (lbf in; lb in)	x 1.152	= Kilograms-force centimetre (kgf cm; kg cm)	x 0.868	= Pounds-force inches (lbf in; lb in)
Pounds-force inches (lbf in; lb in)	x 0.113	= Newton metres (Nm)	x 8.85	= Pounds-force inches (lbf in; lb in)
Pounds-force inches (lbf in; lb in)	x 0.083	= Pounds-force feet (lbf ft; lb ft)	x 12	= Pounds-force inches (lbf in; lb in)
Pounds-force feet (lbf ft; lb ft)	x 0.138	= Kilograms-force metres (kgf m; kg m)	x 7.233	= Pounds-force feet (lbf ft; lb ft)
Pounds-force feet (lbf ft; lb ft)	x 1.356	= Newton metres (Nm)	x 0.738	= Pounds-force feet (lbf ft; lb ft)
Newton metres (Nm)	x 0.102	= Kilograms-force metres (kgf m; kg m)	x 9.804	= Newton metres (Nm)

Power

Horsepower (hp)	x 745.7	= Watts (W)	x 0.0013	= Horsepower (hp)

Velocity (speed)

Miles per hour (miles/hr; mph)	x 1.609	= Kilometres per hour (km/hr; kph)	x 0.621	= Miles per hour (miles/hr; mph)

Fuel consumption*

Miles per gallon (mpg)	x 0.354	= Kilometres per litre (km/l)	x 2.825	= Miles per gallon (mpg)

Temperature

Degrees Fahrenheit = (°C x 1.8) + 32   Degrees Celsius (Degrees Centigrade; °C) = (°F - 32) x 0.56

It is common practice to convert from miles per gallon (mpg) to litres/100 kilometres (l/100km), where mpg x l/100 km = 282

About the MOT Test

In the UK, all vehicles more than three years old are subject to an annual test to ensure that they meet minimum safety requirements. A current test certificate must be issued before a machine can be used on public roads, and is required before a road fund licence can be issued. Riding without a current test certificate will also invalidate your insurance.

For most owners, the MOT test is an annual cause for anxiety, and this is largely due to owners not being sure what needs to be checked prior to submitting the motorcycle for testing. The simple answer is that a fully roadworthy motorcycle will have no difficulty in passing the test.

This is a guide to getting your motorcycle through the MOT test. Obviously it will not be possible to examine the motorcycle to the same standard as the professional MOT tester, particularly in view of the equipment required for some of the checks. However, working through the following procedures will enable you to identify any problem areas before submitting the motorcycle for the test.

It has only been possible to summarise the test requirements here, based on the regulations in force at the time of printing. Test standards are becoming increasingly stringent, although there are some exemptions for older vehicles. More information about the MOT test can be obtained from the HMSO publications, *How Safe is your Motorcycle* and *The MOT Inspection Manual for Motorcycle Testing*.

Many of the checks require that one of the wheels is raised off the ground. If the motorcycle doesn't have a centre stand, note that an auxiliary stand will be required. Additionally, the help of an assistant may prove useful.

Certain exceptions apply to machines under 50 cc, machines without a lighting system, and Classic bikes - if in doubt about any of the requirements listed below seek confirmation from an MOT tester prior to submitting the motorcycle for the test.

Check that the frame number is clearly visible.

> **HAYNES HiNT** *If a component is in borderline condition, the tester has discretion in deciding whether to pass or fail it. If the motorcycle presented is clean and evidently well cared for, the tester may be more inclined to pass a borderline component than if the motorcycle is scruffy and apparently neglected.*

Electrical System

Lights, turn signals, horn and reflector

✔ With the ignition on, check the operation of the following electrical components. **Note:** *The electrical components on certain small-capacity machines are powered by the generator, requiring that the engine is run for this check.*

a) *Headlight and tail light. Check that both illuminate in the low and high beam switch positions.*

b) *Position lights. Check that the front position (or sidelight) and tail light illuminate in this switch position.*

c) *Turn signals. Check that all flash at the correct rate, and that the warning light(s) function correctly. Check that the turn signal switch works correctly.*

d) *Hazard warning system (where fitted). Check that all four turn signals flash in this switch position.*

e) *Brake stop light. Check that the light comes on when the front and rear brakes are independently applied. Models first used on or after 1st April 1986 must have a brake light switch on each brake.*

f) *Horn. Check that the sound is continuous and of reasonable volume.*

✔ Check that there is a red reflector on the rear of the machine, either mounted separately or as part of the tail light lens.

✔ Check the condition of the headlight, tail light and turn signal lenses.

Headlight beam height

✔ The MOT tester will perform a headlight beam height check using specialised beam setting equipment **(see illustration 1)**. This equipment will not be available to the home mechanic, but if you suspect that the headlight is incorrectly set or may have been maladjusted in the past, you can perform a rough test as follows.

✔ Position the bike in a straight line facing a brick wall. The bike must be off its stand, upright and with a rider seated. Measure the height from the ground to the centre of the headlight and mark a horizontal line on the wall at this height. Position the motorcycle 3.8 metres from the wall and draw a vertical

Headlight beam height checking equipment

line up the wall central to the centreline of the motorcycle. Switch to dipped beam and check that the beam pattern falls slightly lower than the horizontal line and to the left of the vertical line **(see illustration 2)**.

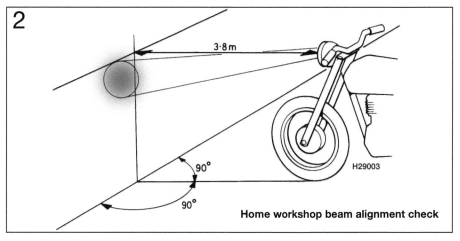

Home workshop beam alignment check

Exhaust System and Final Drive

Exhaust

✔ Check that the exhaust mountings are secure and that the system does not foul any of the rear suspension components.

✔ Start the motorcycle. When the revs are increased, check that the exhaust is neither holed nor leaking from any of its joints. On a linked system, check that the collector box is not leaking due to corrosion.

✔ Note that the exhaust decibel level ("loudness" of the exhaust) is assessed at the discretion of the tester. If the motorcycle was first used on or after 1st January 1985 the silencer must carry the BSAU 193 stamp, or a marking relating to its make and model, or be of OE (original equipment) manufacture. If the silencer is marked NOT FOR ROAD USE, RACING USE ONLY or similar, it will fail the MOT.

Final drive

✔ On chain or belt drive machines, check that the chain/belt is in good condition and does not have excessive slack. Also check that the sprocket is securely mounted on the rear wheel hub. Check that the chain/belt guard is in place.

✔ On shaft drive bikes, check for oil leaking from the drive unit and fouling the rear tyre.

Steering and Suspension

Steering

✔ With the front wheel raised off the ground, rotate the steering from lock to lock. The handlebar or switches must not contact the fuel tank or be close enough to trap the rider's hand. Problems can be caused by damaged lock stops on the lower yoke and frame, or by the fitting of non-standard handlebars.

✔ When performing the lock to lock check, also ensure that the steering moves freely without drag or notchiness. Steering movement can be impaired by poorly routed cables, or by overtight head bearings or worn bearings. The tester will perform a check of the steering head bearing lower race by mounting the front wheel on a surface plate, then performing a lock to lock check with the weight of the machine on the lower bearing (see illustration 3).

✔ Grasp the fork sliders (lower legs) and attempt to push and pull on the forks (see illustration 4). Any play in the steering head bearings will be felt. Note that in extreme cases, wear of the front fork bushes can be misinterpreted for head bearing play.

✔ Check that the handlebars are securely mounted.

✔ Check that the handlebar grip rubbers are secure. They should by bonded to the bar left end and to the throttle cable pulley on the right end.

Front suspension

✔ With the motorcycle off the stand, hold the front brake on and pump the front forks up and down (see illustration 5). Check that they are adequately damped.

✔ Inspect the area above and around the front fork oil seals (see illustration 6). There should be no sign of oil on the fork tube (stanchion) nor leaking down the slider (lower leg). On models so equipped, check that there is no oil leaking from the anti-dive units.

✔ On models with swingarm front suspension, check that there is no freeplay in the linkage when moved from side to side.

Rear suspension

✔ With the motorcycle off the stand and an assistant supporting the motorcycle by its handlebars, bounce the rear suspension (see illustration 7). Check that the suspension components do not foul on any of the cycle parts and check that the shock absorber(s) provide adequate damping.

Front wheel mounted on a surface plate for steering head bearing lower race check

Checking the steering head bearings for freeplay

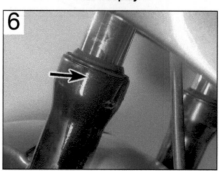

Hold the front brake on and pump the front forks up and down to check operation

Inspect the area around the fork dust seal for oil leakage (arrow)

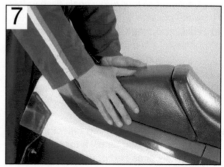

Bounce the rear of the motorcycle to check rear suspension operation

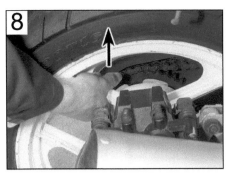

Checking for rear suspension linkage play

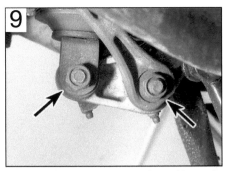

Worn suspension linkage pivots (arrows) are usually the cause of play in the rear suspension

Grasp the swingarm at the ends to check for play in its pivot bearings

✔ Visually inspect the shock absorber(s) and check that there is no sign of oil leakage from its damper. This is somewhat restricted on certain single shock models due to the location of the shock absorber.

✔ With the rear wheel raised off the ground, grasp the wheel at the highest point and attempt to pull it up **(see illustration 8)**. Any play in the swingarm pivot or suspension linkage bearings will be felt as movement. **Note:** *Do not confuse play with actual suspension movement.* Failure to lubricate suspension linkage bearings can lead to bearing failure **(see illustration 9)**.

✔ With the rear wheel raised off the ground, grasp the swingarm ends and attempt to move the swingarm from side to side and forwards and backwards - any play indicates wear of the swingarm pivot bearings **(see illustration 10)**.

Brakes, Wheels and Tyres

Brakes

✔ With the wheel raised off the ground, apply the brake then free it off, and check that the wheel is about to revolve freely without brake drag.

✔ On disc brakes, examine the disc itself. Check that it is securely mounted and not cracked.

✔ On disc brakes, view the pad material through the caliper mouth and check that the pads are not worn down beyond the limit **(see illustration 11)**.

✔ On drum brakes, check that when the brake is applied the angle between the operating lever and cable or rod is not too great **(see illustration 12)**. Check also that the operating lever doesn't foul any other components.

✔ On disc brakes, examine the flexible hoses from top to bottom. Have an assistant hold the brake on so that the fluid in the hose is under pressure, and check that there is no sign of fluid leakage, bulges or cracking. If there are any metal brake pipes or unions, check that these are free from corrosion and damage. Where a brake-linked anti-dive system is fitted, check the hoses to the anti-dive in a similar manner.

✔ Check that the rear brake torque arm is secure and that its fasteners are secured by self-locking nuts or castellated nuts with split-pins or R-pins **(see illustration 13)**.

✔ On models with ABS, check that the self-check warning light in the instrument panel works.

✔ The MOT tester will perform a test of the motorcycle's braking efficiency based on a calculation of rider and motorcycle weight. Although this cannot be carried out at home, you can at least ensure that the braking systems are properly maintained. For hydraulic disc brakes, check the fluid level, lever/pedal feel (bleed of air if its spongy) and pad material. For drum brakes, check adjustment, cable or rod operation and shoe lining thickness.

Wheels and tyres

✔ Check the wheel condition. Cast wheels should be free from cracks and if of the built-up design, all fasteners should be secure. Spoked wheels should be checked for broken, corroded, loose or bent spokes.

✔ With the wheel raised off the ground, spin the wheel and visually check that the tyre and wheel run true. Check that the tyre does not foul the suspension or mudguards.

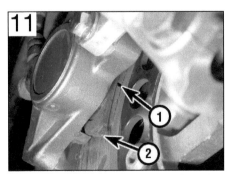

Brake pad wear can usually be viewed without removing the caliper. Most pads have wear indicator grooves (1) and some also have indicator tangs (2)

On drum brakes, check the angle of the operating lever with the brake fully applied. Most drum brakes have a wear indicator pointer and scale.

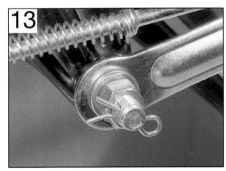

Brake torque arm must be properly secured at both ends

Check for wheel bearing play by trying to move the wheel about the axle (spindle)

Checking the tyre tread depth

Tyre direction of rotation arrow can be found on tyre sidewall

Castellated type wheel axle (spindle) nut must be secured by a split pin or R-pin

Two straightedges are used to check wheel alignment

✔ With the wheel raised off the ground, grasp the wheel and attempt to move it about the axle (spindle) **(see illustration 14)**. Any play felt here indicates wheel bearing failure.
✔ Check the tyre tread depth, tread condition and sidewall condition **(see illustration 15)**.
✔ Check the tyre type. Front and rear tyre types must be compatible and be suitable for road use. Tyres marked NOT FOR ROAD USE, COMPETITION USE ONLY or similar, will fail the MOT.
✔ If the tyre sidewall carries a direction of rotation arrow, this must be pointing in the direction of normal wheel rotation **(see illustration 16)**.
✔ Check that the wheel axle (spindle) nuts (where applicable) are properly secured. A self-locking nut or castellated nut with a split-pin or R-pin can be used **(see illustration 17)**.
✔ Wheel alignment is checked with the motorcycle off the stand and a rider seated. With the front wheel pointing straight ahead, two perfectly straight lengths of metal or wood and placed against the sidewalls of both tyres **(see illustration 18)**. The gap each side of the front tyre must be equidistant on both sides. Incorrect wheel alignment may be due to a cocked rear wheel (often as the result of poor chain adjustment) or in extreme cases, a bent frame.

General checks and condition

✔ Check the security of all major fasteners, bodypanels, seat, fairings (where fitted) and mudguards.

✔ Check that the rider and pillion footrests, handlebar levers and brake pedal are securely mounted.

✔ Check for corrosion on the frame or any load-bearing components. If severe, this may affect the structure, particularly under stress.

Sidecars

A motorcycle fitted with a sidecar requires additional checks relating to the stability of the machine and security of attachment and swivel joints, plus specific wheel alignment (toe-in) requirements. Additionally, tyre and lighting requirements differ from conventional motorcycle use. Owners are advised to check MOT test requirements with an official test centre.

Preparing for storage

Before you start

If repairs or an overhaul is needed, see that this is carried out now rather than left until you want to ride the bike again.

Give the bike a good wash and scrub all dirt from its underside. Make sure the bike dries completely before preparing for storage.

Engine

● Remove the spark plug(s) and lubricate the cylinder bores with approximately a teaspoon of motor oil using a spout-type oil can **(see illustration 1)**. Reinstall the spark plug(s). Crank the engine over a couple of times to coat the piston rings and bores with oil. If the bike has a kickstart, use this to turn the engine over. If not, flick the kill switch to the OFF position and crank the engine over on the starter **(see illustration 2)**. If the nature on the ignition system prevents the starter operating with the kill switch in the OFF position,

remove the spark plugs and fit them back in their caps; ensure that the plugs are earthed (grounded) against the cylinder head when the starter is operated **(see illustration 3)**.

⚠️ *Warning: It is important that the plugs are earthed (grounded) away from the spark plug holes otherwise there is a risk of atomised fuel from the cylinders igniting.*

HAYNES HiNT *On a single cylinder four-stroke engine, you can seal the combustion chamber completely by positioning the piston at TDC on the compression stroke.*

● Drain the carburettor(s) otherwise there is a risk of jets becoming blocked by gum deposits from the fuel **(see illustration 4)**.

● If the bike is going into long-term storage, consider adding a fuel stabiliser to the fuel in the tank. If the tank is drained completely, corrosion of its internal surfaces may occur if left unprotected for a long period. The tank can be treated with a rust preventative especially for this purpose. Alternatively, remove the tank and pour half a litre of motor oil into it, install the filler cap and shake the tank to coat its internals with oil before draining off the excess. The same effect can also be achieved by spraying WD40 or a similar water-dispersant around the inside of the tank via its flexible nozzle.

● Make sure the cooling system contains the correct mix of antifreeze. Antifreeze also contains important corrosion inhibitors.

● The air intakes and exhaust can be sealed off by covering or plugging the openings. Ensure that you do not seal in any condensation; run the engine until it is hot,

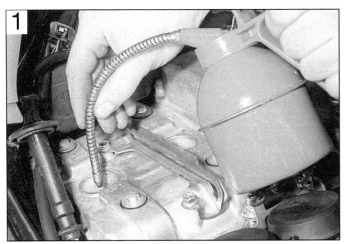
Squirt a drop of motor oil into each cylinder

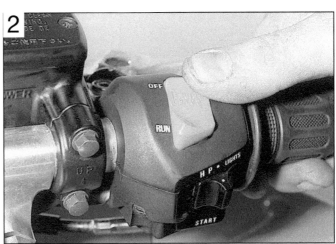
Flick the kill switch to OFF . . .

. . . and ensure that the metal bodies of the plugs (arrows) are earthed against the cylinder head

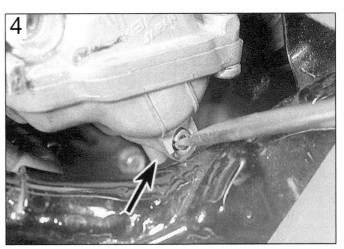
Connect a hose to the carburettor float chamber drain stub (arrow) and unscrew the drain screw

Exhausts can be sealed off with a plastic bag

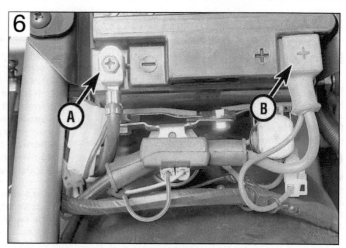

Disconnect the negative lead (A) first, followed by the positive lead (B)

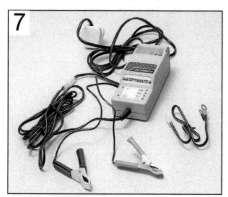

Use a suitable battery charger - this kit also assess battery condition

then switch off and allow to cool. Tape a piece of thick plastic over the silencer end(s) **(see illustration 5)**. Note that some advocate pouring a tablespoon of motor oil into the silencer(s) before sealing them off.

Battery

● Remove it from the bike - in extreme cases of cold the battery may freeze and crack its case **(see illustration 6)**.

● Check the electrolyte level and top up if necessary (conventional refillable batteries). Clean the terminals.
● Store the battery off the motorcycle and away from any sources of fire. Position a wooden block under the battery if it is to sit on the ground.
● Give the battery a trickle charge for a few hours every month **(see illustration 7)**.

Tyres

● Place the bike on its centrestand or an auxiliary stand which will support the motorcycle in an upright position. Position wood blocks under the tyres to keep them off the ground and to provide insulation from damp. If the bike is being put into long-term storage, ideally both tyres should be off the ground; not only will this protect the tyres, but will also ensure that no load is placed on the steering head or wheel bearings.
● Deflate each tyre by 5 to 10 psi, no more or the beads may unseat from the rim, making subsequent inflation difficult on tubeless tyres.

Pivots and controls

● Lubricate all lever, pedal, stand and footrest pivot points. If grease nipples are fitted to the rear suspension components, apply lubricant to the pivots.
● Lubricate all control cables.

Cycle components

● Apply a wax protectant to all painted and plastic components. Wipe off any excess, but don't polish to a shine. Where fitted, clean the screen with soap and water.
● Coat metal parts with Vaseline (petroleum jelly). When applying this to the fork tubes, do not compress the forks otherwise the seals will rot from contact with the Vaseline.
● Apply a vinyl cleaner to the seat.

Storage conditions

● Aim to store the bike in a shed or garage which does not leak and is free from damp.
● Drape an old blanket or bedspread over the bike to protect it from dust and direct contact with sunlight (which will fade paint). This also hides the bike from prying eyes. Beware of tight-fitting plastic covers which may allow condensation to form and settle on the bike.

Getting back on the road

Engine and transmission

● Change the oil and replace the oil filter. If this was done prior to storage, check that the oil hasn't emulsified - a thick whitish substance which occurs through condensation.
● Remove the spark plugs. Using a spout-type oil can, squirt a few drops of oil into the cylinder(s). This will provide initial lubrication as the piston rings and bores comes back into contact. Service the spark plugs, or fit new ones, and install them in the engine.

● Check that the clutch isn't stuck on. The plates can stick together if left standing for some time, preventing clutch operation. Engage a gear and try rocking the bike back and forth with the clutch lever held against the handlebar. If this doesn't work on cable-operated clutches, hold the clutch lever back against the handlebar with a strong elastic band or cable tie for a couple of hours **(see illustration 8)**.
● If the air intakes or silencer end(s) were blocked off, remove the bung or cover used.
● If the fuel tank was coated with a rust

Hold clutch lever back against the handlebar with elastic bands or a cable tie

preventative, oil or a stabiliser added to the fuel, drain and flush the tank and dispose of the fuel sensibly. If no action was taken with the fuel tank prior to storage, it is advised that the old fuel is disposed of since it will go off over a period of time. Refill the fuel tank with fresh fuel.

Frame and running gear

● Oil all pivot points and cables.
● Check the tyre pressures. They will definitely need inflating if pressures were reduced for storage.
● Lubricate the final drive chain (where applicable).
● Remove any protective coating applied to the fork tubes (stanchions) since this may well destroy the fork seals. If the fork tubes weren't protected and have picked up rust spots, remove them with very fine abrasive paper and refinish with metal polish.
● Check that both brakes operate correctly. Apply each brake hard and check that it's not possible to move the motorcycle forwards, then check that the brake frees off again once released. Brake caliper pistons can stick due to corrosion around the piston head, or on the sliding caliper types, due to corrosion of the slider pins. If the brake doesn't free after repeated operation, take the caliper off for examination. Similarly drum brakes can stick

due to a seized operating cam, cable or rod linkage.
● If the motorcycle has been in long-term storage, renew the brake fluid and clutch fluid (where applicable).
● Depending on where the bike has been stored, the wiring, cables and hoses may have been nibbled by rodents. Make a visual check and investigate disturbed wiring loom tape.

Battery

● If the battery has been previously removal and given top up charges it can simply be reconnected. Remember to connect the positive cable first and the negative cable last.
● On conventional refillable batteries, if the battery has not received any attention, remove it from the motorcycle and check its electrolyte level. Top up if necessary then charge the battery. If the battery fails to hold a charge and a visual checks show heavy white sulphation of the plates, the battery is probably defective and must be renewed. This is particularly likely if the battery is old. Confirm battery condition with a specific gravity check.
● On sealed (MF) batteries, if the battery has not received any attention, remove it from the motorcycle and charge it according to the information on the battery case - if the battery fails to hold a charge it must be renewed.

Starting procedure

● If a kickstart is fitted, turn the engine over a couple of times with the ignition OFF to distribute oil around the engine. If no kickstart is fitted, flick the engine kill switch OFF and the ignition ON and crank the engine over a couple of times to work oil around the upper cylinder components. If the nature of the ignition system is such that the starter won't work with the kill switch OFF, remove the spark plugs, fit them back into their caps and earth (ground) their bodies on the cylinder head. Reinstall the spark plugs afterwards.
● Switch the kill switch to RUN, operate the choke and start the engine. If the engine won't start don't continue cranking the engine - not only will this flatten the battery, but the starter motor will overheat. Switch the ignition off and try again later. If the engine refuses to start, go through the fault finding procedures in this manual. **Note:** *If the bike has been in storage for a long time, old fuel or a carburettor blockage may be the problem. Gum deposits in carburettors can block jets - if a carburettor cleaner doesn't prove successful the carburettors must be dismantled for cleaning.*
● Once the engine has started, check that the lights, turn signals and horn work properly.
● Treat the bike gently for the first ride and check all fluid levels on completion. Settle the bike back into the maintenance schedule.

This Section provides an easy reference-guide to the more common faults that are likely to afflict your machine. Obviously, the opportunities are almost limitless for faults to occur as a result of obscure failures, and to try and cover all eventualities would require a book. Indeed, a number have been written on the subject.

Successful troubleshooting is not a mysterious 'black art' but the application of a bit of knowledge combined with a systematic and logical approach to the problem. Approach any troubleshooting by first accurately identifying the symptom and then checking through the list of possible causes, starting with the simplest or most obvious and progressing in stages to the most complex. Take nothing for granted, but above all apply liberal quantities of common sense.

The main symptom of a fault is given in the text as a major heading below which are listed the various systems or areas which may contain the fault. Details of each possible cause for a fault and the remedial action to be taken are given. Further information should be sought in the relevant Chapter.

1 Engine doesn't start or is difficult to start

☐ Starter motor doesn't rotate
☐ Starter motor rotates but engine does not turn over
☐ Starter works but engine won't turn over (seized)
☐ No fuel flow
☐ Engine flooded
☐ No spark or weak spark
☐ Compression low
☐ Stalls after starting
☐ Rough idle

2 Poor running at low speed

☐ Spark weak
☐ Fuel/air mixture incorrect
☐ Compression low
☐ Poor acceleration

3 Poor running or no power at high speed

☐ Firing incorrect
☐ Fuel/air mixture incorrect
☐ Compression low
☐ Knocking or pinking
☐ Miscellaneous causes

4 Overheating

☐ Engine overheats
☐ Firing incorrect
☐ Fuel/air mixture incorrect
☐ Compression too high
☐ Engine load excessive
☐ Lubrication inadequate
☐ Miscellaneous causes

5 Clutch problems

☐ Clutch slipping
☐ Clutch not disengaging completely

6 Gearchanging problems

☐ Doesn't go into gear, or lever doesn't return
☐ Jumps out of gear
☐ Overselects

7 Abnormal engine noise

☐ Knocking or pinking
☐ Piston slap or rattling
☐ Valve noise
☐ Other noise

8 Abnormal driveline noise

☐ Clutch noise
☐ Transmission noise
☐ Final drive noise

9 Abnormal frame and suspension noise

☐ Front end noise
☐ Shock absorber noise
☐ Brake noise

10 Oil pressure warning light comes on

☐ Engine lubrication system
☐ Electrical system

11 Excessive exhaust smoke

☐ White smoke
☐ Black smoke

12 Poor handling or stability

☐ Handlebar hard to turn
☐ Handlebar shakes or vibrates excessively
☐ Handlebar pulls to one side
☐ Poor shock absorbing qualities

13 Braking problems

☐ Brakes are spongy, don't hold
☐ Brake lever or pedal pulsates
☐ Brakes drag

14 Electrical problems

☐ Battery dead or weak
☐ Battery overcharged

1 Engine doesn't start or is difficult to start

Starter motor doesn't rotate

- [ ] Engine kill switch OFF.
- [ ] Fuse blown. Check main fuse and starter circuit fuse (Chapter 9).
- [ ] Battery voltage low. Check and recharge battery (Chapter 9).
- [ ] Starter motor defective. Make sure the wiring to the starter is secure. Make sure the starter relay clicks when the start button is pushed. If the relay clicks, then the fault is in the wiring or motor.
- [ ] Starter relay faulty. Check it according to the procedure in Chapter 9.
- [ ] Starter switch not contacting. The contacts could be wet, corroded or dirty. Disassemble and clean the switch (Chapter 9).
- [ ] Wiring open or shorted. Check all wiring connections and harnesses to make sure that they are dry, tight and not corroded. Also check for broken or frayed wires that can cause a short to ground (earth) (see wiring diagram, Chapter 9).
- [ ] Ignition (main) switch defective. Check the switch according to the procedure in Chapter 9. Renew the switch with a new one if it is defective.
- [ ] Engine kill switch defective. Check for wet, dirty or corroded contacts. Clean or renew the switch as necessary (Chapter 9).
- [ ] Faulty neutral, side stand or clutch switch. Check the wiring to each switch and the switch itself according to the procedures in Chapter 9.

Starter motor rotates but engine does not turn over

- [ ] Starter motor clutch defective. Inspect and repair or renew (Chapter 2A or 2B).
- [ ] Damaged idler or starter gears. Inspect and renew the damaged parts (Chapter 2A or 2B).

Starter works but engine won't turn over (seized)

- [ ] Seized engine caused by one or more internally damaged components. Failure due to wear, abuse or lack of lubrication. Damage can include seized valves, followers/rocker arms, camshafts, pistons, crankshaft, connecting rod bearings, or transmission gears or bearings. Refer to Chapter 2A or 2B for engine disassembly.

No fuel flow

- [ ] No fuel in tank.
- [ ] Fuel tank breather hose obstructed.
- [ ] Fuel pump faulty, or filter is blocked (see Chapter 4).

Engine flooded

- [ ] Starting technique incorrect. Under normal circumstances the machine should start with little or no throttle. When the engine is cold, the choke should be operated and the engine started without opening the throttle. When the engine is at operating temperature, only a very slight amount of throttle should be necessary.

No spark or weak spark

- [ ] Ignition switch OFF.
- [ ] Engine kill switch turned to the OFF position.
- [ ] Battery voltage low. Check and recharge the battery as necessary (Chapter 9).
- [ ] Spark plugs dirty, defective or worn out. Locate reason for fouled plugs using spark plug condition chart and follow the plug maintenance procedures (Chapter 1).
- [ ] Spark plug caps or secondary (HT) wiring faulty. Check condition. Renew either or both components if cracks or deterioration are evident (Chapter 5).
- [ ] Spark plug caps not making good contact. Make sure that the plug caps fit snugly over the plug ends.
- [ ] Ignition HT coils defective. Check the coils, referring to Chapter 5.
- [ ] IC igniter unit defective. Refer to Chapter 5 for details.
- [ ] Pick-up coil defective. Check the unit, referring to Chapter 5 for details.
- [ ] Ignition or kill switch shorted. This is usually caused by water, corrosion, damage or excessive wear. The switches can be disassembled and cleaned with electrical contact cleaner. If cleaning does not help, renew the switches (Chapter 9).
- [ ] Wiring shorted or broken between:

a) Ignition (main) switch and engine kill switch (or blown fuse)
b) IC igniter unit and engine kill switch
c) IC igniter unit and ignition HT coils
d) Ignition HT coils and spark plugs
e) IC igniter unit and ignition pick-up coil.

- [ ] Make sure that all wiring connections are clean, dry and tight. Look for chafed and broken wires (Chapters 5 and 9).

Compression low

- [ ] Spark plugs loose. Remove the plugs and inspect their threads. Reinstall and tighten to the specified torque (Chapter 1).
- [ ] Cylinder head not sufficiently tightened down. If the cylinder head is suspected of being loose, then there's a chance that the gasket or head is damaged if the problem has persisted for any length of time. The head bolts should be tightened to the proper torque in the correct sequence (Chapter 2A or 2B).
- [ ] Improper valve clearance. This means that the valve is not closing completely and compression pressure is leaking past the valve. Check and adjust the valve clearances (Chapter 1).
- [ ] Cylinder and/or piston worn. Excessive wear will cause compression pressure to leak past the rings. This is usually accompanied by worn rings as well. A top-end overhaul is necessary (Chapter 2A or 2B).
- [ ] Piston rings worn, weak, broken, or sticking. Broken or sticking piston rings usually indicate a lubrication or fuelling problem that causes excess carbon deposits or seizures to form on the pistons and rings. Top-end overhaul is necessary (Chapter 2A or 2B).
- [ ] Piston ring-to-groove clearance excessive. This is caused by excessive wear of the piston ring lands. Piston renewal is necessary (Chapter 2A or 2B).
- [ ] Cylinder head gasket damaged. If a head is allowed to become loose, or if excessive carbon build-up on the piston crown and combustion chamber causes extremely high compression, the head gasket may leak. Retorquing the head is not always sufficient to restore the seal, so gasket renewal is necessary (Chapter 2A or 2B).
- [ ] Cylinder head warped. This is caused by overheating or improperly tightened head bolts. Machine shop resurfacing or head renewal is necessary (Chapter 2A or 2B).
- [ ] Valve spring broken or weak. Caused by component failure or wear; the springs must be renewed (Chapter 2A or 2B).
- [ ] Valve not seating properly. This is caused by a bent valve (from over-revving or improper valve adjustment), burned valve or seat (improper fuelling) or an accumulation of carbon deposits on the seat (from fuelling or lubrication problems). The valves must be cleaned and/or renewed and the seats serviced if possible (Chapter 2A or 2B).

1 Engine doesn't start or is difficult to start (continued)

Stalls after starting

☐ Improper choke action. Make sure the choke linkage shaft is getting a full stroke and staying in the out position (Chapter 4).
☐ Ignition malfunction. See Chapter 5.
☐ Carburettor malfunction. See Chapter 4.
☐ Fuel contaminated. The fuel can be contaminated with either dirt or water, or can change chemically if the machine is allowed to sit for several months or more. Drain the tank (Chapter 4).
☐ Intake air leak. Check for loose carburettor intake rubber retaining clips and damaged/disconnected vacuum hoses (Chapter 4).
☐ Engine idle speed incorrect. Turn idle adjusting screw until the engine idles at the specified rpm (Chapter 1).

Rough idle

☐ Ignition malfunction. See Chapter 5.
☐ Idle speed incorrect. See Chapter 1.
☐ Carburettors not synchronised. Adjust them with vacuum gauge or manometer set as described in Chapter 4.
☐ Carburettor malfunction. See Chapter 4.
☐ Fuel contaminated. The fuel can be contaminated with either dirt or water, or can change chemically if the machine is allowed to sit for several months or more. Drain the tank (Chapter 4).
☐ Intake air leak. Check for loose carburettor intake rubber retaining clips and damaged/disconnected vacuum hoses. Renew the intake rubbers if they are split or perished (Chapter 4).
☐ Air filter clogged. Renew the air filter element (Chapter 1).

2 Poor running at low speeds

Spark weak

☐ Battery voltage low. Check and recharge battery (Chapter 9).
☐ Spark plugs fouled, defective or worn out. Refer to Chapter 1 for spark plug maintenance.
☐ Spark plug cap or HT wiring defective – ZX-7R and ZX-9R B models. Refer to Chapters 1 and 5 for details on the ignition system.
☐ Spark plug caps not making contact – ZX-7R and ZX-9R B models.
☐ Incorrect spark plugs. Wrong type, heat range or cap configuration. Check and install correct plugs listed in Chapter 1.
☐ IC igniter unit faulty. See Chapter 4.
☐ Pick-up coil defective. See Chapter 4.
☐ Ignition HT coils defective. See Chapter 5.

Fuel/air mixture incorrect

☐ Pilot screws incorrectly set (Chapter 4)
☐ Pilot jet or air passage blocked. Remove and overhaul the carburettors (Chapter 4).
☐ Air filter clogged, poorly sealed or missing (Chapter 1).
☐ Air filter housing poorly sealed. Look for cracks, holes or loose clamps and renew or repair defective parts.
☐ Fuel tank breather hose obstructed.
☐ Intake air leak. Check for loose carburettor intake rubber retaining clips and damaged/disconnected vacuum hoses. Renew the intake rubbers if they are split or perished (Chapter 4).

Compression low

☐ Spark plugs loose. Remove the plugs and inspect their threads. Reinstall and tighten to the specified torque (Chapter 1).
☐ Cylinder head not sufficiently tightened down. If the cylinder head is suspected of being loose, then there's a chance that the gasket and head are damaged if the problem has persisted for any length of time. The head bolts should be tightened to the proper torque in the correct sequence (Chapter 2A or 2B).
☐ Improper valve clearance. This means that the valve is not closing completely and compression pressure is leaking past the valve. Check and adjust the valve clearances (Chapter 1).

☐ Cylinder and/or piston worn. Excessive wear will cause compression pressure to leak past the rings. This is usually accompanied by worn rings as well. A top-end overhaul is necessary (Chapter 2A or 2B).
☐ Piston rings worn, weak, broken, or sticking. Broken or sticking piston rings usually indicate a lubrication or fuelling problem that causes excess carbon deposits or seizures to form on the pistons and rings. Top-end overhaul is necessary (Chapter 2A or 2B).
☐ Piston ring-to-groove clearance excessive. This is caused by excessive wear of the piston ring lands. Piston renewal is necessary (Chapter 2A or 2B).
☐ Cylinder head gasket damaged. If a head is allowed to become loose, or if excessive carbon build-up on the piston crown and combustion chamber causes extremely high compression, the head gasket may leak. Retorquing the head is not always sufficient to restore the seal, so gasket renewal is necessary (Chapter 2A or 2B).
☐ Cylinder head warped. This is caused by overheating or improperly tightened head bolts. Machine shop resurfacing or head renewal is necessary (Chapter 2A or 2B).
☐ Valve spring broken or weak. Caused by component failure or wear; the springs must be renewed (Chapter 2A or 2B).
☐ Valve not seating properly. This is caused by a bent valve (from over-revving or improper valve adjustment), burned valve or seat (improper fuelling) or an accumulation of carbon deposits on the seat (from fuelling, lubrication problems). The valves must be cleaned and/or renewed and the seats serviced if possible (Chapter 2A or 2B).

Poor acceleration

☐ Carburettor fault. Remove and overhaul the carburettors (Chapter 4).
☐ Engine oil viscosity too high. Using a heavier oil than that recommended in Chapter 1 can damage the oil pump or lubrication system and cause drag on the engine.
☐ Brakes dragging. Usually caused by debris which has entered the brake piston seals, or from a warped disc or bent axle. Repair as necessary (Chapter 7).

3 Poor running or no power at high speed

Firing incorrect

☐ Air filter restricted. Clean or renew filter (Chapter 1).
☐ Spark plugs fouled, defective or worn out. See Chapter 1 for spark plug maintenance.
☐ Spark plug caps or HT wiring defective – ZX-7R and ZX-9R B models. See Chapters 1 and 5 for details of the ignition system.
☐ Spark plug caps not in good contact – ZX-7R and ZX-9R B models. See Chapter 5.
☐ Incorrect spark plugs. Wrong type, heat range or cap configuration. Check and install correct plugs listed in Chapter 1.
☐ IC igniter unit defective. See Chapter 5.
☐ Pick-up coil defective. See Chapter 5.
☐ Ignition coils defective. See Chapter 5.

Fuel/air mixture incorrect

☐ Carburettor fault. Remove and overhaul the carburettors (Chapter 4).
☐ Air filter clogged, poorly sealed, or missing (Chapter 1).
☐ Air filter housing poorly sealed. Look for cracks, holes or loose clamps, and renew or repair defective parts.
☐ Fuel tank breather hose obstructed.
☐ Intake air leak. Check for loose carburettor intake rubber retaining clips and damaged/disconnected vacuum hoses. Renew the intake rubbers if they are split or perished (Chapter 4).

Compression low

☐ Spark plugs loose. Remove the plugs and inspect their threads. Reinstall and tighten to the specified torque (Chapter 1).
☐ Cylinder head not sufficiently tightened down. If the cylinder head is suspected of being loose, then there's a chance that the gasket and head are damaged if the problem has persisted for any length of time. The head bolts should be tightened to the proper torque in the correct sequence (Chapter 2A or 2B).
☐ Improper valve clearance. This means that the valve is not closing completely and compression pressure is leaking past the valve. Check and adjust the valve clearances (Chapter 1).
☐ Cylinder and/or piston worn. Excessive wear will cause compression pressure to leak past the rings. This is usually accompanied by worn rings as well. A top-end overhaul is necessary (Chapter 2A or 2B).
☐ Piston rings worn, weak, broken, or sticking. Broken or sticking piston rings usually indicate a lubrication or fuelling problem that causes excess carbon deposits or seizures to form on the pistons and rings. Top-end overhaul is necessary (Chapter 2A or 2B).
☐ Piston ring-to-groove clearance excessive. This is caused by excessive wear of the piston ring lands. Piston renewal is necessary (Chapter 2A or 2B).

☐ Cylinder head gasket damaged. If a head is allowed to become loose, or if excessive carbon build-up on the piston crown and combustion chamber causes extremely high compression, the head gasket may leak. Retorquing the head is not always sufficient to restore the seal, so gasket renewal is necessary (Chapter 2A or 2B).
☐ Cylinder head warped. This is caused by overheating or improperly tightened head bolts. Machine shop resurfacing or head renewal is necessary (Chapter 2A or 2B).
☐ Valve spring broken or weak. Caused by component failure or wear; the springs must be renewed (Chapter 2A or 2B).
☐ Valve not seating properly. This is caused by a bent valve (from over-revving or improper valve adjustment), burned valve or seat (improper fuelling) or an accumulation of carbon deposits on the seat (from fuelling or lubrication problems). The valves must be cleaned and/or renewed and the seats serviced if possible (Chapter 2A or 2B).

Knocking or pinking

☐ Carbon build-up in combustion chamber. Use of a fuel additive that will dissolve the adhesive bonding the carbon particles to the crown and chamber is the easiest way to remove the build-up. Otherwise, the cylinder head will have to be removed and decarbonised (Chapter 2A or 2B).
☐ Incorrect or poor quality fuel. Old or improper grades of fuel can cause detonation. This causes the piston to rattle, thus the knocking or pinking sound. Drain old fuel and always use the recommended fuel grade.
☐ Spark plug heat range incorrect. Uncontrolled detonation indicates the plug heat range is too hot. The plug in effect becomes a glow plug, raising cylinder temperatures. Install the proper heat range plug (Chapter 1).
☐ Improper air/fuel mixture. This will cause the cylinders to run hot, which leads to detonation. An intake air leak can cause this imbalance. See Chapter 4.

Miscellaneous causes

☐ Throttle valve doesn't open fully. Adjust the throttle grip freeplay (Chapter 1).
☐ Clutch slipping. May be caused by loose or worn clutch components. Refer to Chapter 2A or 2B for clutch overhaul procedures.
☐ Engine oil viscosity too high. Using a heavier oil than the one recommended in Chapter 1 can damage the oil pump or lubrication system and cause drag on the engine.
☐ Brakes dragging. Usually caused by debris which has entered the brake piston seals, or from a warped disc or bent axle. Repair as necessary.

4 Overheating

Engine overheats

☐ Coolant level low. Check and add coolant (Chapter 1).
☐ Leak in cooling system. Check cooling system hoses and radiator for leaks and other damage. Repair or renew parts as necessary (Chapter 3).
☐ Thermostat sticking open or closed. Check and renew as described in Chapter 3.
☐ Faulty pressure cap. Remove the cap and have it pressure tested (Chapter 3).
☐ Coolant passages clogged. Have the entire system drained and flushed, then refill with fresh coolant.
☐ Water pump defective. Remove the pump and check the components (Chapter 3).
☐ Clogged radiator fins. Clean them by blowing compressed air through the fins from the backside.
☐ Cooling fan or fan switch fault (Chapter 3).

Firing incorrect

☐ Spark plugs fouled, defective or worn out. See Chapter 1 for spark plug maintenance.
☐ Incorrect spark plugs.
☐ IC igniter unit defective. See Chapter 5.
☐ Pick-up coil faulty. See Chapter 5.
☐ Faulty ignition coils. See Chapter 5.

Fuel/air mixture incorrect

☐ Carburettor fault. Remove and overhaul the carburettors (Chapter 4).
☐ Air filter clogged, poorly sealed, or missing (Chapter 1).
☐ Air filter housing poorly sealed. Look for cracks, holes or loose clamps, and renew or repair defective parts.
☐ Fuel tank breather hose obstructed.
☐ Intake air leak. Check for loose carburettor intake rubber retaining clips and damaged/disconnected vacuum hoses. Renew the intake rubbers if they are split or perished (Chapter 4).

Compression too high

☐ Carbon build-up in combustion chamber. Use of a fuel additive that will dissolve the adhesive bonding the carbon particles to the piston crown and chamber is the easiest way to remove the build-up. Otherwise, the cylinder head will have to be removed and decarbonised (Chapter 2A or 2B).
☐ Improperly machined head surface or installation of incorrect gasket during engine assembly.

Engine load excessive

☐ Clutch slipping. Can be caused by damaged, loose or worn clutch components. Refer to Chapter 2A or 2B for overhaul procedures.
☐ Engine oil level too high. The addition of too much oil will cause pressurisation of the crankcase and inefficient engine operation. Check Specifications and drain to proper level (Chapter 1).
☐ Engine oil viscosity too high. Using a heavier oil than the one recommended in Chapter 1 can damage the oil pump or lubrication system as well as cause drag on the engine.
☐ Brakes dragging. Usually caused by debris which has entered the brake piston seals, or from a warped disc or bent axle. Repair as necessary.

Lubrication inadequate

☐ Engine oil level too low. Friction caused by intermittent lack of lubrication or from oil that is overworked can cause overheating. The oil provides a definite cooling function in the engine. Check the oil level (Chapter 1).
☐ Poor quality engine oil or incorrect viscosity or type. Oil is rated not only according to viscosity but also according to type. Some oils are not rated high enough for use in this engine. Check the Specifications section and change to the correct oil (Chapter 1).

Miscellaneous causes

☐ Modification to exhaust system. Most aftermarket exhaust systems cause the engine to run leaner, which make them run hotter.

5 Clutch problems

Clutch slipping

☐ Clutch fluid level too high – ZX-7R and ZX-9R B models. Check fluid level (see Daily (pre-ride) checks).
☐ Clutch cable freeplay incorrectly adjusted – ZX-9R C, E and F models (Chapter 1).
☐ Friction plates worn or warped. Overhaul the clutch assembly (Chapter 2A or 2B).
☐ Plain plates warped (Chapter 2A or 2B).
☐ Clutch springs broken or weak. Old or heat-damaged (from slipping clutch) springs should be renewed with new ones (Chapter 2A or 2B).
☐ Clutch pushrod bent – ZX-7R and ZX-9R B models. Check and, if necessary, renew (Chapter 2A).
☐ Clutch centre or housing unevenly worn. This causes improper engagement of the plates. Renew the damaged or worn parts (Chapter 2A or 2B).

Clutch not disengaging completely

☐ Clutch fluid level too low – ZX-7R and ZX-9R B models. Top-up and bleed the hydraulic system (Chapter 2A).
☐ Clutch cable freeplay incorrectly adjusted – ZX-9R C, E and F models (Chapter 1).

☐ Clutch plates warped or damaged. This will cause clutch drag, which in turn will cause the machine to creep. Overhaul the clutch assembly (Chapter 2A or 2B).
☐ Clutch spring tension uneven. Usually caused by a sagged or broken spring. Check and renew the springs as a set (Chapter 2A or 2B).
☐ Engine oil deteriorated. Old, thin, worn out oil will not provide proper lubrication for the plates, causing the clutch to drag. Renew the oil and filter (Chapter 1).
☐ Engine oil viscosity too high. Using a heavier oil than recommended in Chapter 1 can cause the plates to stick together, putting a drag on the engine. Change to the correct weight oil (Chapter 1).
☐ Clutch drum bearing seized. Lack of lubrication, severe wear or damage can cause the bearing to seize on the input shaft. Overhaul of the clutch, and perhaps transmission, may be necessary to repair the damage (Chapter 2A or 2B).
☐ Clutch hydraulic release mechanism defective – ZX-7R and ZX-9R B models. Bleed the hydraulic system (Chapter 2A). If this fails to cure the problem overhaul the clutch master and slave cylinders (Chapter 2A).
☐ Loose clutch centre nut. Causes housing and centre misalignment putting a drag on the engine. Engagement adjustment continually varies. Overhaul the clutch assembly (Chapter 2A or 2B).

6 Gearchanging problems

Doesn't go into gear or lever doesn't return

- ☐ Clutch not disengaging. See above.
- ☐ Selector fork(s) bent or seized. Often caused by dropping the machine or from lack of lubrication. Overhaul the transmission (Chapter 2A or 2B).
- ☐ Gear(s) stuck on shaft. Most often caused by a lack of lubrication or excessive wear in transmission bearings and bushings. Overhaul the transmission (Chapter 2A or 2B).
- ☐ Gear selector drum binding. Caused by lubrication failure or excessive wear. Renew the drum and bearing (Chapter 2A or 2B).
- ☐ Gear selector lever centralising spring weak or broken (Chapter 2A or 2B).
- ☐ Gear selector lever broken. Splines stripped out of lever or shaft, caused by allowing the lever to get loose or from dropping the machine. Renew necessary parts (Chapter 2A or 2B).
- ☐ Gear selector mechanism stopper arm broken or worn. Full engagement and rotary movement of selector drum results. Renew the arm (Chapter 2A or 2B).
- ☐ Stopper arm spring broken. Allows arm to float, causing sporadic shift operation. Renew spring (Chapter 2A or 2B).

Jumps out of gear

- ☐ Selector fork(s) worn. Overhaul the transmission (Chapter 2A or 2B).
- ☐ Gear groove(s) worn. Overhaul the transmission (Chapter 2A or 2B).
- ☐ Gear dogs or dog slots worn or damaged. The gears should be inspected and renewed. No attempt should be made to service the worn parts.

Overselects

- ☐ Stopper arm spring weak or broken (Chapter 2A or 2B).
- ☐ Gear selector shaft centralising spring post broken or distorted (Chapter 2A or 2B).

7 Abnormal engine noise

Knocking or pinking

- ☐ Carbon build-up in combustion chamber. Use of a fuel additive that will dissolve the adhesive bonding the carbon particles to the piston crown and chamber is the easiest way to remove the build-up. Otherwise, the cylinder head will have to be removed and decarbonised (Chapter 2A or 2B).
- ☐ Incorrect or poor quality fuel. Old or improper fuel can cause detonation. This causes the pistons to rattle, thus the knocking or pinking sound. Drain the old fuel and always use the recommended grade fuel (Chapter 4).
- ☐ Spark plug heat range incorrect. Uncontrolled detonation indicates that the plug heat range is too hot. The plug in effect becomes a glow plug, raising cylinder temperatures. Install the proper heat range plug (Chapter 1).
- ☐ Improper air/fuel mixture. This will cause the cylinders to run hot and lead to detonation. Blocked carburettor jets or an air leak can cause this imbalance. See Chapter 4.

Piston slap or rattling

- ☐ Cylinder-to-piston clearance excessive. Caused by improper assembly. Inspect and overhaul top-end parts (Chapter 2A or 2B).
- ☐ Connecting rod bent. Caused by over-revving, trying to start a badly flooded engine or from ingesting a foreign object into the combustion chamber. Renew the damaged parts (Chapter 2A or 2B).
- ☐ Piston pin or piston pin bore worn or seized from wear or lack of lubrication. Renew damaged parts (Chapter 2A or 2B).
- ☐ Piston ring(s) worn, broken or sticking. Overhaul the top-end (Chapter 2A or 2B).
- ☐ Piston seizure damage. Usually from lack of lubrication or overheating. Renew the pistons and renew the cylinders, as necessary (Chapter 2A or 2B).
- ☐ Connecting rod bearing clearance excessive. Caused by excessive wear or lack of lubrication. Renew worn parts.

Valve noise

- ☐ Incorrect valve clearances. Adjust the clearances by referring to Chapter 1.
- ☐ Valve spring broken or weak. Check and renew weak valve springs (Chapter 2A or 2B).
- ☐ Camshaft or cylinder head worn or damaged. Lack of lubrication at high rpm is usually the cause of damage. Insufficient oil or failure to change the oil at the recommended intervals are the chief causes. Since there are no renewable bearings in the head, the head itself will have to be renewed if there is excessive wear or damage (Chapter 2A or 2B).

Other noise

- ☐ Cylinder head gasket leaking.
- ☐ Exhaust pipe leaking at cylinder head connection. Caused by improper fit of pipe(s) or loose exhaust nuts. All exhaust fasteners should be tightened evenly and carefully. Failure to do this will lead to a leak.
- ☐ Crankshaft runout excessive. Caused by a bent crankshaft (from over-revving) or damage from an upper cylinder component failure. Can also be attributed to dropping the machine on either of the crankshaft ends.
- ☐ Engine mounting bolts loose. Tighten all engine mount bolts (Chapter 2A or 2B).
- ☐ Crankshaft bearings worn (Chapter 2A or 2B).
- ☐ Camchain, tensioner or guides worn. Renew according to the procedure in Chapter 2.

8 Abnormal driveline noise

Clutch noise

☐ Clutch outer drum/friction plate clearance excessive (Chapter 2A or 2B).

☐ Loose or damaged clutch pressure plate and/or bolts (Chapter 2A or 2B).

Transmission noise

☐ Bearings worn. Also includes the possibility that the shafts are worn. Overhaul the transmission (Chapter 2A or 2B).

☐ Gears worn or chipped (Chapter 2A or 2B).

☐ Metal chips jammed in gear teeth. Probably pieces from a broken clutch, gear or shift mechanism that were picked up by the gears. This will cause early bearing failure (Chapter 2A or 2B).

☐ Engine oil level too low. Causes a howl from transmission. Also affects engine power and clutch operation (Chapter 1).

Final drive noise

☐ Chain not adjusted properly (Chapter 1).

☐ Front or rear sprocket loose. Tighten fasteners (Chapter 6).

☐ Sprockets worn. Renew sprockets (Chapter 6).

☐ Rear sprocket warped. Renew sprockets (Chapter 6).

9 Abnormal frame and suspension noise

Front end noise

☐ Low fluid level or improper viscosity oil in forks. This can sound like spurting and is usually accompanied by irregular fork action (Chapter 6).

☐ Spring weak or broken. Makes a clicking or scraping sound. Fork oil, when drained, will have a lot of metal particles in it (Chapter 6).

☐ Steering head bearings loose or damaged. Clicks when braking. Check and adjust or renew as necessary (Chapters 1 and 6).

☐ Fork yokes loose. Make sure all clamp bolts are tightened to the specified torque (Chapter 6).

☐ Fork tube bent. Good possibility if machine has been dropped. Renew tube with a new one (Chapter 6).

☐ Front axle bolt or axle clamp bolts loose. Tighten them to the specified torque (Chapter 7).

☐ Loose or worn wheel bearings. Check and renew as needed (Chapter 7).

Shock absorber noise

☐ Fluid level incorrect. Indicates a leak caused by defective seal. Shock will be covered with oil. Renew shock or seek advice on repair from a Kawasaki dealer (Chapter 6).

☐ Defective shock absorber with internal damage. This is in the body of the shock and can't be remedied. The shock must be renewed with a new one (Chapter 6).

☐ Bent or damaged shock body. Renew the shock with a new one (Chapter 6).

☐ Loose or worn suspension linkage components. Check and renew as necessary (Chapter 6).

Brake noise

☐ Squeal caused by dust on brake pads. Usually found in combination with glazed pads. Clean using brake cleaning solvent (Chapter 7).

☐ Contamination of brake pads. Oil, brake fluid or dirt causing brake to chatter or squeal. Clean or renew pads (Chapter 7).

☐ Pads glazed. Caused by excessive heat from prolonged use or from contamination. Do not use sandpaper/emery cloth or any other abrasive to roughen the pad surfaces as abrasives will stay in the pad material and damage the disc. A very fine flat file can be used, but pad renewal is suggested as a cure (Chapter 7).

☐ Disc warped. Can cause a chattering, clicking or intermittent squeal. Usually accompanied by a pulsating lever and uneven braking. Renew the disc (Chapter 7).

☐ Loose or worn wheel bearings. Check and renew as needed (Chapter 7).

10 Oil pressure warning light comes on

Engine lubrication system

☐ Engine oil pump defective, blocked oil strainer gauze or failed relief valve. Carry out oil pressure check (Chapter 1).

☐ Engine oil level low. Inspect for leak or other problem causing low oil level and add recommended oil (Chapter 1).

☐ Engine oil viscosity too low. Very old, thin oil or an improper weight of oil used in the engine. Change to correct oil (Chapter 1).

☐ Camshaft or journals worn. Excessive wear causing drop in oil pressure. Renew cam and/or cylinder head. Abnormal wear could be caused by oil starvation at high rpm from low oil level or improper weight or type of oil (Chapter 1).

☐ Crankshaft and/or bearings worn. Same problems as above. Check and renew crankshaft and/or bearings (Chapter 2A or 2B).

Electrical system

☐ Oil pressure switch defective. Check the switch according to the procedure in Chapter 9. Renew it if it is defective.

☐ Oil pressure indicator light circuit defective. Check for pinched, shorted, disconnected or damaged wiring (Chapter 9).

11 Excessive exhaust smoke

White smoke

- [ ] Piston oil ring worn. The ring may be broken or damaged, causing oil from the crankcase to be pulled past the piston into the combustion chamber. Renew the rings with new ones (Chapter 2A or 2B).
- [ ] Cylinders worn, cracked, or scored. Caused by overheating or oil starvation. Install a new cylinder block (Chapter 2A or 2B).
- [ ] Valve oil seal damaged or worn. Renew oil seals with new ones (Chapter 2A or 2B).
- [ ] Valve guide worn. Perform a complete valve job (Chapter 2A or 2B).
- [ ] Engine oil level too high, which causes the oil to be forced past the rings. Drain oil to the proper level (Chapter 1).

- [ ] Head gasket broken between oil return and cylinder. Causes oil to be pulled into the combustion chamber. Renew the head gasket and check the head for warpage (Chapter 2A or 2B).
- [ ] Abnormal crankcase pressurisation, which forces oil past the rings. Clogged breather is usually the cause.

Black smoke

- [ ] Air filter clogged. Clean or renew the element (Chapter 1).
- [ ] Carburettors flooding. Remove and overhaul the carburettors (Chapter 4).
- [ ] Main jet too large. Remove and overhaul the carburettors (Chapter 4).
- [ ] Choke cable or linkage shaft stuck (Chapter 4).
- [ ] Fuel level too high. Check the fuel level (Chapter 4).

12 Poor handling or stability

Handlebar hard to turn

- [ ] Steering head bearing adjuster nut too tight. Check adjustment as described in Chapter 1.
- [ ] Bearings damaged. Roughness can be felt as the bars are turned from side-to-side. Renew bearings and races (Chapter 6).
- [ ] Races dented or worn. Denting results from wear in only one position (e.g., straight ahead), from a collision or hitting a pothole or from dropping the machine. Renew races and bearings (Chapter 6).
- [ ] Steering stem lubrication inadequate. Causes are grease getting hard from age or being washed out by high pressure car washes. Disassemble steering head and repack bearings (Chapter 6).
- [ ] Steering stem bent. Caused by a collision, hitting a pothole or by dropping the machine. Renew damaged part. Don't try to straighten the steering stem (Chapter 6).
- [ ] Front tyre air pressure too low (Chapter 1).

Handlebar shakes or vibrates excessively

- [ ] Tyres worn or out of balance (Chapter 7).
- [ ] Swingarm bearings worn. Renew worn bearings (Chapter 6).
- [ ] Wheel rim(s) warped or damaged. Inspect wheels for runout (Chapter 7).
- [ ] Wheel bearings worn. Worn front or rear wheel bearings can cause poor tracking. Worn front bearings will cause wobble (Chapter 7).
- [ ] Handlebar clamp bolts loose (Chapter 6).
- [ ] Fork yoke bolts loose. Tighten them to the specified torque (Chapter 6).
- [ ] Engine mounting bolts loose. Will cause excessive vibration with increased engine rpm (Chapter 2A or 2B).

Handlebar pulls to one side

- [ ] Frame bent. Definitely suspect this if the machine has been dropped. May or may not be accompanied by cracking near the bend. Renew the frame (Chapter 6).
- [ ] Wheels out of alignment. Caused by improper location of axle spacers or from bent steering stem or frame (Chapter 6).
- [ ] Swingarm bent or twisted. Caused by age (metal fatigue) or impact damage. Renew the arm (Chapter 6).
- [ ] Steering stem bent. Caused by impact damage or by dropping the motorcycle. Renew the steering stem (Chapter 6).
- [ ] Fork tube bent. Disassemble the forks and renew the damaged parts (Chapter 6).
- [ ] Fork oil level uneven. Check and add or drain as necessary (Chapter 6).

Poor shock absorbing qualities

Too hard:
a) Fork oil level excessive (Chapter 6).
b) Fork oil viscosity too high. Use a lighter oil (see the Specifications in Chapter 6).
c) Fork tube bent. Causes a harsh, sticking feeling (Chapter 6).
d) Shock shaft or body bent or damaged (Chapter 6).
e) Fork internal damage (Chapter 6).
f) Shock internal damage.
g) Tyre pressure too high (Chapter 1).
Too soft:
a) Fork or shock oil insufficient and/or leaking (Chapter 6).
b) Fork oil level too low (Chapter 6).
c) Fork oil viscosity too light (Chapter 6).
d) Fork springs weak or broken (Chapter 6).
e) Shock internal damage or leakage (Chapter 6).

13 Braking problems

Brakes are spongy, don't hold

☐ Air in brake line. Caused by inattention to master cylinder fluid level or by leakage. Locate problem and bleed brakes (Chapter 7).
☐ Pad or disc worn (Chapters 1 and 7).
☐ Brake fluid leak. See paragraph 1.
☐ Contaminated pads. Caused by contamination with oil, grease, brake fluid, etc. Clean or renew pads. Clean disc thoroughly with brake cleaner (Chapter 7).
☐ Brake fluid deteriorated. Fluid is old or contaminated. Drain system, replenish with new fluid and bleed the system (Chapter 7).
☐ Master cylinder internal parts worn or damaged causing fluid to bypass (Chapter 7).
☐ Master cylinder bore scratched by foreign material or broken spring. Repair or renew master cylinder (Chapter 7).
☐ Disc warped. Renew disc (Chapter 7).

Brake lever or pedal pulsates

☐ Disc warped. Renew disc (Chapter 7).
☐ Axle bent. Renew axle (Chapter 7).
☐ Brake caliper bolts loose (Chapter 7).
☐ Wheel warped or otherwise damaged (Chapter 7).
☐ Wheel bearings damaged or worn (Chapter 7).

Brakes drag

☐ Master cylinder piston seized. Caused by wear or damage to piston or cylinder bore (Chapter 7).
☐ Lever binding. Check pivot and lubricate (Chapter 7).
☐ Brake caliper piston seized in bore. Caused by wear or ingestion of dirt past deteriorated seal (Chapter 7).
☐ Brake caliper mounting bracket pins corroded – ZX-9R rear caliper. Clean off corrosion and lubricate (Chapter 7).
☐ Brake pad damaged. Pad material separated from backing plate. Usually caused by faulty manufacturing process or from contact with chemicals. Renew pads (Chapter 7).
☐ Pads improperly installed (Chapter 7).

14 Electrical problems

Battery dead or weak

☐ Battery faulty. Caused by sulphated plates which are shorted through sedimentation. Also, broken battery terminal making only occasional contact (Chapter 9).
☐ Battery cables making poor contact (Chapter 9).
☐ Load excessive. Caused by addition of high wattage lights or other electrical accessories.
☐ Ignition (main) switch defective. Switch either grounds (earths) internally or fails to shut off system. Renew the switch (Chapter 9).
☐ Regulator/rectifier defective (Chapter 9).
☐ Alternator stator coil open or shorted (Chapter 9).
☐ Wiring faulty. Wiring grounded (earthed) or connections loose in ignition, charging or lighting circuits (Chapter 9).

Battery overcharged

☐ Regulator/rectifier defective. Overcharging is noticed when battery gets excessively warm (Chapter 9).
☐ Battery defective. Renew battery with a new one (Chapter 9).
☐ Battery amperage too low, wrong type or size. Install manufacturer's specified amp-hour battery to handle charging load (Chapter 9).

Checking engine compression

● Low compression will result in exhaust smoke, heavy oil consumption, poor starting and poor performance. A compression test will provide useful information about an engine's condition and if performed regularly, can give warning of trouble before any other symptoms become apparent.

● A compression gauge will be required, along with an adapter to suit the spark plug hole thread size. Note that the screw-in type gauge/adapter set up is preferable to the rubber cone type.

● Before carrying out the test, first check the valve clearances as described in Chapter 1.

1 Run the engine until it reaches normal operating temperature, then stop it and remove the spark plug(s), taking care not to scald your hands on the hot components.

2 Install the gauge adapter and compression gauge in No. 1 cylinder spark plug hole (see illustration 1).

Screw the compression gauge adapter into the spark plug hole, then screw the gauge into the adapter

3 On kickstart-equipped motorcycles, make sure the ignition switch is OFF, then open the throttle fully and kick the engine over a couple of times until the gauge reading stabilises.

4 On motorcycles with electric start only, the procedure will differ depending on the nature of the ignition system. Flick the engine kill switch (engine stop switch) to OFF and turn the ignition switch ON; open the throttle fully and crank the engine over on the starter motor for a couple of revolutions until the gauge reading stabilises. If the starter will not operate with the kill switch OFF, turn the ignition switch OFF and refer to the next paragraph.

5 On ZX-9R C and E models, position the ignition coil wiring connectors clear of the head and on ZX-7R and ZX-9R B models, install the plugs back in their caps and arrange the plug electrodes so that their metal bodies are against the cylinder head; this is essential to prevent damage to the ignition system (see

All spark plugs must be earthed (grounded) against the cylinder head

illustration 2). Position the plugs well away from the plug holes otherwise there is a risk of atomised fuel escaping from the plug holes and ignition. As a safety precaution, cover the cylinder head cover with rag and disconnect the fuel pump wiring connector (see Chapter 4). Turn the ignition switch and kill switch ON, open the throttle fully and crank the engine over on the starter motor for a couple of revolutions until the gauge reading stabilises.

6 After one or two revolutions the pressure should build up to a maximum figure and then stabilise. Take a note of this reading and on multi-cylinder engines repeat the test on the remaining cylinders.

7 The correct pressures are given in Chapter 1 Specifications. If the results fall within the specified range and on multi-cylinder engines all are relatively equal, the engine is in good condition. If there is a marked difference between the readings, or if the readings are lower than specified, inspection of the top-end components will be required.

8 Low compression pressure may be due to worn cylinder bores, pistons or rings, failure of the cylinder head gasket, worn valve seals, or poor valve seating.

9 To distinguish between cylinder/piston wear and valve leakage, pour a small quantity of oil into the bore to temporarily seal the piston rings, then repeat the compression tests (see illustration 3). If the readings show

Bores can be temporarily sealed with a squirt of motor oil

a noticeable increase in pressure this confirms that the cylinder bore, piston, or rings are worn. If, however, no change is indicated, the cylinder head gasket or valves should be examined.

10 High compression pressure indicates excessive carbon build-up in the combustion chamber and on the piston crown. If this is the case the cylinder head should be removed and the deposits removed. Note that excessive carbon build-up is less likely with the used on modern fuels.

Checking battery open-circuit voltage

 Warning: The gases produced by the battery are explosive - never smoke or create any sparks in the vicinity of the battery. Never allow the electrolyte to contact your skin or clothing - if it does, wash it off and seek immediate medical attention.

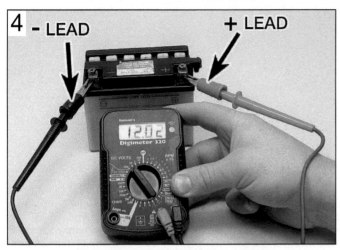

Measuring open-circuit battery voltage

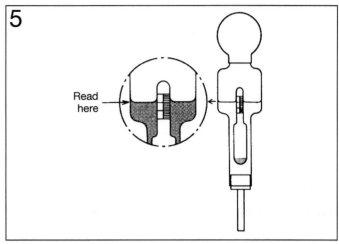

Float-type hydrometer for measuring battery specific gravity

● Before any electrical fault is investigated the battery should be checked.

● You'll need a dc voltmeter or multimeter to check battery voltage. Check that the leads are inserted in the correct terminals on the meter, red lead to positive (+ve), black lead to negative (-ve). Incorrect connections can damage the meter.

● A sound fully-charged 12 volt battery should produce between 12.3 and 12.6 volts across its terminals (12.8 volts for a maintenance-free battery). On machines with a 6 volt battery, voltage should be between 6.1 and 6.3 volts.

1 Set a multimeter to the 0 to 20 volts dc range and connect its probes across the battery terminals. Connect the meter's positive (+ve) probe, usually red, to the battery positive (+ve) terminal, followed by the meter's negative (-ve) probe, usually black, to the battery negative terminal (-ve) **(see illustration 4)**.

2 If battery voltage is low (below 10 volts on a 12 volt battery or below 4 volts on a six volt battery), charge the battery and test the voltage again. If the battery repeatedly goes flat, investigate the motorcycle's charging system.

Checking battery specific gravity (SG)

⚠ *Warning: The gases produced by the battery are explosive - never smoke or create any sparks in the vicinity of the battery. Never allow the electrolyte to contact your skin or clothing - if it does, wash it off and seek immediate medical attention.*

● The specific gravity check gives an indication of a battery's state of charge.

● A hydrometer is used for measuring specific gravity. Make sure you purchase one which has a small enough hose to insert in the aperture of a motorcycle battery.

● Specific gravity is simply a measure of the electrolyte's density compared with that of water. Water has an SG of 1.000 and fully-charged battery electrolyte is about 26% heavier, at 1.260.

● Specific gravity checks are not possible on maintenance-free batteries. Testing the open-circuit voltage is the only means of determining their state of charge.

1 To measure SG, remove the battery from the motorcycle and remove the first cell cap. Draw

Digital multimeter can be used for all electrical tests

some electrolyte into the hydrometer and note the reading **(see illustration 5)**. Return the electrolyte to the cell and install the cap.

2 The reading should be in the region of 1.260 to 1.280. If SG is below 1.200 the battery needs charging. Note that SG will vary with temperature; it should be measured at 20°C (68°F). Add 0.007 to the reading for every 10°C above 20°C, and subtract 0.007 from the reading for every 10°C below 20°C. Add 0.004 to the reading for every 10°F above 68°F, and subtract 0.004 from the reading for every 10°F below 68°F.

3 When the check is complete, rinse the hydrometer thoroughly with clean water.

Checking for continuity

● The term continuity describes the uninterrupted flow of electricity through an electrical circuit. A continuity check will determine whether an **open-circuit** situation exists.

● Continuity can be checked with an ohmmeter, multimeter, continuity tester or battery and bulb test circuit **(see illustrations 6, 7 and 8)**.

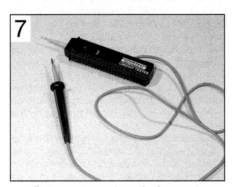

Battery-powered continuity tester

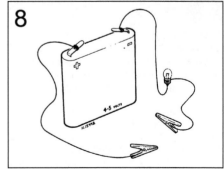

Battery and bulb test circuit

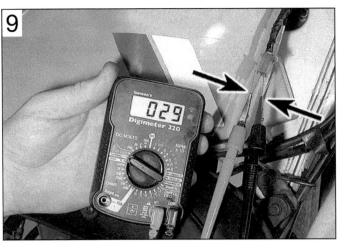

9

Continuity check of front brake light switch using a meter - note split pins used to access connector terminals

10

Continuity check of rear brake light switch using a continuity tester

● All of these instruments are self-powered by a battery, therefore the checks are made with the ignition OFF.

● As a safety precaution, always disconnect the battery negative (-ve) lead before making checks, particularly if ignition switch checks are being made.

● If using a meter, select the appropriate ohms scale and check that the meter reads infinity (∞). Touch the meter probes together and check that meter reads zero; where necessary adjust the meter so that it reads zero.

● After using a meter, always switch it OFF to conserve its battery.

Switch checks

1 If a switch is at fault, trace its wiring up to the wiring connectors. Separate the wire connectors and inspect them for security and condition. A build-up of dirt or corrosion here will most likely be the cause of the problem - clean up and apply a water dispersant such as WD40.

2 If using a test meter, set the meter to the ohms x 10 scale and connect its probes across the wires from the switch **(see illustration 9)**. Simple ON/OFF type switches, such as brake light switches, only have two wires whereas combination switches, like the

ignition switch, have many internal links. Study the wiring diagram to ensure that you are connecting across the correct pair of wires. Continuity (low or no measurable resistance - 0 ohms) should be indicated with the switch ON and no continuity (high resistance) with it OFF.

3 Note that the polarity of the test probes doesn't matter for continuity checks, although care should be taken to follow specific test procedures if a diode or solid-state component is being checked.

4 A continuity tester or battery and bulb circuit can be used in the same way. Connect its probes as described above **(see illustration 10)**. The light should come on to indicate continuity in the ON switch position, but should extinguish in the OFF position.

Wiring checks

● Many electrical faults are caused by damaged wiring, often due to incorrect routing or chaffing on frame components.

● Loose, wet or corroded wire connectors can also be the cause of electrical problems, especially in exposed locations.

1 A continuity check can be made on a single length of wire by disconnecting it at each end and connecting a meter or continuity tester

across both ends of the wire **(see illustration 11)**.

2 Continuity (low or no resistance - 0 ohms) should be indicated if the wire is good. If no continuity (high resistance) is shown, suspect a broken wire.

Checking for voltage

● A voltage check can determine whether current is reaching a component.

● Voltage can be checked with a dc voltmeter, multimeter set on the dc volts scale, test light or buzzer **(see illustrations 12 and 13)**. A meter has the advantage of being able to measure actual voltage.

● When using a meter, check that its leads are inserted in the correct terminals on the meter, red to positive (+ve), black to negative (-ve). Incorrect connections can damage the meter.

● A voltmeter (or multimeter set to the dc volts scale) should always be connected in parallel (across the load). Connecting it in series will not harm the meter, but the reading will not be meaningful.

● Voltage checks are made with the ignition ON.

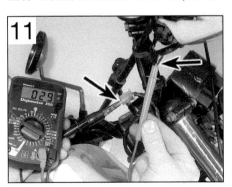

11

Continuity check of front brake light switch sub-harness

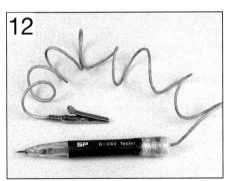

12

A simple test light can be used for voltage checks

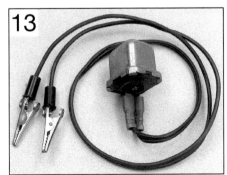

13

A buzzer is useful for voltage checks

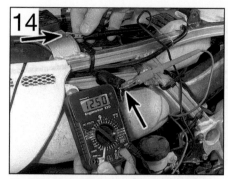

Checking for voltage at the rear brake light power supply wire using a meter . . .

1 First identify the relevant wiring circuit by referring to the wiring diagram at the end of this manual. If other electrical components share the same power supply (ie are fed from the same fuse), take note whether they are working correctly - this is useful information in deciding where to start checking the circuit.

2 If using a meter, check first that the meter leads are plugged into the correct terminals on the meter (see above). Set the meter to the dc volts function, at a range suitable for the battery voltage. Connect the meter red probe (+ve) to the power supply wire and the black probe to a good metal earth (ground) on the motorcycle's frame or directly to the battery negative (-ve) terminal **(see illustration 14)**. Battery voltage should be shown on the meter

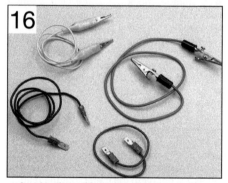

A selection of jumper wires for making earth (ground) checks

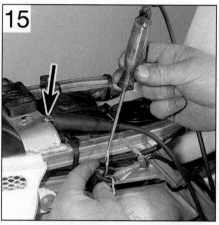

. . . or a test light - note the earth connection to the frame (arrow)

with the ignition switched ON.

3 If using a test light or buzzer, connect its positive (+ve) probe to the power supply terminal and its negative (-ve) probe to a good earth (ground) on the motorcycle's frame or directly to the battery negative (-ve) terminal **(see illustration 15)**. With the ignition ON, the test light should illuminate or the buzzer sound.

4 If no voltage is indicated, work back towards the fuse continuing to check for voltage. When you reach a point where there is voltage, you know the problem lies between that point and your last check point.

Checking the earth (ground)

● Earth connections are made either directly to the engine or frame (such as sensors, neutral switch etc. which only have a positive feed) or by a separate wire into the earth circuit of the wiring harness. Alternatively a short earth wire is sometimes run directly from the component to the motorcycle's frame.
● Corrosion is often the cause of a poor earth connection.
● If total failure is experienced, check the security of the main earth lead from the

negative (-ve) terminal of the battery and also the main earth (ground) point on the wiring harness. If corroded, dismantle the connection and clean all surfaces back to bare metal.

1 To check the earth on a component, use an insulated jumper wire to temporarily bypass its earth connection **(see illustration 16)**. Connect one end of the jumper wire between the earth terminal or metal body of the component and the other end to the motorcycle's frame.

2 If the circuit works with the jumper wire installed, the original earth circuit is faulty. Check the wiring for open-circuits or poor connections. Clean up direct earth connections, removing all traces of corrosion and remake the joint. Apply petroleum jelly to the joint to prevent future corrosion.

Tracing a short-circuit

● A short-circuit occurs where current shorts to earth (ground) bypassing the circuit components. This usually results in a blown fuse.

● A short-circuit is most likely to occur where the insulation has worn through due to wiring chafing on a component, allowing a direct path to earth (ground) on the frame.

1 Remove any bodypanels necessary to access the circuit wiring.

2 Check that all electrical switches in the circuit are OFF, then remove the circuit fuse and connect a test light, buzzer or voltmeter (set to the dc scale) across the fuse terminals. No voltage should be shown.

3 Move the wiring from side to side whilst observing the test light or meter. When the test light comes on, buzzer sounds or meter shows voltage, you have found the cause of the short. It will usually shown up as damaged or burned insulation.

4 Note that the same test can be performed on each component in the circuit, even the switch.

Technical Terms Explained REF•47

A

ABS (Anti-lock braking system) A system, usually electronically controlled, that senses incipient wheel lockup during braking and relieves hydraulic pressure at wheel which is about to skid.

Aftermarket Components suitable for the motorcycle, but not produced by the motorcycle manufacturer.

Allen key A hexagonal wrench which fits into a recessed hexagonal hole.

Alternating current (ac) Current produced by an alternator. Requires converting to direct current by a rectifier for charging purposes.

Alternator Converts mechanical energy from the engine into electrical energy to charge the battery and power the electrical system.

Ampere (amp) A unit of measurement for the flow of electrical current. Current = Volts ÷ Ohms.

Ampere-hour (Ah) Measure of battery capacity.

Angle-tightening A torque expressed in degrees. Often follows a conventional tightening torque for cylinder head or main bearing fasteners **(see illustration)**.

Angle-tightening cylinder head bolts

Antifreeze A substance (usually ethylene glycol) mixed with water, and added to the cooling system, to prevent freezing of the coolant in winter. Antifreeze also contains chemicals to inhibit corrosion and the formation of rust and other deposits that would tend to clog the radiator and coolant passages and reduce cooling efficiency.

Anti-dive System attached to the fork lower leg (slider) to prevent fork dive when braking hard.

Anti-seize compound A coating that reduces the risk of seizing on fasteners that are subjected to high temperatures, such as exhaust clamp bolts and nuts.

API American Petroleum Institute. A quality standard for 4-stroke motor oils.

Asbestos A natural fibrous mineral with great heat resistance, commonly used in the composition of brake friction materials. Asbestos is a health hazard and the dust created by brake systems should never be inhaled or ingested.

ATF Automatic Transmission Fluid. Often used in front forks.

ATU Automatic Timing Unit. Mechanical device for advancing the ignition timing on early engines.

ATV All Terrain Vehicle. Often called a Quad.

Axial play Side-to-side movement.

Axle A shaft on which a wheel revolves. Also known as a spindle.

B

Backlash The amount of movement between meshed components when one component is held still. Usually applies to gear teeth.

Ball bearing A bearing consisting of a hardened inner and outer race with hardened steel balls between the two races.

Bearings Used between two working surfaces to prevent wear of the components and a build-up of heat. Four types of bearing are commonly used on motorcycles: plain shell bearings, ball bearings, tapered roller bearings and needle roller bearings.

Bevel gears Used to turn the drive through 90°. Typical applications are shaft final drive and camshaft drive **(see illustration)**.

Bevel gears are used to turn the drive through 90°

BHP Brake Horsepower. The British measurement for engine power output. Power output is now usually expressed in kilowatts (kW).

Bias-belted tyre Similar construction to radial tyre, but with outer belt running at an angle to the wheel rim.

Big-end bearing The bearing in the end of the connecting rod that's attached to the crankshaft.

Bleeding The process of removing air from an hydraulic system via a bleed nipple or bleed screw.

Bottom-end A description of an engine's crankcase components and all components contained there-in.

BTDC Before Top Dead Centre in terms of piston position. Ignition timing is often expressed in terms of degrees or millimetres BTDC.

Bush A cylindrical metal or rubber component used between two moving parts.

Burr Rough edge left on a component after machining or as a result of excessive wear.

C

Cam chain The chain which takes drive from the crankshaft to the camshaft(s).

Canister The main component in an evaporative emission control system (California market only); contains activated charcoal granules to trap vapours from the fuel system rather than allowing them to vent to the atmosphere.

Castellated Resembling the parapets along the top of a castle wall. For example, a castellated wheel axle or spindle nut.

Catalytic converter A device in the exhaust system of some machines which converts certain pollutants in the exhaust gases into less harmful substances.

Charging system Description of the components which charge the battery, ie the alternator, rectifer and regulator.

Circlip A ring-shaped clip used to prevent endwise movement of cylindrical parts and shafts. An internal circlip is installed in a groove in a housing; an external circlip fits into a groove on the outside of a cylindrical piece such as a shaft. Also known as a snap-ring.

Clearance The amount of space between two parts. For example, between a piston and a cylinder, between a bearing and a journal, etc.

Coil spring A spiral of elastic steel found in various sizes throughout a vehicle, for example as a springing medium in the suspension and in the valve train.

Compression Reduction in volume, and increase in pressure and temperature, of a gas, caused by squeezing it into a smaller space.

Compression damping Controls the speed the suspension compresses when hitting a bump.

Compression ratio The relationship between cylinder volume when the piston is at top dead centre and cylinder volume when the piston is at bottom dead centre.

Continuity The uninterrupted path in the flow of electricity. Little or no measurable resistance.

Continuity tester Self-powered bleeper or test light which indicates continuity.

Cp Candlepower. Bulb rating commonly found on US motorcycles.

Crossply tyre Tyre plies arranged in a criss-cross pattern. Usually four or six plies used, hence 4PR or 6PR in tyre size codes.

Cush drive Rubber damper segments fitted between the rear wheel and final drive sprocket to absorb transmission shocks **(see illustration)**.

Cush drive rubbers dampen out transmission shocks

D

Degree disc Calibrated disc for measuring piston position. Expressed in degrees.

Dial gauge Clock-type gauge with adapters for measuring runout and piston position. Expressed in mm or inches.

Diaphragm The rubber membrane in a master cylinder or carburettor which seals the upper chamber.

Diaphragm spring A single sprung plate often used in clutches.

Direct current (dc) Current produced by a dc generator.

Decarbonisation The process of removing carbon deposits - typically from the combustion chamber, valves and exhaust port/system.

Detonation Destructive and damaging explosion of fuel/air mixture in combustion chamber instead of controlled burning.

Diode An electrical valve which only allows current to flow in one direction. Commonly used in rectifiers and starter interlock systems.

Disc valve (or rotary valve) A induction system used on some two-stroke engines.

Double-overhead camshaft (DOHC) An engine that uses two overhead camshafts, one for the intake valves and one for the exhaust valves.

Drivebelt A toothed belt used to transmit drive to the rear wheel on some motorcycles. A drivebelt has also been used to drive the camshafts. Drivebelts are usually made of Kevlar.

Driveshaft Any shaft used to transmit motion. Commonly used when referring to the final driveshaft on shaft drive motorcycles.

E

Earth return The return path of an electrical circuit, utilising the motorcycle's frame.

ECU (Electronic Control Unit) A computer which controls (for instance) an ignition system, or an anti-lock braking system.

EGO Exhaust Gas Oxygen sensor. Sometimes called a Lambda sensor.

Electrolyte The fluid in a lead-acid battery.

EMS (Engine Management System) A computer controlled system which manages the fuel injection and the ignition systems in an integrated fashion.

Endfloat The amount of lengthways movement between two parts. As applied to a crankshaft, the distance that the crankshaft can move side-to-side in the crankcase.

Endless chain A chain having no joining link. Common use for cam chains and final drive chains.

EP (Extreme Pressure) Oil type used in locations where high loads are applied, such as between gear teeth.

Evaporative emission control system Describes a charcoal filled canister which stores fuel vapours from the tank rather than allowing them to vent to the atmosphere. Usually only fitted to California models and referred to as an EVAP system.

Expansion chamber Section of two-stroke engine exhaust system so designed to improve engine efficiency and boost power.

F

Feeler blade or gauge A thin strip or blade of hardened steel, ground to an exact thickness, used to check or measure clearances between parts.

Final drive Description of the drive from the transmission to the rear wheel. Usually by chain or shaft, but sometimes by belt.

Firing order The order in which the engine cylinders fire, or deliver their power strokes, beginning with the number one cylinder.

Flooding Term used to describe a high fuel level in the carburettor float chambers, leading to fuel overflow. Also refers to excess fuel in the combustion chamber due to incorrect starting technique.

Free length The no-load state of a component when measured. Clutch, valve and fork spring lengths are measured at rest, without any preload.

Freeplay The amount of travel before any action takes place. The looseness in a linkage, or an assembly of parts, between the initial application of force and actual movement. For example, the distance the rear brake pedal moves before the rear brake is actuated.

Fuel injection The fuel/air mixture is metered electronically and directed into the engine intake ports (indirect injection) or into the cylinders (direct injection). Sensors supply information on engine speed and conditions.

Fuel/air mixture The charge of fuel and air going into the engine. See **Stoichiometric ratio**.

Fuse An electrical device which protects a circuit against accidental overload. The typical fuse contains a soft piece of metal which is calibrated to melt at a predetermined current flow (expressed as amps) and break the circuit.

G

Gap The distance the spark must travel in jumping from the centre electrode to the side electrode in a spark plug. Also refers to the distance between the ignition rotor and the pickup coil in an electronic ignition system.

Gasket Any thin, soft material - usually cork, cardboard, asbestos or soft metal - installed between two metal surfaces to ensure a good seal. For instance, the cylinder head gasket seals the joint between the block and the cylinder head.

Gauge An instrument panel display used to monitor engine conditions. A gauge with a movable pointer on a dial or a fixed scale is an analogue gauge. A gauge with a numerical readout is called a digital gauge.

Gear ratios The drive ratio of a pair of gears in a gearbox, calculated on their number of teeth.

Glaze-busting see **Honing**

Grinding Process for renovating the valve face and valve seat contact area in the cylinder head.

Gudgeon pin The shaft which connects the connecting rod small-end with the piston. Often called a piston pin or wrist pin.

H

Helical gears Gear teeth are slightly curved and produce less gear noise that straight-cut gears. Often used for primary drives.

Installing a Helicoil thread insert in a cylinder head

Helicoil A thread insert repair system. Commonly used as a repair for stripped spark plug threads **(see illustration)**.

Honing A process used to break down the glaze on a cylinder bore (also called glaze-busting). Can also be carried out to roughen a rebored cylinder to aid ring bedding-in.

HT (High Tension) Description of the electrical circuit from the secondary winding of the ignition coil to the spark plug.

Hydraulic A liquid filled system used to transmit pressure from one component to another. Common uses on motorcycles are brakes and clutches.

Hydrometer An instrument for measuring the specific gravity of a lead-acid battery.

Hygroscopic Water absorbing. In motorcycle applications, braking efficiency will be reduced if DOT 3 or 4 hydraulic fluid absorbs water from the air - care must be taken to keep new brake fluid in tightly sealed containers.

I

lbf ft Pounds-force feet. An imperial unit of torque. Sometimes written as ft-lbs.

lbf in Pound-force inch. An imperial unit of torque, applied to components where a very low torque is required. Sometimes written as in-lbs.

IC Abbreviation for Integrated Circuit.

Ignition advance Means of increasing the timing of the spark at higher engine speeds. Done by mechanical means (ATU) on early engines or electronically by the ignition control unit on later engines.

Ignition timing The moment at which the spark plug fires, expressed in the number of crankshaft degrees before the piston reaches the top of its stroke, or in the number of millimetres before the piston reaches the top of its stroke.

Infinity (∞) Description of an open-circuit electrical state, where no continuity exists.

Inverted forks (upside down forks) The sliders or lower legs are held in the yokes and the fork tubes or stanchions are connected to the wheel axle (spindle). Less unsprung weight and stiffer construction than conventional forks.

J

JASO Quality standard for 2-stroke oils.

Joule The unit of electrical energy.

Journal The bearing surface of a shaft.

K

Kickstart Mechanical means of turning the engine over for starting purposes. Only usually fitted to mopeds, small capacity motorcycles and off-road motorcycles.

Kill switch Handlebar-mounted switch for emergency ignition cut-out. Cuts the ignition circuit on all models, and additionally prevent starter motor operation on others.

km Symbol for kilometre.

kmh Abbreviation for kilometres per hour.

L

Lambda (λ) sensor A sensor fitted in the exhaust system to measure the exhaust gas oxygen content (excess air factor).

Lapping see **Grinding**.

LCD Abbreviation for Liquid Crystal Display.

LED Abbreviation for Light Emitting Diode.

Liner A steel cylinder liner inserted in a aluminium alloy cylinder block.

Locknut A nut used to lock an adjustment nut, or other threaded component, in place.

Lockstops The lugs on the lower triple clamp (yoke) which abut those on the frame, preventing handlebar-to-fuel tank contact.

Lockwasher A form of washer designed to prevent an attaching nut from working loose.

LT Low Tension Description of the electrical circuit from the power supply to the primary winding of the ignition coil.

M

Main bearings The bearings between the crankshaft and crankcase.

Maintenance-free (MF) battery A sealed battery which cannot be topped up.

Manometer Mercury-filled calibrated tubes used to measure intake tract vacuum. Used to synchronise carburettors on multi-cylinder engines.

Micrometer A precision measuring instrument that measures component outside diameters **(see illustration)**.

Tappet shims are measured with a micrometer

MON (Motor Octane Number) A measure of a fuel's resistance to knock.

Monograde oil An oil with a single viscosity, eg SAE80W.

Monoshock A single suspension unit linking the swingarm or suspension linkage to the frame.

mph Abbreviation for miles per hour.

Multigrade oil Having a wide viscosity range (eg 10W40). The W stands for Winter, thus the viscosity ranges from SAE10 when cold to SAE40 when hot.

Multimeter An electrical test instrument with the capability to measure voltage, current and resistance. Some meters also incorporate a continuity tester and buzzer.

N

Needle roller bearing Inner race of caged needle rollers and hardened outer race. Examples of uncaged needle rollers can be found on some engines. Commonly used in rear suspension applications and in two-stroke engines.

Nm Newton metres.

NOx Oxides of Nitrogen. A common toxic pollutant emitted by petrol engines at higher temperatures.

O

Octane The measure of a fuel's resistance to knock.

OE (Original Equipment) Relates to components fitted to a motorcycle as standard or replacement parts supplied by the motorcycle manufacturer.

Ohm The unit of electrical resistance. Ohms = Volts ÷ Current.

Ohmmeter An instrument for measuring electrical resistance.

Oil cooler System for diverting engine oil outside of the engine to a radiator for cooling purposes.

Oil injection A system of two-stroke engine lubrication where oil is pump-fed to the engine in accordance with throttle position.

Open-circuit An electrical condition where there is a break in the flow of electricity - no continuity (high resistance).

O-ring A type of sealing ring made of a special rubber-like material; in use, the O-ring is compressed into a groove to provide the sealing action.

Oversize (OS) Term used for piston and ring size options fitted to a rebored cylinder.

Overhead cam (sohc) engine An engine with single camshaft located on top of the cylinder head.

Overhead valve (ohv) engine An engine with the valves located in the cylinder head, but with the camshaft located in the engine block or crankcase.

Oxygen sensor A device installed in the exhaust system which senses the oxygen content in the exhaust and converts this information into an electric current. Also called a Lambda sensor.

P

Plastigauge A thin strip of plastic thread, available in different sizes, used for measuring clearances. For example, a strip of Plastigauge is laid across a bearing journal. The parts are assembled and dismantled; the width of the crushed strip indicates the clearance between journal and bearing.

Polarity Either negative or positive earth (ground), determined by which battery lead is connected to the frame (earth return). Modern motorcycles are usually negative earth.

Pre-ignition A situation where the fuel/air mixture ignites before the spark plug fires. Often due to a hot spot in the combustion chamber caused by carbon build-up. Engine has a tendency to 'run-on'.

Pre-load (suspension) The amount a spring is compressed when in the unloaded state. Preload can be applied by gas, spacer or mechanical adjuster.

Premix The method of engine lubrication on older two-stroke engines. Engine oil is mixed with the petrol in the fuel tank in a specific ratio. The fuel/oil mix is sometimes referred to as "petroil".

Primary drive Description of the drive from the crankshaft to the clutch. Usually by gear or chain.

PS Pfedestärke - a German interpretation of BHP.

PSI Pounds-force per square inch. Imperial measurement of tyre pressure and cylinder pressure measurement.

PTFE Polytetrafluroethylene. A low friction substance.

Pulse secondary air injection system A process of promoting the burning of excess fuel present in the exhaust gases by routing fresh air into the exhaust ports.

Q

Quartz halogen bulb Tungsten filament surrounded by a halogen gas. Typically used for the headlight **(see illustration)**.

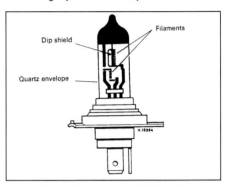

Quartz halogen headlight bulb construction

R

Rack-and-pinion A pinion gear on the end of a shaft that mates with a rack (think of a geared wheel opened up and laid flat). Sometimes used in clutch operating systems.

Radial play Up and down movement about a shaft.

Radial ply tyres Tyre plies run across the tyre (from bead to bead) and around the circumference of the tyre. Less resistant to tread distortion than other tyre types.

Radiator A liquid-to-air heat transfer device designed to reduce the temperature of the coolant in a liquid cooled engine.

Rake A feature of steering geometry - the angle of the steering head in relation to the vertical **(see illustration)**.

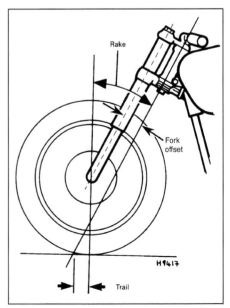

Steering geometry

Rebore Providing a new working surface to the cylinder bore by boring out the old surface. Necessitates the use of oversize piston and rings.

Rebound damping A means of controlling the oscillation of a suspension unit spring after it has been compressed. Resists the spring's natural tendency to bounce back after being compressed.

Rectifier Device for converting the ac output of an alternator into dc for battery charging.

Reed valve An induction system commonly used on two-stroke engines.

Regulator Device for maintaining the charging voltage from the generator or alternator within a specified range.

Relay A electrical device used to switch heavy current on and off by using a low current auxiliary circuit.

Resistance Measured in ohms. An electrical component's ability to pass electrical current.

RON (Research Octane Number) A measure of a fuel's resistance to knock.

rpm revolutions per minute.

Runout The amount of wobble (in-and-out movement) of a wheel or shaft as it's rotated. The amount a shaft rotates 'out-of-true'. The out-of-round condition of a rotating part.

S

SAE (Society of Automotive Engineers) A standard for the viscosity of a fluid.

Sealant A liquid or paste used to prevent leakage at a joint. Sometimes used in conjunction with a gasket.

Service limit Term for the point where a component is no longer useable and must be renewed.

Shaft drive A method of transmitting drive from the transmission to the rear wheel.

Shell bearings Plain bearings consisting of two shell halves. Most often used as big-end and main bearings in a four-stroke engine. Often called bearing inserts.

Shim Thin spacer, commonly used to adjust the clearance or relative positions between two parts. For example, shims inserted into or under tappets or followers to control valve clearances. Clearance is adjusted by changing the thickness of the shim.

Short-circuit An electrical condition where current shorts to earth (ground) bypassing the circuit components.

Skimming Process to correct warpage or repair a damaged surface, eg on brake discs or drums.

Slide-hammer A special puller that screws into or hooks onto a component such as a shaft or bearing; a heavy sliding handle on the shaft bottoms against the end of the shaft to knock the component free.

Small-end bearing The bearing in the upper end of the connecting rod at its joint with the gudgeon pin.

Spalling Damage to camshaft lobes or bearing journals shown as pitting of the working surface.

Specific gravity (SG) The state of charge of the electrolyte in a lead-acid battery. A measure of the electrolyte's density compared with water.

Straight-cut gears Common type gear used on gearbox shafts and for oil pump and water pump drives.

Stanchion The inner sliding part of the front forks, held by the yokes. Often called a fork tube.

Stoichiometric ratio The optimum chemical air/fuel ratio for a petrol engine, said to be 14.7 parts of air to 1 part of fuel.

Sulphuric acid The liquid (electrolyte) used in a lead-acid battery. Poisonous and extremely corrosive.

Surface grinding (lapping) Process to correct a warped gasket face, commonly used on cylinder heads.

T

Tapered-roller bearing Tapered inner race of caged needle rollers and separate tapered outer race. Examples of taper roller bearings can be found on steering heads.

Tappet A cylindrical component which transmits motion from the cam to the valve stem, either directly or via a pushrod and rocker arm. Also called a cam follower.

TCS Traction Control System. An electronically-controlled system which senses wheel spin and reduces engine speed accordingly.

TDC Top Dead Centre denotes that the piston is at its highest point in the cylinder.

Thread-locking compound Solution applied to fastener threads to prevent slackening. Select type to suit application.

Thrust washer A washer positioned between two moving components on a shaft. For example, between gear pinions on gearshaft.

Timing chain See **Cam Chain.**

Timing light Stroboscopic lamp for carrying out ignition timing checks with the engine running.

Top-end A description of an engine's cylinder block, head and valve gear components.

Torque Turning or twisting force about a shaft.

Torque setting A prescribed tightness specified by the motorcycle manufacturer to ensure that the bolt or nut is secured correctly. Undertightening can result in the bolt or nut coming loose or a surface not being sealed. Overtightening can result in stripped threads, distortion or damage to the component being retained.

Torx key A six-point wrench.

Tracer A stripe of a second colour applied to a wire insulator to distinguish that wire from another one with the same colour insulator. For example, Br/W is often used to denote a brown insulator with a white tracer.

Trail A feature of steering geometry. Distance from the steering head axis to the tyre's central contact point.

Triple clamps The cast components which extend from the steering head and support the fork stanchions or tubes. Often called fork yokes.

Turbocharger A centrifugal device, driven by exhaust gases, that pressurises the intake air. Normally used to increase the power output from a given engine displacement.

TWI Abbreviation for Tyre Wear Indicator. Indicates the location of the tread depth indicator bars on tyres.

U

Universal joint or U-joint (UJ) A double-pivoted connection for transmitting power from a driving to a driven shaft through an angle. Typically found in shaft drive assemblies.

Unsprung weight Anything not supported by the bike's suspension (ie the wheel, tyres, brakes, final drive and bottom (moving) part of the suspension).

V

Vacuum gauges Clock-type gauges for measuring intake tract vacuum. Used for carburettor synchronisation on multi-cylinder engines.

Valve A device through which the flow of liquid, gas or vacuum may be stopped, started or regulated by a moveable part that opens, shuts or partially obstructs one or more ports or passageways. The intake and exhaust valves in the cylinder head are of the poppet type.

Valve clearance The clearance between the valve tip (the end of the valve stem) and the rocker arm or tappet/follower. The valve clearance is measured when the valve is closed. The correct clearance is important - if too small the valve won't close fully and will burn out, whereas if too large noisy operation will result.

Valve lift The amount a valve is lifted off its seat by the camshaft lobe.

Valve timing The exact setting for the opening and closing of the valves in relation to piston position.

Vernier caliper A precision measuring instrument that measures inside and outside dimensions. Not quite as accurate as a micrometer, but more convenient.

VIN Vehicle Identification Number. Term for the bike's engine and frame numbers.

Viscosity The thickness of a liquid or its resistance to flow.

Volt A unit for expressing electrical "pressure" in a circuit. Volts = current x ohms.

W

Water pump A mechanically-driven device for moving coolant around the engine.

Watt A unit for expressing electrical power. Watts = volts x current.

Wear limit see **Service limit**

Wet liner A liquid-cooled engine design where the pistons run in liners which are directly surrounded by coolant **(see illustration)**.

Wet liner arrangement

Wheelbase Distance from the centre of the front wheel to the centre of the rear wheel.

Wiring harness or loom Describes the electrical wires running the length of the motorcycle and enclosed in tape or plastic sheathing. Wiring coming off the main harness is usually referred to as a sub harness.

Woodruff key A key of semi-circular or square section used to locate a gear to a shaft. Often used to locate the alternator rotor on the crankshaft.

Wrist pin Another name for gudgeon or piston pin.

Preserving Our Motoring Heritage

< *The Model J Duesenberg Derham Tourster. Only eight of these magnificent cars were ever built – this is the only example to be found outside the United States of America*

Almost every car you've ever loved, loathed or desired is gathered under one roof at the Haynes Motor Museum. Over 300 immaculately presented cars and motorbikes represent every aspect of our motoring heritage, from elegant reminders of bygone days, such as the superb Model J Duesenberg to curiosities like the bug-eyed BMW Isetta. There are also many old friends and flames. Perhaps you remember the 1959 Ford Popular that you did your courting in? The magnificent 'Red Collection' is a spectacle of classic sports cars including AC, Alfa Romeo, Austin Healey, Ferrari, Lamborghini, Maserati, MG, Riley, Porsche and Triumph.

A Perfect Day Out

Each and every vehicle at the Haynes Motor Museum has played its part in the history and culture of Motoring. Today, they make a wonderful spectacle and a great day out for all the family. Bring the kids, bring Mum and Dad, but above all bring your camera to capture those golden memories for ever. You will also find an impressive array of motoring memorabilia, a comfortable 70 seat video cinema and one of the most extensive transport book shops in Britain. The Pit Stop Cafe serves everything from a cup of tea to wholesome, home-made meals or, if you prefer, you can enjoy the large picnic area nestled in the beautiful rural surroundings of Somerset.

John Haynes O.B.E., Founder and Chairman of the museum at the wheel of a Haynes Light 12. >

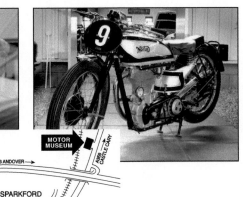

< *The 1936 490cc sohc-engined International Norton – well known for its racing success*

The Museum is situated on the A359 Yeovil to Frome road at Sparkford, just off the A303 in Somerset. It is about 40 miles south of Bristol, and 25 minutes drive from the M5 intersection at Taunton.
Open 9.30am - 5.30pm (10.00am - 4.00pm Winter) 7 days a week, *except Christmas Day, Boxing Day and New Years Day*
Special rates available for schools, coach parties and outings Charitable Trust No. 292048